Dynamics in Document Design

Creating Texts for Readers

Karen A. Schriver

Wiley Computer Publishing

John Wiley & Sons, Inc.

New York • Chichester • Brisbane • Toronto • Singapore • Weinheim

Publisher: Katherine Schowalter
Editor: Terri Hudson
Managing Editor: Carl Germann
Text Design & Composition: Laurette C. Boyer for Karen Schriver Associates, Inc.

Designations used by companies to distinguish their products are often claimed as trademarks. In all instances where John Wiley & Sons, Inc., is aware of a claim, the product names appear in initial capital or ALL CAPITAL LETTERS. Readers, however, should contact the appropriate companies for more complete information regarding trademarks and registration.

This text is printed on acid-free paper.

This publication is designed to provide accurate and authoritative information in regard to the subject matter covered. It is sold with the understanding that the publisher is not engaged in rendering legal, accounting, or other professional service. If legal advice or other expert assistance is required, the services of a competent professional person should be sought.

Endleaves. *The endleaves are a photomontage of the Loughcrew Cairns, an ornamented tomb near the town of Oldcastle in County Meath, Ireland, and the Newgrange Tumulus, a tomb near the town of Slane, also in County Meath. From the Cambridge University Collection. Reproduced with the permission of the Syndics of Cambridge University Library. Newgrange Tumulus by R. Welch (1912) in G. Coffey's* New Grange and Other Incised Tumuli of Ireland *(London: Hodges Figgis and Co., Ltd.).*

Library of Congress Cataloging-in-Publication Data
Schriver, Karen A., 1954–
    Dynamics in document design / Karen A. Schriver
      p. cm.
    Includes bibliographical references and index.
    ISBN: 0471-30636-3 (pbk. : alk. paper)
    1. Technical writing. 2. Graphic design. 3. English-language—
    Rhetoric. 4. Reading, psychology of. 5. Printing—layout. I. Title.
T11.S377   1996
808.' 066--DC20   94-2009
                                   CIP

Printed in the United States of America
10 9 8

To my source of inspiration …

Dick Hayes (also known as John R. Hayes)

Thanks to …

This book has consumed the lives of a few folks over the last year or so. I

cannot thank them enough for their enthusiasm, encouragement, and hard

work. *Thanks* go first to the team that helped make this book a reality:

- **Ann Steffy Cronin**, for her help in analyzing data as well as preparing the figures, tables, bibliography, and index. Ann was tireless and cheerful in seeing the text through its many iterations. She holds a degree in professional writing from Carnegie Mellon and is now working as a freelance document designer in Pittsburgh.

- **Laurette C. Boyer**, for her work in graphic design, drawing, and typography, and for her all around good eye for the visual. She graduated from Carnegie Mellon with a BFA in Graphic Design and is currently president of her own design firm and the Art Director and Chief Designer for Commonwealth Securities and Investments, Inc., an investment banking firm in Pittsburgh.

- **Andrew F. Wheeler**, who played a major role in editing this book. It was Andy who finally convinced me to stop revising and let it go. He took his degree in professional writing at Carnegie Mellon and currently lives in Los Angeles.

- **Dick Hayes**, who read every word and made many suggestions for improvement. I owe a general debt to Dick. His keen sense for getting to the heart of a matter made this a much better book than it would have been—his fingerprints are everywhere. He is Professor of Cognitive Psychology and Director for the Center for Innovation in Learning at Carnegie Mellon. His research focuses on writing, problem solving, and creativity.

Thanks to the following people who played a role in inspiring, developing, revising, and publishing this book:

- David R. Russell, Frank R. Smith, Jonathon Price, Ginny Redish, Carl Jansen, and Nina Wishbow for reviewing early drafts. Thanks especially to Jonathon Price, who encouraged me to keep going when I felt like giving up.

- Craig Borchardt, Liang Chen, Alan Sloan, Lisa Leone, and Susan Stuart—my Research Assistants—for helping me track down historical materials and relevant articles. Thanks especially to Craig Borchardt, now working at Oracle, who fed me chocolate chip cookies and helped me keep my sense of humor.

- Daphne van der Vlist—one of the many excellent "Language and Communication" students at the University of Utrecht I had the pleasure of working with at Utrecht's Centre for Language and Communication—for allowing me to use her case study of navigating a World Wide Web site (in Chapter 6).

- George V. Kelvin—scientific, medical, and techical illustrator—for permitting me to reprint his work, the first technical illustration of the AIDS virus (in Chapter 6).

- My undergraduate and graduate students in *The Nature of Expertise in Document Design* at the University of Utrecht and my students in *Planning and Testing Documents, Integrating Visual and Verbal Texts,* and *Style* at Carnegie Mellon.

- Teachers, writers, graphic designers, managers, and researchers at various organizations I've worked with: Tom Abbott, Hiraku Amemyia, Marc Auerbach, Dan Boyarski, Christina Carey, Debra Carnegie, Karen Cerroni, Leo Delaney, Lois Fowler, Sarah Freedman, Don Freeman, Thea van der Geest, Janet Giltrow, JoAnn Hackos, Akiko Hagino, Seiji Hayakawa, George Hillocks, Michiko Horikawa, Glynda Hull, Nagatoshi Inagaki, Yoshiaki Ishii, Masako Itoh, Japan Society for Technical Communication, Japan Technical Communication Association, Pete Jones, Shiela Jones, Elizabeth Keyes, Koreo Kinosita, Norio Koboyashi, Paul Lorence, John Mackin, Michele Matchett, Kyoko Matsui, Yoshiyuki Matsunaga, George McCulley, Daniel Medvid, Lisa Murray, Judy Leppold, Brad Mehlenbacher, Yasushi Nakajima, Klaus Noack, Dani Oddone, Hideaki Okuma, Eisaku Oshima, Yoji Ozato, Jim Palmer, Norma Pribadi Polk, Mary L. Ray, Mike Rose, Lilita Rodman, Kathy Sayers, Tamara Sargeant, Steve Segal, Noriko Shimada, Erwin Steinberg, Michael Steehouder, STC Tokyo Chapter, M. R. Takahashi, Conrad Taylor, Constance Thomas, Janet Thomas, Mike Vivion, Karel van der Waarde, Gareth Walters, Diana Wegner, Ed Weiss, Piet Westendorp, Wendie Wulff, and Michio Yamamoto.

- The hundreds of people who participated in the various studies I discuss in this book. Without their collaboration, this book would not have been possible. I have tried to enable their distinctive voices to be heard both through my own writing and by presenting documents annotated in their own words. Their substantial contributions give meaning to the subtitle: "Creating Texts for Readers."

- Terri Hudson from John Wiley & Sons for helping me through the book publishing process and for her patience in seeing me through this project.

- John Jay Bonstingl, Helen Hopey, and Cherry and Richard Raymond for encouraging me to to pursue my education.

- Mary L. Baker, Diane Bayer, Louise Bilotti, Susan Eiseman Hays, Robert Lazear, Greg Schriver, Jeff Schriver, Josephine Schriver, Paul Schriver, Robin Snowden, Barbara Whatmough, and Joyce Young for being there when the going got rough.

- Louise Bayer for her love.

- Richard L. Enos, Richard E. Young, Linda Flower, Thomas M. Duffy, and Steve Witte for teaching me about rhetoric, writing, and more.

- Patricia Wright for inspiring me with her work in document design.

About the Author ...

Karen A. Schriver has been a teacher, researcher, and consultant in document design for over ten years. She holds a B.A. in English from Edinboro University of Pennsylvania (1976), an M.A. in English from Carnegie Mellon (1980), and a Ph.D. in Rhetoric and Document Design from Carnegie Mellon (1987). Upon finishing her doctoral work, she was invited to join the faculty of Carnegie Mellon's English Department, serving as Co-Director of its Master of Arts in Professional Writing program, Co-Director of its Communications Design Center, and advisor for doctoral students pursuing a concentration in document design within the Ph.D. in rhetoric degree. Between 1985 and 1995, she was Research Associate for the National Center for the Study of Writing and Literacy (with colleagues from Carnegie Mellon and the University of California at Berkeley). In 1995 she held an endowed full Professorship, the Belle van Zuylen Chair of Language and Communication, at the University of Utrecht in the Netherlands.

She has received several awards for her work. Her dissertation received the National Council of Teachers of English "Promising Researcher Award" for outstanding doctoral research. For research on cognitive processes in revision, she was co-recipient of the College Composition and Communication's 1987 "Richard Braddock Award." In 1990 the Society for Technical Communication awarded her review of the literature on document design research with "Outstanding Article of the Year." In 1994 the National Council of Teachers of English chose an article she wrote as "Best Article on Teaching Technical or Scientific Communication." In 1995 the Association for Computing Machinery's Special Interest Group in Computer Documentation (SIGDOC) presented her and other former directors of the Communications Design

Center with the "Diana Award" for the Center's "sustained and innovative contributions to the field of computer documentation design and technical communication."

Since 1983, she has taught seminars on planning, writing, visualizing, and evaluating documents. She has been an invited speaker and consultant for U.S. companies, government agencies, and academic institutions as well as for audiences in Canada, the Netherlands, and Japan. Some of her clients include Apple Computer, IBM, Bosch, High Technology Communications of Japan, Internal Revenue Service, Sony, Franklin Quest, Japan Society for Technical Communication, AT&T Bell Labs, Fujitsu Ltd., Digital Equipment, Mitsubishi Electric, Sanyo Electric, Booz-Allen & Hamilton, U.S. Postal Service, and the Japan Technical Communication Association.

Karen Schriver recently left her position at Carnegie Mellon to pursue independent research and scholarship. She is president of KSA, a document design research and consulting company. When she is not working, she and Dick Hayes go canoeing with their lovable but wacko dog Mango Mango Brain.

Contents

PART ONE   SITUATING DOCUMENT DESIGN

1

What Is Document Design?   1

2

Evolution of the Field: Contextual Dynamics   13

Left-hand page. *A writer "burns the midnight oil" as he composes a manuscript. From a pen and ink drawing entitled "The Representative," by J. Bancks. Courtesy of the BBC Hulton Picture Library, London, UK.*

4

The Impact of Poor Design: Thinking about   209
Ourselves as Users of Texts and Technology

5

Seeing the Text: The Role of Typography and Space   249

6

The Interplay of Words and Pictures

PART THREE   RESPONDING TO READERS' NEEDS

7

What Document Designers Can Learn from Readers   443

Preface

Many documents fail because they are so ugly that no one will read them or so confusing that no one can understand them. This book aims to help make documents less ugly and less confusing. It explores the design of documents that people deal with routinely, the "forgotten texts" of the everyday world—the stuff we read at our desks, in waiting rooms, in the boardroom, even in the bathroom. Whether it be a textbook, a tax guide, or a timetable for a train, a well-designed document is created to be useful. Good documents get us to read them, and when we do so, they communicate: They help us learn, support us in everyday activities, and enable us to make sense of our world.

At least that's what documents are intended to do. Yet most of us have encountered documents that confuse and confound us, frustrating even highly educated readers. Poor documents are so commonplace that deciphering bad writing and bad visual design have become part of the coping skills needed to navigate in the so-called information age. But bad document design is not inevitable. Documents need not turn us off before reading begins. Documents need not fail to communicate. Something can be done about it—and something is being done. A new field has emerged that explores how good writing and good visual design can improve the documents readers deal with. That field is *document design*.

This book is based on two premises: that readers deserve documents that meet their needs, and that the people who create the prose and graphics play a central role in making this happen. This book is for anyone involved in writing or design—the professional writer, graphic designer, information architect, or communications developer—who already recognizes the importance of designing with an audience in mind,

Left-hand page. A document designer confused by all the things he is expected to remember. From a linoleum print by Joseph Low. Reprinted with the permission of Chronicle Books, San Francisco.

but who seeks a deeper understanding of what people need and want. My aim is to paint a more complex portrait of the audience than has been available, one that puts fresh contours on a familiar subject. I will characterize audiences not as vague abstractions or as constellations of demographic features but as thinking and feeling individuals who actively engage with the prose and graphics of documents. I will offer a view of the audience as people who come to a document with particular purposes in mind, and who not only attempt to understand the prose and graphics but also respond aesthetically and emotionally to the document's design.

I decided to write this book because it has been difficult to find resources devoted to helping document designers reflect on the nature of good writing and design from the perspective of the reader. It is hard to locate books that characterize how people actually experience the documents that professional writers or designers create. The majority of books that are available have a "how to" orientation and are intended for the uninitiated—for the person new to writing and design, who may need ready-to-apply guidelines for producing documents. These books tend to be most useful for inexperienced writers or graphic designers who want advice about how to solve common well-defined problems in document design. Such books clearly serve a valuable purpose, and they have played an important role in developing the field. However, there is also a need for books aimed at an audience who has already mastered the basics and read the introductory literature on writing and design. Indeed, the needs of people who are beyond an elementary understanding of document design—experienced practitioners, advanced students, teachers, and researchers—are rarely addressed. This book is devoted to those who would like to further improve their work with visual and verbal language. My goal is to offer a research-based view of document design that reflects the complexity and difficulty that seasoned writers and graphic designers have experienced.

This is not a guidebook for the choices document designers should make, though I do offer practical advice throughout. I am wary of books that emphasize guidelines for writing and design. It's not that guidelines are intrinsically inappropriate; they are often quite helpful. The problem is that books organized around guidelines tend to trivialize the complexity of decision-making in document design, reducing writing and design to lists of prescriptive and often arbitrary dos and don'ts. Moreover, they tend to underestimate the knowledge, sensibilities, and skills that writers and graphic designers need in order to develop their expertise. In this book, I hope to capture the texture of the choices document designers make and represent the subtlety of the knowledge they rely on in carrying out their work.

Professionals in document design need to recognize, articulate, and build on their strengths. It is my hope that this book will encourage document designers to evaluate their ideas about writing and design as well as their beliefs about how people interact with texts. I want to enable document designers to imagine the readers' world more vividly—to envision people riffling through pages, clicking on hypertext links, ferreting out fact from hype, mapping prose to pictures, wondering what the heck something means. To help, I provide numerous illustrative examples showing why, from the reader's perspective, the moves of writers and designers are sometimes successful and sometimes not.

ABOUT THE STRUCTURE OF THIS BOOK

This book has three broad objectives: (1) to describe how document design has evolved, (2) to characterize how readers think and feel about documents, and (3) to demonstrate the practical advantages of taking the reader's needs seriously. The three main parts of the book reflect these goals. The first part puts document design into perspective by tracing its international evolution in the twentieth century, showing the forces that created a need for document design and the responses to this need from industry and the academy. The second part—the heart of the book— provides a window on the world of the reader by exploring the many facets of people's interactions with words and pictures. And the third part stresses why it is important for document designers to learn from readers, demonstrating the benefits of building a model of readers that can be used while writing or visualizing.

PART ONE, "Situating Document Design," provides a context for the field of document design. Chapter 1 provides a working definition of document design and points to some of the problems the field has had in characterizing itself. History tells us that although the activities of writing and design have much in common, most experienced document designers have developed their expertise primarily in writing or design, rarely in both. In the past, writers were viewed as "word" people and designers as "image" people. However, these traditional separations have been erod- ing. Increasingly, both writers and designers are expected to create both words and pictures—to integrate the visual and the verbal. Today's professional must be flexible enough to cross the disciplinary divide between writing and design, as well as sophisticated enough to make rhetorical choices that are sensitive to the reader's situation.

To provide a context for the book, Chapter 2 presents a historical overview of the field, with a special emphasis on twentieth-century document design. It describes the role that document design plays in society and provides a sense of the breadth of the field. To show why the field looks as it does today, this chapter explores the constellation of social and technological forces that created a need for document design and tracks how industry and the academy responded to meet this need. The chapter reveals some surprising similarities in the ways that the fields of writing and design have struggled toward professionalization in this century. In characterizing the evolution of the field, I take an international perspective and profile five interacting contexts that together shaped modern document design in significant ways:

- Trends in society, particularly those that influenced how people think of themselves as readers and consumers

- Discoveries in science, medicine, and technology (including our understanding of and appreciation for the environment)

- Education and research in rhetoric and writing

- Education and research in graphic design and typography

- Professional developments (e.g., the formation of societies, journals, and publications about writing and design)

Chapter 2 shows why professionals in the field tend to think about writing and visualizing as they do, pointing to some problems in the ways writers and designers have thought about themselves and their work. My contention is that to understand document design, it is important to see how the fields of writing and design have imagined themselves and how these images have influenced the character of the field today. In addition, we need to know how these fields have encouraged their members to imagine the reader—which assumptions govern writers' and designers' judgements about what makes a document good. We must evaluate which assumptions about writing and design result in better documents for readers and which ones do not. Part One puts these issues into per-spective and makes clear why members of the field must be both deliberate and principled in their consideration of readers. At the end of Part One is *A Timeline of Document Design* that chronicles the development of the field. It provides a sense of the context in which document design evolved between 1900 and 1995.

PART TWO, "Observing Readers in Action," explores how readers interpret documents—from their aesthetic responses to typography to their comprehension of prose, pictures, and information graphics. Part Two consists of four chapters.

Chapter 3 characterizes the ways in which people's thinking and feeling come into play as they interpret documents. It evaluates three general approaches to understanding the audience and assesses the implications of each. To illustrate how important it is to take the reader's needs seriously, I present a study of teenagers reacting to the words and pictures of drug education literature. This study shows a glaring mismatch between document designers' intentions and readers' interpretations. The findings suggest that document designers need to rethink their old models of audience analysis. Comprehensible prose or pictures are necessary for good document design but they are not necessarily sufficient. People often do much more than interpret words and pictures when they read. They may also form an impression of the speaker; that is, the words and pictures may give readers clues that encourage them to form an impression of the person or organization who created the document (the persona or organizational identity). This chapter renders a view of the dynamic interplay between cognition and emotions during reading.

Chapter 4 explores the ways in which the design of documents and the design of technology may affect people's beliefs about themselves as users of texts and technology. This chapter provides evidence that "when things go wrong," people have a tendency to blame themselves for problems they experience. I show that poor design may have a negative impact on readers' perceptions of themselves as comprehenders and discuss the possible influence of these negative self-perceptions on people's willingness to use documents in school or at work.

Chapter 5 investigates the role of spatial and typographic cues in documents, examining how space and typography can enable readers to "see the text," its purposes and rhetorical relationships. It brings together the previous literature on typography and presents new research about readers' preferences for typefaces, showing that what people prefer may depend on the genre they are reading and on their purposes for reading. It offers suggestions derived from research for choosing typography, whether designing on paper, computer, or television screen. This chapter also draws on principles of Gestalt psychology to suggest ways in which document designers may use spatial cues to activate rhetorical relationships and promote information access. Additionally, the chapter describes the use of horizontal and vertical space (including ideas about modular grid design) to help readers see the structure of documents. Examples of people trying to decipher manuals, information graphics, forms, tables, and charts reveal how type and space can be employed to meet readers' needs.

Chapter 6 characterizes the interplay of prose and graphics—focusing on the issue of integrating words and pictures. This chapter portrays what people do as they interpret prose and graphics—highlighting the cognitive, social, and cultural dimensions of readers' constructions of meaning. It does so through studies of people trying to use lengthy hardcopy and online documents. These studies evaluate the impact of document design both on how readers search for information and how they understand what they find. What people do in navigating and interpreting depends not only on the design of the words and pictures, but also on the task, the context, and, of course, on whom is doing the reading. To illustrate some of the typical problems readers may experience with poorly integrated documents, this chapter provides an analysis of the unnerving sense of fragmentation that people may experience as they try to put together the words and pictures of World Wide Web sites.

Chapter 6 also features five key ways that words and pictures may interact and offers examples of prose and graphic combinations that typify each. In presenting these examples, I analyze the integration of the words and pictures, pointing out what works and what doesn't for the reader. This chapter tells us that it is a good idea to make documents as visual as possible, but that not all visuals are equal. Indeed, a picture is only sometimes worth a thousand words. It also reminds us that although readers enjoy and have come to expect well-designed visuals, they have equally high expectations for the content presented in prose. This chapter provides specific ideas that document designers can use in planning and revising documents that bring together words and pictures.

Overall, Part Two shows that the message readers construct during their interpretation of documents reflects not only what is said in the document through words and pictures, but also their own knowledge, values, beliefs, and culture. In the four chapters that comprise Part Two, I demonstrate how document designers can employ prose, typography, and visuals in ways that consider readers as thinking and feeling individuals.

PART THREE, "Responding to Readers' Needs," consists of a single chapter that concludes the book. It examines what document designers can learn from readers that will help them improve their writing and design. It illustrates the practical gains that can be achieved by creating texts with people in mind. The chapter provides several studies that reveal the power of readers' feedback for broadening document designers' awareness of what audiences may expect. The studies provide empirical evidence that document design guided by readers' participation can lead to texts that people prefer and that meet their needs for using prose and graphics. A series of before-and-after revisions that were created in response to usability testing show how document designers can translate readers' feedback into textual action. This research makes clear the long-term benefits for document designers in learning about readers by listening to them. In a study evaluating a teaching method that employs commentary from readers during usability testing, I show that document designers with extensive practice in evaluating readers' interpretations can build a model of the reader that will help them anticipate the problems that people may experience with poorly designed prose or graphics. Taken together, these studies show that document designers who take the reader seriously can change the field of document design. They can move it away from the old stereotype that "anyone who can speak and use desktop publishing software" is a document designer. By taking the reader's needs seriously, professionals are creating a modern art and science of document design.

Throughout the book, I draw on research in rhetoric, writing, design, and cognitive science. My assumption is that by embracing a multidisciplinary perspective, members of the field can deepen their understanding of communication and broaden their vision of document design. Moreover, by enlarging their perspective with what can be learned from research, document designers will appreciate more about readers and more about themselves. With this kind of knowledge, they will be able not only to make documents that are less ugly and less confusing, but also to refine their understanding of the rhetorical dynamics that shape their work.

Karen A. Schriver
Pittsburgh, PA
1996

PART ONE
SITUATING DOCUMENT DESIGN

1

What Is Document Design?

This chapter begins by describing the role that document design plays in our

day-to-day activities, presenting examples of readers' personal experiences

with documents. & It characterizes the nature of document design and

discusses why writers and graphic designers have had difficulty both in

defining the field and in naming it. & It then offers a working definition of

document design that integrates the perspectives of those who create

documents with those who use them.

Over the last ten years a number of people have written to me explaining their "close encounters of a strange kind" with documents or technology. The letters I've received show that the frustration people experience is often caused by the poor design of documents or technology, or both. The comments that follow are from those letters.

> *We have an entertainment center in our motorhome. After owning the entertainment center for two years, we still are not able to use it. The remote control has 38 (yes, I said 38) buttons. And as a bonus we get a horrible manual. I find that many professionals at those companies making the gadgets forget who pays their salaries. Help.*

> **Roman Heinzman, age 63**
> **Longview, Washington**

Left-hand page. *Mango Mango Brain (dog on left), explains to her friend Indigo how to find the local Dairy Queen, her favorite place for licking ice cream off the faces of little children. But Indigo's mental map doesn't match Mango's. Cartoon by Laurette Boyer (owner of Indigo) and Karen Schriver (owner of Mango).*

I use my computer to do the books for my small business, so I buy this expensive accounting program that is supposed to be easy. When I type in data into the input boxes of the program and then hit the INPUT key, my data disappears. I ask myself, "Where did it go?" Weirdly, I can see the data when I print it, so I know it's there—somewhere—in the program. I wonder "Is there some data limbo in this program that is preventing me from displaying the data? How can I fix my errors if I can't even see what I just typed in?" So I look in the manual. Nothing. So I call the helpline and after waiting in voicemail land for twenty minutes, their response: "That's not a bug, it's a feature."

Walter Landsberger, age 37
White Plains, New York

Why do medical forms have to be so hard? I have to fill them out for my kids and aging mother, and it takes me so long. Why do they make the words so small and the boxes so short? And they seem to jump around a lot. Why is it harder than it needs to be? I am not stupid but you know, these forms make me feel really dumb.

Lottie Taylor, age 42
Weirton, West Virginia

I love science. I even won a science talent contest. I like to read science books, especially about physics, but the diagrams in my books are sometimes mysterious. I'm not sure where to look and what is the most important thing. I get it usually, but sometimes, I have to keep rereading the words to figure out the picture. Even then I'm not sure if I really got it.... The words are okay I guess, but not always. I don't think it's me.

Josie Elm, age 16
McKeesport, Pennsylvania

We are the elderly sheepish owners of a VCR (VHS - HQ 4-head 050 and other presumably significant letters and numbers). Our grown sons, respectively and separately, visiting from Hawaii and Nashville, have tried vainly to lead us through the VCR—all to no avail. My husband is a physician and I have a Master's in English, but we are obviously too stupid to figure out how to record a program. There is a real watershed between the generations. Do you know if VCR companies are planning any help for folks like us?

Elise Josephson, age 70
Las Cruces, New Mexico

I bought this expensive gas grill because it was supposed to be great, better than charcoal grilling. Well I can't work it. Maybe some spiders got into the pipes. I don't know. I looked in the manual and the drawings look like my kindergarten class made them. The words make no sense and the steps are all jumbled up. What a joke. I called a plumber to fix it, and he said "lady, that's your problem—we don't do gas grills."

Sandra Ostrowski, age 45
Coral Gables, Florida

Every day situations arise in which we must deal with messages in order to act. The messages may be buried in train schedules, government forms, or instruction manuals. They may appear on the screens of banking machines or computers. In some cases, the messages are easy to use. But when the messages are not well designed, we may feel like the people who wrote the comments just presented: frustrated, powerless, and considerably less effective than we might otherwise be.

Documents play a role in almost everyone's daily activities. But surprisingly, knowledge about creating documents for audiences is not yet well developed. Most ideas about writing and design are based on intuition, lore, and personal experience. Of course, a lot of important things can be learned about writing and design in these ways. The trouble is, professionals who depend too heavily on their own experience and intuition may inadvertently ignore other sources of knowledge about document design. They may underestimate the value of finding out how audiences actually interact with their documents. Consequently, they may never know their audiences as readers or as users. Over time they may lose touch with their audiences, especially when those audiences differ from them in age or race or experience.

If writers and graphic designers are to create documents that *take readers seriously,* they will need a more detailed view of readers than they have now—a view which allows them to imagine readers other than themselves actively engaging with words and pictures. Professionals will also need to be able to compare their own writing and design practices to those of others.

In this book, I want to provide document designers with a detailed view of readers and design practices. By drawing on theory and research as well as practical experience, I will characterize both the people who use documents and the people who create them. I hope to help put professionals in a better position to undertake the difficult enterprise of writing and visualizing from the reader's perspective.

PROBLEMS IN DEFINING DOCUMENT DESIGN

There is no perfect name for the field called "document design." As a result, it is often misunderstood. The confusion arises from the meanings we typically associate with "document" and "design." There is little doubt that the word "document" strikes a negative chord for many people. After all, from financial institutions we get "fine print" and incomprehensible "letters of disclosure"; from government, hard-to-understand tax forms; from manufacturers, cryptic instruction guides for computers and electronics. Bad experiences with documents influence not only our thinking about documents we've used but also our attitudes about documents we have not yet seen. People appear to generalize their bad experiences. For example, many refuse to deal with documents that smack of legalese. People also tend to avoid using document types they are not familiar with. Many resist documents that look and feel different from what they're accustomed to, even when those documents may be superior to what they have used before.[1]

Document designers can appreciate why readers may take a wait-and-see attitude before trying out unfamiliar types of documents (such as those not on paper). It is difficult for readers to imagine that these new documents will be any different from the ones they have already experienced: hard to use, boring, and ugly.

Because unfavorable images of documents are so pervasive, professional writers and graphic designers who want to use "document design" to describe their work must clarify its meaning to the public. This sounds easier than it is. For professionals must first clarify what document design means to themselves.

Over the last ten years, the boundaries of document design have expanded, requiring professionals to reconceive the documents they make and their ideas about what may be needed in order to design effectively. Computers, consumer electronics, and technologies for multimedia are radically modifying definitions of documents and books. Document designers who have spent their careers crafting documents such as hardback textbooks are finding themselves challenged by advances that allow them to break conventions and cross genre lines to design hybrid documents (for example, computer-based learning environments in which a traditional book may or may not play a part).

No longer constrained to static and linear formats, document designers can now employ hypertext technologies to design "information landscapes" for practical use. And with the growing affordability of integrating text, animated images, and digital sound, it appears that within this decade,

[1] For example, some people dislike reading procedures displayed in the form of flowcharts. They prefer what they are used to, that is, procedures presented as a list of numbered steps. This aversion may hold even when the flowchart allows users to carry out procedures better and faster than prose does (see Wright & Reid, 1973; Wright, 1982).

most consumers will get hands-on experience with documents that have a decidedly different look and feel than those they grew up with. Such developments in technology provide opportunities for document designers to change people's image of documents as big, bad, and ugly.[2] These new technologies also put professionals in the auspicious position of being able to reinvent themselves and their documents, leaving the word "document" as a placeholder for a text-like artifact composed in print or in mixed media, the combination of which could only be imagined just a few years ago. Thus while using "document" as a key word for the field may create some initial confusion, it also creates an occasion to redefine what a document can be.

As writers and designers try to change how the public thinks about documents, they will have to work on broadening the public's understanding of design. Considerable confusion may be generated by the word "design," particularly its common uses alternatively as verb or noun, as process or object. Design usually evokes images of architects, product designers, or fashion moguls busy in the act of making something, whether it be skyscrapers, espresso machines, or cape coats. As design historian Victor Margolin (1989a) has commented:

> Design is all around us: It infuses every object in the material world and gives form to immaterial processes such as factory production or services. Design determines the shape and height of a shoe heel, the access to computer functions through software, the mood of an office interior, special effects in films, and the structure and elegance of bridges. (p. 3)

While vivid images of design such as these dominate popular culture, they don't convey the idea that documents are also designed, that they too can be infused with mood, structure, even elegance. Because documents serve utilitarian purposes, their design must blend a sense of the aesthetic with certain "ready-to-wear" features: practicality, ease-of-use, and affordability. Document design is just beginning to make itself visibly present in the world of design. For this reason, people may still wince at the idea that creating documents could require a discriminating eye as well as intelligent, deliberate design.

Instead, the design of documents is usually construed as somewhat perfunctory, taking place *after* the important activity of deciding what to say. In this view, design is relegated to dressing up and graphically packaging messages already structured, content already meaningful. Visual design from this perspective demands no planning, no orchestration of competing visions. It simply involves polishing the look of the document—giving

[2] So far, however, if the CD-ROM market is any indication of a trend, document designers (and their colleagues on development teams) haven't done a very good job of changing users' ideas about what documents can be. Many CD-ROM developers simply "dump" books online, reinforcing stereotypes of clumsy, content-poor, hard-to-navigate documents. Market analysts report that the initial enthusiasm for CD-ROMs seems to be waning partly because users are "wising up" about poor design (e.g., see "CD-ROMs That Suck," *Wired*, Jan. 1996, pp. 166–167). Document designers have a key role to play in reinventing how CD-ROMs display, organize, and connect content.

it punch by using a daring typeface or making it sizzle by adding color or illustrations. Much like the wardrobe mistress behind the scenes of a play who at the last minute may be found straightening a tie, adding feathers to a hat, or tying a colorful sash, the graphic designer has been regarded as someone who adds a bit of spice to the scene of a text.

Regrettably, there is a good deal of literature on design promoting this view, particularly in books aimed at newcomers to the field. At the same time, the public is bombarded with ads from printing companies that emphasize, "Before that important business presentation, jazz up those boring black-and-white documents with color," or "Let us format your documents for you while you wait." Books on desktop publishing and professional communication have tended to treat design as mere formatting.[3]

[3] For more detail about the problems with the "design as dress metaphor," see Kostelnick (1994).

This way of thinking relegates the designer to a support role—the one who squeezes content into girdles, who pours messages into templates for smoothing and shaping. This view wrongly separates form and content. It wrongly privileges verbal expression over visual expression. It also wrongly assumes that only visual language is designed. Most important, it prevents document designers from solving communications problems by taking advantage of the powerful ways in which visual and verbal language can give meaning to one another (Barton & Barton, 1993; Bernhardt, 1986).

NAMING THE FIELD: COMPETING VIEWS

These difficulties in defining what is meant by "document" and "design" have led some writers and designers to argue that the name of the field should be changed. Some designers of paper, online, or video artifacts prefer the term "information design" because they view themselves as creators of information structures rather than of documents. These practitioners assert that "information design" more accurately captures the hybrid artifacts they now produce (e.g., scripts for instructional videos, interactive databases for information kiosks, user message systems for graphical interfaces, or information landscapes for CD-ROMs). Using "information design," they believe, signals the activity of building visual and verbal language structures (some writers and designers now call themselves "information engineers" or "information architects").

However, other writers and designers challenge the adequacy of "information design" to characterize the field. Using it reminds them of a theory of communication that was inspired by a model developed by

Claude Shannon and Warren Weaver (1948, 1949) in their *Mathematical Theory of Communication*. The Shannon-Weaver model, developed in the context of their research on information theory, was intended to describe how messages are sent and received as they are transmitted over telephone lines or radio channels. Their model played an important role in the development of statistical theories about electronic communication and engineering. It was designed to predict the capacities for sending signals over phone lines in noisy situations. As such, it symbolized the process of communication with flowcharts of transmitters, channels, receivers, signals, and noise.

Shannon and Weaver did not represent themselves as working on a theory of human interpretation. Even so, in an attempt to better understand and explain the communication process, theorists in communication fields borrowed the language of information theory and applied it to describe the process of communication generally.[4] In its popular usage, the process of communication is one in which a transmitter sends signals to a receiver. Signals may become hazy and unclear if they are mixed with "noise," a term used metaphorically to mean anything that may confuse the message as it travels from transmitter to receiver. For instance, sending e-mail during a thunderstorm may introduce unwanted "phoneline junk" into one's message. Or transmitting a fax composed in a small serif font may make some characters (e.g., the letters "e," "a," and "o") close up to look like black dots, making the message illegible. As Schutte and Steinberg (1983) point out:

> Some communications theorists have even expanded the metaphor to include almost anything that would interfere with or distort a message or distract an audience, including aspects of the message itself. Thus, for example, wordiness may be considered noise if it distorts the kernel of information that a message is intended to carry, or if it distracts or otherwise prevents the reader from understanding the message … in this sense any poorly chosen grammatical structure which interferes with the proper transmission of an idea may be "noise": instead of reflecting an idea and reinforcing it, an inappropriate grammatical structure sets up a dissonance, and works against it. Similarly, an inappropriate layout on the page or even a poorly chosen typeface can create dissonance and thus function as "noise." (pp. 27–28)

Opponents to using the term "information design" point out that while "noise" may characterize familiar phenomena such as foggy writing and cluttered visual design, taken together, the family of concepts—"transmit-

[4] For a discussion of the ways that information theory has been applied to professional communication, see Dobrin (1983, 1989), Doheny-Farina (1992), Waller (1980), and Witte (1992). These authors show why the language of information theory is inadequate and inappropriate to describe the work of professional communicators.

ters," "receivers," and "noise"—fails to capture the interactive nature of communication. Those who oppose basing the field on information theory contend it provides the wrong set of metaphors for describing the intricate process of human-to-human communication. In adopting the language of information theory, organizations become the transmitters of signals. Audiences are the receivers, portrayed as passive recipients of information rather than as people who draw on their knowledge and perception to interpret messages directed at them. Communication is seen as a one-way transmission rather than a complex rhetorical interaction.

Moreover, the process of deciding what to say in words or pictures is reduced to the recording of thought—to the transcription of the message to paper or screen, readying it for transmission—rather than imagining, developing, or shaping it for an audience. Opponents point out that using information design suggests a kind of "Mail Boxes Are Us" image of design, where designers package and ship information rather than create communications. Opponents of "information design" argue that information is the last thing people need more of. Instead, people need communications tailored to their special needs and purposes—communications that enhance their ability to learn, make decisions, and so on.

For these reasons, many in the field favor the term "communications design." To them, it seems broader than either "document design" or "information design." They feel "communications design" shifts the attention to writing and visualizing for people. Instead of emphasizing the products of communication (such as documents or information structures), it focuses on a relationship between a designer and an audience, a relationship that can be achieved, however tenuously, through visual or verbal language. The advantage of communications design is that it underscores human-to-human contact rather than designer-to-subject matter contact.

Even though "communications design" appears to be the most inclusive name for the field, many writers and designers have rejected it for just that reason; that is, "communications" is too general. Opponents argue that "communications" is already strongly associated with the fields of advertising and public relations—areas that overlap with some kinds of document design but which typically have different agendas. Those wary of "communications design" look for a name untainted by the practices of other fields. They want a name that suggests a fresh approach to designing for readers, one that signals their rhetorical stance of bringing together words and pictures in ethical and responsible ways. To them "communications design" signifies designing in order to sell people something rather than designing in order to help people help themselves (e.g., completing a

Medicare form). Furthermore, opponents argue that because "communications design" sounds so familiar, so transparent, hearers may underestimate the requisite knowledges, sensibilities, and skills that writers and designers need in order to be effective.

Members of the field with a background in writing often use the rubrics "technical communication" and "professional communication." However, these names, as familiar as they are to insiders, do not adequately communicate the diverse nature of the field to outsiders. Most outsiders think technical communication means writing computer manuals and that professional communication means corporate communications; both interpretations are too narrow. Even insiders to the field of writing disagree about what "technical" and "professional" mean. Professors who teach courses in advanced writing, for example, have been trying to sort out how to interpret these terms. They have been asking whether the terms reflect important differences about subject matter or simply carve up the world of writing in strange ways—making bogus distinctions between technical and nontechnical, professional and nonprofessional, and technical and professional.

Sorting out these distinctions is important because the interpretations of these terms directly influence what is taught. Writing teachers want to know, for example, what these terms imply about the kind of education a technical communicator needs. Teachers are concerned about the relationship between an education designed to help students become good all-around communicators and an education focused on enabling students to excel in communicating about technical subject matters. Some teachers stress the writer's process (e.g., planning, drafting, revising, evaluating) and the writer's stance toward the audience as the most important things to learn. These teachers argue that if students are good at solving communication problems in general, they can readily bring their talents to bear in situations where they must write about subject matters they know nothing about, technical or not. Other teachers believe that the best education in technical communication involves learning about particular genres (e.g., proposal writing or hypertext design) and subject matters (e.g., engineering or biochemistry). These teachers cite medical writing, scientific journalism, and writing for the computer industry as domains in which knowledge of process and audience is essential but not enough. They argue that if students are to excel in specialized domains such as these, they need to understand the medicine, the science, or the technology. The answers to these arguments matter a lot because they fundamentally shape what college graduates know and can do, as well as what they don't know and can't do.[5]

[5] In Chapter 2, I explore some of the ways that writing and graphic design have been taught at the college level. My concern is with the impact higher education has on how professionals think about what it means to write or design.

From the perspective of document design, however, the most serious problem with "technical communication" and "professional communication" is that these rubrics fail to suggest that writers must be able to think visually as well as verbally. These names do not give an accurate impression of the talents professionals need to cultivate, nor do they suggest the range of subject matters and communication goals that experienced document designers deal with every day.

A WORKING DEFINITION OF DOCUMENT DESIGN

Naming the field is important because it provides a common language and a set of metaphors for talking about what we do. Names also help delineate the territory of the field, giving its members a sense of identity while giving outsiders an idea of what the field is about. But to some extent, naming is arbitrary; the same activity could be described by a variety of names. For example, professionals who see themselves as technical communicators may also, quite appropriately, view themselves as information designers and as document designers.

Understanding the advantages and limitations in the choice of a name, I have chosen to use "document design" in this book because it suggests the *act* of writing and designing—the process of bringing together words and pictures. In 1980, Felker and his colleagues offered this rationale for choosing "document design" over other references to the field:

> The words "document design" are a deliberate choice because they convey the complexity of the field. The terms "clear writing" and "plain English" are not sufficient because useful, understandable documents entail more than easy words and simple sentences. The organization and format of a document may be just as important as its language. The degree to which the document is matched to the capabilities of its users and the setting of its use may affect comprehension as much as clearly written sentences. The broader term "document design" encompasses these added complexities. (p. 2)

Building on this description, I offer the following. Document design is the field concerned with creating texts (broadly defined) that integrate words and pictures in ways that help people to achieve their specific goals for using texts at home, school, or work. As Simon (1981) reminds us, "everyone who designs devises courses of action aimed at changing existing situations into preferred ones" (p. 129). Document design is the act of bringing together prose, graphics (including illustration and photography), and typography for purposes of instruction, information, or persuasion. Good document design enables people to use the text in ways that serve their interests and needs. While documents must also meet the requirements of their clients, the reader's needs should drive design activity. In this way, document design is different from advertising in that advertising focuses on writing and visualizing in order to promote the goals and values of organizations rather than to promote the goals and values of readers.[6] The challenge for document designers lies in developing courses of action that will change existing situations into preferred ones for the people who make use of our work.

Designed for pragmatic purposes, documents help people to learn, use technology, make decisions, and get their jobs done. Documents often concern topics in science and technology, education and training, government and law, economics and finance, health and medicine, risk communication and safety, or public policy and the environment. Since people rely on documents to make decisions that influence their safety, livelihood, health, and education, the highest ethical standards must be brought to bear in making textual choices—in deciding what to say and what not to say, in what to picture and what not to picture. Taking responsibility for these choices is central to the practice of document design. Expert practitioners distinguish themselves by skillfully selecting, structuring, and emphasizing content with the reader's needs in focus.

Document design fuses art and science. The art of document design involves shaping words and pictures in ways that help people to

- Recognize the situations in which using documents might be beneficial (thus inviting and motivating readers).
- Discover how documents can be employed in order to carry out particular purposes and goals (thus supporting readers and their uses for texts).

The science of document design involves judging "what works" by assessing documents in the context of their use by the people expected to use them. Expert practitioners regard the success of a document as an empirical question. They recognize that even when words and pictures appear to be functional and aesthetically engaging, there can be no substitute for observing what readers actually do, think, or feel as they interact with documents. By bringing readers into the process, document designers increase the likelihood of creating medical pamphlets that patients can understand easily, textbooks that enhance student motivation, and computer interfaces that help to reduce errors on the job. Document design, then, is not characterized by genres or subject matters, but by the ways its practitioners envision the reader as an active participant and major stakeholder in the design and evaluation of documents.

[6] It's not that advertisers do not think about their audiences. They definitely do. And they are quite sophisticated about it. And it's not that advertisers don't bring together words and pictures for readers. They typically integrate text and image in clever and unexpected ways. The difference between advertising and document design is one of motivation and focus. The motive of an advertisement is to sell a product or service through words and pictures. The motive of document design is to employ words and pictures to help readers accomplish their personal goals—such as learning (e.g., mastering the operation of a personal computer), doing (e.g., changing the batteries in a smoke detector), or making a decision (e.g., choosing among health-care programs).

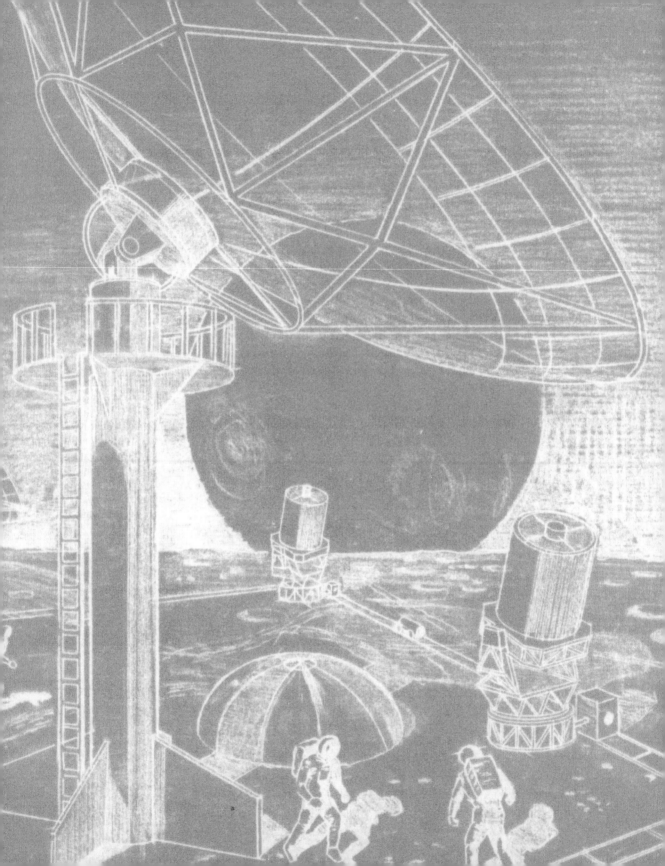

2

Evolution of the Field: Contextual Dynamics

This chapter focuses on the evolution of document design in this century. It first identifies societal and technological forces that created a need for document design. ❧ It then explores the professionalization of document design—from the early part of this century, when practitioners, teachers, and researchers of writing or design had no sense of professional identity, little theory or research to guide their practice, and few places to meet or share ideas—to the present, when members of the field benefit from academic programs and professional societies that are fostering knowledge about document design and developing its research base. ❧ The chapter concludes by presenting a timeline of document design from 1900 to 1995 that chronicles many of the events and developments from around the world that have significantly shaped the field.

Many people in document design think about the field in terms of personal experience. As practitioners, we may have fond memories of the early tools we used: an old Underwood or an oak drafting table. As

Left-hand page. *Scientific discovery plays a significant role in twentieth-century document design. Shown here is a reproduction of a pencil drawing of a plan for a U.S. space station on the moon. The aerospace industry employed many technical writers, illustrators, and designers to meet its needs for well-designed documents, especially between 1957 and 1969— the years of the space race. Drawing by George V. Kelvin, who holds the copyright. Used with his permission.*

teachers, we might remember our first course: the best assignment, lively in-class discussions, or questions we couldn't answer. As researchers, we may recall the widespread interest in differences between readability and usability, arguments about serif versus sans serif typefaces, or indignant reports in the media about how Johnny and Jane couldn't read or write. Individual experience necessarily plays an important role in our image of the field's everyday landscape. But we can develop a broader sense of its terrain by considering the experiences of others and by exploring the field's past. Document design has been enriched by the experiences of practitioners, teachers, and researchers. It is surprising, then, that these interdependent vantage points and their cross-fertilization have not been very well explored.

ACQUIRING A SENSE OF THE FIELD

At present, there are few places to which document designers can turn in order to acquire a sense of the field's geography—its peaks, its valleys, its horizon. Consequently, even though insiders may agree that we have a "rich and revealing past" (Fearing & Sparrow, 1989, p. 1), the lack of historical sources for document design may lead some to conclude just the opposite. Moreover, the absence of histories makes it difficult for both insiders and outsiders to appreciate the breadth of the field and to recognize how far it has come.

Document designers need information about the development of the field, not only in their own country but also in other parts of the world. They would benefit from a fuller understanding of the social and technological forces that are common to countries where knowledge about document design is most advanced (an issue I address later in this chapter). There is almost no literature offering perspective about the contextual factors that have enabled document design to develop in some industrialized countries but not in others. The absence of such a literature makes it difficult to evaluate the state of the field from the point of view of the international document design community.

The contributions made in countries such as Australia, Canada, Denmark, France, Germany, Japan, the Netherlands, New Zealand, and the U.K. are hard to trace. For the most part, the handful of historical accounts that are readily available take a decidedly American point of view.[1]

---

[1] Although the American perspective dominates the historical record, the field of document design did not begin in the United States. Sustained discussion of document design appears to have started in the U.K. in the 1970s, with scholars such as Michael MacDonald Ross, Michael Twyman, Robert Waller, and Patricia Wright leading the conversation. This dialogue has

An awareness of the history of document design—particularly as it has developed cross-nationally—would better allow document designers to reflect on the field's past and to theorize about where it might be going.

There are also practical reasons why writers and designers would be served by knowing more about the field. Such awareness would be especially helpful in dealing with people who are not in the field. Most experienced practitioners, for example, can recount at least one horror story in which the value of document design was challenged or trivialized. Most have heard litanies such as the following:

> We're not going to spend resources on document design when we can just have the secretary "type up something." Customers won't know the difference.

In situations like these, knowledge of the field is critical: Document designers must be able to make cogent arguments based on evidence more persuasive than personal testimony.

Although there is a growing corpus of provocative articles and books about the field, these sources are scattered across diverse literatures. As a result, one tends to find a slice of history about the practice of document design in one literature, a description of pedagogy in another, and a review of research in yet another. These perspectives need better integration. Moreover, the historical sources currently available are also limited by significant omissions. Rarely do they make reference to the relationship between writing and design.[2] To newcomers, the histories of rhetoric and composition, on one hand, and the history of graphic design, on the other, suggest that these areas have little if anything to do with each other. Of course, experienced document designers know that just the opposite is true.

Providing a much-needed critical analysis of the history of document design is not my purpose here. It must be done by a historian, which I am

[2] For some exceptions, see E. Tebeaux and M. J. Killingsworth (1992), who explore technical communication as it existed in the English Renaissance between 1475 and 1640. See also E. Tebeaux (1991a, 1991b), who tracks further the evolution of readable documents in the English Renaissance.

---

continued in a variety of formal and informal venues around the world. For example, from the U.K., there is the influential *Information Design Journal,* the first issue of which provided a sketch of graphic design history in Great Britain (Smith, 1979). A more recent arrival, *The Communicator,* has reported on the development of technical communication programs in England. From Germany, there has been information from the technical communication organization Gesellschaft für technische Kommunikation eV (called Tekom). From Denmark, there is DANTEKOM. From the Netherlands, there have been books in the *Utrecht Series in Language and Communication.* From Japan, there has been the journal *The Technical Writer* (but unfortunately, it is no longer in publication). From Australia, Robert Eagleson's corpus stands out, as do publications from the Centre for Plain Legal Language. Also from Australia is the Communications Research Institute, which hosts conferences and publishes the bulletin *Communication News.*

not. What I would like to provide, however, is "grist for the mill" for such a history.

INTERACTING CONTEXTS THAT SHAPED DOCUMENT DESIGN

As part of the research for this book, I consulted archival sources and conversed with colleagues to obtain a better sense of how the field evolved. My aim was to track the forces that have given rise to document design in this century. I collected historical facts, anecdotes, and observations that might shed light on the contexts in which the field has developed. My research suggests that between 1900 and 1995, document design was shaped dynamically by five interacting contexts:

- Society and consumerism
- Science, technology, and environmental awareness
- Education and practice in writing and rhetoric
- Education and practice in graphic design and typography
- Professional developments in writing, graphic design, and typography

As a heuristic for exploring the relationships among the data I collected about these contexts, I created a timeline in which the events in each of the five contexts for a given decade appear on a two-page spread. This spatial display shows concurrent and sequential relationships among developments in document design—relations that are not readily apparent in the research literature. (*The Timeline* appears at the end of this chapter.)

What follows is an interpretation of some of the trends the data suggested. I organize my discussion by issue rather than by the chronology of the timeline. In presenting my "take" on the issues, I intend not to provide closure, but to stimulate discussion and open the way for other constructions of the field.

THE NEED FOR DOCUMENT DESIGN: SOCIAL AND TECHNOLOGICAL FORCES

In this century, document design developed most dramatically in industrialized, market-oriented countries. It is reasonable to believe that document design emerged largely because these countries shared a need for functional communications and because their citizens asked for them—in some cases, demanded them. Documents of many sorts were needed to help citizens carry out their day-to-day activities on the job or in the home. Indeed, documents provided a vital communications link connecting business, education, government, and the public.

Industrialized nations are similar in the broad sense that their public and private sectors created a demand for documents. However, nations differ markedly in the conditions—social, cultural, political, economic, and technological—that led to the development of document design. For example, in some countries, document design emerged partly as a response to consumer and citizen groups who lobbied their governments for more comprehensible documents (e.g., the U.K. and the United States). In others, it sprang up because consumers outside of the country began to hold higher expectations for product information coming to them from foreign manufacturers, forcing manufacturers to tailor (or localize) their documents for particular languages, cultures, and audiences (e.g., Japan, the United States, and more recently, Korea and Taiwan). In some countries, it arose opportunistically because government or corporate funding was available for certain types of document design projects, such as revisions of income tax forms, legal documents, or product documentation (e.g., Australia, Canada, New Zealand, the Netherlands, and the United States). In others, it grew as a result of a need to devise effective instructional materials used in "distance learning," that is, learning by mail, modem, or television (e.g., the U.K.). More recently, document design has developed in some countries because of economic trade agreements, such as those among partners in the European Economic Community (e.g., Belgium, France, Germany, Italy, and the Netherlands).[3]

As these examples show, there is no single impetus for document design. Understanding the differences among national settings can help us to appreciate the breadth and depth of the field. Consideration of these differences, however, need not lessen our attention to the common forces that have both motivated document design and enabled its development in different parts of the world. Below I characterize some of these common forces, particularly those which have shaped the field since 1900. I focus on the growth of document design in the United States and make reference (as best I can) to parallel developments in other countries. I hope that others will soon fill in the gaps in what appears to be a fascinating intellectual history.

Consumerism Helps Document Design Gain Momentum

The end of the nineteenth century and the beginning of the twentieth marked an era of shifting buying patterns for U. S. consumers. Instead of making cloth and garments, consumers bought clothing; instead of collecting and chopping wood, they purchased coal; instead of butchering their meat in the backyard, they ate meat that had been packed in Chicago (Cowan, 1983). Consumption of goods and services was on the rise,

[3] In particular, industrial and commercial legislation has specified documentation as one of the "deliverables" that must accompany products sold to European Economic Community (EC) countries. The International Standards Organization (ISO) has developed a quality standard, the ISO 9000, which requires companies to demonstrate in writing that a quality process is in place before a company may do business with the EC. For a discussion, see Hunt (1993), Kendall (1988), and Weiss (1993).

▶ Figure 2.1 *Sample pages from the 1900 Spring Edition of the Sears Catalog. Courtesy of Sears Archives, Chicago, IL.*

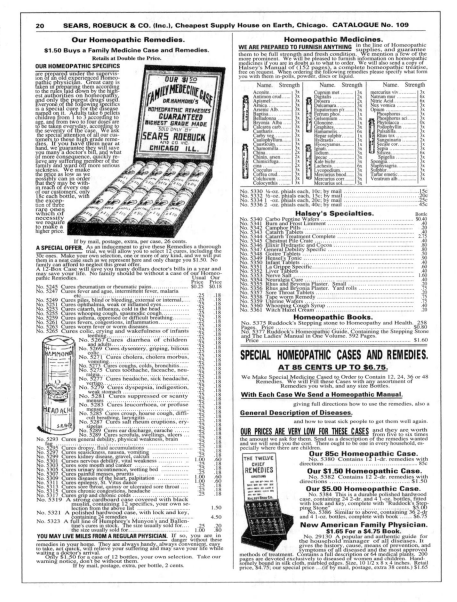

and advertisers spent considerable time and energy trying to convince consumers to purchase particular name brand products.

The postal service expanded free mail delivery to rural America in 1886, making it possible for everyone to receive newspapers, magazines, mail-order catalogs, and, of course, junk mail (Flexner, 1982, p. 535). Farmers and city people alike could now get the *Sears Catalog* delivered to their door. The "Big Book," the "Wish Book," or the "Dream Book"— as the catalog was fondly referred to—was a visual and verbal extrava-

ganza, advertising everything from dinette sets to tombstones. In it, consumers could buy the latest cosmetics and home remedies through the mail—cosmetics that promised to make one's skin beautiful and remedies that claimed to heal an amazing variety of ailments (see Figure 2.1).

According to Brubach (1993), writers of the product descriptions in the "Wish Book" would exaggerate wildly to encourage "the children of immigrants" to buy products (p. 56). Designers filled every inch of the page, creating surrealist juxtapositions of randomly related objects (Patton,

▶ Figure 2.2 *Sample pages from the 1900 Spring Edition of the Sears Catalog. Courtesy of Sears Archives, Chicago, IL.*

4 Kirk Varnedoe, curator of the *High & Low* show at Museum of Modern Art in New York, observes that one person looks at a *Sears, Roebuck Catalog* and sees a total deadpan inventory, while another sees a hallucinatory fantasy of corsets running together with tractors (Varnedoe & Gopnik, 1990, p. 254).

5 For an example of another text that employs similar graphic design practices, but from a British perspective, see *Punch's Almanack*.

6 The *Sears Catalog* showed not only the gullible side of American consumerism, but also its ugly side, with products such as the Lily White Face Wash and, in later editions, "darkey" toys.

1993, p. 21).[4] The idea of substantiating one's claims did not seem to be part of the writer's repertoire. And "functional use of blank space" was apparently not part of the graphic designer's vocabulary.[5]

As the ads from the 1900 edition of the *Sears Catalog* in Figure 2.1 show, consumers could purchase inexpensive medicine kits that promised to cure infirmities from malaria to kidney disorders.[6] The editor of the more recent *Miniature Reproduction of the 1900 Sears, Roebuck and Company Catalog,* Joseph Schroeder (1970) suggests: "With the dozen or so assorted

cures one could try in Sears' 'Family Medicine Case' for $1.50, it was little wonder the average American lived to be only 48!" (p. 2).[7] And if one lived long enough to go bald, no problem. With products such as the Princess Hair Restorer (shown in Figure 2.2), one could easily grow a lovely new head of hair.[8] We can see then that the increase in the availability of consumer products gave people more choices, but the messages written and visualized to help them make decisions among alternatives were fraught with fact, fiction, and fantasy.

[7] Some of the dubious advertising strategies exemplified in the "Wish Book" still persist. For example, today's "Muy Macho" dietary supplement (available in some health food stores) could have been advertised in the Family Medicine Case.

[8] Contemporary ads emphasizing the virtues of "spray-on hair replacement for men" make appeals similar to those made for the Princess Hair Restorer.

Consumer Activism and the Safety of Food and Drugs

The pervasiveness of unsubstantiated claims at the turn of the century made consumers increasingly concerned about the purity and safety of food, drugs, and cosmetics. Not only could companies "get away with" selling the cure of the week, but the level of government control regarding basic food and drug items was primitive at best.[9] Because there were no laws governing what companies could say about their products, they could make almost any claim they wished. Early investigative reporters fueled the debate by writing scathing exposés of unethical practices concerning product safety, food cleanliness, and manufacturing standards.[10] These "muckrakers," as they were called by President Theodore Roosevelt, stirred up the public about corruption in business and government. Their work inspired consumers to lobby government officials to pass the Pure Food and Drug Act and the Meat Inspection Act in 1906.

The ordinary citizens who compelled government and industry to respond to their needs set precedents for the quality of food and drugs and, to some extent, for the quality of the communications that explained them. They also helped generate the demand that documents be simple and truthful. As it turned out, however, even though manufacturers were required by law to describe their products accurately, the government had little power to enforce these laws. The government had to show that consumer deception was intentional in order to prosecute false claims (Mayer, 1989, p. 24). This situation fostered public cynicism about the communications coming from business and government—whether those communications were advertisements or functional documents.

Consumerism and advertising. In the early twentieth century, companies began to mass produce everything from automobiles to toothbrushes. Given the new range of choices, consumers grew to rely on the advertising for brand-name products (e.g., Ivory soap, Kodak cameras, Coca-Cola, or Oreo cookies). Even though consumers paid attention to the accuracy of manufacturers' claims, the task of evaluating these claims was more difficult than it had been. Older Americans can remember the days when

---

[9] For instance, ice was still the principal means of refrigeration. Milk was not pasteurized, nor were cows tested for tuberculosis. Patent medicines could contain opium, morphine, heroin, cocaine, or alcohol (Mayer, 1989, p. 17).

[10] For example, in *The Jungle* (1906), Upton Sinclair painted grim pictures of the food processing methods practiced by Chicago's meat packers—where thousands of rats would die, and then rats, bread, and meat would go into the hoppers together to make sausage. "Sometimes men would fall into the cooking vats, and ... they would be overlooked for days, till all but the bones of them had gone out to the world as Durham's Pure Leaf Lard!" (p. 102).

they knew the people who sold them goods and services. But by the 1920s, industrialized America was taking a different course:

> Mass production had severed the connections between the person who made something and the person who used it. Packaged products were made by strangers working in some distant factory. The only clues to quality were the name on the package—the brand name—and whatever you were told in the product's advertising.[11]

Americans' homes, particularly in the cities, were being wired not only for the light electricity provided but also for the appliances it would run: fans, toasters, irons, hair curling devices, sewing machines, washing machines, vacuum cleaners, and more. Advertisers soon seized the day to inform the public of the new wonders of the industrial age. Advertising "graduated from the promoter of the dubious and glamorizer of the commonplace into a full-fledged partner in the industrial process" (*Consumer Reports,* Jan. 1986, p. 8).

The proliferation of products for the home meant that women became consumers of considerable importance to American business. Advertisers began to target women with an increasing array of visual and verbal messages designed to "educate" them to select the most sophisticated looks, brands, styles, and ensembles for their homes.[12] And as is well known, attention to the improvement of women's appearance became a permanent feature of advertising.[13]

Amidst a climate of puffery, members of the advertising community construed themselves as the "denouncers of fraud," as the ones who could advance society to a higher, more rational level (Higham, 1918). At the same time, they bandied slogans such as "it pays to advertise" and invented the celebrity testimonial, designed to show the masses what a "quality" product could buy them. They construed the audience as "reasonably predictable," "impulsive," "unthinking," and "easily

---

[11] Quoted from *Consumer Reports* (Jan. 1986, p. 8), which profiled the rise of the consumer movement in America in its 1986 edition (the fiftieth year anniversary of the Consumers Union). It offers a discussion of the events between 1920 and 1945 that stimulated consumer activism and of the people who started the Consumers Union.

[12] Mayer (1989) points out that "most people were just getting used to having bathrooms and centrally heated water when they were told by advertisements that plain white towels were a sign of unsophisticated taste" (p. 20).

[13] For example, in 1940, cigarette manufacturers—who were actively trying to enlist more women to smoke—advertised the "red-tipped Debs," a cigarette that left lipstick unsmeared (Flexner, 1982, p. 150).

manipulated" (Scott, 1908; Wadsworth, 1913). Although advertisers were enormously successful in engineering the demand for a wide variety of products, not all citizens were as easily manipulated as advertising dogma suggested they would be.

The birth of the Consumers Union. When American industry moved to mass production, it did so without much planning—resulting in inefficiency, waste, and a lack of quality control. In many cases, companies were producing things without having clear ideas about how well they worked.[14] It was in this context that Stuart Chase and Frederick J. Schlink wrote *Your Money's Worth* (1927), arguing that it was about time that science[15] joined the "buyer's side of the deal." Their book, which has since been described as the *Uncle Tom's Cabin* of the consumer movement, detailed the rather sleazy forces at work in the new mass-marketed world. Chase and Schlink ridiculed made-up brand names (e.g., Lux, Celotex, and Sanitas), gave examples of shortweighting, mislabeling, quackery, or uselessness, and had the audacity to identify products by name. Their most important action, however, would be to recommend that the government set standards for consumer products and establish impartial testing laboratories to compare products. Schlink had been on the staff of the Bureau of Standards, whose practices he took as a model of the sort of scientific testing that might be done to benefit consumers.

After the huge success of *Your Money's Worth*, Chase and Schlink turned a neighborhood consumer's club they had founded into Consumers' Research, Inc. and began a magazine, *Consumers' Research Bulletin*. By 1933, there were 42,000 subscribers. The same year, Schlink and a new partner, Arthur Kallet, published *100,000,000 Guinea Pigs: Dangers in Everyday Foods, Drugs and Cosmetics*, in which they depicted consumers as guinea pigs used in the testing of untried technologies. Their book was a best seller and sparked a wave of consumer-oriented journalism not seen since the muckrakers at the beginning of the century.

Consumers' Research, Inc., however, was shortlived. In 1935, after a bitter strike over working hours and wages, forty employees quit to form their own group, the Consumers Union, and to publish their own magazine, *Consumers Union Reports* (later renamed *Consumer Reports*). The

[14] Herbert Hoover, an engineer by training who was Secretary of Commerce in the 1920s, pointed out that an automobile company might make a different size tire for every model it produced. This resulted in 287 different types of tires available before the war (*Consumer Reports,* Jan. 1986, p. 9).

[15] Chase and Schlink were referring to the legacy of "scientific management," a philosophy in which managers employed scientific methods to boost productivity, speed product to market, and increase sales. For a discussion in relation to business and education, see Berlin (1990, p. 199); Hilgard (1987, pp. 678, 701–707); Killingsworth and Palmer (1992, pp. 164–166); Noble (1977, pp. 264–274); Russell (1991, p. 103); Taylor (1911); Varnedoe and Gopnik (1990, pp. 440–449); and Yates (1989, pp. 1–20).

new magazine was one of the first to criticize manufacturers for overemphasizing the industrial design of their product lines. As "style" and "features" became salable commodities, companies spent enormous amounts of money on ads that hyped the virtues of "new and improved" products. With few exceptions, they paid almost no attention to the quality of "after-the-sale communications" such as owners' guides or warranties.[16] Writers for the Consumers Union helped their members make decisions about these commodities by questioning how much value these new styles and features added to products.

The gadfly spirit of *Consumers Union Reports* was apparent in the first issue, in which the editors commented on the public's newfound enthusiasm for refrigerators. The big attraction? Industrial designers had transformed the old ice box into a modern streamlined shape. The editors took pleasure in pointing out that the streamlining made no functional difference unless one contemplated throwing the box out the window. Along with their commentary about the sleek new shapes, the editors poked fun at the deco-techno names invented by manufacturers (e.g., Eject-o-Cube, Ajusto-Shelf, Handi-Bin, and Touch-a-Bar). By 1939, the Consumers Union had 85,000 members, with citizens from all over America informing themselves about products through the Union's three-tier rating scheme: Best Buy, Acceptable, and Not Acceptable.

In the early 1940s, consumer activism was preempted by the second World War (Mayer, 1989). The tide turned in 1945: The war was over, the GI Bill was passed, and Americans went on a buying spree. They clamored for new homes, appliances, and other consumer goods they had been denied during the war (Flexner, 1982, p. 150). According to the Consumers Union:

> By 1950, subscriptions to *Consumer Reports* had reached nearly half a million. These new subscribers, by and large, weren't interested in product testing as a way to reach a consumer utopia; they just wanted help in choosing among the flood of new products on the market. (*Consumer Reports*, Feb. 1986, p. 79)

Many consumers grew to rely on evaluations of products to help them decide which product features were useful and whether products actually worked in the ways manufacturers claimed. As the demand for new products increased, so too did the need for documents such as brochures, specifications, manuals, warranties, return policies, and other types of consumer information.

During the 1960s and 1970s, a series of federal initiatives led consumers to pay more attention to the documents created by business and industry.

[16] The Singer Manufacturing Company stands out as one of the notable exceptions. Its instruction guides, some as early as 1915, had clear task-oriented information and carefully drawn, beautifully airbrushed technical illustrations. For an example, see Figure 6.11 (p. 420).

Truth in Lending Act (1968). Promotes the informed use of consumer credit. Lenders are required to disclose finance charges and annual percentage rates in language that is clear and well-known. Credit and charge applications plus all solicitations must provide these disclosures in a prominent location or in a tabular format before the first transaction.

Fair Credit Reporting Act (1970). Requires credit agencies to report individual credit information in a fair, confidential, and accurate manner. A consumer report cannot be prepared unless credit agencies clearly and accurately disclose to the consumer that a report is being produced. Credit agencies must also make consumers aware of their right to request this information.

Real Estate Settlement Procedures Act (1974). Directs the government to produce or approve booklets that provide timely information explaining the costs and fees of real estate settlement costs. Booklets must include in clear and concise language a description and explanation of each cost in a real estate settlement, escrow accounts, unfair and unnecessary charges to be avoided, plus a sample of a settlement form.

Fair Credit Billing Act (1974). Promotes the informed use of credit to protect the consumer from unfair credit billing and credit card practices. Before an account is opened, the lender must disclose the finance charge, the method of determining the charge, and any other charges.

▲ **Table 2.1** *Examples of U.S. legislation that have given citizens legal rights and protections regarding goods, services, and communications.*

In 1962 President John Kennedy enunciated a "Consumer's Bill of Rights," which focused attention on consumers' rights to

- Purchase safe products
- Acquire accurate and clear information about products or services
- Choose among a variety of products and services at competitive prices
- Play a role in the formulation of government consumer policy (Mayer, 1989, p. 27)

Table 2.1 presents a number of important acts that were signed into law from the 1960s through the 1990s. Such legislation prompted consumerists to continue lobbying government about issues of product safety and comprehensible product information. Indeed, consumerists would actively champion citizens' rights to clear communication in what has been called "the plain language movement."

An International Plain Language Movement Puts Document Design on the Map

During the latter part of the twentieth century, citizens from around the world began to express their desire for documents they could understand, particularly citizens in the United States, the U.K., Australia, and Canada.

Plain Language in the United States

In the 1960s and 1970s, consumer affairs departments and "action lines" in newspapers and on radio and television sprang up as important re-

Magnuson-Moss Warranty-Federal Trade Commission Improvement Act (1975). Mandates organizations that offer warranties to provide a full and conspicuous disclosure of the terms and conditions of the warranty. The warranty must be simple and easily understood. It must explain the parts that the warranty covers, what the warranty covers if the product is defective, consumer expenses, and the steps that the consumer must follow for the warranty to be carried out.

Consumer Leasing Act (1976). A lease must explain accurately and in a clear and conspicuous manner a property description, cost of rent, other charges, an explanation of insurance, due dates of payments, and an explanation of how the lease can be ended.

Electronic Fund Transfer Act (1978). Requires that the terms and conditions of transferring money through electronic terminals be explained. Financial institutions must explain clearly the types of electronic transfers a consumer can initiate, any charges for a transfer, the right to receive documentation of a transfer, liability for unauthorized transfers, and the person to contact if an unauthorized transaction is made.

Truth in Savings Act (1991). Seeks uniformity in the disclosure of interest rates and fees associated with a bank account in advertisements or solicitations. Information about the account, such as interest rate, minimum balance, initial deposit, regular fees, and early withdrawals, must be explained in a clear and understandable way.

sources through which citizens could lodge public complaints against companies, utilities, landlords, and government agencies. It was a time of tremendous growth in the federal government, coupled with an oppressive increase in the amount of paperwork generated by new government programs. It was a time when people voiced questions about the integrity of government and business (Clive & Russo, 1981, p. 208). This increased activism had many spin-offs.

Beginning roughly at the time President Nixon resigned (1974), proponents of the plain language movement called for an end to "gobbledygook" in government and business documents, demanding communications that citizens could understand.[17] Interestingly, Stuart Chase, who had been so influential in the consumer movement, also played a role in foreshadowing the plain language movement. In *The Power of Words* (1953), Chase deplored the wretched use of language that flourished in bureaucracy, in the law, and in universities.

The plain language movement in the United States got its strongest support in 1978 when President Carter issued Executive Order 12044, designed to make "federal regulations clearer, less burdensome, and more cost effective" (Carter, 1979, p. 561). In it, he required that all major regulations be "as simple and clear as possible, written in plain English, and understandable to those who must comply with [them]" (Carter, 1979, p. 558). The following year, Carter issued Executive Order 12174, which came to be known as the *Paperwork Reduction Act*. In addition to reducing the paperwork coming from government, this act required agencies "to keep forms as short as possible ... elicit[ing] information in a simple, straightforward fashion" (Redish, 1985, p. 129).

[17] For a description of the plain language movement in the United States, see Bowen, Duffy and Steinberg (1991); Clive and Russo (1981); and Redish (1985).

These regulations had positive effects, leading the government to make a concerted effort to streamline its paperwork and redesign its forms for Medicare, Medicaid, tax collection (via documents from the Internal Revenue Service), and some federal programs. It also stimulated state governments to follow the example of New York—the first state in the United States to pass a "Plain Language Law"—and draft their own plain language legislation, particularly in the area of consumer contracts.[18] By 1991, eight states had passed statutes concerned with the plain language of consumer contracts.[19] State governments continue to enact plain language legislation (e.g., *The Plain Language Consumer Contract Act* was signed into law on June 24, 1993 in Pennsylvania).[20]

The momentum for plain language at the federal level declined significantly in 1981 when Carter's regulations were rescinded by President Reagan. As Redish (1985) points out, though, whether administrators in government agencies actually paid attention to these official government positions depended on their level of interest in plain language. Administrators in the Carter days who had no interest in the clarity of their documents paid lip service to the executive orders and did nothing. Those administrators who understood that clearly designed documents could save money for government continued to simplify their documents, even under Reagan (p. 130).

Initially, members of the research community endorsed government administrators who used the plain language approach, largely because they were supportive of *any* government action to improve the quality of what citizens read. Early in the movement, however, studies of the impact of so-called "plain language documents" raised serious doubts about the adequacy of the approach to actually improve documents. Researchers questioned the claims plain language advocates made about readers, particularly the claim that most people have difficulty decoding sentences and need documents that have been "dummied down." (The prototype audience had been the welfare recipient who could not interpret instructions well enough to fill in the requisite forms to receive payments.) Researchers pointed out that the audiences for documents have a variety of reading skills and the working assumption that all document readers were members of a lay audience was not only simplistic but inaccurate.

In addition to taking issue with the rather narrow construction of the reading public, researchers cast doubts on the validity of the methods used for assessing reading comprehension. Under severest scrutiny was an excessive reliance on readability formulas (Charrow & Charrow, 1979; Duffy, 1985; Klare, 1984; Redish & Selzer, 1985; Wright, 1988c). By the mid-1980s, studies in plain language were for the most part abandoned by the research community in the United States and the U.K., replaced by

[18] Felsenfeld (1991) presents an assessment of the plain language experience in New York.

[19] Kimble (1992) offers a comprehensive discussion of plain language legislation in the United States from the legal community's perspective.

[20] Pennsylvania's plain language legislation, House Bill 110 [P.N. 1839], is characterized from the business and legal community's perspective in Bernstein and Paschall (1993).

more broadly conceived efforts in document design. These new efforts examined readers' *actual* comprehension and use of documents, and thus shifted the focus from short words and sentences to larger discourse structures—paragraph, between-paragraph, and whole-text level considerations. Moreover, researchers directed their efforts toward understanding readers' responses not only to prose but also to visual language, including graphic design, typography, and illustration. In effect, during the 1980s researchers refined their methods for evaluating the quality of documents and expanded their definition of which aspects of documents to evaluate.

The United States was not the only country involved with the plain language movement. Researchers and practitioners in several other countries have also been involved with such issues for decades,[21] with the most noticeable activity occurring in the U.K., Australia, and Canada.

Plain Language in the U.K.

In England, the plain language movement, called the "Plain English Campaign," has been waging war on "gobbledygook" since 1979.[22] According to the leaders of the campaign, Chrissie Maher and Martin Cutts, their mission has been to rid the U.K. of forms, leaflets, and booklets "written in impersonal, pompous, or incomprehensible language that confuses and humiliates people" (Moss, 1987, p. 1). Maher—who could not read or write until she was 16 years old—reflects on why she got involved with this grassroots organization and helped cofound it:

> [I] had lived through the pain of being isolated and humiliated because of words. [I] vowed that one day [I] would make the world take notice. [I] did so by taking a truckload of forms to Parliament, setting up in full view of the House of Commons, and shredding the lot. (Kimble, 1992, p. 53)

The campaign for plain language is still going on today, under the aegis of a private company rather than as a public pressure group. Perhaps the most effective activity of the Campaign has been its annual awards competition. Since 1980, organizations have entered their best forms, leaflets, or

[21] For example, Kimble (1992) describes organizations in Canada, England, Australia, New Zealand, and Sweden that have started their own plain language movements, developed documents using plain language principles, or conducted research on the optimal design of documents. There is also a nascent consumer movement in Japan, rumored to have been started by Japanese housewives who were fed up with shoddy appliances.

---

[22] There is some debate over the year the Campaign began. According to a report by Moss (1987), the Campaign started in 1976 rather than 1979. But reports by Eagleson (1991) and Kimble (1992) suggest it was 1979. Although dating the movement is somewhat problematic, we know that from the beginning, the Campaign was closely allied with the National Consumer Council, a government-financed body established in 1975. For details about the origins of the Plain English Campaign, see Cutts and Maher (1986). For an update on plain language activities in the U.K., see Cutts (1993).

23 In the United States, a
similar contest, "The Worst
Manual of the Year," was
sponsored in 1993 by The
Communication Circle, a
company owned by author
and teacher Jonathan Price.

agreements to compete for Plain English Awards. At the same time, the public is invited to nominate examples of the worst documents for Golden Bull Awards.[23] Even the government has endorsed the efforts of the campaigners for plain language. In 1985, for example, the Civil Service and the Plain English Campaign cosponsored a Plain English exhibition, attended by Prime Minister Margaret Thatcher. And in 1986, the exhibit was displayed in the House of Commons (Kimble, 1992, p. 53). Clearly, such backing from the U.K.'s highest officials has been instrumental in keeping plain language before the public eye. This sort of official endorsement, helping to ensure the movement's momentum, has not occurred in the United States since the Carter administration.

For several decades, researchers in the U.K. have guided plain language campaigners away from pithy prescriptions about short sentences and simple words and have encouraged them instead to evaluate empirically readers' understanding of documents (Wright, 1980, 1988a). For an illustration of this "document design approach" in practice, see Cutts (1993), who describes the redesign of a legal document.

Plain Language in Australia

In Australia, the plain language movement began in 1976 when the NRMA insurance company, a subsidiary of the National Road Motorists Association, issued its first *Plain English Car Insurance Policy*. Eagleson (1991) suggests that unlike the movements in the U.K. and the United States, the Australian movement developed in established organizations in the private and public sector, mainly insurance companies, real estate agencies, and, to a lesser extent, government, particularly the Victoria Law Reform Commission (p. 36).

Once plain language documents were introduced, Australian businesses and government agencies found that they yielded considerable economic benefits. In the insurance industry, for example, companies that revised their forms and contracts using plain language principles discovered that the number of invalid claims fell, procedures were followed more efficiently, and employees who processed forms were more productive. It also took much less time to train staff and to provide accurate advice to customers. In government, the revision of one poorly designed summons led to the equivalent of a savings of $400,000 per year (Eagleson, 1991, p. 39). Moreover, litigation declined, demonstrating that plain language could work successfully in law. Plain language documents drew writers and readers together, simultaneously solving the different problems of each.

Plain language issues continue to be debated in Australia (Penman, 1993). For example, the Centre for Plain Legal Language hosted a conference in 1994 on plain language, during which researchers discussed the impact of taking a plain language approach to text revision on the quality of documents. This thorny issue has also been under investigation by the Communications Research Institute of Australia (CRIA). Since 1985, the CRIA has been contributing to knowledge about what makes documents work. Their studies suggest that plain language legal documents are not always superior to quasi-legal writing. CRIA researchers have been developing a set of principles that they believe will help writers produce legal texts that are more usable than those produced using plain language guidelines (Penman, 1990).

Plain Language in Canada

The plain language movement in Canada has been shaped largely by government action rather than by citizen activism. Started in the late 1980s, the movement took a big step forward in 1988 when a Plain Language Centre was established in Toronto by the Canadian Legal Information Centre (CLIC). It received initial funding from legal, corporate, and consumer groups and has been self-sustaining since 1991.[24] A report by Dykstra characterizes the Centre's mission as creating awareness about the movement and providing tools, training, and research needed to adopt the plain language approach (1991, p. 43).

[24] Reported in Kimble (1992, pp. 46–47).

The quality of legal documents has been a prominent catalyzing force behind plain language in Canada (for a discussion, see Jordan, 1994). In 1991 Saskatchewan became the first province to begin a government-wide program in clear language. In British Columbia the Plain Language Institute commissioned research on legal writing and produced a number of reports (however, according to Jordan, 1994, the Institute was recently discontinued). To date, plain language has been supported mainly by businesses involved in creating legal, financial, or insurance documents.

University and industry research labs have been at the forefront of Canadian work that goes beyond plain language to broader considerations of document design. For example, researchers at McGill University's Center for Cognitive Science have been tracking the process of producing technical documents collaboratively (Breuleux & Bracewell, 1994). Faculty from the department of English at the University of Waterloo in Ontario sponsored several international conferences on issues of quality in document design.[25] Cultural, rhetorical, and linguistic approaches to document design are under study by members of the Canadian Associa-

[25] Canadian conferences about document design issues continue to grow in number. Researchers and practitioners in computer documentation came to Ottawa in 1992 for the Association for Computing Machinery's Special Interest Group on Documentation (SIGDOC) Conference. Banff was the site for the 1994 Institute for Electronics and Electrical Engineers (IEEE) conference on Professional Communication.

tion of Teachers of Technical Writing (CATTW), a group that holds an annual conference and also publishes the informative journal *TechnoStyle*. And Bell Northern Research (now called Nortel) has made use of the findings of recent work in document design and has sponsored innovative research.

Practicing technical communicators, particularly in Western Canada, have been active in developing knowledge about document design. For example, Canada's bureau for Western Economic Diversification funded a project to evaluate the need for technical communication in organizations (both public and private sector) in Western Canada. This project, conducted in collaboration with professionals from the Manitoba, Alberta, and British Columbia Chapters of the Society for Technical Communication, has drawn a number of important conclusions about technical communication in Western Canada (see STC Manitoba et al., 1994a, 1994b). And from 1994 to 1996, Simon Fraser University (in Burnaby) and the International Wordsmiths Company (in Vancouver) sponsored the Vancouver Roundtable, a thinktank on technical communication, which focused on identifying international trends and on characterizing what professional communicators need to do in order to prepare for the future.

Consumers as Readers: Readers as Consumers

The trends described in the previous sections provide some perspective on how people's expectations about documents have developed. Since the early part of this century, consumers have become more sophisticated, demanding more from what they read and holding those organizations that design what they read more accountable. Increasingly, *consumers have come to understand that they have needs as readers and that these needs deserve to be met.*

Some readers (although certainly not most) now recognize that unintelligible documents are not natural disasters that have to be accepted like summer squalls or sleet storms. Rather, they know that poor documents are human artifacts produced by organizations that could be encouraged to take readers' needs more seriously. These readers sense that they can have a voice in improving document quality. Unfortunately, there appear to be many more who regard their troubles with poor documents as a reflection of their own failings as readers.[26]

Educating consumers about their rights to well-designed documents and educating organizations about how to create well-designed documents should be priorities in our field. Organizations need to recognize

[26] I will take up this misplaced sense of responsibility in Chapter 4, where I explore the relationship between how people think and feel as they try to understand texts and technology.

that whether they choose to refer to their audiences as "customers," "users," "citizens," or "consumers," their audiences are still readers (at least some of the time). Judging by the flood of poorly designed documents coming from all parts of the globe to consumers, this seemingly obvious point is apparently not so obvious. Yet even with the work that lies ahead, it is clear that the consumer and plain language movements of this century have made an important impact on how organizations think about communication. I turn now to another major impetus for the rise of document design.

Technology Shapes the Practice of Document Design

Document design activity has been growing in this century partly because the technologies for writing and visualizing have enabled it to take place on a larger scale than designers at the turn of the century could ever have imagined.[27] In this section, I trace the development of a few of the technologies that have catalyzed the growth of document design and modified the processes by which documents are composed.

[27] Technologies for printing, displaying, and distributing documents also grew, but here I sketch briefly only those for writing and design.

It may be hard for today's document designers to imagine a time when writers and designers carried around a jar of ink and a steel nib pen. Yet this is what had to be done in the nineteenth century if one wanted to write while away from a desk and use an implement other than a pencil. Steel nib pens not only created unwanted blots and splotches, but also required frequent replenishing of the ink supply, which slowed the writing process. And because users had to exert extra pressure to get the ink to flow, they often experienced cramps in their hands and arms (Foley, 1876, p. 46).

It was not until 1884 that Lewis Edson Waterman developed an effective fountain pen. According to a Presidential Commission on Economy and Efficiency, the Waterman was a success because it recognized that "ink was a difficult and dangerous liquid to carry in the pocket" (Presidential Commission, 1905–13). Although the Waterman did advance technology for writing, its users still had to fill the pen manually using an eyedropper. An improvement came in 1908 when W. A. Sheaffer refined the self-filling mechanism for fountain pens; his mechanism required a simple push of a lever to deflate an ink sack (Daniels, 1980, p. 316). Even with these improvements, though, the fountain pen was not a precision instrument. In design and illustration, areas in which control of line weight is crucial, better technologies were needed. As technologies for writing, design, and illustration developed, they changed the face of document design, both its processes and its products.

From Fountain Pens to Ballpoint Pens and Mechanical Pencils

A technology for writing that remedied the mess associated with fountain pens was the ballpoint pen. John Loud, an American inventor who patented a ballpoint pen in 1888, claimed that the pen was especially useful for, among other purposes, "marking on rough surfaces such as wood, coarse wrapping paper, and other articles where an ordinary pen could not be used" (U.S. Patent 392,046, October 30, 1888). However, because his design was never manufactured, Loud's original ballpoint was quickly forgotten. Fifty years later, two Hungarian brothers—Ladislao and Georg Biró—patented a ballpoint similar to Loud's. But before the Birós could bring their invention to the United States, American Milton Reynolds saw their pen while on a business trip to Argentina and developed his own based on the Birós' model. Reynolds brought his pen to market in 1945 at a cost of $12.50 (Petroski, 1993) and advertised it as "the miraculous pen that would revolutionize writing."[28] The pens used today, including roller balls and precision inking pens, are descendants of the ballpoint invented by John Loud and reinvented by the Birós.

Although many writers prefer pen to pencil, there are some writing and design situations in which only a pencil will do. According to Ernest Hemingway, "wearing down seven number two pencils is a good day's work" (Petroski, 1993, p. 324). And John Steinbeck (1969), whose journal entries attest to his seeming obsession with pencils—their points, shapes, and sizes—put it this way:

> For years I have looked for the perfect pencil. I have found very good ones but never the perfect one. And all the time it was not the pencils but me. A pencil that is all right some days is no good another day. For example, yesterday, I used a [Blackwing, made by the Eberhard Faber company] soft and fine and it floated over the paper just wonderfully. So this morning I try the same kind. And they crack on me. Posts break and all hell is let loose. This is the day when I am stabbing the paper. So today I need a harder pencil at least for a while. I am

---

[28] An entertaining account of the excitement that greeted the marketing of the ballpoint pen appeared in the *New Yorker* on February 17, 1951. Gimbels department store announced that ballpoint pens would arrive on October 29, 1945. By nine-thirty that morning 5,000 people were waiting to swarm through Gimbels' doors, and 50 extra policemen were hastily dispatched to restrain the throng. Inside the store, where ballpoint pens lay heaped in gleaming piles on the counters of two aisles running almost the entire length of the Thirty-second Street side, buying quickly reached the proportions of a stampede. In an attempt to break up the jam, Gimbels set up emergency counters, and during the day fresh supplies of pens were rushed in by plane (see Daniels, 1980, p. 318).

using some [Mongols] that are numbered 2⅜ round. I
have my plastic tray you know and in it three kinds of
pencils for hard writing days and soft writing days. Only
sometimes it changes in the middle of the day, but at least
I am equipped for it. I have also some super soft pencils
which I do not use very often because I must feel as
delicate as a rose petal to use them. (pp. 35–36; quoted in
Petroski, 1993, p. 325)

The quality of a finely crafted pencil was appreciated not only by
Nobel laureates such as Steinbeck, but also by people in other professions.
During World War II, when shortages in raw materials caused a cutback
in the manufacture of pencils made of the best materials, England's
Economist complained:

If the raw materials of pencils are to be limited, the needs
of the accredited pencil users must be safeguarded. The
draughtsman must have his hard pencil to draw the lines
of infinitesimal marking. The staff officer must have the
coloured pencils to mark his map in such a way that he
knows at a glance the course of the battle. The censorial
and editorial blue pencil[29] must not be crowded off the
market by the free distribution pencil advertising Buggin's
Beer. (June 6, 1942, p. 806)

More than anything else, people wanted their pencils to be made with
fine wood casings, erasers that didn't fall off, and hard graphite lead whose
point could be sharpened so finely that it could almost prick the finger.

[29] The blue pencil, appearing
around 1888, used a special
blue lead that made editing
marks invisible on photo-
copies.

Even the mechanical pencil, which by 1900 had more or less reached
its current form, did not seriously threaten the wood-cased kind for
almost a century. In fact, the first mechanical pencils were more like
novelties and pieces of jewelry than serious writing instruments; some
even came with companion toothpicks and ear spoons (Petroski, 1993).
But writers and draftspeople tended not to like them because early versions did not come in the right size, balance, weight, or surface finish to
make them suitable for extended periods of writing, and their relatively
thick leads did not give anywhere near the fine point possible in a sharpened wooden pencil. It would not be until the 1920s that mechanical
pencils began to be viewed as serious writing tools rather than gadgets.
Even then it would take decades of development before "serious" pencil
users would change their practices. Graphic designers, draftsmen, engineers, and architects preferred wood-cased pencils that they could sharpen
themselves. Many enjoyed using a knife to sharpen their pencils and
deliberately cut the wood severely to minimize any obstruction of the
drawing work by the pencil itself. A textbook for a U.S. Navy Draftsman

▶ Figure 2.3 *From the patent application for the first typewriter by Latham Sholes, Carlos Glidden, and Samuel W. Soulé in 1868. Courtesy of the U.S. Patent Office, Washington, DC.*

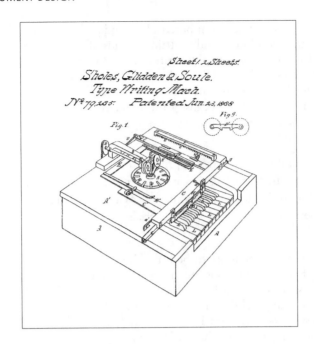

course recommended this practice: "If you use a pencil with a long, exposed lead, you will be able to see around the line as you draw" (United States Bureau of Naval Personnel, 1955, p. 148).

The wood-cased pencil continues to be remarkably popular. Even today, graphic artists who own precision mechanical pencils still keep wood-cased pencils around. Early reports that the typewriter and later the computer would be the end of the wood-cased pencil proved to be false. Petroski (1993) points out that pencils are being manufactured at a worldwide rate of about 14 billion per year (p. 331), suggesting that reports of the pencil's impending demise have been greatly exaggerated.

Twice as Fast as a Pen: The Typewriter

Despite the durability of pen and pencil technologies as "generic wordprocessors" (Schrodt, 1982), there is no doubt that writing with one's own hand cannot be done with great speed. Research on composing suggests advantages for technologies that intrude less into the writing process, that enable writing to proceed more quickly, and that generate more legible text.[30] The typewriter was the first technology to offer such advantages. Invented by Latham Sholes, Carlos Glidden, and Samuel W. Soulé in 1868, the typewriter went through many experimental iterations before a marketable one was produced. The earliest typewriter looked more like a small piano than a writing instrument, leading some to call it the "literary piano" (the photo from the patent is shown in Figure 2.3).

[30] For a discussion of the influence of technology on the writing process, see, for example, the work of Burtis, Bereiter, Scardamalia, and Tetroe (1983), Haas (1996), Haas and Hayes (1986b), and Scardamalia and Bereiter (1983).

The Sholes, Glidden, and Soulé team later collaborated with Philo Remington, who manufactured the first thousand typewriters in a factory built for making sewing machines, farm equipment, and guns. In fact, the Remington Model I, first marketed in 1874, was attached to a sewing machine base (see Figure 2.4). Unlike modern typewriters, it typed only in capitals, and the carriage was returned by means of a foot pedal.

The most striking limitation of the first Remington was that its design obstructed from view what had just been typed. The typist had to wait until the paper scrolled up before the words became visible, usually a few sentences later (Daniels, 1980, p. 321). The other drawback was its price: At $125 in 1874 dollars, it was much too expensive for the average

◀ **Figure 2.4** *The Remington Model I, first marketed in 1874. Courtesy of the Hagley Museum and Library, Wilmington, DE.*

business. But as Mark Twain—the first American author ever to submit a manuscript to a publisher using the writing machine—pointed out:

> It piles an awful stack of words on one page. It don't muss things or scatter ink blots around. Of course it saves paper.[31]

The early typewriter's biggest advantage was that users could type from 30 to 60 words per minute, more than twice as fast as a pen (Current, 1954, p. 86). But as an early advertisement shows (see Figure 2.5), the Remingtons seem to have misunderstood the audience who would want to take advantage of this new speed. Though they did say it was a useful

[31] Reported by Current (1954, p. 72); quoted from Paine (1912, p. 536).

▶ Figure 2.5 *An early advertisement for a Remington appearing in December, 1875. The text has been retyped to enhance its legibility. The writing style and the layout of the type is exactly as it was in the original. Reprinted with the permission of Richard N. Current, author of the 1954 book,* The Typewriter and the Men Who Made It *(University of Illinois Press, Urbana, IL).*

tool for editors, authors, and clergymen—all of whom had to undergo "the drudgery of the pen"—the Remingtons focused their attention on court reporters, "those mere girls who could earn from $10 to $20 per week in courtrooms in the city" (Current, 1954, p. 86). Had they methods for predicting the size of the audience for their new writing technology, improvements might have come more rapidly.

Typewriter technology became more oriented for writing in 1892, when Thomas Oliver patented the first *visible* typewriter. Instead of forcing writers to remember what was just typed (a burden on short-term memory), Oliver's machine allowed writers to use the "text produced so far" (Hayes & Flower, 1980) to "shape at the point of utterance" (Britton, 1975). The visible typewriter made it easier to plan while one was typing, a boon for all professional writers.

However, in most settings, the visible typewriter was used mainly for copying, not composing. It is doubtful that the advantage of the visible typewriter over its predecessors had any effect on the writing processes of professionals who were not writers (e.g., managers, lawyers, or engineers). For the most part, professionals did not use typewriters for composing; they wrote their texts longhand and gave them to office workers for transcribing.[32] (That typewriters were perceived mainly for copying is evident in Figure 2.5; see "Copying Wanted.")

The most successful of the early visible typewriters was the Underwood. Marketed in the early 1900s, it quickly became a favorite among writers; in fact, it is still used by some writers today (mainly by those who hate computers). Surprisingly, electric typewriters, also available around the turn of the century, did not gain wide acceptance until after World War II, when IBM introduced its Executive with proportional spacing. During the decade following the war, electric typewriters became permanent fixtures in office environments.

Another advance came in 1961, when IBM introduced the Selectric I. Designed by Eliot Noyes, it featured a "golf ball" typing element and a stationary paper carriage. Later models of the Selectric, with their correct-

---

[32] The roots of this separation are related to the way corporate America was defining itself, its values for work, and the roles of its workers. The overwhelming enthusiasm for scientific management (see Taylor, 1911) at the turn of the century led business to value the typewriter because it increased the efficiency of producing communications, with skilled typists able to type at rates three to four times faster than the normal handwriting rate (80 to 120 words per minute). Business also valued separating the jobs of those who composed the messages from those who produced them, consciously segregating owners, managers, and executives, usually well-paid men, from typists, stenographers, and secretaries, mainly low-paid women (for a discussion, see Yates, 1989, pp. 42–44).

ing tape and changeable typeface elements (e.g., pica, elite, courier, and orator) would become the most coveted of the modern typewriters. Even with the optional typefaces, however, the designs one could create were still constrained by the physical limitations of the technology itself. Typewriters offered few choices for formatting the text; in fact, single spacing, double spacing, and triple spacing, along with the ability to "set tabs," were the only options. Constraints had the effect of encouraging, perhaps even solidifying, the use of unattractive conventions for design, such as the following:

- Centering headings in uppercase—conveys a dense and hard-to-read look. When headings are long and require three or more lines, centering them can create an ugly negative space around the type.

- Overusing the underscore (i.e., underlining)—flattens the hierarchy of the document. When too much underlining is used, all levels of the text tend to look equally important; thus, nothing seems special.

- Formatting documents in block-style single columns with long lines of tiny type—renders the page an uninviting shade of gray. When long lines of tiny type are set with straight left and right margins, it makes the text look serious and stuffy (see Chapter 5).

▶ **Figure 2.6** *In 1956 graduate students in industrial administration try out the first computer, an IBM 650, at the Carnegie Institute of Technology (now Carnegie Mellon). Manufactured in 1953, the IBM 650 was a digital type machine that used magnetic drum technology. Notice there is no keyboard. It was the "first digital computer installed in over 1,000 locations" (Kidwell & Ceruzzi, 1994, p. 73). The same year,1953, IBM launched its first mainframe, the Model 701. For a discussion of the first IBM instruction manual for the 701 mainframe, see Brockmann (1996). Photo courtesy of Carnegie Mellon University Archives, Pittsburgh, PA.*

Technology for Writing and Design Comes of Age:
The Computer

Eventually, computers would free users from many of the limitations of typewriter technology. However, the transition was not instantaneous. Although computers developed rapidly after World War II, they were viewed primarily as "number crunchers" designed to speed the processing of scientific and engineering calculations. Little about early computers suggested the role they would eventually play in writing and design. For example, early computers were not even supplied with keyboards (see Figure 2.6 on the previous page); instead, they relied on punch cards, tape drives, or manually set switches for inputting data.

Even after keyboards came into use (c. 1967), mainframe computers were still inconvenient for writing and practically useless for design. (Figure 2.7 is an example of a once-popular mainframe system.) Any veteran writer will attest that the line editors that ran on the mainframe systems of the 1960s and 1970s required endless troubleshooting in order to get a document to print as desired. It could easily take pages and pages of "setup" commands just to print a document with numbered procedures, boldface headings, and two or three tab stops (making columns was out of the question). And because it was impossible to predict what the printed page would look like from what was displayed on the computer screen (i.e., no WYSIWYG), writers spent endless hours reprinting.

◀ Figure 2.7 *The IBM System/360 Model 30 mainframe computer was first released in 1965. It represented a new generation of machines with integrated circuits, fully compatible to function as a family. Shown here is a configuration for a university environment in the late 1960s. By the end of 1970, almost 5,000 IBM System/360s had been installed, almost twice the 1964 estimate (Kidwell & Ceruzzi, 1994, p. 74). Like businesses, universities would later abandon mainframes in favor of local area networks. Photo courtesy of Carnegie Mellon University Archives, Pittsburgh, PA.*

The earliest computer intended for writing was called a *wordprocessor*. Introduced in the 1970s, early wordprocessors consisted of a keyboard, a screen, and a central processing unit (CPU). Like using a computer connected to a mainframe, their advantage was the elimination of the need to retype text revisions. Unlike being connected to a mainframe, wordprocessors offered portability, and they were not slowed by other people logged onto the same system. But these advantages did not enhance the design of documents. As Barker points out (1988), the visual format of wordprocessed documents varied little from the typewriter, even though the production methods changed significantly. The design features offered by the wordprocessor included the option to boldface the type, to center and underline automatically, and to "force-justify" the type (that is, to put spaces between the words so that both left and right margins aligned).

From the point of view of document design, the ability to boldface the type was the only improvement. Although the wordprocessor made centering and underlining easier, it did little to provide options for desktop design. Its most touted feature, force justification, operated by inserting uneven blankspaces between words, creating ugly vertical "rivers" through the text. To solve this, users often resorted to hyphenating words at the end of lines, not realizing they were introducing a new design problem (i.e., consecutive hyphens in paragraphs made an unsightly right margin).

Aside from the poor aesthetics caused by force justification, research indicates that uneven wordspacing may have a negative affect on the legibility of the text, requiring the eye to adjust for wide and narrow word spaces.[33] Because force justification adjusts each line of type to be of equal length, it eliminates the desirable characteristic of visual diversity across consecutive lines, making rereading more likely.

[33] See, for example, research reported in Fabrizio, Kaplan and Teal (1967), Gregory and Poulton (1970), Rehe (1981), and Trollip and Sales (1986). Typographic and spatial cues in documents are examined in Chapter 5.

Although wordprocessors did not contribute significantly to improving document design, they did set the stage for computing technologies that would. The first practical personal computers (PCs)—the Apple II in 1978, the IBM PC in 1981, and the Apple Macintosh in 1984—made it readily apparent that computers could enable document design in beneficial ways. However, organizations in the late 1970s and early 1980s tended to purchase computers mainly for accountants and secretaries rather than for writers and designers. Not until the mid-1980s did most organizations dedicate hardware and software to writing and design. Companies that had been reticent about computers made a wholesale shift to composing on PCs, minicomputers, and workstations (for definitions of the various types of computers, see Kidwell & Ceruzzi, 1994). By early

1985, it was apparent that computers had changed not only the ways in which documents could be generated but also the nature of the documents themselves—shifting the focus from paper to the computer screen.

Caught up in the so-called desktop publishing revolution, professional writers eagerly (and uncritically) sought out software that allowed them to integrate text and graphics (see Kalmbach, 1988). However, graphic designers—who understood the complexity of visual thinking—felt that software companies had grossly oversold "easy" design. They scoffed at advertisers' claims that page layout software would lead to better quality in design. They saw the desktop revolution as promoting mediocrity and ugliness (Barker, 1988). Experienced designers and typographers were appalled that so many people (including some of their longtime clients) could be hoodwinked into thinking that the results of "dumping text" into page layout templates and "copying and pasting" clip-art were synonymous with expert design. Although professionals tacitly knew that quality design and illustration were not just a "click" away, very few of them could characterize their expertise in ways that nondesigners could appreciate.[34]

Fortunately, recent developments in hardware and software for desktop publishing (DTP) have provided tangible benefits for professional writers and designers. The 1980s saw many types of new hardware—including two-page color displays, external storage devices, scanners, CD-ROMs, ergonomically-designed keyboards, and laser printers. (Even well-designed chairs and desks have made sitting in front of the screen all day more comfortable). Although the earliest versions of applications such as Pagemaker were not very exciting, they did focus the software industry's attention on refining products for document design. In the 1990s, DTP software has become better adapted to the needs of experienced designers (e.g., Quark Express 3.32, Pagemaker 6.01, Framemaker 5, Adobe Illustrator 6.0, and Adobe Photoshop 3.05). The demand for high-end DTP has led companies such as Adobe and Monotype to redesign hundreds of old and new typefaces for the computer (see Gottschall, 1989). Improvements in software for document design have not only made mundane aspects of the process less tedious (e.g., checking spelling, building indexes, or sizing photos) but have also afforded increased precision in integrating type, image, and sound. Developments in software and hardware continue to influence document design processes—especially planning and revising. Changes have also allowed for global video conferencing, enabling collaboration across national borders. The next section sketches the influence of scientific and technological innovation on the demand by industry and government for professional document designers.

[34] The need for writers and graphic designers to be able to articulate convincingly their sensitivities, knowledge, and skills is one of the most important reasons for taking an advanced degree in writing or design. I discuss this idea more fully in the last section of this chapter.

Science and Technology Create a Need for Document Design

The "Science, Technology and Environment" strand of *The Timeline* (pp. 104–149) overviews some of the developments and innovations that catalyzed the growth of document design in the twentieth century. As activity in science and technology increased, so too did the demand for communications that would help people understand and take advantage of new developments (whether all of those developments were actually helpful is another story). Historians of technical communication often cite two critical periods in the development of professional activity in the field. One of these periods is the 1940s and 1950s, when the defense industry needed easy-to-understand manuals for operating its equipment:

> After the end of the war [World War II], technical writing finally became a genuine profession as wartime technologies were translated into peacetime uses. The giant technological corporations—General Electric, Westinghouse, GM—opened separate departments of technical writing after finding that it was no longer cost-effective to pay engineers both to design and write. (Connors, 1982, p. 341)

The second period, the late 1970s through the present, marks the so-called computer revolution, a time when hardware and software products for the home, school, and industry proliferated. Of course, the development of computer-related technologies generated an enormous need for well-designed documents, a need that has not gone away.

These characterizations, however, do not fully capture the historical record. They paint a picture that is too simple, too tidy. They suggest that document design in the twentieth century can be represented as a post-1940 activity taking shape mainly around the defense and computer industries. But as *The Timeline* makes apparent, the need for document design arose earlier and was much broader. Between 1900 and 1940, for example, hundreds of documents were designed for products such as automobiles, sewing machines, farm tractors, washing machines, cameras, hand tools, phonographs, typewriters, mimeograph machines, dictation machines, shortwave radios, and airplanes. Technologies such as these created a need for communications ranging from instructions and warranties to documents about safety and maintenance. Let's look at a few documents that are illustrative of those used in the early part of the twentieth century.

Figure 2.8 presents a few pages from a guide to the 1922 Hawk-Eye camera by Kodak. It shows a number of writing and design conventions for instructions that were typical at that time. The most striking visual

PART I

THE No. 2 Film Pack Hawk-Eye Camera is of the fixed focus type of camera, therefore objects nearby and at a distance will be sharp without the necessity of focusing. Subjects that are 11½ feet and further from the camera will be perfectly sharp, and objects as near as 8 feet distant, while not as sharp, will be sharp enough for all practical purposes. Do not attempt to take pictures of subjects nearer to the camera than 8 feet, without using a Kodak Portrait Attachment. See page 14.

Kodak
Film Pack
(No. 520)

Loading the Camera

Open the back of the camera. To do this, hold the camera in the manner as shown in illustration (Fig.I), placing the fingers of both hands on the top of the camera. Push up the back about one-quarter of an inch with the two thumbs and then lift it off. Place the thumbs near the middle of the back, as illustrated in Fig. I. The back is secured by means of two projections on the edges.

The back of the camera having been removed, place the film

Fig. I.

1

Important

When making instantaneous exposures with any camera, hold it firmly against the body as shown in

8

illustrations, and when pushing the exposure lever, hold the breath for the instant.

9

feature is the use of high-quality black-and-white photography throughout.[35] Here, we see a young man in his Sunday go-to-meeting clothes presenting the correct way to hold the camera. Unfortunately, although someone paid a good deal of attention to his clothing and hair style, we cannot see precisely which button he is pressing nor exactly where he is looking.

Conspicuously absent from the photos is a sense of context, something one might expect in instructions about shooting pictures. We can only wonder what the creators of this manual were thinking when they posed the young man, photographed him, and then cut away the background, placing his photo in a white box with the caption "Important."

Also worth noting is how similar the layout and typography of the procedural text are to what one might find in a novel. The body text is formatted in traditional block-style paragraphs with centered headings and subheadings; see the first panel, "Loading the Camera." The text is set in a serif font and is wrapped around the smaller pictures. Italic type is used to highlight the procedures, although not consistently so (see the procedure under the pictures; it is in plain type). There also appears to be some borrowing from the conventions of the novel in the way sections are named (e.g., the use of "Part I").

Although the use of most of these document conventions would eventually disappear—paragraphs would be broken up to visually separate procedures, headings would be positioned more strategically, and sections

▲ Figure 2.8 *Pages from a 1922 instruction guide for the Hawk-Eye camera by Kodak. The guide illustrates the procedures for using the camera with many photographs. But the procedures are more difficult to sort out than they need to be. The steps are buried in dense paragraphs formatted in the shape of a block. Here, a young man in formal attire shows the correct way to hold the camera. Thanks to Joyce Young for finding this instruction guide. Used with the permission of the Kodak Corporation, Rochester, NY.*

[35] Although photographs were used in this manual, it was more typical at the time to see line drawings or airbrushed art. The use of photos here may be more related to the product being a camera than a trend in document design.

would be given task-oriented names—there was an unfriendly character-istic of these procedures that would linger. That characteristic was the point of view of the instructions. *The first sentence immediately puts into focus the product and its capabilities rather than the questions and goals the reader might have.* This product-focused approach—with its attention on functions and features—would dominate the design of instruction guides well into the 1980s and even the 1990s.

Lest we believe that all early twentieth-century procedural documents ignored the reader's tasks, consider Figure 2.9, part of a set of instructions for a 1924 Model T Ford. In contrast to the camera instructions, those for the Model T are organized around the reader's questions. Though the phrasing of some of the language could be improved and the questions need not be numbered, overall the orientation is focused on what the reader wants to know, a characteristic of well-designed instructions.[36]

The technical illustration of "what's under the hood" clearly indicates the location of parts and wires, although we might quibble with the naming conventions of these parts and wires. Notice how the illustrator chose a line weight and color value for the leader lines (i.e., the lines

[36] Numbering the questions may have been related to Ford's intent to demonstrate how many questions they anticipated and answered. For a discussion of the writing style of car manuals, see Brockmann (1996), who characterizes the owners' guides for Fords and Chevrolets manufactured between 1912 and 1988.

▶ Figure 2.9 *Part of a set of instructions from a 1924 Model T Ford. Unlike most procedural documents of its time, this operations manual was organized around readers' questions; in fact, dozens of them. The text has been retyped to enhance its legibility. Courtesy of the Ford Motors Corporation, Detroit, MI.*

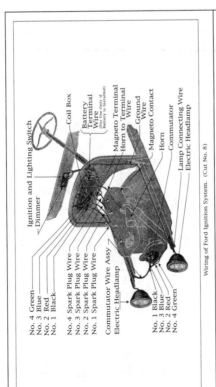

The Ford Ignition System

What is the purpose of the Ignition System?   Answer No. 53

It furnishes the electric spark which explodes the charge in the combustion cham-ber, thus producing the power which runs the engine. It is important that the charge be correctly ignited at the proper time, in order to obtain satisfactory results in running the car. In the Ford car the ignition system is as simple as it is possible to make it.

How does the Magneto generate the current?   Answer No. 54

In revolving at the same rate of speed as the motor, the magnets on the flywheel passing the stationary coil spools create an alternating low tension electric current in coils of wire which are wound around spools fastened to the stationary part of the magneto, and is carried from these coils to the magneto connection (wire) leading to the coil box on the dash.

Should the Coil Vibrator Adjustment be disturbed?   Answer No. 55

The present style of coil unit is properly adjusted when it leaves the factory and this adjustment should not be disturbed unless to install new points. When adjustments are necessary they should, whenever possible, be made by one of our service stations who have special equipment for testing and adjusting units and will gladly furnish expert service. If the points are pitted they should be carefully smoothed with an oilstone or file and the adjusting thumb nut turned down so that the gap between the vibrator and the core of the unit will be a trifle less than 1/32" of an inch. Then set the lock nut so that the adjustment can not be disturbed. Do not bend or hammer on the vibrators, as this would affect the operation of the cushion spring of the vibrator bridge and reduce the efficiency of the unit.

How is a Weak Unit Detected?   Answer No. 56

With the vibrators properly adjusted, if any particular cylinder fails or seems to develop only a weak action, change the position of the unit to determine if the fault is actually in the unit. The first symptom of a defective unit is the buzzing of the vibrator with no spark at the plug. Remember that a loose wire connection, fault spark plug, or worn commutator may cause irregularity in the running of the motor. These are points that should be considered before laying the blame on the coil.

How may short circuit in Commutator Wiring be detected?   Answer No. 57

Should the insulation of the primary wires (running from coil to commutater) become worn to such an extent that the copper wire is exposed–the current will leak out (i.e., short circuit) whenever contact with the engine pan or other metal parts is made. A steady buzzing of one of the coil units will indicate "short" in the wiring. When driving the car the engine will suddenly lag and pound on account of the premature explosion. Be careful not to crank the engine downward against compression when the car is in this condition, as the "short" is apt to cause a vigorous "back kick."

connecting parts to their names) that is distinct from those used for the illustration itself. (The leader lines are slightly thicker and black on an image of mainly gray and white.) This strategy maximizes the contrast among the elements of the illustration and allows readers to distinguish parts and lines easily. It also serves to maintain the legiblity even if the illustrations are printed under less-than-optimal conditions.

A drawback of the Model T manual is that it presents most of the technical illustrations flipped over on their sides, requiring readers to turn their heads sideways in order to read them. The unfriendly practice of presenting illustrations, charts, and graphs in a disorienting way (i.e., vertically instead of horizontally) and of separating illustrations physically from the prose they should be integrated with (e.g., the annoying practice of "see figure X [somewhere] at the end of this report") still plagues many organizations that produce documents.

As we can see from the examples in Figures 2.8 and 2.9, document design conventions for procedural instructions were already well under development prior to 1940, albeit by imitation (e.g., by emulating literary genres) and perhaps by default. Roughly during the same period, genres such as the scientific experimental article (see Bazerman, 1988) and the technical report (see Ray Palmer Baker's 1924 textbook on the topic) became more sophisticated. Unfortunately, the visual conventions for the many types of functional documents used in business and academe developed largely without the benefit of insights from the graphic design community, whose members tended to focus on advertising design (see the "Education & Practice in Graphic Design" strand of *The Timeline,* pp. 106–148).

As scientific discovery and technological innovation spurred the growth of document design, so too did the increasing size of business and government and the consequent needs for technologies of communication. Organizations soon found that documents were excellent vehicles for getting their messages out to employees and customers. Indeed, as Yates (1989) points out, documents such as reports, proposals, instructions, benefits, safety information, policies, and procedures became important technologies for maintaining control through communication in organizations (control in both the positive and negative sense of the term).

Yates suggests that during the early part of the century, companies derived their own genres for written communication—reports, forms, company magazines, memos, even their own company-mandated prose— all without the help of academia. But private business would not be the largest player among organizations that designed their own documents. The U.S. government quickly got into the act and rapidly institutionalized many of this century's worst document design practices. Government publications have been notorious for providing readers with

- Incomprehensible and ambiguous prose, especially in the form of "if-then" constructions (e.g., in Internal Revenue Service instructions for filling out tax forms)

- Hard-to-understand forms, charts, and tables (e.g., in Social Security, Medicare, and Medicaid documents)

- Important information presented in "fine print" or buried in appendices (e.g., in student loan information)

- The institutional "gray page"—created by text set in justifed right "block style" format, small type, tight leading, and little blank space (e.g., the design of many Government Printing Office publications)

- A patronizing tone of voice (e.g., in brochures about AIDS and in procedure manuals for U.S. military personnel)

In 1913, for example, Americans paid their first income tax to the Internal Revenue Service and used what would become a model for later versions of the now infamous U.S. tax forms. As shown in Figure 2.10 (on the next two pages), the IRS distributed information to taxpayers who were anxious to learn what the law required and how much they would have to pay. Although the early form and instructions were much shorter than the one many taxpayers use today (the 1040A), even the first one suffered from problems of legal language and poor design. For example, the instructions to fill out the form advised citizens in this way:

> 14. If debts contracted prior to the year for which return is made were included as income in return for year in which said debts were contracted, and such debts shall subsequently prove to be worthless, they may be deducted under the head of losses in the return for the year in which such debts were charged off as worthless. (IRS Instructions for Form 1040, 1913)

Notice also that the instructions are presented in a justified-right format, the leading is tight, there are no subheadings, and there is little blank space. In the 84 years since this first form was created, the IRS has moved to a three-column format and has started to use ragged-right margins, but it still employs tight leading, few subheadings, and little blankspace. For a more recent IRS form and readers' comments about the features used, see Figures 5.11 (p. 296) and 5.12 (p. 301). Unfortunately, the U.S. government has been much slower than business to improve its document design processes and products.

Examples such as these illustrate that document design in the twentieth century has been more than an appendage to the military or the computer industry. As Brockmann points out, there are "extremely rich areas to investigate that go beyond the military manual mills of World War II, the oft mentioned birthplace of technical writing" (1983, p. 155). In fact, the field was already quite diverse when Joseph Chapline documented the first computer manual for the BINAC (the Binary Automatic Computer) in 1949 (see Brockmann, 1990, 1996). Chapline's achievement, important for launching the field of computer documentation, was made in the context of a long line of activity. The history of twentieth-century document design reminds us that although prior to the 1950s the field had not yet flourished as a named profession, the development of practitioner knowledge was already underway in the early 1900s. Activity in the first half of the century set in motion text conventions, formats, and illustration styles that were later elaborated, revised, or abandoned as knowledge about document design developed. (The section following this one describes how practice in document design moved from a kind of ad-hoc activity to one based more on experience, knowledge, and research.)

The second half of the twentieth century saw the creation of publications departments in many businesses and industries. Organizations that began with a single product or service that required only a small staff expanded and ultimately became some of the largest producers of documents (e.g., organizations in the aerospace, consumer electronics, business machine, computer, and telecommunications industries). The post-World War II period also saw an increase in the need for other types of scientific and technical communications, including scientific journalism, corporate communications, public affairs, proposal writing, and technical illustration. Research and public concern for protecting the environment[37] eventually led to legislation such as the 1969 Environmental Policy Act, which in turn created a need for environmental impact statements and resulted in positions for writers and designers in risk communications and public policy communications (Killingsworth & Palmer, 1992; Lundgren, 1994).

Design historian Victor Margolin (1989b) characterizes the setting for design in the post-World War II era in this way:

> [T]he war's end is a watershed because ... it marks the commencement of a new historical phase in which many of the forces that shape our present economy and culture

---

[37] Research about the environment has not played as large a role as technology and science in the growth of document design, but it has been a vital force since the early 1960s. Since Rachel Carson's *Silent Spring* (1962), which helped expose the damage that could be caused by the indiscriminate use of pesticides, citizens have grown more concerned not only with product quality and safety but also with the health of the planet itself. They have raised questions about the effect of pollutants such as automobile emissions on the environment. What was viewed as a fringe movement in the 1960s is considered part of the mainstream in the 1990s. Document designers have helped to put these issues into words and pictures.

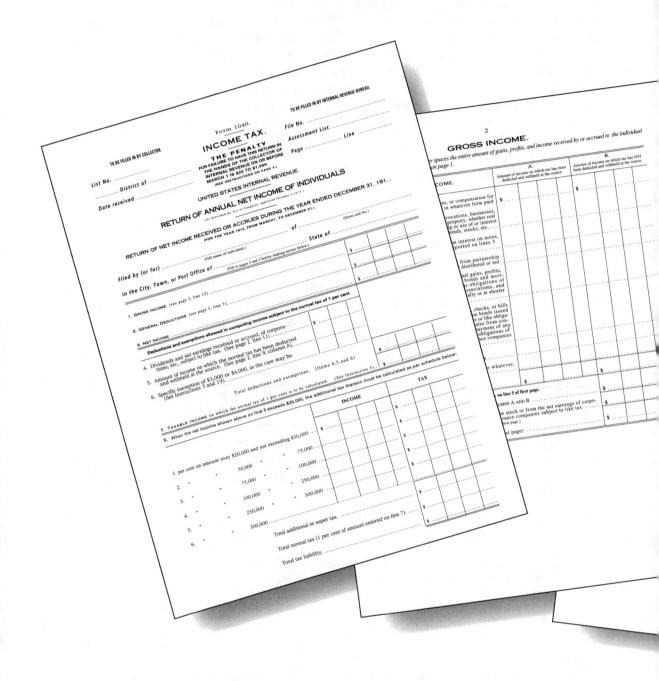

▲ **Figure 2.10** *A reproduction of the first 1040 form printed by the Internal Revenue Service in 1913. It consisted of three pages of questions to fill in and one page of instructions about how to do it. The complexity of today's tax code makes it impossible to have one page of instructions. Another difference between 1913 and today is that Americans can now file their tax returns electronically using online services. By contrast, many people in 1913 stood on line to pay their taxes in person. Courtesy of the National Archives, Washington, DC.*

4

INSTRUCTIONS.

1. This return shall be made by every citizen of the United States, whether residing at home or abroad, and by every person residing in the United States, though not a citizen thereof, having a net income of $3,000 or over for the taxable year, and also by every nonresident alien deriving income from property owned and business, trade, or profession carried on in the United States by him.

2. When an ...

neither shall he be required to include such estimated rental of his home as income.

11. The farmer, in computing the net income from his farm for his annual return, shall include all moneys received for produce and animals sold, and for the wool and hides of animals slaughtered, provided such wool and hides are sold, and he shall deduct therefrom the sums actually paid as purchase money for the animals sold or slaughtered during the year.

When animals were raised by the owner and are sold or slaughtered he shall not deduct their value as expenses or loss. He may deduct the amount of money actually paid as expense for producing any farm products live stock, etc. In deducting expenses for repairs on farm property the amount deducted must not exceed the amount actually expended for such repairs during the year for which the return is made. (See page 3, item 6.) The cost of replacing tools or machinery is a deductible expense to the extent that the cost of the new articles does not exceed the value of the old.

12. In calculating losses, only such losses as actually sustained during the year and the amount of which ...

13. Persons receiving ...
other services, as ...
include all actual ...
which return is ma ...
services, or contin ...
collectible.

14. Debts which w ...
return is made, but fo ...
deducted from gross in ...
not be regarded as wor ...
recover the same have p ...
for the debtor is insolvent ...
year in which said debts w ...
subsequently prove to be wo ...
the head of losses in the retur ...
were charged off as worthless.

15. Amounts due or accrued ...
partnership from the net earni ...
apportioned and distributed or i ...
annual return of the individual.

16. United States pensions shall be ...
17. Estimated advance in value of r ...
to be reported as income, unless the ...
in the books of the individual as an i ...
18. Costs of suits and other legal proce ...
ry business may be treated as an expen ...
ly be deducted from gross income for t ...
ts were paid.

9. An unmarried individual or a married ...
wife or husband shall be allowed an ex ...
husband and wife live together they ...
a total exemption of only $4,000 on their ...
may make a joint return, both subscrib ...
case separate incomes, both make separate returns; ...
o case shall they jointly claim more than $4,000 ...
their aggregate net income there shall be excluded the ...
computing net income of all officers and employees of a State or any ...
on thereto, or if ...
subdivision thereof, except when such compensation is ...
United States Government.

e 2-7357

3

GENERAL DEDUCTIONS.

...essary expenses actually paid in carrying on business, but not including ...es of partnerships, and not including personal, living expenses

...in the year on personal indebtedness of taxpayer.

...ounty, school, and municipal taxes paid within the year (not including those ...al benefits)

...ined during the year incurred in trade or arising from fires, storms, or ...compensated for by insurance or otherwise

...been actually ascertained to be worthless and which have been charged

...reasonable allowance for the exhaustion, wear, and tear of property ...or employment in the business, not to exceed, in the case of mines, ...value at the mine of the output for the year for which the computation ...tion shall be made for any amount of expense of restoring property ...ustion thereof, for which an allowance is or has been made

	$		

...ONS" (to be entered on line 2 of firs page)

...DAVIT TO BE EXECUTED BY INDIVIDUAL MAKING HIS OWN RETURN.

...) that the foregoing return, to the best of my knowledge and belief, contains a true and complete ...income received by or accrued to me during the year for which the return is made, and that I am ...emptions entered or claimed therein, under the Federal Income-tax Law of October 3, 1913

...me this _____

...)

ADDRESS IN FULL.	(Signature of agent.)

...y.)

...INSTRUCTIONS ON BACK OF THIS PAGE.)
...ED BY DULY AUTHORIZED AGENT MAKING RETURN FOR INDIVIDUAL.

...e sufficient knowledge of the affairs and property of
...hereof, and that the foregoing return, to the best of my knowledge and belief, contains
...and income received by or accrued to said individual during the year for which the
...ed, under the Federal Income-tax Law of October 3, 1913, to all the deductions

ADDRESS IN FULL.	(Signature of agent.)

...ONS ON BACK OF THIS PAGE.)

> became dominant. These include advertising, television, life-threatening technology, a realignment of developed, developing, and underdeveloped nations, the swift international circulation of capital, the staking out of global markets, the rise in consumer expectations, the breakdown of distinctions between high and popular culture, and a new wave of intelligent machines. (p. 265)

Over the past several decades, the legacy of these developments has been a move toward specialization. In document design, it has led to a shift in the talents and educational experiences for which employers look. Many organizations now find a bachelor's degree in the arts or humanities to be insufficient preparation for professional communicators in their environment. Instead, they tend to look for new hires who hold bachelor's or master's degrees in writing or design and who also possess domain knowledge in a subfield of education, science, technology, or business. For example, employers may look for students who major in writing or design who also possess

- An "education speciality" in instructional design, adult learning, computer-assisted instruction, distance-learning, or multimedia instruction

- A "science speciality" in biotechnology, biology, chemistry, or physics

- A "technology speciality" in advanced programming techniques, engineering, or information management

- A "business speciality" in marketing, strategic planning, quality control, or localization

The increased need for professional writers and designers in a range of business and organizational contexts has brought about two significant changes in document design:

- A movement toward professionalization—through the growth of journals, conferences, and organizations for the people who practice, teach, or research document design

- The development of academic programs in writing and design—particularly at the community college, four-year college, and university level

The next section examines the professionalization of document design and the academy's response to the need for well-educated writers and designers, with the focus on how the field has developed both in and out of the academy. This context can shed light not only on why the field is the way it is today but also on where document design might be heading in the future.

RESPONSES TO THE NEED FOR DOCUMENT DESIGN: PROFESSIONAL AND ACADEMIC DEVELOPMENTS

As we have seen, a variety of social and technological forces created a need for document design. This section adds to the still incomplete history of the field by examining some of its academic and professional developments.[38] It explores the evolution of educational programs that teach document design, focusing on the influence of the academy and its interpretations of writing and design on the practice of document design.[39] This section relates the professional development of writers, designers, teachers, and researchers to the emergence of societies and forums for sharing and building knowledge in the field. It describes how the building of knowledge and the development of research about writing and design gave professionals—both in and out of the academy—a sense of purpose, identity, and status. Moreover, it chronicles some of the surprising resemblances in the ways that the fields of writing and design struggled toward professionalization. These fields grew up independently but experienced many of the same problems in the academy and the workplace. To understand document design, it is important to see how the fields of writing and design have imagined themselves and how these self-images have influenced the field today.

Practitioners without a Profession: "Nobody Loves Me But My Mother and She Could Be Jivin' Too"[40]

Early in the twentieth century it was difficult for document designers to gain a sense of the field to which they were contributing. There were almost no professional societies in which people working in document design could meet and share ideas. For the most part, writers and designers

[38] See the first three strands of *The Timeline:* "Education & Practice in Writing / Rhetoric," "Professional Development," and "Education & Practice in Graphic Design" (pp. 106–149) for a chronological or synchronous view. Note that the "Professional Development" strand combines writing and design as well as work in academic and nonacademic settings.

[39] I describe the variously named educational programs as "document design" even though individual programs may not describe themselves with this language. Universities employ names such as professional writing, technical writing, rhetoric, graphic design, typography, information design, communications design, or instructional science. These terms, however, are not interpreted in the same way from institution to institution. Consequently, a program in professional writing could focus on scientific journalism or document design; similarly, a program in graphic design could focus on corporate communications or information design.

[40] The line "Nobody loves me but my mother and she could be jivin' too" comes from the song *Nobody Loves Me But My Mother* by the great blues man, B.B. King (Pamco Music, Inc./Sounds of Lucille, BMI, 1972. Reproduced on compact disc in 1987 by MCA Records). B.B. King's lyrics capture the sense of frustration felt by people in writing or design whose "homes" in the academic or business world have often been less than hospitable.

worked in isolation, without a sense of professional identity, without a way to benefit from the accumulated experiences of others. Practitioners spent significant portions of their professional careers completely isolated from others with related interests and activities. Not only did they have little contact with others in their own field, but they also worked as though the fields of writing and design were unrelated. This was the case even though the work of designers and writers often appeared side-by-side in textbooks, journals, magazines, and newspapers.

Because there was little formalized knowledge about what good writing or design actually entailed, practice tended to be guided by organizational habit and managerial whim. Decisions about how to carry out document design activities often had little to do with effective writing or design processes, but rather with what had been done before and how much it cost. Organizations typically asked writers and designers to adhere to specifications and style guides that did little more than codify "the way it had always been done." Especially vulnerable to such influences were new document designers who, if they did not accept the status quo, could risk losing chances for promotion and for working on high-status projects.[41]

41 Of course, the problem of organizations and their resistance to change did not go away by the end of the century. Resisting new ideas for writing and design along with the problem of "design by committee" have hobbled many document design efforts; see, for example, Paul Rand's (1993, May 2) commentary on IBM's "Failure by Design."

Fortunately, some organizations understood the importance of good communication (e.g., early in this century, the Container Corporation of America was known for its forward thinking about graphic design and for sponsoring the development of the first U.S. academic programs in design). Such organizations provided their writers and designers with the freedom and resources to "push the envelope"—allowing them to explore the possibilities of design and to create innovative solutions to communications problems. Those document designers fortunate enough to be employed by organizations that nurtured their work were positioned to help shape the field and often went on to become early "gurus" in the field. But even the gurus of writing and design must have had little beyond personal experience and intuition to guide them. As *The Timeline* makes evident, a number of professional journals and societies were established (especially after the mid-1950s) that enabled professionals in writing and design (in and out of the academy) to broaden their horizons—encouraging them not only to build on personal experience but also to value and draw on the experiences of others.

Today, the field benefits from professional journals and societies as well as from academic programs, which foster knowledge about document design and build its theoretical and research base. However, developing these resources has been difficult, for both the professionals who write and design documents in organizations and those who teach writing and design in institutions of higher education. The history of document design shows that although academics and nonacademics take different professional routes, they run into many of the same obstacles along the way. In this section, I review some of the trends in the development of the field as a profession, point out some of the roadblocks document designers have negotiated, and suggest what road conditions look like now.

Academic programs developed in colleges and universities have been important to document design. In particular, programs developed in English studies and the fine arts have had a great deal of impact on the study of writing and graphic design. How people in English studies and the fine arts have thought about writing and graphic design is an interesting story that should be told in greater detail than the sketch offered here. My aim is neither to conflate the distinct histories of writing and graphic design nor to suggest that they should be linked. Rather, I explore the similarities and differences in the ideas from these fields about teaching, research, and practice—paying attention to the impact of these ideas on workplace practices, beliefs, and myths about writing and design. I begin by outlining three intellectual traditions that influenced the study and practice of both writing and graphic design. I then examine these traditions in more detail, by assessing their impact on writing and examining their effect on graphic design and typography. I conclude by characterizing the legacy of these traditions on document design today, underscoring the important progress that has been made while simultaneously posing some challenges for the field.

THREE TRADITIONS THAT SHAPED THINKING AND BELIEFS ABOUT WRITING AND DESIGN

To understand the evolution of document design in the twentieth century, we must understand three powerful traditions that have shaped peoples' beliefs about writing and design: the *craft tradition,* the *romantic tradition,* and the *rhetorical tradition.*

The Craft Tradition[42]

The craft approach to writing and graphic design cultivates knowledge of guidelines, principles, rules, and procedures that are needed in order to produce visual or verbal products. In this tradition, a teacher helps students to improve their performance by helping them (1) to understand the elements of visual or verbal style and (2) to identify the conditions in which it is appropriate to use them (e.g., when it is a good idea to use the active voice instead of the passive voice, or when it is a good idea to use a

[42] The craft tradition I refer to focuses on helping students acquire fundamental technical skills in writing or design. It should be distinguished from the craft tradition as it emerged in the Arts and Crafts Movement of the 1870s, a movement in the decorative arts and architecture (described later in this chapter).

formal typeface instead of an informal one). To help students learn the craft of writing or design, teachers often supplement their class discussion with handbooks, guidelines, lists of common writing and design errors, techniques, or style guides.

In writing, the craft tradition emphasizes grammatical correctness and proper usage. Students are often asked to complete sentence-level exercises designed to help them write clearly and sharpen their skills in proofreading and editing. The craft approach also encourages students to

- learn the basic formats and conventions of different genres (e.g., the parts of a business report or the parts of a scientific journal article)
- recognize differences among styles of writing (e.g., a formal prose style versus an informal one)
- acquire facility in different modes of writing (e.g., argument versus description)
- master a range of techniques for exposition (e.g., comparison and contrast, summary, etc.)

In graphic design, the craft approach focuses on the "how to" of design, with an emphasis on the steps to take in order to achieve a good final product. Teachers who take a craft approach tend to emphasize the mechanical aspects of design. They may, for example, show how to

- copyfit the type (e.g., specifying how much text will fit in a 4-inch by 2-inch text block using 10-point Times Roman)
- size and crop a photograph
- use software such as Adobe Photoshop
- sketch two-dimensional versus three-dimensional images

The craft approach in design also helps students learn the elements of various genres (e.g., the typical components of a corporate identity package, including logos, stationery, brochures, and business cards). It also familiarizes students with the techniques of design (e.g., working with color, airbrushing, photo manipulation, or prepress techniques).

The craft tradition in both writing and graphic design takes a kind of technical skills approach, in which mastering the fundamentals of style and technique dominates students' instruction.

The Romantic Tradition

In the romantic tradition, writing and design are successful when they express the inner vision of the writer or designer. Creative acts such as writing and designing are viewed as unanalyzable and unteachable.

Individuals either have the ability to write or design well or they do not. Individuals who have the ability are said to have a unique, personal "gift" or to possess "genius." In the romantic view, attempts to teach writing or design directly are believed to be either ineffective or harmful because they impose someone else's view on the "inner vision" of the writer or designer. Thus, worrying about the interests of someone else (such as the teacher or the audience) may distort the integrity of the writer or designer's original vision (which is believed to be true and authentic). The appropriate role for a teacher is to provide a nurturing environment in which the writer or designer's gift can develop according to its own organic logic.

In the classroom, writing teachers who hold a romantic view tend to give assignments in which writers explore topics in ways that suit them personally (e.g., write an essay about a topic that you care deeply about). Often students are advised to keep a diary or journal so they can reflect on their journey of self-discovery. Once a draft is complete, students share their work in the "writing workshop," a nonthreatening environment in which students talk over their concerns about what they've written. Since the operating assumption is that writing is essentially a mystery and it cannot be taught directly, the writing teacher's primary role is to provide an atmosphere in which students feel comfortable to express freely their ideas about writing. As students discuss their writing, the teacher offers advice about issues of language and expression that professional writers often worry about—voice, structure, point of view, selection of detail, or use of imagery.

In the graphic design classroom, the romantic tradition embodies an "art for art's sake" philosophy, where graphics and typography are employed to express the personal feelings and values of the designers. Students are encouraged to develop an individual style that is a kind of signature distinguishing their work. Examples of exemplary work from the "design masters" are often used as models in the classroom, an activity that may suggest to students that design is a solitary activity in which one's personal vision gradually unfolds. The key teaching method in design classes is called the "critique," a dialogue between student and teacher in which strengths and weaknesses of design artifacts are discussed. The teacher's goal in the "crit" sessions—as students call them—is much like that in the writing workshop: to encourage students to develop their capabilities to "evaluate, critique, and coach others, challenging students to define their own standards of evaluation" (McCoy, 1990, p. 20).

Moreover, the romantic tradition in both writing and design is focused on the idea of working by intuition. Writing and design courses taught in the romantic tradition reward students more for displaying personal honesty than for creating texts that people can understand and use for specific purposes.

The Rhetorical Tradition

In classical times, rhetoric was the art of persuasion.[43] Many of our ideas about rhetoric come to us from the writings of Aristotle, Cicero, and Quintilian. A central concern for classical rhetoricians was to identify and formulate strategies for persuasion, especially through public speaking. Twentieth-century rhetoricians have widened their focus to include communication through speech as well as through writing, film, television, and online displays.[44] Courses in rhetoric at the college level now cover almost anything related to the act of saying something to someone in speech, in writing, or through designed objects.[45]

Of the ideas that the rhetorical tradition[46] brings to writing and graphic design, three of the most important are *audience, invention,* and *heuristics.* More than anything else, it is the explicit attention to the needs of the audience that separates the rhetorical tradition from the craft and romantic traditions. And unlike the craft or romantic approach, the rhetorical approach provides document design with a rich theoretical framework for thinking about the complex relationships among the communicator, the audience, the words and pictures, and the context.

The writing teacher working in the rhetorical tradition believes that writing can be taught, that learning to write is as much perspiration as inspiration, and that in order to write well, one need not be born with a "gift." They believe that teachers can do more for the student than create a good atmosphere for talking about writing. Instead, they help students to acquire sophistication in the art of invention—the art of discovering what to say about a subject, of taking a point of view that is sensitive to the reader's knowledge and beliefs, and of finding clear explanations and persuasive arguments.

[43] To many, the word "rhetoric" suggests politicians who manipulate their audiences by using word magic or by telling colorful lies. Popular images paint rhetoric as the art of deceit. Similarly, people who use rhetoric are portrayed as those who trick others through words, pictures, or "infomercials." However, these images of double-talk and deception have almost nothing to do with the rhetorical tradition that has come down to us from classical Greece and Rome. I say "almost" because rhetoricians are concerned with understanding all facets of communication, both the good and the bad. Rhetoric deals with improving the quality of human communication through the ethical use of language. Rhetoricians abhor the idea of using visual or verbal tricks to take advantage of the audience.

---

[44] For a discussion of contemporary rhetoric, see Burke (1950), Perelman and Tyteca (1969), or Richards (1936). For an accessible collection of essays, see Foss, Foss, and Trapp (1991).

[45] For an introduction to the study of rhetoric in writing, see Young, Becker, and Pike (1970). For views about the rhetoric of design, see Buchanan (1985, 1992) or Simon (1981).

[46] The perspective of rhetoric I present here is one of several views. This one is employed by rhetoricians called the "new classicists," named after their interest in reviving classical rhetorical theory (Young, 1980). For a discussion of some other perspectives in the rhetorical tradition, see Berlin (1987, 1990), Bizzell and Hertzberg (1990), or Winterowd (1994).

Teachers in the rhetorical tradition bring to the classroom not rules and prescriptions, but heuristics to kindle students' inventive processes and guide their choices and decisions as they write (Young, 1980, p. 345). Heuristics—as Aristotle tells us in his *"Art" of Rhetoric*—are strategies for effective guessing.[47] Heuristics provide systematic probes that help people draw on the knowledge they already possess and that open up new aspects of the problem to be investigated.[48] Heuristics have been developed to help writers to identify content appropriate to the audience and to evaluate the quality of their drafts en route to a final product.

Like teachers of writing, those in graphic design and typography who take a rhetorical approach encourage students to consider the needs of the audience throughout the design process. In a rhetorically oriented design class, Louis Sullivan's famous dictum "form follows function" is much more than a slogan; it is a way of thinking about design and a way of evaluating designed artifacts (Findeli, 1990, p. 10). Design teachers who advocate a rhetorical approach encourage students to recognize that the visual structure of information must serve the needs of the intended audience. This emphasis during planning and invention helps students to understand the public nature of design. They learn that personal intuition, while essential, is not enough. They learn that an effective design must do more than please the designer. It must first of all meet the needs of the audience. And like their colleagues in writing, design teachers who stress the rhetorical approach challenge their students to assess the adequacy of their designs.

Knowledge of how the craft, romantic, and rhetorical traditions evolved is important because it can help document designers recognize the roots of their assumptions about writing and design. Understanding these traditions can also make document designers better able to empathize with the public's perception of writing and design.

[47] *The "Art" of Rhetoric* was written by Aristotle in about 330 B.C.; see the edition by Freese (1975).

[48] A simple but widely known heuristic is the traditional set of questions used by journalists: Who? What? When? Where? Why? (Winterowd, 1994, p. 113). In Chapter 5, I present heuristics for making decisions about typography (pp. 272–273) and designing grids for page layout (pp. (341–356). See Miller (1985) for some other heuristics developed to help technical and professional writers.

HOW THE THREE TRADITIONS INFLUENCED THE DEVELOPMENT OF WRITING AS A PROFESSION

In order to show the impact of these traditions on the field of writing in the twentieth century, I offer the following as a crude overview of the temporal relationship among the three traditions:

- From 1900 through the late 1940s, the craft tradition was dominant in writing. It began to lose dominance in the 1940s and was subsumed by the rhetorical tradition (which saved many of the craft tradition's good ideas about clear writing but deemphasized its focus on grammar, style, and correctness).

- Starting in the late 1940s, a revival of interest in classical rhetoric led to the development of modern rhetorical approaches to writing. By the early 1960s, the rhetorical tradition had taken the position of dominance in the field, a position it continues to hold today.

- The late 1960s brought a renewed interest in romantic visions of writing. Romantic approaches were mainly embraced by teachers of literature, creative writing, essay writing, and to a lesser extent, freshman writing. However, teachers of rhetoric, professional writing, and technical writing (areas that would be central to the study of document design) rarely shared this enthusiasm.

The Legacy of the Craft Tradition in Writing: Is the Grammar Doctor In?

In the early part of this century, writing teachers who worked in universities were frequently viewed as support people. They helped students from across the university write papers for history or chemistry class. This support role was institutionalized through the freshman composition course. The freshman English teacher was expected to raise the communication abilities of the Johnnys and Sallys who supposedly couldn't read or write at a level called "standard written English."

English teachers also frequently served as advisors for papers written by students across the disciplines.[49] For example, during the 1930s, writing teachers at the University of Minnesota, Carnegie Institute of Technology, and Harvard were asked to take on extra responsibilities in helping teachers in other fields coach students to wed form and content. Though beneficial for the students, this role had the effect of reducing the writing teacher to the level of proofreader (Combies, 1987, p. 97).

Teachers of writing who adopted the craft approach emphasized "correctness" over all else. History tells us that a preoccupation with the craft of writing—grammar, mechanics, spelling, punctuation, and vocabulary—dominated the teaching of English in American high schools and colleges through the late 1940s. Teachers spent more time on correcting students' writing than on helping them think through what they wanted

---

[49] The practice of the English teacher serving as a coach during the early part of the century is different from the English teacher's role in what is called the "writing across the curriculum" movement of the 1980s or 1990s (see Russell, 1991; Walvoord & McCarthy, 1990). While the goals are somewhat similar—to improve students' ability across the disciplines—the focus is different. While the early role of the English teachers was as handmaiden to the economics or physics professor, today's movement tries to get teachers in a particular subject matter to take their students' writing more seriously by giving the subject matter teachers explicit criteria and guidance for evaluating student writing.

to say. This led many students to the reasonable conclusion that an English teacher's mission in life was to correct other people's grammar[50] and that good writing meant not making mistakes. Students were typically required to write a five-paragraph theme a week. Many were horrified to find their themes returned bleeding with red ink and with funny words like "awk" or "dangler" written in the margins.[51] The idea from the teacher's point of view was that frequent practice and close attention to mechanics would make students better writers and more able communicators.

As students practiced their writing, they were encouraged to draw on what were known as the *modes of writing*—description, narration, exposition, and argument.[52] In the writing classroom, teachers elaborated these modes with many examples, putting the greatest emphasis on exposition. Students in advanced writing courses practiced what were called the *techniques of exposition*—comparison, contrast, process analysis, cause-and-effect, induction, deduction, examples, and illustrations. This approach became known as *current traditional rhetoric,* a phrase coined by Daniel Fogarty in 1959 to refer to the practice of teaching the *craft of writing* by focusing on mechanics, modes, and techniques. (Professors who emphasized this way of teaching writing were called the *current traditionalists*.[53]) The idea was that practice in these modes and techniques would give students the building blocks to develop more complex genres. This building-blocks approach introduced students to smaller units of discourse before bigger ones, moving from words to paragraphs to sections and so on.

Although teachers of writing who employed the craft approach actually did much more than simply teach grammar, they became known as the "grammar doctors" on campus. This reputation had politically disastrous consequences. In contrast to most other professors on campus, those who taught writing had two strikes against them.

First, they had low status because other professors regarded their subject as remedial. This attitude led some to characterize the work of writing professors as "teaching bonehead English," an expression that slanders both student and teacher. At the turn of the century, a time when mostly

[50] In actuality, the writing teacher's mission was probably to get through the day without keeling over from exhaustion. Between 1900 and 1910, composition teachers were typically responsible for teaching between 140 and 200 students, making the number of papers each teacher was expected to read and grade staggering (Connors, 1985, p. 66). No wonder they focused only on grammar; how else could they survive?

---

[51] For a list of the "strange" correcting symbols teachers used, see Winterowd and Blum (1994, p. 32). Since teachers' symbols were not the same as proofreaders' marks, they did not help students learn to edit professionally.

[52] For a discussion of the rise and fall of the modes of discourse, see Connors (1981). To see how they got started, see Alexander Bain's *English Composition and Rhetoric* (1866).

[53] See *The Timeline,* the strand "Education & Practice in Writing / Rhetoric," 1900+, 1912, 1935, 1950+, and 1954 (pp. 106, 108, 114, 120, 122).

rich white boys went to college, it was widely assumed that students should arrive at the university knowing "how to write." It was viewed as the job of the high school teacher[54] to teach writing, not the college professor. The idea of freshman composition meant that high school English didn't quite work. Some say that "freshman composition has been a kind of half-way house between high school and college English" (Young, 1995, p. 156).

Second, the craft tradition which formed the foundation of the writing teacher's pedagogy, was not an intellectually rich one. Humanists who valued aesthetic experiences viewed what the writing teacher did as vapid. Scientists who valued empirical research saw what writing teachers did as ad hoc and lacking rigor. Thus, in the eyes of their university colleagues, composition teachers had neither engaging ideas nor research that showed they had a knowledge base or an interesting perspective that they could call their own.

Fortunately, writing teachers have greatly improved their relationships with their university colleagues, but there are still traces of the "grammar doctor on call" in some institutions. For example, professors in business management schools still routinely ask adjunct communications professors who work in their departments to look over their proposals "to make sure the English is good" before they are sent out. Additionally, as I will discuss in the sections that follow, there remain a number of other persistent problems for teachers of writing in colleges, problems related not to the attitudes of business professors but to those of other professors of English. To understand how things got this way, it is important to understand how people thought about writing courses beyond the freshman level, particularly those in professional writing and technical writing.

The Development of Early Courses in Technical and Professional Writing: Solidifying the Craft Tradition

The teaching of professional writing began in American colleges at a time in U.S. history when business, scientific, and news writing were becoming crucial to an expanding nation.[55] The end of the nineteenth century and the beginning of the twentieth saw the demand for professional writers increase dramatically. Publications ranging from magazines and newspapers to professional trade journals (on everything from engineering to forestry) to "how-to" guides (on assembling gadgets, taking care of baby, or repairing farm equipment) needed writers who could communicate effectively to diverse audiences.

[54] The history of education is full of examples of teachers who are blamed for the problems of their students and their students' families. More than other groups, the high school English teacher has taken "the heat" from parents, pundits, and politicians.

[55] Advanced writing courses in the United States began between 1880 and 1910 (Adams, 1993, p. ix). One of the first technical writing courses was offered at Tufts College in 1904 by Samuel Chandler Earle, who some have argued should be considered the "father of technical writing" (Connors, 1982, p. 332). See the histories provided by Adams (1993); Brockmann (1983, 1994); Connors (1982); and Russell (1991).

Pressure to teach technical and professional writing also came from within the academy. For example, engineering schools at the turn of the century complained about the writing skills of engineering students with comments such as: "It is impossible, without giving offense to college authorities, to express one's self adequately on the English productions of the engineering students.... Most of them can only be described by the word 'wretched'" (Connors, 1982, p. 331). Because early courses in technical writing were taught by literature professors, they used poems and works of fiction as models of good writing to improve the writing of engineering students. By 1924, engineering faculty made clear their belief that studying literature did not help engineers write any better. They called for instruction in expository prose and in presenting complex data in an attractive form (Stoughton & Stoughton, 1924). This led to the teaching of business genres, but because literature professors had no interest in business, no knowledge of its practices, and no understanding of the roles documents play in organizations, their advice was severely limited to sentence-level features of style.

Individual courses in technical writing continued to grow in number, mostly in colleges of engineering, mining, or agriculture. Gradually more teachers were hired to meet the demand for writing courses for engineers or other academic majors such as business administration. But the merit of these courses was widely questioned and the status of their teachers was low. English departments considered the technical writing courses a tiresome and dreary service beneath the dignity of literature professors. Engineering schools considered writing a useful adjunct, but of lesser value than engineering (Connors, 1982; Russell, 1991). By the 1930s, most business writing courses were assigned to low-ranking or part-time faculty, often women (Bossard & Dewhurst, 1931, p. 339).[56]

Because there were no professional organizations to disseminate knowledge about technical communication or professional writing, teachers had few resources for classroom ideas.[57] Most felt comfortable with the craft approach and the development of early courses in technical and professional writing had the effect of solidifying the craft tradition. Students who took technical writing classes through the late 1950s— mostly engineering majors—were drilled in prescriptive guidelines for writing reports such as "never use I." In addition to worrying over issues of sentence-level style and paragraph structure, teachers encouraged students to master business genres such as the technical report and its key parts (e.g., the executive summary or the recommendations section).[58]

In practice, teaching genre conventions and stylistic guidelines devoid of a rhetorical context—that is, without reference to the organization, the

[56] As I will explain later in this chapter, the problem of professional writing and technical writing courses being staffed by low-ranking or part-time faculty is a continuing problem. Regrettably, after things got better in the 1970s and early 1980s (more full-time faculty were hired and a record number were tenured), some of the gains started to erode in the 1980s and 1990s (Cunningham and Harris, 1994).

[57] The creation in 1973 of the American Association for Teachers of Technical Writing (ATTW) and its publication *The Technical Writing Teacher,* now *Technical Communication Quarterly (TCQ),* provided a very helpful resource for teachers who had few opportunities to meet one another.

[58] See *The Preparation of Reports: Engineering, Scientific, Administrative* by Ray Palmer Baker (1924), then head of the English department at Rensselaer Polytechnic Institute. Connors (1982) points out that by 1935, most college-level technical communication courses focused on writing reports. Baker's work on reports was so popular that it went through five editions by 1953.

audience, the political climate, and so on—helped students very little. The craft approach reinforced the misguided notion that writers simply "dress up already good ideas" by applying rules and guidelines. A parallel myth has developed around the design of quantitative graphics, where designers are viewed as "decorating the data" by giving it visual organization (see Tufte, 1983, and for commentary, Kostelnick, 1994).

How the Craft Tradition Influenced Views of Writing in Business and Industry

These views of writing, particularly that of "writer as grammar doctor," may have thwarted the professional development of practitioners in the workplace by leading to an unfortunate stereotyping of the writer as "glorified secretary." Unfortunately, it is still the case that managers in many organizations do not understand what writing involves and underestimate writers' capabilities. It's easy to see why. Many of today's managers were in school when the craft approach was in its heyday. Their memory of writing is high school English or freshman composition. To them writing means fixing mistakes rather than creating ideas. These tired old assumptions still govern many managers' ideas about writing, which has meant that when writers are hired, their talents and capabilities are often construed too narrowly. Instead of drawing on writers' abilities to solve complex communications problems, involving them upfront in the development process—an ideal place to consider the audience—they are often brought in at the tail end of development and are relegated to editing the prose of others.

Critiques of the Craft Tradition in Writing

It is now believed that the craft approach to teaching writing was largely ineffective. Early research at Purdue University found no relationship between students' knowledge of grammar and their ability to write well (McKee, 1936). Later research supported this finding. Braddock and his colleagues (1963) hypothesized that writing classes that focus mainly on grammar may have a negative effect on students' learning to write. Later observations proved that Braddock's hunch was right. In a meta-analysis of some 60 studies of written composition, Hillocks (1986) compared the effects of different kinds of teaching on students' writing ability. He found a significant negative correlation between teaching focused on grammar and the quality of student writing (p. 214). This doesn't mean knowledge of grammar and style is irrelevant (good writers do have knowledge about these issues; they "sweat the details"). It means that in becoming a good writer, grammar and style aren't the most important things to learn about. In fact, focusing on them too much appears to hurt more than help.

In retrospect, most writing teachers believe the craft approach to writing helped students, but only minimally. Although it may have improved students' abilities to draft a good section of a document, it helped them neither to conceptualize the whole text nor to organize their writing around a guiding sense of purpose. Consequently, students in a technical writing class with a teacher who emphasized the craft tradition might, for example, learn to write a technically accurate description of a mechanical process without grammatical or stylistic mistakes, but their description might still be rhetorically ineffective because they did not learn ways of selecting and trimming the content to suit the knowledge and goals of the audience. Students might leave such a course thinking that a good writer "says everything" about the topic and then makes sure there are no typos. We can see that the craft approach, while helpful, would not take the student writer very far toward learning to think like a professional communicator.

Renewed Interest in the Rhetorical Tradition

By the end of World War II, the craft approach no longer controlled what writing teachers thought was important. The tradition of rules, grammar, and modes began to be absorbed by an interest in rhetoric. In the 1960s, a group of scholars known as the *new rhetoricians* reintroduced the ideas of the Greek and Roman rhetoricians, igniting a resurgence of interest in the rhetorical tradition. Instead of organizing their courses around modes and techniques, teachers began to draw on ideas from classical rhetoric about the key processes in creating a persuasive message:

- *Invention* (discovering what to say)
- *Arrangement* (selecting and ordering material in order to effect one's purpose)
- *Style* (choosing words, pictures, sounds, or graphic symbols that are effective, appropriate, and striking)
- *Memory* (finding ways to remember the text of an oral speech so that no notes are needed; for example, by using mnemonics and rehearsal techniques)
- *Delivery* (refining the oral presentation of a speech, e.g., pitch, volume, emphasis, pausing, modulation, gestures, body movements, or eye contact)

Since classes were about writing more than speaking, most emphasized the first three canons, especially invention.[59] A great deal of attention was

[59] For textbooks in the new rhetorical tradition, see Corbett's *Classical Rhetoric for the Modern Student* (1965) or Young, Becker, and Pike's *Rhetoric: Discovery and Change* (1970). Unlike textbooks in the craft tradition, these focus heavily on the process of invention, which before the new rhetoricians had all but disappeared from the twentieth-century writing curriculum.

spent on analyzing the audience, the purpose, and the rhetorical context. As the field of composition became more oriented toward the rhetorical tradition, so too did technical and professional writing.[60] In using a rhetorical approach, teachers might, for example, show students ways to analyze the needs of a particular audience, how to deal with more than one audience in the same document, and how to compose parts of a document, such as the executive summary or the recommendation section.

Early courses for technical writers emphasized the importance of considering the audience by writing clearly without insider jargon and by organizing documents in the ways that readers want and expect. According to Souther (1963), this led writers in industry to adopt the practice of

> ... placing conclusions, summaries, and recommendations at the beginning of the report because the administrators are most interested in such material ... and more widespread use of such devices as statements of purpose and background.... [These practices are] ample proof of the writer's growing awareness of the reader. (pp. 225-229)

At Iowa State University, courses began to consider graphic presentations as well as verbal ones (Sweigert, 1956). According to Connors (1982), the 1950s saw the field of technical writing "grow up," moving beyond its focus on grammar, mechanics, and style (p. 342). Over the decades that would follow, technical writing courses for engineers moved toward a more rhetorical focus, a movement that is well documented.[61]

The "New Romantics": A Reemergence of the Romantic Tradition

As mentioned earlier, proponents of the romantic school hold that *writing as an art is essentially a mystery—a journey of self-expression that cannot be taught*. This camp holds that great writers are born, not made. They are inspired by the muse and have a "gift" for writing. Since a mystery can't be taught, the teacher's role is to help students find for themselves their "true" voice (Winterowd, 1994, p. 43). To the romantics, the craft of writing is obvious and pedestrian, and rhetoric should be viewed with suspicion.[62] Historians call this group the "new romantics," after their

[60] We find evidence of the rhetorical approach to writing in a number of early influential textbooks about technical writing (see, for example, Houp & Pearsall, 1968; Nelson, 1940; Mills & Walter, 1954; Souther, 1957).

[61] Compare, for example, Adams (1993), Connors (1982), Grego (1987), and Souther (1989).

[62] For the romantics who viewed the creative act as unanalyzable, the new rhetorician's goal of exposing the process of invention was seen as treading on sacred territory. Romantics scoffed at the new classicists' ideas for teaching writers to plan, generate ideas, or envision ways to move an audience.

nineteenth-century precursors such as Coleridge and Wordsworth[63] (D'Angelo, 1975, p. 159).

The new romantics see the teacher as a coach who designs situations that stimulate the creative process and encourage intuition, spontaneity, and innovation (Young, 1980). Students learn to write by engaging in a master-apprentice relation with their teacher in forums such as the "writing workshop." Students develop an ear for good writing by emulating the "moves of the master" and by reading the works of great authors. This teaching strategy contrasts with ones employed by teachers in the craft tradition, who argue that practice makes a writer good, and with teachers in the rhetorical tradition, who believe that practice and social awareness make a writer good. The romantics contend that their approach helps students cultivate a sense of taste for the art of writing. Students learn to recognize when to revise based on their evolving image of whether the writing "rings true" to their inner vision (Elbow, 1981, p. 283).

In most English departments, the romantic tradition is strongest in creative writing classes and freshman writing classes—the former where want-to-be novelists look for inspiration and guidance, the latter where freshman may keep journals reflecting on their intellectual growth or write essays to celebrate personal discoveries. In contrast, most teachers of professional and technical communication moved from a craft or current-traditional orientation to a rhetorical orientation, paying little attention to the romantic tradition (unless they also taught creative writing). Why?

---

[63] Coleridge provides the philosophical and spiritual basis for the two great splits in English departments: between (1) "imaginative" and "nonimaginative" literature, and (2) "creative writing" and "composition" (Winterowd, 1994, p. 27). In *Biographia Literaria* (1817/1983), Coleridge divided the imagination into the categories of primary and secondary, which set up the conditions for ranking works as primarily and secondarily imaginative. The legacy of Coleridge's ideals and those of other Romantics (see Shelley's *Defense of Poetry,* 1821) was the view that literature embodied the creative expression of the primary imagination, an imagination inspired by genius. Literature was defined as narrative fiction, poetry, and drama. In this view, great writers are born, not made, an assumption which led to the belief that writing could not be taught directly. This encouraged English departments to conceive their role as helping students develop a sense of "good taste" through reading great novels, poems, and plays. A parallel assumption was that composing literary genres calls on the primary imagination while composing nonliterary genres does not; thus, courses in "creative" writing have more value than those in "nonimaginative" writing (e.g., nonfiction essays, arguments, or reports) (Winterowd, 1994, p. 28; see also Berlin, 1984; Crowley, 1990). Moreover, in the hierarchy of "nonimaginative" writing, the activities of professional and technical communication were near the bottom of the aesthetic totem pole, even lower than freshman writing. Why? Because these fields were construed as requiring neither talent nor creativity. Moreover, they dealt with the world of commerce and of ordinary people reading ordinary texts—big negatives in the eyes of the literary elite.

[64] Although teachers of professional and technical writing have mostly ignored the new romantic tradition in their classrooms, their professional lives were still influenced by the ideas of the romantics. Most English departments developed their ideas about writing based on the classical romantic views of what's imaginative and what's not. These views shape which courses (and professors) are judged to be central to the heart and spirit of the department and which ones are seen as marginal. See footnote 63 (p. 67) for information about the legacy of Coleridge's views on English departments.

[65] Veysey (1979) points out that many humanities disciplines at the university level had to wrestle with the intellectual content of their fields while at the same time fighting for status as professions (pp. 52–53). Miller (1991) provides a compelling account of the politics of writing instruction.

[66] The most important of these alliances was the formation of the Conference on College Composition and Communication (CCCC) in 1949. It went on to become the largest organization for teachers of writing, giving them a voice in English studies. In 1950, CCCC started its own journal, College Composition and Communication, providing a forum for disseminating the work of its members.

Because romantic methods that focus only on developing a student's "inner vision" are inappropriate for the unabashedly reader-oriented world of document design.[64] Today's professional writing, technical communication, and business writing teachers often build their entire course around considerations of the audience (for example, see Anderson's 1995 reader-centered approach to technical writing).

PRACTITIONERS FORM A PROFESSION: ARTICULATING A VISION FOR WRITING STUDIES

Experts on how professions are formed suggest that a profession is partly defined by the ability of its members to show that they possess a unique body of knowledge, can demonstrate certain skills, and can specify the training needed to be a member of the profession (Larson, 1977). Others argue that professionalization involves excluding the unqualified (Veysey, 1965, p. 58). Obviously, in order to exclude the unqualified, one must agree on what it means to be qualified. This has not been an easy issue to settle for writing specialists in or out of the academy.

During the first part of the twentieth century, the field of writing failed to meet the criteria that would make it a profession because writing specialists were unable to identify a common identity (Combies, 1987). Until the second half of the century, there really was no *discipline* in the sense of widely shared bodies of readily available scholarship, bibliographies, or groups who identified themselves as writing professionals (Winterowd, 1994, p. 46). The main problem was that members of the field could agree neither on what they meant by the study of writing nor on what knowledge people needed in order to distinguish writing from other enterprises such as literature.[65]

As I mentioned earlier, by the late 1940s the field of writing began to change in significant ways. Teachers began to reexamine their activities from the perspective of rhetoric, a perspective which profoundly changed their thinking about what they were teaching. Members of the field of writing began to value their own expertise about communication processes and recognize that they were much more than proofreaders and grammar doctors. Increasing numbers of writing teachers began to align themselves professionally.[66] In 1963, the theme of the Conference on College Composition and Communication convention was "Toward a New Rhetoric," a slogan that turned into a rallying cry for people in the field of writing. Some scholars refer to 1963 as "the birth of modern composition studies" (North, 1987, p. 15). Others see 1963 as "the culmination of activity that had been smoldering since the 1900s and which heated up during the 1950s" (Young & Goggin, 1993, pp. 26–

31).[67] Both perspectives suggest that the early 1960s was an exciting time for people in the field of writing. The reemergence of rhetoric in English departments connected the field of writing to a body of scholarship and a history going back to the Greeks and Romans.

The renewed interest in rhetoric meant that writing teachers refocused their pedagogy. Instead of teaching rules of grammar and style, teachers helped students work through the writing process. Effective communication moved from "not making mistakes" to "creating texts for readers." For example, students were encouraged to consider their *rhetorical stance,* that is, the position writers assume with respect to their readers, a position that is often reflected by style and tone (see Booth, 1961). They were challenged to find ways to speak to a reader by using the reader's speech, gesture, tonality, order, image, attitude, and idea, as well as identifying with the reader's point of view (see Burke, 1950; Young, Becker, & Pike, 1970).

GROWING THE FIELD: PROFESSIONAL DEVELOPMENT IN DOCUMENT DESIGN

The professionalization of composition had attendant benefits for the study of document design, which would not establish itself professionally until the 1970s. The largest benefit was that the subject of writing was legitimized in the academy as an enterprise worthy of serious intellectual study. Although the major focus of composition studies had been freshman writing, professors in composition did not disparage the study of professional, technical, or business writing (as literature faculty did).

In professional and technical communication, the field shifted from a nonrhetorical view of practice to a rhetorical one. Instead of viewing expertise in writing as the mere application of rules, what constituted expertise was now an open question. Over the next several decades, empirical studies of composing would reveal that good writers are sensitive to the rhetorical situation and to the audience. Studies also revealed the important role that preferences and values play in technical and scientific writing.[68] Teachers strove to show students that the writing they would do in their professional careers was the continuation of a rich, complex, and very old cultural tradition (Rivers, 1994, p. 46).

The Growth of Academic Programs in Professional and Technical Writing as a Response to a Need for Educated Professionals

The "Professional Development" strand of *The Timeline* (pp. 120–128) shows that roughly between 1953 and 1960 practicing technical writers

[67] Compare the historical accounts of authors such as Connors, Ede, and Lunsford (1984); North (1987); Schilb (1989); Vitanza (1987); and Young and Goggin (1993).

[68] No one in technical communication has made these arguments so forcefully and with as convincing data analysis as those scholars working in the rhetoric of science (compare Bazerman, 1988; Gross, 1990; Prelli, 1991; and Zappen, 1987).

began organizing themselves. What would eventually become the world's largest organization for technical communicators, the Society for Technical Communication (STC), began to evolve in 1953 with the founding of the Society of Technical Writers (STW) and the Association of Technical Writers and Editors (TWE).[69] Other signs that the field was organizing itself include the following:

- In 1953, Rensselaer Polytechnic Institute began to offer a Technical Writers Institute, the first of its kind, and continues to offer it each year.

- In 1954, writers in the U.K. joined forces to develop the Technical Communicators Association, which would later become the Institute of Scientific and Technical Communicators (ISTC).

- In 1956, the first meeting of the Council of Biology Editors was held.

- It was also in the 1950s that a number of professional journals started, including *The Society of Technical Writers and Editors (STWE) Review* (later called *Technical Communication*), *Transactions on Engineering Writing and Speech* (later called *IEEE Transactions on Professional Communication*), *Ergonomics*, and *Human Factors*.

Early programs in technical writing and editing were designed to respond to a growing need for well-educated professional writers. The first Master of Science degree in Technical Writing was announced by Rensselaer Polytechnic Institute in 1953, and the first undergraduate Bachelor of Science degree in Technical Writing and Editing was introduced at the Carnegie Institute of Technology (now Carnegie Mellon) in 1958. Only a few programs developed during the 1960s, but by 1976, the first edition of *Academic Programs in Technical Communication* published by the Society for Technical Communication (STC) listed 19 academic programs. That same year, the Modern Languages Association (MLA)—the primary professional organization for professors of literature and modern languages—finally allowed the first technical writing panel to be presented at its convention in over 50 years.[70]

Program development proceeded more rapidly in the late 1970s through the mid-1980s. During this period doctoral programs with an emphasis in technical communication and document design began to develop. These programs followed the lead of Rensselaer Polytechnic Institute, which in 1965 began to offer the Doctor of Philosophy degree in Communication and Rhetoric, and in 1979 added a track in Technical Communication, the first of its kind within the Ph.D. program. In 1981, the STC's second edition of information about programs listed 28 programs, most of which offered Bachelor of Arts degrees. The third edition in 1985 cited 58 programs. By the fourth edition in 1993, there were more than 100 colleges and universities in North America which offered more than

[69] At first, members of the Society for Technical Communication (STC) couldn't agree on what to call themselves. After going through four name changes, in 1971 the organization settled on using "technical communication" rather than "editing" or "writing" to describe its activities. (See the "Professional Development" strand of *The Timeline* in 1953, 1954, 1957, 1960, and 1971, pp. 122–126, 132). By 1996, the STC would have over 20,000 members around the globe.

[70] In the early days the MLA, the major professional organization of college English professors, had a section devoted to pedagogy focusing on the study of issues related to teaching composition or rhetoric. But as the "Education & Practice in Writing / Rhetoric" strand of *The Timeline* (p. 106) shows, in 1903 the MLA disbanded its pedagogical section, the only section concerned with writing instruction. According to Stewart (1985), the last talk on composition was at the 1910 meeting of the MLA.

200 programs, ranging from certificate and associate's degrees to bachelor's, master's, and doctoral degrees. Program development has come a long way.

The Growth of Research about Writers and Readers

During the late 1960s and throughout the 1970s, studies of reading and writing flourished. Although, early in the century, there had been many studies of error and of the characteristics of writing, the first study of the writing process did not appear until 1971. Initially, studies of the writing process focused mainly on "writers at school," but over time, more studies of "writers at work" emerged.[71] Similarly, studies of the process of "reading at work" began to be published about 1977 (see the "Professional Development" strand of *The Timeline*, p. 134, for examples).

From the mid-1970s through the 1990s, research in writing and document design burgeoned (for a review, see Schriver, 1989b). Studies began to appear, for example, that explored reading, writing, and design from various perspectives, investigating the cognitive, social, or contextual dimensions of using documents (and technology). Four strands of document design work evolved:

- Empirical studies of people comprehending and using documents (and of writers and designers creating, revising, and evaluating documents).

- Explorations of social and cultural issues related to the design and use of documents (e.g., What is the effect of e-mail on interoffice communication?).

- Examinations of theoretical issues about the nature of scientific, technical, and professional communication (e.g., What is technical communication? How, if at all, is it different from other types of communication?).

- Arguments about the nature, scope, and province of technical communication—arguments that would help teachers and practitioners be more self-conscious and self-critical of their profession.[72]

Taken together, this work gave people who had been an invisible community a sense of identity. At the same time, it offered them ideas concerning the topics they cared deeply about (writers, readers, texts, contexts, and technology).

During the 1970s several vehicles for disseminating and sharing knowledge were started. For example, in 1970, the *Journal of Technical Writing and Communication (JTWC)* was founded, followed in 1973 by the *Technical Writing Teacher* (renamed *Technical Communication Quarterly* in 1992). Also in 1973, the Association of Teachers of Technical Writing (ATTW)

[71] For a sample of some of the first collections about writing in the world of work, see Anderson, Miller, and Brockmann (1983), Couture (1986), or Odell and Goswami (1985).

[72] Compare, for example, the writings of Britton (1975); Dobrin (1983); Hays (1975); Miller (1979, 1985, 1989); and Stratton (1979).

was formed. Starting as a small group of enthusiastic teachers, the ATTW in 1996 had a membership of more than 900.[73]

[73] Reported in the minutes of the ATTW executive committee, May 29, 1996.

The Growth of International Links in Document Design

The 1970s was a critical decade for document design for another reason. It brought what I call "the British invasion" (no, not the Beatles) of theorists, researchers, and practitioners who emerged to offer ideas about writing, design, and texts. Work from the U.K. inspired document designers around the world. People such as Michael MacDonald-Ross, James Hartley, Michael Twyman, Robin Kinross, Robert Waller, and Patricia Wright became household names in document design circles. Ideas about plain language, document quality, the rhetoric of graphic design and typography, and the interplay between words and pictures were provoked by document designers in the U.K. These ideas were important for broadening the field from the rather narrow conception of technical communication as it had developed in United States departments of English. For example, although U.S. technical communicators always believed that visuals were important, they commonly referred to them as "adjunct aids." This word-centered perspective did not really begin to change until the late 1980s and 1990s, when ideas about visual and verbal rhetoric began to flourish in the U.S. community, much later than in the U.K.

In the 1980s and 1990s, professionals in universities and industry from around the world continued to meet one another, sometimes in person, sometimes via online discussion groups. There are now many active cross-national collaborations among professionals in Australia, Austria, Belgium, Canada, France, Germany, Japan, the Netherlands, New Zealand, the U.K., and the United States. These have resulted in visiting professorships for faculty, educational seminars, consultancies, conferences, freelance document design, Internet discussion groups, jointly written articles, and a variety of joint projects. Some of these cross-national collaborations have resulted in document design research projects (I discuss some of this work in later chapters). As more companies develop their products for international audiences[74] and as more academics become interested in cross-cultural communication,[75] new collaborations are likely to develop even more rapidly.

[74] For approaches to developing documents for products marketed around the world, see, for example, Apple Computer (1992); Hoft (1995); and Jones, Kennelly, Mueller, Sweezy, Thomas, and Velez (1992).

Early Collaborations in the United States: The Document Design Project

One of the early joint efforts involving university and industry professionals was the Document Design Project (DDP)—a project funded by the

[75] See, for example, Bosley (1993) and Sauer (1996).

National Institute of Education,[76] which began in 1978 and lasted until 1981. The DDP brought together three organizations to study document design:

- The American Institutes for Research (AIR) in Washington, D.C., a nonprofit organization known for its Document Design Center (DDC)

- Siegel & Gale, Inc., a New York-based firm that specializes in language simplification and language training

- Faculty from Carnegie Mellon University (from the departments of English and psychology)

The output of the DDP was rather impressive. The Project provided training to government personnel from more than 15 federal agencies. DDP personnel worked directly with federal agencies on at least 13 different projects—for example, advising agencies on how to reorganize their regulations, redesigning financial aid forms for college students, and simplifying instructions for IRS tax forms. Research and evaluation projects included the following:

- Testing the effects of plain English on consumers' understanding of product warranties

- Studying how low-income Hispanic-Americans cope with the documents they must fill out

- Evaluating how people understand logically complex statements (such as the if-thens used in IRS forms)

- Exploring cognitive processes in reading and writing documents

- Developing usability testing procedures such as protocol-aided revision and user edits

The best known product of the DDP was a 1980 two-volume series, *Review of the Relevant Research*, edited by Daniel Felker, and a follow-up monograph in 1981, *Guidelines for Document Designers,* again edited by Felker and his colleagues (Pickering, Charrow, Holland, & Redish). The research from the DDP was quickly put to use by teachers of professional writing and technical communication through the textbook that grew out of the project, *Writing in the Professions* (by Goswami, Redish, Felker, & Siegel, 1981). Unfortunately, after the DDP, federal funding for document design research all but disappeared during the Reagan-Bush era, bringing an end to a highly productive collaboration.

Early Research Centers in Document Design

The activities of the Document Design Project catalyzed the founding of two research centers in document design: the Document Design Center at the American Institutes for Research in Washington, D.C., and the

[76] The National Institute of Education (NIE) has been renamed the Office of Educational Research and Improvement (OERI). Between 1985 and 1995, OERI would fund a National Center for the Study of Writing and Literacy (see *The Timeline,* the "Education in Writing / Rhetoric" strand for 1985, p. 140).

Communication Design Center at Carnegie Mellon University in Pittsburgh. These centers were important because they exemplified the application of reader-oriented research methods to a wide range of practical communication problems. Both centers were active in disseminating research results to the document design community and in sensitizing industry and government to the problems that readers face when they are confronted with poorly designed documents.

The Document Design Center at the American Institutes for Research

The kinds of work that began in the Document Design Project continued over the next few years at the Document Design Center (DDC). Under the very capable leadership of Janice (Ginny) Redish and her colleagues, many companies and organizations were introduced to research in document design and to reader-oriented approaches to solving their communication problems. Significant ties developed with U.S. government agencies such as the Veterans Administration and with companies such as IBM and Hewlett-Packard. The work of the DDC, recently renamed the Information Design Center (IDC) and reenergized under the direction of Susan Kleimann, continues to be disseminated through journal articles and talks at national conferences.

The Communications Design Center at Carnegie Mellon University

Research that began with the Document Design Project continued at Carnegie Mellon through a nonprofit center called the Communications Design Center (CDC). Started in 1979 by an interdisciplinary group of writers, researchers, graphic designers, psychologists, and computer scientists, the CDC was established to study the increasingly serious communications problems in industry, government, and the professions. At the time, the Carter administration's 1978 "plain language" policy (discussed earlier in this chapter) had focused national attention on the need to improve the quality of public documents. The CDC worked with government organizations and industry to find solutions to their problems. Over the next ten years, the CDC would

- Develop new methods for usability testing, such as protocol-aided revision (Bond, 1985; Bond, Hayes, & Flower, 1980; Dieli, 1986; Schriver, 1984, 1989c, 1991a; Swaney, Janik, Bond, & Hayes, 1991).

- Evaluate how headings in documents can mislead readers (Flower, Hayes, & Swarts, 1983; Swarts, Flower, & Hayes, 1980).

- Design and evaluate new methods for helping writers increase their sensitivity to the needs of readers (Schriver, 1984, 1987, 1992a).

- Assess how well people understand "informed consent" when they sign forms upon entering a hospital prior to a medical procedure or operation (Janik, Swaney, Bond, & Hayes, 1981).

- Examine differences between writing with pen and paper and with the computer (Haas & Hayes, 1986).

- Explore how graphic designers use computer-aided design tools (Ballay, Graham, Hayes, & Fallside, 1984).

- Analyze various approaches to plain language (Bowen, Duffy, & Steinberg, 1991; Steinberg, 1986, 1991).

- Study ways in which people read and use computer manuals (Sullivan & Flower, 1986), tax forms (Matchett & Ray, 1989), and legal documents (Stratman, 1988).

- Explore writers and graphic designers as they collaborate on document design tasks (Wulff, 1989).

- Study ways to integrate hardcopy and online documentation (Schriver, Hayes, Danley, Wulff, Davies, Cerroni, Graham, Flood, & Bond, 1986).

- Conceptualize the cognitive activities people engage in when they use online help (Duffy & Langston, 1985; Duffy, Mehlenbacher, & Palmer, 1992; Duffy, Trumble, Isenberg, Janik, & Rogers, 1987).

During its first and only decade, what I call "The Short But Happy Life of the CDC," faculty and students in document design produced more than 50 research reports and worked with dozens of national and international companies.[77] Despite the CDC's international success and even though it had helped to launch the careers of many students who now hold prominent positions in industry, the CDC would see its institutional support disappear as deans and department heads changed. In 1990, the College of Humanities and Social Sciences at Carnegie Mellon and the English department, which jointly governed the CDC, shifted their priorities away from the study of document design, and the CDC was closed. The unfortunate and untimely demise of the CDC illustrates in microcosm a continuing problem for document design: finding a supportive and comfortable home in the university. I will return to this problem at the end of this chapter.

A Challenge for the Rhetorical Approach: Making an Impact on Workplace Thinking about Writing and Design

Although the rhetorical approach to writing dominates the academic writing scene, it has not yet made a large impact on writing in the workplace. Regrettably, some managers still think of writers as glorified

[77] As a former co-director of the CDC, I characterized its "Short But Happy Life" in a talk to accept the 1995 Diana Award in which the CDC and its former co-directors (Thomas M. Duffy, John R. Hayes, Erwin Steinberg, and myself) were honored by the Association for Computing Machinery (ACM) Special Interest Group for Documentation (SIGDOC) for "significant and lasting contributions to the study of computer documentation and document design." For a pointer to SIGDOC, see the "Professional Development" strand of The Timeline for 1983 (p. 138).

secretaries. For example, at a presentation at the 1996 convention of the Society for Technical Communication, a writer lamented that his boss viewed him as "only one step up from a secretary" (he worked for a Fortune 500 company). Even managers who are enlightened often find that getting the resources to support quality efforts in document design requires a "hard sell" to upper management. Those who want to hire full-time writers often find it difficult to convince other managers that their need is genuine and that the cost is justified. The problem stems from the belief that a writer's forte is fixing mistakes of grammar or style. Thus it is hard to justify hiring a writer when some believe a secretary could do the same job with the help of a handbook like Strunk and White (1959). In addition, some managers think that writers perform essentially the same task as a spell checker.

Because the talent and knowledge that writers possess are not well understood, managers tend to believe that the key to being a good communicator is being a subject-matter expert (e.g., an expert in computer programming). Studies tell us, however, that knowing a lot about a subject does not mean one can communicate clearly about it. In fact, research suggests that being a subject-matter expert may actually interfere with one's ability to anticipate how another person without the same knowledge would respond to the text (Hayes, 1989b). Knowledge may "blind" the communicator to another person's potential problems.

Misconceptions about what it takes to be a writer run deep. In many organizations managers seem to have concluded that the best people to hire "right out of college" are the engineering and computer science graduates. Although this practice is a throwback to the bad old days of the 1940s and 1950s when engineers were indentured to write those horrible documents that no one could understand, it is still alive and well in major companies around the world. For example, a recent book on professional writing quotes a personnel director as saying this:

> We're not going to hire any more English majors ...
> They don't know anything.... If writers don't know the
> technology, they can't be more than Kelly Girls.
> (Reynolds, Matalene, Magnotto, Samson, & Sadler, 1995,
> p. 119)

Underlying managers' attitudes is the assumption that writing is merely the mechanistic application of rules—that anyone who can speak can write. In her popular book on editing, Judith Tarutz (1992) from Hewlett-Packard warns:

> Any aspect of editing that can be reduced to a set of rules
> is fodder for artificial intelligence (more specifically,

expert system software). What will you do when software can do your job—or when your manager thinks it can? How will your manager justify your salary plus overhead to senior management when a $50 software package can do the same task—or managers think it can?

Don't say it can't happen. Publishing software keeps getting better and cheaper. Managers will put two and two together and get three, close enough to justify replacing an editor with a spelling and syntax checker. If all you're doing is adding some commas and fixing spelling, you will be replaced by software.... Managers ... don't know the fine points of our job and don't care to. (pp. 364–365)

The overly simple views of writing that were fostered by the teaching of the craft tradition and through the regimentation of business practices during the first half of the century have had a lasting detrimental effect on the professional development of writers in organizations. Because these reductive views are still widely held, writing in some companies is construed as a marginal activity that adds to an organization's costs but that contributes neither to "the bottom line" nor to the quality of products and services. Indeed, writing is sometimes conceived as an annoying necessity, adding nothing and wasting valuable time and resources. Consequently, writers are finding that they must be able to demonstrate how they "add value" to organizations by doing at least one of the following:

- Reducing the investment spent on communication (e.g., more pages written per day for a lower cost, lower costs for printing[78])

- Improving the company's return on the investment (e.g., increasing sales, productivity, or customer satisfaction)

- Reducing the company's "after sales" costs (e.g., fewer customer complaints and returns, lower training costs, fewer requests for maintenance or calls to "help lines," less litigation)

For a number of perspectives on this topic, see articles by Redish (1995) and Ramey (1995b) on "measuring value added." For a set of case histories from government and business that show dollar amounts associated with "the payoff" of quality in document design, see Schriver (1993a). For a discussion of management issues, see Hackos (1994).

The legacy of traditional views creates a special challenge for writers who take jobs in organizations. They must be good at explaining what they do—its complexity and sophistication—in ways that educate managers, colleagues, and clients. They must be experts in their roles as practicing rhetoricians, as the people within organizations who enable others to see

[78] Printing costs can be lowered by hiring experienced document designers who know how to provide the right information at the right level of detail for customers rather than a "core dump" of everything developers know about the product.

[79] For examples of good communication as good business, see the United States Department of Commerce's publication, *How plain English works for business: Twelve case studies* (1984).

that good communication is good business.[79] This means helping organizations define what good communication actually means. Document designers continually face the responsibility of making ethical choices and judgment calls in helping managers and clients achieve their goals, and in helping them to see the advantages of taking readers' rhetorical needs seriously rather than just "going through the motions."

Here is a quick example. A few years ago, a large consumer products company requested some information from me about the financial gains associated with well-designed manuals and interfaces. They had heard that other consumer electronics companies were using their clear manuals and simple interfaces as a selling point and thought it could improve their sales if they did the same. After reviewing their manuals and product designs, I concluded that a major transformation in design was needed before this company could suggest that "good communication" was a reason to buy their products. My cost estimates for the project also suggested that fixing the problem would not be cheap (there were five troublesome product lines and each had 10 to 20 models, with roughly 80 horrible manuals and interfaces to match). After weeks of productive discussion with high-level managers, my colleagues and I submitted a proposal. The company told us the proposed ideas were terrific and the research plan would allow them to quantify their improvement and financial gains. But when managers saw the budget, negotiations came to a rapid halt. They couldn't believe it would cost so much to fix what they called their "annoying problems of communication." They soon convinced themselves that their problems were not bad enough to justify spending the money, and the proposed project was canceled. A few weeks later, the company ran a television ad touting "simple products with user-friendly documents." Although the company had done nothing to improve its communications, the marketing group decided it would be a clever idea to act as though the project had been carried out and had been successful. What was their idea of customer-oriented rhetoric? To tell the customers what they thought they wanted to hear. They had no intentions of "making good" on their promises and shamelessly carried out the idea in print and radio ads as well.

Document designers must figure out how they add value to organizations and how the value they add can promote more responsible corporate citizenry in communicating with audiences. That new hires must be good at representing "who they are" and at negotiating conflicting organizational agendas sets an important educational goal for teachers of document design (see Ornatowski, 1992). It also suggests to educators that we must prepare our students to be skilled in collecting the data they will need in order to make persuasive arguments that are supported by evidence. Students must know how to do the following:

- Collect data by employing quantitative and qualitative methods.
- Analyze data and derive claims.
- Build claim-driven arguments supported by data.
- Contextualize arguments for the rhetorical situation.
- Present arguments (orally and in writing) supported by charts and graphs.
- Disseminate their ideas in electronic and paper channels.

Building arguments about the value of good communication that managers can understand is crucial if document designers are to convince their employers that their talk is not just talk. When professionals in document design get better at doing these kinds of things, those dreary images of the "grammar doctor on call" may slowly fade away.

THE PLACE OF GRAPHIC DESIGN IN THE AMERICAN UNIVERSITY: EUROPEAN ROOTS

American graphic design began in the 1860s with the creation of the first advertising agencies and blossomed further in the 1880s when Linotype and Monotype typesetting machines were developed. American graphic designers followed the lead of the U.K., where graphic design emerged as part of the Arts and Crafts Movement in decorative arts and architecture. The Arts and Crafts Movement was a response to the dehumanizing working conditions and debased products of the Industrial Revolution. Initiated by Socialist reformer William Morris, who was much influenced by the philosophy of John Ruskin, the movement embraced artists, architects, designers, craft workers, and writers. Turn-of-the-century graphic designers were upset with the shoddy typography used in book design, along with inferior paper and poor presswork. They favored a medievalist approach which revered fine craftsmanship, traditional techniques, and the use of natural material (Livingston & Livingston, 1992, pp. 14, 18).

Graphic design became the generic term for the activity of combining typography, illustration, photography, and printing for purposes of persuasion, information, or instruction. William Addison Dwiggins first used the term "graphic designer" in 1922, although it did not achieve widespread usage until after 1945. Prior to this time, the services of graphic designers were carried out by commercial artists mainly working in the advertising industry. From the early 1930s to the end of the second World War, the American graphic design community was enriched by the influx of important European designers[80] fleeing from the deteriorating political situation in Europe. Thus American graphic design—which now encompasses not only advertising design, but also design in the magazine, newspaper, marketing, and publishing industries, and more recently, document design and information design—has strong European roots that continue to influence how designers are taught and what design means.

In colleges and universities in the United States, graphic design is viewed as a practical art that is contrasted with fine arts such as painting. As I mentioned earlier, in most colleges and universities, schools of fine arts became the academic home for the study of graphic design and typography. Much like the status accorded to the study of literature and creative writing as "more worthy" than the study of rhetoric and writing,[81] fine arts subjects such as art history and painting hold higher status than the practical arts of graphic design or typography. Like the literature professors who may accuse professors of technical writing of teaching a vocational subject, those in the fine arts may construe graphic design and typography as mere commercial practices that are better taught in trade, technical, or commercial art schools. And like English professors who may teach writing but publish their scholarly work in literature (their true intellectual work), design professors may teach graphic design but seek to exhibit their work in forums such as the gallery exhibit or the museum show. Here, the parallel between writing and graphic design breaks down. The phenomenon of "one-man shows" stands in stark contrast to technical and professional writing, where the anonymous writer has been the norm (Shulman, 1960) and where growing numbers in the profession are women[82] (O'Hara, 1989).

PRACTITIONERS FORM A PROFESSION: ARTICULATING A VISION FOR GRAPHIC DESIGN STUDIES

Graphic design was influenced by the same three traditions—the craft, the romantic, and the rhetorical—that were important for writing, but in design the romantic tradition has been relatively more important than in writing. To see how the three traditions have affected the ways that graphic designers think about their work, it is important to see how schools of design drew on these traditions. This development shows us that the twentieth century is important in moving graphic design away from a romantic art-for-art's-sake perspective toward one that is human-

[80] American graphic design benefited from the arrival of Bauhaus masters such as Josef Albers, Herbert Bayer, Walter Gropius, Ludwig Mies van der Rohe, and László Moholy-Nagy (Meggs, 1992b, p. 217).

[81] As a respondent in a 1986 survey of composition programs put it, "Composition's status is not an issue on our campus—because it has no status" (Hartzog, 1986, p. 63).

[82] See the "Professional Development" strand of *The Timeline* for 1983 (p. 138).

oriented, that is, directed toward what people want and need. During the latter part of the century, educators and practitioners have taken a more self-conscious and self-critical view of their work and of the position of design in society.[83] Here I provide a brief overview of the most influential movements that shaped design education as it evolved in America.[84]

The Craft Tradition

A focus on "how-to" has preoccupied much of graphic design education. As I mentioned earlier, the craft approach in graphic design emphasizes those routine aspects of design that can be proceduralized (such as using design software, copyfitting, or manipulating photos). Like many professors who teach writing in English departments, design professors may view theorizing or research as activities for the leisure class, not the overworked design teacher who may teach five courses a day.

Another dimension of the craft tradition is its rather narrow focus on traditional paper genres such as the poster or the corporate identity package. To appreciate the history of graphic design, students need to know about these genres. However, knowing only how to create designs that function as a single plane (i.e., one printed surface) dooms the young designer to the subsidiary cleanup role on multiplane documents that require the integration of text and image over pages and pages or screens and screens. Design educators have been concerned about this limitation and have been expanding the canon of genres that get taught. For example, many design programs now have courses in instructional design, interface design, and multimedia design.

Some design educators worry about the trend toward a craft approach, because while students are indeed learning to "make things," they may not be learning to argue why "one approach is better than another" (Giard, 1990, p. 25). Other educators echo this concern:

> Designers need much more than rendering or drawing skills but a language for talking about manipulating form, image, and symbol. This will allow students to articulate, transmit, and interpret the impact of design on culture. (Levy, 1990, p. 49)

[83] I am referring to educators and practitioners who are involved in document design, information design, interface design, and communications design (as opposed to those mainly engaged in poster art or advertising design).

---

[84] I do not discuss some well-known movements in fine arts because they had little effect on document design. For details about the ways in which graphic design has been envisioning itself as a field, see *A History of Graphic Design* by Philip B. Meggs (1992b) as well as back issues of *Design Issues, Design History,* and *Information Design Journal.* For information about journals in design, see Figure 2.11 (pp. 98–99) and Appendix A (pp. 498–501).

Like their colleagues in writing, designers who are educated only in the craft approach are likely to face serious challenges in the workplace. Managers who think graphic design is just a decorating activity don't see why designers should be part of the planning process for products or services. Instead, after things have already been decided, these managers hand things to designers and expect them to "make it pretty."

The Romantic Tradition

In graphic design, the romantic tradition follows the fine arts, where individual creativity is valorized above all else. Fine artists such as painters typically view themselves as participating in something superior to graphic design—something more creative, nuanced, and aesthetic. The fine arts model encourages an art-for-art's-sake view, where design serves no functional purpose, only the fulfillment of an inner vision. In design competitions, exhibitions, and publications which emphasize the romantic approach, the role of audience is reduced to that of spectator. Because many graphic designers take their education in fine arts schools, an environment which tends to celebrate the romantic approach, they often feel torn between an art-for-art's-sake and an art-for-everyday-purposes perspective. For this reason, although designers may appreciate the Bauhaus maxim that "form follows function" intellectually, much of their academic coursework teaches them to value the act of making the form above all else. This conflict of values extends across the design fields. For example, as a 1995 industrial design graduate of Pratt Institute of Design (NY) told me:

> My friends and I went to hear interface designer Donald Norman speak at a conference because we heard in one of our classes that he was famous. But after seeing him, we didn't care that much for what he said. He didn't much talk about design, only about users. He forgot to talk about creativity, about where you get ideas and how you mold them.[85] He didn't move us as designers.

An underlying belief of those who hold a romantic view is that design problems are solved "by intuition ... by the vividness of inner visualization and not by rational or sequential processes" (Findeli, 1990, p. 12). Unlike "process instruction" in writing, which generally means teaching the discrete parts of writing (e.g., planning, writing, revising), process instruction in design refers to teaching methods that lead students to an "inner transformation" (Findeli, 1990, p. 15).

[85] Interestingly, those members of the writing community called the "new rhetoricians" (e.g., Janice Lauer, Ross Winterowd, and Richard Young) have been centrally concerned with helping writers "get ideas," with enabling the process of invention. For some examples of how invention has been taught at the college level, see Miller (1985).

Like the romantic view of writing, advocates of the romantic approach in design believe that design cannot be taught or learned:

> Graphic design constitutes a kind of language with an uncertain grammar and a continuously expanding vocabulary; the imprecise nature of its rules means that it can only be studied, not learnt. (Hollis, 1994, p. 15)

A striking aspect of many graphic design histories is their organization around famous individuals who are prominently associated with particular schools of design. For example, Jan Tschichold's early work is often construed as the embodiment of New Typography (a movement I describe later). In contrast, although historians of writing often mention individuals as exemplars of a tradition,[86] histories of writing tend to focus on the features of the tradition itself more than on the individuals who typify it. That graphic design histories are punctuated by famous individuals may reflect a pervasive romantic view of the field, a view of the designer as artist who struggles against society by "making personal statements" through visual imagery.

De Stijl

An example of an early twentieth-century movement in graphic design that incorporates the romantic philosophy is *de Stijl,* which means "the style." De Stijl was a Dutch movement in fine art and architecture (c. 1917) in which designers repudiated what they considered to be the sentimental, overly decorative, and decadent art of the nineteenth century. Influenced by cubist painters such as Piet Mondrian (1872–1944) and architects such as Jacobus Johannes Pieter Oud (1890–1963),[87] de Stijl designers strove for rationality, using elementary geometric forms (triangles, rectangles, squares) in asymmetrical designs. However, the designs were often concerned not so much with meeting readers' needs as with creating ideal and supposedly objective forms, with expressing the "consciousness of their age," or with elevating life to the level of art.[88]

What made something an "ideal form" was in the eye of the designer, not the viewer. For example, Théo van Doesburg, founder and guiding spirit of de Stijl, was a bit of an eccentric when it came to designing typography and often created interesting but illegible designs. Historians say that Bauhaus leader Moholy-Nagy had van Doesburg in mind when he wrote that "[A]bsolute clarity is the first prerequisite of all typography. Legibility of the message must never suffer from an a priori aesthetics."[89]

[86] For example, Young (1980, 1995) discusses the textbooks of William Coles as an example of the new romantic tradition in writing.

[87] In architectural experiments, de Stijl was realized in the design of the Schroeder House in Utrecht (Netherlands) by Gerrit Rietveld in 1924. It is said that the house was viewed as so radical that neighbors threw rocks at it and the Schroeder children were taunted by their classmates in school (Meggs, 1992b, p. 284). The Schroeder house still stands in Utrecht in splendid visual contrast to its surroundings. It is composed of rectangular planes that appear to be suspended in space.

[88] For a discussion, see Meggs (1992b, pp. 279–285) and Purvis (1992, pp. 25–47).

[89] See Meggs (1992b, p. 291), Ovink (1965, p. 249), and Purvis (1992, pp. 31–32).

Nonetheless, de Stijl was important for establishing the visual vocabulary (e.g., use of asymmetrical designs, color as structural element rather than as ornament, and sans serif typefaces) that would undergird much of the rhetorical tradition in design.

90 That de Stijl did not survive van Doesburg is a sign of the movement's position in the romantic tradition—a movement built around an individual's energy and aesthetic.

Although de Stijl faded away after van Doesburg's death in 1931,[90] its strong sense of avant-garde romanticism remains an undercurrent in design today. The modern romantic tradition tends to portray the audience as an abstraction (e.g., audience as "society") and the designer's art as one of moving, pleasing, or preferably shocking the spectator. In fact, whether the audience "gets the design" seems not to be of concern; that the design "gets noticed" is everything. Designers working in the romantic spirit tend to forget that communication involves working out a shared language and a set of values between the designer and audience (Frascara, 1995). Although the romantic tradition still drives much of design theory and practice, a developing rhetorical tradition may soon supplant it.

The Rhetorical Tradition

Since the second decade of this century, a number of schools and movements in graphic design and typography have in one way or another advocated that designers take a more rhetorical approach to their work. These schools have emphasized the importance of considering the needs, capabilities, and values of the audience throughout the design process. Graphic design historians have tended not to focus on the rhetorical directions that these schools have taken. However, I believe that it is important to do so not only because it provides a way to characterize the developments in design and show how they parallel developments in writing, but also because it helps us to understand how these two fields converge in document design. Below I describe the movements that have contributed to the rhetorical tradition in graphic design and typography, in roughly chronological order.

Constructivism

Constructivism was a radical Russian art movement (c. 1917) born out of the devastation of the Russian Revolution and World War I. It rejected an art-for-art's-sake philosophy of design and directed its energy to socially useful activities such as graphic design, industrial design, photography, and film. The Constructivists, whose work was embraced by designers in Czechoslovakia, Hungary, Poland, and Germany, saw romantic conceptions of art as part of bourgeois society and unsuitable as an expression of the new industrial era. A goal was to link art and technology through functional designs. In practice, Constructivist designs guided the reader through the text by using typefaces and photomontage, and by juxtaposing shapes as visual signals.[91]

The Bauhaus

Without question, the Bauhaus was the most influential of the schools shaping graphic design education. The Bauhaus was founded in 1919 in Weimar, Germany by Walter Gropius, whose work articulated both a vision for design and a method to carry out that vision. It focused on solving problems of visual design created by industrialism and emphasized the principle that "form follows function." Walter Gropius said that their aim was "to breathe a soul into the dead product of the machine" (Meggs, 1992b, p. 289). During the Weimar Republic, Gropius' school provided workshops taught by artists and craftsmen; the idea was modeled along the lines of the medieval Bauhütte, bringing together master, journeyman, and apprentice.

Initially, under the teacher Johannes Itten, the goals of the Bauhaus were quite romantic, "to release each student's creative abilities," but Gropius deemphasized expressionism and instead emphasized searching for "an objective design language capable of overcoming the dangers of past styles and personal taste" (Meggs, 1992b, p. 290). Bauhaus rapidly became world famous for disseminating modernist ideas about art theory and its application to architecture and design. Bauhaus theorists advanced the idea that there should be no distinction between fine art and applied art. However, in 1933, the Gestapo demanded the removal of "Cultural Bolsheviks" from the school, with Nazi sympathizers as replacements. The faculty voted to dissolve the school, ending the most important design school of the twentieth century.

New Typography

The New Typography was a European typographic movement (c. 1920) which promoted a utilitarian typography to meet the needs of the new technological era. Its proponents searched for rational and objective principles to direct the organization and display of design elements such as type, blank space, or forms. Jan Tschichold, an exemplar of the new typography, took many of the Bauhaus principles and applied them to everyday design problems (1928/1987). For example, he argued that the type weight and type size of a word or line of text should be determined by its importance to the overall communication, a decidedly rhetorical point of view.[92]

[91] For a discussion of Constructivism, see Hollis (1994, pp. 44–48), Livingston and Livingston (1992, pp. 46–47), Meggs (1992b, pp. 285–287), or Purvis (1992, pp. 62–98).

[92] For more information about the New Typography, see Tschichold (1928/1987), who devotes a whole book to the subject, or Meggs (1992b, pp. 288–311).

International Typographic Style

International Typographic Style was a Swiss and German typographic movement (c. 1950, also known as Swiss Design), which focused on organizing visual and verbal information in a clear, functional, and precise manner. Its proponents did not perceive graphic design as merely a craft built up around commercial ends such as advertising; rather, they directed their energies toward the design of socially useful artifacts. The work of the International Typographic Style included the design of functional graphics for science. For example, German-born Anton Stankowski worked on a variety of scientific projects in which he transformed concepts such as electromagnetism into visual imagery.[93]

Ulm Hochschule für Gestaltung ("Institute of Design")

The Bauhaus tradition was continued and expanded in post–World War II Germany through the founding of the Hochschule für Gestaltung in Ulm, Germany in 1951. It brought together the lessons of the New Typography movement of Central Europe in the 1920s and 1930s with those of information theory developed at Bell Labs in the 1940s, taking a broad view of design as a rhetorical and problem-solving process. Instead of offering students coursework mainly in the fine arts, the Ulm school provided students with classes in semiotics, rhetoric, psychology, sociology, and cultural history (Meggs, 1992b, p. 334). The result was a marriage of form and appearance with highly developed theoretical interests (Kinross, 1989, pp. 141–142).

In 1996, the Bauhaus tradition has once again reemerged in the place of its birth at the Bauhaus University Weimar.[94] As Jay Rutherford, a professor of visual communications, tells us, he and his colleagues are interested "not so much in the 'posters and CD-covers' kind of design but rather in helping people find their way, take their medications properly, read easily (even if they're not good at it), or find information quickly and easily" (e-mail posted on the *InfoDesign* list, May 8, 1996).

The American Bauhaus School in Chicago

Educators in the United States look to 1937 as a pivotal year for design education. It was the year when László Moholy-Nagy founded the American Bauhaus in Chicago on the principles of its German founders. Under the sponsorship of the Association of Arts and Industries, Moholy-Nagy first headed up a school called the New Bauhaus. (The position was originally offered to Gropius but he had already accepted a position at Harvard and recommended Moholy-Nagy.) Moholy-Nagy headed the

[93] See Craig and Barton (1987, p. 186) and Meggs (1992b, pp. 334–349) for more ideas about the International Typographic Style. There are many good books on Swiss design referenced in these works.

[94] The Hochschule für Architektur und Bauwesen Weimar was renamed the Bauhaus University Weimar on May 15, 1996.

New Bauhaus School until 1938, when it lost its funding, leading him to reopen in a loft in downtown Chicago in 1939 as the School of Design.

With backing from the Container Corporation of America, Moholy-Nagy started the Institute of Design in 1944. His philosophy was "Man, not the product, is the end in view" (Hollis, 1994, p. 129). The school struggled through the war years, and in 1949, under the direction of Serge Chermayeff, the Institute of Design became part of the Illinois Institute of Technology (IIT). The main areas of study were product design, graphic design, photography, and film. Originally it also had architecture, but in 1955 that was dropped in deference to a department established by Mies van der Rohe (Findeli, 1990, pp. 4–7). The program at IIT continues to exert a powerful influence on graphic design education.[95]

Gropius' Bauhaus philosophy was famous for uniting art and technology. Moholy-Nagy added to this a third element: science. As we've seen, the rallying cry for the Bauhaus was "form follows function." To this, Moholy-Nagy (1947) adds that "form also follows scientific, technical, and artistic developments" (p. 33).

[95] There are many good books on the Bauhaus as it was interpreted in the United States. For an introduction, see overviews by Craig and Barton (1987) or Findeli (1990).

The Design Methods Movement

A relatively recent strand of education initiated in the 1960s by Christopher Jones, Christopher Alexander, and other designers from the British Design Research Society was the "design methods movement." These designers sought to bring problem-solving techniques to the world of the design studio, connecting design to studies of ergonomics and human-machine interaction (see Jones, 1970; Jones & Thornley, 1963) and emphasizing issues of planning and production (Margolin, 1989b, p. 277).

Unlike the approach to problem solving as it developed in the writing community, that is, writing as rhetorical problem solving (e.g., Flower, 1989), the problem-solving approach in design sometimes seems a bit hollow. For example, the advice for problem solving laid out by graphic designers such as Craig and Bevington (1989) in *Working with Graphic Designers* seems overly focused on the craft of design, the routine tasks, making it seem as though "anyone could do this." When I used this text in my course "Integrating Visual and Verbal Texts," my undergraduate and graduate students[96] pointed out that missing was a detailed analysis of how designers make rhetorical choices while working under typical pragmatic constraints, such as "with tight deadlines" versus "with a generous time frame." Designers haven't been specific about the relationship between goals and constraints.

[96] Typically this course would have about 25 to 30 students, four-fifths of whom were majoring in technical writing, professional writing, or rhetoric, and one-fifth of whom were majoring in graphic design, history, communications management, or computer science.

The Emergence of Contemporary Rhetorical Approaches to Graphic Design and Typography

According to Kinross (1992), during the late 1960s a new interest began to emerge in Britain and the United States—an interest in information design. The *Journal of Typographic Research* (later called *Visible Language*) was one expression of this interest. Kinross (1989) suggests that the field of information design concerns

> ... discovering what is effective graphic and typographic communication. It has been concerned with the needs of users rather than with the expressive possibilities present in design tasks. This is its point of difference with graphic design as usually practiced and taught. (p. 131)

A complementary perspective comes from Waller (1996), who describes the origins of the U.K.'s *Information Design Journal (IDJ)* and the Information Design Association (IDA) in this way:

> IDJ was started to consolidate a community of interest— an invisible college—that had emerged in the 70s among a number of designers, teachers and researchers.... It had a definite agenda—to get specialists in language and design talking to each other, and to make more research accessible to designers. The origins of the term "information design" are somewhat hazy.... Certainly we had a distinctive meaning for it—to apply the process of design (that is, planning) to the communication of information (its content and language as well as form). It was intended to be a counterpoint to the corporate identity and glitzy graphics that seemed to take over graphic design in the 80s.... IDJ quickly found a small constituency, and we ran five conferences for IDJ readers.... [T]he Information Design Association (IDA) ... [was] started ... to help grow the market, provide a focus for training and career development, and as a lobby group....

> There is a tendency to suggest that ... the whole field of information design may be torn between the differing priorities and approaches of academic, commercial and small business perspectives.... [A]cademics [have] caricatured people in business as unprincipled money-grubbers. You could easily describe some academics as "unprincipled" in their search for grants and career advantage; and many practitioners are as deeply motivated by their interest in progressing the subject area as academics....

> [A] healthy state for information design needs all sorts of ingredients. It needs a flourishing research sector addressing real issues and feeding answers and ideas into education and practice; it needs a professional sector which

takes the concepts to customers, improving the standard
of everyday information and feeding issues back into
research; and it also needs an education sector that links
the two, and trains people to work in information design
practice....

Just what is information design, anyway? It's a question
which is constantly asked of us, and we debate definitions
between us—for instance, recently on the *InfoDesign* list
on the Internet.[97] In the long term, I suspect that ID will
always have something of an identity crisis. To some
extent it exists in contrast to other things as much as in its
own right—by which I mean, it is not graphic design,
nor copy-writing, nor advertising, etc. Information
design is cross-disciplinary and integrative in its approach,
and that is always more difficult to communicate than a
specialism. (pp. 2-3)

[97] To subscribe to the InfoDesign Forum, send email to: majordomo@fwi.uva.nl. Type: subscribe InfoDesign.

Part of the interest in rhetorical approaches to graphic design comes as
a result of design educators realizing that the needs and desires of readers
are frequently at odds with those of designers. Teachers have been grap-
pling with the limitations of the fine-arts model of teaching, asking how
their teaching methods may reinforce a designer-centric model they do
not really intend (e.g., see Frascara, 1995). But not everyone appears to be
convinced that a designer-centric model is such a bad idea. Some still
resist what they may view as being seduced by the reader's aesthetic.
Consider the following criticism of a book written by Heskett (1989) in
which the reviewer derides his positive characterization of a company's
efforts to bring consumers into the design process through usability
testing:

> If what the customer wants is controlling in every case,
> should designers unlearn every notion about form and
> beauty that they might have absorbed from professional
> traditions and from their own academic and artistic
> training? (Marchand, 1990, p. 84)

Frankly, my dear, the idea of designers unlearning what they know
about form and beauty is not the issue. The conflict between the fine arts
and the rhetorical model of design raises concerns about what makes a
design good. For example, which of the following best characterizes a
good design?

- An elegant embodiment of the personal vision of the designer?

- An artifact that meets the client's goals—whatever those goals may be?

- An artifact that meets the needs and desires of the reader?

- An artifact that integrates the vision of the designer, the needs of the
  reader, and the goals of the client?

When answering such a question, design educators have considered how their answers might affect courses in graphic design. Discussing what undergraduates should learn, Frascara (1995) suggests the following.

> Graphic design is first and foremost *human communication*. A graphic designer is a person who constructs a pattern in order to organize the communication link between the piece of design and the viewer. In most cases, graphic designs are meant to be seen or read. These activities happen in time, as well as space. Although designers may work in two dimensions or in sequences of two-dimensional pieces for the most part, the enactment of these pieces happens over time. As with the playwright or the composer, the designer produces a piece (score, play) that only comes into full existence when the communication with the audience takes place. [italics in original] (p. 54)

As we can see, not only have designers moved beyond the view of communication in design as a spectator sport, but they've also moved past the narrow view of communication as decoding (as in the Shannon-Weaver model discussed in Chapter 1). Today's graphic designers recognize the interactive nature of communications design—that designs are intentional acts that invite the audience to accept or reject something (Tyler, 1995). This has led some designers to openly challenge the assumptions about "what works" (e.g., Golsby-Smith, 1996). It has meant that now more than ever before, designers are asking, "How well do audiences interact with our designed artifacts? How can we make our audiences even more active participants in the design of the artifacts themselves?" Questions of value, perceptions, and world view are widening the scope of dialogue about design (Buchanan, 1985). Such questions necessarily place the evaluation of designed things in a position of practical and theoretical prominence. Interestingly, the field of writing has been asking the same questions.

A Challenge for Today's Design Educator: Making Rhetorical Approaches More Explicit for Students

If one uses the Bauhaus movement as a benchmark for design studies, then formal education in graphic design studies has been around for over 75 years; if we begin with its American instantiation at the Illinois Institute of Technology, then more than 50 years. In 1990, there were more than one thousand American colleges that listed design concentrations in their catalogs (McCoy, 1990, p. 20). Even though formal design education has been with us for some time, there remains a question about what constitutes design knowledge, what can be taught, and who is qualified to teach it. Levy (1990) argues that there is almost a total lack of "constitutive knowledge … in the design paradigm" (p. 42).

Today's design educators agree that more discussion about theory, methods, and research needs to take place. Educators are concerned with "developing fundamental knowledge of design" and with "imparting an understanding of the processes of analysis, synthesis, interpretation, creation, evaluation, and judgment" (Levy, 1990, p. 44). However, even with these concerns, many educators still contend that design knowledge develops tacitly, based primarily on the designer's own experience (Cross, Naughton, & Walker, 1981). In fact, design educators tell us that much of what goes on in design programs is not written down, even though there may be a set of common understandings of what should go on.

Although outsiders to design may find it hard to imagine that a reliable design education program could be put together without an underlying model of design, it does seem to be the case that many design programs have not put their purpose in writing. Findeli (1990) admits that "often the models exist but rarely, if ever, are they explicit or conscious" (p. 4). Other educators reiterate this point, telling us that "philosophic beliefs are usually held quietly in the design community, yet they are crucial in determining the direction of practice" (Buchanan, 1990, p. 78). If teachers of design and typography can't tell us what designers know and can do, it is hard to imagine their students will do any better. Design educators might help students discern the key features of design models, their strengths and weaknesses. This will help students to reflect on their own developing model of design.

Writing and Design Education: What's Missing?

In looking over the history of education in writing and design, one thing seems evident: Some degree of congruence in the language that writers and designers use for talking about document design would be helpful, not only for talking to each other but also for talking to the rest of the world. Teachers need to help students consider the relationships between visual and verbal rhetorics. Students in writing and design need more of a shared sense of goals for readers. They need more practice in integrating visual and verbal thinking.[98]

Educators in both writing and design have been trying to decide what the criteria for a profession of document design are. Some in design have argued that professionals "must have a body of knowledge as well as a body of skills" (Giard, 1990, p. 27). Even so, the view of graphic designers "working by intuition" and writers "working by rules" remains deeply

[98] For a discussion of writers and graphic designers working together, see Fleming (1996a, 1996b), Keyes (1995, April 25), and Wulff (1989).

rooted in the field, especially outside the academy. Although these assumptions may have "played well" ten years ago, they have a negative impact on the careers of today's document designers.

It doesn't take a guru in job market analysis to see that young graphic designers must now compete not only with established designers but also with people who learned the latest page layout software in a one-day crash course last week. Similarly, some professional writers are finding themselves competing with people in training and marketing. Writers and designers cannot effectively compete even in their own job market unless they can be persuasive about what knowledge and skills expert practice in design entails. In fact, document designers need to be very good at reading the rhetorical situation so that they will be sensitive to the situations in which they should "seize the moment" to educate others about what it takes to do document design.

To help document design students gain facility in talking about what they do, in finding a shared language for characterizing the nature of design, educators in document design must be more explicit in helping their students answer such questions as:

- What does a document designer know?
- How do document designers acquire their knowledge?
- What knowledge and skills distinguish inexperienced and experienced writers and graphic designers? What is expertise in document design?
- What practical action can a new document designer take in helping nondesigners better understand what they know and can do?

If writers and designers are to distinguish their knowledge from the way it is viewed traditionally and from the way it is being marketed in desktop publishing venues, they will need to articulate document design's tacit assumptions, its "ways of knowing."

THE ACADEMIC ENVIRONMENT FOR DOCUMENT DESIGN: FINDING A COMFORTABLE HOME

If teachers of document design are to build educational programs designed to meet the needs of today's student, they will need a supportive environment in which to work. An important question for document design is where it should live in the university context. Ideally, document design would live in its own department where faculty with expertise in visual and verbal rhetoric would together fashion an interdisciplinary curriculum to meet educational goals such as the ones sketched earlier. So far this type of program does not exist.

As we've seen, writing is usually taught in English departments while design is taught in schools of fine arts. This does not mean that departments of English and fine arts[99] have been the best or the most appropriate homes for writing and graphic design within the university. Historians point out, for instance, that "there was no compelling reason why the teaching of writing should have been entrusted to teachers of English language and literature" (Parker, 1967/1988, p. 11). Many professors of rhetoric and writing hold that the field would be much better off had it left English to form an independent department.[100] Similarly, some graphic design professors believe that the study of graphic design would have made greater strides had it flourished out of the shadow of the fine arts. Although document design has made considerable gains in theory, research, and practice, finding a comfortable home within the university still remains a serious issue for the field at the end of the century. This is especially so for the study of professional and technical communication.

From the 1950s through the 1990s, substantial progress was made in state colleges and universities that emphasized undergraduate teaching as well as in some private engineering institutions. This progress, however, has not been steady. Some academic programs in professional and technical writing, particularly those housed in English departments, have watched the support they gained in the 1970s and 1980s erode as they entered the 1990s. Although it is difficult to say just why things have gone as they have, we can speculate.

Beginning in the 1950s, important groundwork for document design program development in state colleges and universities around the United States began. As I mentioned earlier, the interest in professional and technical communication took root mainly in colleges and universities that emphasized agriculture, mining, and engineering.[101] For the most part, liberal

[99] Here I am referring to departments of English and fine arts in the United States. There are some programs in Australia, Canada, the Netherlands, and the U.K. However, at the time this book was written, information about the development of document design in universities in countries other than the United States was sparse, almost nonexistent. An exception is a report by Graves, McFadden, and Moore (1994), which profiles academic programs in professional writing and technical communication in Canada.

---

[100] Some advanced writing programs have left English departments. For example, there is an independent Department of Rhetoric at the University of Minnesota, which offers degree programs in rhetoric and technical communication from the undergraduate level to the doctoral level. Unlike programs located in colleges of humanities, the program at Minnesota is part of the College of Agriculture, Food, and Environmental Sciences. Other programs, such as one in Technical Communication at the University of Washington in Seattle, have their own department within the School of Engineering. These programs are among the dozen or so exceptions. Unfortunately, few faculties in rhetoric and composition have the institutional support and the financial resources required to sustain a separate department.

[101] For a discussion of how programs got started, see Adams (1993) and Russell (1991).

arts institutions wanted nothing to do with professional and technical communication, as it smacked of the crass world of commerce; neither did the Ivy League schools. One report tells us that in 1959 the status of teaching technical writing "got as little welcome from literary departments as it had in 1929" (Connors, 1982, p. 344).

During the 1960s, teachers of writing and rhetoric began to gain professional respect in English departments, but for those in technical and professional writing, things were still moving very slowly. Historical studies tell us that the place of professional and technical communication in English departments was unstable well into the 1970s. Fortunately, the rise of rhetoric in departments of English during the 1960s had a concomitant positive effect on professional and technical communication. Professors began to be tenured for their work in the 1970s, especially in the latter part of the decade, a trend which continues today.[102] During the 1970s and 1980s, student enrollment in technical and professional communication courses soared (Tebeaux, 1996). It was this climate that led Connors (1982) to paint a rather rosy picture of the field at the end of the 1970s and beginning of the 1980s.

[102] To gain a sense of the persistent difficulties that professors in technical communication have had in getting tenure as well as practical advice, see the anthology edited by Tebeaux (1995).

However, the view became less positive as we moved from the late 1980s to the 1990s. During this recessionary period, many academic institutions suffered severe financial shortfalls and had to cut costs wherever they could. As Kreppel (1995) points out, "all is not well and good on the technical communication floor of the ivory tower" (p. 603). As in any business, the first things to be trimmed were those activities deemed to be less important. Not surprisingly, professional and technical communication programs were vulnerable in departments of English.

In more than a few universities, decisions were made that led professional and technical communication programs to stagnate or backslide. (This appears to be a general trend for composition studies as well.) For example, several colleges that were prepared to develop new master's degrees and doctoral programs canceled their plans. Some institutions cut back the number of courses they offered. Others took the opposite approach and increased student enrollment in order to take in more money but did not increase the number of faculty to teach the larger student body. At a few institutions, advanced writing programs were gutted by literature faculty who refused to tenure their faculty in professional or technical communication. At others, departments quietly "pulled in the reins" on hiring new tenure-track faculty in professional and technical communication and began staffing their courses with poorly paid part-time adjunct professors. (Again, this appears to be part of a more general trend in which the study of writing has been demoted in English departments). Even more worrisome is that some English departments appear to keep their writing programs solely for the purpose of generating revenue to fund other academic programs (such as cultural studies).

The effect has been that professional and technical communication programs housed in departments of English have few tenure-track professors per institution (e.g., from one to four people[103]). Iowa State University is a notable exception. Regrettably, as we move toward the end of the 1990s, it is still common for an individual to be the only person in his or her department with an interest in professional or technical communication.[104] In addition to the stagnation or backsliding that has occurred in established programs, there has been no movement in developing new programs at the nation's most prestigious universities. The field has yet to make inroads in the Ivy League. The doors to these institutions don't appear likely to open.[105] For example, there has been no movement toward developing undergraduate or graduate programs in professional or technical communication at Harvard, Yale, Princeton, Brown, University of Chicago, Cornell, Dartmouth, Duke, University of California at Berkeley, or Stanford. Occasionally such institutions bring in consultants to run weekend courses in "computer documentation" or "hypertext design," but these nondegree courses are viewed as just another source of revenue and have nothing to do with the academic life at these universities.

Professors in technical and professional communication who responded to a survey by Cunningham and Harris (1994) made comments that reflected a deep cynicism about the future of undergraduate writing programs in English departments. Many of the respondents indicate that their gains have been won "at the cost of intense and ongoing struggles" (p. 130). The results of their 1994 survey suggest that "colleagues in literature seem only slightly more likely to accept technical and professional writing as a legitimate, much less equal, discipline than they did 25 or 50 years ago" (p. 132). Some members of the field report that their colleagues in rhetoric and composition—who now compete for the same scarce funding—no longer strongly support them.

Earlier trends seemed to indicate that in the 1990s, colleges and universities would strengthen their programs in professional and technical communication. And fortunately, some programs were strengthened substantially. Especially those not housed in English departments. A 1993 survey found that some departments were expanding and projected "a relatively good outlook for the field" (Allen, 1995, p. 2). This guarded optimism may be related to a sense of shifting priorities in some English departments. More than a few have backed away from their commitment to offer a range of courses in professional and technical writing—courses

[103] Some people would argue just the opposite, that is, they would say "look how far we've come, from no professors to at least a few." It is very difficult, however, to mount an excellent document design program with just a few people. Critical mass is very important to program development.

[104] These individuals may or may not be tenure-track professors. In many cases, they are low-paid adjunct professors or part-time lecturers.

[105] One way things could change is through administrative decision at the highest levels of the university, such as a Dean, a Provost, or the President. Even then, advocacy would not be enough. Administrators need to make long-term financial commitments to fund document design programs (e.g., a guarantee of a certain number of tenure-line positions that cannot be reassigned to other academic programs if the supportive members of the administration leave to take new positions). Industry leaders could be helpful in making university administrators aware of the societal need for document design programs.

that provide students with the breadth and depth they will need to become professionals. Instead, the trend is to offer a set of more general courses:

> Most programs begun since 1980 are broad-based programs that combine courses in composition and rhetoric with courses in creative or technical writing or even journalism. Increasingly, in departments of English, professional and technical writing is taking a back seat not only to literature and creative writing but also to composition and rhetoric. (Cunningham & Harris, 1994, p. 132)

Because the advanced writing curricula at many institutions is weakly structured, just about any course above the freshman level can take the place of another (at some colleges a course in creative writing might readily substitute for a course in professional writing). Without a coherent vision of what students are supposed to learn as a result of taking a sequence of courses, programs in technical or professional communication have no quality control in the education students receive. Courses "add up" only if students do it for themselves.

Although some faculty members in English departments may feel that a random mix of writing courses is good for students, most educators in professional, technical, and scientific communication do not feel this way. Indeed, they have been worried about the issue of how courses should add up. Taking seriously the issue of curriculum design has been one of the very valuable functions of organizations such as the Council of Programs in Technical and Scientific Communication (CPTSC) and the Society for Technical Communication's Trends Forum. Teachers have been trying to move beyond the old model of skill building (Selber, 1994). They recognize that good professionals are created by disciplined practice, that is, practice informed by in-depth knowledge about document design. They want to meet the challenge of the nonacademic community to educate "communications consultants who can handle high-level design and decision-making" (Hackos, 1995, p. 16). They have been identifying the best matrix of courses to give students the depth and breadth they need (Southard & Reeves, 1995). The next generation of academic programs (as well as students and their employers) will benefit from the hard work going on now.

Still, the trend toward staffing programs with adjunct faculty casts doubts on the quality and the long-term stability of the 200 or so professional writing and technical communications programs now on the books. It also suggests that prospective students who are looking for a good school had better do their homework and look beyond the brochures about the programs that interest them. Academic programs vary widely in the caliber of education they offer, and very few have been evaluated formally.[106] Before taking an advanced degree in writing or design, prospective students would be well advised to investigate the program by talking to current and former students.

THE FIELD OF DOCUMENT DESIGN TODAY

Despite the challenges confronting the field, there are many reasons to be optimistic. Document design is growing rapidly and gaining more public attention. In 1995, *Money* cited technical communication as the 18th best profession for the future. In a 1995 survey of growth professions, the *Atlanta Journal-Constitution* listed technical communication as the fifth fastest growing profession. Document design today is supported by a variety of disciplines broadly associated with the study and practice of communication.

The field now benefits from an invigorated sense of purpose as well as from lively forums in which ideas about document design are shared. Figure 2.11 (on the next two pages) presents some of the publications that contribute to the growing body of knowledge about document design. These publications[107] cross disciplinary as well as geographic borders, with publications from Australia, Canada, Japan, the Netherlands, the United Kingdom, and the United States. They provide articles about writing, designing, reading, learning, thinking, and using technology.

The resources now available offer professionals a view of how studies of writing inform those of design (and vice versa). In addition, they offer the very important perspectives of cognitive psychology, human–computer studies, reading and language comprehension, educational research, and discourse analysis. Document designers who are familiar with the interdisciplinary literature will undoubtedly be prepared to take a broader and more informed perspective in solving problems of communication. Furthermore, document designers who can understand and evaluate research (whether or not they do it themselves) are in a better position to make smart decisions and to recognize bad ones. As the history of document design shows, our field cannot progress if we ignore the discoveries of other fields, if we ignore empirical research, or if we ignore what writers and designers (as well as academics and nonacademics) have in common.

THE CONTEXT OF DOCUMENT DESIGN: REFLECTING ON THE PAST, ENVISIONING THE FUTURE

The Timeline that follows this section is intended to provide a context for document design in the twentieth century. It shows some of the events

[106] Many writing professors are interested in evaluating the quality of their programs and have been developing tools both for self-study and for assessments carried out by external reviewers (see Anderson, 1995; CPTSC, 1995).

[107] To avoid invoking personal or disciplinary assumptions about which publications are most important, I arranged them on the basis of their shape and visual contrast.

▲ Figure 2.11 *The field of document design is enriched by interdisciplinary publications from around the world. Photo commissioned by K. A. Schriver. Special thanks to photographer Jeff Macklin from the Carnegie Mellon Research Institute, Pittsburgh, PA. Pictured are:*

(row 1): Technostyle, SIGCHI, Human Factors, International Journal of Human-Computer Studies, Cognitive Science, Metropolis, IDeAs, Journal of Design History, JAC.

*(row 2): Design Issues, Reading Research Quarterly, Journal of Technical Writing and Communication, Human-Computer Interaction, *Journal of Computer Documentation, CSCW 88, Visible Language, AMWA Journal, CCC, Design Issues (note: accidentally included twice), Design Methods.*

(row 3): Written Communication, Technical Communication, Communication News, Design Studies, CPTSC, Design Quarterly, Technical Communication Quarterly, IEEE Transactions on Professional Communication, American Educational Research Journal.

(row 4): Rhetoric Review, IDJ, Computers and Composition, College English, JBTC, RTE, The Technical Writer, tekst[blad].

Journals deserving mention that (regrettably) were not included in this photo: AIGA Journal of Graphic Design; Communication Arts; Discourse Processes; Graphis; ID; Journal of Business Communication; Journal of Experimental Psychology: Applied; and Print. For a brief synopsis of the mission statements of these publications as well as ordering information, see Appendix A (pp. 498–501).

that directly or indirectly contributed to the international evolution of document design—pointing to influences on the field and the social world in which writing and design developed. However, it does not explain why the field took shape as it did. (That is another project.) My aim here is more modest: If document design has any significance, it is within the wider social world in which its projects take on meaning rather than in the closed and elitist subcultures of the academy or in the secretive and proprietary worlds of business and government.

As we have seen in this chapter, document designers have been asking themselves if what they do is an art or a science. There is only one possible answer to this question: "both and neither." The problem is with the dichotomous framing of the question. It reduces the richness of both art and science by flattening them, contrasting them as supposed polar opposites. *Document design blends art and science through the design of textual artifacts that help people take practical action in everyday reading situations.*

One thing *The Timeline* tells us is that the history of document design has been not progressive but adaptive, and sometimes reactive. Our field continues to configure and reconfigure itself, adapting to the changing needs of society and to innovation in science and technology. At the end of the century the field is still trying to define itself, but there is a key difference. The community is no longer invisible. There are academic programs, professional societies, Internet bulletin boards, and journals for sharing knowledge. There are more people than ever before working to push the field ahead, including:

- Experienced document designers who are inventing new approaches to document design.

- Educators who are working on problems of how to teach visual and verbal thinking.

- Researchers who are trying to build a knowledge platform for enriching our understanding of what we do.

- Students who are cross-fertilizing the field, sharing their academic experience during summer internships in industry and returning to universities to share knowledge about their experiences in industry.

However, in some ways these members of the field have been like herds of spirited wild horses, with groups running off in different directions. Collaboration and interaction among the groups has been spotty. For example, there is sometimes animosity and contentiousness between academics and nonacademics.[108] In addition, there has been a good deal of randomness about which interests are worked out, which ones fade away, or which ones, as Connors (1981/1988) said about the demise of teachers' interest in the modes of discourse, "get ignored to death" (p. 32).

[108] As the extended quote cited earlier about the founding of the Information Design Society showed, some academics "caricature people in business as unprincipled money-grubbers while some nonacademics see academics as unprincipled in their search for grants and career advantage" (Waller, 1996). The more common stereotype is that academics believe that nonacademics aren't interested in anything except tomorrow's deadline, while nonacademics believe that academics aren't interested in solving practical problems and spend their time spinning useless theories. This hostility is an old problem; see the first entry of the "Professional Development" strand of *The Timeline* (p. 106). Members of the field of document design need to work on this problem to prevent the gap between academics and nonacademics from increasing.

(Connors was commenting on the gradual disappearance of teachers' emphasis on description, narration, exposition, and argument as the focus of their teaching.) There is also little overlap between the ways that academics and nonacademics talk about what we need to be doing as a field in order to develop further. Hopefully, this will change.

As *The Timeline* shows, document design as a profession has made quite a few gains, especially in the last few decades. But all one has to do is compare the questions asked at the beginning of the century with those posed at the end to see that our field has not solved the problem of its status in industry and universities. Practicing document designers are still not on equal footing with product development engineers, computer scientists, information systems engineers, art directors, marketing directors, or strategic planners—even though their work is every bit as complex and important.

Similarly, after nearly 50 years of academic programs in the field, professors who teach writing or graphic design still lack the status accorded to their colleagues in literature and the fine arts.[109] It would be incorrect to assume, however, that the problem is simply external. As Buchanan (1990) suggests, the field needs better ways to get across its ideas and methods to outsiders and to its own students (p. 75).

[109] See the "Education & Practice in Writing/Rhetoric" strand of *The Timeline* for 1910+, 1930+, 1939, 1948, 1959, and 1994 (pp. 108, 114, 116, 120, 124, 148).

Document design has a perception problem. However, to change the perceptions of outsiders, members of the field need to reenvision themselves. Doing so will require understanding our past and inventing our future—reflecting on how we have imagined ourselves. As a way to enhance this envisioning process, *The Timeline* focuses on the period between 1900 and 1995. It presents historical moments related to the five dynamically interacting contexts discussed in this chapter:

- *Education and Practice in Writing:* The development of knowledge about rhetoric and writing, knowledge that led not only to the publication of articles, books, and dissertations, but also to the creation of academic programs which encouraged further theory, research, and practice in document design

- *Professional Developments in Writing and Graphic Design:* Journals and professional societies that promoted the knowledge-making activities of practitioners, teachers, and researchers in writing and design—providing forums in which members of the field could share ideas and gain a sense of professional identity

- *Education and Practice in Graphic Design:* Academic programs and professional consultancies in graphic design—developments that not only increased the stature of graphic design and typography within the fine arts community but also improved the sensitivity of the general public to the functions of design in society

- *Science, Technology, and the Environment:* Discoveries in science, medicine, and technology (including the events and technologies associated with environmental protection) that generated a need for documents—forces that not only created a demand for well-designed documents but also changed the nature of document design activity itself

- *Society and Consumerism:* Society and its trends, particularly those concerning the need for public information about topics related to consumer products, science, medicine, technology, the environment, and government programs—trends that not only affected citizens' expectations for documents but also influenced their views of themselves as readers and users

In creating *The Timeline,* I came up with roughly 60 entries per decade for each of the five strands. I decided to display 10 to 30 entries per strand for each decade. I did not try to choose an entry for each year for each of the five strands and took liberty in skipping years when little of note leaped out at me. As I said at the beginning of this chapter, I used *The Timeline* as a heuristic for exploring the concurrent and sequential relations in document design, not as a way to nail down the field. I did not strive for equal numbers of entries but for equal space per strand and edited so that strands for each decade ended on the same page. Each two-page spread presents a decade, with some decades spilling over several spreads.

When events had a reasonably firm time frame, my entry for that event has a specific date (e.g., 1901). Alternatively, if the event persists over time or has an approximate beginning, I use a plus sign after the date (e.g., 1901+). It is my hope that each entry is intelligible and that ideas can be explored further through the "Notes" (in the extreme right-hand column of each spread) or the bibliography (at the end of this book).

I expect most readers will use *The Timeline* for reference, rather than reading it from beginning to end. But for those who want to read it, I suggest first looking over the organization of a two-page spread. Notice that the left page of each spread presents entries for education, practice, and professional development in writing and design, while the right page presents the forces that pushed the development of document design in the twentieth century—consumerism, science, technology, and the preservation of the environment. My idea is to allow readers to see events that shaped writing and design both in and out of the academy. As I mentioned earlier, the strand "Professional Development" presents entries for writing and design, bringing together developments for professionals in industry and university settings. The idea is to help people who deal with words and pictures better understand how interrelated their professional lives have been.

For readers interested in events that are particular to one of the five strands, I recommend reading down the columns decade by decade. For those who want a snapshot of a single decade, reading down the columns one at a time will give a better picture of the decade than reading the column entries from left to right. For those who want to use *The Timeline* as a reference, it is indexed.

Although I have tried to be accurate and comprehensive, there may be errors in dates or serious omissions.[110] Clearly the choice of other historical moments than those I've selected would yield a different view. Like any designed artifact, it is biased by the eyes of the designer.

[110] I welcome feedback about *The Timeline,* including ideas for new entries or corrections to those included. Please send suggestions to me by e-mail: ksøe+@andrew.cmu.edu.

A Timeline of
Document Design
1900 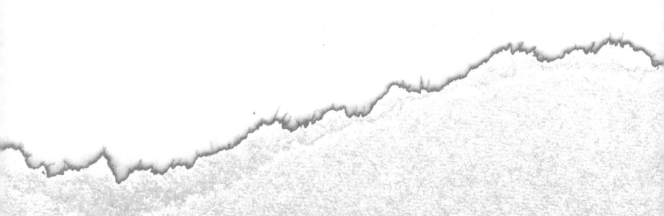 1995

There are no doubt moments about which it is legitimate to say that one thing stopped and another started or that something happened that significantly changes the flow of events.... [E]ven in cases where boundary marking is legitimate, privileging the event may result in overlooking the temporal flow in which the event is embedded.... The effort to identify historical boundaries, then, poses some significant questions of historical interpretation having to do both with the relation of event to context and with the conceptualization of the context itself.

— Richard E. Young & Maureen Daly Goggin (1993, pp. 24–25)

For any classification scheme, there will be disagreement about the categories used, their mutual exclusivity, and about judgments in assigning information to categories. There will also be concerns about the categories and sorts of information that are not included.

— Frank R. Smith, Editor Emeritus of *Technical Communication*
and reviewer of the manuscript for this book (personal communication, 1993)

Education & Practice in Writing / Rhetoric

1900s

1900 +. Writing instruction emphasizes usage, grammar, and mechanics. Students are expected to adapt their texts for an audience and to find an original thesis, but they are not taught explicit ways to do so. Teachers spend most of their time correcting students' grammatical and stylistic errors; this focus on the product of writing rather than on the process of creating it, called "current-traditional rhetoric," dominates writing instruction in the U.S. well into the 1960s.[1]

1900. The pedagogical section of the Modern Language Association (MLA) asks: "Is Rhetoric a proper subject for graduate work? If so, what are the leading problems of Rhetoric as a graduate study? Is reading alone sufficient to develop good writers?"[2]

1902. The first collegiate business-writing course begins at the University of Illinois.

1903. The Modern Language Association (MLA) disbands its pedagogical section, the only section concerned with writing instruction.[3]

1904. One of the first 20th century technical writing courses, "engineering English," is mounted at Tufts College by Samuel Chandler Earle.[4]

1908. T. A. Rickerd's *Guide to Technical Writing* is published; one of the earliest 20th century texts on the subject, it focuses mainly on grammar and usage.

1908. J. Martin Telleen points out that freshman English is not very helpful and that it is not surprising that the *Engineering Record* describes the writing of many practicing engineers as "wretched."[5]

Professional Development

1900s

1900 +. In the U.S., business and industry leaders make known to colleges and universities their needs for workers with practical skills, arguing that education should prepare students for work in this life, not for rewards in the next—an argument made since the latter part of the 19th century.[6]

1900 +. In business and academic contexts, writers are encouraged to consider alternative ways they might influence the audiences for whom they write, but audiences are viewed as passive and static, not contributing to the shaping of meaning.[7]

1900 +. Textbooks on "writing style" continue to appear; most emphasize the need to avoid grammatical impurities, barbarisms, improprieties, and solecisms. In addition to prescribing what not to do, they offer advice on proper diction and grammar; although the tone of their prescriptions is authoritative, their advice is frequently arbitrary, imposing standards that are biased toward the dialects of a particular social class.[8]

1900 +. There appears to be no evidence that professional development in writing has any relation to development in graphic design.

1905. A few faculty from English departments join the Society for the Promotion of Engineering Education; they are the first to advocate that engineering students take writing courses.[9]

1907. The precursor of the Bauhaus school, the Deutscher Werkbund, is founded by design critics, architects, and industry leaders; its goal is to bring the arts, crafts, and industry closer together to produce better-designed and more functional products.[10]

Education & Practice in Graphic Design

1900s

1902. The Essex House Press in London publishes the design masterpiece the *Psalter,* a collection of psalms in vernacular 16th century English from a 1540 translation by Archbishop Crammer of Canterbury.

1903. The Vienna Workshops, a collaboration of carpenters, bookbinders, metalsmiths, and leather workers, are founded; members attempt to elevate crafts to the standards of the fine arts and to offer alternatives to poorly designed and historically trite mass-produced objects.[11]

1905. The German Expressionist movement in fine arts begins, employing woodcuts to express graphic ideas in posters and books, often using bold, simplified forms.

1906 +. Austrian architect Adolf Loos plays a role in shifting the attention in design from a "love of decoration" and "horror of empty space" to a focus on human needs as a standard for measuring utilitarian form.[12]

1906. English type designer and master calligrapher and letterer Edward Johnston publishes the best-selling *Writing, Illuminating, and Lettering.*

1907. The Deutscher Werkbund is formed in Munich, an alliance of manufacturers, retailers, and designers aimed at improving the quality of German products. It was inspired by the Arts and Crafts Movement, which emerged in Britain in the 1870s in response to the shoddy product design of the Industrial Revolution. The Deutscher Werkbund adopts the philosophy "form without ornamentation" and provides inspiration for what will later become the Bauhaus School of Design (see 1919).[13]

▲ **Background Image.** *The mascot of the 1903 Victor Talking Machine listens to "his master's voice"; potential buyers could peruse the Victor's features and functions in the "Talking Machines Department" of the Sears Mail-Order Catalog.*

Science, Technology, & Environment

1900s

1900 +. Underwood's "Visible Typewriter," which allows typists to see what they type, becomes very popular.

1900 +. The Edison Mimeograph machine becomes popular in business.

1900. Max Planck (Germany) proposes the quantum theory of light.[†††]

1901. The first transatlantic telegraphic radio transmission takes place.[†]

1902. The first electric typewriter, the Blickensderfer Electric, is produced.[14]

1903. The Wright brothers launch the first successful U.S. airplane flight.[†]

1904. W. Rubel (U.S.) invents off-set printing.[†]

1905. Guglielmo Marconi works on wireless telegraphy.[†]

1905. The dial telephone is invented.[†]

1905. Albert Einstein formulates a special theory of relativity.[††]

1906. The tungsten-filament light bulb is introduced.[†]

1906. AM radio transmits music and voice for the first time.[†]

1907. The Graphophone, modeled on Edison's phonograph of 1877, is developed as an office dictation machine.

1908. Ford Motor Company introduces the Model T.

1908. French physicist Gabriel Jones Lippmann wins the Nobel Prize in Physics for the invention of a method of color photography.[†]

Society & Consumerism

1900s

1900 +. People who once purchased soap, oatmeal, and crackers now buy *Ivory, Quaker Oats,* and *Uneeda Biscuit.*[15]

1900 +. Time motion studies of workers in industry become a popular way to control workers through "scientific management."[16]

1900 +. U.S. citizens become increasingly concerned about sanitation and safety problems in food, drugs, and cosmetics.[17]

1900. Employees in the United States receive an average wage of 22 cents per hour.[18]

1900. The tenth edition of the *Sears Mail-Order Catalog* advertises more than 1100 pages of products, allowing people across the U.S. to purchase items as diverse as baby carriages and tombstones.[19]

1903. Emmeline Pankhurst founds the National Women's Social and Political Union.[††]

1905 +. More than 10 million immigrants enter the U.S. from southern and eastern Europe (–1914).[††]

1906. Upton Sinclair paints a grim picture of the food processing methods practiced by meat packers in the Chicago stockyards.[20]

1906. The U.S. Pure Food and Drugs Act is enacted.[††]

1906. The first recorded promotional message is presented, announcing, "I am the Edison Phonograph and I will bring crystal clear fidelity and purity of tone."

Notes

1. Berlin, 1984; Young, 1976. Daniel Fogarty coined the term "current-traditional rhetoric" in 1959 to describe an emphasis on the craft of writing—the composing product rather than the composing process.

2. Stewart, 1985, p. 20.

3. Russell, 1991, p. 181.

4. Connors, 1982, p. 332.

5. Ibid., p. 331.

6. Berlin, 1984, pp. 58–76.

7. Ibid., p. 64.

8. Ibid., p. 73.

9. Connors, 1982, p. 331.

10. Craig & Barton, 1987, p. 133.

11. Meggs, 1983, p. 262.

12. Ibid., p. 262.

13. Livingston & Livingston, 1992, pp. 18, 55.

14. Daniels, 1980, p. 32.

15. Consumers Union, Jan. 1986, p. 8.

16. Taylor, 1911. See also Hilgard, 1987, pp. 701–707; Nelson, 1974, pp. 479–500; Noble, 1977, pp. 264–274; Russell, 1991, p. 103.

17. Herrmann, 1970.

18. Schroeder, 1970, pp. 1–3.

19. Ibid., pp. 1–3.

20. Sinclair, 1906.

[†] From Hellemans & Bunch, 1991.

[††] From Grun, 1991.

[†††] From Giscard d'Estaing, 1993.

Education & Practice in Writing / Rhetoric

1910s

1910 +. Technical writing courses continue to develop, mostly in colleges of engineering, mining, or agriculture, but their teachers have low status. English departments consider technical writing courses a tiresome service beneath the teaching of literature; engineering schools consider writing a useful adjunct, but of lesser value than engineering.[21]

1911. The National Council of Teachers of English (NCTE) is formed to fight the use of college-developed Uniform Reading Lists that specify high-school readings necessary to pass college entrance exams. Teachers argue that high schools should make curricular decisions, not colleges; their resolve is intensified by their concern for the learning problems of students not going to college, particularly immigrant students.[22]

1911. Samuel Chandler Earle publishes *The Theory and Practice of Technical Writing,* one of the earliest technical writing texts; Earle will become known as "the Father of Technical Writing Instruction."[23]

1912. Glenn E. Palmer summarizes an argument between Harvard and Yale over how writing should be taught: Harvard advocates that students can cultivate good language habits by reading literature; Yale argues for inspiring students with literature and with what was called "liberal culture," contending that literature ought to be studied for its own sake, and that if writing is to be taught at all, it should be taught to encourage the "gifted" to create literature, not rhetoric.[24]

1914. A course in "report writing" is developed at the University of Michigan's College of Engineering.[25]

Professional Development

1910s

1910 +. As scientific management gains momentum in business, the enthusiasm for efficiency, accountability, and quantification becomes pervasive. These criteria are also applied in evaluating the work of writers, graphic designers, and illustrators, especially those producing advertisements, risk communications, and policy and procedure documents. Scientific management also influences writing classes in high schools and colleges, where the "efficiency of writing instruction" is studied.[26]

1910 +. Members of the advertising community attempt to legitimize their enterprise by using "scientific" methods; advertising is construed as the denouncer of fraud and as an advance toward a higher civilization, but the audience is construed as "reasonably predictable," "impulsive," "unthinking," and "easily manipulated."[27]

1911. The first known airplane flight manual is written, issued with the Glen Curtiss "pusher," thereby helping to establish the tradition of instructional texts in aviation that combine procedures and technical illustrations.[28]

1914. The Speech Communication Association of America (SCA) is founded, representing a formal break between teachers of speech and the National Council of Teachers of English (NCTE).

1914. The American Institute of Graphic Arts is founded; the AIGA is a non-profit organization dedicated to "do all things which would raise the standards, and extend and develop graphic arts in the U.S. towards perfection."[29]

1915. The first Singer sewing machine manual is written and illustrated.

Education & Practice in Graphic Design

1910s

1916. Edward Johnston creates the first modern sans serif typeface for the London Underground, the Johnston's Railway Type.

1917 +. Constructivism—a radical Russian art movement—develops. It rejects "art for art's sake" and directs its energy to socially useful activities like graphic design, industrial design, and film. The constructivist utilitarian ethos will have a profound influence on the Bauhaus School, which later elaborates its ideals and works out its educational implications (see 1919 and 1937).[30]

1917 +. The Dutch movement "de Stijl" ("the Style") becomes popular; in their compositions de Stijl artists strive for dynamic asymmetry rather than static symmetry.[31]

1917. The New York City Telephone Company sponsors research on indenting to improve the legibility of their phone directories.[32]

1917. Guillaume Apollinaire publishes a book of visual poems entitled *Calligrammes* in which he integrates word and image.

1918 +. The Art Deco movement flourishes; its designs are quite different from the florid creations of Art Nouveau (–1939).[33]

1918 +. Maxfield Parrish designs calendars for Edison Mazda; they will make his name a household word (–1934).

1918. Ernst Keller's work in layout, influenced by the de Stijl school's practice of dividing horizontal and vertical visual space, becomes important in the development of grid systems in design.[34]

▲ **Background Image.** *Elegant in design, candlestick telephones gained enormous popularity in the 1910s; using a candlestick phone involved lifting the receiver and listening for the operator to provide service (original models had neither rotary dials nor ringer boxes). Unlike the feature-laden phones of the latter part of the century, the candlestick did not require pages of instructions.*

Science, Technology, & Environment

1910s

1910 +. Photocopying machines, invented in France in 1900, make their first appearance in the U.S.[35]

1910. Electric washing machines are introduced.[†]

1910. Marie Curie's *Traité de Radioactivité* (Treatise on Radioactivity) is published; in 1911, she will win the Nobel Prize in Chemistry for her discovery of radium and polonium.[†]

1910. In *Future of Electricity,* Charles Proteus Steinmetz warns about air pollution from burning coal and water pollution from uncontrolled sewage disposal into rivers.[†]

1910. Chemist Caimir Funk (Poland) isolates vitamin B1 and gives the name "vitamine" to his work.[†††]

1911. Air conditioning is invented by Willis Carrier (U.S.).[†††]

1911. Hieke Kamerlingh Onnes (Netherlands) discovers superconductivity in mercury.[†††]

1912 +. The use of carbon paper to make copies becomes widespread in American business and government.[36]

1913. Henry Ford introduces the first assembly line for manufacturing automobiles.[†]

1913. German surgeon A. Salomen develops mammography.[†]

1914. Edward Kleinschmidt invents the teletypewriter.[†]

1915. The first automatic mechanical pencil is invented by Rokuji Hayakawa (Japan).[†††]

Society & Consumerism

1910s

1912. In the U.S., the first branch of the Better Business Bureau is founded; it is the only national organization that is devoted to handling consumers' complaints about shoddy and unethical business practices.

1913. The first home refrigerator goes on sale in Chicago.[†]

1913. To help spur sales of Life-Saver candies in the U.S., Edward J. Noble invents the counter display, enticing consumers to buy candies displayed next to a retailer's cash register.[†††]

1913. In the U.S., Americans pay their first income tax and use the first IRS tax form.[37]

1913. The first crossword puzzles appear in the *New York World*'s weekly supplement.[†††]

1914 +. The slogan "it pays to advertise" is used by American business to promote the selling of goods.

1914. The Camel cigarette is introduced; three years later, Lucky Strike becomes their competitor; smoking rapidly becomes fashionable and is portrayed as sexy.

1914. World War I begins.

1915. In the U.S., coast-to-coast long distance telephone service is inaugurated; calls take approximately 25 minutes to go through and cost a minimum of $20.70.[38]

1915. Margaret Sanger is jailed for writing *Family Limitation,* the first book on birth control.[††]

1916. In the U.S., the first self-serve grocery store is opened.[39]

Notes

[21] Connors, 1982; Russell, 1991.

[22] Scott, 1901, pp. 365–378; discussed in Applebee, 1974, pp. 49–54; Berlin, 1990, p. 193.

[23] Connors, 1982, p. 332.

[24] Palmer, 1912, p. 488; cited in Berlin, 1990, p. 190.

[25] Nelson, 1931, p. 495.

[26] Berlin, 1990, p. 199; Hilgard, 1987, pp. 678, 701–707; Killingsworth & Palmer, 1992, pp. 164–166; Noble, 1977, pp. 264–274; Taylor, 1911; Varnedoe & Gopnik, 1990, pp. 440–449; Veysey, 1965, pp. 116, 353; Yates, 1989, pp. 1–20.

[27] Higham, 1918; Scott, 1908; Wadsworth, 1913.

[28] AAA Academy, 1911.

[29] Livingston & Livingston, 1992, p. 15.

[30] Ibid., p. 47.

[31] Craig & Barton, 1987, p. 130.

[32] Baird, 1917.

[33] Livingston & Livingston, 1992.

[34] Gottschall, 1989, p. 45.

[35] Yates, 1989, p. 54.

[36] Ibid., pp. 47–49.

[37] IRS historian, personal communication, 1993.

[38] Flexner, 1982, p. 501.

[39] Ibid., p. 494.

[†] From Hellemans & Bunch, 1991.

[††] From Grun, 1991.

[†††] From Giscard d'Estaing, 1993.

Education & Practice in Writing / Rhetoric

1910s *continued*

1914. Psychologists such as Edward Thorndike call for the use of "objective" tests to sort students for specific roles in industry; this new emphasis is part of the "social efficiency" movement, in which schools design curricula to prepare students for future social activities in the workplace and in civic life.[40]

1916. John Dewey lays the groundwork for his philosophy of education; it soon becomes a cornerstone of American public school education.[41]

1918. G. B. Hotchkiss publishes *Business English: Principles and Practice,* a business writing text that introduces the Five C's: completeness, clarity, consideration, courtesy, and correctness.

1920s

1920 +. Technical writing courses in engineering and agricultural schools focus on the mechanics and forms of writing—that is, on issues of sentence-level correctness and on how to write descriptions and instructions—rather than on rhetorical considerations such as attention to the audience's needs and goals.[42]

1921. Edward L. Thorndike publishes a handbook in which he presents the 10,000 most common words in American English; it is used to manipulate the difficulty levels of vocabulary in textbooks, military manuals, and standardized tests. It also gains enormous popularity for estimating the difficulty of texts.[43]

Professional Development

1910s *continued*

1915 +. Companies derive their own genres for written communication—forms, reporting mechanisms, in-house organs, even their own company-mandated prose styles—without the aid of academia.[44]

1917. The first issue of the *Journal of Applied Psychology* is released; it will publish much of the early research on the legibility of typography and the process of reading.

1918. During World War I, many criticize advertising for being dishonest; even so, practitioners defend it as an edifying force in democratic society.[45]

1919. Ford releases a *Users' Guide* for its Model T, one of the early examples of task-oriented writing and design for the automobile industry.

1920s

1920 +. Businesses begin to bring in English professors as consultants on communication problems, claiming that it is cheaper than giving a course in English to executives.[46]

1920 +. Charts, diagrams, tables, and graphs become widely used in American business reports, aiding readability and maximizing efficiency.[47]

1920 +. Commercially available self-help books on writing are published.

1920 +. Family magazines such as *The Saturday Evening Post* and *Colliers* provide a showcase for the works of some of America's finest illustrators.

Education & Practice in Graphic Design

1910s *continued*

1918. An ad for the Club Dada uses typography to create shock.

1919 +. Lazar Markovich Lissitzy, a Russian Constructivist, views the 1917 Russian Revolution as an opportunity to forge a new unity between technology and art; he emphasizes the design of objects that make society and the environment richer.[48]

1919. In Germany, Walter Gropius founds the Bauhaus Movement, revolutionizing the fine arts with the philosophy "form follows function." In graphic design, the emphasis is on the functional use of grids, assymetrical organization of design elements, and sans serif typefaces. Bauhaus launches the New Typography (see 1920 +) and later, the International Typographic Style (see 1942 + and 1950 +).[49]

1920s

1920 +. Few rules pertain to ad copy in magazines; if the ad copy is indistinguishable from the magazine copy (in terms of typeface and design), then the ad may have a better chance of being read; false claims in ads are not punished.[50]

1920 +. The New Typography movement develops in Europe; promoted as a utilitarian typography to meet the needs of the new technological era, its proponents search for rational and objective principles to direct the organization and display of design elements (e.g., type, blank space, or forms.)[51]

1920 +. American E. McKnight Kauffer uses cubism to design posters.

▲ **Background Image.** *Each Model T Ford came with an instruction manual with answers to more than 100 questions new buyers might ask; the introduction of the manual reassured customers that they could learn to use their car without difficulty since "the great majority of Ford owners have little or no practical experience with things mechanical." Shown here is a composite of several of Ford's later models.*

Science, Technology, & Environment

1910s *continued*

1915. The first transcontinental telephone call in North America is made, between Alexander Graham Bell in New York and Thomas A. Watson in San Francisco.[†]

1915. Albert Einstein completes his theory of gravitation, known as the general theory of relativity.[†]

1915. Wireless service is established between the U.S. and Japan.

1917. Duncan Black and Alonso Decker manufacture the first rotary hand drill for do-it-yourself enthusiasts.[†††]

1919. The Radio Corporation of America (RCA) is founded.[††]

1919. Shortwave radio is developed.[†]

1920s

1920. Westinghouse opens the first American broadcasting station, KDKA, in Pittsburgh, Pennsylvania.[††]

1921. Albert W. Hull invents the magnetron.[†]

1924. Vladimir Kosma Zworykin develops the iconoscope, an early type of television system.[†]

1925. Vannevar Bush and coworkers work on the first analog computer, a machine designed to solve differential equations; it is completed in 1930.[†]

1925. The microphone is invented by a team from Bell Laboratories.[†††]

Society & Consumerism

1910s *continued*

1916. Prohibition gains ground as 24 U.S. states vote against the sale of alcoholic beverages.[††]

1917. The first nationwide supermarket chain is established by the Great Atlantic and Pacific Tea Company, later known as A & P.[52]

1918. A worldwide influenza epidemic strikes; by 1920 nearly 22 million people are dead.[††]

1918. The General Electric Frigidaire refrigerator becomes so popular that many people erroneously call all refrigerators "frigidaires."[53]

1918. In the U.S., air mail delivery begins.[††]

1918. World War I ends.

1920s

1920 +. While mass production begins to fill the world with new things, it also severs the connections between producer and consumer; the only clues to quality are the brand name of the product and any information given in advertising.[54]

1920 +. Homes in U.S. cities are wired not only for the light electricity provides, but also for the appliances it runs: fans, toasters, irons, and more.[55]

1920 +. The press refers to women as the "consumers" in American society; advertising firms target women with an increasing array of visual and verbal messages.

Notes

[40] Russell, 1991, p. 138; Spring, 1986, p. 98.

[41] Dewey, 1916.

[42] Connors, 1982; Russell, 1991, p. 123.

[43] Thorndike, 1921.

[44] Yates (1989) suggests that genres such as reports became important because they formed a kind of "organizational memory." For example, in 1841, a series of train collisions prompted the Western Railroad Company to document its activities, which led to the creation of reports, instructions, timetables, and work orders.

[45] For example, see Orman, 1918.

[46] Yates, 1989.

[47] Ibid., p. 91.

[48] Meggs, 1983, pp. 312–313.

[49] Livingston & Livingston, 1992, p. 23; Meggs, 1992, pp. 288–311.

[50] Consumers Union, Jan. 1986, p. 9.

[51] Livingston & Livingston, 1992, p. 145; Meggs, 1992, pp. 288–311.

[52] Flexner, 1982, p. 494.

[53] Ibid., p. 319.

[54] Consumers Union, Jan. 1986, p. 8.

[55] Ibid.

[†] From Hellemans & Bunch, 1991.

[††] From Grun, 1991.

[†††] From Giscard d'Estaing, 1993.

Education & Practice in Writing / Rhetoric

1920s *continued*

1922. Fred Newton Scott attacks the dominant methods used to teach writing in the U.S., especially "the brutality of theme correction," which he believes destroys the student's desire to communicate in writing.[56]

1922. Ferdinand Saussure publishes *Course in General Linguistics,* in which he offers a perspective on language that will influence discussions in linguistics and semiotics throughout the century.

1923. B. A. Lively and S. L. Pressey develop an early readability formula.[57]

1923. C. K. Ogden and I. A. Richards publish a classic text on contemporary rhetoric, *The Meaning of Meaning.*

1924. Engineering faculty express the opinion that literary activity does not help student engineers present complex data in a brief and attractive form; they stress the need for education in expository writing.[58]

1924. Ray Palmer Baker's *The Preparation of Technical Reports* is published, an early technical writing textbook.

1925. High school teacher John T. Scopes goes on trial after he breaks the law by teaching the theory of evolution in his classroom; the outcome has implications for what can be taught or read in public schools.

1929. The "Vienna Circle" (known for operationalism, logical positivism, and behaviorism) is formed by Carnap, Hahn, Neurath, Schlick, and others. Their work stirs debate and influences the development of subsequent theories in philosophy and science.

Professional Development

1920s *continued*

1920 +. The 1920s are dubbed the Advertising Decade, and the career of the "ad writer" develops.[59]

1920 +. The "memo" emerges as a distinct genre in organizations; it takes the place of traditional letter-writing in internal correspondence.[60]

1920. The Art Directors Club of New York is founded.

1923. Henry Luce and Briton Hadden launch *Time* magazine; they are followed shortly by *Newsweek.*

1923. Sada A. Harbarger publishes *English for Engineers*, a book that focuses on technical forms of writing such as reports and letters. Because the publisher of the book feels that many readers might resent being instructed by a woman, only the writer's initials are used.[61]

1924. Ralph Fitting's *Report Writing* is published; it adheres to the product approach to technical writing by emphasizing the types of reports created in engineering professions.[62]

1924. The Linguistics Society of America (LSA) is founded.

1925. Sam Trelease and Emma Yule publish *The Preparation of Scientific and Technical Papers,* aimed at guiding writers through the publication process.

1928. William Addison Dwiggins publishes *Layout in Advertising*, a manual for copy writers; he is the first to write about the work of graphic designers in a major publication.

1929. Carl Gaum and Harold Grave's *Report Writing* is published.

Education & Practice in Graphic Design

1920s *continued*

1920 +. Empirical research on the legibility of typography flourishes; studies show that text set with serif faces are read more quickly and easily than those set with sans serif faces.

1922. William Addison Dwiggins coins the term "graphic design" to describe the act of combining typography, illustration, photography, and printing for purposes of persuasion, information or instruction, but it does not achieve widespread usage until after WWII.[63]

1923. The Surrealist movement in the fine arts is underway in Paris.

1923. Le Corbusier creates *Towards a New Architecture,* helping to establish theoretical and practical links between the design of architecture and the use of grid systems in graphic design.

1926. R.K. Pyke compiles a report on the legibility of print, one of the first of the twentieth century.[64]

1927. The sans serif typeface Futura is created by Paul Renner; its widespread acceptance will help prepare the way for other sans serif typefaces.

1928. Miles Tinker conducts studies of typography, exploring how typeface influences reading speed.

1928. Jan Tschichold's influential book, *Die Neue Typographie,* is published. In it, he lays out the principles of the New Typography movement and develops many of the ideas evolved by the Constructivists and teachers at the Bauhaus.

1928. M. F. Agha becomes art director of *Vogue* magazine; he is one of the first to participate in every stage of design and production.

▲ **Background Image.** *African-Americans created jazz based on ragtime and the blues; characterized by ensemble playing, syncopation, and improvisation, jazz gained initial popularity in New Orleans' brothels and went on to influence popular and classical music around the world.*

Science, Technology, & Environment

1920s *continued*

1926. The movie *The Jazz Singer* introduces the era of talking pictures.[†]

1926. F. W. Went of the Netherlands discovers substances that inhibit the growth of weeds; his discovery introduces the concept of selective herbicides.[†††]

1927. Charles A. Lindbergh flies his "Spirit of St. Louis" nonstop from New York to Paris in 33.5 hours.[††]

1927. Werner Heisenberg (Germany) proposes the uncertainty principle.[†††]

1928. George Eastman shows the first color motion pictures.[††]

1928. Teleprinters and teletypewriters come into limited use in the U.S., the U.K., and Germany.[††]

1928. The *New York Times* installs a "moving" electric sign around its New York City headquarters.[††]

1928. Magnetic recording tape is patented in Germany; it was originally proposed in 1888 by Oberlin Smith of the U.K., who also worked out the theory behind the tape recorder.[†††]

1929. Felix Bloch (Switzerland) describes a theory of conductivity which will become a basis for the invention of the transistor.[†††]

1929. A measure of the spontaneous electrical activity of the brain, an electroencephalogram (EEG), is recorded for the first time by German professor Hans Berger.[†††]

1929. Hubble shows that the further away a galaxy is, the faster it is moving away from Earth (Hubble's Law), confirming that the universe is expanding.[†]

Society & Consumerism

1920s *continued*

1920 +. The American Standards Association and the National Bureau of Standards are formed, providing testing models to benefit consumers.[65]

1920 +. "Conspicuous consumption" (a term coined in 1899 by Thorstein Veblen) is used to characterize buying behavior in which an object's usefulness matters less than the presumed status it confers.

1920 +. The celebrity testimonial is born: the Queen of Romania explains how she entrusts her skin to Pond's cold cream, and Joan Crawford says she uses Lux soap.[66]

1920. In the U.S., the prohibition of alcohol goes into effect.[††]

1920. Women in the U.S. win the right to vote.

1926 +. Ford Motors shortens the work week and helps popularize the "week-end" in the U.S.[67]

1926. Ads for toothbrushes promote dental cleanliness: before World War I, 26 % of Americans brushed their teeth; after advertising, 40% do.[68]

1927. In *Your Money's Worth*, Stuart Chase and Frederick J. Schlink describe the forces operating in the new mass-marketed world; they ridicule made-up brand names such as Lux and Sanitas, giving examples of mislabeling and quackery and naming rip-off products by brand name. They start Consumers' Research, Inc. and the *Consumers' Research Bulletin* (the predecessor of *Consumer Reports*).[69]

1929. On "Black Friday," the Stock Exchange collapses, initiating the Great Depression.[††]

Notes

[56] Scott, 1922, p. 467; cited in Berlin, 1984, p. 78.

[57] Lively & Pressey, 1923; see also Chall, 1958.

[58] Stoughton & Stoughton, 1924; cited in Connors, 1982, p. 336.

[59] Consumers Union, Jan. 1986, p. 8.

[60] Yates, 1989, pp. 95–98.

[61] Connors, 1982, p. 335; Yates, 1989, pp. 92–93.

[62] Fitting, 1924; cited in Souther, 1989, p. 4.

[63] Livingston & Livingston, 1992, p. 90; Meggs, 1992, p.187.

[64] Pyke, 1926.

[65] Consumers Union, Jan. 1986, p. 10.

[66] Consumers Union, Jan. 1986, p. 8.

[67] Flexner, 1982, p. 526.

[68] Consumers Union, Jan. 1986, p. 9.

[69] Ibid., p. 9.

[†] From Hellemans & Bunch, 1991.

[††] From Grun, 1991.

[†††] From Giscard d'Estaing, 1993.

Education & Practice in Writing / Rhetoric

1930s

1930 +. Business writing courses in colleges are assigned to low-ranking or part-time faculty, often women.[70]

1930 +. Studies of semantics and propaganda flourish.

1931. James H. S. Bossard and J. Frederic Dewhurst publish *University Education for Business,* a study in which 92 percent of business college alumni and employers rank their training in the "English language" as the most important part of their business education.

1931. H. L. Creek and J. H. McKee describe the decline of course offerings in the humanities for engineering students, noting that more than one-third of the time given to humane subjects has disappeared from the curriculum; primary declines are reported in languages and literary study.[71]

1931. J. Raleigh Nelson emphasizes that engineers need English instruction that focuses on written composition and public speaking rather than on traditional literary values.[72]

1932. F. C. Bartlett, a pioneer of the constructivist tradition in reading, conducts studies about how people remember and construct meaning from narrative and expository texts.

1935. Most courses in technical writing focus exclusively on the writing of reports; a rigid, mechanical, and technical-forms approach becomes all but absolute by the late 1930s.[73]

1936. *The Philosophy of Rhetoric* is published; in it, I. A. Richards proposes that rhetoric is a study of misunderstandings and their remedies.[74]

Professional Development

1930s

1930. The British Society of Industrial Artists and Designers (later known as the Chartered Society of Designers) is founded, providing a forum for professional debate on design.

1930. *Fortune Magazine* is founded; famous for its exemplary standards of editorial design, the magazine will present complex technical information in an accessible and visually elegant manner for more than 40 years.

1933. W. Sypherd and Sharon Brown publish *The Engineer's Manual of English*, an early influential book designed for practitioners in technical communication.[75]

1934. The first issue of *Communication Monographs* (originally *Speech Monographs*), a rhetoric journal from the Speech Communications Association (SCA), is published.

1934. *PM* (later renamed *AD)* is first published; originally intended for production managers (thus the PM), the journal eventually takes on a much larger international role, informing and sensitizing the European and American design communities to one another and to design activities in different contexts. A casualty of war, *PM* will come to an end in mid-1942.[76]

1934. The collected works of Charles S. Peirce is released. His view of language as a semiotic system has been called a working philosophy for today's electronic writers and designers.[77]

1935. The American Business Communications Association (ABCA) is founded and soon holds conferences and publishes its own journal, books, and position papers.[78]

Education & Practice in Graphic Design

1930s

1930 +. The American graphic design community is enriched by an influx of designers fleeing from Europe.[79]

1930 +. German typographers develop asymmetric typography, a style that rejects the traditional arrangement of type on a central axis (symmetry) and advocates the functional, dynamic placement of typographic and visual elements.[80]

1930 +. Pictorial modernism evolves as a major current in European graphic design; it is influenced by Cubism and Constructivism, but maintains literal pictorial references in order to reach the general public. It communicates ideas about products, services, and political issues through posters and advertising art.[81]

1930 +. O. Neurath develops Isotype (International System of Typographic Picture Education), a system designed to help the public understand complex statistical information. It employs pictographic symbols to represent fixed quantities, with increasing quantities suggested by repeating symbols rather than by changes in perspective or size.[82]

1930. European citizen Alexey Brodovitch comes to the U.S. and establishes an advertising department at the Philadelphia Museum Art School; in 1934, he begins a 25-year reign as the art director of *Harper's Bazaar,* where he will experiment with new ways of combining photography with type.[83]

1931. Stanley Morison creates the typeface Times New Roman. It is at first used exclusively in *The Times* of London; in 1932 it is released for general distribution as Times Roman.

▲ **Background Image.** *In 1933 King Kong and Faye Raye "made it to the top" of the New York Empire State Building in RKO's blockbuster film "King Kong."*

Science, Technology, & Environment

1930s

1930. A tape recorder using magnetized plastic tape is developed.[†]

1930. Hans Zinssner develops an immunization against typhus.[†]

1930. The Big Bang Theory is detailed by George Gamow (U.S.) and Georges Lemaitre (Belgium).[†††]

1931. Ernest Orlando Lawrence develops the first workable particle smasher, the cyclotron.[†]

1932. RCA demonstrates a television receiver with a cathode-ray picture.[†]

1932. The first radio telescope is developed by Karl Jansky (U.S.).[†††]

1933. American engineer Edwin Armstrong perfects FM radio.[†]

1933. Ernst Ruska builds the first electron microscope more powerful than a conventional light microscope.[†]

1934. The first streamlined car, the Chrysler Airflow, is introduced.[†]

1935. The first synthetic insecticide is created by a research team from the U.S. Department of Agriculture.[†††]

1935. Charles Richter and Beno Gutenberg (U.S.) develop the Richter scale for classifying earthquakes.[†††]

1935. British scientists develop radar.[†]

1936. The BBC London inaugurates regular television service.[††]

1936. Alan Turing characterizes the Turing machine and provides the theoretical underpinning for development of computers.[84]

Society & Consumerism

1930s

1930 +. "Style" and "features" in consumer products become saleable commodities. Industrial design flourishes as mechanical "ice-boxes" are transformed into sleek, streamlined shapes with new deco-techno names (e.g., Eject-o-Cube, Ajusto-Shelf, Handi-bin, and Touch-a-bar).[85]

1932. English is proposed as an international language.[††]

1933. The first concentration camps are erected by the Nazis in Germany; by 1945, 8 to 10 million prisoners will have been interned and at least half of them killed.[††]

1933. Frederick Schlink and Arthur Kallet's *100,000,000 Guinea Pigs: Dangers in Everyday Foods, Drugs, and Cosmetics* spawns a wave of investigative journalism not seen since the "muckrakers" (e.g., Upton Sinclair and Ida Tarbell) at the beginning of the century.[86]

1935. Several employees of Consumers' Research (see 1927) are fired after they offer to help organizers from the American Federation of Labor form a union. Forty workers walk out with those fired and form their own group, the Consumers Union.[87]

1936. In the U.S., the Social Security Act is signed, creating a need for information for citizens and instructions for government workers who process employment data.

1936. The U.S. Consumers Union is born, followed shortly by *Consumers Union Reports*. It is a non-profit organization whose main goal is to provide consumers with information and advice on goods, services, health, and personal finance.[88]

Notes

[70] Bossard & Dewhurst, 1931, p. 339.

[71] Creek & McKee, 1931, p. 819; cited in Connors, 1982, p. 331.

[72] Nelson, 1931, p. 45; cited in Connors, 1982, p. 333.

[73] Connors, 1982, p. 338.

[74] Richards, 1936.

[75] Sypherd & Brown, 1933.

[76] Gottschall, 1989, p. 61.

[77] Peirce, 1934. For a discussion, see Bolter, 1991, pp. 197–208.

[78] Russell, 1991, p. 128.

[79] Livingston & Livingston, 1992.

[80] Ibid., p. 19.

[81] Meggs, 1983, p. 292.

[82] Livingston & Livingston, 1992.

[83] Craig & Barton, 1987, p. 157.

[84] Eames & Eames, 1973, p. 124.

[85] Consumers Union, Nov. 1986, p. 709.

[86] Consumers Union, Jan. 1986, p. 10.

[87] Consumers Union, Feb. 1986, p. 76.

[88] Ibid., p. 77.

[†] From Hellemans & Bunch, 1991.

[††] From Grun, 1991.

[†††] From Giscard d'Estaing, 1993.

Education & Practice in Writing / Rhetoric

1930s *continued*

1936. Alfred J. Ayer articulates an influential view of logical positivism in *Language, Truth, and Logic.*

1938. Alvin M. Fountain's report from his dissertation, *A Study of Courses in Technical Writing,* shows that of the more than two dozen English departments that once existed in engineering schools, only five remain.[89]

1938. Writers Robert Penn Warren and Cleanth Brooks describe new criticism in *Understanding Poetry,* a book that will significantly influence how American students are taught to read and interpret literary and other texts.

1938. John Dewey presents a timely and provocative analysis of the interrelationships among education, the community, and the nature of children, giving strong voice to what will come to be known as the "progressive movement" in education.[90]

1938. Charles William Morris publishes his influential text on semiotics, *Foundations of the Theory of Signs.*[91]

1939. Teaching technical writing or composition at the college level is considered "professional suicide"; men who teach such courses in engineering departments are called "effeminate" by some male students who do not see English as sufficiently masculine.[92]

1939. W. O. Sypherd criticizes engineering education, claiming that not enough literature is being taught, that freshman composition is ineffective, that students are not required to write in most engineering courses, and that there is no cooperation between English and Engineering departments. He sees little hope for improvement without radical changes.[93]

Professional Development

1930s *continued*

1935. The WPA's Federal Art Project is instigated as part of the New Deal, providing employment for millions left jobless by the Great Depression. The Project gives work to artists, writers, actors, and musicians; some divisions of the Project are dedicated to presenting public service information on social issues such as health, education, and housing (–1939).[94]

1936. The Royal Designers for Industry (RDI) is founded by the Royal Society of Arts in London; for years to come the Faculty of Royal Designers will confer the honorary title of RDI on many of the U.K.'s most distinguished designers.

1936. The Container Corporation of America (CCA) is one of the first companies to combine precise copy with powerful images, proving that it is possible to combine graphic excellence with success; CCA plays a central role in improving the status of graphic designers in business and industry.[95]

1936. The Ford Foundation is established; it will fund many studies of writing and literacy.

1936. Penguin Books introduces its first paperback books; careers in writing, editing, and illustrating for book publishing industries develop further.

1938. Alvin M. Fountain's research shows that technical writing is a thriving industry in engineering fields, with its own authors, experts, and directors.[96]

1939. Some practitioners in advertising reconsider their ploy of inventing a "disease" (e.g., "razor-blade skin," "halitosis") and then presenting its cure: the product.[97]

Education & Practice in Graphic Design

1930s *continued*

1932. Graphic designer A. M. Cassandre produces a stunning series of posters that helps revitalize French advertising art.

1932. The Vienna Workshops (see 1903) close during the Depression because of financial difficulties.

1933. The Bauhaus School in Germany is closed because it is perceived as a threat to the Nazi party.

1933. Henry C. Beck's *London Underground Map* is published; Beck uses geographical distortion to simplify relations, with all routes as verticals, horizontals and 45° diagonals. It is an icon of British information design.[98]

1935. Jan Tschichold's *Structuring Typographically* is published. Influenced by both the Bauhaus and the Constructivists, Tschichold emphasizes the asymmetric arrangement of graphic elements, sans serif type, and the strategic design of white space.

1937. László Moholy-Nagy establishes the American Bauhaus School in Chicago, based on the philosophy that "form follows function." In 1949 the Bauhaus becomes part of the Illinois Institute of Technology. The forming of the Bauhaus launches formal design education in the U.S. and exerts a powerful influence on graphic design education for the rest of the century.[99]

1938. Caledonia, one of the most popular typefaces for book design, is created by W. A. Dwiggins for Mergenthaler Linotype Company.[100]

1939. The Art Deco movement hits its high point at the World's Fair in New York City, after which its influence slowly declines.

▲ **Background Image.** *In their 1938 film "Carefree," Fred Astaire and Ginger Rogers presented an image of glamour and wealth—an image that was popular with the American public during the Great Depression. Archives of their films reveal that Astaire and Rogers used detailed technical diagrams to choreograph their ensembles in relation to music, singing, dialogue, set design, and camera angle.*

Science, Technology, & Environment

1930s *continued*

1936. George Brown invents the turnstile antenna for TV broadcasting.[†]

1936. A German engineer, Heinrich Focke, develops the first practical helicopter.[†]

1937 +. John V. Atanasoff starts work on the first electronic computer, a machine that is designed to solve systems of linear equations; the first prototype is completed in 1939, and an operational version (known as the ABC) is working by 1942.[†]

1937. American law student Chester Carlson invents xerography, the first modern method of photocopying.[†]

1938. Hungarians Ladislao and Georg Biró patent the ballpoint pen, for the second time; John Loud's 1888 ballpoint, the first one patented, was never developed.[101]

1938. Claude Shannon's *A Symbolic Analysis of Relay and Switching,* a founding document on the mathematical theory of information, is published.[†]

1938. Albert Einstein and Leopold Infeld's *Evolution of Physics* describes physical science to the lay reader.[†]

1938. U.S. engineer T. Ross develops the first machine that can learn from experience.[†]

1938. George Harold Brown develops the sideband filter for use in television transmitters.[†]

1938. Konrad Zuse completes the Z_1, a binary calculating machine.[†]

1939. The complex number calculator is built at Bell Labs.[†]

Society & Consumerism

1930s *continued*

1936. Arthur Kallet, the first director of the Consumers Union, publishes *Counterfeit,* an indictment of shoddy goods, providing the starting point for early reports on products in *Consumers Union Reports.*[102]

1936. Henry Luce begins publication of *Life* magazine.[††]

1937. Many publications, including the *New York Times,* refuse to take the Consumers Union's ads, afraid that they will offend corporate sponsors by advertising a group with the temerity to criticize products by name.[103]

1938. The 40-hour work week is established as a standard in the U.S.[††]

1938. In the U.S., Orson Welles' radio production of H. G. Wells' *War of the Worlds* causes considerable panic.[††]

1938. In the U.S., the Federal Food, Drug, and Cosmetic Act is passed; it is more inclusive than its 1906 version.

1939. The Consumers Union becomes more popular, and its membership hits 85,000; *Business Week* reports that "business cannot afford to overlook the 'organized discontent' because it has already assumed the proportions of a real threat to producers and distributors of organized brands."[104]

1939. The consumer movement is reported to the House Un-American Activities Committee, possibly by William Randolph Hearst (the Consumers Union had attacked Hearst's *Good Housekeeping* Seal of Approval as a fraud). It will not be until 1954 that charges are dropped, ending the "Consumers Union Red Scare."[105]

1939. World War II begins.

Notes

[89] Fountain, 1938; cited in Connors, 1982, p. 338.

[90] Dewey, 1938; described in Applebee, 1974, pp. 48–49, 63–64.

[91] Morris, 1938.

[92] Creek, 1939; described in Connors, 1982, p. 337.

[93] Sypherd, 1939; cited in Connors, 1982, p. 339.

[94] Livingston & Livingston, 1992, p. 73.

[95] Craig & Barton, 1987, p. 154.

[96] Fountain, 1938; cited in Connors, 1982, p. 338.

[97] *Printers' Ink,* 1939.

[98] Livingston & Livingston, 1992, p. 25.

[99] Craig & Barton, 1987, p. 143; Findeli, 1990, pp. 4–7.

[100] Ibid., p. 159.

[101] U.S. Patent Numbers 2,258,841 and 2,265,055; cited in Daniels, 1980, p. 318.

[102] Consumers Union, Feb. 1986, p. 77.

[103] Ibid., p. 78.

[104] Ibid.

[105] Ibid.

[†]   From Hellemans & Bunch, 1991.

[††]   From Grun, 1991.

[†††] From Giscard d'Estaing, 1993.

Education & Practice in Writing / Rhetoric

1940s

1940 +. Influenced by the general semantics school of linguistics and the work of the New Critics—the former originating in response to the use of propaganda in World War I, the latter in response to the complexities of 20th century poetry—high schools and colleges emphasize language study and communication skills. At the college level, this leads to courses in communication that combine writing, reading, speaking, and listening.[106]

1940. *Writing the Technical Report* is written by J. Raleigh Nelson; it is an influential text that emphasizes the process approach to technical communication.[107]

1944 +. The "life adjustment" movement begins; it sees writing as a means to prepare students for specific real-life experiences they will encounter outside of school.[108]

1944. A report entitled *Education for All American Youth,* sponsored by the Progressive Education Association, becomes the major statement of the "life adjustment" movement. Composition courses begin to show concern for basic skills such as conversation, letter writing, and interviewing. The Deweyian concern for progressive education, the improvement of both the individual and society, is submerged and ultimately lost in the formulation.[109]

1947. Courses in written composition are evaluated for their suitability for the flood of war veterans entering U.S. colleges and universities under the GI Bill; enrollment in U.S. colleges triples between 1945 and 1949.[110]

1948 +. Publications that investigate the rhetorical nature of scientific inquiry appear.[111]

Professional Development

1940s

1940 +. In the U.S., the demand for technical communication grows, particularly in the Armed Services, where recruits need written instructions to operate equipment. Most of the writers are male ex-engineers; technical writing as a recognized profession begins.[112]

1940 +. Corporations begin hiring fine artists to design advertisements, creating a stronger link between fine arts and graphic design practice.[113]

1941. The entry of the U.S. into World War II brings attention to the functional aspects of language studies, with a central concern for communication skills; the Army requires men and women in its officer training program to acquire skills in understanding what is read, written, spoken, and heard.[114]

1944. The Council of Industrial Design (later called the Design Council) is formed.

1945 +. Large companies such as General Electric, Westinghouse, and GM establish departments of technical writing after finding that it is no longer cost-effective to pay engineers to both design and write.[115]

1945 +. Scientific journalism in U.S. magazines flourishes, popularizing the peacetime uses of nuclear energy in an uncritical and accepting way.[116]

1947. The Association for Computing Machinery (ACM), the first educational and scientific computer organization in the industry, is founded. By 1992, it will contain 34 special interest groups.

1948. McGraw-Hill hires writers to edit a National Energy Series of books detailing the Manhattan Project.[117]

Education & Practice in Graphic Design

1940s

1940 +. American graphic designers achieve prominence and international recognition, radically changing the direction of graphic design and advertising in America.[118]

1941 +. Ladislav Sutnar, a Czechoslovakian designer, comes to the U.S. to become art director for Sweet's Catalog Services; during his 19-year reign he will popularize the use of the modular grid as a way to organize complex technical information.

1942 +. Max Bill, a Bauhaus-trained designer, plays a major role in evolving a Constructivist ideal in Swiss graphic design; he explores the functional geometry of the page, using raggedright margins in book designs and indicating paragraphs by line spacing instead of indenting.[119]

1946 +. The success of art movements such as Abstract Expressionism helps the public accept a range of modern art, encouraging publishers and advertisers to be more adventurous in their graphic design.[120]

1947. Paul Rand's *Thoughts on Design* is published; his exceptional work will influence many young designers.

1947. One of the first successful women in graphic design, Cipe Pineles Burtin becomes the art director of *Seventeen* magazine; she commissions such artists as Ben Shahn, Andy Warhol, and Richard Lindner to do editorial illustrations.[121]

1948 +. The first generation of practical photo-typesetting systems begins with the Intertype Fotosetter; from two basic fonts and an assortment of lenses, the Fotosetter can set from 4- to 36-point type.[122]

▲ **Background Image.** *World War II dominated the first half of the decade, during which the need for professionals trained in technical communication, illustration, graphic design, and scientific journalism grew significantly. However, few colleges or universities offered coursework in these areas.*

Science, Technology, & Environment

1940s

1941. Konrad Zuse's Z_2 computer is the first to use electromagnetic relays and a punched tape for data entry.[†]

1941. The "Manhattan Project"—to develop the atomic bomb—begins.[††]

1943. A team headed by Alan Turing develops Colossus, the first all-electronic calculating device (using vacuum tubes); Colossus is dedicated to cracking German codes.[†]

1944. The first fully automatic computer, Automatic Sequence Controlled Calculator, or Mark 1, is completed by Harvard's Howard Aiken and a team of IBM engineers; it uses punched paper tape, punch cards, or manually set dial switches for programming and vacuum tubes for calculations.[123]

1944. John W. Mauchly and J. Presper Eckert, Jr. co-invent the Electronic Numerical Integrator and Computer, or ENIAC; it is generally conceded to be the first all-purpose stored-program electronic computer.[124]

1945. Vannevar Bush lays some of the intellectual foundations of hypertext in "As We May Think."[125]

1945. Alexander Fleming (U.K.) wins a Nobel Prize in Medicine for his discovery of penicillin.

1947. Bell Laboratories scientists invent the transistor.[††]

1948. The LP record is invented in the U.S. by Peter Goldmark and introduced by CBS; shortly thereafter, RCA introduces 45 RPM single records.[†]

1948. Edwin Land invents a camera and film system that develops pictures inside the camera in about a minute.[†]

Society & Consumerism

1940s

1940. The first color television broadcast takes place.[††]

1940. Cigarette makers become more aggressive in encouraging women to smoke: the red-tipped "Debs" cigarette is supposed to leave one's lipstick unsmeared; another brand, the "Crane A," is "Made Especially to Prevent Sore Throats."[126]

1941. The U.S. Supreme Court upholds the Federal Wage and Hour Law, restricting working hours for 16- to 18-year-olds and setting a minimum wage for selected businesses.[††]

1942. *Consumers Union Reports* changes its name to *Consumer Reports* after readers express concerns over whether a company's labor policies determine how its products are rated by the Consumers Union.[127]

1942. Assembly lines produce tanks, airplanes, and trucks instead of automobiles, refrigerators, and radios.

1943. Shoe rationing begins in the U.S., followed by rationing of meat, cheese, fats, and all canned goods.[††]

1943. A pay-as-you-go income tax system is instituted in the U.S., accompanied by IRS tax forms.

1944. The Ministry of National Insurance is established in the U.K.[††]

1945. World War II ends. In the U.S., the GI Bill is passed to assist veterans.

1945. In the U.S., the war is followed by economic growth as millions of returning veterans and prosperous workers clamor for the new homes, appliances, and other consumer goods they were denied during the war.

Notes

[106] Applebee, 1974, pp. 139–140; Berlin, 1990, p. 202.

[107] Souther, 1989, p. 5.

[108] Applebee, 1974; Berlin, 1990; Kantor, 1975.

[109] Applebee, 1974, p. 144; Berlin, 1990, p. 202; Hilgard, 1987.

[110] Russell, 1991, p. 259.

[111] Harrington, 1948; for a discussion, see Rubens,1985.

[112] Smith, 1988, p. 84.

[113] Livingston & Livingston, 1992, p. 14.

[114] Applebee, 1974, p. 140; Berlin, 1990, p. 202.

[115] Connors, 1982, p. 341.

[116] Del Sesto, 1981.

[117] Higgins, 1989, p. 261.

[118] Craig & Barton, 1987, p. 173.

[119] Meggs, 1983, p. 381.

[120] Craig & Barton, 1987, p. 173.

[121] Ibid., p. 174.

[122] Ibid., p. 206.

[123] Eames & Eames, 1973, p. 123.

[124] Ibid., pp. 132–133.

[125] Bush, 1945.

[126] Flexner, 1982, p. 150.

[127] Consumers Union, Feb. 1986, p. 77.

[†]   From Hellemans & Bunch, 1991.

[††] From Grun, 1991.

[†††] From Giscard d'Estaing, 1993.

Education & Practice in Writing / Rhetoric

1940s *Continued*

1948. Even as many schools expand their standard engineering curriculum to include more courses in the humanities, courses in technical writing are still not construed as education in engineering or humanities.[128]

1948. Rudolph Flesch develops a readability formula, as does the team of Edgar Dale and Jeanne Chall.

1949. The Conference on College Composition and Communication (CCCC) is formed; it is a coalition devoted to improving the teaching of writing. It becomes the largest organization for teachers of writing and plays an integral role in giving voice to the field and disseminating its work.

1950s

1950 +. There is a growing awareness of the importance of audience analysis and reader-writer relationships in technical and professional writing.[129]

1950 +. The once popular "modes of discourse" approach to composition (i.e., teaching according to the rigid schema of narration, description, exposition, and argument) fades.[130]

1950 +. Ralph W. Tyler's work in curriculum design sets in motion a theory of instruction that will pervade curriculum design for decades.

1950 +. Structural linguistics is used in the classroom to help students learn about the structure of discourse.

1950 +. Robert Gunning creates a readability formula, and William Taylor develops the "cloze" procedure.

Professional Development

1940s *Continued*

1949. Claude E. Shannon and Warren Weaver develop a mathematical model of communication that depicts the process as a unidirectional flow from a transmitter which sends signals, potentially obscured by noise, to a ready receiver. The model is used widely.[131]

1949. The ad agency Doyle, Dane, Bernbach is created; it emphasizes close collaboration between the copy writer and the art director. The result: copy becomes more succinct and more focused to underpin visual images.[132]

1949. Joseph D. Chapline writes a users' manual for the BINAC computer and becomes the first writer of computer documentation.[133]

1950s

1950 +. The growth of technology spurs a huge need for technical and professional writing in many domains, including computers, aeronautics, medicine, risk communication, electronics, agriculture, biology, engineering, and environmental science.

1950 +. Most technical communication is handled by former engineers, usually men who work for the military or defense contractors. Advertisements for careers in the field are often positioned in the "men's" section of the help wanted ads.[134]

1950 +. Madison Avenue in New York becomes the advertising center of the world; popular magazines, including *Look* and *Life,* provide key outlets for illustrators and photographers.[135]

Education & Practice in Graphic Design

1940s *Continued*

1949 +. Herbert Bayer works on *The World Geographic Atlas*, an important milestone in the display of data and the visualization of scientific processes; it is published in 1953.

1949. German typographer Will Burtin begins work for the Upjohn Company, where he makes important contributions to the visualization of scientific processes; he sees the designer as "communicator, link, and inspirer who makes comprehensible the knowledge of science, who gives substance to the invisible."[136]

1949. Herbert Spencer founds *Typographica* and introduces "modern" typographic developments to the U.K.

1950s

1950 +. The International Typographic Style movement (also known as the Swiss Style) emerges in Switzerland and Germany. It focuses on organizing visual and verbal information in a clear and functional manner, free from the exaggerated claims of propaganda and advertising. Its proponents define design as a socially useful activity.[137]

1950. Czechoslovakian graphic designer Ladislav Sutnar continues to make a mark on the design of product information through his functional designs of product catalogs. His philosophy: informational design is a synthesis of function, flow, and form. He explicitly expresses the need to make graphic information easy to find, read, comprehend, and recall, and he calls for the "basic design unit" to be the two-page spread rather than the single page.[138]

▲ **Background Image.** *Regimentation and similarity came to typify the post-war American suburbs; shown here is an adaptation of Levittown, New York. Like other suburbanites during the 1950s, the residents of Levittown clamored to purchase consumer products from cameras to television sets. According to* Consumer Reports, *many of these products came with hard-to-understand instruction guides.*

Science, Technology, & Environment

1940s Continued

1949. Cambridge University's EDSAC (Electronic Delay Storage Automatic Calculator), an early computer, goes into operation.[†]

1949. In the U.S., BINAC, one of the first electronic stored-program computers, begins operation.[†]

1949. The first fax machine is manufactured in the U.K. and installed for Japan's *Asahi Times*, where it becomes enormously successful. Fax machines will become popular elsewhere in the mid-1970s.[†††]

1949. Dorothy Crowfoot Hodgkin (U.K.) is the first to use a computer to work out the structure of penicillin.[†]

1950s

1950 +. The "blue screen" is created; it allows a subject to be filmed against a background of special blue that can then be isolated on a separate film and inserted into another scene. The technique is used to part the Red Sea in Cecil B. DeMille's *The Ten Commandments*.[†††]

1950. John von Neumann, working with a team of meteorologists and ENIAC—one of the first computers—makes the first computerized 24-hour weather predictions.[139]

1950. Einstein proposes the "General Field Theory."

1951. John Mauchly and John Prosper Eckert build UNIVAC 1, the first computer to be commercially available and to store data on magnetic tape; it is first installed in the Census Bureau.[140]

Society & Consumerism

1940s Continued

1945. While America goes on a buying spree, the popularity of *Consumer Reports* increases.

1945. Science-fiction writer Arthur C. Clarke proposes the idea of communications satellites that will be stationary above a particular part of Earth.[†]

1947. The U.S. Congress passes the Labor-Management Relations Act; commonly called the Taft-Hartley Act, it bans unions from making political contributions in elections and places many restrictions on strikes, putting a curb on unionism in the U.S.

1948. The first McDonald's hamburger restaurant opens.[†††]

1950s

1950 +. In the U.S., the average life expectancy is approximately 70 years; "retirement" becomes a common concept; there is much talk of "retirement villages" where the elderly, according to the ads, can happily spend their "golden years."[141]

1950. There are 1.5 million TV sets in the U.S.; one year later, there are approximately 15 million.[††]

1950. *Rashomon* is the first major Japanese film shown in the U.S.

1950. The U.S. recognizes Vietnam, capital at Saigon, and supplies the nation with arms and advisors.[††]

1950. Senator Joseph McCarthy advises President Truman that the State Department is riddled with Communists and Communist sympathizers.

Notes

[128] Fatout, 1948, pp. 715–716; cited in Connors, 1982, p. 340.

[129] Connors, 1982, p. 343.

[130] Connors, 1981, p. 444.

[131] Shannon & Weaver, 1949. For a critique in relation to technical communication, see Dobrin, 1983, 1989; for a brief discussion in relation to design and typography, see Meggs, 1992, p. 3 and Swann, 1991, pp. 10–21; for a critique in relation to the rhetoric of transfer of technology, see Doheny-Farina, 1992, pp. 6–13.

[132] Livingston & Livingston, 1992, p. 58.

[133] Brockmann, 1990, p. 178.

[134] Mitchell, 1989, p. 418; Zook, 1989, p. 415.

[135] Livingston & Livingston, 1992, p. 14.

[136] Meggs, 1983, p. 377.

[137] Meggs, 1992, pp. 334–349.

[138] Lönberg-Holm & Sutnar, 1944; see also Sutnar's later work (1961).

[139] Eames & Eames, 1973, p. 139.

[140] Ibid., p. 162.

[141] Flexner, 1982, p. 478.

[†]   From Hellemans & Bunch, 1991.

[††]   From Grun, 1991.

[†††] From Giscard d'Estaing, 1993.

Education & Practice in Writing / Rhetoric

1950s *Continued*

1950 +. The new critical approach to analyzing the form and meaning of texts dominates the teaching of literature and writing in colleges.[142]

1950. Kenneth Burke, a very influential 20th-century rhetorician, publishes *Rhetoric of Motives.*

1951 +. Technical writing teachers begin to teach students how to design texts such as instruction manuals for consumer products.[143]

1952. In *A Study of Writing,* I. J. Gelb presents the history and evolution of writing, covering systems of communication from pictures to a full alphabet.

1953. Albert R. Kitzhaber explores the growth of rhetorical studies in a dissertation entitled *Rhetoric in American Colleges, 1850-1900.* It is one of the best sources for understanding the roots of rhetoric in U.S. schools.

1953. Rensselaer Polytechnic Institute announces the development of a Master of Science degree in Technical Writing, the first of its kind.

1954. *Technical Writing* is written by Gordon Mills and John A. Walter. An influential, even paradigmatic, textbook, it takes a rhetorical approach rather than one focused on forms.[144]

1955 +. Educators begin to meet with technical communication professionals, engaging in a "dialogue that will enrich the teaching of technical writing for years to come."[145]

1955 +. Technical communication courses begin to consider both visual and verbal texts; there is a great deal of interest in information graphics (e.g., charts, diagrams, and tables).[146]

Professional Development

1950s *Continued*

1950. The journal *College Composition and Communication* first appears.

1951. John E. Warriner's *English Grammar and Composition* is published; it is perhaps the most widely used grammar text ever.

1952. Joseph D. Chapline documents the UNIVAC computer, making use of examples to explain its functioning.[147]

1953. The Japanese magazine *Idea* is formed, illustrating the best in international advertising art.

1953. Rensselaer Polytechnic Institute holds its first Technical Writers Institute (TWI) for professionals.

1953. The Society of Technical Writers (STW) and the Association of Technical Writers and Editors (TWE) are founded on the east coast.[148]

1954. The Technical Publishing Society (TPS) is founded in Pasadena, Cal., by Charles Van Hagan and Ted Tyler.

1954. In the U.K., the Technical Communicators Association is organized by Reginald Kapp and B.C. Brookes; the Association will later change its name to the Institute of Scientific and Technical Communicators (ISTC).[149]

1956. The Council of Biology Editors holds its first annual meeting.

1957. The Society of Technical Writers (STW) and the Association of Technical Writers and Editors (TWE) join forces to become the Society of Technical Writers and Editors (STWE). A journal, the *STWE Review* (later called the *STWP Review* and *Technical Communication),* is founded. By 1959, membership will include 2400 writers and editors.[150]

Education & Practice in Graphic Design

1950s *Continued*

1951. The Ulm Hochschule für Gestaltung ("Institute of Design") is founded in Ulm, Germany, lasting until 1968. It included the study of semiotics, rhetoric, sociology, psychology, and cultural history to undergird the analysis of design problem solving.[151]

1951. The famous exhibitions at the "Festival of Britain" influence British graphic design and typography practices, making many early 19th century display faces popular again.

1951. Alvin Lustig establishes a graphic design program at Yale Univ.[152]

1951. William Golden designs the famous CBS "eye" symbol, representing both the viewer's eye and the lens of a camera.

1953. Russian-born Alexander Liberman combines fashion illustration and photography to create a new visual image for *Vogue* magazine.

1954. Swiss typographer Adrian Frutiger invents the sans serif typeface Univers, one of the most successful typefaces of the 20th century.

1955 +. Corporate design in the U.S. flourishes; art/design departments look at the "big picture," trying to graphically coordinate documents and visual impressions made by a company.[153]

1955. Saul Bass designs the graphic images for *The Man with the Golden Arm* and other films; Bass will also create the logos for AT&T, Quaker Oats, and Warner Communications.

1956 +. Pop Art develops in the U.K. in the late 1950s and in the U.S. in the early 1960s; images are recycled until they become contemporary icons.

▲ **Background Image.** *Rock 'n roll pioneer Elvis Presley gained international recognition in 1956 when he performed on television's "Steve Allen Show," "Milton Berle Show," and "Ed Sullivan Show." Audiences could find out when they could watch Elvis by searching the timetables of* TV Guide, *a weekly magazine that began publication in April, 1953.*

Science, Technology, & Environment

1950s *Continued*

1952. CBS uses a UNIVAC to correctly predict the election of Dwight D. Eisenhower as President of the U.S.; its first prediction of a landslide is accurate but not believed by its operators; after they reprogram it, the machine incorrectly predicts a close contest.[†]

1952. The first commercial product using transistors instead of vacuum tubes (a hearing aid) is introduced.[†]

1952. Sony develops the pocket-sized transistor radio—some say is the beginning of an audio revolution.[†]

1952. The first microwave oven is sold commercially by Tappan.[†††]

1953. IBM releases the Model 650 "magnetic drum" computer, and the Model 701, its first mainframe.

1953. The first phototypesetters, invented in France, go into operation in the U.S.[†††]

1953. James D. Watson and Francis H. Crick develop the double-helix model for DNA, which explains how DNA transmits heredity in living organisms.[†]

1954. Dr. Jonas Salk develops a polio vaccine.

1956. IBM releases its Model 350 mainframe computer.

1956. The first transatlantic telephone cable is put into operation.[†]

1956. John Backus and a team at IBM invent FORTRAN, the first computer programming language.[†]

1956. John McCarthy develops Lisp, the computer language of artificial intelligence.[†]

Society & Consumerism

1950s *Continued*

1950. The Korean War begins.

1950. Credit cards are introduced.[†††]

1952. Cleveland disc jockey Alan Freed—famous for exposing white teens to black music—hosts the first rock 'n roll concert; all of the performers are black. 30,000 black and white teenagers show up. Fearful police pull the plug on the show.[154]

1953. Controls on wages, salaries, and some consumer goods are lifted in the U.S.; all price controls are removed shortly thereafter.[††]

1953. Lung cancer is reported to be attributable to cigarette smoking.[††]

1953. The Korean War ends.

1954. *Consumer Reports* introduces its "Frequency-of-Repair" tables for automobiles.[155]

1954. Consumers Union builds test facilities to evaluate products; although the Union will not formally evaluate the quality of written communications that accompany products, it does provide evaluative commentary on whether products operate as the company literature says they do and on how easy operation actually is.

1954. Senator Joseph R. McCarthy continues his witch-hunting activities, culminating in a nationally-televised hearing in which he seeks to prove Communist infiltration into the U.S. Army; his formal censure and condemnation by Senate resolution follow.

1954. The U.S. Supreme Court rules that segregation by color in public schools is a violation of the 14th Amendment.[†]

Notes

[142] Applebee, 1974, p. 163.

[143] Connors, 1982, p. 342.

[144] Ibid., p. 343.

[145] Sweigert, 1956; cited in Connors, 1982, p. 344.

[146] Souther, 1989, p. 6.

[147] Brockmann, 1990, p. 212.

[148] Pardoe, 1990, p. 188; F. R. Smith, 1993, personal communication.

[149] Mitchell, 1989, p. 418.

[150] Jenks, 1989, p. 84; F. R. Smith, 1993, personal communication.

[151] Livingston & Livingston, 1992, p. 196; Meggs, 1992, p. 334.

[152] Craig & Barton, 1987, p. 184.

[153] Gottschall, 1989, p. 120.

[154] Palmer, 1995, pp. 23, 134.

[155] Consumers Union, Apr. 1986, p. 228.

[†]   From Hellemans & Bunch, 1991.

[††]   From Grun, 1991.

[†††] From Giscard d'Estaing, 1993.

Education & Practice in Writing / Rhetoric

1950s *Continued*

1955. Educators in composition criticize some college technical writing courses for their lack of attention to rhetoric and audience analysis.[156]

1957. Noam Chomsky develops transformational grammar; his work will have an enormous impact on subsequent linguistic theory.[157]

1957. J. W. Souther's *Technical Report Writing* is published; it is one of the earliest textbooks to take a process approach.

1957. The space race leads to federal funding of literature and composition for the first time in American history. This will lead to a reintegration of the efforts of the NCTE and MLA after a separation of nearly 50 years.[158]

1958. In the U.S., the Congress passes the National Defense Education Act (NDEA), legislation that provides funds for research on literature, language, and composition.[159]

1958. Members in the field of English studies convene the Basic Issues Conferences, part of a reform movement to define the province of English studies and to set agendas for curriculum development in schools. As a result, English is finally considered a fundamental discipline.[160]

1958. Carnegie Institute of Technology (which later becomes Carnegie Mellon Univ.) develops the first undergraduate-level program in technical writing and editing in the U.S.

1959. The status of teaching technical writing in the U.S. has not improved since 1929; it is still mainly taught by graduate students and untenured instructors.[161]

Professional Development

1950s *Continued*

1957. The Association Typographique Internationale (ATypI) is formed.

1958 +. The proposal emerges as an important form of technical writing; during the late 1950s and early 1960s, industry will spend more than $1 billion per year on proposals.[162]

1958. The journal *Ergonomics* is started; it will publish many articles relevant to document design.

1958. The Institute of Electrical and Electronic Engineers (IEEE) establishes the journal *Transactions on Engineering Writing and Speech,* later called *IEEE Transactions on Professional Communication.*

1958. The Society of Technical Writing and Editing (STWE) develops a set of canons for ethical conduct.

1958. Bob Gage, of the award-winning advertising agency Doyle, Dane, Bernbach, creates a number of ads that attempt to find a way to present a message artfully without resorting to "visual tricks."[163]

1958. The first book devoted to technical editing, edited by B. F. Weil, is published.

1959. The journal *Human Factors* is founded; it will publish many articles on human-machine interaction.

1959. The first edition of Strunk & White's *Elements of Style* is published; it will serve as a practical reference guide for thousands of writers.

1959. Joseph Racker explains how to write for audiences who differ in expertise in *Selecting and Writing to the Proper Level.*

Education & Practice in Graphic Design

1950s *Continued*

1956 +. Professional practice in the field of graphic design during the late 1950s, particularly in the U.K., signals the demise of the "individual design stars" of earlier decades; more and more designers create interdisciplinary consultancies and work in teams.[164]

1956. Paul Rand and Eliot Noyes develop the corporate identity for IBM; Rand's design manual includes the IBM alphabet, the IBM Logo, along with packaging and signage systems.

1957. Max Miedinger and Edouard Hoffman design the sans serif typeface Helvetica; Helvetica's legible, clear-cut characters will make it popular around the world for decades to come.

1958. Hermann Zapf creates the typeface Optima, a sans serif font with thick and thin tapered strokes, one of the most original type designs of the late 20th century.[165]

1958. Josef Müller-Brockman and other Zurich-based designers found *New Graphic Design (Neue Grafik),* a journal which spreads the Swiss design ethic internationally. The journal, designed on a flexible four-column grid and printed in three languages, is a wonderful demonstration of its own visual ethos; through *Neue Grafik,* Müller-Brockmann and his colleagues disseminate the principles of the International Typographic Style, wedded to the idea that form follows function.[166]

1958. Henry Wolf, one of the most well-known American magazine art directors of the 1950s, succeeds Alexey Brodovitch at *Harper's Bazaar.* At the *Bazaar,* Wolf experiments with page layout and typography, gaining a reputation for designing covers that convey a sense of humor.

▲ **Background Image.** *In the 1950s, Americans adorned their cars with "fins," elaborate body molding, fanciful hood ornaments, and spectacular paint jobs. Publications about cars proliferated, from do-it-yourself-repair guides to consumer information telling how to get the biggest and most luxurious car for the lowest price.*

Science, Technology, & Environment

1950s *Continued*

1956. Stanislaw Ulam's computerized chess program, called the MANIAC 1, becomes the first computer program to beat a human in a game.[†]

1956. William Shockley, Walter Brattain, and John Bardeen (all U.S.) win the Nobel Prize in Physics for their research on semiconductors and their discovery of the transistor effect.

1956. George A. Miller conducts landmark studies about human short term memory, helping to lay the foundation for modern cognitive science.[167]

1957. The first artificial satellite, *Sputnik I,* is launched by the Soviet Union; one month later, they launch their second satellite, carrying a dog. The space race officially begins.

1958. The U.S. opens its first experimental nuclear reactor.[†]

1958. Wernher von Braun and his team launch the first American satellite to reach a successful orbit around the Earth.[†]

1958. The U.S. launches the very first moon rocket; it fails to reach the moon but travels 79,000 miles from Earth.[††]

1959. The British General Election is covered on television.[††]

1959. The first commercial Xerox copier is introduced.[†]

1959. The integrated circuit is developed.

1959. Grace Murray Hopper invents COBOL, a computer language for business; she is also known for coining the word "bug" after a moth became jammed in the computer's circuitry.[168]

Society & Consumerism

1950s *Continued*

1955. Black citizens in Montgomery, Ala., boycott segregated city bus lines.

1955. The "Why Johnny Can't Read" debate begins in the popular press, bringing with it frequent exposés of Americans' "illiteracy."[††]

1956. For the first time in American history, white-collar workers outnumber blue-collar workers; the phrase "high-school dropout" begins to carry a social stigma.[169]

1957. Ford introduces an automobile called the Edsel with great fanfare; the car turns out to be a huge failure and is eventually discontinued.

1958. The Treaty of Rome begins the European Common Market.

1958. Tension grows in the U.S. as the desegregation of schools is attempted in the South.

1958. The director of the Tobacco Industry's Research Committee announces to the public that "efforts to assign a primary causal role to tobacco use [in relation to lung cancer] on the basis of statistical associations ignore all the unknowns and focus undue attention on tobacco use."[170]

1958. Unemployment in the U.S. reaches almost 5.2 million.[††]

1958. Cyril N. Parkinson publishes his satirical exposition of the growth of bureaucracy ("Parkinson's Law").[††]

1959. U.S. Postmaster General Summerfield bans D. H. Lawrence's *Lady Chatterley's Lover* from the mails on grounds of obscenity; his ruling is reversed in 1960 by the Circuit Court of Appeals.[††]

Notes

[156] Wilson, 1955.

[157] Chomsky, 1957.

[158] Berlin, 1987, p. 120.

[159] Applebee, 1974, p. 189; Berlin, 1990, p. 206.

[160] Applebee, 1974, p. 193; North, 1987, p. 10.

[161] Connors, 1982, p. 344.

[162] Ibid., p. 346.

[163] Craig & Barton, 1987, p. 177.

[164] Livingston & Livingston, 1992, p. 34.

[165] Meggs, 1983, p. 349.

[166] Livingston & Livingston, 1992, p. 145.

[167] Miller, 1956.

[168] Barry, 1991, p. 141.

[169] Russell, 1991, p. 239.

[170] Corina, 1975, p. 251.

[†] From Hellemans & Bunch, 1991.

[††] From Grun, 1991.

[†††] From Giscard d'Estaing, 1993.

Education & Practice in Writing / Rhetoric

1960s

1960 +. Teachers and researchers of rhetoric and writing slowly gain respect as composition teachers start to form a greater professional identity.

1960 +. Audience analysis and analysis of the rhetorical situation become principles in most writing courses.

1960. In a report summarizing the events at the influential 1959 Woods Hole Conference of educators, Jerome S. Bruner introduces his notion of the "spiral curriculum," echoing some of John Dewey's ideas and reviving an interest in "discovery" learning.[171]

1960. An Oct. 14 United Press dispatch claims that "Johnny can't read, write, or talk properly," fueling the debate over the presumed literacy crisis.

1961. The National Council of Teachers of English (NCTE) publishes *The National Interest and the Teaching of English,* underscoring the importance of English to the national welfare. The U.S. House Subcommittee on Labor and Education will use this document to determine that English should be funded at higher levels, leading Congress to initiate Project English.[172]

1963 +. The academic community regains interest in the relations among science, rhetoric, and technology.[173]

1963 +. The notion that writers create texts with a specific purpose in mind is widely taught; see, for example, McCrimmon's *Writing with a Purpose.*

1963 +. The field of writing embraces a view of theory, research, and practice which emphasizes a rhetorical approach rather than a craft appoach. Some mark 1963 as the birth of modern composition studies.[174]

Professional Development

1960s

1960 +. Developments in aerospace and aviation create new opportunities for technical and scientific writers.[175]

1960 +. The fields of technical art, illustration, and computer-aided design flourish, with an enormous amount of art produced for NASA and military agencies.

1960 +. The continued growth of technology creates a serious shortage of technical writers; the pay and prestige of technical writing advance as the decade continues.[176]

1960. The Society of Technical Writers and Editors (STWE) and the Technical Publishing Society (TPS) merge to form the Society for Technical Writing and Publishers (STWP). The Society will keep the name STWP until 1971, when it will change its name to the Society for Technical Communication (STC) to better encompass all phases of technical communication.[177]

1960. Because most technical communication and science writing is done by writers who remain anonymous, tracing the history around key individuals who shaped the field is viewed as problematic. This pattern is unlike that in graphic design, where well-known "stars" dominate the field.[178]

1961. The Greater Washington Area chapter of the Society of Technical Writers and Publishers (STWP) sponsors the first Science Writing Contest for area high-school students, a concept that spreads to other STWP chapters across the country; the Washington chapter also develops a brochure entitled *Technical Writing as a Career.*[179]

1962. The Designers and Art Directors Association is established in the U.K.

Education & Practice in Graphic Design

1960s

1960 +. Pop artists such as Roy Lichtenstein, Robert Rauschenberg, Andy Warhol, and James Rosenquist combine advertising images with oversized everyday objects to create a heightened sense of the consumer-oriented society.[180]

1960. In the U.K., Letraset, a design company, invents a dry transfer process which allows designers to create instant headlines; Letraset will later develop "computer Letrafonts" for use on the Macintosh.[181]

1962. *The Sunday Times* (London) issues its first color supplement.[††]

1963. Books that present research on typography begin to appear; for example, see Miles A. Tinker's *Legibility of Print.*[182]

1963. The firm "Total Design" is established in Holland; its members are committed to the International Typographic Style and take an interdisciplinary approach to design problems. Total Design creates awareness of visual design in Holland's public sector and prompts succeeding generations of designers to reshape graphic and typographic practices throughout the country.[183]

1964. Masuru Katsumie, Japanese design critic and journalist, directs the visual design program for the 1964 Tokyo Olympics; he later designs for the Expo '70 in Osaka and the 1972 Winter Olympics in Sapporo.

1964. Yusaku Kamekura, a Japanese designer known for combining Eastern and Western ideas in his work, wins the grand prize from the Japanese Ministry of Education for his symbol of the 1964 Tokyo Olympic Games.

▲ **Background Image.** *In the 1950s and 1960s, Marilyn Monroe became one of Hollywood's most adored stars; shown here is an adaptation of a New York street scene from Billy Wilder's 1956 film "The Seven Year Itch."*

Science, Technology, & Environment

1960s

1960 +. Mainframe computers become popular with government and big business.

1960. Xerox introduces its plain paper copier, revolutionizing photocopying technology.

1960. The first weather satellite, *Tiros 1* (built by RCA), is launched by the U.S.[†††]

1961. Alan B. Shepard, Jr. becomes the first U.S. astronaut in space when the Mercury 3 capsule *Freedom 7* completes a 15-minute suborbital flight.[†]

1961. IBM introduces the Selectric electric typewriter—an important technology for publications departments around the world.

1961. The first time-sharing computer system, the PDP1, is developed at MIT for IBMs 700 and 7090; the system is marketed in 1962.[†††]

1962 +. Douglas C. Englebart builds the first working and usable hypertext system, the Augment system, between 1962 and 1975.[184]

1962. Unimation (U.S.) markets the world's first industrial robot.[†]

1962. Francis H. Crick and Maurice H. Wilkins of the U.K. and James D. Watson of the U.S. win the Nobel Prize for Physiology or Medicine for determining the molecular structure of DNA.[†]

1962. The U.S. space-probe *Mariner 2* becomes the first object made by humans to voyage to another planet.[†]

1962. John H. Glenn, Jr. is the first American to orbit the Earth in the Mercury 6 space capsule *Friendship 7*.[†]

Society & Consumerism

1960s

1960 +. Ralph Nader, American lawyer and consumer advocate, raises U.S. consumers' attention to the sometimes shoddy and unethical practices of business and industry; his followers become known as Nader's Raiders.

1960+. The connections between consumers' attitudes toward products and their values and goals are systematically explored by marketing experts and exploited by advertisers.[185]

1960. In the U.S., historic televised Presidential debates between John F. Kennedy and Richard M. Nixon are held; Kennedy is elected.

1960. The American Heart Association issues a report attributing higher death rates among middle-aged men to the heavy smoking of cigarettes.[††]

1962. Approximately 44 percent of the world's adults are illiterate.[††]

1962. The U.S. and Cuba are involved in the Cuban missile crisis.

1963. Martin Luther King delivers his famous "I Have a Dream" speech at a Washington rally.

1963. U.S. President John F. Kennedy is assassinated in Dallas; Lyndon B. Johnson is sworn in as President.

1964. U.S. President Lyndon B. Johnson signs the Civil Rights Bill, which prohibits racial discrimination in employment, publicly owned facilities, places of public accommodation, and federally funded programs.

1964. In publicity campaigns for the Olympic Games in Tokyo, the world is exposed to some of the best of international graphic design talent.

Notes

[171] Applebee, 1974; Russell, 1991.

[172] Applebee, 1974, pp. 201–204.

[173] Wenzel, 1963.

[174] North, 1987, p. 15. Research suggests that 1963 may actually represent a culmination of activity in composition studies that had been smoldering since the 1900s and which "heated up" during the 1950s. Events taking place in the field between 1950 and 1965 marked the start of the demise of current-traditional rhetoric (see Note 1) and the beginning of the "New Rhetoric," focusing on thought and communication in actual rhetorical situations (Young & Goggin, 1993, pp. 26–31).

[175] Nilsson, 1990, p. 92.

[176] Connors, 1982, p. 344.

[177] Pardoe, 1990, p. 188.

[178] Shulman, 1960; for a discussion, see Moran & Journet, 1985.

[179] Shimberg, 1989, p. 267.

[180] Craig & Barton, 1987, p. 194.

[181] Livingston & Livingston, 1992, p. 119.

[182] Tinker, 1963.

[183] Livingston & Livingston, 1992, p. 59.

[184] Englebart, 1963.

[185] Fisbein, 1967.

[†]   From Hellemans & Bunch, 1991.

[††]   From Grun, 1991.

[†††] From Giscard d'Estaing, 1993.

Education & Practice in Writing / Rhetoric

1960s *Continued*

1963. *Research in Written Composition* is published; it brings together more than 500 studies of reading and writing. It is referred to as the charter of the field of composition.[186]

1963. The theme at the Conference on College Composition and Communication (CCCC) is "Toward a New Rhetoric"; conference participants explore the connections between studies in composition and rhetoric. Most historians cite this conference as the first gathering of the "modern" profession of composition studies.[187]

1964 +. Empirical research in technical writing begins to develop, with studies of error and studies of the variables in writing technical descriptions.[188]

1965 +. Political activism against the war in Vietnam begins to grow on U.S. college campuses; in writing classes, students often express their opinions through journals, essays, and poetry.

1965 +. Edward P. J. Corbett's *Classical Rhetoric for the Modern Student* and Wayne C. Booth's *Rhetoric of Fiction* signal a revival of interest in rhetoric in English departments.[189]

1965. Rensselaer Polytechnic Institute begins to offer a Ph.D. degree in Communications and Rhetoric.

1966 +. The Prague School of Linguistics contributes to the understanding of discourse "beyond the sentence."

1966. The Dartmouth Conference brings together English teachers from the U.K. and the U.S. to consider common problems. While American educators emphasize problem solving, British educators emphasize their students' personal growth.[190]

Professional Development

1960s *Continued*

1962. The first technical art exhibit is sponsored by the Society for Technical Writers and Publishers (STWP) at their annual convention; it is organized by the Technical Art Group (TAG), the first art group in the society.

1963. In the U.K., the International Council of Graphic Design Associations (ICOGRADA) is founded, representing the national societies of professional designers and organizations worldwide who are concerned with raising graphic design standards.

1966. The first major publication of the Society for Technical Writers and Publishers (STWP), *An Annotated Bibliography of Technical Writing, Editing, Graphics, and Publishing*, is written.[191]

1967. *The Journal of Typographic Research*, later called *Visible Language (VL)*, is first published. Dedicated to "all that is involved with our being literate," this journal will publish many research studies in document design and graphic communication.

1967. The journal *Research in the Teaching of English* begins publication.

1967. The first all-woman paper session is presented at the Conference of the Society of Technical Writers and Publishers (STWP).[192]

1967. The STWP permits artists to become part of their organization for the first time, thanks to the lobbying efforts of the Association of Technical Artists (ATA). The first International Technical Art Exhibit (ITAE) is held at the STWP's annual conference; from this time forward, a technical art competition with a graphics stem will be part of the annual conference.[193]

Education & Practice in Graphic Design

1960s *Continued*

1964. In the U.K., outstanding corporate identity programs are created for the British Rail and the Post Office (1966) by the Design Research Unit, a famous British design consultancy that takes a multidisciplinary approach.[194]

1965 +. Psychedelic art gives visual expression to counterculture ideas: type and images are distorted and printed in Day-Glo colors to create hallucinatory effects, and posters are designed to be experienced rather than read.[195]

1965. Swiss typographer Emil Ruder publishes *Typographie,* a seminal work in which he articulates the philosophy that clear typographic legibility is essential to effective visual communication. His designs, which employ grid systems and sans serif typefaces, contribute substantially to the International Typographic Style.

1966. Massimo Vignelli creates the signage for the New York City subway.

1966. The *Times* of London changes its format, putting news instead of advertisements on the front page.[tt]

1967. R. Bass develops CBS News 36, a typeface designed especially for use on TV.

1968. Lance Wyman, a New York-based designer, creates the design for the 1968 Mexico Olympic Games by using pictograms and color coding on signs, kiosks, telephones, and maps to communicate across language barriers.

1969 +. Typographic designer and educator Herbert Spencer takes part in a research project with RCA on the legibility of print, leading to the influential book *The Visible Word.*

▲ **Background Image.** *Young people joined the "peace movement" and organized protest rallies against the war in Vietnam; shown here is an adaptation of Arnold Skolnick's 1969 Woodstock Festival Poster, "3 Days of Peace & Music"—graphic memorabilia from the Woodstock Music and Art Fair.*

Science, Technology, & Environment

1960s *Continued*

1962. Rachel Carson publishes *The Silent Spring,* a book that introduces the public to the dangers of pollution.[†]

1963. The cassette for recording and playing back sound is introduced by Philips of the Netherlands.[†]

1964. IBM introduces the System/360 Model 30 mainframe computer; it is first shipped in June 1965.

1964. Marshall McLuhan's *Understanding Media* foresees electronic media as creating a "global village" in which the "medium is the message."

1965. Thomas Kurtz and John Kemeny develop a computer language for beginners, BASIC (beginners all-purpose symbolic instruction code).[†]

1965. Ted Nelson coins the terms "hypertext" and "hypermedia."[196]

1965. The concept of virtual reality is explored for military applications; the first commercial applications will not be available until the late 1980s.[†††]

1966. The Soviet space-probe *Luna IX* accomplishes the first soft landing on the moon; the first U.S. soft landing is completed by *Surveyor I.*[†]

1966. The U.S. Environmental Science Services Administration launches *ESSA I,* the first weather satellite capable of viewing the entire Earth.[†]

1967. Keyboards, an important technology for writing and calculating, are designed for computers.[†]

1967. Gene Amdahl proposes computers with parallel processors, designed to solve certain problems much faster than ordinary computers.[†]

Society & Consumerism

1960s *Continued*

1965. Ralph Nader's book *Unsafe at Any Speed* provides the impetus for consumer awareness of problems with automobile safety.

1965. Legislative momentum gains for anti-pollution laws in the U.S.[††]

1965. In the U.S., the Medicare bill becomes law.

1966. Color TV becomes popular.[††]

1966. The Fair Packaging & Labeling ("Truth-in-Packaging") Act is passed.

1966. The Child Protection Act is passed in the U.S., banning dangerous toys from interstate commerce.

1967. The U.S. National Highway Traffic Administration is formed; it conducts research on highway safety.

1967. The economist John Kenneth Galbraith critiques the role of corporations in creating and managing the presumed preferences of consumers.

1968. U.S. involvement in Vietnam escalates and young people demonstrate in major cities to protest against the war. Police brutality and riots mark the Democratic National Convention.

1968. Civil rights leader Reverend Martin Luther King, Jr. is assassinated.

1968. U.S. Senator Robert F. Kennedy is assassinated.

1968. There are 78 million TV sets in the U.S.

1968. In the U.S., the Consumer Credit Protection ("Truth-in-Lending") Act and the Radiation Health and Safety Act are passed.

Notes

[186] Braddock, Lloyd-Jones, & Schoer, 1963.

[187] Connors, Ede, & Lunsford, 1984, p. 10; Schilb, 1989; Vitanza, 1987, p. 252. Young and Goggin suggest that 1949 and 1959 are also important boundary markers. The former marks the first meeting of the Conference on College Composition and Communication, which has been said to have triggered "earthquakes that began to dislodge current-traditional rhetoric from its educational dominance." The latter marks a public debate in which Warner Rice proposed that freshman composition should be abolished and in which Albert Kitzhaber argued that composition should not be abolished, but made stronger. In retrospect, it appears that Kitzhaber won (1953, pp. 31, 40).

[188] Connors, 1982, p. 345.

[189] Kinneavy, 1983, p. 169. See Booth (1961) and Corbett (1965).

[190] Berlin, 1990, p. 210; see also Freedman, 1994.

[191] Kleinmann, 1989, p. 263.

[192] Zook, 1989, p. 415.

[193] Nilsson, 1990, p. 92.

[194] Livingston & Livingston, 1992, p. 54.

[195] Craig & Barton, 1987, p. 195.

[196] Conklin, 1987.

[†]   From Hellemans & Bunch, 1991.

[††] From Grun, 1991.

[†††] From Giscard d'Estaing, 1993.

Education & Practice in Writing / Rhetoric

1960s *Continued*

1968 +. Andries van Dam and a team at Brown University develop courses that use hypertext to support instruction.[197]

1968. Kenneth W. Houp and Thomas E. Pearsall publish *Reporting Technical Information,* a very influential technical communication textbook.

1969. The NAEP (National Assessment of Educational Progress) test is used for the first time to assess students' performances in writing; the test uses student writing samples instead of multiple choice problems, but some educators question the types of writing samples used, the length of time students get to write, and the manner in which samples are scored.

1970s

1970 +. Professors of technical communication in the U.S. begin to be tenured for their academic work.[198]

1970 +. Patricia Wright, a pioneer in document design from Cambridge's Applied Psychology Unit (APU) of the U.K.'s Medical Research Council, provides important insights into the cognition of engaging with documents displayed on paper or on a screen.

1970 +. The reading research community begins to seriously question the validity and value of readability formulas for predicting the comprehensibility of written texts.[199]

1970 +. Research in the design of textbooks and computer-based instruction (CBI) flourishes.[200]

Professional Development

1960s *Continued*

1969. The Toronto, Ontario chapter of the Society of Technical Writers and Publishers (STWP) is formed.[201]

1969. The International Council for Technical Communication (Intecom) is founded in Europe; charter members include England, Holland, Sweden, and the U.S. (represented by the STWP). Intecom will grow into a kind of United Nations for professional and technical communication groups and technical art organizations from around the world.

1969. The first International Symposium on Technical Communication is conducted by the STWP in Tel Aviv, Israel.

1970s

1970 +. The U.K. government funds the Civil Service College, which runs a wide range of courses on information design—the process of presenting complex information in ways that people can understand.[202]

1970 +. The *Modern Language Association (MLA) Job List* advertises more tenure-track positions in technical communication than ever before.[203]

1970. *The Journal of Technical Writing and Communication (JTWC)* is founded by members of Rensselaer Polytechnic Institute.

1971. Stello Jordan and his associates edit a collection on technical communication in professional settings, *Handbook of Technical Writing Practices.*

Education & Practice in Graphic Design

1960s *Continued*

1969 +. To counteract Swiss design that has become too formal, too organized, and too predictable, younger generation Swiss designers search for a new visual vocabulary and start "the New Wave," a philosophy in which both intuition and reason determine where graphic elements should be located. Type and illustrations are placed at random with overlapping images, enlarged halftone dot patterns, reversed type, rules, bars, and other elements arranged in unconventional ways.[204]

1969. Under the direction of Muriel Cooper, the MIT Press publishes *Bauhaus* on the fiftieth anniversary of the German school's founding.[205]

1970s

1970 +. Design consultancies become more strongly linked with big business; most graphic design is in the area of corporate identity and advertising.

1970 +. Louis Silverstein redesigns the *New York Times*, introducing a new page grid, larger headlines, a stronger emphasis on photography, and more charts and maps.

1970 +. Some graphic designers begin to use research on the legibility of typefaces to help them make choices.

1970 +. Graphic designers join psychologists, computer scientists, human factors professionals, rhetoricians, and information designers to develop the fields of human-computer interaction and user-interface design.

▲ **Background Image.** *In 1969, U.S. Astronaut Neil Armstrong of the Apollo 11 mission became the first human to walk on the moon.*

Science, Technology, & Environment

1960s *Continued*

1968. One of the earliest empirical studies of virtual reality is reported.[206]

1968. James D. Watson publishes *The Double Helix*.

1968. The U.S. government's Advanced Research Projects Agency (ARPA) creates ARPANET, a computer network that will become the Internet.

1969. Kenneth Thompson and Dennis Richie of AT&T Bell Labs create the UNIX software operating system; it will become the *lingua franca* of open systems by the late 1980s.

1969. U.S. astronaut Neil Armstrong of the *Apollo 11* crew is the first human to stand on the moon.[†]

1970s

1970. The first videocassette recorders are introduced to the mass market; they quickly become the butt of jokes because they are hard to use and their manuals are difficult to understand.

1970. IBM introduces the System/370 Model 155 mainframe computer; it is first shipped in January 1971.

1970. The floppy disk is introduced.[†]

1970. The first of the "jumbo jets," the Boeing 747, goes into service across the Atlantic.

1970. The microprocessor is invented by Gilbert Hyatt (U.S.).[†††]

1971. François Gernelle (France) develops the first microcomputer.[†††]

Society & Consumerism

1960s *Continued*

1969. In the U.S., the National Environmental Policy Act (NEPA) is signed into law; it requires Environmental Impact Statements to be written when corporate or governmental action involves the use of public lands.

1969. GM recalls almost 5 million cars for adjustments of mechanical defects; consumers must deal with the jargon in recall notices.

1969. In the U.S., New York becomes the first state to establish a Department of Consumer Affairs when New York City Mayor John Lindsay appoints Bess Myerson as the Commissioner of Consumer Affairs.[207]

1970s

1970 +. The consumer movement in the U.S. is rekindled, making average citizens more aware of their rights as consumers and more skeptical of communications produced by government and business.

1970 +. Marketers make consumers and their choices a highly researched topic; so-called psychographic studies of consumers' beliefs, lifestyles, and aspirations proliferate.[208]

1970 +. In the U.S., the Department of Consumer Affairs and "Action Lines" in newspapers, radio, and television become important resources where consumers can lodge complaints and grievances with companies, utilities, landlords, and government agencies.[209]

Notes

[197] Yankelovich, Landow, & Cody, 1986.

[198] Connors, 1982, p. 349.

[199] Klare, 1974.

[200] Gagné & Briggs, 1979.

[201] Rhodes-Marriott, 1990, p. 303.

[202] Kimble, 1992, p. 51.

[203] Connors, 1982, p. 348.

[204] Craig & Barton, 1987, p. 203.

[205] Ibid., p. 197.

[206] Sutherland, 1968; discussed in Benedikt, 1991.

[207] Maynes, 1976, p. 328.

[208] Hansen, 1972.

[209] Maynes, 1976, p. 329.

[†]   From Hellemans & Bunch, 1991.

[††]   From Grun, 1991.

[†††] From Giscard d'Estaing, 1993.

Education & Practice in Writing / Rhetoric

1970s *Continued*

1970 +. Issues of open admissions and racial integration force educators to rethink their approach to language instruction. In an effort to better link writing and thinking, teachers initiate Writing Across the Curriculum (WAC) programs.[210]

1971. Janet Emig's *The Composing Processes of 12th Graders* provides an in-depth analysis of students' writing processes; her study marks the approximate beginning of research on "writing as a process" in composition.

1974. According to the results of the National Assessment of Educational Progress (NAEP) test, the writing abilities of secondary school students have declined in some areas since 1969. The American press writes many articles expressing shock and outrage over the apparent decline; educators are skeptical about the meaning of the results.

1974. The Bay Area Writing Project is organized to improve the writing of college freshmen by improving their secondary school writing instruction; in 1977, it becomes The National Writing Project (NWP); the NWP will affect the teaching of writing in schools across the U.S.

1975 +. Academics engage in critical self-examination, defining and redefining the nature, scope, and province of technical communication.[211]

1975 +. Interest in computers and composition increases in the U.S.

1975 +. Writing teachers increasingly recognize the value of studying the reading process, both to help students better understand their audiences and to help teachers better understand how students read their own writing.

Professional Development

1970s *Continued*

1971. *The Journal of Typographic Research* changes its name to *Visible Language (VL)*, reflecting a broader view of communications; *VL* will publish many early studies in writing and document design.

1971. The STWP changes its name to the Society for Technical Communication (STC) to encompass all phases of technical communication; it rapidly becomes the largest organization of its kind in the world.

1972. In the U.K., the Institute of Scientific and Technical Communicators (ISTC), an organization dedicated to the study and dissemination of information about writing and information design, is formed.

1973. The Association of Teachers of Technical Writing (ATTW) is formed to encourage dialogue among teachers of technical communication. Also started is the ATTW's journal, *The Technical Writing Teacher,* which becomes *Technical Communication Quarterly (TCQ)* in 1992.

1973. Herman A. Estrin organizes the first workshop for teachers of technical writing to be held at a meeting of the National Council of Teachers of English (NCTE).

1974. The first annual meeting of the Council for Programs in Scientific and Technical Communication (CPSTC) is attended by program directors and industry representatives from across the U.S.; CPSTC gives program administrators and industry representatives a forum in which they can discuss ways to improve the quality of programs and to build lasting collaborations between people in universities and people in business and government.

Education & Practice in Graphic Design

1970s *Continued*

1970 +. Electronic typesetting systems replace photo-typesetting systems in publishing.[212]

1970 +. The poster craze that erupted in the U.S. during the 1960s (in which posters were used to foster a climate of social activism about civil rights, the Vietnam War, women's liberation, and alternative lifestyles) reaches a peak in the early 1970s, with Peter Max's posters on topics such as "Love."[213]

1970 +. In Japan, graphic designer Tadanori Yokoo rejects the order and logic of Constructivism by turning to Dada for inspiration; Yokoo creates a Pop Art so well liked by Japanese young people that he achieves "cult figure" status in his country.[214]

1970. Herb Lubalin, Aaron Burns, and Edward Rondthaler found the International Typeface Corporation (ITC), an organization that will go on to redraw many standard typefaces such as Garamond, Cheltenham, Baskerville, Century, and Caslon for newer photo-typesetting and digital systems. ITC also commissions new designs for typefaces from leading designers such as Hermann Zapf; its journal *U & lc (Upper and lower case)* will influence the typographic industry for years to come.

1970. The Push Pin Studio—a design group that challenges the dominant mathematical and objective orientation of the International Typographic Style with witty, colorful, and irreverent designs for book jackets, record covers, posters, and magazine illustrations—becomes the first American design group honored with an exhibition at the Musée des Arts Décoratifs in Paris.[215]

▲ **Background Image.** *Inspired by such popular movies as "Saturday Night Fever," the "disco" craze swept America. In an effort to make the best impression on the dance floor, many people took disco lessons and struggled with "learn-at-home" instructions for dances such as the Latin Hustle.*

Science, Technology, & Environment

1970s *Continued*

1971. Patrick Haggerty's Texas Instruments introduces the first pocket-sized calculator, the Pocketronic; weighing about 2.5 pounds, it can add, subtract, multiply, and divide.[†]

1971. The first commercial microchip, the Intel 4004, is created by Marcian E. Hoff, Federico Faggin, and Stanley Mazor.[†††]

1971. Niklaus Wirth develops Pascal (named for Blaise Pascal, who invented the first calculator), a popular scientific language used on home computers.[†]

1972. Xerox PARC develops a computer called the Alto; though it is never commercialized, it spurs ideas for other computer developers, including Apple.

1973. The first *Skylab* is launched by a Saturn rocket.[†]

1973. Canon (Japan) introduces the first color photocopier.[†††]

1974. F. S. Rowland and Mario Molina warn that chlorofluorocarbons, commonly used as spray propellants and in refrigeration, may be destroying the ozone layer in the atmosphere.[†]

1974. Unleaded gasoline is developed to help reduce pollution.[†††]

1975. The VHS format for videotapes is launched by JVC.[†††]

1975. The first personal commercialized computer/microcomputer, the Altair 8800 hobbyist computer, is introduced.[216]

1975. Cray introduces the first of the supercomputers, the Cray-1 Supercomputer; it depends on very large scale integration devices.

Society & Consumerism

1970s *Continued*

1970. Staffan Linder characterizes "harried" consumers, i.e., consumers with a high income who can buy more goods but have less total time available for informing themselves prior to making a purchase.[217]

1970. In the U.S., consumerists push the government to change the automobile insurance system.[218]

1970. The first Earth Day is celebrated.[†]

1970. The U.S. Environmental Protection Agency announces the Clean Air Act. Among its various recommendations, the Clean Air Act requires that unleaded gasoline be available in all gas stations by 1974.

1971. Cigarette advertisements are banned from U.S. television.

1972. In the U.S., the Consumer Product Safety Commission is established.

1972. The "Watergate" affair unravels in Washington, D.C.

1974 +. The "Plain English" movement—concerned with creating documents readers can easily comprehend—gains momentum; it is energized by ordinary citizens who demand their right to clear information from business and government.[219]

1974. The Nationwide Mutual Insurance Company simplifies two of its insurance policies, kicking off the plain English movement in insurance.

1974. President Nixon resigns.

1974. In the U.S., the Equal Credit Opportunity Act and the Fair Credit Billing Act are signed into law.[220]

Notes

[210] Russell, 1991, p. 271.

[211] Britton, 1975; Dobrin, 1983; Hays, 1975; Miller, 1979; Stratton, 1979.

[212] Craig & Barton, 1987, p. 206.

[213] Meggs, 1983, p. 462.

[214] Ibid., p. 473.

[215] Livingston & Livingston, 1992, p. 161; Meggs, 1983, p. 459.

[216] Cringely, 1992, p. 44.

[217] Linder, 1970.

[218] O'Connell, 1971.

[219] Bowen, Duffy, & Steinberg, 1991; Kimble, 1992, p. 2.

[220] For an account of the outpouring of consumer legislation between 1966 and 1976, see Mayer, 1989, pp. 28–30.

[†] From Hellemans & Bunch, 1991.

[††] From Grun, 1991.

[†††] From Giscard d'Estaing, 1993.

Education & Practice in Writing / Rhetoric

1970s *Continued*

1975. *Newsweek's* December 9 cover story, "Why Johnny Can't Write," brings the presumed American literacy crisis (ignited by the 1974 NAEP test scores) to the forefront of a national discussion in the media.[221]

1976. English teachers agonize over the enormous press given to the presumed American literacy crisis. Carl Klaus says, "No matter where I turn … I hear the same feverish cry: Johnny Can't Write (and apparently Jenny can't write either)."[222]

1976. The first edition of *Academic Programs in Technical Communication*, published by the Society for Technical Communication, appears; it lists 19 academic programs.[223]

1977. Scholastic Aptitude Test (SAT) scores of U.S. college-bound students show a steady decline between 1963 and 1977. The media links the trend to a decline in the quality of U.S. educational standards, but it may actually reflect the larger number of students enrolling in colleges.

1978 +. The U.S. National Institute of Education (NIE) funds the Document Design Project (DDP), an extensive research effort shared by the American Institutes for Research, Carnegie Mellon Univ., and Siegel & Gale, Inc. The project produces a textbook on document design, a book of guidelines for document designers, a review of the research, and dozens of technical reports (–1981).[224]

1978. Expressivism, the view that writing is a creative "personal" activity in which the writer expresses a "unique voice," that "writing can be learned but not taught," becomes a popular working philosophy.[225]

Professional Development

1970s *Continued*

1975 +. Summer workshops that contribute to the professional development of teachers of technical writing are held at the Univ. of Michigan, Rice Univ., the Univ. of Washington, Old Dominion, and the Univ. of Minnesota.

1976. The MLA, which for more than 50 years refused to recognize technical writing as a legitimate function of English scholars, caves in and allows the first technical writing panel to appear at its annual convention.[226]

1976. J. C. Mathes and D. W. Stevenson's influential textbook, *Designing Technical Reports*, is published; it contains a detailed procedure for audience analysis.

1977 +. The STC (Society for Technical Communication) removes sexist language from its bylaws. During this period, female members lobby the society to actively support the Equal Rights Amendment (ERA).[227]

1977. The *New York Times* reports that on an average day, the U.S. government prints about 1 million words of regulations and notices in the Federal Register.[228]

1977. In the U.S., studies of reading at work flourish, especially reading while working for the military; see, for example, Thomas Sticht's "Comprehending Reading at Work."[229]

1978. In West Germany, the technical communication association Tekom is founded; it will become the largest European organization for writers.

1979. *Information Design Journal,* an important resource for the international writing and design community, publishes its first issue.

Education & Practice in Graphic Design

1970s *Continued*

1972. Anton Stankowski, a leading German painter and graphic designer, creates the visual design for the 1972 Munich Olympic Games.

1972. Rolf F. Rehe, a specialist in newspaper design, publishes a summary of the research literature on the legibility of typography in *Typography: How to Make It Most Legible.*

1974. The U.S. government sponsors the Federal Design Improvement Project, whose goal is to improve every aspect of design in the public service; the first federal department to gain from the program is the Department of Labor, with a cohesive corporate identity developed by John Massey and the Center for Advanced Research in Design.

1974. The U.S. Department of Transportation commissions the American Institute of Graphic Arts (AIGA), the nation's oldest professional graphic design organization, to create a master signage system consisting of a set of symbols that depict passenger, pedestrian, and first aid information related to transportation facilities; created by Don Shanosky and Roger Cook, this signage system is considered one of the most effective examples of modern graphic communications to transcend cultural and language barriers.[230]

1975 +. Post-modernism is promoted by German designer Wolfgang Weingart, who challenges the rules of the International Typographic Style; he utilizes wide word and letter spacing, step rules, reversed type blocks, unpredictable contrasts of type weights, and diagonal, even random, placement of letterforms.[231]

▲ **Background Image.** *Throughout the 1970s, people in support of the Equal Rights Amendment (ERA) staged rallies for "equal pay for equal work." According to the National Organization for Women (NOW), in 1978 American women were paid on average 59¢ on a dollar for the same work as men; shown here are symbols from the July 9, 1978 "March on Washington," a rally that brought together thousands of women and men who wanted to see the ERA passed.*

Science, Technology, & Environment

1970s *Continued*

1976. A young software entrepreneur named Bill Gates obtains the first UNIX license not granted to a university.

1976. IBM introduces its first ink-jet printer.[†]

1976. The National Academy of Science reports that gases from spray cans can cause damage to the atmosphere's ozone layer.[††]

1977. A fiber optic system is used for large-scale trials in a telephone system for the first time.[†]

1977. Two homosexual men in New York City are diagnosed as having the rare cancer Karposi's sarcoma; in retrospect, they are probably two of the earliest known AIDS victims in the U.S. The disease will not be officially recognized until 1981.[†]

1977. Steven Jobs and Steven Wosniak of Apple Computer launch the Apple II, the first successful microcomputer. It has a full-size comfortable keyboard and a floppy disk drive.[232]

1978. Herbert A. Simon wins the Nobel Prize in Economics for his work on decision making.

1979. Sony introduces the Walkman, a very successful product originally dismissed as not interesting by 8 out of 10 Sony dealers.[†††]

1979. The first compact disc (CD) is developed by Philips and Sony; it makes its debut in 1983.[†††]

1979. Visicalc makes the first spreadsheet program for personal computers; this enables people to use business applications for a personal computer without learning to program.[†††]

Society & Consumerism

1970s *Continued*

1975 +. Concern for the preservation of the environment moves beyond fringe groups who are promoting a "cause" and into the mainstream of politics and social activism.[233]

1975. The U.K.'s National Consumer Council provides a strong independent voice for consumers.[234]

1975. New York's Citibank revises its promissory note, which inspires the first state statute requiring plain English in consumer contracts.[235]

1975. There are 31 periodicals (in 29 different countries) dedicated to informing consumers about the quality, safety, and value of products.[236]

1975. In the U.S., Congress passes the Magnuson-Moss Warranty Act, which establishes that warranties must use language that is free of trade terms, ambiguities, exemptions, and disclaimers. The act raises the expectations of consumers for clarity in document design.[237]

1976. Australia joins the plain language movement when the National Road Motorist Association issues its first plain language policy.

1977. The New York State legislature passes the Sullivan Act, creating the first "Plain Language Law" for contracts and consumer documents; it becomes law in 1978.[238]

1978. On March 23, U.S. President Jimmy Carter signs an Executive Order, *Improving Government Regulations,* which mandates that U.S. regulations be as simple and clear as possible. His attention to the problems created by difficult documents reignites the plain language movement in the U.S.

Notes

[221] Faigley & Miller, 1982; Russell, 1991, p. 276.

[222] Klaus, 1976, p. 335.

[223] Pearsall & Sullivan, 1976.

[224] National Institute of Education (NIE) Grant #G780195; Felker, 1980; Felker, Pickering, Charrow, Holland, & Redish, 1981; Goswami, Redish, Felker, & Siegel, 1981.

[225] Coles, 1978; Macrorie, 1978; Miller, 1978.

[226] Connors, 1982, p. 347.

[227] Cook, 1990, p. 196.

[228] *New York Times*, 1977.

[229] Sticht, 1977.

[230] Meggs, 1983, p. 447.

[231] Livingston & Livingston, 1992, p. 202.

[232] Kidwell & Ceruzzi, 1994, pp. 96–99; see also Kurzweil, 1990, pp. 474–478.

[233] Maynes, 1976, p. 279.

[234] Kimble, 1992, p. 51.

[235] Felsenfeld, 1991.

[236] Maynes, 1976, p. 348.

[237] Black, 1981, pp. 255–300; Kimble, 1992, p. 31; Smith, 1989, pp. MG-49–MG-52.

[238] Felsenfeld, 1991.

[†]   From Hellemans & Bunch, 1991.

[††] From Grun, 1991.

[†††] From Giscard d'Estaing, 1993.

Education & Practice in Writing / Rhetoric

1970s *Continued*

1979. Carnegie Mellon Univ. faculty form the Communications Design Center, a non-profit organization where faculty and graduate students conduct basic and applied research in document design (closed in 1990).

1979. Rensselaer Polytechnic Institute adds a track in Technical Communication to its Doctor of Philosophy degree in Communication and Rhetoric, the first of its kind.

1979. John R. Hayes and Linda Flower develop the first cognitive model of writing processes.[239]

1980s

1980 +. Research on cognitive processes in writing flourishes; a number of studies that grew out of the Document Design Project (see 1978 +) are published, including the first model of the document design process.[240]

1980 +. "Computer literacy" in the classroom and the workplace becomes a concern. Initially the focus is on providing students and employees with the mechanical skills needed to use computers for word processing or calculating spreadsheets; later the emphasis shifts to social, cognitive, and organizational issues that using computers in the classroom or workplace raise; attention is directed to the use of computers to solve problems, invent, learn, collaborate, or design— whether working alone or in a group.

1980 +. Researchers in text linguistics make advances in the understanding of text structure.[241]

Professional Development

1970s *Continued*

1979. The Document Design Center (DDC) of the American Institutes for Research (AIR) is formed. Under the direction of Janice (Ginny) C. Redish, the DDC carries out research and practice in document design, disseminates technical reports, and issues a newsletter entitled *Fine Print* (later changed to *Simply Stated*).

1979. The Society for Technical Communication holds its first Technical Video Competition to recognize excellence in video communications dealing with science, technology, medicine, and government.

1980s

1980 +. The study of usability and iterative design flourishes; eventually, such research is taken seriously by organizations around the world.

1980. In an immigration case involving the occupation classification of a technical publications writer, the U.S. Department of Justice rules that technical writing is a profession.[242]

1981. The Society for Advanced Composition is founded; it is followed in 1984 by the influential *Journal of Advanced Composition (JAC)*.

1982 +. Anthologies on technical and scientific communication flourish; for example, see *The Technology of Text, Volumes 1 and 2*.[243]

1982 +. Industry begins to develop usability testing laboratories to evaluate the quality of its products, user interfaces, and documents.[244]

Education & Practice in Graphic Design

1970s *Continued*

1975 +. Punk, a street culture movement from London, flourishes. In design, the punk movement is characterized by collage, chaotic typography, and shocking slogans.

1977. Paul Davis, a Push Pin Studio designer, becomes known for juxtaposing painterly images with type.[245]

1977. In his book *Image Text Music*, Roland Barthes explores the historical relations between graphics and text, inspiring graphic designers to consider the ways that graphics and text can be orchestrated to sharpen messages.

1980s

1980 +. Digital typesetting becomes an industry standard; every major manufacturer has ceased to make anything but digital equipment.[246]

1980 +. Computer-aided design and laser technology greatly diminish the role of pencil and paper in design and engineering; images can be cropped, silhouetted, distorted, or color corrected with a touch of a key. Some designers resist the computer, but eventually most change their minds.

1980 +. Bringing new typefaces to market becomes more cost effective, continuing a trend that began in the 1970s with the decline of hot-metal typesetting machines; as a result, manufacturers become more willing to introduce new typefaces and full families of faces, enabling designers to emphasize the hierarchical structure in a document while maintaining a unified look throughout.[247]

▲ **Background Image.** *PacMan (and later Ms. PacMan) was an immediate "hit" with boys and girls, many of whom skipped school and spent their lunch money just to play the game. PacMan now seems primitive in contrast to today's more elaborate (and more violent) games from companies such as Nintendo, Atari, and Sega.*

Science, Technology, & Environment

1970s *Continued*

1979. Steve Jobs tours Xerox PARC and gets ideas for the Apple Lisa, ideas that include a graphical user interface and a mouse.

1979. The cellular phone is introduced in Sweden.[†††]

1979. The nuclear power reactor at Three Mile Island, Penn., suffers a partial meltdown.[†]

1979. Hewlett-Packard introduces the HP-41C programmable calculator; it effectively blurs the distinction between a calculator and computer.

1980s

1980 +. The decade of what Donald Norman calls "creeping featurism" begins—that is, the tendency to build too many special-purpose "gee whiz" features on electronics products such as computers and VCRs. The net result for consumers: hard to understand interface designs, unwanted features and functions, and longer manuals.[248]

1980. Apollo Computer unveils its first workstation, a desktop computer with the CPU speed of a VAX 780 mini-computer.

1981. "Post-it" notes, an invention discovered by chance by Spencer Sylver at 3M, become an instant success.[†††]

1981. IBM introduces the PC, its first personal computer. It uses the disk operating system (DOS), which rapidly becomes the industry standard. Within a few years, the PC makes the office typewriter obsolete.

Society & Consumerism

1970s *Continued*

1979. Two class action suits are filed in New Jersey on behalf of clients who could not understand the state's forms for Medicare and mental health services.[249]

1979. In the U.K., the Plain English Campaign is started by a woman who learned to read and write at sixteen and who says she "has lived through the pain of being isolated and humiliated because of words."[250]

1979. The U.S. Department of Defense requires manuals to meet certain readability requirements.[251]

1980s

1980 +. Magazines introducing new technologies become more critical of the poor manuals that often accompany products.[252]

1980 +. Employment trends continue to shift in the U.S., moving away from manufacturing jobs and toward jobs in service industries.

1980 +. War between Iran and Iraq persists through the decade.[††]

1981 +. Eight U.S. states pass statutes concerned with consumer contracts (–1991).[253]

1981. U.S. President Ronald Reagan issues an executive order that revokes former President Jimmy Carter's plain language mandate of 1978, raising questions about the authenticity of the U.S. government's commitment to communicate clearly and truthfully with its citizens.

Notes

[239] Flower & Hayes, 1981; Hayes & Flower, 1980.

[240] For example, see Bond, Hayes & Flower, 1980; Goswami et al., 1981; Holland, 1981; or Swarts, Flower, & Hayes, 1980.

[241] van Dijk, 1980.

[242] Youngblood, 1990, p. 194.

[243] Jonassen, 1982; 1985. See also Anderson, Miller, & Brockmann, 1983.

[244] For example, American Airlines, Apple, Digital, Hewlett-Packard, IBM, Lotus, NCR, and Silicon Graphics; for a discussion of usability labs, see Dumas & Redish, 1993, pp. 383–395.

[245] Meggs, 1983, p. 459.

[246] Craig & Barton, 1987, p. 206.

[247] Gottschall, 1989, p. 101.

[248] Norman, 1988, pp. 172–174.

[249] American Institute for Research, 1979.

[250] Cutts & Maher, 1986; Kimble, 1992, p. 53; *New York Times*, 1982.

[251] Kniffin, 1979.

[252] For example, see *Business Week, Consumer Reports, MacWorld, PC World,* and *Video Review.* See also Davis, 1983.

[253] Kimble, 1992, p. 32.

[†]   From Hellemans & Bunch, 1991.

[††]   From Grun, 1991.

[†††] From Giscard d'Estaing, 1993.

Education & Practice in Writing / Rhetoric

1980s *Continued*

1980 +. The role that writing plays in shaping knowledge gains attention from academics. Research investigating the disciplinary rhetorics in fields such as literary theory, philosophy, history, anthropology, economics, biology, business, law, and physics emerges.[254]

1980. Richard E. Young starts graduate programs at Carnegie Mellon Univ., including a Master of Arts degree in Professional Writing and a Doctor of Philosophy degree in Rhetoric (with an option to concentrate in Document Design).

1981 +. U.S. government funding for document design research dries up during the Reagan-Bush era.

1981 +. Researchers study the variety of genres created by technical and professional communicators as well as the effects specific genres have on readers.

1981. In Sweden, the Research Group for Studies of Texts for General and Specific Purposes is founded at Uppsala Univ.; the group conducts research relating to legal, economic, technical, and medical language.[255]

1981. In the second update of their information on academic programs in technical communication, the Society for Technical Communication lists 28 programs in the U.S.[256]

1982 +. The onset of the computer revolution prompts technical and professional writing teachers to develop courses on computer documentation.

1982 +. Studies of composing in non-academic settings start to appear.[257]

1982 +. Research on the social perspective of writing flourishes.[258]

Professional Development

1980s *Continued*

1982. Researchers at Bell Laboratories develop "The Writer's Workbench," a computer program that employs readability formulas to analyze prose. It gives advice that is intended to be useful for text editing and revision.[259]

1982. The Conference on Human Factors and Computing Systems leads to the development of the Association of Computing Machinery's Special Interest Group on Computer and Human Interaction (ACM/SIGCHI); the focus of SIGCHI is on how people communicate and interact with computer systems.

1983. The Association of Computing Machinery's Special Interest Group for Documentation (SIGDOC) begins holding a yearly conference. SIGDOC is dedicated to advancing computer documentation toward greater technical artistry and to developing knowledge about advanced topics in documentation for and with computers; it publishes the *Journal of Computer Documentation,* which begins as a newsletter called *Asterisk.*

1983. The Plain English Forum is founded. Dedicated to informing major banks, insurance companies, retailers, and Fortune 500 companies of how plain language can improve business, the Forum brings together people from government, universities, and industry, leading to the publication of *How Plain Language Works for Business.*[260]

1983. For the first time since its formation in 1953, females outnumber males in the STC (Society for Technical Communication); this phenomenon is described by some as the "pink-collaring" of the communications fields. However, female members still earn on average only 86 percent of what their male counterparts make.[261]

Education & Practice in Graphic Design

1980s *Continued*

1980. The first issue of the journal of industrial design, *I.D.,* is published.

1980. Adrian Frutiger's seminal text, *Type Sign Symbol,* is published.

1980. The second in the landmark two-volume set *Processing Visible Language* is published. It presents, for example, Robert Waller's argument about the roles that typography and graphics may play in complex texts, showing that type and graphics are not textual decorations but central components of a rhetoric of design.[262]

1981. The first edition of Josef Müller-Brockman's famous text, *Grid Systems in Graphic Design,* provides insights into how grid systems are developed, the principles which underlie their use, and the variety of contexts in which they can be applied.

1982. Ikko Tanaka's *Japanese Coloring* is published; it defines a specifically Japanese attitude toward color.

1982. Renowned English typeface designer Matthew Carter redraws Robert Granjon's 16th century typeface, Galliard, for the computer; it is an Old Style typeface with slightly squared serifs and a large lowercase letterform, making it readable and elegant.[263]

1982. Magazine designer Jan White publishes one of the few books that characterizes the integration of visual and verbal texts—*Editing by Design: A Guide to Effective Word-and-Picture Communication for Editors and Designers.*

1982. Jeremy Campbell's *Grammatical Man: Information, Entropy, Language, and Life* inspires graphic design students.

▲ **Background Image.** *Personal computers revolutionized day-to-day practices in business, industry, and education—with companies such as IBM and Apple Computer leading the development of innovative hardware and software. Although most of the documentation that accompanied the early personal computers was horrendous, there were a few notable exceptions of excellence in document design, particularly from Apple Computer.*

Science, Technology, & Environment

1980s *Continued*

1981. The U.S. Center for Disease Control recognizes acquired immune deficiency syndrome (AIDS) for the first time.[†]

1982. The first camcorder, the Beta-movie, is launched by Sony.[†††]

1982. Compaq Computer introduces the first IBM-compatible computer, launching an industry in IBM clones.[†]

1982. Sun Microsystems releases the UNIX-based Sun Workstations.

1982. The world's first computer featuring parallel architecture, the Cray X-MP, is designed.[†††]

1982. Canada blames U.S. industry for environmental damage to its forests caused by acid rain.[††]

1983. U.S. President Ronald Reagan proposes an antimissile defense system known as the Strategic Defense Initiative (nick-named "Star Wars").

1983. IBM's PC-XT is the first personal computer with a hard-disk drive built into it.[†]

1983. Apple's Lisa brings the mouse and pull-down menus to the personal computer.[†]

1983. The term *virtual reality* (VR) is coined, usually credited to Jaron Lanier of VPL Research.[264]

1984. Apple brings Lisa technology down to an affordable price with its instantly popular Macintosh microcomputer, initiating the desktop publishing revolution. Within a decade, Apple Macintoshes become the most coveted computers for document design.

Society & Consumerism

1980s *Continued*

1981. Michigan forms the first Plain English Committee in its State Bar; it is composed of judges and lawyers.[265]

1981. The American Bar Association's first plain English committee is formed.

1982. *USA Today* newspaper is published for the first time, using color extensively in charts, graphs, and weathermaps; many criticize its design as garish.

1983. The New York state plain language laws are enacted, without the problems that were predicted by opponents from the legal community.

1983. The *Wall Street Journal* reports that hundreds of Coleco's Adam home computers who cannot figure out how the machine works; the manufacturer blames the problem on its incomprehensible manual and later withdraws the product.[266]

1983. The Pennsylvania Citizen's Consumer Council helps convince the government to pass plain language legislation.

1983. In the U.S., approximately 35.3 million people are poor—the largest number since 1964 (a family of four is categorized as poor if its income is below $10,990).[267]

1984 +. In the U.S., 36 states pass regulations regarding the use of plain language in insurance contracts; depending on the state, companies that offer life, accident, sickness, or auto policies must write policies that score between 40 and 50 on the Flesch readability test (–1991).[268]

Notes

[254] Bazerman, 1980, 1988.

[255] Kimble, 1992, p. 58.

[256] Pearsall, Sullivan, & McDowell, 1981.

[257] Faigley, 1985; Faigley & Miller, 1982; Odell & Goswami, 1982.

[258] Bazerman, 1983; Bizzell, 1982; Bruffee, 1984.

[259] Macdonald, Frase, Gingrich, & Keenan, 1982.

[260] U.S. Department of Commerce, 1984.

[261] O'Hara, 1989, p. 310.

[262] Kolers, Wrolstad, & Bouma, 1980; see also the first book in this series, *Processing of Visible Language, Volume 1* (Kolers, Wrolstad, & Bouma, 1979).

[263] Gottschall, 1989, p. 94.

[264] Barry, 1991, p. 80; Caruso, 1990.

[265] Kimble, 1992, p. 42.

[266] Davis, 1983.

[267] Consumers Union, May 1986, p. 283.

[268] Kimble, 1992, pp. 33-35.

[†]   From Hellemans & Bunch, 1991.

[††]   From Grun, 1991.

[†††] From Giscard d'Estaing, 1993.

Education & Practice in Writing / Rhetoric

1980s *Continued*

1983 +. Educators gain interest in using computers in the classroom to improve students' abilities in planning, organizing, and revising text.[269]

1983. Writing and literacy researchers form the Special Interest Group (SIG) in Research on Writing and Literacy within the American Educational Research Association (AERA). It provides a forum for researchers from diverse backgrounds to share their work and obtain critical feedback.

1984 +. Research on collaboration in writing—whether face-to-face or over a computer network—flourishes.

1984 +. Theories of situated cognition begin to make an impact; for example, see Barbara Rogoff and Jean Lave's *Everyday Cognition*.

1984. A Master of Science degree in Technical Communication is proposed by faculty from the Department of Technical Communication at the Univ. of Washington (Seattle, Wash.).

1985 +. The U.S. Office of Educational Research and Improvement funds a National Center for the Study of Writing and Literacy (NCSWL). Led by faculty from the Univ. of Calif. at Berkeley and Carnegie Mellon Univ., NCSWL researchers explore the cognitive and social dimensions of writing and other literate activities (–1995).[270]

1985. Thomas M. Duffy and Robert Waller edit *Designing Usable Texts,* an influential book on document design.

1985. In the third update of their information on technical communication programs, the Society for Technical Communication lists 58 academic programs in the U.S.[271]

Professional Development

1980s *Continued*

1983. Kathleen E. Keifer and Cynthia L. Selfe start the journal *Computers and Composition.*

1984 +. Companies that produce computers become interested in online documentation and online help systems; many expand their publications and information design teams to include professionally-trained writers and graphic designers.

1984. Stephen P. Witte and John Daly start *Written Communication (WC),* an important interdisciplinary journal devoted to research and theory about writing and literate practices in academic and nonacademic settings.

1984. John M. Carroll and his colleagues from the IBM T. J. Watson Research Center develop a theory of minimal manuals, guided by the observation that less can be more.

1984. The U.S. Department of Health releases *Pretesting in Health Communications,* which shows how to conduct reader-focused testing for health communications.

1985 +. The European Community (EC) adopts the ISO 9000, a set of international standards for evaluating and certifying that quality processes are being carried out by companies who sell products to the EC. Since documentation is considered part of the product, there are implications for writers, designers, and their managers.

1985. Izumi Aizu and Hiraku Amemiya are the first Japanese writers to make a speech at the International Technical Communication Conference (ITCC); many other Japanese give speeches in subsequent years.[272]

Education & Practice in Graphic Design

1980s *Continued*

1982. The Vietnam Veterans' War Memorial is dedicated in Washington, D.C. The names of more than 58,000 dead are inscribed on the black granite memorial; created by Maya Ying Lin, it is a masterpiece of sculpture and information design.

1983 +. Many designers become interested in human-computer interface, screen design, and icon design.

1983. Edward R. Tufte's important book, *The Visual Display of Quantitative Information,* is published.

1984 +. With the release of the Apple Macintosh computer, design on the computer flourishes and graphic artists develop new ways of working.

1985. Paul Brainerd, president of Aldus, introduces the slogan "desktop publishing."[273]

1985. Articles on "do it yourself desktop publishing" appear, leading to the belief that anyone can become an instant designer. Design tasks normally contracted to professional designers are sometimes assigned to non-professionals, resulting in many poorly designed documents.

1985. *The Journal of Graphic Design* publishes a symposium on the current state of magazine design; most articles lament the lessened impact of the art director and the overtaking of design by advertisers who are concerned only with "selling lame ideas."[274]

1985. Instructional designers and cognitive psychologists consolidate the research literature on the visual display of functional texts, including work in graphic organizers, typographic cues, diagrams, flowcharts, and tables.[275]

▲ **Background Image.** *Home electronics products such as Sony's Walkman and the camcorder proved popular with consumers. Research by the Electronics Industries Association shows that in 1979 only 1% of Americans owned VCRs; by the late 1980s, more than 70% owned them. Unfortunately, because many electronics products suffered from poor interface design and atrocious document design, consumers could only rarely take full advantage of the features these products offered.*

Science, Technology, & Environment

1980s *Continued*

1984. Hewlett-Packard introduces its LaserJet printer.

1984. IBM introduces a megabit RAM memory chip with four times as much memory as earlier chips.[†]

1984. IBM's PC AT is the first personal computer to use a new chip to expand speed and memory in an existing personal computer architecture.[†]

1984. William Gibson's science-fiction novel *Neuromancer* suggests some ideas for researchers in virtual reality.

1984. U.S. and French teams independently identify the AIDS virus; the first case was reported in 1977.

1984. The European Space Agency launches the world's largest telecommunications satellite.[††]

1985. AT&T Bell Labs achieves the equivalent of sending 300,000 simultaneous telephone conversations or 200 high-resolution television channels over a single optical fiber.[†]

1985. The CD-ROM, a laser-read compact disc with a read only capability, is invented by Philips.[†††]

1985. The first digital video recorder is introduced by Sony.[†††]

1985. Video Display Units, designed specifically for playing video games, become an instant success.[†††]

1985. Apple introduces the Laser-Writer, a 300 dpi Postscript printer, helping to launch the desktop publishing industry.

1985. The first version of Microsoft Windows is released.

Society & Consumerism

1980s *Continued*

1984 +. The Australian plain language movement, led by Robert D. Eagleson, becomes prominent in the reform of banking and legal documents.[276]

1984. In Australia, the government establishes the Law Reform Commission of Victoria, which will become the leader of the movement toward plain English in legal documents.[277]

1984. In the state of Washington, the Legal Writing Institute is founded at the University of Puget Sound Law School.

1984. The American Heart Association lists smoking as a risk factor for strokes.[†]

1985 +. Interactive fiction enables readers to modify the plots of books as they read; some call it the beginning of a new literary genre.

1985. New York requires a plain language format for residential gas and electric bills.[278]

1985. In New Zealand, the parliament creates the Law Commission, which advises government on ways in which the law can be made more understandable.[279]

1985. In the U.K., the Plain Language Campaign and the Civil Service sponsor a Plain English exhibition, which is attended by Prime Minister Thatcher; in 1986, the exhibition is moved to the House of Commons.[280]

1985. The U.S. Congressional Budget Office reports that one out of every five children comes from a family where at least one person holds a full-time job but does not earn enough to meet the child's basic needs.[281]

Notes

[269] For an account of the growth of interest in using computers to teach writing, see Hawisher, LeBlanc, Moran, & Selfe (1996).

[270] For back issues of reports of research produced by the National Center for the Study of Writing and Literacy, write to: NCSWL, School of Education, University of Calif., Berkeley, CA 94720 or visit the site on the World Wide Web at http://www-gse.berkeley.edu/research/NCSW/csw.homepage.html. For an example of research sponsored by the NCSWL, see "'Just Say No to Drugs' and Other Unwelcome Advice: Teens Speak Out" in Chapter 3 (pp. 167–207).

[271] Kelley, 1985.

[272] Aizu & Amemyia, 1985.

[273] Kalmbach, 1988, p. 277.

[274] Gottschall, 1989, p. 121.

[275] Jonassen, 1985.

[276] Eagleson, 1991; Kimble, 1992, p. 54.

[277] Kimble, 1992, p. 54.

[278] Ibid., p. 36.

[279] Ibid., p. 57.

[280] Ibid., p. 53.

[281] Consumers Union, May 1986, p. 283.

[†]   From Hellemans & Bunch, 1991.

[††]   From Grun, 1991.

[†††] From Giscard d'Estaing, 1993.

Education & Practice in Writing / Rhetoric

1980s *Continued*

1986. The Central Intelligence Agency (CIA) wins the National Council of Teachers of English "Doublespeak Award" for its *Psychological Warfare Manual,* which explains to Nicaraguan rebels how to "neutralize government officials."

1986. The teacher-researcher movement in composition studies flourishes, encouraging teachers to reflect on their classroom practices in order to design student-centered rather than teacher-centered instruction.

1986. Representatives from Japanese computer and electronics industries visit technical communication programs in U.S. colleges and universities to get ideas for starting their own academic degree programs.

1987 +. A number of excellent textbooks on technical and professional communication are published, many of which build on research on the cognitive, social, and rhetorical dimensions of writing and design.

1987 +. Over a decade of "writing as a process" research makes a significant impact on the classroom practices of writing teachers; process-oriented methods dominate the teaching of all aspects of writing, from planning to editing.

1987 +. Professors of technical, scientific, and professional communication explore what constitutes "advanced" knowledge in upper-level undergraduate and graduate curricula.

1987. E. D. Hirsch's *Cultural Literacy* and Allen Bloom's *Closing of the American Mind* are published amidst skepticism about whose culture the authors intend to represent.

Professional Development

1980s *Continued*

1985. The first Japanese Study Group in Technical Communication (TC) is formed, the TC Kenkyu-kai; technical communication begins to gain national attention within Japanese industry.

1986. Writers use a number of hypertext programs, including *Hypercard, Guide, HyperTIES, KMS, Document Examiner,* and *Notecards.*[282]

1986. The first Japanese journal in technical communication, *The Technical Writer,* is started.

1986. The first conference on Computer-Supported Collaborative Work (CSCW) is held.

1986. The American National Standards Institute releases the Standard Generalized Markup Language (SGML), which soon becomes the international standard for describing and tagging electronic texts, allowing their parts to be reconfigured and reused.

1986. The *Washington Post* reports "Technical Fields Hiring More Women to Rewrite Jargon."[283]

1986. *The Journal of Business and Technical Communication* begins publication.

1987. The first Japanese chapter of the Society for Technical Communication (STC) is established in Tokyo.

1988. A Centre for Plain Language is established in Toronto by the Legal Information Centre.[284]

1989 +. Professionals in companies try to avoid product liability lawsuits by employing principles of user-centered design.

Education & Practice in Graphic Design

1980s *Continued*

1986. The International Typeface Corporation (ITC) acknowledges the work of typographers who design typefaces for use on the computer by paying them an upfront lump sum for delivery of a typeface and then a percentage of all revenue earned by the design.[285]

1987. Scientific illustrator George V. Kelvin creates the first technical illustration of the AIDS virus; it is featured on the cover of the January issue of *Scientific American.*

1987. The Communications Research Institute of Australia (CRIA) begins to conduct document design research, especially on the design of forms; the CRIA publishes a newsletter entitled *Communication News.*[286]

1987. *The Psychology of Illustration,* an important two-volume text on the psychological and instructional issues surrounding textbook illustrations, is published; this summary of the basic research details the range of functions that illustrations play in educational materials.[287]

1988. Articles critiquing the idea that "anyone can be a designer with a computer and desktop publishing software" begin to appear, most of which detail the proliferation of poor quality documents designed by nonprofessionals.[288]

1988. The first Stanford Design Forum is held; it is an invited gathering of CEOs, design managers, and cultural leaders with an interest in promoting international design awareness.[289]

1988. Donald A. Norman, called the "guru of workable technology," publishes a book that presents a theory of human-centered design.[290]

▲ **Background Image.** *Although the first case of AIDS was reported in 1977, the U.S. government did not officially recognize the disease until 1981 (after it had already reached epidemic proportions); throughout the 1980s men and women from the gay and lesbian communities championed the rights of AIDS victims, stressing the importance of research about the virus; shown here is the AIDS awareness ribbon and a slogan created by activists to make the point that silence about AIDS can be lethal.*

Science, Technology, & Environment

1980s *Continued*

1985. Aldus introduces *Pagemaker* 1.0; it rapidly becomes the most popular page layout software program.

1985. The first touch-screen is created for computers.[†††]

1985. The British Antarctic Survey detects a hole in the ozone layer.[†]

1986 +. Adobe Systems develops hundreds of typeface (font) families for personal computers.

1986. Compaq introduces computers that use an advanced 32-bit chip, the Intel 80386.[†]

1986. *Ventura Publisher* 1.0 is released for the IBM PC.

1986. OWL International releases the first commercially viable hypertext program, *GUIDE*.

1986. The space shuttle *Challenger* explodes 73 seconds after launch, killing everyone on board; the next U.S. space mission carrying astronauts will not launch until 1988.[†]

1987. Digital audio tape (DAT) is developed in Japan by Matsushita and Sony; it produces outstanding audio.[†††]

1987. Compact disc video (CDV) is developed by Philips and Sony.[†††]

1987. Workstations employing RISC architecture are announced.[291]

1987. Apple introduces three new laser printers; the Laser-Writer II NTX quickly becomes the printer of choice for desktop publishing.

1987. The IBM PC version of *Pagemaker* is introduced.

Society & Consumerism

1980s *Continued*

1985. The first televised home shopping channels are introduced.[†††]

1986. The U.S. Congress honors the Consumers Union for continuing contributions made in aiding, informing, and protecting consumers.[292]

1986. In Australia, the Office of Parliamentary Counsel begins following a policy of drafting bills and amendments for the Federal Parliament in plain language.[293]

1986. 25,000 AIDS cases are diagnosed in the U.S.[††]

1986. The Chernobyl nuclear reactor, in the U.S.S.R., explodes on April 26, leading to a catastrophic release of radioactivity that kills dozens of people, forces the evacuation of 133,000, and creates clouds of fallout all over Europe.[†]

1986. Radon is linked to the contamination of homes, posing the same risk of lung cancer to inhabitants as if they had smoked half a pack of cigarettes every day of their lives.[†††]

1988. Amendments to the Truth in Lending Act, the Truth in Savings Act, and the Fair Credit Reporting and Billing Act are passed in the U.S. Federal Court, all requiring clear, conspicuous, or understandable language in various consumer transactions.[294]

1989 +. In the U.S., consumers sue companies over products whose manuals have inadequate instructions or warnings.

1989. New York requires plain language in notices, forms, and bills for water service.[295]

Notes

[282] Conklin, 1987.

[283] *Washington Post*, 1986.

[284] Dykstra, 1991; Kimble, 1992, p. 46.

[285] Gottschall, 1989, p. 101.

[286] Kimble, 1992, pp. 56–57; Penman, 1985.

[287] Willows & Houghton, 1987a, 1987b.

[288] Barker, 1988.

[289] Kleinman, 1989.

[290] Norman, 1988.

[291] Kidwell & Ceruzzi, 1994, p. 131. RISC stands for Reduced Instruction Set Computer. RISC computers can execute their instructions much faster than computers having a complex instruction set.

[292] Consumers Union, Aug. 1986, p. 429.

[293] Kimble, 1992, p. 55.

[294] Ibid., p. 31.

[295] Ibid., p. 36.

[†]   From Hellemans & Bunch, 1991.

[††] From Grun, 1991.

[†††] From Giscard d'Estaing, 1993.

Education & Practice in Writing / Rhetoric

1980s *Continued*

1987. The Research Network is established at the Conference on College Composition and Communication convention; it provides a day-long forum in which writing teachers share ideas about conducting research on writing.

1988. In the U.K., the first conference on "Computers and Writing" is held.

1988. Charles Bazerman's *Shaping Written Knowledge* is published; it is an important book on the rhetoric of scientific activity.

1989 +. Studies of the ethical dimensions of designing risk communications, public service messages, and environmental impact statements increase.

1989 +. Across the U.S., colleges begin to offer courses in document design, usability testing, computers and writing, and desktop publishing.

1990s

1990 +. Academics are concerned with integrating social, cognitive, cultural, and feminist perspectives into writing and document design.

1990 +. Studies of visual rhetoric and visual literacies increase; the term "visual aids" becomes antiquated. Visual and verbal rhetoric are construed as having a symbiotic textual relation.

1990 +. Constructivist approaches to instructional design and computer-assisted instruction flourish; hypermedia textbooks are proposed.[296]

Professional Development

1980s *Continued*

1989. The negative press surrounding the announcement of the alleged "discovery of cold fusion" contributes to a growing awareness of ethics in scientific journalism.

1989. In Japan, various technical communication study groups meet to hold the first annual Technical Communication Symposium.

1989. 16 percent of the members of the Society for Technical Communication describe themselves as self-employed; the number of freelance professionals increases, often with the same person responsible for writing, designing, illustrating, and printing.[297]

1989. Early versions of multimedia, with the capability of using hypertext technology to link text and analog audio, appear; unfortunately, they are impractical for most publications departments because they are quite expensive.[298]

1990s

1990 +. In the U.S., continued recession, downsizing, cutbacks, and layoffs lead industry to reduce investment in writing and design. The decline of the mainframe computing business results in job losses in some publications departments. There is a growing tendency to use subcontractors for document design work, and more writers and designers turn to freelancing. There is also less of a need to document products made by defense contractors, a trend related to the fall of the Berlin Wall (1989) and the end of the Cold War.[299]

Education & Practice in Graphic Design

1980s *Continued*

1989. James Craig and William Bevington describe professional fields for communications designers, including corporate design, computer graphics, advertising, AV presentation, editorial design, exhibition design, illustration, environmental design, film and video graphics, package design, photography, and public relations.[300]

1989. Richard Saul Wurman's *Information Anxiety* provides an argument for good design.

1989. Edward M. Gottschall publishes *Typographic Communications Today,* a compendium on the evolution of typographic trends.

1989. *Graphic Design in America* is published; it is the first large-scale effort to depict American graphic design, focusing on the ways in which graphic art raises public consciousness about social issues and the ways in which technology affects design.[301]

1990s

1990 +. The pervasiveness of color during the 1980s stimulates a revival of black-and-white photography in advertising and commercials.[302]

1990 +. Budget-conscious companies cut back on graphic design; at times, this means collapsing the once separate job categories of writer and designer by seeking to hire those who can both write and design using a computer. However, the curricula of academic programs that educate writers and designers typically do not prepare them for doing both.

▲ **Background Image.** *In the 1980s and 1990s, concern for recycling and preserving the environment entered American mainstream culture; Americans followed the lead of European citizens who had formed lasting grassroots organizations focused on ecological issues decades earlier and who had called for reforms in how government and industry communicated to the public about the environment.*

Science, Technology, & Environment

1980s *Continued*

1988. The first transatlantic optical fiber telephone cable links France, the U.K., and the U.S.; it is capable of processing up to 40,000 simultaneous conversations.[††]

1988. Sony introduces a video version of the Walkman; it is a television and an 8 mm format video recorder.[†††]

1988. The NeXT computer system is released.

1989. Meteorologists pronounce this year the warmest on record; some see this as a sign of the greenhouse effect.

1989. Eighty nations adopt a declaration agreeing to stop producing chlorofluorocarbons (CFC's) by 2000 A.D.[††]

1989. The University of Wuppertal in Germany develops a system that can monitor changes in the ozone layer by satellite.[†††]

Society & Consumerism

1980s *Continued*

1989. Federal and state governments in the U.S. pass a variety of statutes regarding ways to write instructions that will help jurors understand the law (–1991).[305]

1989. The Exxon Valdez causes the world's largest oil spillage (11 million gallons) when it runs aground in Alaska's Prince William Sound; in 1993, the clean-up is still not fully complete to the satisfaction of Alaska's Department of the Environment.[††]

1989. Time Inc. buys Warner Communications for $13 billion to create the world's largest entertainment group.[††]

1989. Chinese pro-democracy students rally for government reform in Tiananmen Square, Bejing; some are killed by the Chinese government.

1989. Sky Television, the U.K.'s first satellite station, begins transmission.[††]

Notes

[296] Cognition and Technology Group at Vanderbilt, 1991; Cunningham, Duffy, & Knuth, 1993; Duffy & Jonassen, 1991; Spiro et al., 1991.

[297] O'Hara, 1989, p. 312.

[298] Cole, 1993.

[299] Hayhoe, Kunz, Southard, & Stohrer, 1993.

[300] Craig & Bevington, 1989.

[301] Walker Art Center, 1989.

[302] Livingston & Livingston, 1992, p. 64.

[303] Cringely, 1992.

[304] Cole, 1993.

[305] Kimble, 1992, p. 339.

[†] From Hellemans & Bunch, 1991.

[††] From Grun, 1991.

[†††] From Giscard d'Estaing, 1993.

1990s

1990 +. Mainframe business is well on its way to becoming obsolete; most mainframe computers are being replaced by workstations and networked PCs. Robert X. Cringely, a computer-industry guru, predicts that mainframe computing will die by 1999.[303]

1990 +. Interactive multimedia continues to grow, using object-oriented technologies to link text, graphics, animation, and sound. Several products for end users appear, but the price is still prohibitive for most organizations.[304]

1990s

1990 +. Consumers continue to become more sophisticated about the features they do and do not want in consumer products. "Ease of use" is regarded as one of the key factors influencing purchasing decisions. Ease of use includes the documents that may accompany the product.

1990 +. After some studies find a link between carpal tunnel syndrome and the frequent use of computer keyboards, users become increasingly concerned with the ergonomic issues related to the design of keyboards.

Education & Practice in Writing / Rhetoric

1990s *Continued*

1990. The Univ. of Waterloo (Ontario, Canada) holds the first in a series of international conferences on the topic of "Documentation Quality."

1991. David R. Russell publishes *Writing in the Academic Disciplines: 1870-1990*, one of the few histories of writing in the academy to mention the development of technical, professional, and business writing.

1991. The Univ. of Utrecht (the Netherlands) hosts the first in a series of international conferences on the topic of "Functional Text Quality."

1992. In the U.K., *The Communicator* describes a number of polytechnics, colleges, and universities at which students can work on a degree or take courses in technical communication or information design. The Univ. of Reading (the oldest research-oriented information design program in the U.K.) and Coventry Polytechnic Univ. (which combines work experience and classwork) offer degree programs; among the schools that offer courses are Humberside, Middlesex, Wolverhampton, and South Bank.[306]

1992. A report indicates that the number of U.S. academic institutions offering doctoral studies in rhetoric and/or technical communication is on the rise. The report also cites 74 institutions (from the U.S., Canada, and the U.K.) that produced 170 dissertations between 1963 and 1990 related to technical communication or document design.[307]

1992. A report from the Netherlands indicates that Dutch research in text design and text quality is done mainly at the universities of Utrecht, Twente, Delft, Eindhoven, and Tilburg.[308]

Professional Development

1990s *Continued*

1990. The Japanese government sponsors a survey of U.S. technical and professional communication programs at the university and college level.

1990. In the U.K., the Plain Language Campaign sponsors the first International Plain English Conference.[309]

1990. In Canada, the Bar Association and the Bankers Association release a widely-publicized report, "The Decline and Fall of Gobbledygook: Report on Plain Language Documentation."[310]

1991 +. Publications departments attempt to define "quality" and "customer satisfaction" in relation to their efforts in writing and design. Some manufacturers develop "metrics" for assessing the relative effectiveness of document design. Writers and designers who work for companies that do business with the European Community develop ways to meet ISO 9000 certification standards (see 1985).

1991. The Communications Research Institute of Australia (CRIA) holds the first Australian symposium on information design.[311]

1992 +. As more companies conduct international business, the need to translate and localize documents escalates; interest in document "re-use" and machine translation increases.

1992. The Association of Teachers of Technical Writing (ATTW) journal, *The Technical Writing Teacher,* gets a new name and an elegant redesign as *Technical Communication Quarterly*.

1992. Japanese technical communication groups announce that they will work to initiate technical communication programs in Japan's universities.

Education & Practice in Graphic Design

1990s *Continued*

1990 +. Recession around the world results in a decline in the business of design consultancies.

1990 +. Some designers believe the phrase "graphic design" does not fully describe what they do. As alternatives, they propose "user interface design," "interactions design," "information design," or "communications design." Although these alternatives more fully suggest current theory and practice, they create ambiguity because other professionals may use the same terms. Designers tend to view the ambiguity as positive because it provides an occasion for redefining their work.

1990 +. Information designers and human-computer interaction specialists develop interfaces, keyboards, and peripherals for special populations of users, such as those with limited motor, visual, or auditory abilities.

1990. Edward R. Tufte's *Envisioning Information* is published, providing principles for structuring well-designed charts, graphs, diagrams, and maps.

1990. Teachers of design reflect on the structure and content of design education. Using the Bauhaus as a benchmark, they ask what it means to teach design and wrestle with issues of what designers ought to know.[312]

1990. Dennis Doordan argues that people who write about the history of design need to do more than merely identify prominent individual designers and award-winning or money-making designs; instead, they should conduct case studies of the role design plays in corporate culture, the people involved in setting design agendas, and the practical problems that visual identity programs attempt to solve.[313]

▲ **Background Image.** *After continued reports linked body pain with the frequent use of standard computer keyboards, companies responded by creating ergnomic designs that offered comfort and ease of use. Some companies also took up the challenge of designing computing technologies for people with special needs, such as those who use wheelchairs or who may need additional assistance in using a mouse, pushing keys, or hearing system feedback.*

Science, Technology, & Environment

1990s *Continued*

1990 +. Open software systems continue to develop, enabling users to successfully mix and match different vendors' hardware and software and thus operate across computing platforms; most systems use the UNIX operating system.

1990 +. Laptop and portable computers proliferate; cellular telephones and fax machines increase in popularity.

1990. Laserdiscs, a new application of compact disc video (CDV) technology, are marketed.†††

1990. Japanese research teams from Mitsubishi and the University of Osaka innovate the field of ceramics by developing superplastic ceramics.†††

1990. The Hubble space telescope, put into orbit by the U.S., transmits photos of Pluto and Saturn.

1991. Panasonic unveils the first VCR that can be programmed orally; it confirms by voice synthesis all the instructions received: channel selection, date, time, and so on.†††

1991. NASA announces mission "planet Earth," a vast satellite observation program that will study the Earth's environment and upper atmosphere.†††

1992. Nikon invents the first self-focusing underwater reflex camera.†††

1992. Cellular phones are linked with cancer, even though the link is not proven.

1992. Kodak launches its Photo CD, a system for storing photographs digitally on a compact disc which can then be played back on television screens.†††

Society & Consumerism

1990s *Continued*

1990. The Americans with Disabilities Act (ADA) is signed into law, providing civil rights for people with disabilities and setting standards for making public places and information more accessible. Enforcement of the ADA takes effect in 1992.

1990. The U.S. Congress passes the Nutrition Labeling and Education Act, requiring the development of new food labels that specify the sodium, fat, and cholesterol levels in all foods; the Act takes effect in May 1994.

1990. Consumers herald voicemail as the new "rude" technology.[314]

1991 +. *Newsweek, Time,* and *Business Week* feature articles about consumers' frustrations with technology that is getting more difficult to use, with interfaces that are cumbersome and cluttered, and with documents that make readers "weep."[315]

1991. The U.S. National Conference on Uniform State Laws passes an act recommending plain English principles for bills and legislation.[316]

1991. Government officials in Saskatchewan, Canada, take initiatives to become the first province with an official government-wide Clear Language Program.[317]

1991. The idea of computers leading to the "paperless office" is construed as "a laughable utopian notion that has been entirely discredited as people drown in a sea of documents."[318]

1992. Ross Perot, a candidate for the U.S. presidency, runs televised "infomercials" in which he shows charts and graphs of the growing U.S. federal deficit; Bill Clinton wins the election.

Notes

[306] Kirkman, 1992, pp. 2–4. See also Hunt, 1993, p. 323.

[307] Rainey & Kelly, 1992.

[308] Jansen, 1992; 1994.

[309] Kimble, 1992, p. 53.

[310] Ibid., p. 45.

[311] Communication Research Institute of Australia, 1992.

[312] *Design Issues*, 1990; Levy, 1990.

[313] Doordan, 1990.

[314] Beale, 1990; Shrage, 1990.

[315] Nussbaum & Neff, 1991; Rogers, 1991; Zoglin, 1992.

[316] Kimble, 1992, p. 40.

[317] Ibid., p. 50.

[318] Barry, 1991, p. 42.

† From Hellemans & Bunch, 1991.

†† From Grun, 1991.

††† From Giscard d'Estaing, 1993.

Education & Practice in Writing / Rhetoric

1990s *Continued*

1993. Nell Ann Pickett, a professor at Hinds Community Col. (Raymond, Miss.) wins a "Lifetime Distinguished Service Award" from the American Association of Teachers of Technical Writing (ATTW).

1993. Tokyo Univ. of Science and Technology announces Japan's first university course in technical writing.

1993. James W. Souther, Myron L. White, and John H. Mitchell win the STC's first Jay R. Gould Award for Excellence in Teaching.

1993. The Univ. of Minnesota's Rhetoric Department starts a Ph.D. program in Rhetoric and Scientific and Technical Communication.

1993. In the fourth update of their information on U.S. and Canadian academic programs in professional and technical communication, the STC lists over 100 programs—ranging from certificate programs and associates degrees to bachelor's, master's, and doctoral degrees.[319]

1994. Academic and industry experts question whether technical and professional communication programs are suitably housed in departments of English, underscoring problems associated with literature professors making decisions about the tenure and promotion of writing, rhetoric, or technical communication faculty. They suggest either moving programs to other departments or setting up independent interdisciplinary programs.[320]

1995. Professors from around the world exchange ideas about writing, rhetoric, and document design by using email and bulletin boards on the World Wide Web (WWW).

Professional Development

1990s *Continued*

1993. The Council for Programs in Technical and Scientific Communication (CPTSC) celebrates its 20th anniversary with a meeting devoted to "Technical Communication: Strategies for the Next 20 Years."

1993. The STC sponsors a research project to measure the "value added" that expert technical communicators bring to corporations and government agencies, a value that other experts do not bring.

1993. In Winnipeg, Manitoba, the government sponsors a study of *Practices of Technical Communication in Western Canada,* a large research project to study the activities and needs of people who write on the job.

1993. In Wales, Scotland, a conference on "Computers and Writing" is held.

1993. The STC reports approximately 17,000 members worldwide. It estimates that there are more than 100,000 technical communicators in the U.S. and predicts that the number will grow to 140,000 by 1998. The STC actively supports new research by increasing the funding allocated for research grants and scholarships.[321]

1994. Simon Fraser Univ. at Harbour Centre (Vancouver, Canada) and International Wordsmiths, Ltd. host an invited thinktank on business and educational trends in "International Technical Communication."

1995. The International Council for Technical Communication (INTECOM) sponsors a conference, "Disappearing Borders," held in Dortmund, Germany; it attracts document designers from around the globe.

Education & Practice in Graphic Design

1990s *Continued*

1990. The graphic design community begins to evaluate its roots using historical and semiotic methods, showing how good graphic design can be a false index of the quality of a consumer good, a political candidate, the news, or any other commodity.[322]

1990. Richard Buchanan reflects on the possibility that the 1990s will rival the 1930s as a design decade; he argues that the field needs better ways to get across its ideas and methods to outsiders and to its own students.[323]

1993. Paul Rand critiques the decline of IBM as a "failure by design," noting the short-sightedness of American CEOs who lacked the vision to see that good design is good business.[324]

1993. The Duxbury Braille font allows users to compose documents for people who read Braille, enabling the creation of texts that conform to the Americans with Disabilities Act (ADA).

1993. *The Information Design Journal* publishes new research about what makes maps and diagrams memorable and usable.[325]

1993. The *New York Times* announces that it will use four-color processing in its Sunday supplement and eventually in the daily edition; critics complain that the *Times* has "sold out" to the *USA Today* glitzy image.[326]

1994. The Museum at the Fashion Institute of Technology (N.Y., N.Y.) hosts a European exhibition on "Visual Instructions and User Manuals."

1995. A dissatisfaction with the traditional emphases in MFA programs in graphic design leads to new programs in "communications design."

▲ **Background Image.** *Multimedia, virtual reality, and the "information superhighway" captured the public imagination. For the most part, however, the excitement was among people already familiar with computers. These technologies made people more aware of the gap between those with computing skills and those without, accentuating the need for better public access to technology and the need for well-designed interfaces, documents, and communications about technology.*

Science, Technology, & Environment

1990s *Continued*

1992. Philips introduces its CD-I, a compact disc-interactive system operated by remote control handsets that allows CDs to be played on a deck that plugs into a TV and stereo system.[†††]

1992. Digital printing is introduced, providing the capability of printing on two sides of a paper simultaneously without printing plates.[†††]

1992. AT&T reports the successful testing of a new fiber-optic communications system that may revolutionize underwater cable technology.[†††]

1992. High definition television (HDTV) is previewed.[†††]

1992. Apple introduces the concept of palmtop computing and its Newton.

1992. The Earth Summit is held in Rio de Janiero, Brazil.

1993 +. New technologies become available for computer users who are challenged in their ability to learn, use language, use a mouse, hear system feedback, or push keys; innovations include touch-sensitive (rather than pressure-sensitive) keyboards, "point and puff" (rather than "click and point") mouses, wheelchair mounted powerbooks, and talking icons.[327]

1993. The creation of a global "information highway" is advertised widely.

1994. Questions regarding public access to the information highway are debated, as are issues of copyright protection and invasion of privacy.

1995. Microsoft releases Windows '95 with much hype and fanfare. It provides PC users with an interface that looks more like a Macintosh.

Society & Consumerism

1990s *Continued*

1993. Guy Kawasaki chides U.S. computer companies for what he calls the "Akihabara Syndrome." Named after Tokyo's famous electronics district, the Akihabara Syndrome refers to creating product lines in which different models are so close in features and functionality that the uniqueness of particular models is no longer apparent, leaving consumers confused and frustrated.[328]

1993. Ralph Nader argues that "talking heads" on television raise punditry to new levels, but that the range of debate and the diversity of people who get to enter it is severely limited.[329]

1993. *Consumer Reports* wins a National Magazine Award for General Excellence for its July 1992 coverage of the U.S. health care system.[330]

1993. Virtual reality and cyberspace become part of mainstream pop culture, complete with cyberpunks who "surf the edges" of information, science, sex, fiction, and art.[331]

1993. The U.S. Food and Drug Administration (FDA) questions outlandish claims made by makers of health foods and dietary supplements, claims similar to those made by snake oil salespeople at the turn of the century.[332]

1994. U.S. food manufacturers are required to label their products with explicit consumer-oriented nutrition information (see 1990); many companies balk, but eventually comply.

1995. In Beijing, China, delegates to the United Nations Fourth World Conference on Women draft a document about human rights for women; there is significant controversy among the delegates over the meanings of "equity" and "equality."

Notes

[319] Geonetta, Allen, Curtis, & Staples, 1993.

[320] Hayhoe, Stohrer, Kunz, & Southard, 1994.

[321] Society for Technical Communication, 1993, p. 2.

[322] Craig, 1990.

[323] Buchanan, 1990.

[324] Rand, 1993.

[325] *Information Design Journal,* 7(1), 1993.

[326] Stanberg, 1993.

[327] Apple Computer, 1993.

[328] Kawasaki, 1993.

[329] Nader, 1993.

[330] Consumers Union, July 1992.

[331] Elmer-Dewitt, 1993.

[332] Arnot, 1993.

[†]   From Hellemans & Bunch, 1991.

[††] From Grun, 1991.

[†††] From Giscard d'Estaing, 1993.

PART TWO

OBSERVING READERS IN ACTION

3

How Documents Engage Readers' Thinking and Feeling

This chapter characterizes the ways in which people's thinking and feeling may come into play as they interpret documents. ❧ The chapter begins by exploring what it means to analyze the audience and profiles three ways to consider the reader. ❧ Next it discusses how people's feelings may influence their decisions about when to read documents and when to ignore them. ❧ These ideas are illustrated through a study of teenagers interpreting brochures about the dangers of taking drugs. Their interpretations illustrate how readers may form impressions not only of the message but also of the messenger—portraying how thoughts and feelings interact as readers make sense of content and as they construct ideas about whom may be presenting the content (the persona, organizational voice, or corporate identity). These findings suggest that "catching the reader in the act" of interpretation can provide important clues about how readers think and feel. Most of all, this chapter provides a sense of the dynamic interplay between cognition and emotion during reading.

Left-hand page. *Samantha Krampf is an eighth-grade student at Carlynton Junior High School (Rosslyn Farms, PA) and a participant in a study described in this chapter. Samantha read and evaluated several brochures that were designed to encourage teenagers to "Just Say No to Drugs." Shown here is a still from a videotape as she chose a brochure to read.*

To create effective communications—ones that are sensitive to the needs of audiences—document designers must understand how readers might think and feel as they interact with documents. They must anticipate what their audiences need and expect. Although these ideas are hardly new to experienced professionals, just what they mean has been difficult to translate into action. Over the last few decades, members of the reading and writing communities have been trying to better understand what readers "do with texts" and how communicators can be more sensitive to readers' needs. Much has been learned (I outline these developments in the next section), but we don't yet know the whole story. We still have theoretical and practical problems in making connections between audience analysis and textual choice, in linking what readers may need or expect with textual moves that use those analyses to improve the design of prose and graphics.

In this chapter, I explore these issues, paying particular attention to the interactive role that cognition and affect play in interpretation. I do so by

- Presenting an analysis of readers' thoughts and feelings as they engage with documents, showing how interpretation may be influenced by attitudes, values, knowledge, experience, age, race, class, or culture (an analysis continued in the remainder of this book)

- Reflecting on possible differences between document designers and their readers that may make it difficult for communication to take place

- Showing that readers form impressions not only of what a document says, but also of who they believe may be presenting the message, of the people or organization they imagine delivering the content (i.e., the persona, the organizational identity, or the corporate voice)

- Demonstrating that when document designers analyze the audience, the model of the reader they construct matters a great deal

ANALYZING THE AUDIENCE: COMPETING VISIONS

Imagine the following scenario:

> Three document design teams are given the task of revising an article on "global warming" from *Scientific American* so that it meets the needs of a junior high school audience. The original article, aimed at college-educated adults, presents ideas in prose and reinforces them with technical illustrations and graphs. The goal of the revision is to redesign the article so that it informs boys and girls

in junior high school, particularly in grades seven and
eight, about the problems of global warming.

In carrying out this goal, what might the document design teams do in
analyzing the needs of the audience? The following vignettes depict
alternative paths the teams might take.

Document Design Team 1: The Classifiers

The first document design team approaches the problem by brainstorming
characteristics of the audience. Their aim is to distinguish junior high
school students from college-age students. They begin by classifying the
features of the younger audience. The team spends considerable upfront
time cataloging all the facts they can dig up that might be relevant to
know about boys and girls in grades seven and eight: their age, attitudes
about science (and whether these attitudes differ by gender), hobbies that
might be science related, average vocabulary level, and their interest in the
environment. Once the team gathers what they deem to be enough
information concerning these issues, their audience analysis is complete.
They next make an outline that incorporates the audience information.
The outline helps them to keep the facts about the audience in mind as
they draft the new version of the article. After their first draft is complete,
they make sure the language isn't too hard by running the text through a
style checker (it conducts a grammar analysis and computes values for
several readability formulas, such as the Gunning-Fog Index and the
Flesch test).[1] The style checker tells the team that the language is suitable
for a ninth-grade audience. Since their revision is for seventh and eighth
graders, they adjust the vocabulary "down" to make it simpler. Once their
draft gets a score for a seventh-grade student, the team knows that they
are done.

[1] For a discussion of these and other readability formulas, see Klare (1984).

Document Design Team 2: The Intuitors

The second document design team begins by reading the original article
carefully and making notes about what might interest a junior high school
student. Team members then share with each other their personal reflec-
tions about global warming and swap stories about the science classes they
took in junior high. As they reminisce, they generate ideas for pictures for
the article, exploring their intuitions about what would make the topic
interesting to junior high school students. Next the team turns to drafting
the new version, at which point document designers try to imagine how
junior high school students might interpret their ideas. One document
designer remembers how she responded to environmental topics at the

same age. Another recalls his younger cousin talking about a TV program on the greenhouse effect and tries to imagine what kind of graphics might engage his cousin. Once the first draft is ready, each team member critiques it individually by trying to put himself or herself in the shoes of a junior high school student. Their critiques lead the team to argue over their choices of examples and visuals, over what "rings true" to their image of the audience. Some members of the team feel the illustrations are too childish while others feel the examples require too much knowledge of science. Their disagreements stimulate a number of fresh ideas for creating their final draft.

Document Design Team 3: The Listeners

The third document design team begins by calling people who might know where to find a group of junior high school students who could critique the team's drafts. Members of the team want to know what seventh and eighth grade boys and girls understand about the science of global warming. They are concerned with creating visuals that will both help students to understand the science and motivate them to learn about the topic. Initially, the team collects a set of articles written for young people about topics such as photosynthesis and the effects of deforestation. Next they visit several junior high schools to elicit students' feedback about the language and pictures employed in these articles. They also talk with teachers about "what works" with science topics. The students and teachers give the team members many ideas they can use for generating a new version of the article. After discussing a number of alternatives, the team decides to organize the revision around a set of illustrations rather than around prose. Once they complete a draft, they again seek the feedback of the audience. This time they listen to students as they read their draft, paying attention to how students use the illustrations, work through the concepts, and map pictures to text. The team members pay attention to what students find interesting and to what confuses or bewilders them. Drawing on this moment-by-moment view of the real reader, the team creates their final draft.

DIFFERENT VISIONS, DIFFERENT MODELS OF THE AUDIENCE?

The actions of these three document design teams typify three distinct visions of how document designers may analyze their audiences. The first view focuses on classifying audiences by identifying their features. I will call this approach *classification-driven audience analysis*. The second view emphasizes the powers of self-reflection and personal experience to imagine an audience. I will call this approach *intuition-driven audience analysis*. The third view focuses on gathering feedback from the real audience to find out how readers actually interact with the text. I will call this approach *feedback-driven audience analysis*.

In practice, document designers tend to internalize their views about how best to proceed in analyzing the audience. Rarely do they stop to choose one model or another. Rarely do they realize that what they do "naturally" is a choice among alternatives. Over time, these visions of the reader can become working mental models, providing document designers with cues about when to think about the reader and how. In the next section, I overview these three audience analysis models: (1) *classification-driven,* (2) *intuition-driven,* and (3) *feedback-driven.* Understanding them can help document designers make more perceptive choices about when to rely on one model or another.

Classification-driven Audience Analysis

Developed during the 1960s,[2] classification-driven audience analysis provides professional communicators with methods for creating profiles of their anticipated readership, often called the "target audience." Communicators begin their analysis by brainstorming about the audience and by cataloging audience demographics (e.g., age, sex, income, educational level) or psychographics (e.g., values, lifestyles, attitudes, personality traits, work habits). These audience profiles are then used to classify the audience into groups, for example, nontechnical or technical, general or specialized, novice or expert.

[2] Prominent educators in technical communication such as Kenneth Houp and Thomas E. Pearsall (1968, 1969) and J. C. Mathes and Dwight Stevenson (1976) pioneered innovative methods for classifying the audience.

Although these categories may suggest what sort of prose and graphics the audience might want, the leap between audience analysis and textual action is quite large. Authors of books about writing and design that present a version of the classification model tend to skirt the issue of how professionals actually put these analyses to use. Authors make it seem as though document designers move effortlessly from producing audience profiles to making audience-sensitive decisions during writing and design. Many books suggest that classifying the target audience can, for example, help communicators to select a proper tone, adjust their prose or graphics to the reading level of the audience, or provide the kind of information readers most need. But these books rarely give explicit advice about how this can be done.

A strength of classification-driven models is that they prompt communicators to think about the needs and expectations of different groups for their documents. For example, classifying the audience may tell document designers that novice users of computers may need more detailed procedures while expert users may need only quick-reference information.

The weakness of classification-driven models is that they encourage a rather narrow and static view of readers. They tend to lead communicators to focus on the similarities within reader groups and to ignore their diversity. *A key feature of the classification-driven models is that they "fossilize the reader" as a static compilation of demographics and psychographics that document designers somehow "keep in mind" as they compose.* This tendency to stereotype the reader may lead the communicator to draw faulty inferences about the audience's needs. As Long (1990) points out,

> [T]he writer might decide that his or her audience consists primarily of white, middle class (whatever that may mean to the writer) Americans who live in the southwestern region of the United States. This may be true, but how can such information be applied other than by taking an unjustifiable inductive leap to conclusions about the tastes, political preferences, religious or moral inclinations, or general interests from this group? What could be legitimately concluded from such information? This audience tends to be politically conservative? It distrusts divorce as an easy solution to marital difficulties? It knows little about science? It is quite knowledgeable about the history of the southwestern states? Clearly none of these are certainly valid or viable conclusions. (pp. 74–75)

Despite its limitations, audience-classification models offer document designers "a method—composed of a series of questions about the reader's background, education, position … to make their writing [and design] appropriate for the reader" (Allen, 1989, p. 53).

Intuition-driven Audience Analysis

Described by rhetoricians and writers of fiction since the 1950s,[3] the intuition-driven model of audience analysis is one in which communicators *imagine* the audience and draw on their internal representation of the audience as a guide to writing and design.[4] In using this model, document designers look inward to "visualize the audience" or to "listen to their inner voice" as they compose.[5] The image of the audience that emerges from this careful introspection can take various shapes: (1) a wholly fictitious reader with no correspondence to any real person, (2) a constructed reader, based at least in part on memories of real people, or (3) an imagined ideal reader, that is, the reader the document designer most wants to read his or her text. There are many terms that have been used to

[3] For example, see Booth (1961), Gibson (1950), and Ong (1975).

[4] The intuition-driven model appears to have links to Romantic notions of writing in which authors are guided by an evolving inner vision of the text. For example, in the nineteenth century, see Coleridge (1817); in the twentieth, see Elbow (1973, 1981). Both were discussed briefly in Chapter 2, the section "Three Traditions that Shaped Thinking and Beliefs about Writing and Graphic Design" (pp. 55–68).

[5] Interestingly, writers tend to talk about visualizing the reader while designers tend to talk about listening to their inner voice; compare, for example, Elbow (1981, p. 71) on writing and Rand (1993, p. 46) on design.

portray the reader that may be constructed—"implied reader," "invoked reader," "fictionalized reader," "created reader," "audience invoked," "imagined reader," or "ideal reader."[6] (In this chapter, I use "imagined reader.") Despite a lack of consistent terminology, the ideas about how the reader is created in the mind's eye are roughly the same. Communicators are said to first imagine their readers and then to use this representation dynamically as they write or design. That is, they move dialogically from text to thought, from reflecting on what they have written or visualized so far to projecting or role-playing the audience's possible reaction to those words or pictures, from thinking about their personal vision for the text to making textual decisions that take that interaction into account.

The intuition-driven model then operates by using *a mental construct of imagined readers* rather than of actual readers (even though the imagined readers could be based on memories of real people). In other words, when document designers imagine their readers, they may think not of actual people but of a composite of human characteristics (e.g., a reader who is curious, intelligent, technically minded, critical). Or they may think of people they have met before who could be like the intended audience (e.g., someone like my Aunt Sally who has never used a computer). Or they may use themselves as a model of the reader (e.g., I know nothing about investing in the stock market and here's the important thing I'd want to know). Document designers may even imagine an ideal reader they hope to interest in the text (e.g., as they might if they were generating an article to the op-ed section of the *New York Times,* a brochure about mutual funds, or a marketing piece about a new technical product). As we can see, the construct of the imagined reader that document designers may hold in consciousness is a complex set of "estimations, implied responses, and attitudes" (Park, 1982, p. 251).

With a representation of their imagined reader in mind, communicators choose words and graphics to invite the audience to engage with the text. They rely on the semantic and syntactic resources of language to provide cues for the reader—cues that not only encourage the audience to read, but also help to define the role that communicators wish the audience to adopt in responding to the text (Ede & Lunsford, 1984). Theorists call this rhetorical move "invoking" a reader through textual choice (thus, some describe the imagined audience as "invoked readers" or as the "audience invoked"[7]). The idea is that through the careful orchestration of textual or graphic cues (e.g., tone, typeface, illustrations, examples) and textual conventions (e.g., choosing the most appropriate genre and medium), document designers can suggest to readers a role[8] they might take on as they read, for example, "an informed user of page design software who

[6] For a discussion of implied and created readers, see Booth (1961), Ede and Lunsford (1984), Gibson (1950), Gragson and Selzer (1990), Iser (1978), McCormick (1994), and Tompkins (1980).

[7] See, for example, Long (1980, 1990) and Ong (1975).

[8] For a discussion of some of the roles readers may take on, see Coney (1992).

wants to separate fact from hype" or "an expert in cold fusion research who is skeptical of faddish trends in scientific journal articles." *A key feature in the success of using the intuition-driven model of audience analysis lies in the communicator's ability to keep the internal representation or mental sketch[9] of the audience in mind during composing and to draw on it to create ideas that connect with and motivate their imagined readers.*

[9] Berkenkotter (1981) explores this issue in an interesting case study of the thinking that underlies the work of a professional editor.

The literature from the writing and graphic design communities that speaks to the intuitive model stresses the communicator's personal creativity in invoking a reader through textual cues and conventions. However, the literature is quite vague about how communicators actually do this. Much of the literature in graphic design, for example, treats intuition as an inexplicable personal trait and seems to valorize the idea that the creative process can't be characterized. Take the following extended quote from eminent graphic designer Paul Rand (1993) as an illustration:

> [T]here is really no one definition of intuition. For the sake of this chapter ["Intuition and Ideas"] we can settle on: a flash of insight. Intuition cannot be willed or taught. It works in mysterious ways and has something to do with improvisation. It has nothing to do with intentions.... It simply happens—an idea out of the blue—characterized sometimes by surprise, elation, and a release of tension. Intuition is conditioned by experience, habit, native ability, religion, culture, imagination, and education, and at some point, is no stranger to reason.
>
> The question is really less a matter of *experiencing* than of *listening* to one's intuitions, following rather than dismissing them.... The ability to intuit is not reserved to any special class of individuals, although many painters, writers, designers, dancers, or musicians believe that this ability is something special, something God-given.... Except in a most general sense, one cannot prove the validity of color, contrast, texture, or shape.... This is one of the reasons it is so difficult to understand or teach art.... The designer works intuitively.... There is always an element of choice, sometimes called good judgment, at others good taste.
>
> Aside from practical considerations, in matters of form the typographer must rely on intuition. How else does one select a typeface, decide on its size, line width, leading, and format? The alternatives are to repeat one's previous performances, to imitate what others have done, or simply to make arbitrary decisions. (pp. 45–47)

Rand portrays a romantic vision of design: that art cannot be taught, that artistic talent comes from God, that intuition somehow just happens, and that artists cultivate good taste.[10] Rand is hardly alone in the design community. An ample literature likens good design to good choreography. A good designer (or typographer) is someone who has an intuitive sense of when to use which move—when to be graceful and delicate, when to be rough and raunchy, or when to be witty and playful. Judging from its dominance in the literature, intuition-driven audience analysis continues to hold enormous appeal for the graphic design community.

The strength of intuitive models is that they capture, in ways that other models do not, the phenomenon that skilled communicators are good at "doing things with words and pictures" that get the audience's attention and keep it—that good communicators are sensitive to visual and verbal rhetorical moves that resonate[11] with readers. The limitation of intuitive models is that they lead document designers to not question the adequacy of their own judgments about the reader. Intuitive models do not encourage document designers to check their imagined reader against a real reader. In fact, the only test of effectiveness for the intuitive model is the document designer's personal review, during which he or she might say "Yes, it reads the way I intended" or "No, that's not quite what I was trying to visualize." Intuitive models don't help communicators to discriminate ideas that will actually resonate with readers from those which will fall flat (or that resonate only for themselves or their clients). Just how professionals get to the point where they can readily make wise or rhetorically sophisticated choices while imagining the reader remains enshrined in mystery, perhaps not so surprising for a model of audience built on intuition.

---

[10] Young (1980) provides an illuminating discussion of the romantic tradition in modern thought about writing. He suggests that writers who hold the romantic view believe that the composing process should be free of deliberate control (what Rand calls intentions), that the act of composing is a kind of mysterious growth fed by what Henry James called "the deep well of unconscious cerebration" (1934, pp. 22–23). "Above all, this view insists on the primacy of the imagination ... [in] the mystery of language ... [in] art as magic" (pp. 343–344). As I discussed in Chapter 2, the romantic view holds that writing cannot be taught, that good writers are born with the right stuff, and that with the right stuff they can (as Rand tells us) cultivate good taste. Winterowd (1994) tells us that the romantic view of acquiring taste means that "some people are just genetic slobs and there's not much we can do about them" (p. 22).

[11] Meggs (1992a), for example, describes the nature of graphic resonance. He says that graphic designers bring a resonance to visual communication through the interaction of the connotative qualities of type and images and the expressive power of the visual vocabulary, that is, color, shape, texture, and the interrelations between forms in space (p. 117).

Feedback-driven Audience Analysis

Feedback-driven audience analysis provides a view of real readers engaged in the process of interpreting texts. Studies of readers-in-action show in considerable detail that audiences come to texts with knowledge, needs, values, and expectations that dramatically influence how they interpret what they read. The image of the audience that emerges from feedback-driven methods is of people who engage with documents in order to understand, access, and use them for pragmatic purposes.

The literature that speaks to feedback-driven audience analysis comes from two broad research traditions. One is from disciplines that focus on how people read and interpret text—such as reading comprehension, cognitive psychology, psycholinguistics, discourse analysis, and linguistics. Researchers working in this tradition have been characterizing in rather precise ways what readers do (e.g., their cognitive and linguistic moves) in making sense out of visual or verbal language. A second tradition has been developed by fields that focus more on how people read and interpret texts in particular contexts (e.g., professional, institutional, organizational, technological). Researchers in areas such as rhetoric, document design, technical communication, human factors, ergonomics, organizational behavior, cultural studies, sociology, anthropology, and the rhetoric of science have provided a view of people as they interpret messages directed at them (whether spoken, on paper, or on a screen).

Researchers in these fields stress the importance of studying the impact of the situation on the audience's interpretation. They suggest that document designers need to "catch the reader in the act" of interpretation by listening to them as they use prose and graphics in everyday situations (van der Meij, 1994). Feedback-driven audience analysis has been especially important in developing empirical methodologies for evaluating the design of artifacts—textual or otherwise.[12] These methods offer document designers ways of collecting quantitative and qualitative information about people's thinking and feeling as they engage with texts and technology. Feedback-driven accounts of audience have become increasingly concerned with studying communication as it unfolds in real time.

As *The Timeline* in Chapter 2 shows, during the 1980s and 1990s "understanding the user" gained worldwide attention from professionals working in usability testing, human-interface design, and user-centered design of products.[13] This trend led many professionals away from the traditional way of testing the quality of texts or technology, that is, by "crash testing" them on the audience after they were finished. Instead, professionals invited the audience to participate in evaluating their documents or products, in what has been called *participatory design*.

[12] A number of books and articles describing practical methods for assessing the quality of documents and products are available for newcomers to feedback-driven audience analysis (e.g., Dumas & Redish, 1993; Landauer, 1995; Nielsen & Mack, 1994; Rubin, 1994; Schriver, 1989a, 1991a; Schuler & Namioka, 1993; Schumacher & Waller, 1985; Suchman, 1987; U.S. Department of Health, 1984; Velotta, 1995.) For a bibliography of source materials about usability testing, see Ramey (1995a).

[13] For a view of user-centered design, see Casey (1993); Duffy, Mehlenbacher, and Palmer (1992); Duffy and Waller (1985); Landauer (1995); Norman (1988); Norman and Draper (1986); Redish (1985); Shneiderman (1987); or Wright (1980).

Professional communicators who employ feedback-driven audience analysis begin by thinking about ways to bring the audience into the design process in order to draw on their ideas to guide invention. A working assumption in using feedback-driven methods is that the audience should be part of the document design process as early and as often as possible during planning and revising. A second assumption is that as one elicits feedback from the audience, one is considerate, unobtrusive, and honest. Document designers rightly worry about the influence of their presence on the reader's interpretation. Feedback-driven approaches stress listening as carefully and as empathetically as possible, taking care not to assume the stance of judge or critic. Readers who provide document designers with feedback should be made aware that it is the text or the technology under evaluation and not their intelligence, their reading ability, or their cleverness in using technology. In responding to the audience, document designers try to do more of what readers like, while at the same time finding ways to solve problems readers may experience.

Like intuition-driven models of audience analysis, feedback-driven models operate dynamically. That is, the mental image communicators construct about the reader is used interactively during writing and design. *The key difference between intuition-driven models and feedback-driven models lies in how the image of the reader is built—on where ideas about the reader come from. Intuitive models of readers spring from the document designer's imagination, while feedback-based models derive from representations of real people.* Seeing the audience engage with prose or graphics allows document designers to build a mental representation of the reader which can be brought to bear during writing and design. By representation I do not mean a mirror-image rendering of the reader; document designers using feedback-driven audience analysis still consolidate their impressions of readers, still interpret their readers, still imagine them, and yes, still fictionalize them.

A strength of feedback-driven models is that the representation a document designer forms about the audience is likely to be much more oriented toward real people reading and comprehending than it would be if the document designer were using other models. *Feedback-driven models allow document designers to get a detailed view of how particular people interpret sentences, paragraphs, illustrations, diagrams, and so on. Watching people read provides firsthand insight into what makes documents easy (or hard) to understand. Listening to readers also alerts document designers to the differences among readers and to differences between readers and themselves.* Communicators who have observed someone trying to untie their tortured prose or decipher their use of "way cool" layered typefaces are more likely to have a better sense of the moments in the creative process when they should resist their writer-centered or graphic designer-centered tendencies. This is quite a different view of the audience than one can glean by classifying or imagining people. Indeed, document designers can classify or imagine their audience and never once think of someone tripping over sentences. Instead, their attention is directed toward imagining readers engaging with the ideas they are supposed to *take away* from the text. The classification-driven and intuition-driven models tend to ignore the very real fact that what people take away from text depends on their process of interpretation—processes which may differ from those of the document designer.

A weakness of feedback-driven models is that like the other models, there is still a gap between forming an image of the audience and taking action based on that image. Feedback-driven methods can provide communicators with a veritable mountain of data to sort through. Not all of it is relevant. Not all of it will lead to improvement in the text. Some of the things members of the audience may say are idiosyncratic; others are just plain weird. Up to this point, however, there has been almost no research on how document designers move from the data they collect (e.g., during usability testing) to interpretations about those observations and then to revisions that reflect those interpretations. We need to know much more both about how to interpret what readers may say about prose and graphics and about how to take action on those interpretations.[14]

Classifying, Imagining, or Listening: The Collision of Ideas about Audience Analysis?

Theories of audience analysis suggest that experienced professionals may analyze their audience in different ways—classifying them, imagining them, or listening to them. Although some of the literature argues implicitly or explicitly for one model or another, these visions needn't be viewed as being on a collision course. Instead, they can be used alternately, depending on what the rhetorical situation calls for.[15] Experience in document design can enable professionals to develop their sensitivity to moments in the creative act when it may be appropriate to shift gears and redirect their attention, using one vision of the audience or another. Experience also provides insight about how to employ these models interactively—that is, moving back and forth, for example, between imagining and observing the reader, allowing a model of the real reader to anchor the reader imagined, while at the same time calling on the document designer's personal creativity and intuition to help make design moves that resonate.

Experience in document design also helps professionals learn to recognize when they need to put off thinking about the audience[16] and

[14] I provide examples of how document designers may move from collecting readers' interpretations about prose and graphics to making audience-sensitive revisions in Chapters 5, 6, and 7.

[15] Compare, for instance, the depictions of audience found in the writings of Berkenkotter (1981), Coney (1987), Ede and Lunsford (1984), Elbow (1987), Flower (1979), Iser (1978), Lunsford and Ede (1996), Park (1982), Roth (1977), Selzer (1992), and Young, Becker, and Pike (1970).

[16] For a discussion of when it may be appropriate to ignore the audience, see Elbow (1987).

concentrate on their own understanding of the subject matter about which they are writing or visualizing. Document designers frequently work with subject matters that are new to them, requiring them to learn about the topic from scratch. These situations call on document designers to get the content straight for themselves before imagining or observing how someone else may understand it. Working with the subject matter allows document designers to develop a better understanding of it. The act of writing or designing may also inspire them to see new relationships, make fresh connections, and develop a better plan for the document. As document designers write or design, they form a mental representation of the text itself, a working image of its content, its structure, of what the text says so far. In a real sense, the "text produced so far" provides cues about how well the design is going (see Hayes & Flower, 1980). Each time document designers review their prose or graphics, the text itself speaks to them.

With experience, professionals learn to gauge for themselves when to listen to the text and when to listen to the audience. They become more responsive to the rhetorical situation, alternately working out the content—getting it straight—for themselves, classifying readers with special needs and interests, invoking readers they hope to converse with through the text, or listening to the flesh-and-blood people who may actually use their document. In this way, professionals develop a good sense of timing, calling on the right audience model at the right time and turning it off at the right time.

ANALYZING AUDIENCES/ANALYZING OURSELVES

As we have seen, there are considerable differences among the three approaches to audience analysis I just discussed. However, all three agree on an important point: Audience analysis should include a comparison of the communicator and the audience, an assessment of their respective knowledge, values, and beliefs about the subject matter. A comparative analysis can put document designers in a more informed position to make visual and verbal decisions that may bridge the gap between themselves and their audience. Young, Becker, and Pike (1970) put it this way:

> The writer frequently takes too much for granted, assuming that merely by speaking his mind he can change the reader's. If he fails, however, to utilize available bridges or to create new ones, his writing will not be effective. Thus it is not enough that bridges exist; they must be used—and therein lies much of the art of rhetoric. (172)

A comparison of perspectives may help document designers to see more clearly—in sometimes startling ways—that documents routinely present points of view that are neither anonymous nor objective. Indeed, all documents—whether they are designed to move, please, inform, or teach—project the knowledge of a knower, of an interested party. As Eagleton (1983) comments,

> There is no possibility of a wholly disinterested discourse…. All of our descriptive statements move within an often invisible network of value-categories, and indeed without such categories we would have nothing to say to each other at all…. [Our] interests are *constitutive* of our knowledge, not merely prejudices which imperil it. [italics in original] (pp. 13–14)

By exploring differences between themselves and their audience, document designers can become more reflective about the biases that can be created by knowledge and values. Such an awareness can make them more considerate of the reader's perspective, allowing them to generate ideas about how to address the differences between them and their readers. However, as I will show later in this chapter, there are cases in which the communicator and the audience live in such different worlds that the gaps between them may not easily be bridged. The audience, for example, may make radically different assumptions about why the document was written and about whose interests were meant to be served by the selection of content.[17] In the remainder of this chapter, I discuss what people do in choosing whether to read documents and how thinking and feeling come into play as they make these decisions.

TO READ OR NOT TO READ: WHY BELIEFS MATTER

The first decision people make when confronted with a document is whether or not to read. Anecdotal evidence suggests that many people prefer not to read at all unless they have to. People learn quickly that reading documents—whether they are textbooks or tips on investments—takes effort. Redish (1993) points out that people read as much as they think they have to and no more. If a document "puts us off" when we first look at it, the likelihood that we will read it closely is greatly reduced. In some situations, such as filling out income tax forms, we are forced to read every word no matter how ugly the text seems. In most situations, however, we choose not only *whether* to read, but also *how* to read.

Many people find they must do a lot of reading on the job, making it essential for them to adjust their reading processes to the task at hand. For

[17] This is especially true with persuasive documents in the domain of risk communication and public policy. A few years ago, risk communicators from Los Alamos National Laboratory in New Mexico (the place where the atom bomb was built) carried out a mock town meeting in which they showed how difficult it is to change people's minds through documents when your organization is known "as the company that brought you the seven-eyed trout" (Durbin, Wahl, Molony, Klein, & Wade, 1993).

example, a 1986 study of 150 research and development companies found that managers spend roughly 30 percent of their time reading documents such as research reports, memos, proposals, or technical articles (Sageev, 1994, p. 143). Similarly, in another study, managers at Exxon were found to spend an average of 35 percent of their time dealing with documents (Paradis, Dobrin, & Miller, 1985). Some managers of Fortune 500 companies have reported coping with as many as 142 pieces of mail in one day (Mintzberg, 1975). Obviously, with reading loads this high, managers need to reduce the time they spend dealing with documents and develop strategies for getting to the main points without reading the details. As Wright (1988b) has argued, we need to develop theories of NOT reading as well as theories of reading—theories that explore people's motivation for reading some documents carefully while ignoring others completely.

Since not all reading is of equal importance, skilled document readers develop ways of sizing up the material to be read—deciding what to browse, skim through, examine with full attention, or skip altogether. Skilled document readers behave opportunistically, getting what they want from documents and no more (as long as the document is designed in ways that make it convenient for them to do so). Although there is considerable informal evidence that individuals employ a range of strategies when dealing with documents, only recently have researchers started to explore how people make decisions about reading and using texts.

Researchers are just beginning to study how the particular situation or context shapes what people do when they read. Although there is widespread agreement that old models which assumed that individuals read in the same way across situations are wrong—in fact, dead wrong—we still have little empirical evidence about how the context influences what people do. Much of the early work on reading was done in university labs where college students were asked to respond to short narratives rather than to lengthy documents with real rhetorical functions such as informing, teaching, or persuading. Student participants in these studies were usually asked to carry out contrived tasks rather than their own tasks and imagine that they had the researcher's purpose in mind while reading.[18] Recently, researchers have begun to conduct naturalistic studies that explore reading and composing processes in everyday situations (see, for example, Stratman's 1990 study of court clerks interpreting legal briefs, Dauterman's 1993 study of nurses revising hospital documents, Mirel's 1989 study of office workers avoiding the use of computer manuals, Charney's 1993 study of biologists interpreting scientific writing, or Ackerman and Oates' 1996 study of architects using visual images to solve design problems). Studies of the reading habits of scientists, for example,

[18] Dumas and Redish (1993) point out that evaluating tasks from the user's perspective rather than from the manufacturer's perspective is crucial. Companies often discover that once they release a product, customers use it in ways they did not anticipate (which may contribute to the rise in third-party documents, for example, *DOS for Dummies*.) Document designers need to study users as they carry out their own tasks in their own environments in real situations and not simply document the tasks that the company's engineers find interesting.

have found that scientists typically read articles in professional publications in the following way:

> First they read the title and the abstract. Then they look for the most important data, usually in graphs, tables, drawings, and other visual aids. Next they typically read the Results section. (Berkenkotter & Huckin, 1995, p. 30)

Berkenkotter and Huckin note that this pattern is "strikingly similar to that displayed by newspaper readers … [in which people] look for the most surprising, most newsworthy information first (i.e., the headline statement). Then, if interested, they read further…." (p. 31). Their research offers observation-driven support for the use of a "conclusions first" organizational structure in articles and proposals. Document designers should frame their texts so that the main points are presented "upfront" in a brief and engaging way; they should avoid recapping the inductive process of discovery that may have led to their scientific claims. As Harmon and Gross (1996) point out:

> Readers of scientific articles are an impatient lot. Of those who read the title and byline, only some will peruse the Abstract. Of those who read the Abstract, still fewer will read the Introduction. Many will skip from either the Abstract or the Introduction to the Conclusion…. And some will jump from the front matter directly to the reference list to see if their name was cited. (pp. 62–63)

What we know now is that most people choose to read and to keep reading only when they believe there will be some benefit in doing so and only when they cannot get the same information in easier ways (for example, by asking someone else). In order to help readers recognize the documents (or the sections thereof) that deserve their consideration, document designers must do at least two things. They must visibly structure the document so that the main ideas catch the attention of busy readers. At the same time, they must use language (both visual and verbal) that connects with the readers' knowledge, experience, beliefs, and values. The examples I present in this chapter show how this can be done and how hard it is to do well.

THE DOCUMENT DESIGNER'S DILEMMA: BALANCING THE READER'S NEEDS AND THE ORGANIZATION'S NEEDS

Up to this point, I have been talking as though the intended audience is the only group of readers document designers need to worry about. But as experienced professionals know all too well, there are other important readers of documents besides real audiences, imagined readers, or end users—namely, the people who sponsor the document (e.g., the boss, the client, the manager) or those who distribute the document (e.g., gatekeepers,[19] marketing groups, teachers, sales personnel, bureaucrats). Unlike creative writers who get to compose exclusively for themselves, invoking imagined audiences when the mood strikes them, document designers must negotiate among the needs of multiple real audiences—juggling allegiances, mindsets, and agendas of competing stakeholders.

Part of being an expert in document design[20] means being able to write and design a single document that will satisfy the needs of multiple audiences. For example, when creating texts intended to persuade, document designers need to develop ideas in ways that show readers their perspective has been understood and represented fairly. At the same time, document designers must orchestrate the visual and verbal content so that it encourages readers to seriously consider the position put forth through the document, a position held by the sponsoring organization, even if it is as mundane as "use our equipment in this way." It would be naive to believe that organizations that sponsor document design do so without particular aims (e.g., educational, informational, political, or economic). The document must meet their needs and reflect their values (in effect, create an identity for them) as well as those of readers. This rhetorical situation—in which document designers must take into account the readers' knowledge and values while at the same time furthering the goals of an organization—is one that professionals deal with often. The study below illustrates how difficult it can be to strike the balance between readers' needs and the organization's needs. It shows how document designers are sometimes stuck in the middle.

"JUST SAY NO TO DRUGS" AND OTHER UNWELCOME ADVICE: TEENS SPEAK OUT

Recently my colleagues and I[21] studied a context in which good writing and visual design have the potential to make an important difference: the design of drug education literature. We were concerned with how teenage audiences interpret brochures intended to discourage them from taking drugs, and more broadly with how readers may respond to the visual and verbal messages presented through brochures that aim to inform and persuade. We felt that the area of drug education literature would provide a challenging rhetorical situation to study because it is a context in which the audience's knowledge and values may stand in stark contrast to those of professionals employed to write and visualize the documents. Professionals who design drug education literature typically differ from

[19] Gatekeepers are people who control access to information and who, in some cases, have the authority to require revisions of documents before they are released to the intended audience—people such as school board members, health authorities, supervisors, budget officers, personnel officers, corporate legal teams, military strategists, or public relations managers.

[20] The nature of expertise in document design is an important topic that needs much more exploration.

[21] My collaborators in this study were John R. Hayes and Ann Steffy Cronin. We gratefully acknowledge the sponsor of this research: The National Center for the Study of Writing and Literacy under the administration of the Office of Educational Research and Improvement (OERI), U.S. Department of Education. We also thank Patricia Chi Nespor and Michele Matchett for their contributions in the early phases of this project. An early version of this study appeared in Schriver, Hayes, and Steffy Cronin (1996).

their audiences in age, in point of view, in experience with drugs, in education, and sometimes in race, culture, and social class. Designing documents that communicate across these social and cultural boundaries is complex because professionals may have difficulty in anticipating how someone who may be quite unlike themselves will interpret their ideas.

Furthermore, even when professionals are good at "getting on a level" with their readers, the organization sponsoring the document may constrain the "voice" document designers can create by controlling (and in the worst cases, censoring) what may be said or illustrated.[22] This study showed us how critical it is to consider the possible interactions and conflicts among the values of the document designer, the organization, the gatekeepers, and the intended audience. It also made us aware of how important it is to learn about what audiences believe and value by listening to them as they interpret documents.

Where Our Research Team Started

We began by collecting over 100 brochures and handouts from national and local drug prevention agencies.[23] Many of these materials were funded by U.S. taxpayer dollars or through grants to nonprofit organizations during the Reagan administration. From this collection, we selected a

---

[22] Consider the U.S. government's abysmal track record in designing effective brochures about AIDS prevention. The first brochure from the Surgeon General that was mailed to all households in the U.S. failed to include the word "condom" because conservatives thought its use encouraged sexual activity. Unfortunately, almost 10 years later, the design of AIDS brochures continues to be perverted by political agendas. For example, the New York Times (Berke, September 13, 1995 and September 17, 1995) reported that when Senator Bob Dole decided to make a bid for the 1996 presidential election, his wife, Elizabeth Dole, president of the Red Cross, called a halt to the release of already-designed AIDS brochures to be distributed nationwide. The reason was that the illustrations were too explicit about how to put on a condom. Although writers could use the word "condom," illustrators had their hands tied regarding the type of drawings to make. Illustrators had wisely chosen to depict realistic images of people putting on condoms. But out of fear that these drawings could be construed as sanctioning illicit sex, illustrators were sent back to the drawingboard to make more technical, medical-looking illustrations. The consequence was the wrong revisions implemented for the wrong reasons. As this study will show, teenage readers tend to "tune out" illustrations that look like they came from their biology textbooks.

[23] Agencies such as the U.S. Department of Health and Human Services, the National Office for Substance Abuse Prevention, the National Crime Prevention Council, the Do It Now Foundation, Campuses Without Drugs, and the Pittsburgh Police Drug Abuse Resistance Education (DARE) Program. Our research team respects these organizations for their continued excellent efforts to communicate effectively with their intended audiences. Our goal was not to criticize the work of these organizations, but to better understand how readers respond to drug prevention literature in order to improve it.

subset of brochures intended for a junior high school, high school, or college audience. Among the brochures we studied were the following:

- *Don't Lose a Friend to Drugs*
- *Here Are Some Snappy Answers to the Question: Want Some Alcohol or Other Drugs?*
- *Smokeless Tobacco: It's Not as Safe as You Think*
- *Crack: Cocaine Squared*
- *Crack: The New Cocaine*
- *Ice: Crystal Methamphetamine*
- *Pot: A Guide for Young People*
- *Marijuana: Health Effects*
- *The Effects of Alcohol*
- *Inhalants*
- *Facts About Anabolic Steroids*

To learn about how these documents were designed and interpreted, we looked at the situation from three perspectives:

- Teenagers' interpretations of messages directed at them through the brochures
- Gatekeepers' (e.g., teachers or guidance counselors)[24] opinions about what they look for in drug prevention messages, particularly in brochures
- Document designers' ideas about what they were trying to do in creating the drug prevention messages (and what the organizations they worked for were trying to do)

I now describe what our research team did and what we found out about these perspectives.

Exploring Teenagers' Interpretations of Drug Education Literature

We investigated students' responses to the drug education brochures by asking them to participate in focus groups, surveys, and one-on-one interviews, or to provide think-aloud reading protocols.[25] A total of 297 students from western Pennsylvania, West Virginia, and eastern Ohio, ranging in age from 11 to 21, took part in the project.[26] These students came from diverse educational settings: inner-city and suburban junior high schools and high schools, private prep schools, parochial schools, community literacy centers, karate schools, business schools, vocational-education schools, and private colleges.

[24] In the context of drug education literature, gatekeepers disseminate communications such as brochures or public service announcements, choosing which brochures get put in waiting rooms, counselors' offices, and the like. Gatekeepers exert influence over whether audiences ever see the communications its organization may have bought, commissioned, or received from other organizations. For a discussion, see the U.S. Department of Health (1984).

[25] For readers of this book who are not familiar with these methods for evaluating texts, I recommend reading the sources mentioned in footnote 12.

[26] Special thanks to the teachers and students at Pittsburgh's Gateway Technical Institute, Riverview High School of Oakmont, the Community Literacy Center of Pittsburgh's Northside, the Jewish Community Center of Squirrel Hill, the Baptist Youth Group of Allegheny County, the Defense Tactics Institute of West Virginia, the Karate School of Pittsburgh, Robert Morris College, Carnegie Mellon University, Westinghouse High School of Pittsburgh, Shadyside Academy of Fox Chapel, and Carlynton Junior High of Rosslyn Farms, Pennsylvania.

We chose our methods for collecting data—surveys, think-aloud protocols, interviews, and focus groups—with several goals in mind. In particular, the surveys were designed to evaluate students'

- Understanding of the facts about the drugs (e.g., how many times can a person smoke crack before becoming addicted?)
- Opinions about the writing and visual design of the brochures
- Beliefs about the persuasiveness of the brochures

The think-aloud protocols provided a detailed view of students' sentence-by-sentence, picture-by-picture comprehension of the brochures. The interviews and focus groups elicited students' general impressions of the content presented in the brochures. With the permission of students, their parents, and their teachers, we videotaped the focus groups, interviews, and think-aloud protocols.

We visited classrooms where teachers allowed us to talk with their students for a few hours in the morning or afternoon. We began by asking students to read a drug brochure and then evaluate its quality by responding to a survey. From each class, we asked a few students to provide think-aloud reading protocols or to take part in one-on-one interviews while the other students read silently and filled in the survey. After the surveys, protocols, or interviews, the entire class participated in a focus group session, during which we prompted students to respond to the features of the brochures that struck them as effective or ineffective. We posed questions such as these:

Overall impression

- What is your impression of the brochure?
- What about this brochure makes you want to read it?
- If you saw this brochure on a rack in a guidance counselor's office, would you pick it up? Would you take it home?

Interpretation of the main ideas

- What ideas does the brochure tell you about?
- What are the main points of the brochure?
- Does this brochure help you make an opinion about its main points?
- Does this brochure change your mind about anything?

Impression of the visual design

- Do you like the way this brochure looks?
- What do you think of the pictures, tables, or diagrams?
- What about the appearance of this brochure catches your eye and makes you want to look it over?

Impression of the author

- Did you imagine an author when you read this?
- If you did imagine an author, what is the author like?
- Can you point to places in the brochure that make you feel this way?

Impression of the intended audience

- What does the author think the reader is like?
- Does the author have a point of view about the reader?
- Can you point to places in the brochure that make you feel this way?

Students told us several important things about the drug education literature: how well the writing "spoke" to them, how well the graphics and visual design worked, who they believed might have produced the drug literature, and who they thought the author was writing to. They also provided feedback regarding the effectiveness of the brochures, that is, would these documents actually have any effect on someone who is considering taking drugs?

Teenagers Respond to the Text and Graphics

Students' responses revealed that although most of the brochures were clearly written and visualized in terms of sentence structure, choice of language, and ease of understanding the graphics, they did not work very well for the intended audience. We found that students' interpretations developed partly in response to the main ideas of the drug education literature and partly from their perception of who they believed wrote the text and why. In general, students understood the facts about the drugs discussed in the brochures, that is, they had little trouble comprehending the main points. They also had few problems figuring out what the pictures were intended to represent, at least on a literal level; they could

readily see that a diagram of a heart was supposed to be a heart. But importantly, students' understanding of the main ideas and the intended meaning of the graphics did not appear to have much to do with whether or not they were persuaded by the document.

Students' interpretations of the "just say no" rhetorical stance often ran counter to the expectations of the organizations sponsoring the brochures. Students were quick to infer an authorial agenda in presenting the message, an agenda that document designers and the organizations they worked for may or may not have intended. Teenagers displayed considerable rhetorical sophistication in evaluating the text and graphics directed at them. They were astute in making inferences about the author and in identifying textual clues that suggested the author's beliefs about them. An examination of students' responses to several of the brochures vividly makes these points.

Don't Lose a Friend to Drugs (shown in Figure 3.1) is a trifold brochure aimed at middle school students and high school freshmen. Of the 90 students who evaluated this brochure, only two students liked it. One student remarked that the pictures in the brochure made the whole thing seem "too kiddy," and, as one ninth-grader said, "If I looked at the picture, I'd think it was for eight-year-olds and I wouldn't read it." Another told us, "If I saw this on a rack, I'd pass it by."

Some students zeroed in on how outdated the character portrayed in the brochure was; one student described him as "a seventies kind of guy," while another scoffed, "Is that [his hair] supposed to be an Afro? What a throwback to Jheri curl or my dad's Afro-sheen days." Students were insulted by the character's implied ethnicity; one asked: "Why is a black man on the inside in the middle? Why do they show black males in all these brochures?"[27]

[27] Interestingly, not all students in our study believed the picture in Figure 3.1 was of an African American. Interviews with writers on the document design team revealed that they were worried about the organization's choice of illustrator, reporting that "he always draws pictures of blacks that look like they're from that old TV show, *The Mod Squad.*"

Students' comments in the focus groups and think-aloud protocols showed they were accustomed to judging visuals, readily inferring meanings (intended or not) from the choice and design of graphics. Students remarked that many of the illustrations across the set of the brochures were "insulting," "corny," and even "pitiful." One student offered this sobering suggestion:

> I think they should take actual photographs of people on drugs. My friend's cousin is on drugs, well … he just sits there and laughs.… That's how gone he is.… I think they should use pictures of people just looking into space. I mean that cover with the hand pulling away the other hand with the pill in it, that's just lame. The story is dumb. Give us some credit.

Some guy's trying to take a pill and another's trying to stop him. It's good but, it needs more detail and more colors to draw your attention to it ... or a picture of a guy who's really messed up. As is, you're like what's up with this guy?

This sounds so typical ... person uses drugs, person gets help, person gets life back on track. It's like whenever you get one of these pamphlets that's all it is. Person gets help at some center and he's OK. Tell about him dying or him destroying his life.

Maybe if you explain more facts about drugs or what they do to you. Or even when you're under the influence what kinds of things happen to you. Many teenagers don't know all the effects of drugs, so like you could tell true stories of what happened.

I think that you could just give them the facts and it's their decision whether they want to try them or not. You should like have a list of drugs and effects—just state the facts. This is too long, nobody's going to read it.

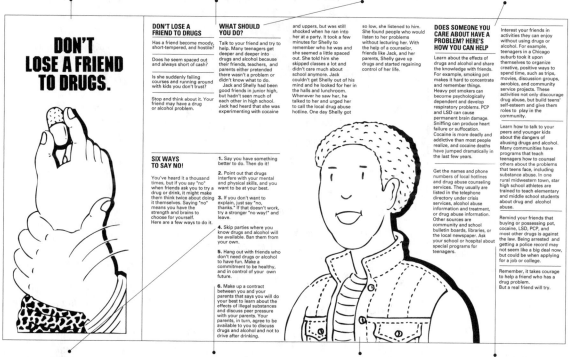

How about #4 of the six ways to say no, skip parties. Well, parties aren't the only place drugs are available. How about school and everyday life, so maybe we should start skipping school (giggles).

The sixth way to "say no" is corny ... you'd say hey mom, how about a contract? She'd say, how about a slap? This looks like it was written by someone who's in some Washington office building all the time and never gets outside.

Oh that picture is so cheezy. Plus is he supposed to be black? Why are black men always shown in these brochures? I resent this crap! Like why is he smiling and why doesn't he have normal eyebrows ... his jacket I mean, it's like gross. Is he supposed to be happy? They should get input from other young people.

I think the part "If someone you know has a problem here's how you can help" is good because there's some abbreviations in there that catch your eye ... PCP, LSD. I like that cause it makes you want to read it ... maybe they could also tell true stories like how somebody on drugs gouged out their eyes.

▲ **Figure 3.1** *Teenagers' responses to a brochure about helping a friend on drugs. Courtesy of The National Crime Prevention Council, Washington, DC.*

The title makes it sound like when you open this box the flyer asks you if you want some drugs or alcohol. Sick. And they don't say stuff we could really do, just "say no" with one of these "snappy" answers … which are lame at best.

It sounds more like a joke. Some people would just say "not with you," but these say, "I have to walk my python (laughs)." These answers are kind of stupid. It sounds like the author is a nerdy white guy that was cooped up in his office too long. Maybe they should tell why taking drugs is bad. They could say blow-by-blow what happens to you.

This is aimed at kids pretty much because it says "No thanks, my coach will keep me on the bench." But, it's not very interesting. They should use more pictures … if they really wanted to make an impact they should use pictures of a dead guy.

Here are some SNAPPY ANSWERS
to the
QUESTION . . .

Want Some?

Alcohol
or other
Drugs

▲ No thanks, I'd rather walk my pet python.

▲ No way, I'm in a skateboarding contest today.

▲ Uhuh, I need all my wits about me to write my new rap song.

▲ With YOU??

▲ No thanks, I'm saving my bad breath for pepperoni pizza.

▲ You must be kidding! If I'm going to ruin my body, I'd rather do it with a hot fudge sundae.

▲ No thank you, I need all my brain cells, so I'd rather have noodle soup.

▲ No thanks, my coach will leave me on the bench.

▲ I'd rather not. I'm too special.

▲ No thanks, I don't like the taste.

▲ No thanks, I'm all-American. I'll stick to milk.

OSAP

U.S. DEPARTMENT OF HEALTH AND HUMAN SERVICES
Public Health Service Alcohol, Drug Abuse, and Mental Health Administration
Office for Substance Abuse Prevention

Nobody says "Want some alcohol or other drugs?" That "or other" sounds really weird.

What are these little triangles? Oh no, I guess this is supposed to be acid. Why do they use drugs to decorate the letters if they are not trying to make using drugs seem fun? It seems odd to me.

This one's OK, but I'd say "boarding."

This one's funny. You could say it like in a "smart" way. Like you could say it with an attitude. It's the only one I could say. The other ones would get you beaten up.

Get a grip! Only "goodie-goodies" talk like this.

Was this written by someone's grandma?

I like this one "I better not, I'm too special." NOT!

People never admit to drinking milk in front of friends. This is strange.

▲ **Figure 3.2** *Teenagers' responses to a flyer intended to give them ways to "say no to drugs." Courtesy of the Office of Substance Abuse Prevention and the U.S. Department of Health and Human Services, Washington, DC.*

A one-page pamphlet, *Here are Some SNAPPY ANSWERS to the Question: Want Some Alcohol or Other Drugs?* (shown in Figure 3.2 on the opposite page), advises preteens how to "just say no" when offered drugs. At best, students found the idea of "snappy answers" dumb and condescending. Students ridiculed answers such as "No thanks, I'm all-American. I'll stick to milk"—identifying them as glaringly inadequate for coping with the reality of America's playgrounds and streets.

One student reasoned, "A pusher would have a more powerful comeback if someone was dumb enough to say one of these." Another student pointed out the danger of using inappropriate responses like "I'd rather have a hot fudge sundae," predicting "You'd get beat up if you said this." Students suggested that writers should "create a realistic scenario, maybe put themselves in a situation … like a realistic play, but just don't have a hokey script." Rather than offering "snappy answers," students advised prompting teens to "really think about drugs and what can happen…. Make 'em really think about their lives."

Again and again, students pointed to differences between their perspective and the author's (that is, their inferences about the author). Some recommended bridging the gap by involving the audience directly in the document design: "We [the students] should write it…. We should have a say." Students seemed to have an implicit model of the benefits of usability testing and participatory design (see Schuler & Namioka, 1993). They felt that either "teenage drug users" or "kids who have had firsthand experience with someone who has had a problem with drugs" would reach the intended audience better because "adults can't really see."

Students were more impressed with *Smokeless Tobacco* (shown on the following page in Figure 3.3). They found the message compelling and were very positive about the author's attitude toward them as readers. They responded favorably to the author's "it's your decision" rhetorical stance. They thought the facts about what smokeless tobacco does to the body were effective and that imagining the gruesome effects made the topic real.

Although students liked the way the brochure was written, they criticized its ugly appearance. The original was printed on yellow-gold paper. Students thought the paper looked cheap and said that illustrations and graphics were needed "so you don't have to imagine what it looks like to have your mouth destroyed." As one student put it:

> I would include graphic pictures of actual tissue damage. This is what your mouth is going to look like in so many years … you know, stuff that is going to make the kids cringe … I think that might work.

Looking at the cover you don't get any idea of what this is about. The coffee cup and pouch don't have any effect on me. A little more color would be good. It reminds me of a Jehovah's Witnesses brochure and you always try to slam the door in their face.

I think that they should make this more interesting. If I picked this up and looked inside I wouldn't want to read it. It's a lot of writing all close together. They should put those bubbles around it like the ones in cartoons.

It is good that instead of just telling you that you can get oral cancer they describe it. White lesions—that sounds horrible, sickening … but a picture would be more convincing. The words have big spaces between them. Why is that?

These facts say there are chemicals in chewing tobacco that you don't think about being in there. That's good. People who do it think it's just a thing you put in your mouth. By the way, this brochure looks typed—like they used a really old typewriter. It's ugly. Get a computer.

SMOKELESS TOBACCO....... *it's not as safe as you might think*

Do you use smokeless tobacco--commonly called snuff or chewing tobacco?Are you thinking about using it because your friends do it or because advertisements feature a popular athlete who promotes chew and says it's safe, clean, convenient and cool? You've heard of the dangers of smoking and you think smokeless tobacco will let you enjoy tobacco safely. Well, although smokeless tobacco is not as lethal as smoking, it is a definite health hazard that can cause visible damage in just a few months. Chewing or sniffing is also as habit forming as smoking.

A wad of snuff, finely ground tobacco, is placed between the lower lip and gum where it mixes with saliva, and the nicotine is absorbed through the lip, gum, tongue and throat. Snuff can also be inhaled through the nose.

Chew, coarsely cut tobacco, is placed in the cheek, next to the teeth and gums and is sucked or chewed. Nicotine penetrates the lining of the mouth and is absorbed into the body. Excessive spitting usually occurs whether chewing tobacco or dipping snuff.

All smokeless tobacco is believed to cause oral cancer, dental problems and nicotine effects.

Oral Cancer--Most snuff and chew users develop a soft, white lesion in the mouth. This lesion, called leukoplakia, is caused by irritation from direct contact with tobacco juice. Five percent of leukoplakia cases develop oral cancer.

Dental Problems--occur because the tobacco causes shrinking of gum tissue. Shrinkage exposes the tooth and root and leads to decay, tooth abrasion and tooth loss.

Nicotine--causes constriction of blood vessels which increases blood pressure thereby increasing the risk of heart attacks and strokes. Tobacco products also decrease the senses of taste and smell which could lead to an increase in salt and sugar intake.

Nicotine is also believed to be habit forming. It directly affects the nervous system causing a feeling of euphoria and stimulation which is followed by a psychological depression. Your brain only remembers the positive feeling, that is why you want to use nicotine again. To feel good, a person with a nicotine habit needs a "boost" about every thirty minutes while awake.

So, now you see that smokeless tobacco is far from harmless. Look at the facts. It's your decision.

This cover is boring. A gruesome picture on the front would be an attention-getter. I saw a brochure with a picture of a guy who used chewing tobacco and his face was all destroyed—it was really gross. It was really effective. I'd never touch chew now.

I think sometimes just showing what it will do might show people how to use it. If the brochure tells what chew will do or where to put it in your mouth, kids will understand how to use it better. So if more people read this, more people might do it.

These facts are good. Even though you could say, "I use a brand that's not as harmful," you're still influenced by this message. It might even convince me more if there was a testimonial from a baseball player who used chew.

Here they say it is your decision—you can use chew and get cancer or you can ignore it and you won't. It's good that they're clear about giving you a choice. They respect us and think we have a mind! But they should show what it does to your mouth.

▲ **Figure 3.3** *Teenagers' responses to a brochure about the dangers of smokeless tobacco. Courtesy of the Allegheny County Health Department, Pittsburgh, PA.*

Some felt that a famous baseball player who had tissue damage should be featured (a strategy often used in videos about the dangers of drugs). A number of students thought that a well-known and respected spokesperson would add credibility to the brochures. Others felt the focus should be on making the tobacco companies "the enemy," arguing "they don't care about us … they just want our money."[28] As one ninth-grade female said to another,

> Those tobacco companies don't care if we die, girl. But we're not the fools they make us be.

In addition to pointing out problems caused by the lack of illustrations in *Smokeless Tobacco,* students made judgments about its graphic design and typography. Students did not have insider language for graphic and typographic features such as layout, typeface, word spacing, kerning, leading, or format. But even so, they readily saw these features. As one student observed:

> Once you read *Smokeless Tobacco* you like it, but when you glance it over, you think, boy, this is really cheap looking. Look at the letters and the spaces there between the words, like it was done in somebody's basement. It's so ugly you don't want to read it. If you didn't ask me to read it, I wouldn't have … even though I did like it.

In other brochures we tested, we found that students' interpretations of pictorial graphics, especially representational illustrations and cartoon-like line art, were influenced by associations they made between what was pictured and their personal lives. For example, in *Pot: A Guide for Young People* (part of which is shown in Figure 3.4 on the following page), students commented that the cartoons of a "stoned guy with the munchies watching TV" made pot smoking "look like fun." One student, a freshman in college, thought that it looked like an "ad for pot which featured the celebrities, Cheech and Chong, from those classic stoner films of the 1960s." To probe his interpretation further, we repeated his comments in our focus groups with junior high school students and were met with blank stares. Younger teens had never heard of Cheech and Chong. One eighth-grader asked, "who is this old guy with the long hair supposed to be? He's weird."

Members of the document design team may have been teenagers in the 1960s; the illustration style appears to be influenced by Robert Crumb of *Zap Comix.* Clearly, document designers need to be more aware that the same graphic can mean very different things to readers from different age groups. Readers' comments about the graphics made us realize the importance of paying attention both to the connotations of graphics and to their visual tone.

[28] By contrast, some students had not yet formed an opinion and seemed highly susceptible to messages directed at them. The twelve-year old boy pictured at the bottom left on page 170 (wearing a Kool cigarette T-shirt) said this as he read *Smokeless Tobacco:* "I guess I don't know what I think. If I read this and it shows me how to put it behind my lip, then I know how to use it. So some people might try it out. It says that the snuff is not as bad as the smoking…" Impressionable young people such as this boy seem likely targets of tobacco advertising. A survey in 1996 of teenage smoking by the Center for Disease Control indicated that 34.8 percent of high school students age 17 and under said they had smoked in the previous month, up from 27.5 percent in 1991. Says Dr. Michael Eriksen, head of the Center's Office on Smoking and Health, "teenage smoking is almost a mathematical function of adult disapproval" (Mansnerus, 1996). In August 1996, President Clinton announced new steps by the Food and Drug Administration to limit the marketing of tobacco to minors.

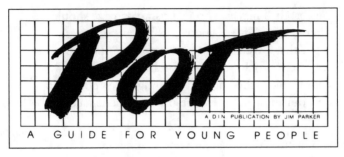

Are we having fun, yet?
The 'spectator drug' strikes again.

Up in Smoke:
Homo erectus meets Stono perplexus.

'Munchie Mania': THC tickles the taste
buds and thickens the waistline.

Bang for the buck: Today's strains pack more
punch and potential problems.

▲ **Figure 3.4** *Pictures from a brochure intended to educate students about the effects of marijuana on the body. Reprinted with the permission of Jim Parker, DIN Publications, Tempe, AZ.*

Readers found the words and pictures in the brochure *Marijuana: Health Effects* (see Figure 3.5 on the next page) to convey mixed messages. Some students believed it simultaneously encouraged and discouraged drug use. On one hand, they thought the picture of the marijuana leaf on the cover was attractive and that it presented a positive image of the drug. One tenth grader commented: "you could wear the leaf on your T-shirt or cap." On the other hand, they thought the fact-like presentation of the health effects made using marijuana seem harmful. They thought the words and pictures were "out of sync."

Students' responses to *Marijuana: Health Effects* were unlike those to *Smokeless Tobacco* in that students who read the marijuana brochure thought the health effects were dull and unpersuasive while students who read about smokeless tobacco found the health effects fascinating and interestingly gory. Our research team got the impression that citing health effects might be persuasive if the teenager could look in the mirror and imagine himself or herself looking different because he or she used a particular drug. For example, students mentioned how turned off to drugs they would be if they looked in the mirror and saw rashes, pimples, blisters, canker sores, or swollen (or missing) body parts (as could be the case in an alcohol-related traffic accident).

Alternatively, students "tuned out" almost immediately when the brochures depicted "inside the body" diagrams of the heart, lungs, or brain. This was especially so when the diagrams were of disembodied body parts such as line drawings of the heart, lungs, or brain. Several junior high school students mentioned that the pictures of body parts reminded them of their "boring biology books" or "Mr. Hall's health class."

To really get people's attention, show pictures of people who get high. Maybe little cartoon characters . . . well no, not actually the regular kind of cartoon characters. That would be dumb, but not black and white pictures, colorful pictures.

A lot of this writing won't have any impact. They should have a celebrity more in touch with kids telling them don't do drugs, like Madonna and show pictures (laughter). Well, maybe not Madonna but a celebrity—a heroine everybody could relate to.

This does not look interesting. I'd like to see the government come out with a brochure that is more on the offensive. Like how about showing a drug user as an astronaut to show how you can't do a good job if you're high.

This won't influence kids. Is this brochure aimed at parents? So parents can talk to kids? This medical stuff is boring. Who cares about the immune system? There should be more stuff parents could say to make kids care.

MARIJUANA
HEALTH EFFECTS

Micrograph of emphysema-related lung damage.

A D.I.N PUBLICATION BY CHRISTINA DYE

THC is particularly tricky: It breaks down into at least 25 different by-products before it's eliminated. And along the way, the metabolites never seem to stop moving.

They race out of the bloodstream within minutes and zero in on high-fat parts of the body, including the brain, sex glands, and heart.

Once there, they take their time in leaving. Unlike many drugs, which exit the body within hours, pot's breakdown products stick around for 3-5 days—even weeks, in heavy users.

What this build-up means isn't altogether clear. But researchers think it may contribute to many subtle, long-term problems, particularly in people who smoke often.

What sorts of problems?

Take the heart and lungs, for example. In the heart, pot can speed things up like a fast 50 minute hour in an aerobics class.

Heart rate can jump as much as 50 percent, making the heart work harder and blood pressure to build

The increase may only last minutes, but it can be a strain for users with heart problems or high blood pressure.

Problems in the lungs are even more clear-cut. That's where pot does its most visible work. Why? Because it
▶ Contains up to 50 percent more tars and cancer-causing chemicals than cigarettes.
▶ Disrupts the lungs' pumping and filtering, so less oxygen gets where it needs to go.
▶ Triggers major lung diseases, such as emphysema and bronchitis.

It's still too early to tell whether pot smokers will be as vulnerable to lung cancer and other problems as cigarette smokers. But common sense (and a few centuries' experience with tobacco problems) says it's just a matter of time.

Are any other body systems affected?

It sure looks that way.

Evidence is piling up about pot's ability to impair the immune system—the system that fights off infections and disease in the body.

This effect seems only temporary in most users, but it may explain frequent colds and sniffles in less-fit smokers.

Hormones, the internal chemicals that shape and control how and when our bodies develop, are more directly—and seriously—affected.

For example, it's now known that pot:
▶ Produces a short-term drop in the hormones that direct growth and development.
▶ Slows sperm production in males, resulting in fewer, less-healthy sperm cells.
▶ Upsets the balance of hormones that control the menstrual cycles of girls and women.

In adults, most hormonal changes seem only temporary.

But researchers say that young people in particular should avoid pot to prevent possible problems in growth and development.

What about the brain? Isn't that where pot does most of its work?

That's about the biggest question of all. Because no one's completely sure yet of how, exactly, marijuana works in the brain. Still, researchers think they're closer to real answers than they've ever been before.

And what they're learning is that marijuana alters the way thoughts and perceptions are processed in the brain.

And it does that in a number of ways:
▶ Pot tilts the balance of chemicals that control mood, energy, appetite, and concentration.
▶ It disrupts learning and memory-making in the brain, causing forgetfulness and problems in concentrating.
▶ Marijuana also seems to reduce brain cell sensitivity. Some researchers think that heavy

use may eventually damage connections between nerve cells.

That much is already known. But uncovering all of pot's effects in the brain is probably years away.

But this much is known right now: Heavy users in general and long-time smokers in particular are more likely to suffer ongoing problems than occasional smokers and non-smokers.

And that should give even the most confirmed pot smoker something to stop and think about.

Evidence is piling up about pot's ability to impair the immune system—which fights off infections and disease in the body.

Does marijuana cause birth defects?

Maybe.

Because marijuana and impending motherhood don't mix very well, either.

According to the best available evidence, a pregnant woman's pot use can cause unnecessary problems for her unborn baby, even raising levels of miscarriage and stillbirth.

That's because marijuana metabolites can cross the placenta to the developing fetus, and that can result in lowered birth weight, nervous system problems, and delayed learning.

And for most mothers-to-be, risks like those are just too high to justify getting high.

GETTING OFF GETTING HIGH

For most people, getting off marijuana isn't a big deal. All they need to do is stop—and stay stopped. Quitting isn't fun, but it rarely requires much more than a little time and a lot of willpower.

For others, it's more complicated. That's because some people let pot become a main part of life, like going to the bathroom in the morning or to bed at night.

For them, quitting is just the first step in an ongoing process, one that will involve finding alternative activities to fill the holes that giving up marijuana leaves behind. Places to start:
▶ Exercise. Any activity will boost your spirits and clear your mind. Running and aerobics, in particular, seem to turn on the same feel-good brain chemicals that pot does—without the risks.
▶ Diet. A junk-food-free diet (less fat, more fresh foods and whole grains) can help tone down the blues that can come with giving up pot. Avoiding caffeine and sugary drinks can help, too.
▶ Relaxation. Learn to relax. Try an activity or a skill that you may have forgotten for a while.

Now is as good a time as any to experiment with who you're going to be from here on out.

If you think you need help, get it. And if you've thought about it before, do something about it now. It's the best time we've ever heard of for doing anything.

I think kids will pick up this brochure. I picked up brochures like this a few times. It's attractive—you could wear a hat with this leaf on it, you know (laughter). The picture of the marijuana leaf is cool. It might make them want to try it.

Pretty much anybody could have wrote this. All they had to do was to look up information about pot, put it all together and you have something that they think is informational. But that's only if you read it. This looks like someone was given an assignment. They went to the library. Then they put it together in this and photocopied it by the thousands.

When I read this it seemed that they didn't know the answers to the questions they asked. What they should do is try to get kids' attention in the beginning. Then have stories of people of different ages. With pictures telling the bad things that happened to them when they took drugs—stories of people who got killed or died while using drugs.

You get out of this what you want to get out of this. I mean if you're a pot smoker and you're trying to quit, sure, you can find out how to quit. You know, stuff like that. But if you don't care about quitting. You're just going to blow off this brochure and not get anything out of it.

▲ **Figure 3.5** *Teenagers' responses to a brochure about the potential hazards of smoking marijuana on health. Reprinted with the permission of DIN Publications, Tempe, AZ.*

A one-page handout, *Inhalants* (see Figure 3.6), was designed to offer older students (particularly freshmen in college) advice about the effects of sniffing aerosols and solvents. It came as part of a package of six one-page handouts on drug education topics such as alcohol or cocaine. Students in our study rated it "the best" of the six. They thought the topic was interesting and wanted to know more about the effects of inhalants, particularly what happens moment by moment. This handout promoted a lot of positive discussion of the sort "it makes you really think about it."

Yet as the comments in Figure 3.6 show, some students were ambivalent about the effectiveness of the message. Students' criticisms arose mainly from the picture of the body. As one student questioned,

> I already know where my brain, heart, and lungs are. Do they think we're dumb? Can't they think of a better picture?

These students wanted content about drugs that was different from what they had seen already in brochures for younger audiences. As one college freshman student put it:

> I learned this stuff in high school. Now I want more depth about what inhalants do. You know, make me really want to read this with some new stuff.

Teenagers Construct an Image of Who May Be Speaking to Them

Although worrying over issues of writing and design are crucial, a key to composing persuasive documents may lie in anticipating readers' perceptions of who may be speaking, of the persona projected through the text. Much like document designers who may imagine their audience, readers may construct an image of the speaker as an individual or as an organization comprised of people—for example, an organizational identity or a corporate voice. Of course this image may or may not bear any resemblance to the actual author(s) of the text.[29] And it may or may not be the image that authors intend to project. Walker Gibson—one of the best prose style

---

[29] Research suggests that readers may also consider the *actual* author a critical piece of information. For example, readers have been known to judge the merit of scientific articles and proposals, at least in part, by who wrote them and by who is cited in the bibliography or references. Even when articles and proposals are judged using blind peer reviews, it is still sometimes easy to figure out who the author is by making inferences about who "shows up" in the references. Experts use these clues to develop hypotheses about what the author knows, what the text might say, what point of view it might take, how novel the arguments might be, or how truthful it might be (see, for example, Bazerman, 1985; Berkenkotter & Huckin, 1995; Blakeslee, 1993; Bobbitt-Nolen, Johnson-Crowley, & Wineburg, 1994; Charney, 1993; Wineburg, 1991).

There shouldn't be so much text. Images and symbols are much stronger. The stacking of text into blocks is a good idea. But the "Inhalants" paragraph turns me off. It's obviously aimed more toward people with backgrounds like in science or math.

Here they highlight the word "perceived" but then they don't highlight the categories of inhalants. It's like inconsistent.

You know, I like the way that they have the big blocks of type that have important information other than just the facts like people die in alcohol accidents. I mean most people already know that. But I think they could say a little more. They could have more indepth info about what inhalants are, and then go down to the diagrams and stuff.

I think that sometimes the diagrams like this are kind of effective. What if they used actual photos of things that happen that go along with drugs? Like things that happen, I mean, where the drugs come from, who's in danger, you know actual footage of what happened.

This looks to me like a health form, a handout you get at the nurse's office and never read. And putting these on this colored paper is like low budget. Even if you folded it like a brochure it would be more interesting than, you know, just simply giving the person a hand-out like it was torn off a bulletin board with frat announcements. It's much more interesting to have some kind of fold-out. Even in white and black.

I didn't even bother to read the long, involved paragraphs at the top of the page. I was more interested in reading the diagram and the lists. I wanted more diagrams and pictures and less text. And I mean text that went together with the visuals.

You know, when they're talking about volatile nitrates, they list amyl nitrate, and, I mean, why are we supposed to know what these are? Am I getting anything extra by reading this? NO!

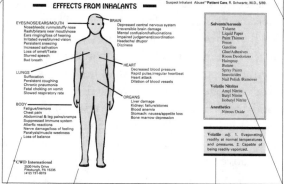

It went downhill in the diagram. I think they could have improved on the diagram and not made it such an eyesore. The way there's dots in there is kind of an eyesore. The picture is, well … it has no, it's just kind of a figure. It has no value.

They give you a definition of "volatile" way down at the bottom there and in the corner. And when it says "volatile" in the text, you have to go way down to the bottom to see what it means. And they don't define other terms at all, like "nitrates." What do I think they mean by that? I have no idea.

▲ Figure 3.6 Teenagers' responses to a flyer intended to warn them about the dangers of inhalants. Courtesy of Campuses Without Drugs, International, Inc., Pittsburgh, PA.

analysts of the twentieth century and someone who has written extensively on persona (1966, 1969)—suggests that opening a text is like meeting a new person you've never met who wants to convince you of something. When readers meet someone or some organization as they do through a document, they may try to bring a neutral attitude to the meeting.

> But we are bombarded with impressions of such power … that the most we can do is reserve our impressions with as much readiness for correction as possible.

> [W]hen someone tells us something, no matter how well we may know him, how adjusted to his appearance we may be, our understanding of *his* meaning is almost certainly more than verbal, involving a sense of the him that is talking, at the moment, in the flesh, before us. [italics in original] (Gibson, 1966, pp. 6–7)

Research tells us that readers may indeed construct an image of the person or organization talking, an image of someone trying to make an impression on them. Hatch, Hill, and Hayes (1993), for example, found that the essays high-school seniors write to gain acceptance to college are judged by university admissions counselors—at least in part—by the persona the student applicant projects. Admissions counselors in their study were asked to judge a set of 20 essays written by high-school students who wanted to enroll in a private university in the Northeast. Before the admissions counselors made their judgments, the essays were first evaluated by a group of writing teachers who agreed on which essays projected a positive or negative image of the person who wrote it. Counselors were told that all 20 essays were written by students who had been wait-listed (that is, they were at the top of the list as the next best candidates to admit). Counselors were advised that all 20 students were about equal from an academic point of view—that is, they had comparable grades, recommendations, and Scholastic Aptitude Test (SAT) scores. Their task was to admit 10 of the 20 students. The key difference in who the counselors chose to admit was the persona students projected through their writing.

Hatch and her colleagues found that the personality students projected was significantly correlated with the counselors' decisions. Counselors voted to admit students who conveyed a positive persona twice as often as those who projected a negative one. A positive persona was related to traits such as sincerity, sensitivity to other people, and eagerness to accept diverse perspectives. A negative persona was associated with insincerity, egocentrism, and insensitivity to diverse perspectives.

It is reasonable to believe that the persona projected by a document may play a powerful role in readers' acceptance of the message. Unfortunately, document designers typically have no way of introducing themselves and the organizations they work for beyond what they can make the reader see by means of words and graphics in various arrangements.[30] The visible language of a document invites the reader to make guesses about who is speaking, to infer a personality just as they might in a social situation.

But unlike a face-to-face encounter—where conversants get multiple cues for assessing how the communication is going through gesture, intonation, facial expression, the setting, and so on—the reader of a document has only words and images to go on. As document designers introduce themselves through a document, their choices of words and graphics have an absolute importance and finality. Unlike the give-and-take of face-to-face interaction, in which conversants can repair a failing conversation, document designers have no backup resources for fixing a bad interaction with a reader. Document designers get only one chance to dramatize themselves and the organizations they work for, one chance to communicate effectively with the reader. When evaluating a document, a reader is by no means ready to reserve judgment, to wait and see. "A reader can shut the book at any moment, at the slightest displeasure" (Gibson, 1966, p. 8).

Because our research team was interested in the persuasiveness of the drug education brochures, we wanted to know not only whether the message was presented in a convincing way, but also whether students constructed an image of the persona. Moreover, if readers imagined a person or organization behind that text, could that image influence their acceptance of the message? We uncovered these perceptions in three ways. First, during the protocols and interviews, we found that students made comments about their impressions of the message and the author without being asked. Second, in the focus groups, we asked students directly whether they imagined an author as they read. Third, in the surveys, we asked students to rate the persuasiveness of the brochures and, if they imagined an author, to characterize the person or organization.[31]

[30] Persona or voice is usually engendered by a combination of visual and verbal cues which suggest tone, point of view, and rhetorical stance (the attitude of the speaker toward the listener). People commonly identify the persona or the voice with the character of the speaker. The concept we use here corresponds to what Elbow (1994) calls "resonant voice," that is, "the relation of textual features to an inferred person behind the text" (p. xxxvii). The resonant voice has no necessary relation to the real person, group, or organization who wrote it; nevertheless, that voice may influence in powerful ways how the listener, viewer, or reader imagines the author. In some cases, the persona may be projected explicitly by mentioning the name of the author, by providing biographical information about the people who worked on the document, or by profiling the organization's history or philosophy. In these cases, although the author tries to manage the reader's image of who is speaking, readers construct their own image, sometimes agreeing with the image the author intended to project but at other times dimissing it as exaggerated, self-serving, or hypocritical.

[31] Our methods may seem a bit intrusive in that we prompted readers to think about the author, something they may or may not have done ordinarily. By asking students about whether they imagined an author, we may have inadvertently influenced them to imagine one. However, in the interviews and think-aloud protocols, conditions in which we did not prompt students to address issues of persona, we found that students more than occasionally made remarks in reference to a person or a group they imagined speaking. We hypothesize that documents routinely present readers with images of organizational or corporate identity (e.g., about values, knowledge, credibility, politics, trustworthiness, attitudes toward customers, and so on). Learning how readers make judgments about an organization's identity is a difficult area to study for it requires choosing research methods that do not lead the reader. This study suggests that, indeed, there is some psychological reality to the concept of persona.

Students reported that they sometimes pictured an individual writer, but more often saw the author in terms of an institutional "they," citing health agencies or the government as author. One student put it this way:

> I think the writer is someone who is, you know, higher up … someone who would never come to my neighborhood, but who wants to control us … someone like very detached.…

> They might have a purpose, but they're doing it just because they need to put out information someone told them to put down.

For the most part, students alternately referred to the author as "someone" or "they." For example, "the writer is *someone* who thinks we're dumb, so *they* talk down to you like you can't think, can't decide on your own." Or, "I hear *someone* like the drug czar talking behind this" (pointing to prose that says "Just say no, I'm too special"). In a few cases, students wondered if there was more than one author:

> Well, I'm not sure who wrote it because *maybe there was somebody who wrote the words and someone else who did the pictures*. I'm not sure if they're the same. It seems like *they* had a purpose but yet … though, I can't point to it. I don't know. [italics added]

Students made reference to their image of the persona in various ways, sometimes with remarks indicating they felt the author really cared about teenagers, other times indicating that the author seemed distant and out of touch. Here are some of the positive and negative characterizations of the author students generated in their own words.

Positive

- A kind and helpful person
- Someone who cares, who knows the pain of drugs
- A religious person with a sincere mission for other people
- Someone who has seen the trouble drugs can get you into
- A policeman who doesn't have an attitude that young people are jerks
- An organization trying to give some decent advice
- A person who wants to tell it like it is
- A person with a little sense of humor and loves children
- A doctor, a person who knows what the actual health effects would be

Negative

- An earthy kind of weird white person
- Not a person, a faceless organization
- Somebody paid minimum wage who is completely shut off from the outside world with outdated books and encyclopedias to work from
- A "big nurse" type, out of touch, no kids, and never talks to teenagers
- A bureaucrat in some big office in Washington who is dealing with out-of-date information
- A Nancy Reagan "wanna-be"
- A person we wouldn't like to meet
- A white hippie who thinks he's cool, but he's not
- One who may know the facts, but nothing of real life

Teenagers Imagine How the Speaker Views Them

Students' reactions to the drug brochures revealed that the selection, organization, and visual display of the content shaped not only their interpretation of the message but also their image of the audience they believed was being invoked through the text. In other words, real readers may use textual cues, both visual and verbal, to construct an idea of the imagined or "implied reader" (Booth, 1961, p. 138). Readers rely on the words and pictures to make guesses not only about what the text may mean but also about who is speaking to whom, about who is being "hailed" or "called out to" by the text, about the social relations between the speaker and the reader (Althusser, 1971). For example, in reading a brochure that presented a cartoon character of a girl sitting on a chair with a cat curled up next to her, one seventh-grade student said, "This must be written for first or second graders. Look at that kitty cat—it's too cute for someone my age."

Impressions created through the choice of content. From the point of view of an outside observer (that is, from our research team's perspective), document designers' writing suggested that they hoped teenage readers would adopt the role of "a thoughtful person who cares about being healthy, especially about the long-term health of their internal organs." Teenagers, however—from junior high to college—seemed "unfazed" by discussions of the long-term health effects of drugs such as anabolic steroids or alcohol, rarely commenting on them. They were interested in the immediate effects of drugs on the body, especially in physical damage they could see. The communicator's interest in getting students to ask questions about the long-term effects of drugs for themselves went largely unheeded.

Document designers also presented short narratives designed to depict "drug scenes" in which a smart teenager does the "right thing." These scenarios often went like this: boy goes to party, meets new friend, new friend offers drugs, boy "says no," and everyone lives happily ever after. Although these scenarios were designed so that the reader would imagine himself or herself in the situation of being asked "Want some alcohol or other drugs?" they were often viewed by students as "somebody else, not me" or "fake and unrealistic." Students did not take on the empathetic "that could be me" role the writers hoped for. Instead they said things like:

> I kind of hear Nancy Reagan's voice there. "Just say no,"
> boys and girls. That's all you need to do.

Students' interpretations showed that readers may ignore (and in some cases resist) the roles that communicators may hope they will take on during their reading. For teens in this study, the "just say no" message failed miserably.

Impressions created through the visuals. Many of the brochures our research team reviewed used simple line drawings that seemed to caricature teenagers, unintentionally or not. The style of a good proportion of these drawings was reminiscent of the bad cartoons in early military manuals, in which artists depicted strange-looking sergeants with pointy noses who gestured knowingly at a blackboard while forcing a smile. Another poor drawing style presented readers with Pillsbury Doughboy-like "pillow people" with friendly but personless snowman faces.

Some students asked if artists first drew a generic person and then made it a boy or a girl, depending on what was needed.[32] Other students who knew about "clip art" asked if the people who made the brochures used it at the last minute. Students commented repeatedly on the need for realistic photographs of young people in authentic situations; students exhibited no particular bias toward four-color photography, but realism seemed essential.

Recently some organizations that design drug education literature have moved toward more representational renderings they call "real style" (for example, companies such as Channing-Bete). Unfortunately, because the real-style brochures were unavailable when we carried out this study, we did not test them to see if students liked them better. What became evident to us from the brochures we assessed was that teenage readers

[32] Teenagers may be onto a strategy practiced by the communications departments of some organizations. For example, a revision of a 1991 brochure by the Ford Motor Company (Ford U.K., Dagenham, England) changed the race of its company's employees. In the original version, which presented a view of Ford U.K.'s forward-thinking hiring policies, 18 smiling employees stood side-by-side. Of the 18 workers, 5 were from minority groups: 4 blacks and 1 Indian with a beard and turban. In a revision, all of the black employees turned white, and the Indian executive lost his beard and turban. Citing an error by its ad agency, Ford paid each retouched worker $2,300. (CNN Prime News, February 21, 1996 and *Newsweek*, March 4, 1996, p. 55).

were already seasoned consumers of graphics. They knew what they liked—they wanted visuals that showed teens who were smart, savvy, and in control.

   Impressions created by attitude and tone. In the survey, we asked students if they could tell where the author thought the reader lived. Students checked suburbs (52%), rural (25%), and inner city (23%). Students tended to believe that the author viewed the reader as a teen from the suburbs who had never taken drugs and needed to "just steer clear of it" rather than "deal with it." In some cases, students from the inner city responded angrily to the idea that a brochure could make a dent on the problems people have with drugs. One African-American female said this:

> That brochure is insulting to my intelligence because if they really wanted to do something about crack, they should take the money they are wasting on these dumb brochures and on studies like yours and go find out who's bringing it [the crack] here. These are the people who you should be targeting this to. Not one person in the projects, not one poor person manufactures crack. That's the bottom line. I don't have nothing to say about that brochure, it's insulting.

> Tell them to take the money and go stop the government. They know where this mess is coming from and who brings it here. It's people making money on other people's problems and that's exactly what they are doing. This is a business.

> What about the money for treatment centers? Where are they going to get the money for taking care of all these babies that are messed up behind this mess. This brochure does not lift their spirits, does not give them a job, doesn't give them money, doesn't give them respect—none of that. That's what causes people to go to drugs, because they don't have a life worth living.

   Another focus group participant, building on her comments, captured why people from the African-American community may respond indignantly to the "idea of solving drug problems through a brochure":

> I want to say this as diplomatically as possible … and I don't want to hurt anybody's feelings, but for such a long time … heroin, cocaine, and all the rest of that drug mix (crack has been the most notable) … but for so many years they were in the cities and ghettos, black areas. With it tucked away in the ghettos, the rest of society just sort of covered it over, saying "well, it's not affecting me." Now

crack is affecting the nucleus of our society, you know, the brains of our society. Now our society is becoming afraid. Don't you think those people that it's been affecting for all these years don't notice this?

Comments like this one show that readers may respond as much to the idea of a document as to the actual text. Whether a document will be a good vehicle for conversing with readers depends on the reader's situation, making it important for document designers to be sensitive to the rhetorical appropriateness of the genres they choose (see Berkenkotter & Huckin, 1995). Inner-city students in this study tended to reject the brochure as a legitimate form of discourse for building bridges between the communicator and the reader.

These results also tell document designers that readers' interpretations of content may be deeply entangled with their personal conditions and social position (with either their actual situation or the one they presume the speaker wants them to take on). We found that many teenage readers were unwilling to buy into the implicit social and rhetorical contract the document invited them to take on, refusing to accept the not-so-subtle ideology that told them "let us show you how to act."[33] Students did not accept their assigned role[34] as the imagined reader and were skeptical of the rhetorical tactics used to invoke (even inscribe) them. Moreover, students' perception of the imagined reader and the persona seemed to interact. Many students didn't like "who they were supposed to be" and didn't want to listen to someone who in their words "thought they were superior and who knew what was good for teenagers."

These data show that readers' interpretations of documents may arise dynamically on the basis of their

- Knowledge, personal experience, values, and feelings
- Ideas about what the text says, about the visual and verbal content
- Impressions of who is speaking through the words and pictures (i.e., the persona, the organizational identity, or the corporate voice)
- Beliefs about who the speaker is addressing by the choice of words and pictures (i.e., readers' impression of the speaker's intended audience)
- Perceptions of the speaker's tone and attitude toward the audience
- Feelings about "the idea" of the document as an appropriate medium for communication about the content

While it is difficult to predict the particular mix that may be brought into play for any given document, this study makes clear that readers'

[33] For an interesting discussion of the social and ideological contracts between writers and readers that may be established through texts, see Brandt (1990), McCormick (1994), and Nystrand (1986).

[34] Reflecting on their previous work on audience, Lunsford and Ede (1996) point out that although they recognized the possibility of readers rejecting the role or roles that the writer wished them to adopt, they "consistently downplayed the possibility of tension and contradiction ..." (p. 170). Long (1990) hypothesizes that readers of fiction may be more willing to play or to accept a wider variety of roles than readers of non-fiction, especially when that nonfiction is addressing issues about which the reader already has strong opinions (p. 83). The findings of this study support his hypothesis.

constructions of meaning extend well beyond the ideas presented "in the text." Readers' interpretations of documents are shaped by thinking and feeling, by the subtle interplay of cognition and affect.

Why Evaluating Readers' Comprehension of Documents May Not Be Enough

This study makes clear how difficult it is to take the readers' point of view, especially when readers differ from document designers in age, race, culture, or experience. Readers' comments displayed sensitivity to the selection of content and to its presentation, to both informative and persuasive aspects of the brochures. In order to better understand the relationship between what student readers understood and what they viewed as persuasive, our research team evaluated a subset of the drug education brochures further.

In particular, we compared students' comprehension of brochures with their judgments of how effective the brochures were. We evaluated an original and a revised version of two different brochures, one about crack and another about marijuana. These brochures were produced by a single nonprofit organization, the original versions in the early 1980s, the revisions in the early 1990s. Of interest was whether the revisions influenced either students' understanding of the main points or their evaluations of the brochures' effectiveness.

A problem in making the comparison was that the content of the original and revised versions was not exactly the same. The revision of the brochure about crack made many of the same points as the original text, but had a new layout and different photos. In the revised version of the marijuana brochure, document designers cut the text from eight panels to four and reconceived the drawings and layout. Since the brochures had changed in significant ways, our analysis provides only a crude index of the differences between them. We were interested only in comparing them for how well their main points were understood and how effective students thought they were. Having two versions of the same text allowed us to make a more reasonable comparison than assessing brochures that differed in topic, goals, and so on.

Our research team evaluated how well students understood the main points by comparing the original and revised versions of the brochures on content items that were very similar. We first analyzed the claims (e.g., drugs can ruin your life) and facts (e.g., crack enters the bloodstream on your first puff) presented in each of the four brochures.[35] Based on this analysis, we designed two questionnaires that could be used for comparing the original and revised versions, one for testing both versions of the crack

[35] We found that the crack brochures made 24 claims and presented 30 facts, while the marijuana brochures made 7 claims and 15 facts (independent raters agreed 82 percent of the time about which were claims and facts).

brochures and another for the set of marijuana brochures. In addition to the comprehension questions based on the claims and facts, we asked questions about the effectiveness of the brochures (e.g., how much of an effect might the brochure have on someone thinking about taking drugs?).

The 140 students who participated (part of the same group as the main study) were between the ages of 17 and 21. They were enrolled in vocational or business schools; most were working toward a high school diploma or its equivalent. Students read a brochure silently to themselves and then answered the questionnaire; no student read both versions of the same brochure.[36]

Table 3.1 shows how students understood and assessed the brochures. As shown, the students understood the brochures quite well, scoring roughly 80 percent on each of the four versions. Students apparently had few difficulties with comprehending the main points—either the claims or the facts presented in the brochures. (Another possibility is that they already knew these main points, but in a separate question about this issue, students reported that they did not.) At least for the questions we asked, the revisions were equally good in terms of the clarity of main ideas. In fact, although the content had changed from the originals to the revisions, the revisions were remarkably consistent in helping students comprehend the same main ideas.

[36] We planned to randomly assign the four brochures within each class so that equal numbers of the "befores" and "afters" would be tested. However, some teachers whose students participated did not want students in the same class to read different versions of the brochures (they thought one group of students was getting the "bad" or "incorrect" information about drugs, and though untrue, this meant we could not test equal numbers of the original and revised versions).

▶ Table 3.1 *How teenagers understood the message of drug education literature in relation to how they rated the persuasiveness of the message. Teenagers took an objective test about the claims and facts presented in original or revised versions of brochures about crack or marijuana. They also rated how well the brochures communicated to them by responding to the question, "If a teenager was thinking about trying crack (or marijuana), what effect do you think this brochure would have?" Results show that although most students were quite able to under-stand the claims and facts, about half of them did not find the brochures very effective.*

Comprehending a Message Versus Judging Its Persuasiveness: A Comparison of Brochures About Crack and Marijuana

	Comprehension[a]	Persuasiveness[b]			
	Percent Correct	A Lot of Effect	Some Effect	Little Effect	No Effect
Original					
Crack (n = 53)	82	3	48	33	16
Marijuana (n = 49)	78	3	35	31	31
Revised					
Crack (n = 15)	81	7	53	13	27
Marijuana (n = 13)	81	5	45	27	23

[a] Students who read the crack brochures answered a 21 point multiple-choice questionnaire; students who read the marijuana brochures answered an 18 point multiple-choice questionnaire.

[b] Values represent students' responses in percentages.

Although students understood the brochures, their assessment of how well the brochures worked was mixed. As Table 3.1 shows, students were split in their opinions about how effective the brochures were. About half of them thought the brochures had "some effect" or "a lot of effect," while the other half rated both original and revised versions as having "little effect" or "no effect."

That so many readers rated the brochures as having "some effect" should please the document designers who worked on them. Generally speaking, the revisions improved readers' attitudes about how well the brochures were working (though not significantly so). But these findings also suggest that for at least half of the readers, their ability to understand the brochures seemed unrelated to their assessment of effectiveness. In a separate analysis, we found no significant differences between the comprehension scores of students who rated the brochure as having "no effect" and those who rated it as having "a lot of effect." In other words, students tended to score about 80 percent in their comprehension whether they liked the brochure or hated it.

Had we evaluated the brochures only by exploring readers' comprehension of the main points, we would have likely overestimated how good the brochures were. Conversely, had we asked questions only about the persuasiveness, we could not have learned that the main points were, in fact, well understood. These results point to the value of employing feedback-driven audience analysis and of collecting multiple views of what may be going on. In this way, document designers will have a better idea, for example, of whether to do one of the following:

- Keep the content but develop a new rhetorical strategy for presenting the ideas visually and verbally (given that readers understand it, but dislike it).

- Rethink the content and clarify the main points while keeping the presentation basically the same (given that readers don't understand it, but seem to like it).

- Throw out the document and start over (given that readers don't understand it and don't like it).

Exploring Gatekeepers' Views of Drug Education Literature

We interviewed teachers, guidance counselors, and drug prevention advocates to learn their opinions of the characteristics of the best brochures they had seen. We asked them how drug education brochures fit into the context of drug education, that is, one-on-one counseling, class discussion, group therapy sessions, and so on. We focused mainly on their opinions about the visual and verbal features that were effective in communicating with young people. Of the five people we interviewed, all had over eight years of experience in their areas. (These interviews lasted between one and three hours.)

All of the gatekeepers we spoke with mentioned the role of documents in giving students something to take home, something to reread. All thought drug education literature was useful and that it stimulated discussion. A second-grade elementary school teacher we interviewed, for example, felt the brochures were a good "motivator" and could be used as a "teaching aid to promote class conversation." While she felt the brochures could be "good food for thought," she pointed out:

> Often the brochures seem aimed at someone else rather than the kids. Maybe the parents. So I send them home with the kids to give to their parents. I don't know if they read them.

Interestingly, her comments about the visual design of the drug education literature echoed the sentiments of students:

> The only thing bad is some of the pictures. I often choose not to use the brochures or posters because of them. Now the other day, I got posters in the mail of people drinking at a party and smiling—not what I want to teach. I also got a poster of a bum drinking out of a paper bag and lying in the alley. You can't generate a good discussion from one of those things. And many times, the information that comes with these posters doesn't say how to use them in the classroom. We need that. Besides, I think they have a tendency either to make drinking look like fun or like it's something that only derelicts do. My coworker and I wind up devising our own materials.

A high school teacher who taught ninth grade commented on the writing of the brochures, particularly the scenarios. Again, this teacher's interpretation reiterated some of the students' points about the need for more thoughtfully imagined stories about teens:

> I think using little stories to draw in the reader is pretty effective. To me, a story is better than listing a bunch of symptoms. But then again, I find that the stories in the brochures too often seem contrived and the kids really react negatively to them. So instead of the brochures, I clip out stuff from the newspaper or Ann Landers or *Readers' Digest*. This way we can use something more real. The kids always ask, "Is this a true story?" And even if I have no idea in the world I generally say, "Yeah, I think it is based on a true story." Then they'll read it. Like if I use something from the *Readers' Digest* First

Person Drama Awards, they love it, because those stories are true. Look at television, I mean we've got *Emergency Rescue* and *Cops,* all those scene-type shows. Kids watch those. If the story feels like something made up, they ignore it. If the story feels real and has a little drama to it, the kids tune in. I find you really have to do something spectacular to get their attention these days.

Unlike the teachers, the counselors we spoke with seemed to stress that drug education literature "should not give a school-type feeling." They mentioned using brochures or posters on the first day of counseling, typically when the parent or guardian is present. As one counselor told us: "I read the brochures together with the parent and student, using them as a way to initiate a conversation and some reactions to what might happen to somebody on drugs." He saw the brochures as fitting into the larger context of human-to-human counseling:

To be honest, the brochures just aren't as effective as group discussion about stuff kids bring up themselves. I find if the brochure or poster has too much to do with school things, it becomes too much like work. They especially don't like those ones that seem like health class. To them, it's just more stuff to learn. Then they just won't talk. They don't buy into the game.

Exploring Document Designers' Feelings about Writing and Visualizing Drug Education Literature: The Dynamics of Action and Constraint

When it was possible to track down the individuals who worked on the brochures (as it turned out, this was incredibly difficult), we interviewed members of the document design team by telephone. We posed a set of open-ended questions about what they did in writing, illustrating, and designing the brochures. The questions dealt mainly with their work, their process in designing documents, and their organizational context (e.g., who had control over the text). These interviews lasted between 20 minutes and two hours each.

We found that writers and graphic designers of drug education literature were sometimes reluctant to talk about their work. On six different occasions, the response to our request for interviews went something like this:

That brochure is not attributable to anyone. We receive lots of assignments, that was just one of them. We can't say who wrote it. There are so many hands in the process. And we can't say that what was printed was what anyone in this office wrote. We have to go now.

We suspected that some document designers were unwilling to talk about their work because they were either too busy or too embarrassed by the outcome of the final brochures. Perhaps their writing and design had been "improved" by so many supervisors that they couldn't (or wouldn't) recognize their work anymore. As experienced professionals know all too well, many a good design is ruined in the final stages of development when people without expertise in document design feel compelled to put their mark on the text. These people often introduce inconsistencies, sometimes changing the original text so much that its originator may no longer feel comfortable saying that he or she worked on it.

We spoke with five document designers; all had seven or more years of experience. Two were subcontractors, that is, part-time employees hired to create or update particular brochures. Three were full-time staff; they conceptualized the writing and design of a variety of documents in the area of health education and risk communication, from persuasive brochures about the dangers of drugs to medical forms for the elderly to instruction guides on breast feeding.

The five document designers we did speak with were very informative. They characterized their writing and design process, their thoughts about the audience, and the difficulties they faced in carrying out their work. One writer described the process of designing documents and of analyzing the audience in this way:

> Five or six of us begin by sitting around a table and throwing out ideas. The group talks about the goals and objectives and then one person sits down to grind it out. We spend most of the group sessions trying to figure out how to get the reader to see the point, you know, what would get through to them. Once a draft is ready, the rest of us review it, fixing it here and there. Then we send it outside for review. Anything can happen to the text from then on. We're not really responsible for what happens after we send it out.

Another writer explained how she imagined the audience during the planning of a brochure she worked on:

> When writing this, I realized kids worry more about their friends than they do about themselves. So we created this scenario where we tried to show how a person can care about another person of the opposite sex without there being any sexual feelings. We also wanted to let the kids know that if you approach someone about drug abuse you may not get the result you want. We chose a boy helping a girl because it is less common.

This writer seems to be saying that drug education brochures may be most effective when readers are encouraged to think about helping their friends rather than themselves. The writer is also sensitive to not being trite in depicting boy-girl relationships. Though these considerations are not unreasonable and show a concern for the audience, they do not address the main problems students had with the brochures, that is, with the selection of information about drugs, the portrayal of teenagers, and the persona the organizations projected.

Document designers were also concerned with the type of illustrations presented and expressed difficulties with finding good illustrators[37] who were sensitive to teenagers' needs. As one team leader said,

> The art work was done by a free-lance artist. My team showed a bunch of illustrations to kids age 10 to 20. They picked this guy's work. One of my partners had a little trouble with the artist, well, he did some bizarre things with African-American hair that was 20 years out of date. We usually try to make our illustrations either of generic people[38] or to show diversity. I have to admit that the artist's newer stuff is better.

We found that for the most part, document designers had only general ideas about their audience(s). For example, they would describe their audience as "middle school kids" or "younger elementary school children." As one writer put it,

> After we figure out the target audience, we research the subject through our clearinghouse that carries a lot of information about what drugs are used and which ones are more popular. Then we try to think of some specific ways a kid could avoid using drugs. To find this we talk with people like policemen who go into schools and give presentations. Sometimes, we use feedback from teachers, pediatricians, and even parents. This way we can compile anecdotes about how drug education literature can be effective. Once we have the best stuff, we write it up, passing the draft back and forth until we are happy with it. Then it is reviewed for technical accuracy by many people both inside and outside the agency. They can suggest changes wherever they like. Sometimes what we get back is very different from what left.

We asked the writer how her group knew if the audience would like the brochure and how the document design team gauged whether teens would respond positively to their selection of content and design. She responded, "We rely on our experts—they know better than we do."

[37] With few exceptions, the illustrators were freelancers who were brought in at the tail end of the development of the brochures. As this study shows, when the illustrations are not well integrated with the text, they can cause problems for readers.

[38] Notice that the team leader thinks that projecting generic teenagers is a good idea, although our data suggests that teenagers hated this.

Our team found that the organizations that produce drug education literature mainly employed classification-driven or intuition-driven audience analysis. Rarely did they evaluate their materials with the intended audience.[39] One writer told us that they had conducted focus groups to choose among line drawings. Another said they occasionally do surveys about what students know about drugs. None of the document designers we spoke with collected teenagers' moment-by-moment responses to their drafts, such as by asking teenagers to provide think-aloud protocols.[40] As far as we could tell, most of the brochures were printed without any direct input from the intended audience. Even when student readers' feedback was collected, it was typically too vague to be very helpful in making the nitty-gritty document design decisions such brochures entail.

In some cases, we found that document designers' attention was focused entirely on issues other than the reader. One writer explained it in this way:

> There are some things we do that have nothing to do with the reader. We decide how many ideas to include not based on the reader, but on how long the document can be. For example, a threefold brochure can't explain more than two or three ideas. It's a crap shoot. You can't overpower the reader with ideas. If you give them three things you're lucky if two will work.... I rely more heavily on the experienced writers in my office for feedback on the brochures I write.... Another criteria for judging a good brochure is that it should be easily reproduced and laid out so it could be folded to be included in a mass mailing.

Although this writer talks as though experienced professionals regularly include only three ideas in a short brochure, we found that most of the short brochures that we examined contained 10 or more ideas; none contained as few as three. How many ideas readers can handle in a short brochure depends on what readers know, how many of the ideas are new to them, and how related those ideas are—that is, how coherent the text is—

[39] Surprisingly, the same situation exists for textbooks used in the schools from the elementary grades through college. Textbooks are rarely evaluated with students, only with gatekeepers such as teachers and members of school boards (see Chall & Squire, 1991). Moreover, the instructional materials used in thousands of corporate training classes are rarely evaluated for their effectiveness before they are "crash tested" on company employees.

---

[40] Although focus groups proved a useful method for gathering general impressions, the think-aloud protocols and the one-on-one interviews provided more detailed information about readers' interpretations. Unlike focus groups, these methods avoid the problems of peer influence on responses (see Kreuger, 1988). For example, some teenagers in our study appeared to be concerned with "acting cool" in front of other students. In testing a brochure about steroids with ninth-grade students, we noticed one boy who looked like he was trying out for the Pittsburgh Steelers. As students read the brochure, a number of them turned around and looked at him. During the focus group, students seemed reluctant to be very specific, as though they were holding back ideas. In an interview, a different young man asked, "Didn't you guys notice how uncomfortable questions about steroids made the class feel? He's popular, everybody likes him" [the athletic young man].

not on how many panels the brochure is.[41] If it were true that students could understand no more than three ideas in a short brochure, students in our study who read brochures with 10 or more ideas should have scored less than 30 percent on the comprehension questionnaires they completed.

Furthermore, contrary to the belief of the writer (just quoted) about the best judge of a text, research has shown that "experienced writers in the office" are typically not very good at simulating readers' interactions with a document (Bond et al., 1980; Hayes, 1989b). In fact, professionals may never consider the reader as a comprehender who engages with the document moment by moment. Writers we spoke with in this study did not imagine the audience as a reader, only as a stereotypical teen. When they tried to imagine someone interacting with the text, they used themselves as a model, remembering what it was like when they were teens. This strategy is worrisome given that today's teenagers face challenges about drugs that are unlike "the way it was" when document designers were growing up, even for document designers in their early 20s.

Document designers we interviewed may have gotten a false sense of security about how well their messages were working because the brochures complied with in-house guidelines about the best way to compose drug education messages. Figure 3.7 presents a set of U.S. government-developed guidelines for designing written materials for federal, state, or local drug prevention programs. Notice how the advice focuses writers'

[41] For a discussion of how readers make judgments about the coherence of text, see, for example, Halliday and Hasan (1976), Sanders (1992), and Witte and Faigley (1981).

Alcohol & Other Drug Terminology

Do Not Use	Use
Drunk Driving	Alcohol-impaired driving (because a person does not have to be drunk to be impaired)
Liquor (to mean any alcoholic beverage)	Beer, wine, and/or distilled spirits
Substance Abuse	Alcohol and other drug abuse
Substance Use	Alcohol and other drug use
"Abuse" when the sentence refers to youth, teens, or children (anyone under 21)	Use (OSAP aims to prevent use-not abuse-of alcohol and other drugs by youth)
Hard or Soft drugs	Drugs-since all illicit drugs are harmful
Recreational use of drugs	Use-since no drug use is recreational
Responsible use/drinking	Use-since there is risk associated with all use
Accidents when referring to alcohol/drug use and traffic crashes	Crashes
Drug Abuse Prevention or alcohol abuse prevention	Except when referring to adults. Use the phrase, "to prevent alcohol and other drug problems"
Mood-altering drugs	Mind-altering
Workaholic	(Since it trivializes the alcohol dependence problem)

Source:
Office of Substance Abuse Prevention, Prevention Plus II
US Dept of Health & Human Services, 1989, p. xvii.

◀ Figure 3.7 *Suggested words and phrases for designing drug education literature. This handout is intended to provide guidelines for authors of drug education literature so that they do not inadvertently encourage their audiences to try alcohol or drugs. (Capitalization inconsistencies were in the original.)*

attention on words and phrases rather than on the big picture. There is certainly no guarantee that composing a text using the "do" phrases will produce a rhetorically effective text. One writer we interviewed told us that "his writing process always begins by checking the mandated lists of allowable words and phrases." We also found that writers received training in identifying phrases that may send mixed messages to teenagers. The following examples provide an idea of the differences between "mixed" messages and "clear" ones.

Mixed message

> I was stupid to do drugs. I almost threw away my whole career. But now that I'm off drugs, I've been able to turn out hit records just like I used to.

Clear message

> Taking drugs lessens your chance of succeeding at whatever career you would choose to pursue. Drugs close the doors of opportunity.

Mixed message

> Several crack addicts have compared the sensation they derive from the drug to sexual orgasm.

Clear message

> People who snort cocaine frequently develop nasal problems, including holes in the cartilage separating the nostrils.

Guidelines such as these may be helpful, but only marginally so. The guidelines completely miss the major problems that we found—problems that stemmed from document designers' failure to understand the differences between themselves and their readers and the reality of their readers' lives. Instead, the guidelines directed writers' attention to choosing the "right words" and to saying things in the "right way." Although avoiding the use of examples that glamorize drugs is no doubt an important consideration, this study shows that other rhetorical considerations should take priority. These other considerations—tone, register, persona, rhetorical stance, choice of content, believability of scenarios, quality of writing, and quality of illustrations—have a significant impact on whether teenagers read and on their acceptance or rejection of a document's message.

In the words of one document designer we interviewed, "the guidelines were intended to eliminate the chance for misinterpretation and to ensure that messages actually reach their intended audiences."[42] We found that, instead, the guidelines seemed to act as mental straitjackets,[43] focusing document designers' attention rather narrowly—on "not getting it wrong." The guidelines reinforced the misguided idea that if document designers choose precisely worded "just say no" slogans, teenagers will be left with only one interpretation of the message. This myopic focus on crafting phrases appeared to take writers' attention away from creating realistic portrayals of the difficult drug-related situations that teenagers often face.

Be Smart! Don't Start! (Figure 3.8) illustrates this point. This brochure is a revision of Figure 3.2, *"SNAPPY ANSWERS."* As shown, the document designers use the same poorly phrased question (i.e., "Want Some

[42] In Chapters 5 and 6, I discuss why it is impossible to eliminate the chance for misinterpretation. I argue that instead we can constrain interpretation through our visual and verbal moves.

[43] For analyses of the limitations of guidelines and their possible negative effects on creativity, see Duffy, Post, & Smith (1987); Flower, Schriver, Haas, Carey, and Hayes (1992); Steinberg (1986); or Wright (1988c).

◄ **Figure 3.8** *A revision of the brochure presented in Figure 3.2, "Here are Some SNAPPY ANSWERS to the Question: Want Some Alcohol or Other Drugs?" (p. 174).*

Alcohol or Other Drugs?") to organize the brochure's content (see the top of the second panel). Document designers seem concerned with inviting readers to imagine themselves responding to questions about drugs by saying, "No, I'm smart! I'd rather...."

Although the revision has a more positive tone in that it encourages readers to "be nice to themselves" instead of telling them to say "No thanks, I'd rather walk my pet python," the revision introduces a number of new audience-related problems. For example, it is unclear what age group this brochure is intended to reach. The picture of the little boy under item #4 (who is supposed to "Draw a dream!" in the cloud and fill in "My Name" on the blank line) seems aimed at a young child, perhaps in grades one or two. However, the girl illustrated next to item #1 is doing something that teenagers do, talking on the phone. The teen who might write in the phone numbers of her friends might not be interested in writing her name on a blank line under item #4 nor in seeing herself depicted with a rat-tail hairdo (a style more suited for a five-year old).

On the first panel of the brochure, there is a picture of a boy being served a Thanksgiving turkey. At least it looks this way until one examines the illustration more closely. Actually, the boy is helping his mother set the table, but he looks like he is sitting down because his legs are not shown. Either way, one wonders what this picture has to do with not taking drugs; does it mean "eat your turkey" or "help mom set the table instead of taking drugs"? Although presenting illustrations of young people in various situations is a good strategy that is likely to increase younger students' interest in the brochure,[44] older students might interpret these particular illustrations as poking fun at young people, given that they depict noses, ears, chins, and hair in an odd, even ugly way. (The illustrations of the mother are equally ugly.)

Unfortunately, we have no student feedback[45] about this revision. Our own intuition suggests to us that readers would find that this brochure conveys "mixed messages" of a different sort than designers were being trained to avoid. In other words, the mixed message is not in generating what drug prevention counselors call "pro-drug ideas," but rather in presenting a confusing message about who the audience is. Unfortunately, as we have shown, intuitions can be unreliable. An audience analysis in which document designers considered teenagers' actual responses to the original brochure could have helped them identify how young people of different ages interpreted the illustrations and could have suggested ways to tailor the revision for a particular age group. As is, it appears that the revision is certainly an improvement over

[44] Legenza and Knafle (1978) report three key components of illustrations that may have the greatest appeal to elementary school children: the number of actions in the illustration, the number of children presented, and the number of people presented. Similarly, babies often like to watch videos that present other babies.

[45] We had already completed the study when I picked up the revision at a street fair in my neighborhood; local police officers were passing it out to children and parents.

the original, but until we try it out with a real audience, we won't know for sure.

The Document Designer's Dilemma Revisited: Standing between the Reader and the Organization

The document designers we spoke with worked in a rather volatile environment. They had to deal with frequently changing mandates and directives from their superiors, many of whom had political ties to the U.S. Congress. The document designers we interviewed who were full-time staff had experienced several reorganizations, which often left the team demoralized and worried about the security of their jobs. Sometimes reorganizations meant that the boss and the chain of command changed. One designer told us:

> One day you are working for someone who has an enlightened view of communication, the next day you work for someone who only cares about not offending people on the Hill [referring to Capital Hill in Washington DC]. We have to watch our backs now. You never know when the ax will hit.

Several writers commented that they felt "overworked and underpaid" and that "things had been better before the cutbacks." In the words of one writer:

> I don't always do my best work, I can't. There isn't time to think around here. I got reamed for taking time to plan a poster I worked on last month. My supervisor said planning was a waste of time. He just wants me to hurry up and get it out.

Moreover, we found that the social and political context in which document designers worked appeared to reward them more for "not making textual waves" than for learning about their readers and inventing ways to talk with them. This made us rethink our early attitudes about what the problem with these documents was.

Early on in the project, members of our research team speculated that the problem was with the document designers' education—perhaps they had no formal training in writing or design. If true, the number of rhetorically ineffective decisions they made about the content, tone, persona, illustrations, and visual design were at least understandable, though still unfortunate for readers. We wondered if the document designers had any firsthand experience in usability testing or participatory design. Our assumption, we admit, was that bad writing or design could probably be traced back to bad writers and designers. But as these results show, writers and designers may not have always made the textual decisions that introduced the problems into the brochures. Writers and designers were "stuck in the middle" between the reader and the organization, and often it seemed the organization's ideas about content, tone, and persona took priority over finding out what readers wanted and expected.

These results suggest that only by examining the context in which documents are produced is it possible to get an idea of "where things may have gone wrong." We imagine that any of the following might adequately characterize the problem:

- The document designers were not very skilled in writing and design; they also had little understanding of the needs and expectations of a teenage audience.

- The document designers were skilled in writing and design, but their intuition-driven audience analyses gave them ideas about what teenagers needed and expected that were too vague and sometimes wrong. Given information about how teenagers actually read the brochures, the same document designers could have done a much better job.

- The document designers were skilled in writing and designing for a teenage audience, but their original high-quality drafts of the brochures were "redesigned by committee," making the final drafts less effective than the originals.

We suspect that the real answer lies between the second and the third possibilities, that document designers were "up to the task," but they needed better information about the audience, less rigid constraints, more control over the text, and less micromanagement of the text by supervisors. Our study also suggests that in order to do a good job, document designers need adequate funding and a supportive atmosphere in which they can be creative. It's hard to produce an engaging brochure for an audience as critical as teenagers when working with a shoestring budget. These findings suggest "missed opportunities" as well as outright losses for several important stakeholders in drug education literature:

- *First,* and most important, teenage readers miss the chance to read something that could potentially discourage them from taking drugs.

- *Second,* the taxpayers whose dollars funded the brochures lose because stacks of brochures sit in teachers' closets and guidance counselors' stock rooms unread. Gatekeepers selectively filter what readers see.

- *Third,* the individual writers and designers lose because no matter who could be blamed for the design of a poor document, the document design group usually "takes the heat." Not exactly the way to make a document design group secure against threats of downsizing and outsourcing. Clearly, document designers need to assert themselves as reader advocates, demonstrating how everyone wins if the reader wins.

- *Fourth,* the organizations who produced the brochures lose. They not only forfeit the opportunity to promote a positive organizational identity, but also miss the chance to communicate effectively with their readers about a real social problem they could have a positive impact on.

LESSONS LEARNED
ABOUT ANALYZING THE AUDIENCE
AND CONSIDERING THE READER

This study shows us that when it comes to designing documents that inform and persuade, it is critical to consider the real readers' thoughts and feelings. It tells us that the model of the reader that document designers build matters a lot. If document designers who composed the brochures erred, it was in placing too much faith in the adequacy of intuition-driven audience analysis, in relying only on the ideas about readers they created in their minds. As the teenagers' comments made apparent, there was a significant gap between the readers document designers imagined and the real readers. This is not to say that document designers should not or will not construct an imagined reader (even if they try not to). As Walter Ong (1975) has said, "the writer's audience is always a fiction," even when the representation of the audience is constructed on the basis of real readers (p. 17). Even so, document designers overlooked the benefits of talking with teenagers, of finding out how young people felt about drug education. Instead, they relied on personal reflection, experts, peers, guidelines, and source materials. They never anchored their intuitions by listening to teenagers talk about their actual dealings with drugs, pushers, or the drug culture. Many never heard the voice of a teenage boy or girl reading a drug education brochure and forming an opinion about it.

The study also demonstrates that teenagers' interpretations of the brochures involved more than comprehending the words and pictures, more than simply understanding the content and structure. Although a document's content and design provide important, even crucial, "instructions" for readers, instructions that allow readers to construct a coherent mental representation of the text,[46] they fall short of fully explaining

[46] Early research about how people understand text tended to emphasize the primary influence of the text's structure on comprehension, assigning little importance to the influence of what may happen "outside of the text" (e.g., see Kintsch & van Dijk, 1978; van Dijk & Kintsch, 1983). More recent accounts (e.g., Kintsch, 1990) suggest that people use cues from the situation to assign meaning to the text. Kintsch shows that readers of stories may produce a "situational model" of a text that is independent of their mental representation of the text. For implications of this work for writing, see Greene and Ackerman (1995).

whether people are moved by what they read. Moreover, they do not predict what sort of dialogue the text may provoke the reader to engage in. Analyzing the audience, then, means considering how readers may

- Construct the meanings of the prose and graphics on the basis of their thinking and feeling (cognition and affect).

- Interpret the role they are expected to take, a role established through rhetorical clues set up by the design of the prose and graphics.

- View the messenger of the text (e.g., the persona, organizational voice, or corporate identity) and the messenger's attitude about the reader.

- Feel about the way the visual and verbal message constructs them as an intended audience.

- Respond to "the idea" of the text as a legitimate form of communication.

As we saw, teenagers in this study had problems not only with document designers' ideas about the imagined reader, resisting the role the text assigned them to take on, but also with the persona the brochures projected. These difficulties rendered many of the documents ineffective, even when students comprehended them. From the perspective of the audience, the drug education literature seemed to present an ethos that showed "someone had noticed the problem" rather than "someone was doing something about it." Students' comments revealed that readers do not view documents as neutral dispensers of information. Teenagers recognized the content as value-laden and didn't necessarily appreciate the values which were being presented.

These findings also raise the issue of management in document design. Failing to see the value of taking the reader seriously, of taking the time to plan the content around the audience's needs, can bring negative consequences, not only for readers—the most important constituency—but also for document designers and for the organization itself. Failing to consider the knowledge and values of the real audience can create a lasting negative identity for the organization that may take years to shake.[47] Building a positive identity (and here I am talking about more than just logos, product naming, or graphic style) requires organizations to develop a distinctive voice—through the interplay of text and graphics—that makes evident to audiences that their knowledge and values are understood, respected, and not taken for granted.[48] Whether we call our audiences readers, users, customers, or stakeholders, they all want the same thing: to feel that someone has taken the time to speak clearly, knowledgeably, and honestly to them.

[47] Consider, for example, the IRS. Even when their document designers create well-designed tax forms and instruction guides, the media and taxpayers want to "take aim" at tax forms sight unseen.

[48] Figuring out how people construct ideas about organizational or corporate identity warrants the attention of document design researchers, for it may determine substantially whether people choose to read. Experts in the graphic design community have argued this point for a long time (see Meggs, 1992b, pp. 380–409); however, few graphic designers have provided empirical support for this argument.

Organizations can separate themselves from their competition by projecting their unique organizational ethos in all of their communications, from routine correspondence to the most important documents. Figure 3.9 presents a form letter I received after requesting a catalog of collector's stamps from the United States Postal Service. In addition to not saying why the Postal Service did not stock the stamps that were advertised at my local post office, they "apologize for any customer service" they offered (see the letter's closure section); not exactly the way to make customers feel confident in the speaker.

PHILATELIC FULFILLMENT SERVICE CENTER

**UNITED STATES
POSTAL SERVICE**

December 28, 1995

Dear Philatelic Customer:

Thank you for your Philatelic order. We must return your order for the following reason(s). Please resubmit in the enclosed return envelope.

XXX The Philatelic item(s) you ordered or inquired about are no longer available from this facility. These items may be available through a stamp dealer.

____ Shipping and handling fee for foreign orders is $8.20 (orders $20.00 and under. Add $5.00 to progressive values per domestic rate schedule in catalog).

____ Make remittance payable to the Philatelic Fulfillment Service Center or U S Postal Service.

____ Your order was received without payment. Please resubmit your order with a check, money order, or you may choose to authorize a charge to either your Visa, MasterCard or Discover credit card.

____ Your personal check is not signed.

____ Your check was received without an order for Philatelic items or instructions for deposit to a subscription account.

____ Foreign collectors must remit payment with a check drawn on a U.S. Bank or an international money order.

____ Remittance/funds are insufficient for the cost of the items ordered plus shipping and handling. A catalog is enclosed for your convenience.

____ The credit card number provided has been rejected as invalid. Please compare the number for verification and return your order for processing.

____ We accept Visa, MasterCard and Discover. Please resubmit your order using one of these credit cards, of a check or money order.

        We apologize for any
Customer Service
1-800-STAMP-24

Enclosures

8300 NE UNDERGROUND DR PILLAR 210
KANSAS CITY MO 64144-9998

◀ **Figure 3.9** *A form letter from the U.S. Postal Service that suggests someone isn't "minding the store" when it comes to communicating with the customers. (Inconsistencies in the writing and design were in the original.) Notice the final sentence of the letter is cut off, the format of which, unfortunately, becomes visually associated with the name "Customer Service," making the letter appear to "apologize for any customer service."*

Organizations need to figure out what makes their personality unique and devise an integrated approach that puts that identity into prose and graphics—from planning to production. However, it will not be possible to create a voice that speaks honestly, consistently, and clearly to audiences unless managers give document designers the time, financial resources, and intellectual and artistic freedom to do their best work.

Moreover, these findings suggest that document designers themselves must take more responsibility for what happens to their documents. That some of the professionals we interviewed in the drug education study seemed unconcerned about what happened to their text "after it left their desk" raises questions of personal integrity.[49] Document designers must stand up for the reader, making certain that they know what happens to the documents they work on. They must ensure that the readers' needs are indeed met in the final printed document. *In a real sense, all document designers—no matter where they work—stand between the organization and the reader. As the best and sometimes only link with the audience, document designers must take the responsibility for worrying about whose vision underlies the communications they create.* Implicitly or explicitly, this issue comes into play in the design of every document.

The study also shows, however, that even well-intentioned document designers who try their best to meet the reader's needs may still produce prose and graphics that evoke anger or ridicule. This observation underscores how essential it is to "catch readers in the act of interpretation"—to test what we write and illustrate. In addition, these results point to the very real need for education and training programs that can help document designers increase their sensitivity to readers' cognitive and affective needs.

Written materials are only one component of effective drug prevention campaigns, but they are important because they provide the audience with something to hold in their hands, with something to take home. These results suggest that the written materials used in many antidrug campaigns may be failing because the documents are not designed with an awareness of the audience's knowledge, needs, and values. A deeper understanding of the audience is crucial if document designers are to be effective in anticipating how members of culturally diverse audiences may construct visual and verbal messages directed at them.

This chapter has shown that when readers come to documents, they may respond not only to the message but also to the messenger. As readers construct ideas about the message or the messenger, they engage in a dialogue with the words and pictures, bringing their thoughts, feelings,

[49] See Dragga (1996) for a survey of writers' opinions about ethical practice in document design.

and values into play. Document designers who are sensitive to the
dynamic interplay between cognition and affect during interpretation are
much more likely to create documents that people will actually read.

...AND CONNECT THE H-73DB DEEBLE SIGNAL AMP TWIXT THE VCR AND THE LBD DESCRAMBLER BOX ZH-310B ...

4

The Impact of Poor Design: Thinking about
Ourselves as Users of Texts and Technology

This chapter explores the ways in which design can influence how people think about themselves. ❧ It begins by asking how design may affect people's beliefs about their ability to use texts or technology. ❧ It illustrates these issues with a study of where people assign the blame when "things go wrong" while they are using documents or products, showing that documents and products can make people feel incompetent about themselves as users and as comprehenders. ❧ A second study of people trying to use home electronics equipment examines how poorly designed documents and poorly designed products may conspire to create serious cognitive difficulties for users. ❧ This study also explores the idea of "problem space," that is, the set of plausible alternatives that people may need to consider in figuring out how to solve a problem. ❧ Overall, the chapter provides empirical evidence that poor design may have a negative impact on readers' perceptions of themselves.

Left-hand page. *Opus of "Bloom County" discovers he is "technologically-challenged" when he tries to program his VCR. Created by Berke Breathed; reprinted with permission of Little, Brown and Company, Boston, MA.*

Companies that manufacture consumer electronics assume people buy fax machines and microwave ovens because these products make life easier and more enjoyable. Rarely do companies consider that their products may not be as fun or as easy to use as the engineers who designed them may believe. In fact, almost every consumer has purchased at least one electronics product—from a calculator to a camcorder—that now sits idly collecting dust because learning to use it was simply too frustrating. Consumers can easily recount stories about products that have either more features than they want or features they would like to use but for some reason cannot. The source of the problem is twofold. On one hand, many products are designed to impress engineers. Although technically elegant, such products may baffle the intended audience.[1] On the other hand, the documents that explain the use of products are often put together (one can hardly say designed) as an afterthought at the end of the product development process. To make matters worse, the people putting together the documents often have neither experience nor interest in document design.[2]

[1] For a number of true tales about the relationship between design, technology, and human error, see Casey (1993).

The prevalence of poor product design and document design partly explains why people have so many problems in learning to use technology. But it does not explain how people think about the problems they experience while using texts and technology. It is important to study how people represent the troubles they experience because their beliefs may affect how they approach new situations; similarly, beliefs about documents or products in one setting may influence people's beliefs about another. It is likely that positive experiences will motivate people in ways that could make learning from texts or about technology easier, while negative encounters may leave them apprehensive.

It is also important to study how people interpret the problems they experience because the ideas people hold about the source of the problem may be wrong. For example, when we have difficulty understanding, we may interpret our trouble in a variety of ways. We may blame the text and mumble to ourselves: "This is really badly written." We may blame the topic: "The tax code is so complex that no one could make it clear." We may blame the manufacturer: "I'm never going to buy another

[2] For example, it is still common in some consumer electronics companies to assign the task of writing and designing the instruction guides to (1) engineers (so they can learn the company's line of products or because they know the technology) or (2) members of the marketing staff (because they know the audience demographics). These specialists are thrust into the situation of writing and designing for users, when most have not even had as much as one hour of education about document design. As more companies become aware of academic programs in document design, perhaps this worrisome (and dumb) practice will come to an end.

product from that company because data entry in a spreadsheet program should be easier than this." Or we may blame ourselves: "I'm not technical enough to understand computers." Locating the source of the problem accurately is part of the path toward its solution. User-interface design advocate Donald Norman (1988) recounts a number of anecdotes about how users of technology assign blame when "things go wrong" (p. 40).

However, there have been few systematic investigations of how readers assign blame for the troubles they experience. Moreover, there are almost no studies of how people think *and* feel as they engage with consumer products and the documents intended to explain them. In the two studies that follow, my colleagues and I explore people's interactions with texts and technology, showing that poor design may not only prevent people from accurately making sense of products and documents, but may also influence people's ideas about themselves.

WHY CAN'T I GET THIS THING TO WORK? THE BLAME STUDY

The "blame study" came about in response to a request from a large Japanese consumer electronics manufacturer to help improve the quality of its design. The company's marketing department had received hundreds of complaints from customers about the poor design of products such as video cassette recorders (VCRs) and stereo systems. Customers reported that these products were confusing and hard to understand. The company's marketing department had also received many irate letters about the incomprehensibility of their instruction guides. The company's managers were not certain why customers were having so many problems, but they suspected that the source of the difficulties was not related to the design of the products but to the design of the documents that explained them. Their request was to find out what was going on.

Our research team approached the problem with a two-part study. In the first part, we focused on four types of products that the company had received the most complaints about, asking consumers about their experiences with such products and the instruction manuals that accompanied them. In the second part, we explored how people learned to operate three of the company's top-selling products; here, we asked consumers to learn the products by using the instruction guides provided by the company. What first began as an attempt to find out "what was going wrong with the products and the instruction guides" ended up revealing in some rather unexpected ways the importance of people's thinking about themselves as users of technology and comprehenders of instructions.

Investigating People's Attitudes about Texts and Technology Based on Their Past Experiences

[3] My collaborators in this study were Michele Matchett, Norma Pribadi Polk, Mary L. Ray and Liang Chen. I am greatly indebted to them for their assistance. I also thank Marc Auerbach of Apple Computer (formerly of Mitsubishi Electric Sales of America), Remi Audoin from Thompson Consumer Electric (France), Richard King of Panasonic of America, owned by Matsushita (Japan), and Yoji Ozato and Michiko Horikawa of Sony (Japan) for posing to me questions about how consumers actually use instruction guides, questions that stimulated my thinking about the problems people have with instructional texts and technology.

Our research team[3] began by meeting with our corporate sponsor, who selected four consumer products that had caused the company a lot of headaches:

- Video cassette recorders (VCRs)
- Telephone answering machines
- Cordless telephones
- Stereo systems

To find out more about why consumers were having problems with these types of home electronics, we generated a survey for each of the product categories. The four surveys were aimed at tapping people's ideas about home electronics generally as well as their ideas about the design of the products and the instruction guides for one of the four product categories. The surveys were composed of eight pages of close-ended and open-ended questions and had two sections. The first part of each survey posed the same questions (e.g., "Generally speaking, how do you read instruction guides?"). The second explored consumers' memories about using the particular features of one of the four products (e.g., How often do you use "auto redial" on your cordless phone? or, If your stereo has a "shuffle play" feature, how often do you use it? For what purpose?)

We recruited participants for the survey as they walked out of video rental shops and electronics stores located within a 50-mile radius of Pittsburgh, Pennsylvania. Our aim was to survey 50 people for each of the four consumer products with roughly equal numbers of men and women for each product in each of six age groups: under twenty, twenty to twenty-nine, thirty to thirty-nine, forty to forty-nine, fifty to fifty-nine, and sixty and over. We canvassed customers as they exited these stores about whether they had recently acquired one of the four products, and if so, asked if they'd be willing to answer some questions about two things:

- Their habits in using the consumer product and the instructions that came with it
- Their attitudes about the problems they experienced "when things went wrong"

Participants self-selected which survey to fill in based on the product they had acquired most recently. In total, 201 people volunteered to participate (107 men and 94 women).[4] Participants varied in education and socioeconomic background; their occupations ranged from postal worker to waitress to ballet dancer to software engineer.

[4] All participants were paid $12 for their time (which was about half an hour).

What We Found Out about People's Past Experiences in Using Products and Documents

Table 4.1 shows how participants responded to the question: "Generally speaking, how do you read instruction manuals?" Roughly 80 percent of the consumers reported they scanned their manuals or used them as reference, while 15 percent said they read manuals cover-to-cover and 4 percent claimed they never read them at all.

How Consumers[a] Read Documents	
Cover-to-Cover	15%
Scan	46%
Read as Reference	35%
Never Read	4%

[a] There were 201 respondents.

◀ Table 4.1 *How consumers responded to the question: "Generally speaking, how do you read instruction guides?"*

Since this question required participants to generalize their experience across the various manuals they had encountered in the past, we thought it could also be informative to ask a similar question about the manual that accompanied the consumer product they had acquired most recently. In particular, we asked if they read the manual

1. Before they used the product

2. During their use of the product

3. Only when they got stuck using the product

4. Not at all

Table 4.2 (on the next page) presents participants' responses for each of the four products. (The participant groups were independent, that is, no one filled out more than one survey.) As shown, across the four groups of participants, most people say they read the manual before using the product (23 percent) or while they try it out (41 percent); thus, 65 percent of participants report they use manuals in order to learn about their new product. In contrast to their responses to the previous question about using manuals generally (see Table 4.1), fewer people (17 percent vs. 35 percent) say they used their most recently acquired manual as a reference guide but more report not using the manual at all (19 percent vs. 4 percent).

We were surprised by consumers' responses to both questions because we expected they would report overwhelmingly: "I do not use instructions." The anecdotal literature gives the impression that people never use instruction guides and has led to articles such as "Nobody Reads Documentation" (e.g., Rettig, 1991). Some companies justify not spending much money on their instructional documents based on the premise that people never read them. But data from this study as well as from a recent survey of people's use of computer manuals (DeTienne & Smart, 1995) suggest that the facile assumption that no one reads documents is simply wrong. If anything, as Grech (1992) points out, users are telling companies that they want better documents and that they contribute significantly to customer satisfaction. As the data show, even in the worst case (using the manual to learn about a telephone) 68 percent of consumers report they used the manual either before they started, while they were trying it out, or when they get stuck. With VCRs, 92 percent of consumers report using the manual at some point. It is clear that the design of the manual is something manufacturers need to worry about and take more seriously. Across the four product categories, more than 80 percent of consumers report using the manual some of the time. The distribution of responses indicates that the higher rate of not reading is associated with instruction guides for telephone answering machines (TAMs) and cordless phones.

Why might people be less likely to read manuals for some products than others? Wright, Creighton, and Threlfall (1982) found that British

▶ Table 4.2 *How consumers responded to the question: "How did you read and use the instruction guide that came with your product?" (referring to the last product they acquired in one of four categories). As shown, more than 80 percent of consumers report using manuals. Most people try out the product while reading the manual, suggesting that a well-designed manual can help consumers take full advantage of the features and functions a product offers. Given the fact that consumers do read manuals, companies might consider the manual as a good way to help reinforce a positive corporate identity after the sale of a product or service has been made.*

How Consumers Reported Using Their Most Recently Acquired Instruction Guide

	Product				Average
	VCR (n = 51)	TAM[a] (n = 52)	Phone (n = 47)	Stereo (n = 47)	
Read the instructions through BEFORE trying a new function	22	23	23	24	23
Tried the new function WHILE reading the instructions	49	40	30	47	42
Referred to the instructions only when confused	22	13	15	18	17
Did not use the instructions	8	23	32	12	19

Note. Values represent responses in percentages (n = 197; 4 of the 201 participants did not respond). To enhance the discriminability of the data, percentages have been rounded to the nearest whole number; due to rounding, column totals may not equal 100 percent.

[a] TAM stands for telephone answering machine.

consumers' decisions about whether to read were based on whether they thought the product needed instructions. Consumers who participated in their study believed they should not have to read instructions for a product such as a TV because they expected to simply plug it in and switch it on. Perhaps consumers didn't read the manuals for telephone answering machines and cordless phones because they felt such products should be easy to figure out without any instructions.

The findings in the study by Wright and her colleagues and in this one remind us that reading instructional documents is not a monolithic process that is always executed in the same way. Consumers' reading habits of documents will necessarily vary, depending on the type of product the document accompanies, on how familiar they are with the product category, on how the product "speaks to them" through the design of the interface, and on the context in which the product will be used. (For example, people seem more likely to read at home than at work; they also seem to read more when the product is their own rather than someone else's.) As I discussed in Chapter 3, people tend to read documents only when they have the time and believe that reading will benefit them.

In talking with the consumers who participated in our survey, we found that even when people read their instruction guides—believing the information would be helpful—they were not always rewarded for their effort. Many reported having problems with the products and being unable to solve them by rereading the manual. Consumers reported exasperation with some products, particularly VCRs. As one young man put it:

> I have a master's degree and I work with high-end computers all day, but when it comes to my VCR, I never seem to be able to program it. I read the manual and I saw the onscreen menus. They were useless. I had to ask for help. I hate that feeling.

Shoe   By Jeff MacNelly

"Shoe" created by Jeff MacNelly; reprinted with the permission of Tribune Media Services, Chicago, IL.

This man is not alone in his feelings of inadequacy. Many people find that reading documents can be a kind of punishment, a loathsome activity that produces confusion, frustration, and downright resentment. The survey asked consumers to describe the difficulties they had experienced with electronics products and manuals. After asking participants what they liked and disliked about the products and the instruction guides, we posed the question, "If you experienced a problem of any sort while you were trying to use your product, where did you assign the blame?":

1. To the manual

2. To the machine

3. To the manufacturer

4. To myself

5. Don't remember

▶ Figure 4.1 *Where survey participants attributed the blame for the difficulties they experienced while using a consumer electronics product.*

Note. Values represent responses in percentages (n = number of respondents).

Results shown in Figure 4.1 indicate that of the 201 votes, 127 people—or 63 percent of the participants—said they blamed themselves for errors they made with consumer electronics. Participants' bias toward blaming themselves is statistically significant by chi-square test ($p < .001$).

Our team then explored the data to identify how respondents differed based on their age and sex. We suspected that older participants might show tendencies to blame themselves more often than younger ones. And if common wisdom was accurate, females would blame themselves more than males. However, contrary to stereotypes, all participants, young and old, male and female, were about equally likely to blame themselves (roughly 60 percent of the time) for the troubles they experienced (see Tables 4.3 and 4.4). We found no significant differences for age or gender.

Attribution of Blame by Age

	Age Group						Average
	under 20 (n = 30)	20 - 29 (n = 37)	30 - 39 (n = 39)	40 - 49 (n = 30)	50 - 59 (n = 33)	60 plus (n = 32)	
To the Manual	10	8	13	13	18	13	12
To the Machine	20	16	5	7	21	13	13
To the Manufacturer	3	3	10	0	12	3	6
To Myself	67	65	67	70	42	69	63
Don't Remember	0	8	5	10	6	3	6

◀ Table 4.3 *Where survey participants of various age groups attributed blame for the difficulties they experienced with using consumer electronics products. Values represent responses in percentages (n = number of respondents).*

Attribution of Blame by Gender

	Male (n = 107)	Female (n = 94)	Average
To the Manual	12	13	12
To the Machine	14	13	13
To the Manufacturer	6	5	6
To Myself	62	65	63
Don't Remember	7	4	6

◀ Table 4.4 *Where male and female survey participants attributed the blame for the difficulties they experienced with using consumer electronics products. Values represent responses in percentages (n = number of respondents).*

Investigating People's Attitudes about Texts and Technology Based on Their Use of Consumer Products and Manuals

These findings were interesting and surprising enough that we felt it important to verify them in a more focused study. We were concerned that the survey was based on people's memories of reading, memories that may underestimate or overestimate the original experience. It could be, for example, that a single good or bad experience with a manual might color a reader's attitude about manuals generally. We wondered if the same results (i.e., the tendency for readers to blame themselves) would obtain *while* readers were engaged in using instruction guides.

To explore this question, we recruited 35 people (20 women and 15 men) to participate in an evaluation of three consumer products and the instruction guides that explained their operation. Participants ranged in age from twenty-two to seventy-three. We did not attempt to control for age or sex and recruited participants based on their availability. The three products we tested (selected by our corporate sponsor) were:

1. A telephone system—consisting of three parts: (a) a desk-model telephone, (b) a telephone answering machine, and (c) a cordless telephone. The system was equipped with the latest features. For example, users could pick up a call using the desk-model, press a button to put the caller "on hold," and press another button to switch the call to the cordless. Users could also record their own conversations by turning on a feature called "two-way record."

2. A video cassette recorder (VCR)—providing the latest features for copying and editing videotapes in the home. For example, users could copy a television program, complete with annoying commercials, and then edit out all of the commercials by using one of the special editing features.

3. A stereo system—including an AM/FM tuner, a CD player, a double-deck cassette player, a graphic equalizer, and speakers. For example, users could play the radio to record a broadcast on a cassette tape and then "mix" that tape with "cuts" from their favorite CD. Users could also set the clock to wake them up with their favorite radio show, tape the show that woke them up, and shut down the system at the end of an hour.

Participants first completed an entrance survey in which they provided information about their (1) background, (2) experiences with consumer electronics equipment, (3) experiences with instruction guides for consumer products, and (4) memories of where they usually assigned the blame when they experienced problems in using products or instruction guides: to the manual, to the machine, to the manufacturer, or to themselves.

Participants were then randomly assigned to use one of the three products along with the corresponding instruction guide. Because we were interested in the usability of the product and the manual, we prompted participants to try to use the manual as they carried out a series of typical tasks for the product, such as "setting the clock on the VCR." We asked participants to talk aloud,[5] saying whatever came to mind as they worked and reminded them that we were testing the technology and the instructions, not them. We told participants that we would draw on their feedback to give the company advice about future versions of the products and manuals. Participants gave us permission to videotape their activities as they interacted with the product and the instruction guide.[6]

[5] Our procedure was modeled on the think-aloud protocol methodology described by Ericsson and Simon (1991).

[6] Initially, some participants felt self-conscious about the videotaping, and worried about whether they would "look dumb" on tape. But after about ten minutes, participants became quite comfortable about the videotaping. Most had to be prompted "to keep talking" because they got so absorbed in their task at hand that they would forget "to say what they were thinking aloud."

After participants completed the usability test, they filled out an exit survey in which they characterized their attitudes about the product and the manual they had just used. The exit survey repeated the "blame" question, this time asking participants where they assigned the blame if they experienced difficulties while carrying out the tasks for the product they had used in the study.[7]

[7] The three parts of the study—the entrance survey, the usability test, and the exit survey—took about an hour and a half to complete; each participant was paid $25 for his or her time.

The data were analyzed to identify readers' attributions of blame *prior to*, *during*, and *immediately after* using one of the consumer products. The results (see Table 4.5) indicate that *before* participating in usability testing, readers tended to blame themselves 52 percent of the time, *during* usability testing, about 51 percent of the time, and *after* usability testing, about 53 percent of the time. Thus, whether we explored users' attitudes before, during, or after using a product and its instruction guide, the results were the same—users blamed themselves for the problems they experienced more than half the time.

Attribution of Blame Before, During, and After Usability Testing

	Before[a]	During[b]	After[c]	Average
To the Manual	23	35	33	30
To the Machine	2	14	5	7
To the Manufacturer	7	0	7	5
To Myself	52	51	53	52
Don't Remember	15	n/a	1	8

◄ Table 4.5 *Where readers placed blame before, during, and after using a consumer electronics product with its instruction guide.*

Note. Values represent responses in percentages. "Before" and "after" usability testing, the 35 participants choose the response categories that best fit their experience; some participants checked more than one answer in these entrance or exit surveys. Evaluative comments participants made during usability testing were coded using the categories shown except for "don't remember."

[a] Participants made 40 responses to the entrance survey before they took part in usability testing.

[b] Participants made 331 responses during usability testing.

[c] Participants made 57 responses in the exit survey after they took part in usability testing.

Participants' responses to the entrance survey indicated that *before* participating in usability testing, users blamed the manual 23 percent of the time, *during* testing about 35 percent of the time, and *after* testing, about 33 percent of the time. The lower proportion assigned to the manual in the "before" results, which presumably reflects previous experiences, suggests that problems attributable to the manual tend to fade somewhat in memory, but not problems that readers attribute to themselves.

When participants blamed the machine, they were most likely to do so *as* they were using it. In contrast, when they blamed the manufacturer, they tended to do so before or after using a machine.

The main finding was that—in all of the conditions—readers attributed more than half of the problems they experienced to themselves. In some cases, of course, they were right. In about a third of the cases in which readers blamed themselves, they made errors even though the appropriate information was readily available. For example, readers may have

- Misread the text even though it stated what to do clearly and correctly (e.g., they might read "do not do X" as "do X")
- Read the text correctly and then performed the wrong action (e.g., they may have pushed "button B" when instructed to "press button A")
- Become impatient and acted without reading

However, in the majority of cases (about two-thirds of the time) in which readers blamed themselves for troubles, the fault was not with the reader, but with the manual, the equipment, or both, as the following examples illustrate.

Example 1. A woman was reading about how to insert a cassette tape into a telephone answering machine (see Figure 4.2 for an excerpt from her protocol). After looking at a poorly drawn technical illustration that obscured the correct way to angle the tape so it would fit into position, the woman worried that it was her fault that she couldn't get the tape in: "I'm gonna break this thing.... I must be stupid."

Example 2. An instruction guide for the stereo system described more parts than were actually needed or provided in the box. When a woman assembling the stereo system ran out of parts, she said, "Oh my God. I've lost something. I'm so dumb. What did I do with those parts?"

Example 3. A man was reading a stereo instruction guide to learn how to work the "shuffle-play" function of a CD player. In fact, some essential information that should have been in the instruction guide about this function was missing. After trying the procedures that were presented and

Excerpt from a User Protocol

"Installing the microcassette happens to be right here on page 7. Side for recording. Where's the side? What's the side for recording?"
Muriel read the manual about how to insert a cassette tape into the device. She carefully studied a technical illustration that did not specify how to angle the tape so it would fit into position.

"I can't see how to put the tape in there. It's just ... I mean, it doesn't say how. It just says make sure there is no slack in the tape. I'm gonna break this thing."
She looked at the manual. With the cassette still in her hand, she began turning the tape with her little finger, trying to make the tape inside the cassette taut. She tried

again to insert the cassette into the machine but it didn't work.
"I must be stupid. I can't get this thing in. Oh, come on ... should I quit now? Don't you want this to work for the next person? I mean you might need this tape. I'm gonna break it.
Muriel flipped through the manual, trying to find more information on how to insert

the cassette. But there were no more instructions.
"All it says here is make sure there's no slack in the tape. I guess I'm too stupid to figure this out."
Muriel sighed and tried once more to insert the tape, but it would not snap into place.
"I can't get this tape in the machine. I told you I'm gonna break it."

▲ Figure 4.2 *Participant Muriel as she tries a procedure for inserting a cassette tape into a telephone answering machine. To view parts of the manual she read and a revision, see Figures 7.8 and 7.9 (pp. 466–467).*

finding that the shuffle play function failed to work, the man said "I'm not usually this stupid, but I guess it's my own fault."

Example 4. A woman read this ambiguous sentence in a VCR instruction guide:

> This VCR employs direct function switching where any playback mode may be directly entered from any other playback mode (normal playback, still frame, speed search, etc.) simply by pressing the appropriate buttons.

After reading the sentence, the woman said, "But I don't care what *direct function switching* is and I don't know what the *appropriate buttons* are. I'm ignorant about these technical things. You guys aren't trying to trick me, right? I don't get it. Well, it figures."

Example 5. A man was trying to set the clock on the VCR using the buttons on the front of the machine. The manual directed him to "Press the menu button" but it did not say that unlike other buttons, the menu button was available *only* on the remote control. After searching carefully on the front of the VCR, the man said "It says 'Press the menu button' but I can't find it. Why can't I find this darn thing? I must be blind. Well, if I had just bought this VCR, I'd take it back to the store. I'll tell you what, how about if I take this manual home and read it real good tonight, you know, look it over. Then I'll come back tomorrow. I just can't do this cold. I'm sorry."

This study convinced us of two points. First, that reported difficulties with electronics devices and their instruction guides are distributed fairly uniformly across individuals irrespective of age or gender (as was shown earlier in Tables 4.3 and 4.4). Second, when instruction guides mislead readers, as they often do, readers tend to blame themselves for their confusion. *Contrary to popular belief, young people and old, males and females, are about equally likely to blame themselves for the troubles they experience.* The situations in which we blame ourselves are obviously unpleasant and certainly time wasting, but they are more worrisome because of their potential cumulative effects. Over time, peoples' repeated experiences with badly designed products and instruction guides may convince them that they are incompetent as both readers and users of technology.

Manufacturers might take people's tendency to blame themselves as a license for "business as usual." Since they aren't blamed, companies might interpret these results to mean they are "off the hook." I believe, however, that this is a mistaken and short-range view. Manufacturers should be concerned with the long-range effects of self-blame, with the cumulative results of repeated frustration and humiliation that poorly designed products and manuals can cause.

Companies that acquire reputations for products or documents that make people feel stupid (or that make them work harder than they believe they should) may lose sales because consumers will stick with their old model—even if it was initially aggravating—rather than spend money on an unfamiliar and potentially even more frustrating new model. This partly explains why many computer users resist updating their software. As computer users readily attest, learning to use software can be an enormous "time sink" with slow and sometimes questionable payoff. Users often have the experience that once they get comfortable and productive with their software, a new release comes along, rendering the old one obsolete—then they have to work hard just to get up to their former speed. This phenomenon, called the *productivity paradox* (see Keyes, 1995; Landauer, 1995), refers to new technology that is designed to make us work faster and smarter, but actually only makes us work slower and with less confidence. More generally, the productivity paradox has been used by economists to describe why massive investments in technology often result in flat profits and stagnant gains in productivity.

The main point is that no matter whom the user blames, if the experience of using new technology is predictably unpleasant, then users may resist change and feel less enthusiasm for making new purchases. As a result manufacturers are going to make less money. We can see then that the consequences of people's attitudes may be significant even if the company is not blamed.

To probe the issue of the relationship between a document's quality and people's purchasing decisions, we asked our 201 survey participants a number of questions about their likelihood of purchasing a product from a company if they knew it had a clear manual. Figure 4.3 shows that 79 percent of users report they would buy from a company they thought had clear communications. These data also suggest that more than half of participants would consider paying more for a product if they knew it had a clear manual (while the dollar amounts we proposed are admittedly arbitrary, the main point is that people recognize that quality communications are valuable and might even be willing to pay something extra for them).

These findings remind us that the ways in which users think and feel about documents is important. We need to be careful to attend to readers' attitudes and motivation. Memories of documents that readers have encountered in the past may shape their beliefs about texts they have not yet read and may determine whether reading will take place at all.

1. Do you believe consumers have the right to clear instruction manuals?

    86 = yes
    12 = maybe
    2 = no

2. Do you believe most companies care about your ability to understand and use the products they sell?

    29 = definitely
    41 = somewhat
    30 = no

3. Do you believe companies should advertise "user friendly" manuals if they have them?

    84 = yes
    15 = don't care
    1 = no

4. Would advertising "user friendly" manuals influence your purchasing decision?

    35 = definitely
    40 = maybe
    25 = no

5. Would you be willing to pay more for a product if you knew it had a clear manual?

    27 = yes
    36 = maybe
    37 = no

6. If you answered "yes" or "maybe" to question 5, how much more would you be willing to pay?

    20 = $1.00 to $2.99
    42 = $3.00 to $4.99
    13 = $5.00 to $6.99
    25 = $7.00 or more

7. If you bought a product that had a clear manual, would you buy from the same manufacturer again (assuming the product was of high quality, competitively priced, and something you wanted)?

    79 = yes
    14 = maybe
    4 = no
    3 = don't know

Note. Values are percentages based on a group of 201 respondents, except question 6, for which there were 79 respondents. Some respondents who answered "yes" or "maybe" to question 5 did not answer question 6.

▲ **Figure 4.3** *Consumers' perceptions of the value of quality in document design.*

DO WE BLAME OURSELVES FOR PROBLEMS WE EXPERIENCE WHEN READING AT SCHOOL OR ON THE JOB?

These observations also raise several other serious questions: Is the tendency of readers to blame themselves restricted to instruction manuals and products? Or is it more general? For example, does it apply to students reading textbooks? To people learning from texts on the job? When students fail to understand a science or history lesson, we typically attribute their problem to the difficulty of the subject matter and not to the inadequacy of the textbooks. It is easy to see why. The texts usually look quite attractive. They are often lavishly produced, with lots of pictures and four-color printing. However, these appearances may be deceiving. A rather substantial body of research shows that not all or even most textbooks are well designed. Even good ones are uneven in how well they explain and visualize ideas.[8] Garner and Hansis (1994) identify a number of features that poorly designed textbooks have in common:

[8] The work of reading researchers such as Britton, Gulgoz, and Glynn (1993) or Chall and Squire (1991) make the problems of textbook design quite clear.

> They introduce too many concepts in too few words (Beck, McKeown, & Gromoll, 1989); they rarely contain interesting or entertaining material "written in any rhetorically purposeful way" (Hidi & Baird, 1988, p. 468); and they often contain topically irrelevant information (Garner, Alexander, Gillingham, Kulikowich, & Brown, 1991). Perhaps worst of all, they are anonymously authoritative. [citations in original] (p. 71)

As Benson (1994) has shown, textbooks may also create serious comprehension problems for students—problems that experts who design them may never see. Benson studied college students reading science textbooks and found that students had troubles with poorly written text, confusing illustrations, and mismatches between text and illustrations (e.g., information was presented in text but not connected to illustrations, or labels that appeared in illustrations were never referenced in the text). Benson then asked experts (in writing, graphic design, and science) to judge the same texts that students judged. Her findings were that experts not only failed to identify the problems that the textbooks posed for students, but also disagreed among themselves about what the problems were.

Benson found that experts collaborating on textbooks tend to work in isolation. For example, first a team of biologists may compose the content, each one taking a different chapter, then an editor improves the writing style, and then a graphic artist and illustrator are "called in" to visualize the subject matter. Rarely in this process do authors, editors, graphic designers, and illustrators meet face-to-face and discuss what students need. Even more rarely do they talk directly with students themselves. In fact, experts in her study were just as likely to worry about impressing their colleagues as they were to worry about the audience. Benson argues that the context of writing textbooks creates a kind of institutionalized separation between writers and readers. Her results suggest that the failure of experts to understand the point of view of students can severely impede their ability to predict problems that students may experience either with the text, its illustrations, or its combinations of prose and graphics (p. 74). Her work underlines the importance of collaborating to fashion a coherent image of readers and of testing draft materials with students.

Could poorly designed textbooks lead students to believe that they are not competent enough to understand the subject matter? Students may be in a more vulnerable position than the adults who took part in "the blame study." From the primary grades through college—to corporate training and adult education programs—students are taught to respect the authority of the textbooks. Students who tell their teacher that they do not under-stand their textbook are typically advised to "read it again, try harder this time, take your time." Garner and Alexander (1994) suggest that students' beliefs about text, "about what text is, who created it, and how to evalu-ate it are an influence, often a profoundly important one, on how they use text" (p. xvii). Parents' and teachers' views about textbooks as "the authority" on the subject are often reinforced by the authoritative voice of the texts themselves. Seldom do they offer hedges to indicate that they are presenting one perspective selected from a world of perspectives, whether the topics be black holes, the Revolutionary War, or sonnets. Indeed, textbooks give few clues about the social world in which they originate. They appear to present authorless unquestionable truth.[9]

As Brent (1992) astutely points out, the process of reading creates an illusion that we are "simply absorbing information from a text rather than conversing with, and being persuaded by, another human being" (p. 12). Learners may not believe they have "the right" to argue with the author(s) about the way they are being taught or about the point of view they are being asked to consider. They may see their role as one of understanding rather than of questioning or challenging. This tendency appears to be more pronounced in the education of children in Asian countries than in Western countries.[10] The possibility that students may resist criticizing their textbooks with the same vigor as they do other texts (e.g., drug education brochures) raises the question: Should students be taught to argue with their textbooks?

A study bearing on this issue was carried out by Beck, McKeown, and Worthy (1993), who designed a teaching method called "questioning the author." It was developed to enhance fifth-graders' active engagement

[9] See, for example, Apple (1992) and Luke, de Castell, and Luke (1983).

[10] See, for example, descriptions of Japanese schooling by Kitagawa and Kitagawa (1987) or comparisons of Japanese, Chinese, and American children by Stevenson, Lee, and Stigler (1982).

with their social studies textbooks. In this method, students are told that textbook authors are not perfect, and that if they as readers do not understand, perhaps the authors failed to make their point clear. The students are then encouraged to explore carefully the clues that suggest the author's intended meaning. Dole and Sinatra (1994) have commented that "this instructional strategy clearly fosters a deeper processing of the text than students would have undertaken on their own. It may also promote a sense of 'ownership' on the part of readers, that is, a sense that they are in control of their own comprehension process" (p. 260).

The study I presented in Chapter 3 about teenagers' interpretations of drug education literature would affirm that teaching methods which challenge students to make use of their already keen sense of the social world may help them take a more active rhetorical role in learning from texts. Methods such as those developed by Beck and her colleagues are a step in the right direction for teachers as well as for students. In the classroom, teachers' beliefs about textbooks and about how students should interact with them may play as large a role in shaping what students believe about textbooks as do their personal experiences with reading (Anders & Evans, 1994).

Poorly designed textbooks can create more than one kind of problem for readers. While sometimes we may blame ourselves for the problems we experience, at other times we may overestimate how well we understand. We may think we understand even when we don't. Glenberg, Wilkinson, and Epstein (1982) studied a phenomenon they call the *illusion of knowing,* referring to a reader's belief that comprehension has gone smoothly when comprehension has actually failed. College students in their study, who read texts in which experimenters had "planted" contradictions, failed to notice the contradictions. Surprisingly, after having read contradictory material, students rated themselves as feeling "very certain" they understood the text. In fact, students had overlooked the contradictions and had answered many of the comprehension questions incorrectly.

Glenberg and his colleagues point out that there may be "serious discrepancies between a person's self-assessment of their understanding and their actual understanding of what they read" (p. 587). Teachers would readily agree with this claim, for it is common to hear students report, "I studied for the exam, I was prepared, I knew the material, but I still got a D." Research on the illusion of knowing suggests that readers may need to be taught explicit strategies[11] for monitoring and reflecting on "how things are going" as they try to understand a text. Better ways of gauging the process of understanding would be very helpful.

[11] See Chi, Bassok, Lewis, Reimann, and Glaser (1989) for a study of how "self-explanations" can help students monitor their problem solving.

Taken together, these findings suggest that researchers are just scratching the surface in their investigations of (1) why people blame themselves when it is not their fault, and (2) why people think they "got it" when they did not. One thing seems clear. There needs to be more research on the design of instructional texts and instructional experiences (from manuals to textbooks)—research that takes peoples' thoughts and feelings seriously. As it stands now, we know that cognition, motivation, and emotions interact in important ways when people attempt to learn from instructional text, but not how, to what extent, or under which circumstances.

Additionally, it is important not to forget that when people use instructional texts, there is often a machine or a device involved as well. Users must simultaneously monitor their understanding of a machine and its responses along with a manual that describes its functionality. If we are to understand this complex situation, it will be essential to examine documents in the context of their use. In this way, we can evaluate how the document design helps or hinders people in learning to use technology. Of course, it will also be important to assess the usability of the product itself. A well-designed device may not need a good manual and a well-designed manual may allow readers to use a badly designed device. However, if both the manual and the device are poorly designed, readers may experience the sorts of problems that are illustrated in the following study.

"CREEPING FEATURISM"—THE MONSTER IN OUR VCRs: PROBLEMS FOR USERS CREATED BY PRODUCT DESIGN

This is an account of two people who tried to learn to use some new technology quickly. In it my colleague John Hayes and I narrate our experience of trying to set up two VCRs so we could copy and edit the videotapes that were shot for the "blame" study just presented. Our purpose here is to illustrate that people's difficulties in using consumer electronics have their origin not only in problems such as ambiguous language or hard-to-find buttons but also in problems that are more fundamental—namely, getting the thing to work and understanding why it worked or didn't. We will argue that the problems people experience with technology are often related to the number and complexity of the features the products offer. To describe manufacturers' seeming obsession with adding newfangled features to their products, Donald Norman (1988) coined the phrase "creeping featurism." The idea is "the more features the better." With each new model or release, manufacturers

[12] Users are often shocked to find that a new release of their favorite old software now takes up to four times the hard disk space it used to and needs twice the RAM to operate. Devoting so much space for two or three features one "might use" hardly seems wise. In corporate and educational contexts, for example, bosses and teachers routinely ask their employees and students to use old versions of software because they still run with minimal hard-disk space and RAM. Thus, companies lose repeat sales because they assume that everyone wants lots of new features and that everyone can afford to buy memory upgrades (or CD-ROM drives) just to run a new release. There is room in the market-place for new companies that take the opposite philosophy: that less can be more.

increase the number of features, often providing more bells and whistles than people will ever use.[12] Some manufacturers, particularly in the electronics industries, tout the number of new features added over what the features do. Others manufacturers, such as software companies, try to hide how much complexity they've added to their products by not saying how much disk space and RAM their new releases actually require.

As this study will show, the thinking demanded by some consumer products just to get them "up and running" can be quite significant. People who need to accomplish a task that requires them to use more than one product at the same time, such as connecting two VCRs together in order to edit, are left to figure out a very complex set of relationships among the many features these products may provide. Moreover, this study provides empirical evidence that some problems posed by consumer electronics are genuinely hard and that the confusion people experience can be attributed to causes other than generation gaps, poorly written manuals, or simple idiocy.

Our goal was not an unusual one. We wanted to connect two VCRs, a cable outlet, a converter box, and a TV so that we could copy and edit tapes from one VCR to the second, and at other times watch TV or record cable TV programs. Certainly this is not an exotic use of such equipment. Accomplishing that goal, though, proved surprisingly difficult. In fact, it took about ten hours of joint effort before we found a configuration that worked.

Why did we find the problem so difficult? After we finally managed to connect the VCRs properly, we began analyzing this question by collecting our sketches of the various connections that we tried, writing down our recollections of where we looked for help (in manuals, by calling other people), and documenting the possibilities we considered and the assumptions we made. From this evidence, we pieced together the following account of the problem and our attempts to solve it.

Making the Right Connections: An Analysis of Problem Difficulty

In order to make the right connections, we had to consider two interacting parts of the problem: (1) hooking the components together and (2) setting the various switches that control the internal states and modes of the components. When we say that the parts interact, we mean that it is impossible to tell if either part has been solved until both have been solved. For example, at several points, we had correctly connected the components. However, when the system didn't work because of an incorrectly set switch, we could not tell that we had already solved the problem of hooking the components together. Because we got no feedback from the equipment, we assumed the connections were wrong and started over. Let's look first at the problem of connecting the components.

The First Part of the Problem: Connecting the Audio/Video Components

There were five things that we had to deal with: a cable TV outlet, a converter box (required to descramble the cable signal), a TV, and two VCRs—one we wanted to edit *from* (VCR-1), and another we wanted to edit *to* (VCR-2). Based on our previous experience with audio/video equipment (we had each connected a VCR to a TV about ten times), we did not think this would be a hard task.

We started by reading the instruction guides for the VCRs and TV. However, the VCRs were made by different manufacturers and the manuals were of little help. Manufacturers typically don't say how to hook their machine to another manufacturer's machine. In this case, neither manual contained instructions for connecting two VCRs together—from our perspective, a major procedural omission. Although the manuals explained how to connect the VCRs to camcorders by the same manufacturer, neither of the VCR back panels looked like the ones illustrated in the manuals. After four hours of connecting and reconnecting the components, if we pressed "play" on either VCR and looked at the TV, we got either: (1) a "snowy" picture and no sound, (2) sound but no picture, or (3) the most aggravating of all—the dreaded blue TV screen with no sound accompanied by both VCR clocks blinking "12:00, 12:00, 12:00."[13]

To figure out what was wrong, we first reread the beginning sections of the manuals (about 25 pages in each instruction guide). We were met with arcane discussions of "flying erase heads" and cryptic references to "U/V Band Separators" and "F-type Connectors"; no mention of the blue screen. Assuming the manuals might still offer some help, we turned to the "Troubleshooting Sections"; still no mention of blue screens. Here's what we found:

Troubleshooting advice about "no picture"

- Press ANT TV/VTR[14] so that the VTR indication appears in the display window.
- The TV's channel is not set to 3 CH or 4 CH, or the video input has not been selected on the TV.

[13] In a 1989 "State of the Union" address, then-President George Bush set a national goal that "By the year 2000, all U.S. citizens will be able to set the clock on their VCRs." However, it doesn't seem likely that we will make it.

[14] "ANT" means antenna to the TV; VTR means video tape recorder, the same as video cassette recorder (VCR). We don't know exactly why this button was not called TV/VCR given that VCR, not VTR, was the product's name and since the button was the main switch to toggle from the TV to the VCR.

Troubleshooting advice about "no sound"

- The tape is defective.
- Use a new video cassette.

Troubleshooting advice about the blinking 12:00, 12:00, 12:00

- There has been a power interruption.
- Reset the date, clock time, and timer settings.

This troubleshooting advice is written from the point of view that the VCR is already connected and "up and running." We do not know why document designers made this assumption, but it does suggest they predicted the audience would have "no troubles" with setting up the VCR and with making connections to other audio/video equipment.

Although none of the troubleshooting information appeared directly relevant to our situation, we thought perhaps the second piece of advice under "no picture" was something to check. We looked to see if both the VCR and the TV were set to the same channel, that is, both set to channel 3 or 4.[15] They were. So we checked the second part of the advice, that "the video input has not been selected on the TV." Our interpretation of this idea was that we should switch on the TV's "video input" to take the VCR signal. In trying to use this recommendation, we looked for a button or a switch on the TV with the name "video input." There was no such button on the TV. Frustrated, we recabled the equipment again. Still the blue screen. We then turned to inspect all of the buttons on the VCR. Here we found a button with a similar name: "input select." It appeared on both the fold-down front panel of the VCR and on the remote control. We pressed the "input select" button on the remote control and the word "tuner" flashed in a little LCD display window on the front of the VCR.

As it turned out, "input select" told VCR-2 where to look for its signal, which could be coming from a cable TV, a compact disc player, a cassette tape player, a videodisc, a TV with an antenna, a simulcast radio station, a stereo tuner, or another VCR. Users were expected to press the "input select" button repeatedly until the name of the source they wanted to record from, such as a cable TV, appeared in the VCR's LCD display window on the front panel. But in order to use "input select," we had to know that there were a set of values (i.e., the options for the signal) that we would see if we pressed the input select button again and again. We also had to know that we would get a new option for the signal every time we pressed the button until it came full circle through all options and started over.

[15] Notice the instructions do not say that the settings for the TV and the VCR channels need to match. Instead, the instructions only suggest checking that the TV is set to channel 3 or 4. If the TV and the VCR channels are not set on the same station, that is, both to channel 3 or both to channel 4, then a signal other than the VCR will come through on the TV (e.g., a simulcast radio station). We had set both the TV and the VCR to the same channel, but did so only because we were experienced with VCRs. This important fact was not clearly described in the manuals.

At this point, we recognized the problem that led us to wasting time reading the manual, talking about what it meant, pressing buttons, and recabling. The troubleshooting advice contained a major ambiguity. It recommended checking whether the video input had been selected "on the TV." This prepositional phrase led us to look for a button to press *on* the TV. In fact, the button was *on* the VCR and its remote control. The advice actually meant "check to see if the VCR is ready to receive the cable signal by making sure the 'input select' button is set *to* cable TV." As this example shows, poor writing led us to make an incorrect assumption about how to solve the problem, about where to direct our attention. It gave us the illusion of knowing—that we knew "what was going on," even though we were completely wrong and were in fact searching the wrong piece of equipment. We can see that all choices document designers make, even those at the phrase level, can matter a great deal. The poorly worded advice cost us another 45 minutes. And even after we had correctly selected VCR-1 to be the input of VCR-2, the configuration still gave us a blue screen.

We had to conclude that none of the troubleshooting information was relevant to our problems. In fact there was no information in either manual about the problems users might encounter as they tried to make connections. At this point, our self-confidence was waning rapidly and we began to call electronics stores. In fact, we called three of them. The people we talked with were very helpful and provided us with detailed instructions for cabling the components together. Not surprisingly, the three sets of instructions were completely different; and unfortunately, none of them worked. At this point, we knew we were on our own.

Although we couldn't claim any concrete progress at this point (now more than five hours into our marvelous adventure), working though the problem and talking with electronics experts led us to three assumptions about the correct flow of the "inputs and outputs" among the components. These assumptions guided the remainder of our search for a workable configuration.

- We had to start with a cable coming out of the wall as the input to the system (that is, as input to the family of components).
- VCR-1 had to be upstream from VCR-2, that is, VCR-1 had to be an input to VCR-2 or to other components that supplied input to VCR-2.
- The TV, because it had no output, could not be an input to any of the other components.

We didn't clearly recognize it at the time, but these assumptions narrowed our attention to the three configurations for connecting the components

Three Configurations for Connecting the Components

Configuration A: The components can be connected in 4 to 24 different ways.

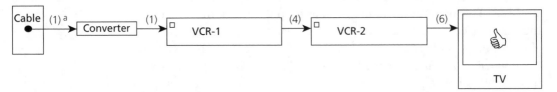

Configuration B: The components can be connected in 1 to 6 different ways.

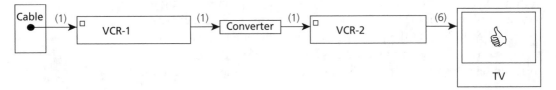

Configuration C: The components can be connected in 3 to 18 different ways.

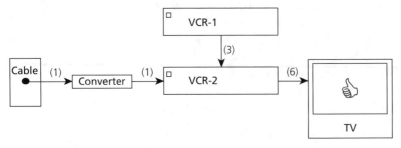

[a] Numbers in parentheses between pairs of components represent the maximum number of ways to connect the components.

▲ **Figure 4.4** *Three configurations for connecting common consumer electronics products. Each configuration has a minimum and a maximum number of possible ways to connect the components. Across configurations A, B, and C, there were between 8 and 48 possible alternatives for connecting the components.*

shown in Figure 4.4. The numbers in parentheses between pairs of components in this figure indicate the number of alternatives for connecting the components that we regarded as plausible. In Configuration A, we identified four ways to connect VCR-1 to VCR-2 and six ways to connect VCR-2 to the TV. If the choice about how to connect VCR-2 to the TV was independent of the choice for connecting VCR-1 to VCR-2, then there would be 4 × 6 or 24 distinct ways to realize Configuration A. Similarly, there would be 1 × 6 or six ways to realize Configuration B, and 3 × 6 or 18 ways to realize Configuration C. In total, then, there would be between 8 (i.e., 4 + 1 + 3) and 48 (i.e., 24 + 6 + 18) plausible alternatives for connecting these components.

Three Panels for Connecting Two VCRs and a TV

◀ Figure 4.5 *The back panels of the three consumer products used in this study.*

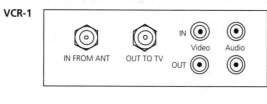

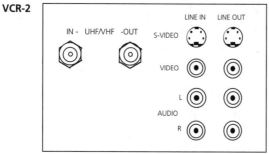

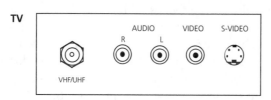

When we looked at the back panels of the components, we realized that some of the components could be connected to others in only one way. For example, the converter box had just one input connector and one output connector. Three of the components, however, had multiple connectors for input or output. These are shown in Figure 4.5.

As the back panels in Figure 4.5 show, the two VCRs and the TV can be connected to each other in many ways. In making input and output connections, we believe that most people with prior knowledge of how electronics are usually connected would adopt certain sensible constraints on what can be connected to what. For example, people familiar with electronics would connect outputs to inputs, not to other outputs; they would connect video to video and audio to audio, and they would connect left to left and right to right. We suspect that these people might construct a mental model of the typical path of the signal flow through a set of audio/video components.[16] In Figure 4.6 (on the next page), we present a crude sketch of what this flow might look like based on our own model.

If the technical writers who created the VCR manuals we used had worked more closely with illustrators to design a visual model for helping

[16] For a discussion of mental models and of how people imagine electricity works, see Gentner and Gentner (1983).

▶ **Figure 4.6** *A sketch of how the audio/video equipment could be connected, showing the path of the signal as it flows through the components.*

The Path of a Cable TV Signal Through a Set of Audio/Video Components

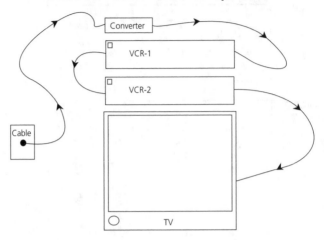

users to conceptualize key activities in using the VCR, writers could have reinforced these visuals with explanations of the key features to attend to, the things to watch out for. (In our case, this would have meant a visual overview of the idea of signal flow, depicting it moving through a set of components.) A visual model of the signal flow could have been elaborated with callouts to focus the user's attention on the idea of inputs and outputs. It could also prompt the user to keep in mind the need to keep the signal flowing in the same direction. It seems likely that a conceptual model presented visually along with carefully designed verbal explanations would have allowed users to make fewer conceptual errors in connecting equipment.

However, even a well-designed conceptual model may not help users accomplish their specific goals if their ability to draw on the model is compromised by additional product complexities that may render the model useless. As Figure 4.7 shows, even if one observes the logical "input and output" constraints, there are still nine ways to connect VCR-1 to VCR-2. When we were choosing among alternative connections for the components, we were using slightly more severe constraints than these. Based on our experience with connecting VCRs and TVs, we regarded only the first four alternatives in Figure 4.7 as plausible.

Let's take a look at Figure 4.4 again to examine some of the features of the product design that made it hard to use a model like that in Figure 4.6. As I mentioned earlier, there were as many as 48 plausible alternatives for connecting the components. However, this number is based on the assumption that the choice of connecting VCR-1 to VCR-2 would be independent of the choice for connecting VCR-2 to the TV. We think

◀ **Figure 4.7** *Nine ways to connect VCR-1 to VCR-2.*

1.   VCR-1 coax out to VCR-2 coax in

2.   VCR-1 video out to VCR-2 video in

3.   VCR-1 video out to VCR-2 video in +
       VCR-1 audio out to VCR-2 audio L in

4.   VCR-1 video out to VCR-2 video in +
       VCR-1 audio out to VCR-2 audio R in

5.   VCR-1 coax out to VCR-2 coax in +
       VCR-1 video out to VCR-2 video in

6.   VCR-1 coax out to VCR-2 coax in +
       VCR-1 audio out to VCR-2 audio L in

7.   VCR-1 coax out to VCR-2 coax in +
       VCR-1 audio out to VCR-2 audio R in

8.   VCR-1 coax out to VCR-2 coax in +
       VCR-1 video out to VCR-2 video in +
       VCR-1 audio out to VCR-2 audio L in

9.   VCR-1 coax out to VCR-2 coax in +
       VCR-1 video out to VCR-2 video in +
       VCR-1 audio out to VCR-2 audio R in

the independence assumption seems a bit extreme, given our previous experience with connecting VCRs. It is more reasonable to assume that experienced people would try to be consistent in the way they connect components. That is, they may base their choice of inputs and outputs to VCR-2 on their choice of inputs and outputs for VCR-1. Thus, if they use a coaxial cable[17] as the output of VCR-1, they would tend to use a coax as the output of VCR-2 as well. See Figure 4.5 (the back panels of the components). Notice the parts of the drawing labeled IN FROM

---

[17] A coaxial cable, called "coax" for short, carries both audio and video signals. To connect a set of components, users can choose between two types of cables: (1) coax cables (referred to in our manuals using the technical term, "75-ohm coaxial cables"), or (2) standard audio/video cables (red and black cords with 2 plugs on each end that match up with plugs on the back of audio/video equipment). The same connections can be made with either kind of cable. Neither manual explained why someone might want to use one kind or the other. After talking with audio/video experts, we discovered that standard cables were better for stereo separation during playback. In fact, they recommended using expensive gold-tipped cables for (1) the best sound and picture, or (2) in situations in which the original tape had less-than-perfect audio or video and you didn't want to degrade it even further by copying it. This happened to be our situation with some of the videotapes we wanted to edit for the "blame study." Some participants in the usability study had soft voices and it was hard to hear them during playback. Thus, in editing the tapes we needed the best audio we could get. This very useful advice was never hinted at in the manuals.

18 "ANT" means antenna. VHF/UHF are frequency bands for TV signals and are placeholders for the antenna or cable.

ANT, OUT TO TV, IN - UHF/VHF - OUT, and VHF/UHF are places to plug in coax cables.[18] Now let's look at Figure 4.4 again. Strict adherence to a consistency rule would reduce the total number of alternatives to eight (four for Configuration A, one for Configuration B, and three for Configuration C). Although we did not adhere strictly to a consistency rule, 8 rather than 48 is probably a more accurate estimate of the number of alternative connections we considered.

Our mental model of what to do in choosing the right connection is reasonably represented by Figure 4.6. We concluded that of the three configurations we sketched out in Figure 4.4, "Configuration A" was the best solution. We believed this until we turned the machines around and had to sort out the range of alternatives presented by the design of the back panels.

In Newell and Simon's (1972) terms, the set of plausible alternatives in solving a problem—that is, in getting from where you are to where you want to be—is called the "problem space." *The problem space is important for this analysis because the size of the problem space influences the difficulty of the problem.* Generally, the bigger the problem space, the harder the problem. We can establish a reasonable benchmark for problem space size by considering the problem of opening a combination lock. A lock with ten numbers on each of three dials entails a problem space of $10 \times 10 \times 10$ or 1000 alternatives, a lock with five dials, 100,000. In comparison, a problem space of 8 or even 48 alternatives seems small, but it's important to recognize that it represents the problem space only for the first part of the problem in connecting the two VCRs.

The Second Part of the Problem: Setting the Switches

The components we were connecting were well equipped with switches for enabling or disabling features and functions. VCR-1 had 9 switches and VCR-2 had 27. In addition, the remote control for VCR-2 had more than 80 buttons.[19] Some of these were redundant and others obviously served no function for our task. However, we did identify 17 switches that we thought might be critical. Of these 17, only 6 actually were. The

19 The remote control for VCR-2 had 34 buttons on its top panel. This panel acted as a flip-top lid that when opened exposed another 53 buttons on an inside panel (a whopping 87 buttons to set the VCR in various states and modes). Using the remote with the VCR was even more complex because some buttons that appeared on the remote did not appear on the fold-down front panel on the face of the VCR. Sometimes the same feature was labeled with different acronyms, one on the remote and a different one on the VCR front panel. In addition, two of the 87 buttons on the remote had the same name: "REC MODE." Moreover, users could do some tasks *only* by pressing buttons on the front panel of the VCR; other times *only* with the remote control. The manual never mentioned these "helpful" design features.

"Bloom County," created by Berke Breathed; reprinted with the permission of Little, Brown and Company, Boston, MA.

other 11 had no effect on our task and served only to distract us. If someone had simplified our task by telling us beforehand which 6 switches to pay attention to, we would have been faced with a problem space of 704 alternatives (4 switches with 2 alternatives each, that is, 2^4; one switch with 4 alternatives; and one switch with 11 alternatives).

Because we had to solve both parts of the problem before we could tell whether we had solved either part, the problem space size for the whole problem was the product of the problem space sizes for the two parts.

Since there were eight ways to cable the configuration (using the conservative estimate) and 704 ways to set the switches, our problem space could be calculated as 8×704 or 5,632 alternatives. *Thus, the size of the problem space for our task falls between that for a three-dial and a four-dial combination lock.*

Of course, the difficulty of the problem does not bear a one-to-one relation to the size of its problem space. As Kotovsky, Hayes, and Simon (1985) have shown, there are many factors that influence problem difficulty. For example, one factor is how familiar the problem solver is with the material in the problem context. Another is whether the problem solver has ready access to external memory supports—that is, do problem solvers have something they can see to help them navigate through the problem or do they have to imagine it? A factor that would tend to make combination lock problems more difficult than other problems of comparable size is that all of the alternatives in a combination lock problem are equally likely to be the right one.

The alternatives in our task probably were not all equally likely to be correct. A factor that tended to make our task more difficult than comparable combination lock problems was the welter of distracting switches. The 11 plausible but irrelevant switches had 2 alternative settings each and would have an effect roughly equivalent to adding two irrelevant dials to the combination lock.

More importantly, we may not have accurately assessed all of the constraints on our decision processes. Although we tried to be complete in assessing our decision processes, we may have overlooked some knowledge or rule that helped us to avoid bad alternatives. Even if our estimates were off by as much as a factor of ten, though, the problem space for our task is still large enough to account for the difficulty we experienced.

PROBLEMS FOR USERS CREATED BY TOO MANY FEATURES

Manufacturers work hard to add new functions to modern electronics products. Some users are pleased to be able to record one TV program while watching another or to record a TV program while they are away on vacation. However, extra functions usually bring with them increased complexity: more switches to set, more alternative connections to consider. As we have seen, the difficulty of the task tends to grow geometrically as options increase, lending confirmation to Norman's (1988) insight about the problems created by "creeping featurism" in product design:

Creeping featurism, one of the deadly temptations of designers, is the tendency to add to the number of features that a device can do, often extending the number beyond all reason. There is no way that a program can remain usable and understandable by the time it has all of those special-purpose features.... [E]ach new set of features adds immeasurably to the size and complexity of the system. More and more things have to be made invisible, in violation of all the principles of design. (pp. 172–173)

This case study shows that consumer electronics products can pose genuine problems for users—difficulties that arise from the nature of the tasks themselves, tasks made inherently more difficult by poor product design. This study also makes apparent that manufacturers should avoid making the assumption that the problems people have with texts and technology can be attributed to not reading the manual, not trying hard enough, acting like a technophobe, or being just plain stupid. Manufacturers should resist "blaming the user" for problems people experience with technology.

This study highlights the fact that products laden with features can be intrinsically hard to use. Even so, the temptation to add new features has been difficult for the electronics and computer industries to resist—what self-proclaimed computer guru Guy Kawasaki (1993) calls the "Akihabara Syndrome." Named after Tokyo's famous consumer electronics district—where customers are greeted with thousands of square feet of VCRs and other electronics wizardry, most of which are black boxes with lots of buttons—the Akihabara Syndrome refers to the tendency of manufacturers to plan new technologies with an eye toward "out-featuring" their competitors. Some market analysts argue this is a good practice because consumers want new features whether they use them or not—that more is better. Of course, consumers may buy products with "gee whiz" features because they are "neat"[20] or because they want to "impress someone."[21] But consumers may also resist making purchases based on their recognition that the features are ones they would only use "in their next life." Products that have either too many features or ones that are difficult to

---

[20] For example, in a classroom demonstration of new products for "today's consumer," one of my students did a presentation in which he touted a watch he "invented." He began his talk, "Look at this watch: It can tell time, calculate an equation, play a song, or tell me my global positioning. Are you impressed yet?" About half the class raised their hands.

[21] One of my friends said this to me as he described his new computer, "I've never used a computer except Super Nintendo if that counts. You should see the computer I bought. It is really cool. I can play video games and everything. I got a lot of RAM; I'm not sure what RAM does for the color and sound, but the guy in the store said it's good."

learn and burdensome to remember are "drowning consumers in a sea of features they can't use and will never need" (Flipczak, 1994, p. 52). As one woman from the survey of consumers I discussed earlier put it:

> When I opened the box for the cordless phone my son got me, I saw all those buttons and all those things to learn. I didn't want to place people on hold, switch lines, memorize nine zillion numbers, and other stuff. The fanciness just wasn't my idea of good. I felt "licked" just looking at it. I just wanted a phone I could walk around with and not trip over the cord. So I returned the dumb thing.

Apparently, a growing number of American consumers have returned products they consider too cumbersome for their needs.[22] These consumers "do the right thing" by returning badly designed products and by complaining about badly designed manuals (although it appears that more "hang in there" and learn to use their feature-laden products even if they don't use all of the functionality). Product returns are obviously not a good thing for manufacturers. Unfortunately, instead of facing the problem squarely and doing something about it, manufacturers tend to justify product returns by blaming the user. For example, in 1992 a director of international marketing from one of Japan's consumer electronics companies flew to Pittsburgh to interview me about my research. During our conversation, he said that his company had a warehouse outside of Chicago filled with thousands of cordless phones and answering machines that consumers had returned as defective. He argued that the phones were not defective, but that consumers were lazy and never bothered to read the manual to figure out how the product worked. Upon evaluating the products and the manuals, however, it became clear that neither the interface design of the products nor the design of the manuals could have led users to conclude that using the product was going to be easy.

As we saw in the study earlier in this chapter, for some products—such as phones—consumers may believe they should not need to read. Companies that go overboard in adding new features to what were once simple products (like phones and TVs) do so at high risk, especially when features are not obvious to users. Companies that violate users' expectations of how hard it should be to learn to use their products not only run the risk of increased product returns, but may also lose old customers, miss opportunities for repeat business, and generate negative word-of-mouth publicity.

In the last few decades, many companies have been trying to reduce the complexity of their products.[23] Progressive companies have embraced a definition of quality in product design that encompasses all dimensions of the product, including the human interface and the product informa-

[22] That Americans are ready to return technology "they can't figure out" gained widespread attention after the case of the Coleco Adam Computer, a computer supposedly so easy "that even a child could use it." But when parents couldn't, consumers returned hundreds of Adam computers, causing it eventually to be withdrawn from the market. See the *Wall Street Journal,* "Hundreds of Coleco's Adams are Returned as Defective: Firm Blames User Manual" (Davis, 1983).

[23] For pointers to the rise of ergonomics, human factors, and computer and human interaction design, see *The Timeline* in Chapter 2 (particularly the "Professional Development" strand: 1947, 1958, 1959, 1980+, 1982+, 1982, pp. 118–138). For some of the journals in these areas, see Figure 2.11 (pp. 98–99).

tion. However, most are not tackling the problem of the interaction between product design and document design based on systematic analyses of users' cognitive and affective needs. This kind of research is needed because users are increasingly demanding products that not only help them perform tasks quickly and easily, but also make learning less burdensome.[24] Many people on the job find themselves in situations in which they must learn a technology quickly, not for the sake of learning the technology, but for doing their real work.

As this study shows, ten hours of frustration hardly puts one in the mood to keep trying. To get a working configuration of the components, we spent almost seven hours of fussing with cables, about an hour on the phone with experts, and more than two hours of fiddling with the switches and modes to guess which combination might get rid of the blue screen. The cabling connection that finally worked turned out to be Configuration A (shown in Figure 4.4), a configuration we had tried early on. In fact, we had tried it seven different times with different cables and different settings for the switches, but we could never monitor what was going on to tell that "we had it right." By the end of our ordeal, we were so tired we didn't want to edit anymore (our original task).

WHAT WOULD HAVE IMPROVED THE DESIGN?

The difficulties we had with this audio/video equipment raise three issues that have general implications for the design of consumer electronics products. These issues concern standardizing the user interface, allowing users to monitor their progress, and helping users to constrain their search.

Standardizing the User Interface

Connecting pieces of electronics equipment designed by different manufacturers need not be as hard as it is. If the labeling and the arrangement of inputs, outputs, switches, and settings were clear and consistent, there would be benefits to both consumers and manufacturers. The obvious benefit for consumers would be intelligible procedures for using machines from different manufacturers (document designers would also find it easier to create pictorial instructions). If users were able to master the core tasks easily, they might be willing to attempt tasks that are currently beyond their range. Consumers who participated in the survey described earlier in this chapter reported that the perceived complexity of consumer electronics equipment both discourages them from exploring the more advanced features and affects their future purchasing decisions. On average, respondents reported using less than 50 percent of the functionality of their consumer products.

[24] Judging from the media attention given to this issue by journalists around the world, it seems apparent that consumers in many countries have been searching for usable products and usable documents. See, for example, Van Alebeek (1995) in *Brabants Dagblad* (the Netherlands); the Associated Press in *The Japan Times* (1990); Nakamura (1990) in *InfoWorld;* Nussbaum and Neff (1991) in *BusinessWeek;* Rogers (1991) in *Newsweek;* Smith (1990) in the *Los Angeles Times;* Van Vliet (1995) in *Utrecht's Nieuwsblad* (Netherlands); and Zijlmans (1995) in *DeVolkskrant* (Netherlands).

Learning how to use new products could be made easier if consumers could depend on using their prior knowledge productively. In our case, for example, while prior knowledge of connecting electronics equipment helped us to eliminate several blind alleys in connecting inputs and outputs, our knowledge also led us to believe that getting the components connected was the only problem to solve in order to make things work. As I explained earlier, the two parts of the problem interacted. Consequently, even though we had connected the equipment correctly at least seven times, we could not monitor the state of the connections because a number of the modes and switches were set incorrectly, the combination of which made the screen blue. Thus, our knowledge and assumptions about "what should work" actually got in our way.

What We Saw and Wanted to See on the TV Screen
While Recording from One VCR to Another
A Comparison of Helpful and Unhelpful Features of VCR Interfaces

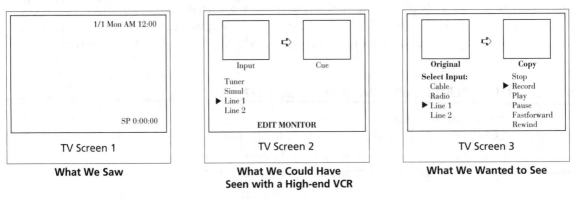

▲ **Figure 4.8** *Three VCR interfaces that might be displayed on a TV connected to two VCRs. The screens show a progression from unhelpful to helpful, both in visual and verbal design.*

Allowing Users to Monitor Their Progress

When we were searching for the appropriate settings for the six critical switches (that finally made it possible to view a videotape with sound), we had to get all of them right before we knew if we had any of them right. If the manufacturer had provided us with some indication displayed on the TV screen that we were making progress toward our goal, it would have made our task much simpler. What kind of indication would have been helpful? Let's consider a few displays that users might see on a TV screen when the TV is connected to a VCR. Although "what's going on" with the VCR is typically presented cryptically, it needn't be that way. Figure 4.8 shows three VCR interfaces (as displayed on a TV screen), progressing from unhelpful to helpful both in visual and verbal design.

Screen 1: What we actually saw on the screen of the TV used in this study. Notice in the first TV screen that the VCR interface shows the date and time (at the top right). In addition, the display offers an indication of the tape speed (in the bottom right). The speed of a video tape can be adjusted to standard play (SP), long play (LP), or extended play (EP). The time displayed to the right of the tape speed is the time elapsed during the recording or playback. These items are presented in white on a blue background. The question is: Are these pieces of information relevant to the user's task when connecting a VCR? The answer is no. None of them are relevant until recording or playback is ready to begin. Thus, until "everything works" nothing on the interface is helpful for the user.

Screen 2: What is currently available on some high-end VCRs. The second TV screen shows an interface that has been available on some high-end VCRs since the early 1990s. Notice that it displays two small windows that allow users to monitor their progress as they record from one VCR to another. This design allows the user to divide the problem into two independent problems that can be solved separately: (1) the problem of whether VCR-1 is connected properly, and (2) the problem of whether VCR-2 is recording a signal from VCR-1. The first window, called "Input," allows users to see if the first VCR is connected properly. If the picture in the first window also appears in the second, called "Cue," the user knows the first VCR is "talking to" the second one and that recording can begin.

Breaking up search in this way narrows the problem space for the user and allows for considerable savings in effort. Importantly, this design enables users to act without searching blindly. Users don't have to "keep pressing buttons," hoping the next one pressed will make one VCR or the other "do the right thing." Users can simply select (from a menu) which input source they prefer (e.g., VCR, TV, or cable). Once they do this, they can readily tell how things are going because a picture of the signal from their videotape or cable channel appears in miniature in the display window. Similarly, when a videotape is being copied from VCR-1 to VCR-2, users can see the picture of what is being recorded in the second display window, allowing them to monitor exactly what is being recorded (that is, knowing a videotape is recording from VCR-1 and not the TV channel or simulcast radio). The second display window also helps users monitor the audio and video of the recording, avoiding the familiar problem of recording a whole tape only to get either: (1) nothing, (2) picture but no sound, or (3) sound but no picture.

But notice that the labels "Input" and "Cue" under the windows are not easily understood. The first window, "Input," shows the signal, if there is one, that is coming into VCR-1. The second window, "Cue," shows what, if anything, is happening to VCR-2. Magically, the name of the label under the second window changes depending on the status of the videotape; for example, if fastforwarding, it reads "Cue," if playing, "Play." The list under the "Input" window (Tuner, Simul, Line 1, Line 2) is a menu for selecting the signal to be recorded. Unfortunately, none of the menu choices is easy to figure out. The label "Tuner" means "cable," not "stereo tuner." This may surprise people who have owned audio equipment for the last 20 years. The label "Simul" means radio (not closed caption TV for the hearing impaired). "Line 1" and "Line 2" mean that users can connect any component they wish to the video and audio input jacks labeled "Line 1" (e.g., a VCR) or "Line 2" (e.g., a camcorder) and record that input signal. For the configuration used in this study, that is, two VCRs connected to the TV, the cursor arrow next to "Line 1" means that VCR-1 is selected to be the input signal to VCR-2 via Line 1. (Whew!) Overall, this visual display is quite helpful because it divides the problem into two parts, allowing the user to tell if a signal is coming through and if it is reaching the second piece of equipment. Still, the interface is poor because the language used to label it is engineering-speak.

Screen 3: What would have been ideal (as least as far as we could imagine it based on the technology we had seen at the time). The third window is what we hoped to see in a VCR interface for the early 1990s. Notice that the visual design is the same; the only change is the wording of the labels. The first window is called "Original" while the window for the new recording is called "Copy." The menu now has a heading "Select Input" to guide the user to make a choice (given that it still doesn't look like a menu). The list of the menu items for the input signal is written in more everyday language (e.g., "Cable" and "Radio" are used instead of "Tuner" and "Simul"). However, the labels "Line 1" and "Line 2" cannot be revised without also changing the labels for the input and output jacks on the back of the TV and VCRs. Under the second display window, instead of the labels changing "magically" as the machine changes states, the user can see the state of the VCR: stop, record, play, pause, and so on. In addition, the more common "Fastforward" is used instead of "Cue." This third version has a helpful visual and verbal interface design.

Although providing performance indicators such as these may be technically difficult for manufacturers, any aids of this sort would be greatly appreciated by consumers. In addition, some of these aids could be handled in the documents, providing, of course, that document designers knew which problems to anticipate. The manuals we used contained no information about how to monitor one's progress. We were connecting in the darkness of the blue screen.

Helping Users Constrain Their Search

Hours of aggravation could be avoided if instructions provided a little guidance to help users constrain their search. Unfortunately, many manuals are designed in unhelpful ways, and like the ones we used, tend to be comprised of features such as these:

- *Topic-oriented Organization*—headings and subheadings written from the point of view of the topic (e.g., around technical features, button names, and mode settings) rather than from the point of view of users and their tasks.[25]

- *Missing Index* (this omission is inexcusable in a guide that should support users' search, both during their initial learning and when they use the document as a reference).[26]

- *Poor Graphic Design*—thick horizontal rules between each text chunk coupled with thick black "reversed–out" bars for major headings and subheadings, inconsistent typographic and graphic signals, ugly page design, and dull grid system.

- *Poor Writing*—excessive use of technical jargon, passive voice, and acronyms, along with no conceptual information, few examples, badly written procedures, and incomplete troubleshooting information. In addition, there were many word- and phrase-level problems, presumably related to the writer's first language not being English (e.g., problems of prepositions, articles, case, verb tense, number, and pronoun reference).

- *Technical Illustrations Presented in an Engineering Style*—illustrations that look like circuit diagrams decorated with a dizzying array of wires and connectors.

In addition to avoiding design flaws such as these, it would have been helpful if document designers had created a visual display such as a table that presented the modes and switches that were critical for obtaining a VCR signal and those that were not. This would have eliminated about two hours of tinkering with irrelevant alternatives. Similarly, if we had been advised to limit our experimentation to "coax connections" until we found a working configuration, we could have reduced our search space by an order of magnitude.[27]

Document designers need to anticipate those critical juncture points in carrying out a task that may lead users to a cognitive impasse—to a breakdown in completing the task. They need to give users a clear idea of the consequences of their choices, especially when choices are either nested with or contingent on other choices. (As was our case with the switches, "if X was on, then

[25] See the work of Kern and his colleagues (1976, 1985) and Sticht (1977, 1985).

[26] As one manager of a "small appliance" division of a major consumer electronics company said to me, "Well, it's like this. If the manual is too long, we cut the index. They can use the table of contents."

[27] In this way, we could have found a working configuration with a coax connection and then switched to the cables we wanted to use, that is, to the gold-tipped audio/video cables (see footnote 17, p. 235).

Y must also be on." But these choices are only apparent if the user knows what "Y" is.) And as mentioned earlier, we believe that many VCR users would be helped by a discussion of the direction of signal flow provided through pictures and words, emphasizing the visual.

This study demonstrates that consumer electronics equipment as currently designed can pose serious cognitive problems for users. We have suggested some ways in which manufacturers might help to alleviate these problems. More studies would very likely reveal additional ways to help users. However, if manufacturers continue to add features without attending to the human consequences, while at the same time designing documents that omit critical information, the problems that users now face will get worse.

POSTSCRIPT ON THE IMPACT OF POOR DESIGN

In this chapter, I have illustrated how both cognition and affect may interact as people use texts and technology. The two studies show that the design of documents and products is critical to people's ability to use texts and technology. We've seen that poorly designed documents and products may conspire to negatively influence people's ability to interpret texts and technology, as well as their interpretations about themselves as readers and users. Taken together, this chapter makes two important points.

Document Design and Product Design Must Be Integrated

Learning to use a device quickly and easily depends on both the design of the document and the device. Document designers and product designers should work collaboratively to create products that people can use. This means planning communications as a team from the onset of the development process (see Hackos, 1994). This study suggests that document designers and product designers did not work together. In fact, it appears that the various teams of product designers (e.g., VCR engineering team, remote control engineering team, and menu design team) did not work together either. For example, as I pointed out in the second study, we found major inconsistencies between the labels used on the VCR interface and the remote control. These inconsistencies reveal that the engineering teams did not conceptualize the user in the same way with the same language. As document designers learn to create a more unified vision of the user, they will need to organize their instructional texts around users' tasks, not around the buttons, features, modes, and so on designed by the company's engineers. Had the document designers for the VCR manuals carried out a task analysis,[28] they would have anticipated the many

[28] For a discussion of task analysis, see Gagné and Briggs (1979); Jonassen, Hannum, and Tessmer (1989); Kern (1985); or Newell and Simon (1972).

troubles we ran into while connecting the VCRs. Had document designers been part of the product planning, the problems of inconsistent
language would have been noticed immediately. Companies need to
embrace the idea that good communication starts with good planning.
They need to move beyond the antiquated view of "documentation as a
nuisance activity" (Glushko & Bianchi, 1982) and bring their best communicators into the front end of product development.

Bad Documents and Bad Products
May Have a Long-Term Negative Impact on People

When people experience difficulty in understanding either texts or
technology, they tend to blame themselves much more often than they
should. Unfortunately, this tendency appears rather resilient even in the
face of the real culprit: poorly designed texts and/or poorly designed
technology. As we saw in the first study presented in this chapter, before
consumers participated in the usability test, they held the belief that the
problems they had experienced in the past were their own fault. Their
tendency to blame themselves both during the study and after it show that
taking part in "a test of a machine and a manual" made no difference in
changing their minds. Indeed, we must assume that participants carried
away with them the same negative attitudes about themselves to the next
instructional text.

People's bias toward blaming themselves has potentially serious long-
term consequences—perhaps leading them to believe that they are
incapable of dealing with complex technology and reducing their interest
in new technology. This is a serious worry in documents and technologies
designed for the elderly or the physically challenged. A wider problem,
however, is the real possibility that students of any age may be led to
believe that they are too incompetent to understand either the subjects
they study in school or the topics and technologies they must learn on the
job. Clearly, teachers need to develop ways to help students identify more
accurately what may be causing their troubles. As greater demands are
placed on people to use technology to solve problems at school and work,
they will need better skills in monitoring their understanding of texts and
technology. Learners need not be extremists in their point of view about
how things are going—blaming themselves for not understanding or
happily overestimating their understanding. They need better ways to
distinguish problems that are their own fault from those that are not. They
need better ways to recognize when they are learning and when they are
not. Document designers and product designers should work hand-in-
hand to create products and documents that help people in these efforts.

suo qui sedet super thronum. no. Et omnes angli stabant
cuiui throni ⁊ ceciderunt ⁊ ado runt deum dicentes. amen. B

5

Seeing the Text: The Role of Typography and Space

In this chapter, I explore how typography and space can be employed to help readers "see the text"—its structure and the relation of parts to the whole. The chapter has four sections that explore different aspects of the role that typography and space play in document design. ❧ Section 1 discusses two critical features of good typography: legibility and rhetorical appropriateness. ❧ Section 2 examines how readers' purposes in using texts may shape their ideas about what makes typography rhetorically appropriate. ❧ Section 3 draws on principles of Gestalt Psychology to suggest some ways that document designers may use spatial cues to activate rhetorical relationships and promote information access. ❧ Section 4 investigates how vertical and horizontal space interact in document design and presents ideas about designing modular grids to make part-whole relationships evident to readers. ❧ Throughout the chapter, I suggest ways that document designers can better employ typographic and spatial cues.

Left-hand page. *Top: A writer using a wide-nib pen (Courtesy of the Newberry Library, Chicago). Bottom: A thirteenth to fifteenth century typeface called Gothic Textura Quadrata, a late Gothic style with rigorous verticality and compressed letterforms.*

The famous architect Ludwig Mies van der Rohe once observed, "God is in the details." His comment is apt for thinking about the role of typography and space in document design. By training one's eye to notice the details, the document designer can learn that type and space work together to:

- Set the mood, look, and feel of a document (e.g., formal or informal, urgent or relaxed).

- Make the structure of a document apparent (e.g., hierarchy, part-whole relationships, clusters of related ideas).

- Invite readers to scan and navigate the document in certain ways (e.g., top-to-bottom, left-to-right, column-by-column).

- Give clues about the type of document, that is, its genre (e.g., the graphic clues that distinguish a business letter from a bus schedule).

- Suggest how to interpret and use the text (e.g., take this seriously or not, use it in procedural fashion or not, keep it or throw it away).

- Reveal what the designer and/or editor thought was important (e.g., amount of space devoted to certain items, the position and emphasis given to certain words and pictures, the amount of graphic contrast used to set off certain ideas).

The best way to appreciate these issues is through careful study of many documents, paying attention to their typographic and spatial patterns. No explanation of type and space can substitute for the perceptual knowledge that can be acquired by close personal scrutiny of document after document. In this chapter, I offer some ideas about what "details" to look at and suggest some criteria for evaluating what we see. In particular, I explore how type and space work together, enabling readers to see the text. Since the topic of typography and space in document design is complex, worthy of an entire book, my intent here is modest.[1] The following four sections present ideas about how type and space interact:

- *Section 1* provides an introduction to typography and its key terminology (its jargon), with the idea of providing a foundation for talking about type and space in later sections. Here, I integrate ideas about legibility from typographers and researchers in order to suggest a constellation of typographic features that tend to have the most impact on readers when they are reading hardcopy or online documents.

- *Section 2* presents a study of the relationship between readers' preferences for type and the genre of the document they are reading. This study shows that genre and context play an important role in the typefaces readers prefer and deem appropriate for their situation. It argues that we need rhetorical theories about how type and space work together for readers.

[1] My initial discussion of type may be more basic than is warranted for experienced document designers, but because typography is a completely new topic to many writers, I felt the need to discuss it at an introductory and technical level. It may be difficult to understand, for example, why anyone would fret over the relationship between the size of a typeface and its x-height if x-height is unfamiliar. Readers of this book who are experienced with typographic terminology will want to skim Section 1 and focus on the later sections.

- *Section 3* offers a view of how document designers can make use of principles of Gestalt Psychology in order to activate rhetorical relationships through the deliberate structuring of spatial cues. This discussion extends previous work in this area and provides a number of illustrative examples that show how document designers can draw on what has been learned about human perception to help focus readers' attention and guide the order in which they scan the text.

- *Section 4* delves further into the use of space and typographic cues to structure the reader's visual field. It discusses ways to employ horizontal and vertical space to help readers recognize intended distinctions among parts of the text. These spatial cues serve not only to provide visual contrast but also to meet rhetorical goals for the reader's interaction with the content. This section also presents ideas for designing modular grids as a way to organize the visible language of documents.

Taken together, the sections of this chapter show how type and space can be employed by document designers to help them meet their rhetorical goals by articulating the visual field for the reader.

I begin with a basic question that concerns every professional, student, or teacher of document design: In what ways does the design of the document help the reader see the text[2] and recognize its structure? The answer requires knowing how typographic and spatial cues can be employed to help readers get the "big picture" of the document—to see the text's hierarchy, the relation of parts to the whole, and the distinction between main ideas and details (whether on paper or online). Since many readers come to documents without enough time to read them fully, they hope the structure will "leap out" at them. In order to develop information structures that help readers meet their goals for rapid access, document designers need to make their typographic decisions with two key considerations in mind: (1) legibility and (2) rhetorical appropriateness.

SECTION 1
THE LEGIBILITY OF TYPOGRAPHY:
ITS ROLE IN SEEING THE TEXT

Legibility was first studied in the late 1800s by Parisian Jean Anisson and has been a concern for many (though not most) typographers and graphic designers for more than one hundred years.[3] It has also been of interest since the 1920s to psychologists who studied human processes of perception and reading (Huey, 1908; Pyke, 1926). According to Tinker (1963), legibility concerns the features of typography that make it easy for people to read text—whether in short bursts as on road signs or billboards or over extended periods as in the continuous text of a novel. Studies of legibility

[2] Here I borrow the phrase "seeing the text" from Bernhardt (1986), who challenged writers to learn more about ways to employ visual cues (e.g., blank space, graphic patterning, and enumerative sequences) to signal the organization of texts.

[3] For an account of legibility from the perspective of typographers, see Kinross (1992). See also *The Timeline* in Chapter 2, the strands "Education & Practice in Graphic Design" and "Professional Development," especially 1917 through 1970 (pp. 110–130).

investigate how the shapes of letters (including numerals) enable people to read text quickly, effortlessly, and with understanding (p. 8). Figure 5.1 presents some of the key features of typefaces that typographers and researchers concern themselves with in thinking about legibility. These characteristics make one typeface look different from the next (or one paragraph look different from another). I first offer definitions of these features and then elaborate their role in considerations of legibility.

The Anatomy of a Letterform

The idea in Example 1 of Figure 5.1 is that all typefaces share a basic anatomy comprised of a few key features. All *letterforms* (that is, uppercase letters and lowercase letters) sit on an imaginary line called the *baseline*. The height of the uppercase letters is called the *cap height* (they touch the *cap line*); the height of lowercase letters is the *x-height* (they touch the *mean line*). For every typeface, parts of some letterforms extend below the baseline (e.g., the tail of a "g" or "y"); these are known as *descenders*. The vertical parts of lowercase letters such as "d" and "l" that extend above the mean line are called *ascenders;* they are usually the same height as upper-case letters, but in some cases they are slightly taller than the cap height (e.g., the lowercase "f"s in Example 2 of Figure 5.1 are taller than the uppercase "S"). Enclosed spaces such as those found in the letters "a," "e," "g," or "o" are called *counterforms* or *counters,* as are the partially open spaces in the uppercase "G." The body of a letterform is the *stem;* it is created by making a *stroke*. The cross of a "t" or an "f" is a *cross stroke*.

Type Size

The standard measuring unit for type size in most English-speaking countries is the *point* (there are approximately 72 points to an inch). Typefaces may be set in sizes from 4 to 144 points, but are generally used in 6 to 72 points. As shown in Example 3 of Figure 5.1, type size (also called the point size) is measured from the top of the highest ascender to the bottom of the lowest descender. In addition, the type size includes a little extra vertical space above ascenders and below descenders (my example shows this extra space below the descender). This way of mea-suring is a holdover from the days of handset metal type. Early printers set type using rectangular metal blocks, each of which had a raised letterform on top. The raised letterform (called the *face*) was inked and came into contact with the printing surface to produce the image. Each letterform's block had a little frame of metal around the face. The frame did not print but simply helped to position the letterform in relation to others for that typeface. Enough framing was needed above and below the letterforms to

Example 1: Anatomy of a Letterform

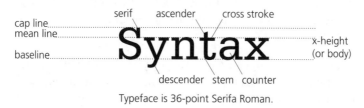

Typeface is 36-point Serifa Roman.

Example 2: Two Styles of Type and Their Contrasting X-heights

Typeface is 22-point Monotype Bembo.   Typeface is 22-point Frutiger Light.

Example 3: Illustration of Leading and Line Length

Typeface is 24-point Bauer Bodoni with 28.8-point leading (24/28.8).

Line Length
17 picas and 9.3 points (or 213.3 points)
2.97 inches
75.25 millimeters

Around 1500, the humanistic Renaissance, through the work of Aldus Manutius, its chief exponent, established a completely different visual ideal … The new style originated in Italy about 1450, but did not spread to other countries until considerably later. Aldus Manutius was the first to recognize that printed books had a character of their own and were different from manuscripts. Aldus can therefore be seen as the beginner of the new typographic age in book design. (Tschichold, 1928/1987, pp. 15–18)

Monotype Bembo
10/11 (type size is 10 point with 11-point leading)

Around 1500, the humanistic Renaissance, through the work of Aldus Manutius, its chief exponent, established a completely different visual ideal … The new style originated in Italy about 1450, but did not spread to other countries until considerably later. Aldus Manutius was the first to recognize that printed books had a character of their own and were different from manuscripts. Aldus can therefore be seen as the beginner of the new typographic age in book design. (Tschichold, 1928/1987, pp. 15–18)

Monotype Bembo
10/14 (type size is 10 point with 14-point leading)

▲ **Figure 5.1** *Three examples that show the relationships between type and space that make typefaces and paragraphs look different from one another.*

accommodate capital letterforms and those letters with ascenders or descenders. This ensured that the letters would not touch when they were set over consecutive lines of type. Type size (or *point size*) is a measure of the face plus the frame.

Strangely enough, even with today's digital typefaces, the typographic community still uses the point system for measuring type.[4] Since point size is not measured by the physical size of the face, it is impossible to determine the actual size of type just by measuring the printed letters (Craig, 1980, p. 24). This becomes especially problematic when trying to judge the point size of capital letters set in large sizes. For example, the face of a 36-point letter may measure only 30 points. Although a trained eye can often make an educated guess, even experts must often use a type specimen book to identify the size of a typeface they evaluate on paper or onscreen. Hopefully, typographers of the future will derive a system for measuring type that relies on what is visibly printed and that allows the viewer to accurately compare typefaces against one another. More than 20 years ago, Rehe (1974) argued that typographers should develop methods for measuring type that are sensitive to the differences readers see. Unfortunately, his call went unheeded. (And even if someone had invented a new system, getting the typographic and printing communities to adopt it would be another effort.) Although there are limitations to the point system of measurement, it is the lingua franca of the printing industry. Thus when a document designer talks to a printer about measurements in inches, the printer will assume that the document designer is a novice.

Families, Fonts, and Faces

A *type family* consists of a group of related typefaces unified by a set of similar design characteristics. Most of today's type families such as Caslon, Futura, Bodoni, or Sabon have a range of styles—varying from light to medium to bold to extra bold to black. In addition, most faces are designed with a complete set of italic letterforms as well as special characters and symbols. The commercial success of desktop publishing has led to the development of thousands of type families for the computer. While many of these type families are entirely new designs, others are digital updates of classic faces such as Bembo, the face used for the body text of this book.

Today the terms *font* and *typeface* (or *face*) are often used interchangeably. But technically speaking, in the world of computer-based typesetting a *font* is the "source" of the typeface. In general, there are two types of fonts: (1) screen fonts,[5] the jagged-looking bitmapped characters comprised of pixels that are displayed on a computer screen, and (2) printer fonts, the smooth characters that are printed.[6] The *typeface* refers to the

---

[4] The point system was invented in France in 1737 and updated in America in the 1870s (Carter, Day, & Meggs, 1985, p. 34).

[5] Whether screen fonts are needed depends on the computing platform (e.g., Macintosh or IBM) and the kind of fonts used (e.g., PostScript or TrueType). Screen fonts are relevant only when using a Mac, and in particular, only when using Macintosh PostScript fonts. In contrast, Macintosh TrueType fonts use a single file that stores both screen and printer fonts. When using an IBM, only a single file is needed for either PC PostScript or PC TrueType fonts.

[6] There is a good bit of technical detail about the Byzantine world of fonts and it is not my purpose here to explain it. Suffice it to say that some typefaces will require that you install two separate files on your computer, a set of screen fonts and a set of printer fonts (e.g., Macintosh PostScript fonts). Other typefaces have both screen fonts and printer fonts built into one file (e.g., TrueType or PC PostScript fonts). For more detail, see Fenton (1996) or Shushan, Wright, and Lewis (1996).

complete set of characters, punctuation, and symbols that share a common design. As font expert Fenton (1996) points out, you might say "I'm going to load this Garamond font into my printer," but you wouldn't say, "What do you think of this brochure that's set in the Garamond font?" In the second case, you're referring to characteristics of the design of the printed type, so you'd speak of the Garamond typeface (p. 2). As a practical issue, in order to see or print a typeface, one must have the appropriate fonts installed on the computer; else the text will default to an unwanted font both in displaying the document and/or in printing it.

Two Basic Styles of Type: Serif and Sans Serif

Figure 5.1 illustrates two[7] of the major styles of typography: *serif* and *sans serif*. As shown in Example 1 (see the uppercase "S"), a *serif* is a line or curve that finishes off the end of a letterform. It projects from the top or bottom of the main stroke of the letter. Serifs originated with Roman masons who terminated each stroke by chiseling the edges of the letterforms with a serif in order to correct the uneven appearance made by their tools (Craig, 1980, p. 17). For this reason, serif typefaces are sometimes called Roman faces. Serifs are said to be useful because they help the reader's eye distinguish individual letters and provide visual continuity across words.

The typeface so aptly named Serifa in Example 1 of Figure 5.1 shows a type of serif called a *slab* (or Egyptian serif); it is characterized by a strong monotone stroke weight and thick square horizontal serifs. In contrast, the serifs in Example 2 (which shows Monotype Bembo) are called *bracketed,* in which each serif has a diagonal stroke emphasis in relation to the stem, reminiscent of calligraphy. Notice that Bembo has little contrast in the thickness of the strokes that comprise the letterforms, providing an evenness of weight to the eye. At the same time, the strokes have a light touch. A third type of serif, called *hairline,* is presented in Bauer Bodoni in Example 3; see how its serifs are thin, square, and horizontal.

Serif typefaces may be found in almost any book, magazine, or newspaper (in Western countries). They have been employed by typographers and book designers since Johann Gutenberg[8] and his colleagues introduced moveable type in 1450 and the first Textura style typeface (see the bottom portion of the opening spread of this chapter for an illustration). Textura lettering (from the Latin *texturum,* which means woven fabric or texture) was later called Black Letter. This style simulates the handwriting practiced by the scribes during the late medieval era. It looks a little like a picket fence with its rigid repetition of verticals capped with pointed serifs, giving an overall effect of a dense black texture (Meggs, 1992b).

[7] There is a third style called "Script" (sometimes called cursive), which looks like handwriting with the letters connected. I do not cover it here because it is usually unsuitable for document design except in cases such as invitations or menus. In addition there are decorative faces for special purposes. More recently a number of avant-garde faces have been developed; these appear to have been designed to express the individualism of the designer and to be hard to read (see Shushan et al., 1996). Using typefaces that deliberately make it difficult for people to recognize the letterforms is not consistent with the goals of document design.

[8] It is important to consider Gutenberg and the work of his colleagues in context. They were important in extending the idea of printing in European countries, but they did not invent printing. Gough (1968) points to evidence of widespread printing in China by 980 A.D. In addition, there is ample evidence of hand-printed documents with many of the same qualities we value in documents printed with moveable type.

9 See Twyman (1970) and
Kinross (1992) for discussions
of the evolution of modern
printing and modern
typography respectively.

Type designers in Gutenberg's day incorporated the variations in stroke weight, the angular quality of characters, and other calligraphic flourishes of hand-drawn letters (Fenton, 1996). The serif faces that are ubiquitous in today's publications have their roots in the Black Letter tradition.[9] (In fact, we still see offshoots of the Black Letter tradition on the CD-covers of heavy-metal bands or on the mastheads of newspapers).

As the name suggests, a *sans serif* face is one without serifs. See the second style of typeface in Example 2 of Figure 5.1. Sans serif faces were introduced by English typefounder William Caslon IV in 1816. In the early 1800s, sans serif faces were called Gothic or Grotesque—a term which meant primitive and barbarous. In contemporary design, Gothic simply refers to a group of anonymously designed sans serif typefaces. Today's typefaces (both serif and sans serif) are mostly named after typographers, design groups, or corporate entities. Though the term Gothic has for the most part fallen out of use, we still have some sans serif faces with names such as Franklin Gothic or News Gothic. Moreover, typographers sometimes use the terms *Roman* and *Gothic* instead of serif and sans serif. As *The Timeline* in Chapter 2 shows (see the "Education and Practice in Graphic Design" strand), sans serif faces became popular around 1919 when architect Walter Gropius started the Bauhaus school of design.[10]

In fact, part of the practical contribution to typography of the Bauhaus, and its descendent movements in the New Typography and the International Typographic Style (also called Swiss Design),[11] was a proliferation of many new sans serif faces. A key feature of most sans serif faces is little variation in the stroke width of the letterforms, providing a uniform, clean, modern appearance. A notable exception is the typeface Optima, which has some contrast in the stroke. (If you haven't seen Optima, turn ahead to Figure 5.6; see the fourth example under sans serif faces.) Sans serif faces are geometric in their construction and almost always have a strong vertical stress. Another distinctive feature of sans serif faces is that they generally have better contrast between the plain and bolded versions of their letterforms than do seriffed typefaces. Thus, sans serif may allow

---

[10] To get a sense of the development of the Bauhaus school of thought and its legacy on graphic design and typography, see *The Timeline*, the "Education & Practice in Graphic Design" strand, particularly 1907 through 1975 (pp. 106–136).

[11] The International Typographic Style Movement (or Swiss Design) emerged in Germany and Switzerland in the late 1940s and 1950s. For illustrations of Swiss Design, see Max Bill (1945), Adrian Frutiger (1980), Anton Stankowski (1966), or Emil Ruder (1982). Ruder and Frutiger, for example, discuss the design of the famous sans serif face Univers. Frutiger was the designer of the sans serif typeface used for the footnotes of this book, a face that bears his name, and the seriffed typeface employed in Example 1 of Figure 5.1, Serifa.

better visual distinctions among parts of the text and may signal the hierarchy of the text more easily. When the New Typographers and the Swiss Design[12] movements were at their zenith, they deemed the use of serif faces as close to heretical (see the sidebar below). Today many designers advocate using a serif and a sans serif face in the same document. Together, they offer the best of both worlds: the visually rich texture of the serif faces (typically used for body text) and the sparse, uniform look of the sans serif (often for headings, captions, and marginalia).

[12] For a characterization of the Swiss Design aesthetic, see Hollis (1994), Kinross (1992), Livingston and Livingston (1992), or Meggs (1992b).

The Politics of Sans Serif Typefaces in Twentieth-Century Graphic Design

A rallying cry for the Bauhaus movement in typography (as well as in other arts such as painting, architecture, and furniture design) was "form follows function." To Bauhaus designers in the 1920s this was more than a catch phrase. It was a politics of design. Antecedents of Bauhaus thinking can be found in an earlier German design movement, the 1907 Deutscher Werkbund, which developed as a response to the shoddy product design of the Industrial Revolution. The Werkbund values were centered on the idea of quality ("Qualität") and simplicity: they prized bringing the highest craft standards to industrial production (Kinross, 1992, p. 68). A similar organization, formed in London in 1915, was called the Design and Industries Association. This early activity spread the message that "nothing need be ugly" (Livingston & Livingston, 1992, p. 54). The Bauhaus elaborated these ideas to embrace the philosophy of "form without ornament." The Bauhaus employed the concept in designing chairs and buildings as well as in their approach to typography. In typographic design, proponents of the Bauhaus "stripped letters of calligraphic embellishments such as serifs in favor of simple shapes and lines" (Fenton, 1996, p. 4).

From the Bauhaus evolved what became known as the New Typography, a movement which took a utilitarian approach to graphic design (described in Jan Tschichold's seminal book, *Die neue Typographie*, 1928/1987). The New Typography and the subsequent movement, the International Typographic Style (also called Swiss Design), had a profound influence in changing the text features designers paid attention to, an influence which is still felt today.

Whereas turn-of-the-century graphic design and typography had embraced what Austrian architect

Adolf Loos called "a love of decoration" and a "horror of empty space," Bauhaus-inspired designers searched for functional principles to direct the organization and display of graphic elements (Meggs, 1983, p. 262). See *The Timeline*, the "Education & Practice in Graphic Design" strand for 1906+. See also the pages from the *Sears Catalog*, Figures 2.1 and 2.2, which typify the designer's "horror of empty space." Like the Bauhaus, the New Typographers and those in the Swiss Design Movement held the principle that sans serif faces should be employed over serif faces. Their contention was that sans serif was more modern, functional, and clean looking (Tschichold, 1927/1987, p. 208). The New Typographers and their protégés also showed how blank space could be employed as an active design element. But one thing about the New Typographers was that their rhetoric was rather messianic. Either you believed in their politics or you were damned. Designers who used serif faces were seen as violating the new rational "machine age" aesthetic. (In today's jargon, using a serif typeface was politically incorrect.)

Design historians argue that the New Typographers and their counterparts in the International Typographic Style Movement went overboard in their quest for organized designs, that they were obsessed with trying to make design a completely rational and objective enterprise. And sometimes even though they claimed their emphasis was on functionality, it seemed more on personal aesthetics. As Fenton (1996) suggests, "just as a chair made of steel tubing might be more beautiful but less comfy than its overstuffed counterpart, certain sans serif faces are a pleasure to look at but difficult to read" (p. 4). Even with their excesses, though, there is no question that the attention to functionality catalyzed by the Bauhaus designers made a lasting contribution to human-centered design. The legacy of their emphasis on using type and space to structure functional communications was important in laying a foundation for modern document design.

▲ *Today's art and practice of typography has a rich history from which documents designers can draw.*

As we can see, document designers in the West inherited the Roman alphabet, a symbol system with a number of styles that developed over many centuries. The letters we use today (especially the seriffed typefaces) maintain many of the visual properties of the implements used as writing evolved—from the strong geometric look of the capital letters found chiseled on the faces of Roman monuments to the graceful curves of the lowercase letters that evolved from the reed pen used by scribes in the medieval monasteries.[13] Capital letters, for example, still employ the same simple forms of the ancient Greeks—the square, circle, and triangle (Carter et al., 1985). Indeed, although some of the new digitally-mastered typefaces of today are unique, most owe a big debt to those long lost (but not forgotten) typographers without computers.

Typefaces and X-height

One of the distinctive characteristics of typefaces is the *x-height* (also called the body height). As shown in Examples 1 and 2 of Figure 5.1, it is the height of the lowercase "x" for a given type family, excluding the ascenders and descenders. The lowercase "x" is used to measure typefaces because in most faces it has no ascenders or descenders and—unlike rounded letters such as "a," "o," or "e"—sits squarely on the baseline. X-height affects a face's perceived size and has an unexpected way of interacting with the point size of type.[14]

As Example 2 in Figure 5.1 shows, typefaces with large x-heights look bigger than faces with small ones, even when both faces are set at the same point size (thus the Frutiger Light looks like a different point size than the Monotype Bembo). This example and many more that could be shown indicate that a typeface with a small x-height set in a large point size may look as small as another typeface with a large x-height set at a smaller size. In choosing a typeface, document designers must consider the x-height as well as the point size, as the x-height is a more sensitive indicator of its visual size. Rehe (1974) argues that typographers should reclassify type according to x-height because it, unlike point size, precisely distinguishes two typefaces set at the same size (p. 27).

Contrary to appearances, typefaces with a greater x-height do not occupy any more vertical space on the page. In a sense, "the x-height transfers some of the 'wasted space' from between the ascenders and descenders to the main body of the letters, giving them an enlarged and easier-to-read look" (White, 1988, p. 16). A face with a large x-height can usually be set at a smaller size than a face with a small x-height with no loss of legibility (Fenton, 1996, p. 11). A document set in a face with a greater x-height may appear more approachable to read because it looks

[13] Medieval monks who copied thousands of manuscripts by hand found that curved strokes reduced the number of strokes needed to write many of the letterforms. Using lowercase letters enabled them to copy the manuscripts more quickly (Carter et al., 1985, p. 26). Interestingly, some of today's Cistercian and Benedictine monks as well as some Dominican nuns work in what has been called the "electronic scriptorium," where monastics use computers to transfer information from paper to digital form—preserving our collective memory by archiving and indexing the hardcopy texts of libraries (Millar, 1996, pp. 94–104).

[14] For a discussion of how x-height affects the visual impact of a face, see Black (1990) or Craig (1980).

larger. Typefaces with larger x-heights tend to have a modern and friendly look. For example, the typeface used in the catalog design of the J. Peterman Company, shown in Figure 6.13 (p. 422) is a custom-designed large x-height font, albeit nameless except to those inside the company. Using a typeface with a large x-height is also a good idea when designing documents for children or for people with poor vision (see Appendix C for some guidelines, pp. 506–517).

If You Don't Like the Way the Typeface Looks, You Can Change It

Until recently, it was not possible to adjust the proportions of a typeface without distorting the letterform (that is, when using desktop publishing software). However, recent technologies for digital type such as Adobe's *Multiple Master* typefaces[15] allow document designers to adjust several aspects of type, including:

[15] For an explication of the features of Multiple Master typefaces, see Adobe (1995), Brady (1996), or Fenton (1996).

- Character weight (up to 11 weights from light to extra black)

- Optical size (scalable x-heights, enabling the change of a typeface with a small x-height to a large x-height or a large-size face with an overly generous x-height to one with a smaller x-height)

- Width (10 optional widths that range from condensed style characters, that is, narrow and skinny, to extended characters, that is, fat-looking letters)

- Style (serif and sans serif in the same typeface, permitting the user to morph the letterforms from serif to sans serif or vice versa)

The added control that Multiple Master faces offer, however, demands considerable sophistication in perceiving the micro details of letterforms and their interactions in order to make wise decisions. Even though advocates of Multiple Master faces, such as Fenton (1996), claim they can be used by the aesthetically challenged and have been designed especially to avoid squashing, stretching, or otherwise manipulating a typeface beyond the bounds of legibility, it's not necessarily true that "the rest of us" who don't have an advanced degree in typography can use them well.

If the situation calls for a custom-designed typeface, I recommend hiring a professional typographer with an advanced degree who believes in attending to the needs of the audience and in getting their feedback. These folks have studied dozens (sometimes hundreds) of typefaces which even most experienced document designers have never seen. Bartram (1982) found large differences in the attitudes of designers and nondesigners in how they perceive the mood and suitability of typography. The perceptual knowledge of experienced typographers should not be taken lightly, for they will usually make better first guesses than will most document designers about what may work with the audience.[16] However, even experts need to check their intuitions with readers; thus, it is important to choose a typographer who believes the audience should have a say in what works. This is not always so easy. As Shushan, Wright, and Lewis (1996) point out:

> The "democratization" of typography has led to one of the most creative—and confusing—periods in the history of design. It used to be that good design employed typography as a vehicle for the message. Headlines might be treated as a graphic element; but in body text, well-designed type was transparent and didn't call attention to itself. Today's cutting edge designers have turned their back on balance and harmony and neat columns of evenly spaced text. They go for odd shapes; they change the column width (or line spacing or typeface) in the middle of a paragraph; they overlap the columns, blur the edges, run the type up to the edge of the page. If you look at the trendsetters in type design—magazines like *Raygun* and *Emigre*—you'll find that type, far from being the vehicle for the message, is the message. (p. 10)

Clearly the avant-garde romantic approach to typographic design, that is, "type as personal radical statement" (discussed in Chapter 2), is still alive and thriving in the design community.

Two Key Features of Legibility: Leading and Line Length

Example 3 of Figure 5.1 shows the concepts of *leading* and *line length*. Leading (rhymes with "sledding") is the amount of vertical space between lines of type. The term leading is another holdover from the days when the lines of type were hand set. Because type can be hard to read without some breathing space, typesetters inserted one or more thin strips of lead between the lines. Each of these strips was one point in size. It was common practice to insert two points of leading.

If no space was inserted between the lines, the type was said to be *set solid*. Type set solid gives a dense appearance (like the "terms of disclosure" in credit card agreements). At the opposite extreme is text set with overly generous leading (usually five points or more). This is a common practice in magazine and newspaper advertising where one paragraph might be leaded to take up the whole length of the page (as in ads for cosmetics or cars). Typographers design their typeface families so that even when set solid, the face will still be legible. As mentioned earlier, they do this by building a little frame around the letterforms. The extra

[16] See Tschichold (1928/1987) for a fascinating account of the evolution of a modern typographer's thinking. By the end of his career, Tschichold abandoned his strict adherence to sans serif type and asymmetrical designs, acknowledging that in some cases, such as designing books for children or for the elderly, serif faces may be more readable.

vertical space of the frame ensures that letterforms on one line won't touch those on the next. But this default vertical space is rarely ever enough for designing documents that are comfortable on the eye.

Leading is expressed as two numbers: the first is the typeface's point size, and the second is the *baseline-to-baseline measurement* (see Example 3 in Figure 5.1). Like type size, leading is also measured in points. A document set in 10-point type with 12-point leading is written 10/12 (which translates as 2 points of leading between every two lines of 10-point type). In talking about leading, one reads the fraction 10/12 as "10 on 12" or "10 over 12."

A 10-point typeface set solid has no extra space between the lines of type. When type is set solid, the first number (the type size) and the second number (the baseline-to-baseline measure) are the same; thus, 10 point set solid is 10/10, or "10 over 10" or "10 on 10." This may be confusing because it may seem to be saying there are 10 points of blank space between the lines of type. Not so.

To determine how many points of leading there are between the lines, one must subtract the first number from the second number (in this case 10 minus 10 = 0, which means set solid). It is tricky because naming conventions use the phrases "10-point leading" and "10 points of leading" to mean different things. In the first case, 10-point leading is used to describe a baseline-to-baseline measurement (it would be easier if this term had a different name like "vertical distance"). In the second case, 10 points of leading means the difference between the type size and the baseline-to-baseline measurement is 10 points (like Times Roman 20/30). To take another example, the body text for this book is set at 11 over 13; the footnotes are 8 over 11. This means the type is 11 point with 13-point leading, which means 2 points of leading. Similarly, the footnotes are at 8 point with 11-point leading, or 3 points of leading. (Whew, what a system!)

Even though typographers design the type so that it will still maintain a legible appearance when set solid, document designers should avoid setting their texts solid (unless the line length is very short, as in a newspaper). Tinker (1963) found that readers tended to dislike type that is either set solid or that has too much leading; too much in this case was 4 points of leading with 10-point type (p. 92).

While some word processors automatically adjust the leading incrementally, depending on the size of the type, others set solid by default. Most are set to default at 12-point type size with 2 points of leading, or 12/14. Most typographers recommend that the leading for hardcopy documents should add about 20 percent to the face's point size; thus, for software such as Pagemaker, the default leading is set at 120 percent of the font size (for suggestions about choosing the leading for online documents, see Appendix C, pp. 506–517).

One of the more common problems associated with poor document design is tight leading. Insufficient leading renders a page of hardcopy a forbidding shade of gray. It can also give a computer or television screen of text a vibrating and busy look. A different problem is that when lines are set too tightly, the ascenders and descenders of letterforms in consecutive lines may touch, making the type blurry and giving the page a muddy look. In general, body text needs more leading, while headings need less, often much less. Why? Because headings are easy to see without much space around them; in fact too much space between consecutive lines of a heading set in a large size can make the text look choppy, spread apart, even fragmented. When setting lines of large type it may even be necessary to use *negative leading,* that is, a point size that is smaller than the size of the type. Many corporate logos exploit the dramatic effects that can be created by negative leading, such as stacking words and making them touch to form an interesting visual mark (e.g., the logo for New York Life).

Although strict guidelines about leading can be misleading—since it interacts with typesize and line length—Fenton (1996) makes a few handy suggestions:

- 9-, 10-, or 11-point type needs between 1 and 3 points of leading.
- 12-point type needs between 2 and 4 points of leading.
- 14-point type needs between 3 and 6 points of leading.
- 16-point type needs between 4 and 6 points of leading.
- 18-point type needs between 5 and 6 points of leading.

These guidelines correspond roughly with the "safety zones" suggested by Tinker (1963) and his colleagues, who studied the relationship among type size, leading, and line length (pp. 106–107).

As shown in the bottom portion of Example 3 in Figure 5.1, the *line length* is the distance between the left and right margin of the type. Line length is also called *measure* or *column width.* When measuring the length of a line, a larger unit of measure than the point is used called the *pica* (12 points make a pica and there are roughly 6 picas to an inch). Line length is an important visual characteristic of documents because it affects both legibility and tone. The third example in Figure 5.1 shows the *line length* of the first paragraph in points, picas, inches, and millimeters. In general, longer lines of type require a larger point size and more leading.

When lines of type are too long (more than 70 characters), readers may find that the text makes them weary. They may also have trouble locating the beginning of new lines, and thus may accidentally reread lines of type they just read. People tend to lose their place more often when they are reading documents in which the text is set solid at 10 point or less (Tinker, 1963, p. 86). Conversely, when lines are too short, roughly three words or less, readers may find the text difficult because the visual display tends to break up the syntactic groupings of words, a cue which readers use to comprehend clusters of words[17] (Paterson & Tinker, 1940, 1942). *Generally speaking, in order for lines of text presented on paper to be easy to read, they should be about 40 to 70 characters, or roughly eight to twelve words per line.*[18] *On a computer screen, a shorter line length is more desirable—about 40 to 60 characters.*[19] In situations where it is necessary to use a long line length, the leading should be increased to maximize legibility.

It is important to adjust leading not only for line length but also for the style of the letterform. For example, boldface type, faces with large x-heights, faces with a strong vertical emphasis, or sans serif faces typically require an extra bit of leading (Fenton, 1996, p. 46). As a general principle, when using sans serif typefaces, it is a good idea to insert more leading between the lines of type as the uniform line weight and similarity of letterforms may make it more difficult for readers to track the text smoothly. It's also wise to use narrower columns (a maximum of roughly 60 characters per line on paper and 50 on a computer screen) with sans serif faces. One of the important conclusions from expert typographers and from research on typography is that leading, point size, and line length interact to influence a document's legibility. To make the best decision for the situation, document designers need to try out alternatives in which they systematically vary combinations of these features (there is really no other way to do it).

[17] When designing texts for readers with impaired vision, it is important to provide a larger size of type and shorter line length. However, readers may have trouble getting an accurate sense of the structure of sentences if syntactic units are chopped up, forcing readers to double back in order to identify phrases or clauses. When formatting text with short columns, it is important to preserve the syntactic units of the text or, as editors say, "break for sense." This principle applies to headings and subheadings as well.

---

[18] This advice is intended for body text set between 9 points and 12 points. Because the optimal line length depends on the point size and leading, typography experts hesitate to make guidelines about line length. When they do make guidelines, they tend to disagree. Generally speaking, book design leans toward the higher end of line length (it is common to see 12 to 14 words per line), while the design of instruction guides leans toward the lower end. White (1988) suggests that it is better to stick with the low end of the scale (8 or 9 words per line) with sans serif faces and the higher end (10 or more) for serif faces (p. 25).

[19] In designing online documents, it is better to aim for text toward the lower end, that is, about 40 characters of text per line. Horton (1994) points out that longer lines may make the screen look crowded or may overlap with the labels of icons on the desktop (p. 198). Alternately, Galitz (1989) suggests avoiding long lines by using double columns of text (p. 75). For more information about designing online, see Appendix C (pp. 506–517).

Characteristics of Type: Size and Slant

One way readers make distinctions among the parts of a document is through paying attention to typographic cues such as the size and slant of the text elements. There are two categories for describing the size of a typeface in relation to its purpose in the document: text type and display type. In addition, there are two slants of type: roman and italic. Let's look at each of these basic characteristics.

Text Type Versus Display Type

In general, typefaces are used to compose either continuous text (the body text) or noncontinuous text such as headings, subheadings, headlines, or titles. Type chosen for the body text is often called *text type,* and for noncontinuous text, *display type.* The distinction between text type and display type, while not hard and fast, is usually made in terms of type size (Craig, 1980, p. 24). Text type (or body text) is usually set at 9, 10, 11, or 12 point, with heads and other display type set at 11, 12, 14 or higher.

However, type size is only one of several cues that could be employed to signal distinctions among continuous and noncontinuous text. In addition to being set off by size, display type may be distinguished from text type by outdenting (i.e., by shifting the *position* of the type), bolding (i.e., by changing the *weight* of the type), capitalizing (i.e., changing the *case* of the type), or by employing a different typeface (i.e., changing from one *style* of type to another). Experimenting with the interaction among these five cues—size, position, weight, case, and style—is one of the best ways to develop perceptual knowledge in document design.

One thing to note about type size. Although 12-point type is usually the default for most wordprocessors, it is often too large and not the best size for body text. Again, it depends on the x-height. Rehe (1974) recommends the following for choosing a type size for the body text: "For typefaces with a small x-height, 11 or 12 point should be used, while for those with a large x-height, a 9 or 10 point is more appropriate" (p. 29). When formatting the body text of reports, for example, a typeface with a large x-height, such as Palatino, looks much better set at 10 or 11 point than at 12 point.

Slant of Typefaces: Roman and Italic

Within most serif and sans serif type families there are two *angles* or *slants* of type: *roman* (the upright or plain style of type) and *italic* or *oblique* (the elegant forms that tilt to the right). In desktop publishing or wordprocessing programs, roman type goes by the names Normal or Plain Text. The use of roman to describe the vertical orientation of both serif and sans serif type is sometimes confusing because serif typefaces are called Roman-style typefaces. Used in this sense, Roman contrasts with Gothic or sans serif style.[20] Generally speaking, typographers call the inclined versions of serif typefaces italic and the sans serif oblique.

Italic faces have their origins in the slanted handwriting style[21] that was favored among Italian scholars of the late fifteenth and early sixteenth centuries. They liked its informality and found they could write slanted letters more quickly (Meggs, 1992b, p. 96). Humanist and scholar of the Italian Renaissance Aldus Manutius (1449–1515) is credited with using the first italic face in 1501.[22] Manutius published the major works of Greek and Roman thinkers, editing a five-volume edition of Aristotle. To make books more economical, he published them in a small size, a kind of prototype paperback (only 3.75" by 6"). Manutius found that italic letterforms were narrower than roman letterforms and he could put 50 percent more words per line when the text was set in all italics than he could with roman type. To save space, Manutius used italic to set entire books. His reasons were more than economic, however. Inspired by the writing of Petrarch, Manutius thought that the slanting cursive script of italic letterforms were more beautiful than roman ones. In addition, Manutius experimented with the relationship between prose and graphics, the use of leading, uppercase and lowercase letterforms, letterspacing of type,[23] and more. He was an early document designer extraordinaire. Today Manutius is known to document designers as the "guy on the Aldus Pagemaker logo." (Example 3 in Figure 5.1 provides a short paragraph about Manutius.)

The practice of using italic to set whole books ended when it was recognized that continuous prose set in italics is hard to read. Today the

[20] Note that when describing serif faces, the word Roman is capitalized; when describing vertical letters as distinguished from italic ones, roman is lowercase (Shushan et al., 1996, p. 13).

[21] The handwriting style was called Cancelleresca Script, often shortened to Chancery. Today's document designers can use the beautiful italic typeface, Zapf Chancery, designed by Hermann Zapf.

[22] Manutius didn't actually cut the italic typeface himself. That was done by his assistant at the Aldine press, Francesco da Bologna, surnamed Griffo. It was Griffo who actually made the italic (a font called Aldine), but Manutius was the first to print them in his prototype of the paperback book. Slanted letters were from then on referred to as italic (Jean, 1992).

[23] Letterspacing means adjusting the space between characters to make them look wider or tighter. Manutius used letterspacing in his books to make headings more spacious looking. When widening the space between the letters, one must also widen the space between the words (the wordspacing). In addition to making headings more prominent, letterspacing can be used to enhance the legibility of type that is "set reverse," that is, white type on a black or colored background. Because dark backgrounds have the effect of making white characters look thinner and tighter, reversed type often looks better when the letterspacing is adjusted to make it wider than normal.

use of italic is generally restricted to providing emphasis within a text set in roman (i.e., plain) type.[24]

Typographic Personality: Stress and Weight

In addition to the unique characteristics of the roman and italic letterforms, there are a variety of features that give a face its overall feel, its typographic tone. Choosing a type based on the mood one is trying to create is important, and the possibilities are seemingly endless—from serious to playful, nostalgic to futuristic, delicate to brash, and much more (for example, Adobe Systems Inc. offers more than 2000 typefaces—and it is one of dozens of companies). Two characteristics of type that contribute to its personality are stress and weight.

Type Stress

The angle of the thickest part of the curved strokes in a letterform reveals the *stress* of a typeface. Stress can be either vertical (that is, straight up and down) or oblique, that is, slightly angled to the left. The stress of a typeface captures some of the visual properties of writing with a nibbed pen. Compare, for example, the "o's" in Figure 5.2. Note that the seriffed typeface, Monotype Bembo (the second example), has an *oblique stress*. See how the "o" is slightly thicker on the bottom-left and top-right edges of the curve, making the letterform tilt slightly to the left in a diagonal fashion. In contrast, the "o" in Bauer Bodoni has a strong vertical stress, with symmetrical sides, even in its italic.

A typeface with an oblique stress in its roman version also has an oblique stress in its italic. When designing italic letterforms for a new face, typographers are scrupulous in maintaining the same stress as the roman version (whether that stress is oblique or vertical). For an illustration, see Figure 5.2; this time compare the Bodoni Italic and the Bembo Italic. Typographers suggest that the stress of a typeface may influence the tone of a document. Fenton (1989), for example, says that seriffed type with a strong vertical emphasis tends to convey a more formal and serious tone than do faces with an oblique emphasis, but I have seen no studies that evaluate whether readers respond in this way to the stress of a letterform. To the untrained eye, stress may go unnoticed.

It seems more likely that readers may respond to the "overall feel" of a typeface. The feel is conveyed in part by its stress, but a more dramatic cue to the eye may be the thickness and thinness of the strokes. Look at Figure 5.1 again for some examples of typefaces that differ in this regard.

[24] Desktop publishing has enabled the gradual disappearance of underlining, a signal used by typists to tell the printer to italicize the underlined portion. As a general rule, underlining should be avoided. It distorts letterforms by cutting across their descenders and rarely looks nice. Document designers should use italics instead of underlining.

"What do you read, my lord?"
Polonius
Hamlet, Act II: Scene II, Lines 192–193

vertical stress	oblique stress	vertical stress	oblique stress
words O	words O	*words O*	*words O*
Bauer Bodoni	Monotype Bembo	Bauer Bodoni Italic	Monotype Bembo Italic

▲ **Figure 5.2** *Some visual differences between typefaces with vertical and oblique stress.*

Notice that the thickness of the strokes can be relatively uniform, or some parts may be thick (such as the stems) and others thin (such as the cross strokes, curves, and serifs). In Example 1, the typeface Serifa has very little contrast in the thickness among its strokes. However, the typeface Bauer Bodoni in Example 3 has what typographers refer to as classic *thick-thin proportions* (Black, 1990).

Type Weight

Many of today's digital typefaces have a range of *weights* available (such as light, light italic, semibold, semibold italic, bold, bold italic, black, black italic, ultra black, ultra black italic). When document designers select a type family to use in desktop design, it is a good idea to choose a typeface that offers a range of weights (e.g., five or more). In this way, one can be fairly certain that there is sufficient contrast between the light and bolded versions of the face to allow readers to make visual distinctions among text elements. As a practical matter, it is also important to be sure the needed fonts are installed on the computer. For example, if using Macintosh PostScript fonts, make sure screen fonts and printer fonts for the full type family—including roman and italic versions and their range of weights—are available.[25]

Optional weights for type (in addition to the contrast among the strokes of the plain version of a face) offer document designers a way to *color the page through type* and to provide helpful visual cues for readers about the hierarchy among text elements. Although most people don't pay much attention to the many shades of gray that lie between a light gray and a black, the weight of the type has a direct impact on the color of the text on white paper or on a computer screen—from a light delicate look such as the Garamond developed by the International Typeface Corporation (ITC), called ITC Garamond,[26] to the heavy black look of Serifa, developed by Swiss typographer Adrian Frutiger.

[25] In styling a text with italics, use only typefaces that have been designed with their own italic version. Typefaces that do not have their own italics (such as Geneva) should be avoided because selecting italic for such faces results in a mathematically "tilted to the right" letterform. When typographers design the italic version of their typefaces, they redraw every stroke of the letterform to enhance the aesthetic proportions, never merely "slanting the plain version." Don't make Aldus Manutius roll over in his grave by using fake italics (as mentioned earlier, Manutius was the first printer to publish a book using type designer Griffo's italic letterforms). See Hermann Zapf's work for exemplary italic designs such as Palatino Italic (Society for Typographic Arts, 1987).

[26] For an example of ITC Garamond, see Figure 5.9 (p. 292), the fourth example in the column of seriffed faces.

27 To compare the color of various typefaces, mock up six to twelve paragraphs of text (enough for a two-page spread) at a size of 10 or 12 points. Set the type with fairly tight leading (say 1 to 1.5 points), then print out the text using different faces, comparing the samples side by side. The color differences will be quite apparent.

28 Dpi stands for dots per inch and is a handy way of talking about the resolution of an image on hard copy or on a computer screen. Resolution is the clarity or fineness of detail visible on-screen or in the final printout. In printed material, the resolution depends on the printer's capacity, which in the current desktop technology ranges from 300 dots per inch in most laser printers to 2540 dpi in Linotronic 300 imagesetters.

The color of a typeface is most apparent when the type is employed in continuous text.[27] As a general principle, it is best to choose typefaces that have a lighter look when formatting continuous text. This way the headings will stand out better. Also, unless you print at a high resolution, even light type will look darker than it should when printed at 300 dpi.[28] For some typeface families, the contrast between the plain and bold styling is strong enough that it is unnecessary to emphasize bolded items using additional cues—such as by increasing the size, shifting the position, or changing the case. For other type families, the contrast between the plain and bold is so slight that one needs to use a double cue—such as size and weight, position and case, or weight and position—to get the reader's attention.

TYPOGRAPHIC FLEXIBILITY, CONTRAST, AND DISTINCTIVENESS

In choosing a set of typefaces for everyday purposes, three criteria need to be considered: flexibility, contrast, and distinctiveness. A typeface with *flexibility* is one that can be used in a variety of genres (e.g., reports and newsletters) with reliable results. A face with flexibility is sometimes called a "workhorse" because it holds up well across a range of genres and printing conditions (Times Roman is known as the workhorse among workhorses). It is important to build a personal type library that includes both workhorse faces and those designed to suit special purposes (e.g., Poetica or Tekton).

Contrast refers to the amount of visual difference among versions of the typeface within a given family, especially among the plain, bold, and extra bold (or black). There is a continuum of typographic contrast from low contrast (in which only slight differences are perceptible) through medium contrast (in which differences are perceptible but not pronounced) to high contrast (in which differences are dramatically apparent). Because many documents are designed for rapid access, it is important to strive for high contrast between the body text and the display text. In this way, headings and subheadings will be visibly salient, allowing readers to scan quickly to retrieve the information they want. Contrast can also be achieved by mixing serif and sans serif styles of type. However, in situations where getting the maximum impact from a single face is desired, either a serif or a sans serif face with good internal contrast can perform just as well as mixed faces.

The *distinctiveness* of a typeface refers to how well the face stands out from the crowd. A distinctive typeface need not call attention to itself by shouting "I'm different." Instead, it ought to make a more subtle state-ment by helping the document take on a character that readers have not seen previously for that genre. In this sense, even an old familiar face can be distinctive, particularly when it is employed in a unique way or set in a size readers haven't seen much of. One of the current trends in advertising design, for example, is to use faces that look as though they were created with an old manual typewriter. These faces emulate the look of the typewriter's ribbon going dry—complete with the broken uneven appearance of the strokes and with the counters (e.g., in the "e's and "o's") clogged up with ink. This new "typewriter look" represents a departure from the tradition of using typewriter faces such as Courier or American Typewriter, the regimented faces that look as if they came from an IBM Selectric. And instead of using these new faces to set the body text, they are often employed to set big splashy headlines. For some examples of these digitally mastered "grunge" faces, check out the ads for Broadway shows in the Sunday *New York Times* during the summer of 1996. You will find the choice of faces distinctive even though you may have seen their previous incarnations many times before.

Document designers might consider alternatives to workhorse typefaces that have been overexposed (such as 12-point Times Roman, Helvetica Regular, and Palatino Roman). Although these faces are flexible, they have lost their ability to appear distinctive (at least in this size and in these styles). Moreover, document designers will profit from careful study of the features of typefaces, for this will allow them to develop their perceptual knowledge—improving their eye for choosing a face that is legible and that conveys the most appropriate character and personality.[29]

TO JUSTIFY OR NOT TO JUSTIFY?
MAY BE THE WRONG QUESTION

An important consideration in the design of documents is *justification*, which refers to the visual display of the left and right margin. To justify a text means to arrange it so that it has straight vertical edges on both the left and right margin, like a block. *Ragged-right* text (also called ranged-right text) is text aligned on its left margin with a ragged right margin. (This book is designed using a ragged–right margin, as are the footnotes.) *Ragged-left* text (also called ranged-left text) is text aligned on its right margin with a ragged left margin. Ragged left is usually reserved for "special case" situations in documents, such as the masthead for a magazine, the credits in a movie, or the characters in a playbill.

Some studies have shown that justified text may be hard for poorer readers to comprehend quickly (Gregory & Poulton, 1970). However, the results across the research literature are inconsistent. For example, some studies find no difference between justified and unjustified type in either

[29] A good way to study the differences between typefaces is to assess them in relation to one another. It is important to evaluate the entire alphabet (uppercase and lowercase), including numerals and special characters. There are many books which display popular text typefaces with various degrees of leading. Seeing typefaces side-by-side allows one to inspect the details that one might otherwise miss. For some examples of special symbols and characters, see Appendix B, pp. 502–505).

reading speed or comprehension (Fabrizio, Kaplan & Teal, 1967; Hartley & Burnhill, 1971). The inconsistency in the literature may be related to another factor more important than the straightness or raggedness of the right margin. That factor is *word spacing,* the amount of horizontal space between words. It is well known that justified texts often have unequal spaces between the words (both among the words on the same line of type and from one line to the next). This creates a disturbing visual illusion known as "rivers"—paths running vertically through the text that connect the blank spaces between words on adjacent lines. For an example, look again at Figure 3.3, *Smokeless Tobacco* (p. 176). The irregular and uneven spacing disrupts the visual rhythm of each line. Moreover, rivers may distract the reader and slow the rate of reading.

Research by Campbell, Marchetti, and Mewhort (1981) found that reading speed was significantly faster with a right-justified text with equal horizontal spaces between words[30] than a justified text in which there were large and unpredictable spaces between the words (the "river" condition).[31] Similarly, comprehension was significantly less accurate with the river condition. In a second study, they found that reading speed for "justified text with equal word spacing" was faster than both "justified text with rivers" and "ragged right." When justified texts are formatted using word spacing that has been adjusted so there is relatively equal horizontal space between the words, then the difference between justified and ragged right disappears. We can conclude that quarreling over the issue of justifying the text or not is probably the wrong concern. The right concern is how to achieve a text without rivers and excessive hyphenation.[32]

When using the ragged–right setting in desktop design, computer software programs automatically put the same amount of space between each word on every line. However, when using the justified setting, "all hell may break loose" when trying to get equal word spacing. The

[30] Right-justified text with equal horizontal spacing is called the *variable character full-justified technique.* This technique distributes space proportionally between the characters and the words on a line.

---

[31] Text that has rivers or unpredictable spaces between the words is called *fixed character full-justification technique.* The unpredictability lies in how many fixed characters between the words the justification algorithm will permit. The algorithm works by calculating the space from the right margin to the end of a line of text in blank-character units and distributes the space in character units between the words on that line. The character spacing within a word is fixed; this technique does not put extra spaces within the word (i.e., no extra letterspacing to even out lines of type).

[32] Thanks to Conrad Taylor, a British designer who trades under the name Ideography and who edits the U.K.'s Information Design Association newsletter, *IDeAs,* for setting me straight on the complicated issues of parameters and algorithms for digital type (E-mail, July 23, 1996).

problem for document designers is that software programs use bewildering algorithms to do three things at the same time: (1) put a little extra space between the characters, (2) put extra space between the words, and (3) decide when to break lines by using hyphenation. Not surprisingly, the algorithms differ in how they consider these factors. Some offer complete control (even though the user needs to be a mathematician to figure out the complicated numbers he or she is expected to set); others offer no control. This makes it hard to know what the justified document will look like when ported from one platform to the next. With most word-processing programs, choosing to justify the text effectively means "give me rivers" and while you're at it, "give me excessive hyphenation."

Consequently, document designers who insist on justifying their text must worry about letterspacing, word spacing, and hyphenation as three parts of the same problem. (This is why most desktop publishing software programs designate letterspacing as a paragraph-level attribute.) To get equal word spacing in a justified text, one must first adjust the parameters for word spacing and letterspacing. One must then set the hyphenation to limit the number of consecutive hyphens to two.[33] Without adjusting the word spacing, letterspacing, and hyphenation, one risks the typographic nightmare of a body text with huge rivers that also has 15 or more hyphens per paragraph.[34] Practically speaking, it is much easier to use a ragged-right setting and to limit hyphenation than it is to justify the text with equal word spacing while maintaining a limit on hyphenation. Even after taking the extra trouble to set the word spacing, letterspacing, and hyphenation to achieve the desired effect, often the designer must go back into the file and manually space some of the lines. Moreover, this process makes editing cumbersome. What a pain!

There seems no real advantage for the reader in taking all this trouble. But avoiding justified text in documents may also be a sound idea for another reason that has to do with the relationship between documents and readers' feelings. Because justification has been used for centuries in the design of Bibles, sacred texts, medical documents, government documents, and legal texts, readers may perceive the severe rectangular look of justified texts as formal, distant, even unapproachable. This may be true even for readers in highly technical and scientific domains. For example, in a survey of the preferences of readers at NASA, researchers found that 61.5 percent of survey respondents preferred ragged-right margins over justified margins when reading technical reports (Pinelli, Glassman, & Cordle, 1982). When composing documents that people may already dislike (e.g., manuals, instructions, forms, and reports) it is a good idea to present the prose and graphics using text features that readers prefer.

[33] For some advice on using hyphenation and other typographic cues, see Appendix B (pp. 502–505).

[34] Unfortunately, some well-known academic book publishing houses pay no attention whatsoever to ugly document design, routinely publishing books with rivers running through the body text coupled with excessive hyphenation. Such ghastly typographic practices by organizations that should set the standards for publishing erode their own reputations and do their authors a disservice.

A HEURISTIC FOR DECISION MAKING ABOUT TYPE

In evaluating what typeface to use, document designers need to consider typographic and spatial factors as interactive elements within a visual field.[35] That is, they must judge how various features of the typography and space—size, weight, width, case, letter spacing, word spacing, line length, leading, position, and manner of justification—may interact on the page or on the screen. Given the difficulty in making all of these decisions at once (or worse, just letting the computer scientist who designed your word processor or page layout software make the decision for you), document designers need what Aristotle called a *heuristic*. As I mentioned in Chapter 2, a heuristic is a way of thinking systematically about the key features of a problem.

A helpful rule of thumb for thinking about the interactive nature of type, space, and text features has been set out by Black (1990). She recommends beginning the document design process by taking an inventory[36] of the range of text elements the particular document requires (e.g., body text, headlines, marginalia, captions, and so on). For example, a proposal may employ body text, headings, and footnotes. On the basis of this inventory, the document designer should "mock-up" a prototypical document—one that includes long and short paragraphs of body text, long and short headings, and long and short footnotes. Next experiment with the prototype by varying its typographic features, starting with those that may matter most to the reader. Start by choosing several suitable type families[37] and then "put them through their paces." Look for typefaces that look well together side-by-side and that support the intended tone of the content. Next, find a satisfactory type size for each of the main text elements. Then vary the line length to find what lengths work best for each of the text elements. Finally, vary the leading so that each text element is attractive to read and that all of the text elements work together in an aesthetically pleasing way.

To see how the document will actually look to the reader, format at least one page or screen to specification and print out (or display) the variations—placing the competing samples side-by-side on a big table (or screen). This way you can evaluate the effect of each change. You must literally "see the text" to judge it critically. Avoid relying on memory: It's never quite the same.

In putting the type through this sort of "test drive," examine how it looks when employed for the biggest chunks of continuous discourse (such as the longest paragraph of the body text). Ask yourself how well the face works for the special cases (such as the longest heading or the

[35] For a discussion of the interactive nature of typographic elements, see Black (1990), Keyes (1993), or Van der Waarde (1993).

[36] I am interpreting and summarizing ideas that Black presents over the course of several chapters in her book; thus, she may not have viewed herself as presenting the heuristic I took away from my reading.

[37] Writers with little experience in choosing typefaces might consider the advice of graphic designers. An informal survey by Fenton (1996) in which she asked design experts to choose their top ten favorite all-purpose typefaces revealed the following (in alphabetical order): Bodoni, Caslon, Futura, Galliard, Garamond, Goudy Old Style, Janson Text, New Baskerville, Optima, and Univers. Runners-up were: Adobe's Stone family (Stone Serif, Stone Sans, Stone Informal), ITC Cheltenham, Franklin Gothic, Gill Sans, Helvetica, and Berkeley Oldstyle (p. 71).

shortest paragraph, and whether special characters such as mathematical or musical symbols will be needed). If tradeoffs have to be made, prioritize your "giving in" points. Like all heuristics, Alison Black's heuristic is not a guarantee of success. However, such heuristics can be very effective in helping document designers make better decisions in the very complex situations that they must face. In particular, Black's heuristic provides a systematic way to base typographic decisions on an analysis of the whole document.[38] This is a good idea not only for choosing type, but also for making decisions about which text elements the layout will require, especially which text elements need to "talk directly" to others.

In my experience, writers and graphic designers tend to have different kinds of troubles in envisioning the possibilities for documents. On one hand, inexperienced graphic designers may have difficulty designing a coherent set of typographic and spatial cues for lengthy complex documents. They may excel in the design of posters and one-page flyers, but tend to falter with multileveled documents that require the considered design of special cases. They forget that all of the special cases need to be considered "up front" and that the strategy of "figuring out as you go" can be disastrous with big documents.

On the other hand, too many writers still use computers as typewriters. Their idea of horizontal space is using the "tab key." Just tab over for columns. Just hit a few "returns" between the paragraphs. They have trouble visualizing their words set on a page and tend to miss opportunities for using space in creative ways (discussed later in this chapter). Many writers are not only oblivious to the graphic possibilities for their texts, but also tend to be more conservative than graphic designers in their willingness to take textual risks. For example, as I mentioned earlier, writers tend to rely on typographic standbys: Times,[39] Helvetica,[40] and Palatino.[41] Both writers and graphic designers would do each other a favor if they developed their facility in considering the whole document before making decisions about the type and space.

[38] Research on writing provides consistent evidence that experienced writers take a whole-text view of what they are working on while inexperienced writers tend to take a linear, "whatever strikes them at the moment" approach (Flower et al., 1986; Hayes & Nash, 1996; Schriver, 1993b).

[39] Designed for the London *Times* in 1931 by Stanley Morrison, Times is somewhat condensed, so it can fit a lot of text into a small space. It has a large x-height and bold even strokes. These features have made it the choice in the newspaper industry, as it holds up well even under poor printing conditions. But, as they say in the movie industry, Times is "overexposed." Fenton (1996) advises, "Don't use this ubiquitous face if you want your publication to stand out from the crowd" (p. 53). An example of Times is shown in Figure 5.9 (p. 292), the third typeface under "Serif."

[40] Helvetica, designed by Max Meidinger of Switzerland, is an easy-to-read, simple typeface. Unfortunately, it has been used in so many areas that it no longer has a special or interesting feel. Some even say Helvetica is "short on personality, but long on versatility" (Fenton, 1996, p. 53). For an example of Helvetica, see Figure 5.9 (p. 292), the third typeface under "Sans Serif." Times and Helvetica may be the two most widely used faces in the western world.

[41] Palatino is a classically beautiful face designed by renowned typographer Hermann Zapf. Unfortunately, Palatino is now so overused that it looks nearly as familiar as Times or Helvetica. When used for body copy, avoid 12 point or higher as it looks too large. Palatino looks better set at 10 or 11 point. For an example of Palatino, see Figure 5.9 (p. 292), the second typeface under "Serif."

WHAT RESEARCH SAYS ABOUT THE LEGIBILITY OF TYPOGRAPHY

The research literature on typography, while not extensive, provides the following guidelines:

- Serif and sans serif typefaces are likely to be equally preferred by readers (Hartley & Rooum, 1983; Tinker, 1963) and read equally quickly (Gould et al., 1987; Hartley & Rooum, 1983; Zachrisson, 1965). Serif faces may be easier to read in continuous text than sans serif faces (Burt, 1959; Hvistendal & Kahl, 1975; Robinson, Abbamonte, & Evans, 1971; Wheildon, 1995).

- The x-height of a typeface matters as much if not more than the size of the type in affecting its legibility (Poulton, 1955).

- People read faster when text is set with 1 to 4 points of leading than when the type is set solid (Becker, Heinrich, van Sichowsky, & Wendt, 1970; Bentley, 1921; Paterson & Tinker, 1932).

- When the lines of type are either too long or too short, readers may be forced to slow their normal rate of reading (Paterson & Tinker, 1942). (See the suggestions for line length presented earlier in this chapter.) It is easier for readers to see the structure of the text when the number of different line lengths that comprise a document is kept to a minimum. It is a good idea to provide contrast in the line lengths employed—with some longer and others shorter—but all textual material with the same rhetorical function should have the same line length throughout the text (Bonsiepe, 1968).

- When italic type is used for continuous prose, reading speed can be reduced substantially (Foster & Bruce, 1982; Tinker, 1955). Extensive use of italic in continuous prose may make nonitalicized words stand out more than italicized words (Glynn, Britton, & Tillman, 1985).

- When text is set in all capital letters, reading speed is slowed about 13 to 20 percent (Breland & Breland, 1944). Reading speed is optimal when uppercase and lowercase letters are used (Poulton, 1967; Rickards & August, 1975). When extra emphasis is needed, bold has been found to be a better cue than uppercase (Coles & Foster, 1975).

- Readers pay attention to contrast among typographic elements. Changes in the weight of type (e.g., light, medium, bold, extra bold, black) may be noticed more than changes in the typeface (Spencer, Reynolds, & Coe, 1974).

- By "reversing the type"—making white letters on a black or colored background—designers can call attention to textual elements (shown in Figure 5.3). Reversed type may be used for headings, pull-out quotes, or section tabs (e.g., reversed bars along the right-hand side of pages as in phone directories). In general, reversed headings should be used cautiously; they are such a strong cue that they may make the rest of the text appear unimportant.

> *"Contextual Inquiry is based on the premise that the inquirer and the participant are equals."*

◀ **Figure 5.3** *An example of "reversed out" type with too little leading (14-point Sabon Italic with 11.7 point leading). Notice that the ascenders and descenders of some letterforms touch. In addition, the italics seems to vibrate a bit. Under normal circumstances, that is, when printed without being reversed, the sharp serifs of Sabon are beautiful. Here, partly because they are reversed out and partly because the leading is too tight, they look busy and are not the best choice for this situation. The use of more leading along with slightly expanded letterspacing (about 5% expansion) would have increased the legibility of the text. From* The Journal of Computer Documentation, *20(1) 1996, p. 3. This quote appears in Raven and Flanders' (1996) interesting article about contextual inquiry, a form of reader-feedback audience analysis.*

- Reversed headings can create an ugly striped look when employed in the design of two-page spreads with multiple heads and subheads. Also consider the following about reversing the type:

  ○ When typefaces are reversed, the dark background makes the strokes appear thinner than they actually are. Typefaces need to be chosen for their strong strokes and cross strokes as well as for sturdy ascenders and descenders. This is also true for setting type on a dark computer screen or dark television screen (Rehe, 1974).

  ○ Sans serif faces usually look better than do serif faces when re-versed, but this depends on the type size. A large serif typeface can work well, especially if the serifs are horizontal or slab serifs. Many seriffed faces at small sizes are hard to read when reversed. Avoid thinly seriffed faces and serifs with pointed tips, as in Figure 5.3.

  ○ When reversing type, it is best to use uppercase and lowercase letters in the medium weight or bolded versions for the face. Avoid the use of all capitals (Wheildon, 1995) as the letterforms tend to make a square shape that is boxed by another square.

  ○ In small amounts, reversing can be a dramatic cue, but never set continuous text by reversing it as it may reduce reading speed up to 15 percent (Holmes, 1931; Taylor, 1934) and readers may dislike it (Paterson & Tinker, 1932).

- Blank space around paragraphs and between columns of type helps increase legibility (Smith & McCombs, 1971). In columns of type that are designed with a screen running behind them (such as a 10 percent shade of gray), the line length should be shorter than the width of the screen. In this way, the screen provides a frame around the type on both the left and right sides of the screen.

- Text with generous amounts of blank space may attract and hold the reader's attention longer than text with little blank space (Strong, 1926). A rule of thumb in publishing is that textual material should occupy about 50 percent of the page (Tinker, 1963; see also, Pinelli, Cordle, & McCullough, 1986).

Criticisms of the Research on Typography

Several studies of legibility have shown that people read serif-style faces with greater ease than sans serif-styles; the finishing strokes of serif typefaces has been said to help the eye to distinguish individual characters and to recognize words (Robinson, Abbamonte, & Evans, 1971; Hvistendahl & Kahl, 1975). Serifs are also believed to improve tracking in horizontal lines of text, enabling rapid movement from one line to another. Although early research such as Burt's (1959) suggested advantages for serif type in continuous text, more recent investigations have found no clear patterns suggesting that serif is always superior to sans serif (Gould et al., 1987; Hartley & Rooum, 1983). These mixed results are partly an artifact of the scant and incoherent state of typographic research; it's hard to draw conclusions about a literature that has few benchmarks for quality or validity.

Many of the presumed advantages of serif over sans serif may have been statistically significant but suffered from a lack of ecological validity (that is, the results of these studies may not apply in typical reading situations). As Kinross (1992) points out, the research on typography prior to the 1930s suffered from a persistent unreality in what was tested. Much work was done on "testing the recognizability of isolated letters—as on an optician's card—instead of the legibility of words or passages of text" (p. 32). However, even the research in the 1930s through the 1980s was not always persuasive.[42] Some of the results were confounded by using ugly sans serif faces with small x-heights. MacDonald-Ross and Waller (1975) point out that the stimulus materials used in many studies failed to meet the basic standards of clarity achieved by most professional graphic designers; that is, the materials researchers considered to be examples of "good typography" were considered less than adequate by typographers.

More importantly, researchers tended to study the effect of component parts of the letterform without looking at the big picture. They often studied one feature (such as type size) without looking systematically at how that feature worked with other ones. Thus, we find few studies that explore the interaction among what are perhaps the three most crucial features of type that influence its legibility: (1) x-height, (2) line length, and (3) amount of leading. A notable exception was a series of landmark studies carried out by Tinker and Paterson which explored the interplay of type size, leading, and line width. They carried out 11 studies in which more than 11,000 readers took part (described in Tinker, 1963, pp. 90–107). Their work forms the basis of the existing guidelines for type size, line length, and leading (mentioned earlier). However, even their work measured type according to point size (the less sensitive measure of type) rather than x-height.[43]

[42] Sadly, there has been very little empirical research on typography during the 1980s and 1990s.

[43] In fairness to Tinker and other researchers, they should not have to invent a system for measuring x-heights. It is the responsibility of typographers to derive a system for measuring type that will replace the point system.

A more serious problem was that researchers ignored the rhetorical role of type and the reader's context for reading. They tended not to ask whether a face was suited for the particular message, given the audience and the situation. Their idea of context was whether there was enough light in the room to see the letterforms. Because many researchers have been insensitive to these contextual issues, many typographers and graphic designers dismiss the typographic research as irrelevant to making typographic decisions. Although their dismissive attitude is understandable, in my opinion it is a mistake.

Why Should Document Designers Bother with the Research on Typography?

Instead of dismissing typographic research as irrelevant, document designers should work to improve it, to contextualize it—to show where it has value and where it does not. The document design community should foster typographic research because it provides valuable assistance in making design decisions. Often such decisions are made primarily on the basis of personal preference (e.g., for small type) or on the basis of cost (the lower the better) because solid evidence about the effects of typographic decisions on readers is not available. If, for example, we relied only on the opinions of graphic designers, readers might have to decipher text set at 7 and 8 points because the individual letterforms are pleasing to the designer's eye. If, on the other hand, we relied on the opinions of writers, then readers might have to get used to justified-right margins because writers think they look tidy. Left to managers, who may favor outsourcing typographic decisions to printers, readers might find themselves reading typefaces that were chosen so that as much text could be crammed on the page as possible.

My point is that empirical studies can serve a very useful corrective function to document design practice. The findings of research needn't be turned into guidelines in order to be useful. (It is nice if they can be, but this isn't a necessary condition for their value). In fact, studies that merely act to redirect practical action can be the most valuable. For example, researchers who found that people read body text more slowly when it is set in uppercase didn't tell designers precisely how to display the type, merely what to avoid. Research helps us to steer the course. Like a set of buoys guiding a ship's captain to a harbor, it prevents us from crashing into rocks we can't see.

Research can help us to think more creatively about the writing and design problems that concern us. For example, there is evidence from both research and anecdotal experience that readers do prefer some typefaces over others and that these preferences are associated with legibility (Tinker & Paterson, 1942). In fact, preference often agrees with reading speed as well (Tinker, 1963, p. 51). The complication is that what readers prefer and what is most legible depends on the situation. But just because research hasn't specified which features of typefaces make them most preferred and legible, this doesn't mean that "anything goes" or that research is worthless. Instead, it reminds document designers of the need to evaluate their typographic choices with the intended audience(s) in the context in which the documents will be read or used.

Research helps us to expand our ideas about which parts of the context might be important. For example, if the text is usually read at a desk while the reader's fingers are on a keyboard, research suggests we should evaluate legibility and preference in those conditions. Research gives us systematic procedures for taking the local context into account. In this way, we can avoid gross stereotypes, such as Americans prefer serif faces while Europeans like sans serif. Research can also help us make more reasonable guesses about why readers like what they do. For instance, preferences may correlate with the reader's familiarity with the face. Moreover, what readers like may align with the publishing practices of where they live (not surprisingly, documents in the United States have had a tradition of using serif faces while those in Europe have used sans serif). I will come back to this issue of preference at the end of this section with a study on the effect of genre on readers' preferences.

LEGIBILITY AND PRINTING: AN OVERLOOKED BUT IMPORTANT ISSUE

Most typographic research has studied hardcopy materials that have been produced using high-quality printing (as I've mentioned, the materials were not always up to the standards of expert typographers, but researchers did make an effort to use clearly printed output). However, many of the texts that people read every day are not of the highest production quality because they have been copied, faxed, or output using a printer on the last leg of its toner cartridge. Each of these common practices provides an occasion for the type to lose some of its integrity and may compromise the legibility of certain typefaces (particularly those set at small sizes). For example, when documents that are set with serif typefaces are copied many times, the serifs may start to break down (and if the toner of the copier is going, even disappear). The typeface Bauer Bodoni (shown in Example 3 of Figure 5.1) is one of those typefaces in which the hairline serifs might fade out under poor printing conditions.

A common problem for desktop designers is not that they are using a 300-dpi laser printer, but that the toner cartridge is not up to par. Cartridges that are very new or very old tend to produce uneven ink coverage and generally should not be used to print important documents. The typographic integrity of the letterforms can also be jeopardized when the text is printed using recharged toner in a laser printer. Because recharged toner cartridges may distribute ink unevenly, the type may "heavy up," making it look bolder than it should be. (I discovered this after downgrading my students' document design projects, reminding them that it was a bad idea to use boldface for the whole document, only to find out the problem was the toner cartridges used in the university's computing clusters.) When too much toner comes out of the cartridge for each letterform, the ink spreads, causing the letterforms to get slightly bigger than they should be. Thus, consecutive lines of type may look fine on a computer screen but if set with tight leading may touch once printed. Similarly, if typefaces have tight letter spacing, the characters within words may touch.

A related problem with poor toner cartridges may occur when the counters of a typeface are small. That is, the space inside of letters such as "o," "e," or "a" may close up, looking like old typewriter output (see Example 1 in Figure 5.1 for an illustration of a letterform's counters). The result is a document that looks sloppy and careless. Unless the designer is seeking the "grunge look" (a trend I mentioned earlier), it's better to avoid having one's typographic choices compromised during the printing process.

How the text is printed (or displayed) is an important variable affecting legibility and tone (Black, 1990). Poorly printed documents send the reader a message that the content is unimportant. Research needs to take the effects of faxing,[44] copying, low resolution displays, and nonoptimal printing conditions into account. Such findings could help document designers make arguments about the added value of good design, showing that quality of printing contributes to the customer's image of products and services.

LEGIBILITY AND QUANTITATIVE GRAPHICS

Research from psychology suggests that it is important to keep the reader's cognitive load as light as possible. Work by Kosslyn (1994) shows a number of ways to reduce the reader's burden during comprehension of quantitative displays. In Figure 5.4 (on the next page), I present an application of his work to show the effect of two sets of symbols that could be used in the design of a line graph. The first set of symbols,

[44] Adobe Systems (1989) conducted an informal study of typefaces for faxing. They printed the same letter 12 times, using a dozen different fonts. The letter was then faxed "across the street and across the country" (p. 14). Using volunteer judges, including members of the Adobe's Type Development department, each fax was ranked by how well the typeface maintained clarity of its letterforms and on how legible the text was. The winners in order were: (1) Lucida Roman, (2) Lucida Sans, (3) ITC Stone Sans, (4) ITC Bookman Light, (5) Corona, (6) Utopia, (7) Frutiger, (8) Melior, (9) Century Expanded, (10) News Gothic, (11) Glypha, and (12) Clarendon. The top two winners, Lucida Roman and Lucida Sans, were designed for low-resolution electronic publishing. Although we might quibble with their choice of faces to test (they may have been interested in selling them), the results suggest that typefaces with a consistent thickness in all parts of the letterform work the best under the duress of faxing.

because they are so close in visual design, color, weight, size, and shape, may be hard to discriminate if the reader is looking at a graph where some of the data aggregate and plot lines pile up on one another. Perceptual research indicates that filled symbols such as triangles, squares, and circles often become difficult to discern when clustered at small sizes (Chen, 1982; Cleveland & McGill, 1984; Schutz, 1961). For example, Schutz (1961) found that black-and-white displays with highly discriminable symbols were almost as good as displays that used color. The negative effects of poor discriminability increase when graphics are reduced or reproduced without consideration for maintaining the distinctive shape of all symbols.

The important consideration in the easy-to-discriminate symbols is not the choice of symbol itself (for instance, an X may not be the best choice in many situations), but the selection of the symbol in relation to other

▶ **Figure 5.4** *A comparison of hard-to-discriminate and easy-to-discriminate symbols that can be employed to plot the data for line graphs (based on the work of Kosslyn, 1994).*

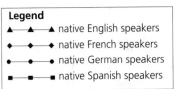

Hard-to-Discriminate Symbols

Easy-to-Discriminate Symbols

▶ **Figure 5.5** *A poorly designed line graph. Notice the lack of discriminability among the symbols employed to plot the data. Also note that the reader must expend extra effort to map the labels in the legend to the graphic. In addition, the captions are set too wide in relation to the width of the graph.*

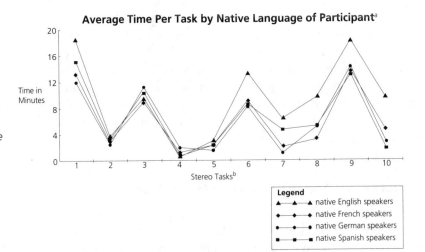

[a] There were 29 participants: 6 native English speakers; 8 native French; 7 native German; and 8 native Spanish.

[b] Each participant completed 10 tasks: (1) connect the stereo components together, (2) set the clock on the tuner, (3) program a series of radio stations, (4) listen to the radio, (5) listen to a cassette tape, (6) record some music on one side of a tape, (7) listen to a song on a CD player, (8) program the CD player to play songs in a certain order, (9) create a mixed cassette tape in which particular songs are recorded in a certain order, and (10) program the timer to begin recording at a specified time.

choices in proximal relation to it. Here, the X is clearly distinct from the filled triangle; similarly, the filled circle and the open square are different from one another. Moreover, all four symbols are visually discrete from each other, making them readily perceptible even at a small sizes.

To put these ideas into practice, I used them to redesign a graph from a usability study in which participants were native speakers of English, French, German, and Spanish (the study is described in Chapter 7). Figures 5.5 and 5.6 present a "before" and "after" line graph in which the symbols employed to plot the data were revised to enhance their visual discriminability. Notice that for tasks 2, 3, 4, 6, and 9, the data pile up and it's hard to see the differences among the symbols in the first graph, while it is easier to see them in the second. (Hard-to-discriminate symbols can create similar difficulties online, and in some cases, the problem may be much worse, if the screen resolution is low.)

Also note that in Figure 5.6 the position of the legend has been moved; I followed the work of Milroy and Poulton (1978) who found that placing labels directly next to the plot lines enabled people to find information on the graph more quickly than when a legend or a key was used. They attribute the advantage to fewer processing steps and a lighter load on short-term memory. In the first graph, the reader not only has to figure out which symbol is which, but must also map the symbols to the legend (doubling the mental effort just to get the point).

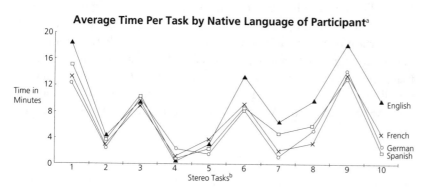

Average Time Per Task by Native Language of Participant[a]

◀ Figure 5.6 *A line graph after revising the symbols employed to plot the data in order to enhance their discriminability. Also revised is the location of the data labels (i.e., placing them directly on the graph rather than in a legend or key). In addition, the line length of the captions is the same as the width of the graph.*

[a] There were 29 participants: 6 native English speakers; 8 native French; 7 native German; and 8 native Spanish.

[b] Each participant completed 10 tasks: (1) connect the stereo components together, (2) set the clock on the tuner, (3) program a series of radio stations, (4) listen to the radio, (5) listen to a cassette tape, (6) record some music on one side of a tape, (7) listen to a song on a CD player, (8) program the CD player to play songs in a certain order, (9) create a mixed cassette tape in which particular songs are recorded in a certain order, and (10) program the timer to begin recording at a specified time.

LEGIBILITY AND ONLINE DOCUMENTS

Readers often experience problems with the legibility of type on a computer screen. While some typefaces presented on a computer or a television may have an ugly, jagged[45] look (see Figure 5.7), others have a tight, cramped appearance. Either way, poor legibility slows down readers in their attempts to interpret the text. In fact, studies of writers and editors working online have found that reading online may take people 20 to 40 percent longer than reading on paper. Writers and editors are also more likely to experience fatigue and eye strain when proofreading lengthy documents online than when editing lengthy documents on paper. Moreover, proofreaders have been found to miss errors in texts when they edit online, errors that they otherwise would see on paper.[46] These findings imply that if writers and editors are to work accurately and efficiently while maintaining their mental alertness, they should edit on paper and not online. It also suggests that inexperienced writers (such as high school or college students) should never edit online, since they have been found to miss a high proportion of errors when revising on paper (Flower et al., 1986; Hayes et al., 1987; Hull, 1987) and would likely miss even more when editing online.

Recent research[47] suggests that the differences researchers in early studies found between hardcopy and online text may no longer be an issue. These newer studies tested numerous variables, including screen resolution, antialiasing of fonts, leading, and spacing to understand why reading online tends to be slower. (Antialiasing[48] is a technique used to improve the legibility of jagged fonts or line art on a computer screen; see the top portion of Figure 5.7). They found that with high-resolution monitors and digital typography, the speed and accuracy differences tend to disappear. But document designers need to ask, "What population of users will reap these benefits in the near future?" Not everyone can afford a high-resolution monitor. Most organizations I've consulted with don't have them, not even for writers.

[45] Fortunately, the problem of the "jaggies" can be solved by using type manager software such as Adobe Type Manager. The technical term for the problem of jagged type is called "aliasing," referring to the stair-step appearance of diagonal lines and curves on a computer screen. To get rid of the jagged look in type, a technique called antialiasing is used (see footnote 48). Although anti-aliasing can solve the problem of jaggies, the difficulties of reading online when type has tight letterspacing or small x-height cannot be solved except by changing the font.

[46] See the research of Gould and Grischkowsky (1984), Haas and Hayes (1986b), Muter, Latremouille, Treurniet, and Beam (1982), or Wright and Lickorish (1983).

[47] See the work in the area of reading online versus on paper by Gould, Alfaro, Finn, Haupt, and Minuto (1987) and Osborne and Holton (1988).

[48] Antialiasing works by rendering the pixels around the edge of a letterform in intermediate shades of gray so that the pixels seem to blend together, creating a smoother look. Antialiasing blurs the boundaries of letterforms in order to make their jagged edges less distinct. Paradoxically, by blurring their edges, letterforms appear smoother to the eye. Figure 5.7 shows what fonts can look like when bitmapped and what images can look like after scanning. The letter "a" was repaired using antialiasing with Adobe Type Manager; the cartoon was modified with Adobe Streamline. Rather than using antialiasing, Streamline works by vectorizing raster images into curves, a technique that smooths out the jaggies that can result from scanning.

◀ Figure 5.7 *A bitmapped "a" and a bitmapped line drawing, the cartoon "Shoe." Notice the "jagged look" of the first "a" versus the smooth look when presented with type manager software, Adobe Type Manager. Note also the improved look of the illustration when "cleaned up" with Adobe Streamline, a software program that can smooth the rough edges of line art. "Shoe" created by Jeff MacNelly. Reprinted with the permission of Tribune Media Services, Chicago, IL.*

At some point, differences between reading online and on paper might disappear, but for now there are still plenty of hard-to-read online texts. Fortunately, there has been considerable research on ways to make the design of online displays (including World Wide Web pages) more legible and aesthetically pleasing. In fact, the research is more extensive than the work available on designing hardcopy texts. This work covers issues such as choosing a typeface, type size, leading, type style, text density, and line length. It also provides recommendations regarding the use of italics, uppercase, and letterspacing. Moreover, it provides advice on setting margins, grouping content with itemized lists, and formatting subheadings. Because this literature is somewhat lengthy, I present it separately in Appendix C, "Guidelines for Designing Online Displays" (pp. 506–517).

THE RHETORICAL APPROPRIATENESS OF TYPOGRAPHY: ITS ROLE IN SEEING THE TEXT

Up to this point I've characterized the importance of providing readers with legible type in hardcopy and online documents. As we've seen, legible typography is necessary for good document design. But designing legible documents is not enough. A second important characteristic of well-chosen typography is rhetorical appropriateness—the relationship between the typeface, the purpose of the document, its genre, the situation, and the audience's needs, desires, and purposes. This calls on document designers to employ typography in ways that influence how readers perceive, organize, and remember the content. Although typographers tend to focus on the aesthetic functions of type, emphasizing that it provides mood, personality, and tone—all of which are essential to a rhetorically effective artifact—an equally and perhaps even more important consideration is the rhetorical role that typography plays in readers' engagement with and interpretation of the content. Well-chosen typography helps to reveal the content and its structure, enabling readers to see the text in ways that help them to interpret its meanings.[49]

49 For ideas about the rhetorical nature of typography and graphics, see Barton and Barton (1985), Bernhardt (1986), Kostelnick (1996), Twyman (1979), and Waller (1980).

Experienced designers recognize the need to know *what* is to be read, *why* it is to be read, *who* will read it, and *when* and *where* it will be read. On this basis, designers select typography that will make it easier for readers to see the relationships among the parts of the document. Good typography can enhance the reader's ability to infer the purpose and organization of the document. The rhetorical role of typographic design can be seen in how it provides perceptual clues for the reader. In particular, typography gives readers clues about two key features of documents:

1. *Text structure* (the hierarchy, organization, and divisions among levels of the content; e.g., the structure of a book may have several levels of headings below a chapter level)

2. *Roles of text elements* (the purposes and relations among the text elements, and their functions to one another; e.g., in an instruction manual, the relationships among illustrations, labels, and captions)

As Waller (1980, 1982, 1985, 1987) has pointed out on a number of occasions, the typographic organization of a text may signal the structure of the content in several ways:

50 Waller refers to "argument" in its largest sense, that is, any piece of discourse designed to inform, instruct, or persuade.

- *Typography can provide information about the argument*[50] by delineating text features which serve particular purposes. For example, the executive summary of a report serves the purpose of abstracting the main ideas. Rhetorically effective typography makes the executive summary visually distinct (through choices such as typeface, leading, point size, and line length), allowing the reader to immediately draw the appropriate inference that this content serves a different role than does the rest of the document.

- *Typography can provide information within the argument* by emphasizing text parts. For example, to make some content items more prominent, designers might use italics to highlight words and phrases. They might also employ leading to signal transitions in the text's content (e.g., by putting extra leading around headings or between paragraphs). They might also present some content in the form of itemized lists in order to draw the reader's attention to particular parts of the argument.

- *Typography can provide information about supplements or addenda to the argument*. For example, typography may be employed to indicate which text elements play a subordinate role to the body text, through elements such as footnotes, appendices, references, and captions.

In these ways, typography plays a fundamental role in visualizing the message.[51] Choices document designers make about typography influence how readers interpret the text's structure, what they view as the most important points, how they believe ideas are related, and which ideas they represent as subordinate. Typography works in concert with spatial cues. A striking example of the way in which typographic and spatial cues interact is in the design of tables, matrices, and lists—all of which depend on visible structure to render the text meaningful. (Later in this chapter, I discuss how the structure of tabular information can reveal the document designer's rhetorical purpose.)

Without typographic and spatial cues, documents demand more mental work of readers, forcing them to relate text parts and to figure out part-whole relationships. For example, the loss of typographic and spatial cues may happen when a formatted text is inserted into an e-mail file and shipped to an address where it winds up stripped of its formatting and typographic emphasis (and accompanied by unnatural line breaks). This can leave the reader with a document that is very hard to read. To illustrate this point, I present Figure 5.8 (on the next page). It is an excerpt from an e-mail message sent to me while I was developing the content for a proposal to design a multimedia learning environment for organ transplant patients. One of my collaborators sent me a file via e-mail with some suggestions to include in the proposal. When I downloaded the message and printed it, somehow the file defaulted to the typeface Mesquite, shown in the first part of Figure 5.8 (a face normally used in rodeo ads and labels for barbecue sauce). Note how the typography renders the text barely legible, confused in tone, and devoid of rhetorical purposefulness. It is no longer possible to see its simple but important structure, signaled by a heading followed by an itemized list. It is not easy to infer the rhetorical function of items in the list. That is, the visual display obscures the sender's intent that each item have a parallel relationship. Instead, we can't see where items begin and end. Even after the text has been reformatted in a more legible face, Frutiger (see the second part of Figure 5.8), we cannot see the embedded questions that were linked to particular points. What the message should have looked like is presented in the third part of Figure 5.8.

Although my example is obviously an extreme case, it aptly illustrates what can go wrong when type is chosen by default. It can wind up illegible and rhetorically inappropriate. When type is chosen to suit the structure of the text, it allows readers to make reasonable inferences about "what is going on" and to attend selectively to the parts of that structure they most want to see, while bypassing other parts (Glynn, Britton, & Tillman, 1985). A number of studies have shown that readers make use of

[51] Typographic design was exploited by poets such as Apollinaire, George Herbert, and William Blake who composed both poems with pictures and "pattern poems" in which the structure and the layout of the type formed a picture. For examples, see Ernst (1986) or Higgins (1986).

Example 1

THE ORGAN TRANSPLANT MULTIMEDIA ENVIRO
NMENT: WHAT IT WIL
L CONTAIN
A VIDEO LIBRARY OF PO
ST-TRANSPLANT PATIENTS RELATING THE
IR PERSO
NAL STORIES OF WHAT THEY HAVE GONE THROUGH.
   A VIRTUA
L MEDICAL LIBRARY CONTAINI
NG INFORMATION ON TERMINOLOGY
SPECIFIC TO THE PATIENTS' INDIVIDUAL ILL
NESSES. TWE
LVE MINI-DOCUMENTARI
ES ON THE DIFFERENT TYPES OF MEDICAL TES
TS THAT ARE REQUIRED TO BE ACCEPTED ON THE TRANSPL
ANT LIST. THIS WILL ALSO
REDUCE ANXIETY BECAUS
E IT EXPOSES THE UNKNOWN.
            A MODULE ON DRUG THERAPY. THE
PERSON WILL LEARN THE PHYSICA
L APPEARANCE OF THE DRUGS, T
HEIR SIDE EFFECT
S, AND THEIR
BENEFITS. IT WILL ALSO GIVE THE P
ATIENT HELPFUL HINTS ON HOW TO
REDUCE SOME OF THE SIDE EFFECTS OF THE MEDICINES.
                ANIMATION WILL B
E USED TO EXPLAIN HOW THE ORGAN IN QUESTION WOR
KS
AND HOW THE PATIENT'S SPECIFIC ILLNESS IS AFFECTING
HIS OR HER BODY. THIS WILL BE A
CCOMPLISHED BY USING 3-D IMAGES OF THE HUMA
N BODY ALONG WITH ANIMATED
SEQUENCES OF THE INNER WORK
INGS OF THE SYSTEM (E. G., HEART OR KIDNEY).
   ART FOR LIFE WILL BE A VIRTUAL ART GALLERY. T
HE ART CONTAINED IN THIS AREA WILL BE
DONE BY TRANSPLANT
PATIENTS. BENEATH EACH PIC
TURE WILL BE A
N ICON THAT CAN BE CLICKED ON BY
THE USER AND A VIDEO OF AN ARTIST EXPLAININ
G HIS OR HER THOUGHTS WHILE CREATING
THEIR ART.

Example 2

The organ transplant multimedia environment: What it will contain A video library of post-transplant patients in which they tell their personal stories about what they have gone through. A virtual medical library containing information on terminology specific to patients' individual illnesses. Twelve mini-documentaries on the different types of medical tests that are required to be accepted on the transplant list. This will also reduce anxiety because it exposes the unknown. A module on drug therapy. The person will learn the physical appearance of the drugs, their side effects, and their benefits. It will also give the patient helpful hints on how to reduce some of the side effects of the medicines. Animation will be used to explain how the organ in question works and how the patient's specific illness is affecting his or her body. This will be accomplished by using 3-D images of the human body along with animated sequences of the inner workings of the system (e.g., heart or kidney). Art For Life will be a virtual art gallery. The art contained in this area will be done by transplant patients. Beneath each picture will be an icon that can be clicked on by the user and a video of an artist explaining his or her thoughts while creating their art.

Example 3

The organ transplant multimedia environment: What it will contain

- A video library of post-transplant patients in which they tell their personal stories about what they have gone through.

- A virtual medical library containing information on terminology specific to patients' individual illnesses.

- Twelve mini-documentaries on the different types of medical tests that are required to be accepted on the transplant list. This will also reduce anxiety because it exposes the unknown.

- A module on drug therapy. The person will learn the physical appearance of the drugs, their side effects, and their benefits. It will also give the patient helpful hints on how to reduce some of the side effects of the medicines.

- Animation will be used to explain how the organ in question works and how the patient's specific illness is affecting his or her body.

  ☛   This will be accomplished by using 3-D images of the human body along with animated sequences of the inner workings of the system (e.g., heart or kidney).

- Art For Life will be a virtual art gallery. The art contained in this area will be done by transplant patients. Beneath each picture will be an icon that can be clicked on by the user and a video of an artist explaining his or her thoughts while creating their art.

▲ **Figure 5.8** *An example of what can happen when spatial and typographic cues are degraded. Example 1 is a text downloaded and printed from an e-mail message (which accidentally defaulted to the cowboy font, Mesquite). Example 2 is the same text in Frutiger Light with all the line breaks taken out. Example 3 is what the sender of the e-mail intended. The message was a set of suggestions to revise a proposal for the development of a multimedia program for organ transplant patients.*

typographic cueing (or signaling) in their understanding of text. These studies suggest that cueing is helpful as long as there aren't too many signals competing for the reader's attention.[52] Clearly, document designers need to know more about the rhetorical nature of typographic and spatial cues for readers.

---

[52] Investigations of the effects of visual cues in texts and of oversignaling have been carried out by various researchers (Coles & Foster, 1975; Foster, 1979; Foster & Coles, 1977; Phillips, 1979; Spencer, Reynolds, & Coe, 1974, 1975). For a review of signaling in texts, see Spyridakis (1989a, 1989b).

SECTION 2
MAKING TYPOGRAPHIC DECISIONS
THAT ARE SENSITIVE TO THE SITUATION

Although research offers advice about choosing type to enhance the legibility of hardcopy and online documents (as I've outlined earlier), the literature is impoverished when it comes to providing hints about making typographic and spatial decisions that are appropriate for the rhetorical situation. Many articles suggest that type conveys mood, but they usually stop at this point—failing to connect mood to genre, purpose, and context. Document designers need much more information about the role of typography and space in shaping how people engage with documents in particular situations. This information would put them in a better position to make decisions about how best to provide typographic and spatial cues that are sensitive to the reader's needs.

Widening the scope of typographic research beyond legibility is important because choosing a legible type is usually not the most difficult problem document designers face. Most of the classic typefaces have been redesigned for desktop design to maximize their legibility, thus minimizing the worry in using them. Document designers still need to concern themselves with legibility because they will create problems for their readership if they choose an overly decorated typeface, one that has been stretched, or one that is not supported by PostScript technology. Document designers will also thwart their goals if after choosing a generally legible face, they set the leading too tight or make the lines too long or too short. But as Bartram (1982) points out:

> The problem [for today's designer] is not in choosing between legible and illegible alternatives, but rather of choosing the most appropriate typeface from a set of legible ones. Indeed, in certain instances, where the designer is trying to create a particular effect with the type (such as the evocation of the atmosphere of a Parisian restaurant) he may be willing to sacrifice some degree of legibility in order to achieve that affect.

> Such "effects" are produced by the semantic properties of the typeface. The semantic properties are those which affect its apparent "fitness" or "suitability" for different functions, and which imbue it with the power to evoke in the perceiver certain emotional and cognitive responses. It would seem more appropriate, for example, to use a plain bold face rather than a florid decorative one for a warning sign. Not only might it be more legible, but it also has a more authoritative effect. In contrast, a decorative Art Nouveau face might create the right "feel"

for the menu in a French restaurant but seem out of place in an instructional manual for a washing-machine.

These semantic properties modify the explicit message of the text (the actual words) and provide an implicit context within which the message is understood. The overall effect of a piece of text will be a function of the words used and the style of writing and also of the semantic properties of the "vehicle" used to represent those words. (pp. 38-39)

Following Bartram's ideas that more study needs to be done of the effects of type on readers in context, it is important to ask what role typeface plays in enhancing the semantics of a text. In addition, the question needs to be sharpened beyond the one that Bartram asked. Here we can draw on work in genre analysis (e.g., Berkenkotter & Huckin, 1995), which suggests that people may have different expectations for text, depending on the genre. Although Bartram's example of the French menu hints at choosing the best typography for the situation, he still takes the point of view of the designer, that is, of what the designer wants and of what the designer is willing to sacrifice. I contend that it is important to look at this question from the point of view of the reader. In an attempt to explore whether the genre of a document has an effect on readers' preferences for serif or sans serif typefaces, my colleagues and I carried out the following study.[53]

[53] My colleagues in this study were Alan Sloan, Malavika Arunachalam, and Ann Steffy Cronin, former students at Carnegie Mellon. Special thanks to Alan Sloan, who insisted that we do this study, and to Cynthia Atman, a faculty member of the Department of Industrial Engineering at the University of Pittsburgh, who helped us in carrying out the study and who made it possible to locate and pay participants.

THE ROLE OF RHETORICAL CONTEXT IN SHAPING READERS' PREFERENCES FOR TYPE (OR THE "TYPOGRAPHY UNDER DURESS STUDY")

Our study investigated whether a document's genre makes a difference in the typeface readers prefer. This issue is relevant because document designers must make decisions about typography that span a wide variety of genres. Typography that may work well for one type of document may be rhetorically disastrous for another. Up to this point, there has been little research about how readers respond to the typography of common document types. Evidence from such inquiry could be useful in helping document designers make better choices and better arguments about typography. In this research, we explored four related questions:

1. Do readers have preferences for serif or sans serif typefaces in documents? Or do they like both styles equally well?

2. Do readers' preferences depend on what they are reading? That is, do readers' preferences for serif or sans serif typefaces depend on the genre?

3. Do men and women differ in their preferences for typeface? If so, how? Do they differ depending on what they are reading?

4. How do readers talk about the differences they may see between typefaces? What features do they notice?

To make our study responsive to the kinds of documents readers typically see, we printed our stimulus materials using everyday low-resolution production techniques and then photocopied them. As I mentioned earlier, low-resolution printing may be further worsened by a low-quality toner cartridge. Depending on how the ink spreads, the serifs may not be as pronounced (or conversely, they may be too thick). In addition, the definition of letters may not be as clean, and the contrast between bold and plain may not be as noticeable because both plain and bold may look dark (see Black, 1990). In this study, we used a 300-dpi laser printer with a recharged toner cartridge. This result was a rather heavy ink spread, but since we printed all of the materials using the same toner cartridge, all of the typefaces we tested were made uniformly more bold. In fact, the plain and the bold had close to the same color value. The typefaces were further compromised because we duplicated the materials 100 times by using a standard office copy machine.

My colleagues and I subtitled this study "Typography Under Duress." We wondered whether readers would notice the less-than-optimal printing and whether they would mention anything about the legibility of the type.

Selecting Documents for the Typeface Study

In choosing documents to evaluate, our aim was to choose four genres delineated mainly by the purposes for which people might read or use them.

Considering Purpose and Genre in Choosing Typography

We hypothesized that perhaps some of the confusion in earlier typographic research was related to the worrisome assumptions that "all texts are alike," and that either serif or sans serif typography will prove most legible and most preferred in all rhetorical situations. Unlike studies that presented participants with a few randomly chosen paragraphs, rhetorically disembodied from their textual context, we used rhetorically complete texts. That is, we provided readers with enough context that they could easily recognize what type of text it was and what the relationships among its parts were. We were concerned with the sorts of documents people read at home, school, or work—everyday contexts in which they may form preferences for typography. We looked for genres that people use for four common purposes: (1) reading to enjoy, (2) reading to assess, (3) reading to do, and (4) reading to learn to do.

Reading to enjoy. This purpose for reading is characterized by the satisfaction one gets in the experience of interacting with the text, the pleasure of engaging with the content (see Rosenblatt, 1978). This stands in contrast to reading in order to do something as a result of reading, such as when using a set of instructions. Genres for which readers have the goal of reading to enjoy are often, though not always, characterized by continuous narrative prose. Common "reading to enjoy" texts include novels, stories, poems, magazines, newspapers, or tabloids. Some of these genres employ precise typographic cueing (such as poetry) while others may not (novels). The reader's goal with such texts is often pleasure or aesthetic engagement—from the cerebral to the escapist (though these are not mutually exclusive.) As an example of a "reading to enjoy" text, we selected a two-page spread from a short story.

Reading to assess. This purpose for reading is characterized by the goal of evaluating the relevance or value of the document's content. When people read to assess, they make a judgment about how, if at all, to use the content or to act on it (Diehl & Mikulecky, 1980). The assessment can be as quick as what direct marketers call the "three-second lookover" to an extensive evaluation of the content. Texts that call on readers to assess the value of their content (before committing to reading them) include business correspondence, junk mail, proposals, reports, catalogs, feasibility studies, marketing communications, risk communications, newspapers,[54] and even Web pages. Genres such as these are often comprised of short paragraphs and itemized lists. Many employ graphics (pictorial or quantitative). For the purposes of our study, we selected a text without graphics (as we wanted to emphasize the typography). We also wanted to evaluate a typical business document. We chose a one-page business letter from a bank telling the recipient of an increase in his credit limit.

Reading to do. This purpose for reading is characterized by the intention of using the document in order to perform a task. In reading to do, people engage with the content in order to put it to immediate practical use, usually to carry out a job (Kern, 1985; Sticht, 1977, 1985). In contrast to reading to enjoy, the most important thing is what readers take away from their interaction with the document. Texts that enable "reading to do" include instruction manuals, forms, employee handbooks, online help, quick reference guides, bus schedules, and cookbooks. Such documents are often comprised of telegraphic prose, enumerated procedures, itemized lists, and tabular displays. Key features also include overviews, scenario headings,[55] and illustrations.[56] When people use

[54] People may bring multiple purposes to bear when they engage with a genre, or they may bring a single purpose. For example, when reading newspapers, we sometimes read them for enjoyment, other times to assess their political orientation, and at other times to learn about a particular event. In contrast, when reading the instructions on the side of a fire extinguisher, we have only one purpose: to put the instructions to immediate use.

[55] Scenario headings are written in the active voice with verbs that enable the reader to see the topic in relation to their personal intentions (e.g., "How Do I Apply for Food Stamps?")

[56] These illustrations range from the cutaway drawings of an air conditioning system of a skyscraper for an engineer, to the exploded parts diagrams of a sewing machine for a seamstress, to the "how to avoid scratching your compact discs" Illustrations for a teenager.

"reading to do" documents, they often shift their attention between the document and the object or piece of equipment they are reading about; thus, well-designed typographic cues are critical. For this genre, we selected a two-page spread from an instruction manual for a microwave oven. It was comprised of numbered steps, short examples, boldfaced headings, and technical illustrations. It was set in three columns.

Reading to learn to do. This purpose for reading is characterized by engaging with the content of a document in order to acquire the background knowledge needed in order to do something else (Redish, 1989). For example, it would be inappropriate for an aspiring new gardener to learn about the world of plants by beginning with procedural information about how deep and how far apart to plant seedlings. Instead, it would be better to start with a text that explained the differences between annuals and perennials. Readers often need background information—concepts, models, explanations, arguments, heuristics—in order to make use of the document's content in an intelligent manner. "Reading to learn to do" is often contrasted with the purposes of "reading to learn"[57] and "reading to do." However, although it is a simple matter to specify which types of texts are prototypically "reading to learn" (e.g., textbooks, journal articles, essays) or "reading to do" (e.g., procedures, decision memos, forms), it is not easy to say which documents are usually "reading to learn to do." A question arises over what is meant by "doing." Narrowly construed, it means reading in order to perform tasks (such as using a software product after working through the tutorial). But conceived more broadly, "doing" can also mean (1) making an informed decision (e.g., investing in the stock market after reading an investment guide explaining the "ins and outs" about stocks and bonds), or (2) taking practical action (e.g., developing a policy for reducing teen pregnancy as a result of reading a book about why young women may have low self-esteem).

[57] Reading to learn is characterized by reading with the goal of understanding and remembering the content, as in studying a textbook.

The documents that may "fit this bill" are often hybrid genres that mix continuous prose (previews, definitions, explanations, arguments, examples, summaries), telegraphic prose (procedures and itemized lists), and visuals (charts, graphs, pictures, and illustrations). Documents that promote "reading to learn to do" usually combine declarative information (e.g., "What is it?" or "What makes it work?"), decision-making information (e.g., "Why is it useful to me?"), and procedural information (e.g., "How is it done?"). In cognitive terms, texts that promote "reading to learn to do" help readers acquire a mental model of "how it works" and a procedural model of "how to do it."[58] In social terms, they help readers acquire an understanding of how to employ what they learn in achieving personal agendas.

[58] See the work of Bovair and Kieras (1991), Kieras (1985), and Redish (1989).

In choosing a "reading to learn to do" document for our study, we selected a two-page spread from a workbook designed to help U.S. citizens estimate their taxes. The typography of this document was dense looking (it was set at 8/8.5). Boldface was used for cueing, but the contrast between the plain type for the body text (Helvetica) and bold type for the headings (Helvetica Bold) was not very strong. The text consisted of explanatory paragraphs (mixing facts, procedures, and complex "if-then" conditionals[59]). It also included a form for making calculations. Its purpose was to help citizens understand the facts about taxable income (a kind of "tutorial on tax law") in preparation for filling out the 1040 tax form.

[59] For a discussion of conditionals, see Holland and Rose (1981) or Wright and Reid (1973).

We chose these genres with the idea that readers might differ in their preferences for typography, depending on what they were reading. If, as Miller (1984) has suggested, genres are a kind of "social action," fusing form and purpose to meet a rhetorical need, it would be useful to know whether readers respond to their different typographic conventions. We hypothesized that readers might have different expectations for typography when "reading to enjoy" from when "reading to do." We suspected that readers may have grown to notice (perhaps unconsciously) that the typographic cueing in a short story is different from that in a manual, and that readers may have acquired preferences for the typography employed in these genres.

▼ Figure 5.9 *Examples of the typefaces employed in the study shown at 20 points to illustrate their differences. For reproductions of the materials used in the study, see Figures 5.10 and 5.11.*

To carry out the study, we scanned in a typical two-page spread from the short story, the microwave manual, and the IRS workbook on taxes. Since business letters are often only single page, we used the one-page

	Serif	**Sans Serif**
Manual	Typeface & Genre 20-point Bauer Bodoni	Typeface & Genre 20-point Univers 45 Light
Credit Letter	Typeface & Genre 20-point Palatino	Typeface & Genre 20-point Futura Book
Tax Form	Typeface & Genre 20-point Times	Typeface & Genre 20-point Helvetica
Short Story	Typeface & Genre 20-point ITC Garamond Light	Typeface & Genre 20-point Optima

credit letter as it was. In each case, we maintained the language and look of the original document, making no writing or design improvements (or degradations). We then styled each document using the serif and sans serif typefaces shown in Figure 5.9.

We maintained the same point size as the original documents for the first version of each text and then adjusted the point size of the second document to make the two versions of each document appear equivalent. Specifically, we adjusted the type size so the x-heights of the serif and sans serif faces were roughly the same. For example, with the IRS document, the original, which was set with 8-point Helvetica, required a slightly larger point size (9 point) when set with Bauer Bodoni in order to achieve a similar x-height. In mocking up the documents, we also pre-served the line length and the leading of the original documents. We mounted the two-page spreads for each document on 11" × 17" paper so readers could see a full-size spread for the serif and sans serif versions of the three longer documents (manual, tax form, and story). With the one-page credit letter, we copied the serif version on one side of the page with the sans serif on the other. Using these originals, we copied each spread 100 times.

We employed a within-subject design. Thus all participants saw both serif and sans serif versions of all four documents. To minimize the effect of the order of the documents on readers' preferences, we made 50 packets using one order (story, manual, letter, tax form[60]) and 50 using another order (letter, tax form, story, manual). We also randomized the order of the serif or sans serif typefaces. Half of the participants were given the first order, the other half the second. One-page excerpts from the materials we used are shown in Figures 5.10 (the manual and the letter) and 5.11 (the form and the short story).

[60] I truncate the phrase "IRS workbook and form" to "tax form" in the rest of this discussion.

Participants in the Study

To carry out the study, we employed a convenience sample (that is, an opportunity arose in which we could recruit a number of people who were assembled in one place). In particular, we learned of a high school in a small town about 50 miles east of Pittsburgh where parents and friends were trying to raise money for the high-school band. These "band parents and friends" were willing as a group to come to a high-school auditorium and take part in the study for a lump sum contribution of $500 to the band. In total, 67 people (29 women and 38 men) volunteered. The distribution of ages was between twenty and seventy, with most people between the ages of thirty-five and sixty.[61]

[61] In total, 49 people were between the ages of forty and fifty-nine; there were 5 people over sixty and 13 under forty.

▶ Figure 5.10 *Excerpts from documents used in the typeface study. The typeface was the only aspect of the documents that was changed; the language and design were unaltered from the original documents. A larger type size was employed in the serif versions of the documents shown here (and in Figure 5.11) to "even out" the apparent differences in x-heights between the serif and sans serif typefaces used. Before participants were asked to read them, the documents were xeroxed 100 times, resulting in more "clotty" looking type than appears here.*

An Excerpt from a Microwave Oven Manual

The body text is 11.5-point Bauer Bodoni with 12-point leading; the heading is 18-point Bauer Bodoni Bold; the subheadings are 13-point Bauer Bodoni Bold.

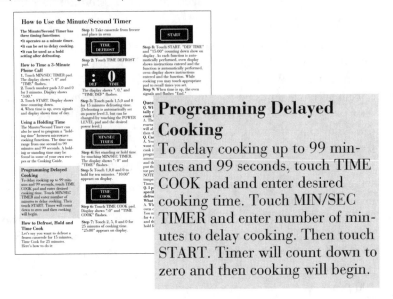

An Excerpt from a Microwave Oven Manual

The body text is 11-point Univers 45 Light with 12-point leading; the heading is 18-point Univers 65 Bold; the subheadings are 13-point Univers 65 Bold.

A Credit Letter

The body text is 9.5-point Palatino with 11-point leading.

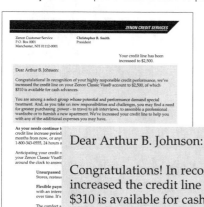

Dear Arthur B. Johnson:

Congratulations! In recognition of your highly responsible credit performance, we've increased the credit line on your Zenon Classic Visa® account to $2,500, of which $310 is available for cash advances.

You are among a select group whose potential and performance demand special treatment. And, as you take on new responsibilities and challenges, you may find a need for greater purchasing power—to travel to job interviews, to assemble a professional wardrobe or to furnish a new apartment. We've increased your credit line to help you with any of the additional expenses you may have.

A Credit Letter

The body text is 10-point Futura Book with 11-point leading.

Dear Arthur B. Johnson:

Congratulations! In recognition of your highly responsible credit performance, we've increased the credit line on your Zenon Classic Visa® account to $2,500, of which $310 is available for cash advances.

You are among a select group whose potential and performance demand special treatment. And, as you take on new responsibilities and challenges, you may find a need for greater purchasing power—to travel to job interviews, to assemble a professional wardrobe or to furnish a new apartment. We've increased your credit line to help you with any of the additional expenses you may have.

▶ Figure 5.11 *Excerpts from documents used in the typeface study. The typeface was the only aspect of the documents that was changed.*

An Excerpt from a Tax Form

The body text is 9-point Times Roman with 9.5-point leading; the headings are 13-point Times Roman Bold; the subheadings are 11-point Times Roman Bold.

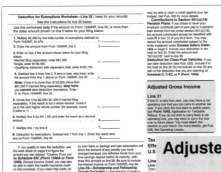

An Excerpt from a Tax Form

The body text is 8-point Helvetica with 8.5-point leading; the headings are 12.5-point Helvetica Bold; the subheadings are 10.5-point Helvetica Bold.

An Excerpt from a Short Story

The body text is 10-point ITC Garamond with 13.5-point leading; the title is 17-point ITC Garamond Bold Italic.

He rose at six, read for two hours, and walked another hour—three miles—to work. He dictated poems to his secretary. He ate no lunch; at noon he walked for another hour, often to an art gallery. He walked home from work—another hour. After dinner he retired to his study; he went to bed at nine. On Sundays, he walked in the park. I don't know what he did on Saturdays. Perhaps he exchanged a few words with his wife, who posed for the Liberty dime. (One would rather read these people, or lead their lives, than be their wives. When the Swedish aristocrat Wilhelm Dinesen shot birds all day, drank schnapps, napped, dressed for dinner, he and his wife had three children under three. The middle one was Karen, later known as Isak Dinesen.)

An Excerpt from a Short Story

The body text is 9.5-point Optima with 13.5-point leading; the title is 18-point Optima Bold Italic.

He rose at six, read for two hours, and walked another hour—three miles—to work. He dictated poems to his secretary. He ate no lunch; at noon he walked for another hour, often to an art gallery. He walked home from work—another hour. After dinner he retired to his study; he went to bed at nine. On Sundays, he walked in the park. I don't know what he did on Saturdays. Perhaps he exchanged a few words with his wife, who posed for the Liberty dime. (One would rather read these people, or lead their lives, than be their wives. When the Swedish aristocrat Wilhelm Dinesen shot birds all day, drank schnapps, napped, and dressed for dinner, he and his wife had three children under three. The middle one was Karen, later known as Isak Dinesen.)

What We Asked of Participants

The task was simple and took about 20 minutes. We began with an explanation that we were interested in "what people prefer to look at when they read materials such as letters, stories, or instructions." We advised participants to "Notice there are two versions of each kind of material. Look over the two versions and pick the one you would most prefer to read if you were in a situation where you needed or wanted to read them." (We did not mention anything about genre, purpose, or typeface.) Participants were given three categories from which to choose: serif, sans serif, or neither. For each document, we also asked participants to complete the sentence "The reason for my choice is…"

What We Found About Typeface and Genre

A summary of the 67 readers' responses across the four document types is shown in Table 5.1. There were no significant differences for gender (though a slightly higher proportion of men preferred sans serif over serif than women). Analysis also revealed no significant overall preference for serif or sans serif. That is, averaged across the four genres, readers were about equally likely to choose serif as sans serif typefaces.

▶ Table 5.1 *The relationship between participants' gender and their preference for serif or sans serif style of typefaces.*

Readers' Preferences for Style of Type: Does Gender Matter?

	Male (n = 29)	Female (n = 38)	Average
Serif	26	36	31
Sans Serif	44	39	42
Neither	30	25	27

Note: Values represent responses in percentages.

However, when we evaluated readers' preferences according to the genre/purpose (shown in Table 5.2), we found that preference was significantly influenced ($\chi^2 = 68.19$, df $= 6$, p $\leq .001$). *In particular, when reading continuous prose in a short story, people preferred serif faces, but when reading the more telegraphic prose found in instruction manuals, they preferred sans serif.* We found no strong preference for either face on the credit letter. Participants who did express a preference for a face in the tax form leaned toward serif, but as shown, many people chose "neither" (perhaps more a reflection of their attitude about paying taxes than anything else).

Readers' Preferences for Style of Type: Does Genre Matter?

	Manual	Letter	Tax Form	Story	Average
Serif	9	25	40	51	31
Sans Serif	81	37	19	28	42
Neither	10	37	40	21	27

Note: Values represent responses in percentages.

◀ Table 5.2 *The relationship between genre of document and participants' preference for serif or sans serif style of typefaces. (There were 67 participants.)*

This quantitative picture was illuminated by readers' responses to the open-ended question in which we asked participants to comment on their choices. These data, summarized in Figure 5.12 (on the next two pages), shed light on why people felt as they did about preferring serif, sans serif, or neither typeface for each genre. Although readers' comments were quite general, they revealed that preferences may arise from a constellation of factors in the rhetorical context. These factors include:

- *The mood or tone of the text.* In the manual, the sans serif type makes the text "seem easy." In the letter, the sans serif appears "more businesslike." In the tax form, the serif face is "somehow softer to look at," but the long sentences with the "ifs" are "deadly" and the type for both faces "cramped." In the story, the dark type seems "gloomy."

- *The density of the text.* In the manual, the sans serif type is good for "glancing over the text." In the tax form, there are "too many words in a little space," "the words look squashed," and "they need more space between the paragraphs." In the story, the serif type lets one read "without getting a headache."

- *The contrast among parts of the text.* In the manual, the sans serif face makes "the headings 'pop' right out," allowing readers to "pick out the sections faster." In the letter, the serif has a nice "lightness," while the sans serif is "too dark." In the tax form, both serif and sans serif faces seem "too dark." In the story, both versions seemed "glary."

- *The legibility of the type and the quality of the printing.* In the manual, "both seem like bad copies." In the letter, "both have poor printing" and "blotchy" type. Readers suggest "it would be nicer if they were typeset" and recommend increasing "the printing budget." In the tax form, the serif helps to avoid "losing my place," but "the printing is blurry, too jammed together," and it "looks like it was photocopied." Moreover, the "letters look smeared." In the story, the sans serif "looks too bright" and "they are both ugly and bad reproductions."

MANUAL

I preferred the serif because ...
- Everything looks nicer with these letters.
- The lettering is good.
- I like its print.

I preferred the sans serif because ...
- The print is easier to read; it seems bigger.
- The headings "pop" right out at you, easier to read the directions. That's good with these steps.
- Picking out the sections with the blackened headings is faster.
- The typing is more legible and in focus.
- The letters are pronounced and make it easy to read the steps without getting mixed up.
- Better letters, less eye strain. The enlarged spacing is good for glancing at only the parts I care about.
- I like the bigger printing; it makes me feel like this microwave is easy to understand.
- It would be easier to use the microwave with these letters. It's nice to see the parts quickly.
- I see the headings stand out from the instructions; that's good for doing the steps to make the microwave work. It must be a nice model.

I preferred neither because ...
- I don't use a microwave.
- Both seem like bad copies of the same instructions.

LETTER

I preferred the serif because ...
- It is nicer, more friendly and personal for a form letter.
- The other one is too dark and blotchy looking.
- This one is bigger and says the company is friendly.
- It's a form letter, but it's nice to have it on one page.
- It's more restful on my eye. I like the lightness too.

I preferred the sans serif because ...
- It looks more computerized and the type is clear.
- The type is professional but a little dark.
- It looks simple, no-nonsense, and more spread out.
- It's not fussy like the other one, more businesslike.

I preferred neither because ...
- They were identical to me; my copies were poor.
- The letters would be nicer if they were typeset.
- They are form letters so I never read these.
- The ideas are wordy, no one reads all these things.
- The letter should be more personal; it looks like a machine wrote it.
- The differences are too minor to notice.
- Both letters have poor printing. Increase the printing budget so they look nicer.
- These two are exactly the same unlike the other samples.

▲ **Figure 5.12** *How readers responded to the design of different genres composed of serif and sans serif typefaces.*

- *Their attitudes about the topic or the writing.* In the manual, "I don't use a microwave." In the letter, "it should be more personal." In the tax form, "I can't read sentences like this for more than a few minutes" and "they should simplify the tax code." In the short story, "it is boring."

- *Their likely uses of the text.* In the manual, the sans serif type "allows you to see the parts quickly, to read the steps without getting mixed up." In the letter, "I never read these form letters." In the tax form, "it would be hard to use the paragraphs to fill in the form, too many cross referrals." In the short story, the "scripted letters are appealing in stories" and "I can relax while I read."

- *Their knowledge of genre conventions.* In the manual, the sans serif type makes "the headings stand out from the instructions" and you can "see the parts of the microwave quickly." In the letter, readers comment that "in a form letter, it's nice to have it on one page." In the tax form, the serif type was recognized as the same "lettering as in the newspaper." In the story, "this kind of lettering [serif type] is used in paperbacks."

TAX FORM

I preferred the serif because ...

- There is more space around the words. The print is somehow softer to look at. The subtitles stand out.
- The type is easy on my eye though crammed.
- The little paragraphs are more spread out, they are quicker to read but who knows what they mean.
- Those long, long sentences with the "ifs" are deadly, but I can read the sentences without losing my place.
- I'm used to reading this lettering in the newspaper.

I preferred the sans serif because ...

- It takes up less space. So maybe this form is shorter.
- The titles are bigger and it's not as busy as the other one, but they are both too dark, small, and squashed.

I preferred neither because ...

- I can't read sentences like this for more than a few minutes. So many words in a little space.
- I couldn't get it. The IRS should simplify the tax code.
- The first one is small and ugly. The other one is blurry.
- Both look awful. Is this due to photocopying?
- It would be hard to use the paragraphs to fill in the form at the top of the page, too many cross referrals.
- I would ask someone else to read this, the printing is too jammed together and the letters are smeared.
- They need more space between the paragraphs and little sections. I can't find the right parts easily.

STORY

I preferred the serif because ...

- The print is easy to read and the inking is not so heavy.
- The letters are thinner which makes it nice on the eyes.
- The other one looks too bright—it strains my eyes.
- It's clear. I like stories this way. I can relax while I read.
- The story seems good and it doesn't blur together.
- I'm used to this kind of lettering in paperbacks, it's nice.
- I could read this without getting a headache.
- The scripted letters are appealing in stories.
- It gives me the illusion of taking less time to read.
- This bigger print and clear type is important to me.

I preferred the sans serif because ...

- The bolder print is nice to look at. It seems bigger.
- It is easy on the eyes even though it is very black.
- I like the plain letters, but they could be less dark.
- I like this one because the type is larger and bold.

I preferred neither because ...

- They look the same to me. Not pleasing to the eye.
- They were both too dark.
- They are ugly and both look like bad reproductions of pages out of a book. You should try a printer.
- The stories are boring and the pages are gloomy.
- My eyes are feeling like both versions are glary.

Reflecting on the Results

First of all, these findings suggest that the widely held assumption about Americans preferring serif typefaces is a myth. We found no across-the-board preference for serif faces. This may be an artifact of the changing face of contemporary typography, which in many publishing areas has been moving more toward sans serif. It could also be an artifact of our "mixed grill" of genres. On one hand, our results stand in opposition to research in which readers were found to prefer serif typefaces over sans serif (see Burt, 1959; Hvistendal & Kahl, 1975; Robinson et al., 1971). We suspect that the superiority of serif in these earlier studies is related to the popularity of serif typefaces in the publications earlier in this century. On the other hand, our results support and replicate studies of typography that found no differences in readers' preferences for serif and sans serif (Gould et al., 1987; Hartley & Rooum, 1983; Tinker, 1963; Zachrisson, 1965). Taking together our findings and those of earlier studies, it appears that either serif or sans serif typefaces are likely to be equally legible and equally preferred.[62] This study suggests that people find serif and sans serif typefaces equally pleasing but that the situation in which they are reading may lead them to prefer one style over the other. This study adds a new dimension to the picture by suggesting that genre may play a role in shaping readers' expectations and preferences for typography.

One additional finding is of note. The typeface Univers was preferred by more people than any of the eight typefaces we studied. We suspect this was because it has excellent contrast and legibility between its light and dark values even "under duress." It seems likely that for documents that require quick access and retrieval, readers will choose high-contrast faces over low-contrast ones, whether serif or sans serif.

What we do not know from these results is whether readers' preferences would have been different if the type had been produced using high-resolution output on good-quality bright white paper. These results suggest that people do not like to read type that is overly dark. The faces that held up best "under duress" were those with sturdy but clean letterforms and large x-heights (i.e., ITC Garamond and Univers).

These findings also tell us that readers do notice poor typographic output and are bothered by it. Even though we said nothing about how we produced and copied the materials, people noticed the poor legibility of the documents. However, there is another side to this story. People may also notice when the typographic design is working. We found that readers were often generous in making favorable attributions about what they were reading when they felt the design of the document was helpful. Notice how the readers who preferred the sans serif face of the microwave manual made positive comments about a product they had never seen. The microwave seemed "easier to use" even without it being present, an impression created through the document.

This finding lends empirical support to the idea that good design of written and visual communications can enhance readers' images of the product or service they are reading about. Some readers assumed that the microwave would be easy to use because the manual made it look that way. This study suggests that people are responsive to the design of documents and that it may have a positive "halo effect"[63] on their attitudes about products and services.

This study contributes to the growing research literature that suggests there may be some psychological reality to readers' expectations for genre. As we saw, expectations may come into play even at the level of typeface. That readers clearly preferred sans serif for "reading to do" documents but serif for "reading to enjoy" documents suggests that these faces—in

Bartram's (1982) terms—were a good semantic fit between the genre and the reader's purpose. More studies are needed to better understand the role of the rhetorical context in shaping readers' preferences for document design features such as typography.

SECTION 3
USING GESTALT PRINCIPLES TO UNDERSTAND READERS' INTERPRETATIONS OF SPATIAL CUES

As we have seen, typography can be used to reinforce or to mute the message of a text. The same is true of the spatial arrangement of the text. The use of blank space, the arrangement of rows and columns, and the juxtaposition of words and graphics can influence the way readers see the text; that is, the things they attend to, the order in which they scan the text, and the relations among text elements that "pop out" at them.

Naturally, document designers want to create spatial arrangements that lead readers to see the text in particular ways. Doing this is not at all easy. However, some useful guidance has been provided by psychologists working in the Gestalt tradition who studied how people group and organize what they see.

▲ Figure 5.13 *A shape is understood as a relation among parts.*

Gestalt Psychology developed in Germany at about the same time as Behaviorism developed in the United States—the second decade of the twentieth century. In contrast to the Behaviorists, who were interested primarily in learning, the Gestalt psychologists were concerned with the study of perception, particularly visual perception. A major objective of the Gestalt psychologists was to explain why the world looks the way it does to ordinary people in natural settings. Led by Max Wertheimer, Wolfgang Köhler, and Kurt Koffka, the Gestalt psychologists systematically studied how the properties of the visual world shape our perceptions.[64] One of the earliest discoveries of Gestalt psychology was that the way things look depends not just on the properties of their elementary parts, but also, and more importantly, on their organization. They pointed out that we can't find the shape of a square such as the one shown in Figure 5.13 by examining its parts one at a time. Readers see a square even though none of the parts are square. Our perception of squareness depends on the relation among the parts.

Squareness is just one example of a quality that depends on the relationship of parts within a whole; melody is another. A melody depends not on any of the individual notes but on the relationships among the notes. Qualities such as squareness and melody that depend on the relationship of parts are called "form qualities." The fact that Americans can

[64] For a detailed discussion of Gestalt Psychology, see Koffka (1935), Köhler (1947), or Wertheimer (1922, 1923). For a review, see Hilgard (1987).

recognize "Yankee Doodle" whether it is sung by a soprano or a bass, whether it is played on a tuba or a piccolo, indicates that tunes depend on the relationship among notes rather than on the notes themselves. The Gestalt psychologists pointed out that the things we deal with in the practical world (e.g., landscapes, buildings, automobiles, and chairs) speak to us visually as organized wholes and that the most interesting properties of these things are their form qualities. A chair reduced to its parts is no longer a chair but rather a heap of sticks.

The Gestalt psychologists sought to understand the relationships among the parts of organized wholes and, in general, among elements in the visual field—asking how these relationships shape the way things look. Their extensive research program yielded a number of principles that can be very useful for document designers. Occasional pointers to the work of the Gestalt psychologists can be found in the graphic design literature (e.g., Frascara, 1995), but a more detailed discussion has grown in the interface design (e.g., Mullet & Sano, 1995), professional writing, and technical communication communities.[65] The next section integrates and extends the previous literature by presenting seven Gestalt principles for describing how people may interpret the visual field of a document. It explores how the relationships among elements of documents both structure the visual field and influence readers' interpretations of what they see.

[65] Ideas about applying Gestalt psychology to document design have been discussed in the rhetoric and writing community over the last ten years (e.g., Barton & Barton, 1985; Bernhardt, 1986; Campbell, 1995; Gribbons, 1992; Moore & Fitz, 1993a, 1993b).

GESTALT PRINCIPLES FOR DOCUMENT DESIGN

1. Perception Is an Active Process

Gestalt psychologists studied the act of seeing as a dynamic process involving both the viewer and the viewed. When people look at a page, a picture, a computer screen, or the environment around them, they actively organize what they see. They resolve ambiguities, impose structure, and make connections. Many of the problems in document design occur because, although the designers want the reader to see the text in one way, the structure of the text leads readers to see it differently. Figure 5.14 shows some of the different perspectives readers may take while engaged in the process of interpretation. It is a graph created by the *New York Times* intended to show some of the key events that took place in 1992 during the United States presidential campaign.

My colleague Ann Steffy Cronin and I asked a group of 10 people to provide us with feedback about "Bush's Bumpy Ride to Defeat." Participants were high-school graduates from a working-class neighborhood in Pittsburgh between the ages of thirty and sixty. All had expressed some

This is a percentage poll, how favorite or unfavorite he is. This doesn't make it clear what the numbers on the left side are. So, I don't know what these horizontal thin lines represent, how much percentage Bush has in the polls? Why do the numbers only go up to 50?

First of all I guess I am supposed to be reading pages before this to tell me about this chart. So previous to this it would tell how they came to all these conclusions, where the data is, what's it based on, stuff like that. If I just look at this chart it is mass confusion to me.

What do these little white dots mean? Or are they just points to make it more definite? The tiny white dots … are they the dates when the other states held their primaries (like New Hampshire)?

Oh favorable, unfavorable, I see the two lines, one is a darker black and one is kind of grayish. Is that a shadow or are there two lines together? I expected favorable to be the top line. It's the first thing up here, but it's not first on the graph.

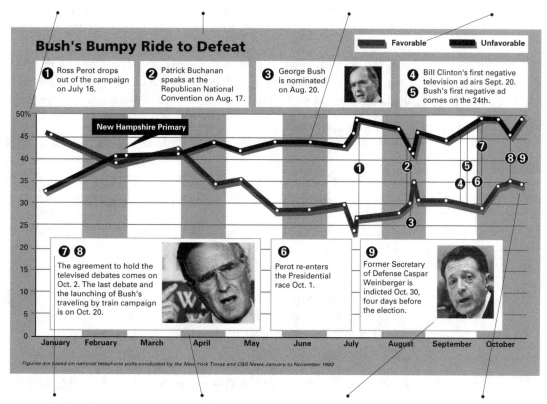

I am reading 1, 2, 3, 4. It is an easy guideline—you know what to look at. You can see when Ross Perot drops out of the campaign that he had pulled votes away from Bush. OK, 5 then 6, no, next is 7 and 8, that's wrong. It's out of order.

Unfavorable are darker, favorable are gray. But, these gray bars stay the same throughout. So I'm confused. I do see a little bit of gray that follows the black, I also see that the gray goes up, it follows right along with the black, but these bars, what do they mean?

I don't understand from the two lines who are we comparing here. We've got all these different names, Ross Perot. I don't know what I am looking for. I don't think you need the pictures. Caspar Weinberger, don't they call him Cap?

Right here at #9 Caspar Weinberger is indicted. He looks like he's at the peak of his unfavorable rating. I expected the favorable line to drop a lot more than it does. Where are the lines connecting #9 to the favor-able and unfavorable lines?

▲ **Figure 5.14** *Participants' responses to a graph depicting the events of the 1992 election that contributed to George Bush's defeat. Reprinted from the* New York Times, *November 29, 1992 (used with permission).*

interest in the events that surrounded the 1992 presidential election. Each person read the graph aloud and told us what they thought its it meant. After they had made their interpretation, we prompted participants to say more about what they thought during their reading.

As the comments in Figure 5.14 show, readers found the organization of this graph confusing. It was hard for them to decide what to focus on. They had trouble judging the intended meanings of the various graphic symbols and cues (e.g., the white dots on the plot lines, the shaded bars which separate the months, the drop shadows on the plot lines). They were mystified by the chaotic out-of-order numbering scheme employed to map the numbers on the graph to the rectangles along the top and bottom of the graph. They also wondered "Why these pictures rather than others?" The biggest problem, however, was that most of the readers couldn't infer the main point—that is, they couldn't make heads or tails of the favorable and unfavorable ratings that led to Bush's defeat.

Gestalt psychologists argue that people tend to impose meaning and structure on things they see. As readers' comments about the Bush graph show, people will attempt to generate meanings for the content even when the structure is haphazard and works against a consistent reading. (But most readers will try to work with a poorly designed document for only a short period.) Despite readers' very active efforts to resolve the ambiguities between the "favorable" and "unfavorable" ratings, most were left without a clear idea of its main point, thus defeating the designer's rhetorical purpose. An implication of Gestalt psychology for document design is that readers may make use of all of the cues in the visual field to help them in constructing meanings for the content. If the cues are not carefully orchestrated, it is highly unlikely that readers will create the meanings for the content that the document designer intended.

2. People Organize What They See into Figure and Ground

The figure-ground principle captures the idea that the visual field is normally divided into two parts, figure and ground. "Usually the figure is at the focus of attention ... is surrounded by a contour ... and is seen as a whole. The rest of the field is the ground ... [It] is apt to be in the margin of attention and is usually seen as further away [or behind] the figure" (Boring, 1929, p. 605). Look at Figure 5.15. It presents a famous figure-ground illusion that was studied by Danish psychologist Edgar J. Rubin (1915/1921). One can see the figure as either a white vase on a black background or as two black faces on a white background. In either case, the edge between figure and ground is seen as bounding the figure but not the ground. The figure is perceived as being in front of the ground

◀ **Figure 5.15** *An ambiguous figure illustrating the principle of figure-ground relationship (based on the work of E. J. Rubin, 1915/1921).*

and the ground is perceived as continuing behind the figure. In examining Figure 5.15 from the perspective of figure and ground, we notice how the function of the boundary changes as the figure changes from vase to faces.

The figure-ground principle is very much a part of our everyday experience. If we notice a book on a table, we see the book as a figure and the table as its ground. The edge that divides the book from the table bounds the book but not the table. The table is assumed to continue under the book. We would be very surprised if, when we lifted the book, we discovered a hole in the table the size and shape of the book. Figure 5.16 (on the next page) shows a two-page spread from an instruction manual for a stereo system designed in Japan that was intended for an American and European audience. It presents four languages at once. The central horizontal rectangle (with the pictures) may be seen as a figure lying on top of the vertical columns of text, which may be perceived as continuing underneath (the ground).

We might be tempted to view figure and ground as a relationship between just two levels. However, what serves as ground in one relationship can serve as figure in another. The table that was ground for the book may also be a figure that has a whole room as its background. Figure-ground relationships, then, may involve multiple levels. In addition, the figure-ground effect does not require the viewer to look at already meaningful figures in order for the phenomenon to operate. It works for meaningless blobs such as clouds as well as for meaningful objects like traffic signs.

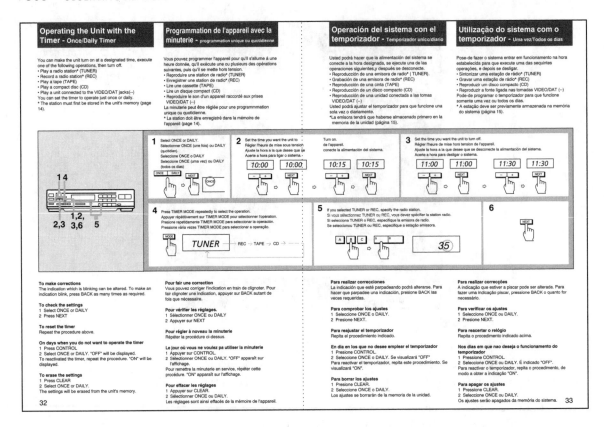

▲ Figure 5.16 *A two-page spread from a multilanguage stereo manual. This spread provides a set of procedures for programming a stereo to play for a certain amount of time (e.g., a half-hour) and then to turn off.*

Some writers (Porter & Goodman, 1988) have conflated the concept of "ground" with the concept of "negative space." We should be careful to distinguish between these concepts because they are quite different. To illustrate their difference, let me ask you to imagine a large black "X" drawn on a blank sheet of paper. The area on the page not covered by the X is the blank space. When we focus on the X as figure, the blank space is seen as the ground continuing behind the figure. As ground, it is not shaped by the contour around the X. In comparison, when we focus on the blank space as figure, we do not see it as continuing behind the X. Rather, we see its shape, perceiving its contour, which is the reverse of the contour of the X. When the blank space is perceived by the viewer as figure, it acts as "negative space." Negative space is blank space that has been brought to the visual fore. For example, many logos and posters are designed using the technique of "reversing the type" (white letters on black or colored background) or of suggesting the shape of a letterform (by using the negative space to render visual clues about the figure). In contrast, the ground is blank space that runs behind the text, where the type and graphics act as figure. This does not mean, however, that ground cannot be an active element in the design. For the space around, between, and within the figure can be employed to show rhetorical relationships among the content elements as well as to provide continuity, emphasis, and an elegant appearance.

An issue for document design is how to make the ground a more active and purposeful element in the design. Gombrich (1961) argues that artists are trained to increase their sensitivity to the effect of space and shape by "half closing one eye … switching attention from the meaningful objects [figures] to the shapes they leave empty against a background. These negative shapes … have no meaning in terms of things" (p. 306). Here the strategy is to deliberately foreground the negative space in order to sense how positive (i.e., deliberate and intentional forms) and negative design elements (i.e., the accidental forms created by the ground) speak to one another. The idea is that even the ground can still convey a sense of purpose, closure, and of aesthetically pleasing forms. Conversely, the ground can appear chaotic, choppy, and haphazard. (I discuss the idea of creating effective spatial cues in Section 4 of this chapter).

Document designers would profit from evaluating the possible figure-ground relations in their texts because these relationships are likely to effect the order in which people read the text and graphics. Keep in mind that both blank space and text can act as ground (as we saw in Figure 5.16). Because figures are by definition in the focus of attention, they tend to be examined first.[66] Thus, an ad that features dramatic pictures of people may completely overshadow the message presented through the text (e.g., consider cigarette manufacturers' colorful pictures of smokers "alive with pleasure" juxtaposed with the visually indistinct text-only warning label). If readers start with the "wrong" information, they may miss the information they need most, assume it is not there, or conclude it is too much of a hassle to find and give up. Anticipating how people will interpret figure-ground relations is important for document designers.

[66] Even when document designers take care to create figure-ground relations that are consistent with their rhetorical goals, readers will not necessarily pay attention. Inevitably there will be situations when people's habits, goals, or personal preferences for reading text and graphics will override the designer's intentions, a point I demonstrate later in this section.

3. How People Group Figures Depends on the Visual Properties of the Figures

When people perceive a visual field, the patterns that emerge depend on the unique characteristics of the elements of the field and the relationships among the elements within the field. For example, the array of identical circles in Figure 5.17a (on the next page) can be seen in groups of rows or columns. However, we can lead the reader to see columns (or rows) by varying the size (Figure 5.17b), the color or contrast (Figure 5.17c), the shape (Figure 5.17d), or the separation (Figure 5.17f). We can also group the circles by providing connecting cues (Figure 5.17e). These cues that

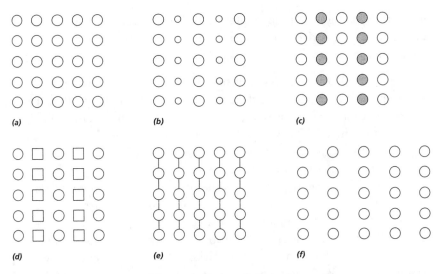

▲ Figure 5.17 *The grouping of figures depends on their visual properties.*

encourage visual grouping can be very powerful (Bertin, 1983). If they are used appropriately, they can help the reader to understand the internal relationship among the text parts.

The principle of visual grouping can be employed in many practical document design situations. For example, Figure 5.18 shows how dotted lines can be used to group elements on a page. The three illustrations are successive iterations of an instruction manual for a combination telephone plus answering machine.[67] In their revisions, document designers explored different ways of visualizing the steps in order to help readers better see the relationships among the steps.

The initial concept uses blowups of the buttons to show which ones to press, but it does not show their relationship to the tasks or to each other (the blowups are too far away from the steps, weakening visual proximity cues). Though the blowups of the buttons are neatly aligned, they are rhetorically ineffective because they require the reader to do the work of mapping which step goes with which button (most of the procedures to operate this device required more than one button per step). The second draft clusters the blowups of the buttons closer to the verbal instructions, using a staggered layout. It was intended to show the back and forth motion of completing the steps. However, a usability test showed that users were confused about when one step ended and the next one started. Furthermore, they still did not know which blowup went with which step. The third draft solves this mapping problem by visually clustering the blowups through the use of dots to connect the related steps, making the steps easy to track as a series of nested actions.

[67] This example is from a project carried out by Mary L. Ray, Dan Boyarski, Carlos J. Peterson, Norma Pribadi Polk, Michele Matchett, Ann Steffy Cronin, and myself. The ideas presented in this example were the result of collaborative brainstorming, usability testing, and redesigning. Details of this project are presented in Chapter 7.

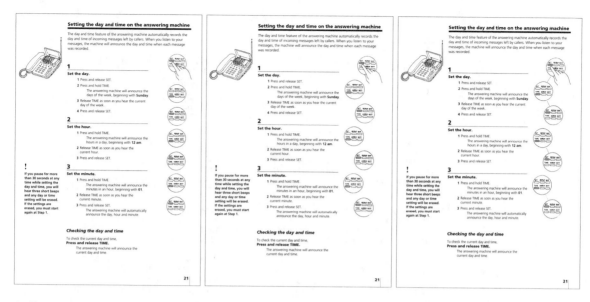

▲ **Figure 5.18** *Successive iterations of the design of an instruction manual for a combined telephone and answering machine. The design explores visualizing the steps by using proximity cues to help readers see the relations among the sequences within the steps. Document design by Dan Boyarski, Norma Pribadi Polk, Mary L. Ray, and Carlos Peterson for Karen Schriver Associates, Inc., Pittsburgh, PA. (To see an example of the original manual upon which these revisions are based, see Figure 7.8, p. 466.)*

Another device that can help promote grouping of related text elements is shading. (Like the visual clustering achieved by using dots to connect items, shading can be employed even in black and white publications.) Figure 5.19 (on the next page) shows how shading can be used to help readers search the columns more quickly and disambiguate the numbers in the columns. Notice how the margins between the columns can be tight when the columns are shaded. It is important that the shading is applied lightly, here using only a 15 percent gray screen.

However, if cues such as shading are used inappropriately, they can be quite misleading.[68] The use of shading in Figure 5.20 could lead readers to overlook half of the rows in the figure or it could convey the unintended message that the shaded and unshaded rows represent two distinct groups of diseases. The problem here is that the use of the 80 percent gray screen is much too strong. It not only disambiguates the rows but may encourage readers to assign meaning to the visual distinctions.

In his discussion of the design of quantitative graphics, cognitive psychologist Kosslyn (1994) observes that any sharp contrast will draw the reader's attention. Moreover, the greater the contrast, the more salient the effect. Typographers and graphic designers have made similar observations since the 1920s. In fact, Jan Tschichold (1928/1987, 1967) argued that contrast is perhaps the most important element of all modern design. He

[68] In his *Semiology of Graphics,* Bertin (1983) suggests that readers typically attend to visual cues in the following order: size, value, pattern, color, orientation, and shape.

▶ Figure 5.19 *A sample revision of an IRS instruction booklet. Created by document designers Mary L. Ray and Michele Matchett, former students at Carnegie Mellon, in collaboration with tax experts at the Center for Taxation Studies in Akron, Ohio.*

IRS version

If 1040A, line 17, OR 1040EZ, line 7 is—		And you are—			
At least	But less than	Single (and 1040EZ filers)	Married filing jointly	Married filing separately	Head of a house-hold
		Your tax is—			

32,000

32,000	32,050	7,063	5,207	7,754	5,877
32,050	32,100	7,080	5,221	7,771	5,891
32,100	32,150	7,098	5,235	7,789	5,905
32,150	32,200	7,115	5,249	7,806	5,919
32,200	32,250	7,133	5,263	7,824	5,933
32,250	32,300	7,150	5,277	7,841	5,947
32,300	32,350	7,168	5,291	7,859	5,961
32,350	32,400	7,185	5,305	7,876	5,975
32,400	32,450	7,203	5,319	7,894	5,989
32,450	32,500	7,220	5,333	7,911	6,003
32,500	32,550	7,238	5,347	7,929	6,017
32,550	32,600	7,255	5,361	7,946	6,031
32,600	32,650	7,273	5,375	7,964	6,045
32,650	32,700	7,290	5,389	7,981	6,059
32,700	32,750	7,308	5,403	7,999	6,073
32,750	32,800	7,325	5,417	8,061	6,087
32,800	32,850	7,343	5,431	8,304	6,101
32,850	32,900	7,360	5,445	8,051	6,115
32,900	32,950	7,378	5,459	8,069	6,129
32,950	33,000	7,395	5,473	8,086	6,143

Revised version

If 1040EZ Line 7, or 1040A Line 17 is:		And your filing status is:			
At least	But less than	Single	Married filing jointly	Married filing separately	Head of house-hold

$32,000

32,000	32,050	7,063	5,207	7,754	5,877
32,050	32,100	7,080	5,221	7,771	5,891
32,100	32,150	7,098	5,235	7,789	5,905
32,150	32,200	7,115	5,249	7,806	5,919
32,200	32,250	7,133	5,263	7,824	5,933
32,250	32,300	7,150	5,277	7,841	5,947
32,300	32,350	7,168	5,291	7,859	5,961
32,350	32,400	7,185	5,305	7,876	5,975
32,400	32,450	7,203	5,319	7,894	5,989
32,450	32,500	7,220	5,333	7,911	6,003
32,500	32,550	7,238	5,347	7,929	6,017
32,550	32,600	7,255	5,361	7,946	6,031
32,600	32,650	7,273	5,375	7,964	6,045
32,650	32,700	7,290	5,389	7,981	6,059
32,700	32,750	7,308	5,403	7,999	6,073
32,750	32,800	7,325	5,417	8,061	6,087
32,800	32,850	7,343	5,431	8,304	6,101
32,850	32,900	7,360	5,445	8,051	6,115
32,900	32,950	7,378	5,459	8,069	6,129
32,950	33,000	7,395	5,473	8,086	6,143

▶ Figure 5.20 *An ineffective use of shading to promote grouping. The contrast is so great that readers may be led to conclude there are two main groups of cancers. In addition, there is no rhetorical reason to orient the shaded bars horizontally. Vertical shading used lightly would have been a more effective cue. From* Time, *April 25, 1994 (used with the permission of Time, Inc., New York, NY).*

THE BIG KILLERS
Estimates in the U.S., 1994

Cancer		Deaths	New cases	Five-year survival rate	Risk Factors
Lung		153,000	172,000	13%	Cigarette smoking; exposure to asbestos, chemicals, radiation, radon
Colon/Rectum		56,000	149,000	58%	Family history; high-fat, low-fiber diet
Female Breast		46,000	182,000	79%	Age, family history; no pregnancies; late menopause; early menarche
Prostate		38,000	200,000	77%	Age; family history; possibly fat intake
Pancreas		25,900	27,000	3%	Age; smoking; fat intake
Lymphoma	Hodgkin's Non-Hodgkin's	22,750	52,900	78% 52%	Reduced immune function; exposure to herbicides, solvents, vinyl chloride
Leukemia		19,100	28,600	38%	Genetic abnormalities; exposure to ionizing radiation, chemicals; viruses
Ovary		13,600	24,000	39%	Age; family history; genetic disorders; no pregnancies
Kidney		11,300	27,600	55%	Smoking
Bladder		10,600	51,200	79%	Smoking
Uterus	Cervical Endometrial	10,500	46,000	67% 83%	Intercourse at an early age; multiple sex partners; smoking Early menarche; late menopause; obesity
Oral		7,925	29,600	53%	Smoking; excessive use of alcohol
Skin Melanoma		6,900	32,000	84%	Sunburn; fair complexion; exposure to coal tar, pitch, creosote, arsenic, radium

Source: American Cancer Society

suggests there are many ways to achieve contrast, the simplest of which reveals a form by using its opposite: large/small, light/dark, horizontal/vertical, square/round, smooth/rough, closed/open, colored/plain (p. 70). Document designers need to consider how the design of contrasting visual cues encourages readers to group the content. They need to evaluate whether the grouping helps readers to make reasonable (and appropriate) inferences about the internal relationships among the parts of the document. They need to answer: Do the visual cues support the rhetorical goals for understanding and making use of the content? If document designers succeed in doing this, readers won't have to deal with documents that have the "gratuitous grays"—screens of gray that decorate while they obfuscate.

4. How People Group Figures Depends on "Good Continuation"

The Gestalt principle of "good continuation" says that graphic elements that suggest a continued visual line will tend to be grouped together. In addition, visual patterns with good continuation may suggest to the viewer that the pattern continues beyond the end of the pattern itself. That is, we mentally "fill in" or "paint in" the rest of the pattern. Let's take an example. In Figure 5.21, viewers tend to see the coyote's footprints labeled "(d)" as a continuation of those labeled "(a)" and the footprints labeled "(b)" as a continuation of those labeled "(c)." The footprints at (d) are said to provide a good continuation of the footprints at (a) because they line up reasonably well. Moreover, the good continuation allows us to mentally trace the path that the coyote took through the pond, and we can also picture the footprints walking off the page. The footprints at (b) do not provide good continuation to those at (a) because of the sharp angle between the two paths.

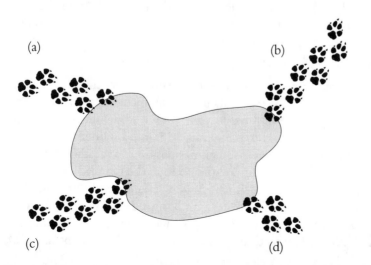

(a)

(b)

(c)

(d)

◀ Figure 5.21 *An example illustrating "good continuation." When good continuation is working, there is little ambiguity about what is connected to what.*

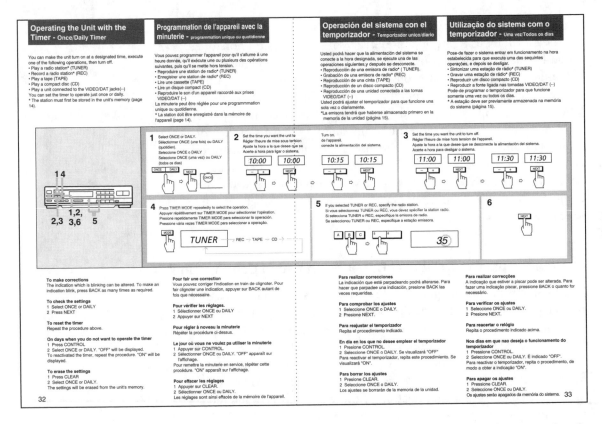

▲ **Figure 5.22** *How Figure 5.16 would look without "good continuation." Notice that shifting the bottoms of the columns to the right breaks the continuity of their alignment with the tops of the columns. Bad continuation may cause people to read the top of a column as a separate chunk from the bottom. They might also read the bottom segments as supplementary to the top segments since the bottom chunks are visually indented under the top.*

The example of the stereo manual shown earlier is another example of good continuation. Look again at Figure 5.16. Notice that the columns of text above the horizontal rectangle seem to be grouped with the columns of text below it because the left margins of these text blocks align visually. The justified-left margin provides for good continuation. In contrast, Figure 5.22 shows how the columns would appear if the text blocks were not lined up. Notice how the break in the margin destroys the continuity in the alignment of the columns. The layout of the columns could encourage readers to assume that the content presented along the bottom of the page is rhetorically different from that along the top.

Moore and Fitz (1993b) point out that good continuation is important in the design of tables, especially in the alignment of columns. They suggest that readers should not look down a column to see the good continuation broken by a rule line that is intended to frame a subheading. Inexperienced document designers sometimes position subheadings in a centered position over the columns and then bound the subheads with horizontal rule lines above and below them. When designed in this way, the horizontal lines may "inadvertently create areas of strong closure … [which may] interfere with the reader's ability to connect the column headings with the data" (p. 398). In effect, this strategy carves up the content into parts which are marked by the rule lines. Unless the content of the columns changes from one section to the next, horizontal cues should not compete with vertical ones. To avoid this problem, subheadings should appear in the leftmost column of the table as side headings (called *stubs*). Document designers can conclude that unless they want to signal a rhetorically distinct text element, it is a good idea to maintain good continuation.

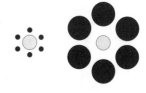

▲ **Figure 5.23** *A size illusion.*

5. How a Figure Looks Depends on Its Surroundings

Gestalt psychologists carried out numerous studies in which they showed that the various parts of the visual field interacted with one another. For example, the perceived size, brightness, and shape of a figure depends on its surround, on other figures in its neighborhood. A general Gestalt principle is that everything in the perceptual field influences everything else. Figure 5.23 shows two gray disks of the same size (measure them if you are not convinced). They appear different in size because of their different surroundings.

Figure 5.24 shows two gray disks of exactly the same color. Again, they don't look the same because of their different surroundings. A phenomenon called *simultaneous contrast* makes the gray surrounded by a dark background appear lighter than the gray surrounded by a light background. Thus, the perceived color of the disk depends not only on the disk but also on its environment.

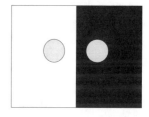

▲ **Figure 5.24** *A brightness illusion.*

Figure 5.25 shows a perfect square that doesn't look square because of its surroundings. Thus, the size, color, and shape of a figure can be modified substantially by its surroundings. Figures that work well in isolation may not work well when they are put in the context of a complete page or screen design.

Because every element within the visual field interacts with other elements, it is important to flesh out the major and minor text elements early in the document design process. Document designers must consider the interactions among the elements and orchestrate their interplay so that the main points of the content can be inferred quickly and easily. The principle that a figure's appearance depends on its surroundings—that everything in the visual field influences everything else—suggests avoiding the all-too-frequent practice of changing major elements of the design after it has been deemed finished. One last minute change *can* ruin the whole thing. It is not that last minute changes should not happen (they inevitably do). Rather, it is that time must be allotted to assess the effect of changes on the whole. Moreover, time must be allocated to make other modifications to the design in the event that the strength, cohesiveness, and continuity of the design is diminished by changes.

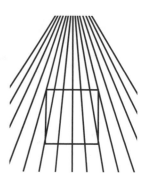

▲ **Figure 5.25** *A shape illusion.*

6. Strong Figures Are Stable

Although everything in the perceptual field does influence everything else, it is also true that some figures are more resistant to contextual influences than others. Figures that tend to resist such influences—called strong figures or "good gestalts"—generally share the properties of simplicity, regularity, and symmetry. In addition, such figures tend to be "closed," that is, they are surrounded by a continuous, unbroken contour—a property called "closure." For example, a circle, because it is simple, regular, symmetrical, and closed, is a very strong figure. Squares, rectangles, and triangles (which are also simple, regular, symmetrical, and closed) are also considered strong figures. However, these figures are not as simple as the circle (because they have corners). Neither are they as symmetrical (circles are symmetrical with respect to any axis but squares, rectangles, and triangles are not). Strong figures resist change or disintegration under poor viewing conditions or variations in the viewer's attention. Further, strong figures tend to win out in competition with weaker figures. For example, Figure 5.26 shows two line drawings. Each drawing could be seen either as two figures side-by-side or as a single figure with a line through it. In the top drawing, we tend to see two hexagons side-by-side rather than a more complex figure with a line through it. In contrast, in the bottom drawing, we see a single rectangle with a line through it rather than two asymmetric figures side-by-side. In both cases, the stronger simpler figures win out in the viewer's eye.

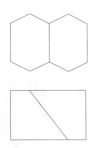

▲ Figure 5.26 *In ambiguous situations, people tend to see stonger rather than weaker figures.*

The spread at the top of the next page above Figures 5.27 and 5.28 is the one shown earlier as Figure 5.16, from the multilanguage instruction guide for the stereo system. The Japanese document design team was a group of writers, graphic designers, and technical illustrators who first wrote an English version of the text and then employed a European contract firm to translate it into different languages. Once the translations were finished, the texts were returned to Tokyo, where the Japanese team completed the design. The final layout of the guide was based on the team's intuitions about how people would read it. Conversations with members of the team revealed that document designers expected users would read the text in the order shown in Figure 5.27. That is, document designers anticipated that readers would start with the leftmost (shaded) box of the central horizontal rectangular block and then move through the subsections within that block in numerical order. Next, they expected that readers would spot the column written in their native language, begin with the label at the top of that column, read the chunk immediately below it, and then move to the bottom of the column (below the figure) to finish the text.

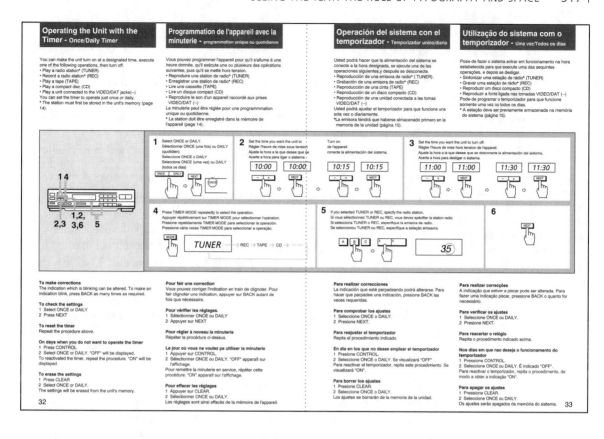

How Document Designers Thought Bilingual Readers Would Scan the Text

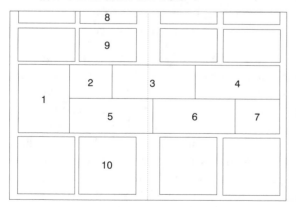

▲ Figure 5.27 *The order in which document designers predicted that bilingual readers would navigate the two-page spread for the stereo manual (shown at top).*

How French-English Bilingual Readers Tended to Scan the Text

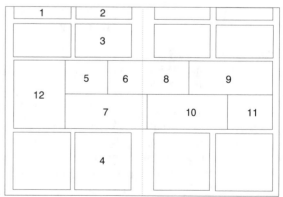

▲ Figure 5.28 *The order in which French-English bilingual readers actually navigated the two-page spread. The path readers took had little in common with designers' predictions.*

The designers anticipated that the layout of the spread would lead people to perceive the central rectangular block as its focal point, inviting readers to attend to it first. They expected the central rectangle in Figure 5.27 (boxes 1 to 7) would operate as a single unified figure. They felt that readers would be drawn to consider the instructions with the pictures before the "text only" sections in the columns.[69] They assumed the text displayed in columns (e.g., boxes 8, 9, and 10) would be construed as the ground and would be read after inspecting the content of the rectangle.

However, the Gestalt principles I have been discussing suggest that what people do may be more complicated. In fact, as shown in Figures 5.28 and 5.29, French bilingual readers apparently did not view the central rectangle as a single figure. Why might this happen? A design feature that works against reading the block as a unified whole is the two vertical lines which transect the rectangle, visually carving it into pieces. The first line, roughly in the middle of the left-hand page (i.e., the right edge of the shaded box), invites the reader to see the shaded box as separate from the other boxes in the group. (The shaded box is a strong figure because it is nearly square, uniformly shaded, and bigger than other boxes.) The second vertical line, created by the stapled binding of the manual (indicated by the dotted line) leads the reader to divide the remaining part of the rectangle into two smaller rectangles—one including boxes 1, 4, and half of 2 and the other including boxes 3, 5, 6, and the other half of 2 (these numbers refer to the numbered boxes in the actual spread from the manual, not to the ones in the diagram at the bottom of the page). We can see, then, that there are at least three figures readers may consider. These interacting elements may lead readers not to see the figure as a whole. Moreover, they may not know where to start because there are essentially two competing grids for the reader's attention, one moving left-to-right (boxes 1 to 6, each of a different width) and another moving top-to-bottom (the columns).

Figure 5.28 shows the reading order[70] that was most typical of five French-English bilingual readers as they tried to use the guide. (Comparable accounts could be provided for the other nationality groups—English-only, German-English bilinguals, and Spanish-English bilinguals—who took part in the study. The study from which this excerpt is drawn is presented in Chapter 7. This manual was translated into six different languages, three of which are shown here. My colleagues and I studied how different language groups used the guide and revised it based on their feedback. For examples from the revision, see Figures 7.12 and 7.13, pp. 470–471. To see participants' performance, see Table 7.2, p. 456.) The French-English bilinguals, and indeed all nationality groups, started reading in the location that Western readers usually start, the upper-left corner—moving left-to-right. Perhaps it would have been possible to make the central block a stronger figure that would have led users to start reading in a place different

[69] It is widely held among Japanese document design groups that Japanese consumers prefer visual instructions and feel comfortable with complex technical illustrations. The document designers' strategy was to make the document more verbal than they would for their home market but to maintain an emphasis on pictorial instructions, using prose only when necessary.

[70] The idea for this analysis came from Goldsmith (1987), who found that the layout of science textbooks for British middle-school children made it difficult for students to figure out the order in which to read the materials. She also found a large gap between the order of reading document designers anticipated and what readers actually did in navigating the text.

from the one they normally choose. In this case, though, it is not clear why the designer would want to compete with the readers' habitual preference. If the designer wants the reader to read the information in the central block first, why not place it at the top of the page?

Let's look at Figure 5.28, which shows the order in which French-English bilinguals scanned the spread:

- *First:* The heading in the first column at the top left, written in English.
- *Second:* The heading in the second column (it was written in French).
- *Third* and *Fourth:* The top and then the bottom of the second column of text.[71]
- *Fifth:* The box labeled 1 in the horizontal bar.
- *Sixth:* The left half of the box labeled 2 in the horizontal bar.
- *Seventh:* The box labeled 4 in the horizontal bar.[72]
- *Eighth:* The right half of box 2 in the horizontal bar.
- *Ninth* through *Eleventh:* The boxes 3, 5, and 6 in the horizontal bar.
- *Twelfth:* The shaded box on the left (the one that the document designers hoped that readers would start with).

[71] The column functioned well as a unit even though it was divided by the central block, presumably because of the good continuation of the left margins.

[72] The order in which the text was read certainly suggests that readers were treating the rectangular forms on the left page as distinct from those on the right page. Apparently, the cues dividing the central rectangular block and box 2 were stronger than the cues unifying them.

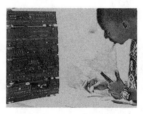

Laurent looks at pages 32 and 33 in the stereo manual. The two-page spread describes how to program the timer on the stereo to turn the radio on and off at designated times. *"Okay I have to do the clock thing again. I'd rather my language be isolated. I don't like the way it keeps switching languages while I read. I like my own French version. Operating the unit with the timer, okay, Programmation de l'appareil avec la minuterie … All right here we go."* He continues to read the text under the French heading.

"Vous pouvez programmer l'appareil pour qu'il s'allume à une heure donnée, qu'il exécute une ou plusieurs des operations suivantes, puis qu'il se mette hors tension.… I can program the stereo to turn on and off. La minuterie peut être réglée pour une programmation unique ou quotidienne. I can program the timer once or more than one time. I need to keep reading." Laurent follows the column down to the bottom of the page, stopping at the next French section of text.

"Hmm. Pour faire une correction, no, I don't need to correct the program yet. Pour vérifier les réglages, I don't need to repair the program. This is not helping. Let me check the graphics." Laurent looks at the picture in the middle of the two pages. *"Okay, one, sélectionner une fois ou quotidien. 'ONCE' and 'DAILY.' Where are those buttons? I can't find them."* He reads the manual, then looks at the radio on the stereo. *"I don't know, maybe I'll understand if I keep reading."*

Régler l'heure … Set the time" Laurent presses buttons while continuing to read the manual. *"I'm trying to set the time. Appuyer règpétitivement sur TIMER MODE pour sélectionar la opération. First I set the time and then pick the component that is going to play. Next, de l'appareil. Hmm? Oh, this is part of number two from the other page. I missed it before."* Laurent continues to read the manual while pressing buttons. *"This task is too hard—the manual is confusing. Is there a French version?"*

▲ Figure 5.29 *Laurent, a French-English bilingual usability testing participant, tries to program the stereo to turn on and then off again after playing for 10 minutes. Unfortunately, because the visual and verbal design of the manual is confusing, he becomes frustrated and is unable to get the timer to turn off the stereo.*

To provide a feel for the user's experience with these instructions, Figure 5.29 (on the previous page) presents a transcript of a French-English speaker as he tries the task, along with a few "freeze frames" from a video of his usability test. (The text in roman type shows notes taken by the usability tester as the participant tried out the procedures and the bold italic displays the participant's comments.) His comments show that he did not scan the text in ways that designers expected. Instead, he (and other participants) found the layout confusing and tried to read it one page at a time. He found the four languages on one page difficult (the problem is not so much that there are four languages but that they are presented using a competing horizontal and vertical organization). The chaotic design and ambiguous writing led him to conclude that the task was too hard and prompted him to ask if there was another manual designed for French speakers.

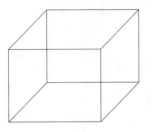

▲ Figure 5.30 *Viewers tend to see this 2-D drawing in 3-D.*

A knowledge of Gestalt principles might have helped the designers of this spread avoid some of the problems it created for them and for their readers.

7. The Reader May Add a Dimension: 2-D to 3-D

People tend to see two-dimensional drawings in three dimensions—moving from the flatland of 2-D to the solid representation of 3-D. For example, Figure 5.30 (called the Necker cube) consists of lines on a flat piece of paper. Yet, most people see it as a cube in three dimensions. In fact, it can scarcely be perceived as a flat figure on a 2-D page unless its orientation is adjusted so it takes the shape of a symmetrical 2-D hexagon (Hilgard, 1987, p. 154).

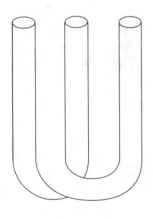

▲ Figure 5.31 *A drawing that provides contradictory 3-D cues.*

Figure 5.31 also consists of lines on a flat piece of paper. As long as we see it as a 2-D drawing, it is unproblematic. It is only when we interpret it in 3-D that we run into trouble. The visual cues in the top half of the drawing and the bottom half of the drawing lead to different and incompatible spatial representations. (Try covering up the bottom half with your hand, then the top half; each time predict how you expect the completed drawing to look.) The fact that most viewers regard this figure as uncomfortable to look at or "weird" testifies to the commonness of the tendency to see 2-D figures in 3-D.

This illustration is not simply a toy exercise. People have a strong inclination to translate 2-D representations into three dimensions even when those figures are formed by lines on a two-dimensional page or computer screen. What does this have to do with document design? Look at Figure 5.32 (especially the first box and the ones numbered 3 and 4).

These technical illustrations are quite typical of drawings in consumer electronics manuals. It is from the same multilanguage stereo system manual presented in Figures 5.16, 5.27, and 5.28. This two-page spread is intended to show users how to connect the components (e.g., stereo, CD player, tuner, and tape deck).

The designer appears to have modeled the technical illustrations on the engineer's 2-D circuit diagram using a minimum of 3-D cues. The representation of the key components in the first box and in boxes 3 and 4 are crucial for the user's success in hooking things together. Yet these key components appear flattened, like bugs pinned to a board in a biology project. Why did document designers eliminate 3-D cues when users must make the connections in a 3-D environment? Perhaps they believed that users would find the 2-D drawings simpler to understand. But if users try to represent the components in three dimensions—as they must when they are connecting them—it makes sense to provide lots of 3-D cues.

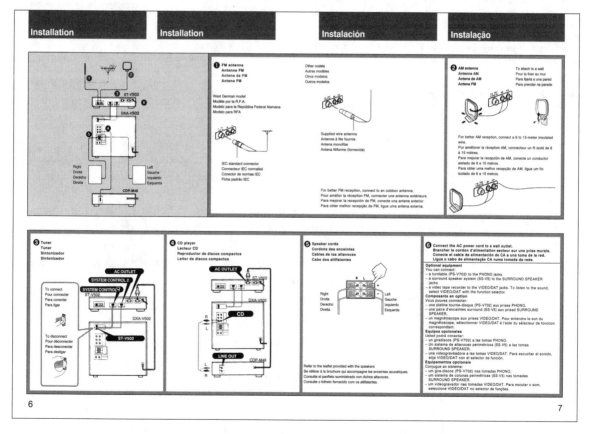

▲ Figure 5.32 *A diagram for connecting together the components of a stereo system. Notice that among other problems of design, it provides readers with few 3-D cues.*

Martha looks at the Table of Contents in the stereo manual to find instructions describing how to connect the stereo components.
"I am looking in the 'índice.' The task you want me to try is 'connect the radio, cassette player, and speakers together.' In the 'índice' ... I don't see any Spanish 'conectar,' which means to connect. That is the first thing I would look for if I'm connecting something."
She scans the Table of Contents one more time.
"'Instalación.' I guess that could mean connecting the stereo."

Martha turns to pages six and seven and begins reading the text under the Spanish heading.
"Otros modelos, antena monofilar, para majorar la recepción de FM, conecte una antena exterior. No, I don't see the instructions to connect the stereo."
She points to the first two pictures on page six. [See Figure 5.32, top-left and bottom-left pictures.]
"These pictures look strange. I mean the lines, they look like a box ... I can't tell if the lines are wires or is that the edge of the stereo? What part am I looking at?"

Martha continues to scan pages six and seven, trying to decide what to focus on.
"Okay, well, I think I will try to follow the pictures."
Martha takes a deep breath.
"I don't know if the same pictures are repeated for the different languages or if the translation is done but it is the same pictures for all languages. Because under Spanish, I see just this little portion of information."
She points to the two boxes under the heading in Spanish, "Other models" and number 5, "Speaker cords," and continues scanning the spread.
"Oh okay, numbers one, two,

three, four, five. So hopefully, if I follow these numbers I will be able to do this. One, Antena de FM, modelo para la República Federal Alemana, conector de normas IEC ... Otros modelos, I don't care about other models ... I have this one. Para mejorar la recepción de FM, conecte una antena exterior. Hmm ... I don't know why they are talking about 'improving the reception.' At this point, I don't want to improve anything, I just want to make the stereo work...."

▲ Figure 5.33 *Martha, a Spanish-English bilingual usability testing participant, tries to connect a set of stereo components together. Unfortunately, because the technical illustrations in the manual are hard to understand and the language is not procedural (nor always relevant to her task), she is unable to connect the components.*

Figure 5.33 provides a transcript from a Spanish-English bilingual usability testing participant who tried, unsuccessfully, to connect the stereo components using the spread shown in Figure 5.32 (on the previous page). Notice that among other things, she has trouble distinguishing the lines on the drawing that are wires from the edge of the stereo itself. Her problem stems partly from the 2-D diagram, but also from the similarity between the line weight for the edge of the components and the wires (which are rendered with squared-off edges, the right angles of which form another set of competing rectangles).

In addition, because the procedure in Figure 5.32 is not organized according to her task, she must figure out which boxed steps are most relevant to her goal of connecting the components together. Notice the box labeled 1 describes how to connect the FM antenna. However, at this point, she doesn't need to attach the antenna; she needs to hook the CD player and tuner to the main unit. When she gets to step 2, she is given information about how to get "better AM reception by connecting a 6- to 15-meter insulated wire." This little factoid is also irrelevant to her immediate goal. In her words, "I don't know why they are talking about improving the reception. At this point, I don't want to improve anything. I just want to make the stereo work." In fact, the insulated wire was not even provided with the stereo. She tries to sort things out in step 3, but cannot tell what to do because the cartoon bubbles in boxes 3 and 4 are labeled with acronyms such as ST-V502 and DXA-V502 instead of tuner, CD player, and tape deck. The bubbles were intended to indicate where to plug in the various components but this idea is unintelligible because the labels are cryptic. As we can see, the information is not task oriented; it neither presents the content consumers expect nor organizes the steps according to when they need them.

From the user's perspective, this spread violates a number of the principles I've been discussing, especially those of size, position, and dimensionality. For example, the most important parts are the smallest; the most important procedures are not presented in the focal position of the first steps; and the most important things to render in 3-D are drawn in 2-D. The Spanish-English usability participant is also confused by the ambiguous visual signals about how to navigate the content. Notice that the vertical columns seem to suggest: Find your language and then read down the column. But when she turns to the Spanish heading "Instalación," looks down the column, and sees only the second half of box 1 and box 5, she wonders aloud:

> I don't know if the same pictures are repeated for the different languages or if the translation is done but it is the same pictures for all languages. Because under Spanish I see just this little portion of information.

She then recognizes that she should read all of the boxes, not just the ones under the column for Spanish speakers. Like the earlier spread shown in Figure 5.16, this one also employs a design with competing horizontal and vertical cues.

Figure 5.34 (on the next page) shows an alternate 3-D approach for instructing users to connect these same components. Data I report in Chapter 7 indicate that people of four language groups (English-only, Spanish-English, French-English, and German-English) had much more success in connecting electronics components when the instruction manual used a 3-D rather than a 2-D approach (see Figure 7.2, p. 453, and Table 7.2, p. 456). When they can, people tend to represent a situation in three dimensions rather than two. Rather than working *against* this inclination, document designers should try to work *with* people's tendency to transform the flat world of the page or screen to the 3-D world they live in.

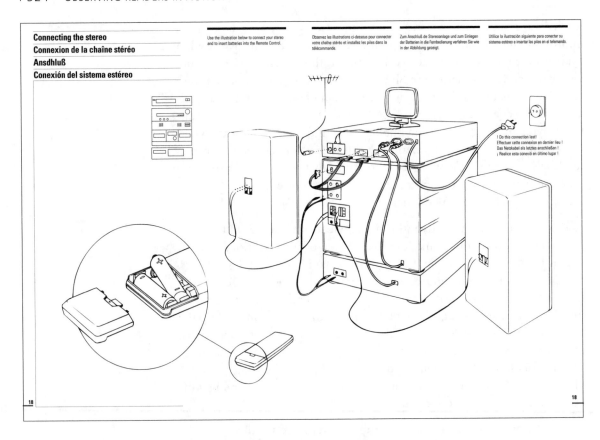

Connecting the stereo
Connexion de la chaîne stéréo
Ansdhluß
Conexión del sistema estéreo

Use the illustration below to connect your stereo and to insert batteries into the Remote Control.

Observez les illustrations ci-dessous pour connecter votre chaîne stéréo et installez les piles dans la télécommande.

Zum Anschluß de Stereoanlage und zum Einlegen der Batterien in die Fernbedienung verfahren Sie wie in der Abbildung gezeigt.

Utilice la ilustración siguiente para conectar su sistema estéreo e insertar las pilas en el telemando.

! Do this connection last!
Effectuer cette connexion en dernier lieu !
Das Netzkabel als letztes anschließen !
¡ Realice esta conexió en último lugar !

18

18

▲ Figure 5.34 *A revision of the instructions for connecting the stereo shown in Figure 5.32. Notice it has more effective 3-D cues. Document design by Carlos Peterson, Norma Pribadi Polk, Dan Boyarski, Mary L. Ray, and Michele Matchett for Karen Schriver Associates, Inc., Pittsburgh, PA.*

GESTALT PRINCIPLES ARE TOOLS RATHER THAN RULES FOR DOCUMENT DESIGN

The Gestalt principles are valuable tools that document designers can use to help them accomplish their rhetorical goals. However, the Gestalt principles are not intrinsically rhetorical, and they were not intended to tell designers what their goals ought to be. The Gestalt psychologists were not advocating that designers make every figure as strong as possible. Nor were they saying that symmetrical designs are better than asymmetrical ones. Rather, the Gestalt psychologists were describing the effects that closure, symmetry, asymmetry, proximity, similarity, continuity, grouping, hierarchy, and balance would have on the appearance of figures. Their principles are descriptive, not prescriptive.

This is an important point because some articles that apply Gestalt principles to document design—though helpful in raising awareness about the applications of Gestalt ideas—have introduced confusions. And sometimes these articles tend to restate the author's misunderstandings prescriptively. For example, some authors have cautioned document designers to avoid asymmetrical layouts, claiming that symmetrical organizations are intrinsically better. This is nonsense. It is simply not true that "an asymmetrical page or graphic appears esthetically unpleasing and it may appear to give the reader the impression that something is missing or wrong" (Moore & Fitz, 1993a, p. 143). It is also imprecise to say that "asymmetrical elements on a page seem unstable, and they distract readers from the content of the message…" (Moore & Fitz, 1993b, p. 391). As the history of typography (discussed in Chapter 2) shows very clearly, most of twentieth-century graphic design has worked toward perfecting the art of asymmetry as a means of articulating complex rhetorical relationships.

It is important to distinguish the concepts of *symmetry* and *balance*. They are not the same! In *Designing Visual User Interfaces,* Mullet and Sano (1995) describe how balance can be realized with either symmetrical or asymmetrical designs.

> The quality of *balance* ensures that the display remains stable in its position on the page or screen. Balance can be achieved by using either symmetric or asymmetric layout.… Classic display typography, which evolved over centuries from conventions originating in monumental inscriptions and other forms of public proclamations, is simple, centered, and perfectly symmetrical. In the 20th Century, typographic designers discovered the greater vitality and inherent visual interest provide by active, asymmetric layouts.…

> Balance in display design [e.g., paper documents, online documents, or computer interfaces] is analogous to balance in everyday physics. A composition is balanced when the visual weight of design elements on either side of the composition is approximately equal. The visual weight of the composition is distributed across the center of balance (the "fulcrum" in the physical analogy) like the weights on a scale. When the visual weight and distance from the center of elements on each side of the axis are physically equal, the impression of balance is guaranteed. Symmetrical layouts provide this visual equilibrium automatically. Asymmetrical layouts can achieve equilibrium as well, but their tenser, more dramatic form of balance depends on careful manipulation to compensate visually for differences in the size, position, and value of major elements. As with a physical balance, lighter elements can balance heavier elements if their size or value (visual weight) is increased or if they are moved farther from (or the heavier element is moved closer to) the center of balance.… The axis of symmetry can be vertical or diagonal, so long as elements are balanced properly about it. (pp. 102–103)

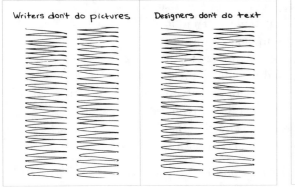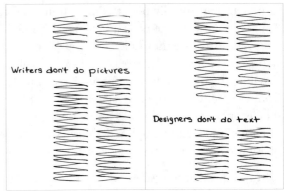

▲ **Figure 5.35** *A comparison of a two-column text designed using symmetry and asymmetry. Notice that the symmetrical layout appears more formal, the asymmetric more relaxed. In the asymmetrical layout the headings stand out.*

[73] See Mullet and Sano (1995) for many interesting examples of interface designs which employ Gestalt principles.

[74] For example, Gestalt principles don't address readers' emotional or affective responses to texts, as I discussed in Chapters 3 and 4.

As Gribbons (1992) points out, any principle of organization, symmetrical or asymmetrical, must complement the linguistic and rhetorical aims of the text (p. 64). Symmetry is an extremely useful organizational device for many documents, both paper and online.[73] However, when overused, it can make documents look dull and uninteresting. Often, asymmetry can have a very welcome enlivening effect. Figure 5.35 contrasts a simple two-column text using symmetry and asymmetry.

Gestalt principles are important for document deign because they can help us guide the reader's focus of attention, emphasize certain groupings, and organize sequences of the content. In effect, they can be employed rhetorically. Moreover, the Gestalt principles, although not telling the whole story,[74] do help us in profitable ways to organize the visual field in ways that support our rhetorical goals and intentions.

SECTION 4
CREATING EFFECTIVE SPATIAL CUES FOR READERS: THE RHETORIC OF THE VISUAL FIELD

As we have seen, document designers can use typographic cues and Gestalt principles to design more effective texts. In this section, I discuss how the spatial organization of the text can be used to increase its rhetorical impact. As the Gestalt psychologists pointed out, there are various strong figures—such as circles, triangles, squares, and rectangles—that can be used to organize the visual field. For example, many ads and works of art use the triangle as a principle of organization (Gombrich, 1961). In some special cases—such as the Mayan calendar, star charts, and diagrams of polar coordinates—the circle serves as the principle of organization.

However, for most print and online documents, the most common form of organization is the rectangle—appearing either as rectangular columns, rectangular rows, or both. In this section, I discuss how document designers can make use of the dynamic interaction of vertical and horizontal space. I first explore some ideas about spatial cues in documents from the graphic design and typography community.[75] Then I examine why document designers need to be rhetoricians in their approach to the design of space. A few definitions about what I mean by vertical and horizontal spacing set the stage.

[75] In particular, I draw on the writings and designs of Lönberg-Holm and Sutnar (1944), Müller-Brockmann (1985), Rüegg (1989), Tschichold (1928/1987, 1967), Ruder (1982), and Sutnar (1961).

Vertical Space and Horizontal Space as Interactive Cues

Vertical space refers to (1) the up-and-down perpendicular distance between the elements on a page or screen, and (2) the top-to-bottom size of visual or verbal elements. As explained earlier in this chapter, vertical space is usually called leading (sometimes linespacing); it is the distance from baseline-to-baseline among lines of text. However, vertical space is not only the space between consecutive lines of text, but also the space between paragraphs, the space between the bottom edge of a picture and its caption, the space between subheadings and text regions. In traditional book design (see Wilson, 1993) the generous vertical space below a chapter title is called *sinkage,* that is, the amount of vertical space the text "sinks" before the first line of the text begins. In its second sense, vertical space refers to the physical depth of a text block (measured in points and picas or sometimes by the number of consecutive lines the space permits; e.g., this book has a 40-line vertical space for the body text, give or take a few lines). Vertical space can also point to the depth of a picture or a table (in common parlance, we sometimes call vertical space "depth" while at other times "length").

Gestalt principles suggest that any vertical space in a visual field will interact with other vertical spaces in that field. To illustrate this point in the context of a document, look at Figure 5.36 (on the next page), two versions of the first page of a proposal. Both versions employ the same point size (10-point Frutiger Light), line length (about 26 picas), and horizontal space. Both versions also employ the same between-paragraph leading (22 point). Yet the paragraph breaks are more striking in Example 1 than in Example 2 because the within-paragraph vertical space is tighter in Example 1 (11 point) than in Example 2 (15 point).

As we can see, changing the vertical space can have a dramatic effect on the visual appearance of text. This simple case shows us that the vertical space employed in any part of a document will interact with other vertical spaces in the reader's visual field. It is important for document designers to consider the visual contrasts they can create by using vertical space. These contrasts can give powerful clues to the reader about the hierarchy of the document. For example, vertical space can be employed to (1) signal parallel text elements, (2) set off one text element from another, or (3) show internal relationships among text elements. Document designers need to find ways to employ vertical space to emphasize their rhetorical goals.

Horizontal space describes the left-to-right measurement of (1) the visual or verbal elements, and (2) the space between the elements on a page or screen. In the first sense, horizontal space refers to what is commonly called the "width" of the type or graphic. As I said earlier, the distance between the left and right margin of a line of type is called *line length or measure* and is usually expressed in points and picas. The second sense of horizontal spacing refers to areas of blank space (measured from left-to-right) between elements of the document. The distance between characters in a word is called *character spacing;* between words, *word spacing;* between two columns of type, an *alley;* between two pages, the *gutter.* Horizontal space, then, is used to characterize the width of objects as well as the distance between them (e.g., indenting is horizontal spacing, as is the distance between a bullet and the text that goes with it).

▼ **Figure 5.36** *How vertical spatial cues may interact within the visual field. Notice the vertical space between paragraphs for this proposal is the same in Examples 1 and 2, but it looks more generous in Example 1 because of the tighter leading within paragraphs.*

The Problem

As of January 1996, there were more than 44,000 individuals on the United National Organ Sharing (UNOS) national patient waiting list. Each year more than 18,000 patients receive organ transplants at the 277 transplant centers–around the country. Patients–pre-transplant and post-transplant–and the families who support them have very special needs. They require education that promotes both the physical and mental health of the patient. It is essential that the patient and family recognize how important it is that the patient comply with prescribed schedules of medication and diet. Non-compliance poses a very serious health problem for patients. It has been estimated that up to 40% of transplant patients are seriously non-compliant with their medical recommendations. At least some of this non-compliance can be attributed to lack of understanding patients and their families may have about the consequences of non-compliance.

To understand issues of compliance and the nature of the patient's medical problem, patient and family must understand, at least at a practical level, the function of the diseased organ, the nature of the pathology, the purposes of diet and drug therapy, and relevant medical vocabulary. In addition, it is useful for patient and family to know the roles of the various people on their transplant team, to be aware of financial options that may be available to them, and to understand how patients are ordered on the UNOS patient waiting list. Further, since the transplant experience may subject patients to unusually high levels of stress, training in stress reduction methods can increase patient comfort and facilitate both treatment and learning.

The purpose of this proposed project is to develop the Organ Transplant Education System, a comprehensive, computer-based, multi-media, training package for transplant patients and their families.

The Problem

As of January 1996, there were more than 44,000 individuals on the United National Organ Sharing (UNOS) national patient waiting list. Each year more than 18,000 patients receive organ transplants at the 277 transplant centers–around the country. Patients–pre-transplant and post-transplant–and the families who support them have very special needs. They require education that promotes both the physical and mental health of the patient. It is essential that the patient and family recognize how important it is that the patient comply with prescribed schedules of medication and diet. Non-compliance poses a very serious health problem for patients. It has been estimated that up to 40% of transplant patients are seriously non-compliant with their medical recommendations. At least some of this non-compliance can be attributed to lack of understanding patients and their families may have about the consequences of non-compliance.

To understand issues of compliance and the nature of the patient's medical problem, patient and family must understand, at least at a practical level, the function of the diseased organ, the nature of the pathology, the purposes of diet and drug therapy, and relevant medical vocabulary. In addition, it is useful for patient and family to know the roles of the various people on their transplant team, to be aware of financial options that may be available to them, and to understand how patients are ordered on the UNOS patient waiting list. Further, since the transplant experience may subject patients to unusually high levels of stress, training in stress reduction methods can increase patient comfort and facilitate both treatment and learning.

The purpose of this proposed project is to develop the Organ Transplant Education System, a comprehensive, computer-based, multi-media, training package for transplant patients and their families.

Example 1: The vertical space (leading) within paragraphs is 11 point and the leading between paragraphs is 22 point.

Example 2: The leading within paragraphs is 15 point and between paragraphs is 22 point.

Like vertical space, horizontal space interacts with other horizontal space. In Figure 5.37, I present two versions of a page from a computer hardware manual. Note that Examples 1 and 2 differ in their use of horizontal space. Both of these versions employ the same point size (10-point Times Roman body text with 12-point Univers 67 Condensed headings), line length (about 25 picas), and vertical space (12 point). The only difference is the shift in Example 2's horizontal space that makes the "warning" and "important" stand out from the rest of the text (these text elements are outdented about 3 picas). When document designers use horizontal space to signal the structure of the content, it is important to provide the reader with a clear cue. Readers should not mistake a shift for an error in alignment. The contrast in horizontal space needs to be seen as intentional. Dramatic horizontal cues are often more effective than subtle ones.

▼ **Figure 5.37** *How the horizontal spatial cues may interact within the visual field. Notice the horizontal space in Example 1 presents all text elements similarly, while Example 2 outdents the "importants" and "warnings," making them stand out from other text elements.*

As these two examples (Figures 5.36 and 5.37) show us, vertical and horizontal spatial cues can interact to give the reader an impression of the structure of the document. But that impression is not created by first analyzing the vertical elements and then the horizontal ones or vice versa. Rather, as the Gestalt psychologists remind us, we perceive the visual field

DRAM, VRAM, and cache configurations

You can have memory–dynamic random-access memory (DRAM) or video random-access memory (VRAM)–added to your computer in packages called Dual Inline Memory Modules, or DIMMs. You can also upgrade your computer's cache by installing a DIMM.

WARNING To avoid damage to your computer, Computers, Inc. reccomends that only a certified technician install additional DIMMs. Consult the service and support information that came with your computer for instructions on how to contact an authorized service provider or Computers for service. If you attempt to install additional DIMMs yourself, any damage you may cause to your equipment will not be covered by the limited warranty on your computer. See an authorized dealer or service provider for additional information about this or any other warranty question

DRAM configurations

Your computer can use any DRAM configuration with DIMMs of these sizes: 8, 16, 32, or 64 MB. The exact configuration depends on the density of the DRAM chips that are mounted on the DIMMs. (The DIMMs support both 2K and 4K refresh rates.)

You can increase your computer's DRAM to up to 512 MB. The main logic board has eight slots where DIMMs can be installed. To increase DRAM to the maximum of 512 MB, have an authorized dealer or service provider fill all eight slots with 64 MB DIMMs. You can also fill slots with 8, 16, or 32 MB DIMMs.

Note: 128 MB DIMMs are available and can fit in the computer's memory slots to increase DRAM to as much as 1 gigabyte (GB). These DIMMs have not been tested for use with some computers, however.

IMPORTANT The DIMMs should be 64-bit-wide, 168-pin fast-paged mode, with 70-nanosecond (ns) RAM access time or faster. The Single Inline Memory Modules (SIMMs) from older computers are not compatible with your computer and should not be used.

Example 1: One horizontal position is used, with the same left margin for all text elements.

DRAM, VRAM, and cache configurations

You can have memory–dynamic random-access memory (DRAM) or video random-access memory (VRAM)–added to your computer in packages called Dual Inline Memory Modules, or DIMMs. You can also upgrade your computer's cache by installing a DIMM.

WARNING To avoid damage to your computer, Computers, Inc. reccomends that only a certified technician install additional DIMMs. Consult the service and support information that came with your computer for instructions on how to contact an authorized service provider or Computers for service. If you attempt to install additional DIMMs yourself, any damage you may cause to your equipment will not be covered by the limited warranty on your computer. See an authorized dealer or service provider for additional information about this or any other warranty question

DRAM configurations

Your computer can use any DRAM configuration with DIMMs of these sizes: 8, 16, 32, or 64 MB. The exact configuration depends on the density of the DRAM chips that are mounted on the DIMMs. (The DIMMs support both 2K and 4K refresh rates.)

You can increase your computer's DRAM to up to 512 MB. The main logic board has eight slots where DIMMs can be installed. To increase DRAM to the maximum of 512 MB, have an authorized dealer or service provider fill all eight slots with 64 MB DIMMs. You can also fill slots with 8, 16, or 32 MB DIMMs.

Note: 128 MB DIMMs are available and can fit in the computer's memory slots to increase DRAM to as much as 1 gigabyte (GB). These DIMMs have not been tested for use with some computers, however.

IMPORTANT The DIMMs should be 64-bit-wide, 168-pin fast-paged mode, with 70-nanosecond (ns) RAM access time or faster. The Single Inline Memory Modules (SIMMs) from older computers are not compatible with your computer and should not be used.

Example 2: Two horizontal positions are employed, one for "importants" and "warnings," another for other text elements.

as a perceptual whole (Wertheimer, 1923). When we first glance at a page or screen, we respond to its vertical and horizontal space in dynamic interaction. *An important goal for document designers is to consider the interplay of the horizontal and vertical dimensions of the page or screen to help readers infer the intended structure of the text. We can think of this as the design of the architecture of the page or screen.* The idea is to make deliberate use of vertical and horizontal space so that together, they define and articulate one another.

Although it is clear that the spatial features of a document must be designed, the popular literature in document design (and desktop publishing) talks about space in rather trivial and arhetorical ways. It is commonly held, for example, that white space and itemized lists (or bulleted lists) are things one "adds" to documents to make them friendly. This idea is wrong in two ways.

<aside>[76] Blank space is a better term than white space because it does not suggest that the background is always white. As I discussed earlier, blank space can be used as either figure or ground.</aside>

1. Blank space[76] is not something document designers add—it is something they orchestrate.

2. Although well-designed blank space can be a powerful rhetorical tool in document design, there is no necessary relationship between blank space and effective document design. Common lore suggests that if we just add blank space to page or screen designs, readers will automatically get the benefit of a more effective document. This assumption, however, needs to be reconsidered.

To see why adding blank space need not be effective, look at Figure 5.38. Here I present a form designed by an inexperienced document designer. The purpose of the form is to record data about employees of a university in order to assess their eligibility for benefits. The intended users of the form are administrative assistants to departments; the administrator records the employee's data, has the employee check it and sign it, and then submits it to the central benefits office. At the benefits office, a data-entry clerk takes the form and enters the information into a database.

The creator of the form thought that adding blank space would make the form friendly and dutifully added about an inch of horizontal space between each item in the bottom half of the form (see items 8 through 18). But notice that the overall use of horizontal space is choppy and uneven. Practically every blank space has a different width, making for a chaotic appearance. The appearance of the form suggests that someone simply "tabbed over" to the next fixed position using a typewriter (this text was created on a computer; it just looks typed). Vertical space was created by inserting line spaces between the items (just hit the carriage return twice). From the inexperienced document designer's point of view, once the blank space had been added and the spell checker had been run, the document was finished. But as we can see, the visual organization fails to establish or reinforce relationships among the content, making for a haphazard layout. It is hard to tell the intended relations either within sections of the form or across them. This organization destroys any sense of "good continuation" as there are no clean vertical margins that invite the eye to scan the content by looking down a column.

Notice that the horizontal position of subheadings shifts from line to line. In addition, the horizontal location of items to fill in and check off varies uncomfortably. The poor continuation and nonrhetorical grouping of the content items may lead the form-filler to skip some items. These same perceptual problems will make it hard for data-entry clerks to rapidly input the information into a database, increasing the likelihood of errors since they must slowly scan each line, hopping from item to item. Poor design can lead not only to more errors in filling in the form but also to increased errors in retrieving information from the form. Thus, poor design slows down "both ends" of the process. Clearly, poor design has economic penalties, requiring extra time for administrative assistants and data-entry clerks.

Figure 5.39 is a revision of the Employment Data form by an experienced graphic designer, Laurette C. Boyer. There are several things to notice. One of the most important is the reorganization of the informa-

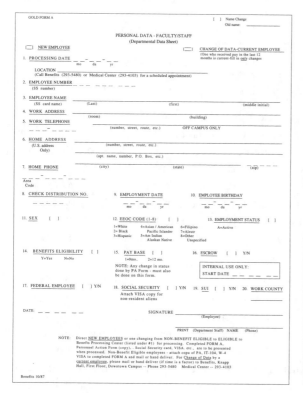

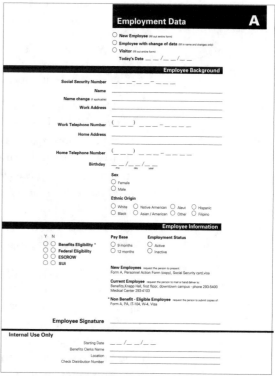

▲ **Figure 5.38** *A form designed by an inexperienced document designer.*

▲ **Figure 5.39** *A revision of the form by an experienced graphic designer, Laurette C. Boyer.*

tion into functional categories (e.g., employee background, employee information, and information for internal use). These categories are clustered visually and separated by vertical space. This strategy is coupled with the use of horizontal rules, the thickest ones for the two main sections, accented with reversed-out headings.

The revision employs vertical and horizontal space in an asymmetrical layout to meet the rhetorical goal of helping users see the main sections of the document. Notice the design is improved considerably by logically grouping the elements. It also establishes stronger ties among related items through the use of a consistent line width. The revision aligns the sub-headings under "Employee Background" and "Employee Information" against the right-hand margin of the first column, making them stand out. This alignment creates a strong vertical axis to the form, providing for good continuation. The consistent use of horizontal space forms an alley between the two main columns, giving a clear cue about where to fill in information and where to retrieve it. The deliberate use of blank space—both vertical and horizontal—helps the reader to see the structure and scan its parts. As White (1982) puts it:

> Blank space is emphatically NOT the random nothing-area that is left over after the 'important' stuff has been imposed on the page. Rather, it is an active participant in the design of the page ... it organizes groups of ele-ments.... It is not how many square inches of blank space there are, what matters is the shape of the blank space and where it appears [capitalization in original]. (pp. 59–60)

This example reminds us that when blank space is added without regard to how horizontal and vertical spatial cues work together, the effect may be a more spacious document, but the overall result is nonetheless rhetorically inept because the space doesn't articulate the document's structure. *It is not enough just to add blank space; it must be orchestrated to signal structural relationships.* As the Gestalt psychologists suggested, spatial cues are crucial in both organizing perception and influencing the reader's interpretation of the visual field. It is up to document designers as practic-ing rhetoricians to make deliberate use of these cues.

Although many organizations have been slow to wake up and realize that bad document design is costing them money, some organizations have provided evidence that quality in document design pays. For example, in 1991 the Motorola Corporate Finance department found that after they made changes to speed the "closing of their books" by revising, among other things, the directions on their forms and the format for entering data on computer screens, they were able to save $20,000,000 a year (Therrien, 1991, p. 60). Similarly, in Holland, a division of the Dutch Department of Education and Science reported that a form for applying for educational grants created so many difficulties for form-fillers that each year an average of 60,000 forms had to be returned to respondents because of incorrect or missing answers. A revision led to such a decrease in errors that only 15,000 to 20,000 forms continued to be reprocessed per year, saving enormous clerical costs, postage, and handling (Jansen & Steehouder, 1992, p. 166). For other examples, see Schriver (1993a).

Employing Spatial Cues Rhetorically: A Fish Story about the Design of Tables

As we've seen so far, the interaction of horizontal and vertical cues can shape how readers see the structure of a document. But as important as it is, it doesn't tell the whole story. Spatial cues not only give structure to the content but also invite the reader to consider the content in a particular way. Spatial cues may be employed to encourage readers to see the text in ways that allow them to use the content for their personal purposes. In fact, research in the design of quantitative graphics shows that effective spatial cues can both structure an argument visually and help readers make reasonable judgments about the data (MacDonald-Ross, 1977a, 1977b; Waller, 1980; Wright, 1982). Let's look at an example of how spatial cues can be employed rhetorically in the design of a table.

Table 5.3 is an original version of a table intended to provide customers at the fish counter of a grocery store with information about the nutritional value of various types of fish. Despite its neat appearance, the grid does not add to the information display. Instead, its excessively heavy rule lines overwhelm the data. Tufte (1983) would call its design an "information prison." But more importantly, even if we removed the rules lines, the display is not organized to make it informative. It is simply an unordered list. This is worse than boxing in the numbers. This means the reader must do all the work in guessing the structure of the data. There is no attempt to organize the information to answer questions that readers might bring to this topic. Document designers need to keep in mind that data do not speak for themselves; they must be interpreted both by the document designer and by the reader. Document designers must give structure to quantitative displays so that readers can construct appropriate inferences about the data. A well-designed quantitative graphic both creates a context for interpreting the data and provides a visual argument. The document designer's job is to put the argument into focus by helping the reader see the relationship between the "big picture" and the details.

Wright (1982) points out that whenever people use tables, they nearly always have to do at least three things: (1) grasp the logical principles on which the information has been organized; (2) find the required information within the table; and (3) interpret the information once it has been found.

Readers of the original version of the Fish Market (Table 5.3) found it difficult to discern a logical principle which organized the data. Indeed, its design makes finding information difficult because the numbers within cells do not align—bad continuation. The type is set in all capitals and each cell entry is centered, making it hard to scan. There is also unnecessary redundancy. For example, since the cells in the first column contain identical values, the information should be presented just once. There is a similar problem with the repeated abbreviations MG and GR. The poor design makes it difficult to search for information and make comparisons among the cells. Moreover, the structure of the data do not show that the document designer has anticipated how readers will make use of the information.

Ehrenberg (1977) suggests arranging numbers in tables in some meaningful order (e.g., greatest to smallest). The next two examples show that reordering the numbers can improve the rhetorical effectiveness of this information. Tables 5.4 and 5.5 are successive revisions of Table 5.3. In the first revision, document designer Ann Steffy Cronin removed the ugly grid. But more importantly, the information was regrouped in ways that may have significance for the reader; shellfish were separated from other types of fish.

FISH MARKET

NUTRITIONAL INFORMATION

FEDERALLY LOT INSPECTED — ALL OF OUR FRESH SEAFOOD IS FEDERALLY LOT INSPECTED BY THE US DEPARTMENT OF COMMERCE FOR ONLY THE BEST QUALITY AND FRESHNESS

SEAFOOD	SERVING SIZE	CALORIES	FAT GRAMS	CHOLESTEROL MILLIGRAMS	SODIUM MILLIGRAMS	PROTEIN GRAMS	IRON MILLIGRAMS
ROCK FISH	3 oz.	100	1.7 GR	36 MG	64 MG	20 GR	.4 MG
SHRIMP	3 oz.	113	1.8 GR	163 MG	157 MG	22 GR	2.6 MG
COD	3 oz.	87	.7 GR	39 MG	76 MG	19 GR	.3 MG
CATFISH	3 oz.	116	4 GR	50 MG	60 MG	14 GR	.15 MG
CLAMS	3 oz.	126	1.7 GR	57 MG	95 MG	22 GR	24. MG
FLOUNDER	3 oz.	77	1 GR	45 MG	74 MG	14 GR	.08 MG
ATLANTIC SALMON	3 oz.	151	6.7 GR	61 MG	46MG	21 GR	.9 MG
SCALLOPS	3 oz.	150	1.3 GR	56 MG	274 MG	29 GR	.5 MG
CRABMEAT	3 oz.	78	1 GR	90 MG	337 MG	14 GR	.02MG
HADDOCK	3 oz.	87	1 GR	60 MG	88 MG	14.9 GR	.06 MG
HALIBUT	3 oz.	116	2.4 GR	34MG	58 MG	22 GR	1.0 MG
MACKEREL	3oz.	218	15 GR	75 MG	95 MG	20 GR	1.7 MG
ORANGE ROUGHY	3oz.	134	7.4 GR	23 MG	71 MG	16 GR	.2 MG
PERCH - OCEAN	3 oz.	100	1.7 GR	45 MG	80 MG	20 GR	1.MG
RAINBOW TROUT	3 oz.	125	3.6 GR	60 MG	29 MG	22 GR	2.0 MG
SOLE	3 oz.	100	1.3 GR	58 MG	89 MG	21 GR	.3 MG
LOBSTER	3 oz.	96	.9 GR	101 MG	323 MG	20 GR	.3 MG
OYSTERS	3 oz.	117	4.2 GR	93 MG	190 MG	12 GR	11. MG

▲ Table 5.3 *A poorly designed table before revision.*

The internal organization within each category of fish—moving from the most caloric and to the least caloric—was designed to help readers make comparisons. The new structure grew out of interview data about what consumers wanted to know about eating fish. Subsequent usability testing revealed that consumers were surprised to find salmon high in calories and fat in relation to other fish. As one participant put it, "I am shocked that salmon is not one of the healthiest choices." Thus, unlike the original, the new design allows readers to draw inferences about the data. Other changes include properly aligning the numbers in their columns and placing labels that are common to each entry in a column in headings (e.g., grams). The text now uses uppercase and lowercase type. The new design makes it easier to scan the information and compare fish.

The second revision employs a visual design similar to the first but reorganizes the content to allow readers to focus on the fat content of different fish. Usability testing of the initial revision indicated that consumers cared more about fat than calories. To meet this concern, Steffy Cronin recalculated the cell entries to determine the calories from fat for each fish. She also determined the proportion of fat in relation to the

FISH MARKET
Health Conscious Guide to Popular Seafood
(based on a 3 oz. serving size)

Fish	Calories	Fat (in grams)	Cholesterol (in milligrams)	Sodium (in milligrams)	Protein (in grams)	Iron (in milligrams)
Mackerel	218	15.0	75	95	20	1.7
Atlantic Salmon	151	6.7	61	46	21	.9
Orange Roughy	134	7.4	23	71	16	.2
Rainbow Trout	125	3.6	60	29	22	2.0
Catfish	116	4.0	50	60	14	.2
Halibut	116	2.4	34	58	22	1.0
Perch - Ocean	100	1.7	45	80	20	1.0
Rock Fish	100	1.7	36	64	20	.4
Sole	100	1.3	58	89	21	.3
Haddock	87	1.0	60	88	15	.1
Cod	87	.7	39	76	19	.3
Flounder	77	1.0	45	74	14	.1
Shellfish						
Scallops	150	1.3	56	274	29	.5
Clams	126	1.7	57	95	22	24.0
Oysters	117	4.2	93	190	12	11.0
Shrimp	113	1.8	163	157	22	2.6
Lobster	96	.9	101	323	20	.3
Crabmeat	78	1.0	90	337	14	.0

All of our fresh seafood is federally lot inspected by the U.S. Department of Commerce for only the best quality and freshness.

FISH MARKET
Health Conscious Guide to Popular Seafood
(based on a 3 oz. serving size)

Fish	Fat (in grams)	(% Daily Value)	Calories (total)	(from fat)	Cholesterol (in milligrams)	(% Daily Value)	Sodium (in milligrams)	(% Daily Value)	Protein (in grams)	(% Daily Value)	Iron (in milligrams)	(% Daily Value)
Mackerel	15.0	23	218	135	75	25	95	4	20	40	1.7	9
Orange Roughy	7.4	11	134	67	71	8	71	3	16	32	.2	1
Atlantic Salmon	6.7	10	151	60	46	20	46	2	21	42	.9	5
Catfish	4.0	6	116	36	50	17	60	3	14	28	.2	1
Rainbow Trout	3.6	6	125	33	29	20	29	1	22	44	2.0	11
Halibut	2.4	4	116	22	45	11	58	2	22	44	1.0	5
Perch - Ocean	1.7	3	100	15	34	15	80	3	20	40	1.0	5
Rock Fish	1.7	3	100	15	36	12	64	3	20	40	.4	2
Sole	1.3	2	100	12	58	19	89	4	21	42	.3	2
Haddock	1.0	2	87	9	60	20	88	4	15	30	.1	1
Flounder	1.0	2	77	9	45	15	74	3	14	28	.1	1
Cod	0.7	1	87	6	39	13	76	3	19	38	.3	2
Shellfish												
Oysters	4.2	6	117	38	93	31	190	8	12	24	11.0	61
Shrimp	1.8	3	113	16	163	54	157	7	22	44	24.0	133
Clams	1.7	3	126	15	57	19	95	4	22	44	2.6	14
Scallops	1.3	2	150	12	56	19	274	11	29	58	.5	3
Crabmeat	1.0	2	78	9	90	30	337	14	14	28	0	0
Lobster	.9	1	96	8	101	34	323	13	20	40	.3	2

All of our fresh seafood is federally lot inspected by the U.S. Department of Commerce for only the best quality and freshness.

[a] The % Daily Values for the nutrients listed are based on a 2,000-calorie diet. The % Daily Values adhere to the United States Food and Drug Administration's Recommended Daily Allowances (RDA). RDAs and % Daily Values show the minimum nutritional requirements needed by most people to maintain good health.

▲ Table 5.4 The "Fish Market" table after an initial revision by Ann Steffy Cronin.

▲ Table 5.5 The "Fish Market" table after a second revision by Ann Steffy Cronin.

Daily Value (the dietary standard developed by the U.S. Food and Drug Administration). In addition, she provided more information about cholesterol, sodium, protein, and iron in relation to the Daily Value. This allows readers to see, for example, that although shrimp is high in cholesterol, it is a rich source of iron. This final design not only makes it easier to search the content and compare fish, but also helps readers to make judgments about the content within a familiar framework.

Complexity without Chaos in the Design of Tables: The Evolution of the *Morningstar Report*

In their attempts to improve documents during revision, document designers sometimes conceive of their task as one of adding spatial cues (e.g., shading, rule lines, blank space, and so on). However, sometimes removing such cues can be the most effective way to improve a design. To illustrate the development of a document design team's ideas about spatial cues and how "less can be more," I present the evolution of the *Morningstar Report,* a widely respected financial page on the stock market. Figure 5.40 provides three successive iterations of a portion of a page about stocks. The design team was constrained by the need to present a great deal of financial information on a single page. As we can see in the first iteration, the complex information was made even more complicated by the heavy-handed use of rules, boxes, and uppercase.

Notice that the second revision removes most of the vertical rules and many of the horizontal rules. This simple strategy makes the columns and rows come into focus, inviting the eye to scan the data. It helps to put the numbers in the "figure" position rather than the rule lines, inviting readers to focus on the relationships among the data. By the third iteration, even the shaded bars used for the headings have lost their unnecessary borders. These deletions improve the design and at the same time reinforce the intended rhetorical relationships among the data clusters. This example shows that even in situations in which document designers must fit as much data as they can on a page, there is often much that can be done to make even dense information displays accessible. Clearly these designers had their work cut out for them and did a great job.

The Modular Grid as a Way to Organize Space in Documents

The examples just presented show how spatial cues can be employed to articulate the rhetoric of the visual field. Not surprisingly, graphic designers and typographers have talked more about how to employ spatial cues than have writers. Important ideas were developed by the Bauhaus

Version 1:
September 30, 1990

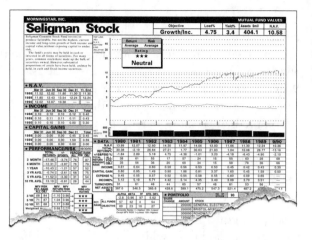

▶ **Figure 5.40** *Three iterations of a financial report on Seligman Common Stock from Morningstar. Courtesy of Morningstar, Inc., Chicago, IL.*

Version 2:
August 31, 1992

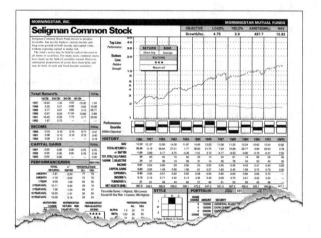

Version 3:
June 30, 1993

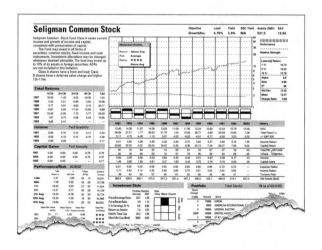

masters as well as by the typographers and graphic designers who were influenced by them. Interestingly, the proponents of the Bauhaus and their protégés in the New Typography and the International Typographic Style were operating at roughly the same time as the Gestalt psychologists.[77] While the Gestalt psychologists were developing principles of human perception and to a lesser extent a theory of aesthetics (see Arnheim, 1969), the Bauhaus designers were developing principles to organize designs in ways that emphasized form and structure. An important idea for document design from the Bauhaus is the modular grid, a way to signal the architecture of a document through the design of its horizontal and vertical space.

The idea of a grid is quite simple. It organizes the space by dividing it into columns and rows which specify where visual or verbal elements can be placed. A key feature of a grid is its modularity. As columns and rows intersect, they form a series of standardized spatial units called *grid fields* (also called *modules* or *modular units*). These grid fields divide a two-dimensional plane or a three-dimensional space into rectangular or square compartments that have a precise horizontal and vertical dimension (Müller-Brockmann, 1985). Standardizing the modules provides a consistent depth and width for the body text and pictures (what is called the *type and picture area*). The grid also separates text elements with vertical and horizontal space between columns and rows. In this way, text and pictures can be placed so that they do not touch other text, pictures, or captions.

Let's take a look at the grid for this book as an example. Figure 5.41 shows the shape of the pages for a typical spread. The design, a four-column grid, provides eight columns for the type and picture area across a spread. The four-column grid is a flexible one for book design, since it allows the text and graphics to be positioned in columns two through seven, leaving columns one and eight free for marginal information. It also makes it easy to size illustrations as small as a single grid unit or as large as two pages.

---

[77] The Gestalt psychologists were most active from 1912–1950. The Bauhaus designers and their protégés in the New Typography and the International Typographic Style (often called Swiss Design) were prominent from about 1917 to 1960. Sadly, key figures in both Gestalt psychology and Bauhaus design were compelled to leave their native Germany in the 1930s to emigrate to the United States. As I mentioned in Chapter 2 in my discussion of the "Rhetorical Tradition" in graphic design, the Nazis perceived the work of the Bauhaus school as a threat and closed it in 1933. Consequently, the U.S. design scene was immensely enriched by the influx of designers fleeing from Europe (see *The Timeline* in Chapter 2, the strand "Education & Practice in Graphic Design," especially between 1919 and 1950, pp. 110–122).

◄ Figure 5.41 *A sample two-page spread from the grid design of this book.*

In designing a grid, document designers strive for an aesthetically interesting layout that also reveals the rhetorical relationships among the parts of the document. Grids can assist document designers in organizing the visual field by making the structure and hierarchy apparent to the reader.[78] The horizontal and vertical position of visual and verbal elements—along with their contrast, juxtaposition, sequence, continuation, and grouping—can suggest to readers how to scan and make sense of the content. A well-designed grid provides a sense of nested (that is, part-within-part) relationships.[79] Modular grids play a role in punctuating the visual field, in helping readers parse the "big picture"—the syntax of macrolevel relationships. Waller (1980) refers to the graphic aspects of complex documents as a kind of macropunctuation. And like the punctuation of prose, signalling the structure of the text with a grid can be used either effectively or ineffectively. In other words, *using a grid won't hide problems in thinking, writing, visualizing, or organization. Document designers must consider the architecture of the content while they develop the architecture of the page or screen.*

Using Grids to Unify the Visual Field

The most important goal in employing a grid is to unify the visual field, whether it be the single plane of a bus schedule, the two-page spread of a printed book, or a series of computer screens for a World Wide Web site. Some have suggested that document designers "see the page as a grid" (Kramer & Bernhardt, 1996, p. 39). Such ideas can be made more precise. Document designers need to see the page (or sets of pages or screens) as a visual field. The goal is to organize that field by using visual and verbal cues that prompt readers to see the content as related in harmonious ways.

[78] The visual field can be two-dimensional, as in a brochure, or three-dimensional, as in architectural planning documents. We can also think of 3-D grid designs for museum exhibits that may use the space of the built environment (e.g., walls, columns, lighted cases, or items suspended from the ceiling) as an active part of the visual field. I limit my discussion to two-dimensional documents.

[79] For exemplary examples of grids in action, see the designs of Bayer (1953), Lönberg-Holm and Sutnar (1944, 1950), Müller-Brockmann (1985), Ruder (1982), or Sutnar (1961). For suggestions about grids for desktop design, see Shushan et al. (1996) or White (1987); for advice about grids for computer interfaces, see Mullet and Sano (1995).

Here a grid can be helpful, but a grid is not required to create visual unity. As we've seen, artists, designers, and psychologists have shown that strong shapes can be used to organize the visual field (e.g., triangles, circles, squares, and rectangles) and can be employed with or without a grid. In this section, I show how grids can be used to unify the rectangular shapes so typical of documents.

Some of the most engaging ideas about structuring the visual field come from Czechoslovakian designer Ladislav Sutnar (Lönberg-Holm & Sutnar, 1944, 1950), a pioneer of grid design. During the 1940s and 1950s, Sutnar urged designers to make their information designs more functional and visually interesting. He argued that the "basic design unit" should be the *two-page spread* rather than the single page, a strategy called *designing in spreads*. Sutnar and his fellow designers, Herbert Bayer and Will Burtin,[80] contended that designing in spreads creates optical unity (for any text joined in the middle by a binding). Design historian Philip Meggs (1992b) characterizes Sutnar's philosophy as a synthesis of *function*, *flow*, and *form*.

[80] Ladislav Sutnar, Herbert Bayer, and Will Burtin were among the early pioneers in information design. Sutnar designed innovative catalogs for industrial products and furniture. Bayer was involved in many projects for which he created beautifully designed yet functional information graphics such as maps, charts, and technical illustrations (see Bayer, 1953). Burtin was among the innovators in the visualization of scientific processes, taking technical illustration and medical illustration to new heights (for some examples, see Meggs, 1992b, p. 327).

[81] Bleed is a term for graphics, photographs, illustrations, shaded regions, or colored regions that run off the edge of the page (the side and the bottom). The left-hand page of the chapter dividers in this book use bleeds.

Sutnar defined *function* as utilitarian need with a definite purpose: to make information easy to find, read, comprehend, and recall. *Flow* was his term for the logical sequence of information. He felt the basic unit to be not the page but the "visual unit," which is the double-page spread. He rejected traditional margins as rigid containers creating barriers to visual flow and employed bleeds[81] extensively. He used shape, line, and color as functional elements to direct the eye as it moves through the design seeking information.... As he approached problems of *form*, static and uniform arrangements of catalogue information gave way to dynamic information patterns and clear, rational organization.... Visual articulation of type—underlining, size and weight contrasts, spacing, color, and reversing—was used to aid searching, scanning, and reading. A simple visualization language with emphasis upon graphic charts, diagrams, and pictures was used to clarify complex information and save the reader's time. The upper-right corner, which he considered the visual entry point for each layout, was used for identifying information. Optical unity was achieved by a systematic use of signs, shapes, and color. [italics in original] (p. 325)

As we can see, the concepts that underlie the functional use of space in document design are older than we might think. Sutnar's concern with the reader's "visual entry point" represents a radical departure from designers whose primary concerns were aesthetics, style, and personal expression. An understanding of Sutnar's advice may have helped the designer of the stereo manual in Figure 5.16. The competing orientations of the columns and rows could hardly pass a test for simplicity or for considering the reader's visual entry point.

Despite the advantages in using a grid, designers often worry about recommending their use. Their concern is reasonable, for a grid may act as a straitjacket, encouraging the same design on every page. Dull, dull, dull. This can happen when document designers choose ready-made grids that come packaged with page design software or when they use grids sold by consultants. These "one-template-fits-all-situations" grids *are* dull. When one organization uses the same grid as the next, it's hard for readers to distinguish among organizations because their public faces look the same.

Although grids may be employed in a formulaic manner, they need not restrict thinking. As Müller-Brockmann (1985) argues, using a grid design can encourage designers to think more creatively about the content, allowing them to imagine possibilities that would otherwise be missed. In teaching document design, I find that students usually begin using grids rather mechanically, in cookie-cutter fashion. However, after some practice, students discover that grids can act heuristically—that is, they can use them to systematically explore how the content "looks and feels" when presented through the lens of different visual structures. Whether a grid suits the content well depends on a number of interrelated factors:

> Whether the printed page looks harmonious and is pleas-
> ant to read depends on the clarity of the typeface, its size,
> the length of lines, the leading of the lines, and the size of
> the margins.... The general aesthetic impression created
> depends on the quality of the proportions of the page
> format, the size of the type area, and the typography....
> Just as every problem is novel and different from others,
> so the grid must be conceived afresh every time so as to
> meet requirements. (Müller-Brockmann, 1985, p. 50)

A Heuristic for Decision-Making in Constructing Grids

As a way of summarizing ideas about unifying the visual field, here I present a heuristic for grid design that focuses on using grids in order to help the reader see the structure of the content. Grids can be used rhetorically—that is, as inventional tools for working through alternatives for structuring a document visually. In using heuristics, be aware of their "potentially dynamic characteristic of energizing thought by shaping meaning" (Enos & Lauer, 1992, p. 81). Working with a heuristic for grid design is an interactive process—it can change the way the document designer thinks about the content (both visually and verbally). Similarly, the content can suggest changes to the grid. Which comes first, the content or the grid? There is no simple answer. Although it is most common to flesh out the words and pictures first, the grid itself often serves as a catalyst for new ways of integrating the words and pictures, which in turn may change the structure of the content.

The visual structures created through document design enhance and constrain a particular way of reading the content, one of many possible ways. Meanings are constructed transactionally, that is, as an artifact of a person engaging with the document. We should expect that readers may form different interpretations of ideas presented in our documents. Since audiences tend to read selectively, there is no guarantee that readers will even look at the same words and pictures (especially with online documents). *In a metaphoric sense, readers create their own text because they vary in what they read, in the order in which they read, and in what they bring to the text (e.g., values, beliefs, attitudes, culture, and knowledge).*

As a matter of discipline, we document designers aim to constrain the meanings readers create. But we cannot control the process of interpretation; we can only guide it through careful design of words and pictures. With a well-designed grid, we can make the hierarchy and the internal relationships of the text visible, giving readers signals about the intended structure and meaning. What a heuristic for grid design or any arrangement tool can do best is enable its operator to develop a number of visual solutions for the content—solutions that differ in how they invite and constrain interpretation. As Neel (1988) points out, a heuristic is "an endless generator … a good heuristic never stops until the operator turns it off while it is still humming along, still unfinished finding something new" (p. 61). With this in mind, I present a ten-stage iterative heuristic for structuring content visually by using a grid. To show how it works, I describe the evolution of the grid for this book.

1. Take an Inventory of the Text Elements the Document Requires

[82] When evaluating a document in need of revision, document designers often begin with a *features analysis,* an assessment of the quality of the various visual and verbal elements and their integration.

Brainstorm the text elements the document will need. A *text element* is a part of a document, visual or verbal, which is distinct in its nature, purpose, or function (such as a photograph, description, or caption). In contrast, a *text feature* is a characteristic of a document that usually pervades more than one element[82] (e.g., organization, repetition, coherence, style, or use of space). Documents are comprised of various text elements which often depend on their genre (e.g., reports have executive summaries, online help has procedures, forms have "fill-in the blank" sections, and World Wide Web sites have home pages). In taking an inventory of the text elements the document requires, characterize all components readers will expect or need—everything from the main parts down to the details. Be thorough. By the end of the grid construction process, each text element must have a "home on the grid."

In taking an inventory for this book, I found that the grid would need to accommodate these elements: headings, subheadings, body text, footnotes, pictures, tables, figures, charts, graphs, references, itemized lists, enumerated lists, indented quotes, sidebars, abstracts, special symbols, headings for the timeline, dates for the timeline, entries for the timeline, footnotes for the timeline, index, table of contents, front and end matter, colophon, page numbers, page headers, and chapter divider pictures.

2. Organize the Text Elements into Rhetorical Clusters

Group the text elements into rhetorical clusters by deciding which ones need to "talk to each other" by being positioned close to one another spatially. By *rhetorical cluster* I mean a group of text elements designed to work together as a functional unit within a document. Rhetorical clusters act as reader-oriented modules of purposeful and related content. They are comprised of visual and/or verbal elements that need to be grouped (or put in proximal relation) because together they help the reader interpret the content in a certain way. Most documents require several key rhetorical clusters. Here are four common examples:

Illustrations with annotations and explanations

- illustrations (small, medium, or large)
- leader lines and callouts (i.e., labels that identify elements)
- figure numbers, captions, and credits

Body text with footnotes

- body text (including paragraph styling)
- footnote text
- headings and subheadings
- itemized lists
- indented quotes

Procedural instructions with visual examples

- scenario (overview/goal of procedure)
- procedures (enumerated step-by-step)
- visual example of machine/device responses
- captions for examples

Front matter of a feature article

- headline (main point)
- byline (author, division)
- tagline, exploded quote, or attention-grabbing lead
- photograph (medium to large)
- caption (under photo if needed)

Rhetorical clusters may differ in scope (i.e., size) and they are often multiply embedded (e.g., a picture cluster within a body text cluster). The key feature of a rhetorical cluster is that its elements interact as a Gestalt; the elements have structure and the parts are interdependent. Every element in a rhetorical cluster influences the interpretation of others (e.g., a caption for a picture significantly constrains the world of interpretations for the picture).[83]

[83] In a series of landmark studies of the relationships between words and pictures, cognitive psychologists Bransford and Johnson (1972) showed that a caption (or lack thereof) can change completely how readers represent the meaning of the picture.

We can think of a document as a field of interacting rhetorical clusters. If the document is well designed, the clusters orchestrate a web of converging meanings, which enable readers to form a coherent and consistent idea of the content. When documents are not well designed, the rhetorical clusters may seem unrelated. They may compete for attention, contradict one another, or have so many gaps between them that readers find it hard to form a coherent and consistent interpretation of the content. Rhetorical clusters operate dynamically—on single pages, on spreads, or over screens.

In organizing text elements into rhetorical clusters, make rough sketches that show them in optional arrangements, exploring different horizontal and vertical arrays for the content. Experiment with the internal organization of each cluster and with the position of the clusters in relation to one another. Consider the hierarchy of the content, asking "What is the main point of this spread?" Position the clusters so that the most important ideas are in focal position (the most prominent or perceptually distinct) on the spread. Make sure text elements of subsidiary importance are in a position of less visual prominence.

In working on the grid for this book, I began with these rhetorical clusters in mind:

- *Cluster 1:* body text with footnotes.
- *Cluster 2:* chapter-opening spreads which included a left page with a chapter-divider picture and a right page with a chapter title, an abstract, and a picture caption.
- *Cluster 3:* charts, tables, figures, sidebars, and captions.
- *Cluster 4:* headings, text entries, dates, and notes for *The Timeline*.

3. Measure the Actual Print Area or Display Area

Before making firm decisions about size and position, it is important to know just what size the text can be. Calculate the exact length and width of the print area or display area by using the same scale that will be employed for designing the grid (e.g., inches, millimeters, or points and picas). Although the print area for paper documents is often taller than it is wide, online documents are usually wider than they are tall. The grid should accommodate either a vertical orientation (i.e., portrait) or a horizontal display (i.e., landscape). In addition, make certain any constraints on printing or displaying the document are considered. For example, in using a laser printer, one usually can't print to the edge of the paper. In many online displays, the design must give room for application/system icons. Plan the grid by taking these spatial constraints into account.

In designing this book, I worked with a standard size for books published by Wiley Computer Publishing. After the book pages are trimmed at the printing plant (called the *trim size*), the pages are 7½" wide by 9¼" tall. For pages with images that bleed off the page, such as the left-hand page of chapter opening spreads, I needed to extend the image past the trim area by ¼" (thus, pictures needed to be sized at 7¾" × 9½"). The text and picture area could be roughly 6" by 7¾" on each page. These dimensions became the guide for the outside edges of the grid.

4. Divide the Print or Display Space into Columns and Rows

The idea in employing a grid is to unify the visual field in order to evoke a sense of proportion, regularity, structure, and rhythm as the reader engages with the content. This requires standardizing the width of the columns and rows (though for some designs, rows may be unnecessary). It also means specifying the width of the gutters (the space between pages) and alleys (the space between columns). The grid units (or modules) are the basic units in the composition of the visual space. Most documents employ the same number of columns as rows, generally from one to six (e.g., from a simple one-column grid, which has no rows, to a 2 × 2 grid, a 3 × 3 grid, a 4 × 4, and so on; this book uses a 4 × 4). In laying out content using the grid, one can "respect individual columns or aggregate them into larger units, providing a pleasing contrast in the layout" (Mullet & Sano, 1995, p. 135). Thus, a six-column grid can readily be redivided into three columns or vice versa.

To help decide how many columns you will need, choose a simple ratio for organizing the key elements on the page. It is often useful to divide the page into two groups, items that need the most space and items that require less space. Some common ratios of main elements to supplementary text elements include the following:

5-column grid: 4:1 or 3:2

4-column grid: 3:1 or 2:2

3-column grid: 2:1

2-column grid: 1:1

1-column grid: 1

In designing the grid for this book, graphic designer Laurette Boyer and I started with a 4 × 4 grid, where each grid module unit was roughly 1⅜" wide × 1¾" tall (about 8 picas × 10 picas). We strove for a 3:1 ratio between the body text and the footnotes (i.e., 3-grid units to 1-grid unit). To see the grid we used, look back at Figure 5.41 (p. 339).

5. Evaluate the Elements within Each Rhetorical Cluster in Terms of the Minimum and Maximum Space They Will Require

[84] By a subordinate rhetorical cluster, I do not mean unimportant, but subsidiary to a major one.

[85] Sometimes important items are signaled by using a dramatically shorter width. Just as a short sentence can be dramatic (e.g., "I do"), a text element with a short width can take on visual prominence by juxtaposing it with wide text elements.

Experiment with alternative widths for major and minor elements. Develop ideas by comparing how the major and minor rhetorical clusters look when they are shifted in and out of focal position. Items of subordinate status[84] in the textual hierarchy should be in a subsidiary visual position. Typically, though not always, subordinate items get a shorter width.[85] Generally speaking, text elements that require more width (such as the body text) are allowed to span multiple grid units. Those that can have short width (e.g., marginalia) should begin and end on a grid boundary. It's a good idea to identify two or three possible widths for grid units that will accommodate the major and minor rhetorical clusters.

In designing this book, we first considered the rhetorical cluster comprised of the body text and footnotes (since it would be the most dominant feature of the book). To avoid the monotonous look of foot-notes always at the bottom of the pages, we decided to use two positions: on the same line as the reference in the body text and at the bottom of the page. This gave us the flexibility of placing long or short footnotes in either position, depending on what was needed. In addition, we consid-ered alternatives for the line length when the body text was set at different point sizes and with different amounts of leading. After several iterations, we settled on Monotype Bembo at 11/13 and chose a line length of roughly 10 to 14 words per line. As I said earlier in footnote 18, book publishing leans toward 12 to 14 words per line, a bit higher than the generally recommended 8 to 12 words per line. We also wanted the footnotes to have roughly 4 to 6 words per line. These goals led us to a line length for the body text of about 4½" (or 27 picas) and a footnote length of about 1⅜" (or about 8 picas). These dimensions gave us enough of an alley to separate the text from the footnotes by about ⅛" (or a little less than 1 pica). We experimented with alternative sans serif typefaces and type sizes for the footnotes, looking for one with a warm tone that complemented the humanistic look of Bembo. We chose Frutiger 8/11. It met our criteria for line length and tone.

6. Consider the Rhetorical Clusters That Contain Exceptions or Deviations

Further iterate the grid by considering how well key rhetorical clusters work when they vary in size or continue over pages or screens. The question is: "Does the design hold up under normal circumstances as well as when there are exceptions?" Determine whether the grid accommo-dates the norm and the exceptions, but keep in mind that it is more advisable to make the exceptions fit the norm than to redesign the grid to fit the exceptions and risk making the norm look poor.[86] The design of the exceptions should not weaken the structure of the whole.[87] When all else fails, get rid of the exceptions by redesigning or rewriting the content.

However, if the content is strong and does not warrant major redesign or rewriting, plan to "break" the grid by modifying it (e.g., shifting from a

[86] For example, Mullet and Sano (1995) point out that in sizing the windows for messages that appear on graphical user interfaces (GUIs), designers have a tendency to size items for the worst case (i.e., the largest amount of information) (p. 104). The design strategy of making the most typical text elements use a space designed for "exceptions" means that 90 percent of the messages will appear in a box that is too big, where the message looks unbal-anced and perhaps as though content is missing.

[87] The principle of using spatial cues to show structural relationships is important to the design of all documents, even routine business reports, a genre comprised mainly of paragraphs and itemized lists. For example, in designing itemized lists—a spatial array in which the content is formatted to stand out from the body text—it is important to evaluate the nature of the content that will appear in lists since it will be visually prominent. Because readers tend to skim lists before paragraphs, information that does not need visual segregation and prominence should not be displayed as a list. For some guidelines about maintaining consistency in the content of itemized lists, see Appendices B and C (pp. 502–517).

three-column to a six-column grid) or by creating an entirely new one (e.g., moving from a five-column to a three-column grid). But before creating a new grid, clearly define how much prominence the exception deserves in the context of the rhetorical whole. If the exception is supplementary to the main structure, it should not be positioned using a spatial array of maximum contrast. In other words, don't break the grid with content that is not a major text element. Doing so will promote less important content into a focal position where it will stand out within the rhetorical structure.

In designing this book, our trial runs with the typefaces Bembo and Frutiger met our goals for the body text and footnotes. We did run into a problem, however, when it came to designing *The Timeline*. We found that even after considerable tinkering with the line length of text entries, the 4 × 4 grid just didn't suit the nature of the content. A key feature of the rhetorical approach to grid design is that decision-making is driven by (1) analyzing the content and (2) anticipating how the reader will want to use the content. It is important *not* to think of grid design as merely arranging text blocks or gray blobs of copy.

The main grid for this book was designed with continuous text, pictures, and footnotes in mind, but the content for *The Timeline* was tabular and needed special consideration. It became important to know how much text the grid would accommodate. I had the goal of making each timeline entry meaningful and independent, while keeping each entry as short as possible. As an exercise in developing the content, I asked students to read an entry and tell me what it meant. For example, in response to the entry, "1958 *Ergonomics* started," one student asked, "Is that a club or a field?" To give readers a better clue of my intent, I wrote: "1958. The journal *Ergonomics* is started; it will publish many articles relevant to document design." This simple elaboration made the difference between mysterious and obvious (even without defining ergonomics). The recognition that very brief entries might be unintelligible suggested that more space for each entry was needed than I had originally anticipated. This led me to worry about how many words would fit on each line for an average timeline entry.

The act of composing raised the question of how to make the grid handle deviations in the length of timeline entries. Some could be skeletal sentences, while others needed to be closer to mini-paragraphs. We worried about the adequacy of the four-column grid because the columns were narrow; thus, longer timeline entries would have a long and skinny appearance (see Iteration 1 of Figure 5.42 on the next spread). One option was to reduce the size of the type, which would fit more words on each line and shorten the vertical space required for each text entry. But this had the drawback of reducing the already small 8-point type. For the sake of legibility, we chose instead to design a new grid that suited the content of *The Timeline*. We needed a wider grid unit so we could have a longer line length without reducing the type size. This led us to conclude that each page should have three columns instead of four.

7. Try Out Optional Spatial Orientations for the Document

Think of the layout as a guide for the reader to scan the text. Plan a typical path for the reader's eye to travel through the page, spread, or display. Decide whether the overall layout should be horizontal, vertical, or a mix of both. As we saw earlier in this chapter with the example from the multilanguage stereo manual (Figures 5.27 and 5.28), competing grids should be avoided unless the mixed design is warranted by a clear demarcation of the function of the rhetorical cluster.

In evaluating optional spatial orientations for the grid, designers recommend creating a series of small sketches called *thumbnails,* which allow one to see the rough layout of the whole and the relationships that build between the text and graphics—both within and across a sequence of pages.[88] (Most page layout software allows for printing miniature pages of the document; thumbnails make it easy to compare the relative goodness of alternative concepts.) The eight mini-spreads shown in Figure 5.42 are slightly enlarged versions of thumbnails. According to Shushan, Wright, and Lewis (1996), thumbnails can give you a sense of the texture and continuity of the pages and often help you spot opportunities and problems, both in editorial continuity and format consistency.

As I mentioned earlier, in designing the grid for *The Timeline,* we decided to move from a four-column grid to a three-column grid. Still, there was the issue of which spatial orientation would be best to present the flow of history: horizontal or vertical?

Option 1. Time runs left to right, that is, with events related to the context of document design presented in rows. The practical impact of this idea can be seen in Iterations 1 through 3 in Figure 5.42. As shown, the five strands of *The Timeline* would not fit on one spread unless the entries were edited severely as in Iteration 3. We rejected this option because it worked against the goal of providing more detail for ideas that warranted explanation or were more important. In looking at the horizontal design spread-after-spread, the alignment grew monotonous. The

[88] One of my favorite books on this topic is Jan White's *Editing by Design: A Guide to Effective Word-and-Picture Communication for Editors and Designers* (1982). He also has a little book entitled *The Grid Book* (1987). Both are extremely accessible and will help you to think through the task of integrating words and pictures.

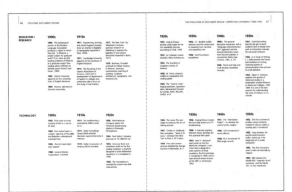

Iteration 1: Horizontal organization

Allows reader to view 2 of 5 timeline strands per spread; can see a portion of 7 decades per spread. Each strand requires 3 spreads to finish one decade. A drawback is that 3 of 5 strands cannot start until first 2 are finished (6 pages later). This makes for a choppy view of history. Does not meet the goal of having all 5 strands visible at the same time. Readers might read down the columns even though *The Timeline* is designed to be read from left to right. A lot of uninteresting blank space.

Iteration 2: Horizontal organization

Allows 3 of 5 strands per spread; can see 1 decade per spread. Each strand requires 2 to 3 spreads to finish decade. A drawback is that 2 of 5 strands cannot start until the first 3 are finished (6 pages later). Still presents a choppy view of history. Even though one more timeline strand fits on this spread than the last, it still doesn't allow all 5 of the strands to be viewed at once. The horizontal rule line across the top ties the spread together but is nothing special, kind of routine. The layout seems to emphasize the differences in length among the text blurbs.

Iteration 3: Horizontal organization

Allows 5 of 5 strands per spread; can see most of 1 decade per spread. However, text blurbs must be shortened substantially to fit, which truncates the content too much. The design inhibits meeting the rhetorical goal of saying more about some historical events and less about others. The layout looks clear but a bit dull.

Iteration 4: Vertical organization

Allows 5 of 5 strands per spread; can see an entire decade on one spread. "Notes" for each entry fit on the same two-page spread. However, the Frutiger Black used for the dates is too dark. It emphasizes the dates over the content—bad rhetorical move. The pages seem too regimented in appearance; the spreads need some dynamism. The columns look "stripey."

▲ Figure 5.42 *Eight iterations of the grid design for* The Timeline of Document Design *in Chapter 2.*

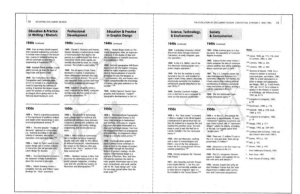

Iteration 5: Vertical organization

Allows 5 of 5 strands per spread. The Frutiger Roman used for dates is much better than the Frutiger Black used in Iteration 4 because it makes the dates less dominant. The background image is light enough so that it doesn't obscure the typography. The left page's picture of "hula hoopers" makes a playful pattern that breaks up the columns, but they may be a little "busy" looking. The atomic energy symbol on the right page typifies the era. But when these images are juxtaposed on the same spread, they read poorly together and invite unintended resonances. Poor integration of the visual images.

Iteration 6: Vertical organization

Allows 5 of 5 strands per spread. The larger dramatic images seem better than the smaller somewhat "busy" patterns created by the hula hoopers in the previous version. The ADA symbol is strong and bold, inviting to look at. The AIDS symbol "Silence = Death" is powerful and evocative. Even the words are legible beneath the type. Separately, both images work quite well. But together, they suggest a number of unintended relationships and do not work well on the same spread.

Iteration 7: Vertical organization

Allows 5 of 5 strands per spread. The image of Ginger Rogers and Fred Astaire dancing is elegant. The "close to symmetrical" design works well to integrate the columns. The image offers a view of the social context that complements the "Society & Consumerism" strand of *The Timeline*. The curved lines break the rigidity of the rectangles. The joining of the dancer's hands unites the two pages in a pleasing way and makes the spread interesting to look at.

Iteration 8: Vertical organization

Allows 5 of 5 strands per spread. The image of the Candlestick phone evokes a bygone era. The telephone cord stretches across the columns to connect them—nice dynamic asymmetry. The negative space created by the enlarged dial is handsome. The image is not too dark, so it doesn't obscure the typography of *The Timeline* entries. The image contributes to the sense of history and adds a dimension not available in the prose.

text seemed to unfold like a long straight ribbon. It didn't hold our interest. The design had to work for at least 20 spreads; we wanted every spread to give the reader reason to pause, even if just for a second.

Option 2. Time runs top to bottom, that is, with events related to the context of document design presented in columns. The use of a vertical orientation is explored in Iterations 4 through 8 in Figure 5.42. We began to lean toward the vertical orientation after working with the content in more detail. In particular, we tried to make each decade fit on one spread (i.e., ten decades spanning ten spreads), but discovered that some decades had much more document design activity and required two or three spreads. We decided to include a second or third spread for a decade only if all five strands had enough content to complete a new page. In this way, the strands for each decade would still end together visually. We didn't want big holes of nonfunctional blank space.

The vertical grid seemed the better choice because it helped us achieve our rhetorical goals more easily than did the horizontal orientation (which constrained the writing too much). In fact, once we saw the options the vertical orientation gave for the content, there was no turning back, only successive refinement. As the iterations of *The Timeline* show, *goals for writing influenced the visual design and goals for the visual design influenced the writing—each dynamically shaping the other. Importantly, both goals for writing and design were motivated by ideas about how readers might engage with the content.*

8. Standardize the Dimensions of the Grid Unit and Finalize the Number of Columns and Rows

En route to completing the grid design, it will be important to settle on which option from those explored is most promising. At this point, document designers should narrow their options to one and specify the size of the grid unit. The idea is to iterate the best version until it meets the rhetorical goals for the project.

In designing *The Timeline,* we had settled on a three-column grid with a grid unit that allowed one to three more words per line than the grid unit for the rest of the book. We then turned our attention to making the spreads more visually interesting from one to the next. Our main goal was to pique the reader's interest in the history of the field. We saw this might be difficult because although the vertical orientation did meet the goals for content, the spreads took on a visibly heavier look than in previous versions. We felt the darker pages were dreary. So did one of my editors, who suggested that we change the dates for each entry from Frutiger Bold to Frutiger Black. Her idea was that black dates would add visual contrast and interest.

However, once we implemented the idea (shown in Iteration 4), the contrast between the Frutiger Black for the dates and the Frutiger Light for the blurbs proved to emphasize the wrong rhetorical goal. The dates took visual prominence over the flow of events—not what we wanted. We then changed the numbers from Frutiger Black to Frutiger Roman, scaling back the boldness by three shades (between the Roman and Black were Bold and Extra Bold). This typographic change meant that the numbers were a little darker than the blurbs, but not overwhelmingly so. Still, we had a gray page.

In trying to come up with another way of "livening up" the gray pages, we thought it could be engaging to present an image running across the two pages underneath the type. We looked for striking curved and rounded images that had strong bold shapes (see, for example, the background image for the 1930s spread, "King Kong and Faye Raye," in *The Timeline*). Our aim was to break up the monotonous rigidity of the rectangles and tie the spreads together as a single visual field. We searched for images with a solid silhouette that wouldn't make the text entries hard to read by looking "blotchy" or "lacy" behind the text. The goal was to make certain we kept the typography legible while lightening up the stodgy look of the columns.

To carry out this idea, we collected photos of dozens of symbols and visuals for each decade, most of which were from American popular culture. We rejected clip art on the grounds that most of it was trite or ugly (often both). Our very first exploration was to place one image in the center of each spread. (This draft is not shown.) The problem with this initial exploration was that most of the image was in the gutter. In addition, most of the images we found were not wide enough to span all six columns; this meant that once placed on the grid, the images were bounded by columns 1 and 6. The centered solution didn't meet the goal of tying the columns together.

Our next drafts developed the concept of using two images per spread, one on each side (see Iterations 5 and 6). As shown, these images, though true to the spirit of their decade, don't speak well to one another when juxtaposed. In Iteration 5, we thought that showing kids with hula hoops from the 1950s was a playful idea and could make a unique and lively pattern. However, when we put the hula hoopers next to the symbol for atomic energy, things got really strange. The hula hoops seemed to take on a somber resonance from their similarity to electrons orbiting around an atomic nucleus; not exactly what we intended.

Iteration 6 is another story of poor integration of images. Here we tried the international symbol for buildings or places that are accessible for people who use wheelchairs; it also spoke to the Americans with Disabilities Act (ADA), a clear and engaging icon. For the same decade, we considered alternative AIDS symbols. Though each image worked well separately, put together they were disastrous. The orientation of the wheelchair made it seem to ride across the page to the right, crashing into the AIDS symbol. As the Gestalt psychologists showed, images that have "good continuation" allow readers to "mentally fill in" the direction of the movement. Good continuation as well as the overall semantics of the ADA/AIDS spread suggested a variety of unintended relationships between the images.[89]

These problems of poor integration prompted us to look for images that suggested a single theme and that were composed of elements that could be placed on each side of the spread. Our goal was to tie the columns together with an image from the era without the image leaping out at the reader (thus, we chose a 10 percent screen rather than anything darker). We looked for images that could unify the visual field by joining the two pages as they crossed the gutter. Elements such as the hands and shoes of the dancers (in Iteration 7) and the winding telephone cord (in Iteration 8) became important to the design.

9. If Designing in Spreads, Explore Optional Relationships Between the Left-hand and Right-hand Pages

In exploring how well the grid works, consider its flexibility in allowing for different displays of the content from spread to spread. Depending on the rhetorical situation, document designers may want to display the content using the same pattern throughout the document or a range of complementary patterns which are unified by the underlying grid. In making choices, evaluate how effectively the dimensions of the grid afford different patterns for the content. These variations might include, for example, using (1) the same pattern for each page, (2) a mirror-image pattern, or (3) two different but complementary patterns.

The same grid for the whole spread. For example, a left-hand page with a 5-column grid in which column 1 is used for marginal information and columns 2 through 5 for body text and illustrations. This pattern is repeated on the right page.

A mirror-image grid. For example, a left-hand page with a 5-column grid in which column 1 is used for marginal information and columns 2 through 5 for body text and illustrations. This pattern is reversed on the right page; that is, columns 1 through 4 are for body text and illustrations and column 5 for marginal information.

[89] Care must be taken in using images that imply direction. When looking at pictures of people, readers tend to follow the direction of the eyes in the picture (sometimes called "gaze motion"). Always position faces looking into the body text, never looking away off the page. A similar idea is called "sequence direction," or the way in which the eye is led through the layout. Ads often use a layout in the shape of a reverse "S" or a "Z" pattern. The idea is to take advantage of readers' propensity to read from left to right, inviting them to traverse the page by following a pattern (e.g., car ads often use a road in the shape of an inverted "S" or a "Z," leading the eye to the name of the car company). But it's not that people read in the Z pattern, it's just that readers in western countries are used to it. For a discussion, see Starch (1966).

Two different but complementary grids. For example, a left-hand page with a 6-column grid in which column 1 through 4 are used for a large photo and columns 5 and 6 for a single column of text. On the right-hand page, this pattern is changed. Instead, a 3-column grid is used, each column for text (as in a magazine layout).

In the design of *The Timeline,* we used the same grid for the whole spread. In order to avoid a monotonous appearance, we selected images that could be employed to create symmetrical and asymmetrical layouts. For example, while the image of Ginger Rogers and Fred Astaire[90] in Iteration 7 is relatively symmetrical, the image of the Candlestick Telephone in Iteration 8 is asymmetrical. We think the spreads could still use improvement, but they came a long way toward meeting our rhetorical goals for the content.

[90] Notice that although the image itself is fairly symmetrical, we off-centered the image so the feet and hands wouldn't get lost in the gutter of the book.

10. Iterate the Design of the Rhetorical Clusters to Optimize How the Grid is Employed

Evaluate how well the grid holds up during the layout of extended sections of the content. Put the grid through its paces until a satisfactory set of visual and rhetorical relationships have been established. "Tweak the grid" by making final adjustments. Once all of the rhetorical clusters "have a home on the grid," fine-tune the design of text features (organization, style, horizontal space, use of leading, and so on). Focus on structuring the prose and graphics so that their design is enhanced by the visual display. Consider the content that might be featured as a purposeful deviation from the grid. Work iteratively, improving the integration of the visual and verbal content. Make time to evaluate the design with the intended audience. If the structure doesn't help readers use the content in purposeful ways, either revise or start over.

In addition to creating a new grid for *The Timeline* over several iterations, we refined the main grid employed to display the body text. Once the two grids were finalized, we scrutinized the details of the layout of the body text for the book. Notice the paragraph breaks in the body text are signaled by using indentation and extra leading between the paragraphs. In the view of most book designers, one should employ either indenting or vertical space to signal paragraph boundaries, but never both, as it amounts to "double signaling." However, on the basis of an informal study of readers' preferences I describe next, we decided to ignore the double signaling taboo.

91 Participants were upper-level undergraduate (juniors and seniors) and graduate students in writing and graphic design. Advanced students are part of my intended audience.

In particular, I showed 18 readers[91] mock-ups of three alternative layouts for the book design (presented in Figure 5.43) and asked them which they would prefer to read:

- Extra leading between paragraphs, with no indentation, justified left, and ragged right (Style 1).

- The same leading between paragraphs and within them, paragraphs indented, and ragged right (Style 2).

- Extra leading between paragraphs, paragraphs indented, and ragged right (Style 3).

Students who participated had the following preferences about the three layouts:

- Thirteen preferred the double-signaled layout using both indentation and leading (Style 3).

- Three chose the layout using flush left, ragged right, with extra leading between paragraphs—today's most popular style for reports, articles, business correspondence, and technical and scientific books (Style 1).

- Two chose the layout that employed indented paragraphs without extra leading—the traditional layout for most books, especially fiction and academic books (Style 2).

Readers who chose Style 3 made comments such as these: "It looks easier," "There are fewer words," "It looks shorter," "It's more airy," "It doesn't seem like as much to read." Based on readers' responses, I opted for a design using both indenting and extra leading to signal paragraph boundaries. I felt it was the best option because readers preferred it and it gave the text a lighter appearance.

I am not, however, recommending this type of layout as a guideline for documents more generally. It worked for this situation, but if the paragraphs were short (they usually are not), the text would look choppy with both indenting and linespacing. Here, the double-signaled layout helped me meet a rhetorical goal of lightening up the density of my paragraphs.

These findings are based on a small sample (and to be generally applicable would need to be tested across a number of documents with a larger, more diverse population), but they do suggest that the spatial design of paragraphs contributes to a reader's first impression. This case adds to the literature which suggests that the visible structure of language plays a role in readers' reception of text.[92] As I said in Chapter 4, if on their initial pass readers are left with a lukewarm first impression, they may avoid reading altogether. Document designers must do what they can to encourage reading by using spatial cues for rhetorical purposes.

92 See, for example, the work of Foster (1979), Garofalo (1988), Kolers, Wrolstad, & Bouma (1979, 1980), Twyman (1981), and Waller (1980).

[23] In the United States, a similar contest, "The Worst Manual of the Year," was sponsored in 1993 by The Communication Circle, a company owned by author and teacher Jonathan Price.

agreements to compete for Plain English Awards. At the same time, the public is invited to nominate examples of the worst documents for Golden Bull Awards.[23] Even the government has endorsed the efforts of the campaigners for plain language. In 1985, for example, the Civil Service and the Plain English Campaign cosponsored a Plain English exhibition, attended by Prime Minister Margaret Thatcher. And in 1986, the exhibit was displayed in the House of Commons (Kimble, 1992, p. 53). Clearly, such backing from the U.K.'s highest officials has been instrumental in keeping plain language before the public eye. This sort of official endorsement, helping to ensure the movement's momentum, has not occurred in the United States since the Carter administration.

For several decades, researchers in the U.K. have guided plain language campaigners away from pithy prescriptions about short sentences and simple words and have encouraged them instead to evaluate empirically readers' understanding of documents (Wright, 1980, 1988a). For an illustration of this "document design approach" in practice, see Cutts (1993), who describes the redesign of a legal document.

Plain Language in Australia. In Australia, the plain language movement began in 1976 when the NRMA insurance company, a subsidiary of the National Road Motorists Association, issued its first *Plain English Car Insurance Policy*. Eagleson (1991) suggests that unlike the movements in the U.K. and the United States, the Australian movement developed in established organizations in the private and public sector, mainly insurance companies, real estate agencies, and, to a lesser extent, government, particularly the Victoria Law Reform Commission (p. 36).

Once plain language documents were introduced, Australian businesses and government agencies found that they yielded considerable economic benefits. In the insurance industry, for example, companies that revised their forms and contracts using plain language principles discovered that the number of invalid claims fell, procedures were followed more efficiently, and employees who processed forms were more productive. It also took much less time to train staff and to provide accurate advice to customers. In government, the revision of one poorly designed summons led to the equivalent of a savings of $400,000 per year (Eagleson, 1991, p. 39). Moreover, litigation declined, demonstrating that plain language could work successfully in law. Plain language documents drew writers and readers together, simultaneously solving the different problems of each.

Plain language issues continue to be debated in Australia (Penman, 1993). For example, the Centre for Plain Legal Language hosted a conference in 1994 on plain language, during which researchers discussed the

impact of taking a plain language approach to text revision on the quality of documents. This thorny issue has also been under investigation in Australia by the Communications Research Institute of Australia (CRIA). Since 1985, the CRIA has been contributing to knowledge about what makes documents work. Their studies suggest that plain language legal documents are not always superior to quasi-legal writing. CRIA researchers have been developing a set of principles that they believe will help writers produce legal texts that are more usable than those produced using plain language guidelines (Penman, 1990).

Plain Language in Canada. The plain language movement in Canada has been shaped largely by government action rather than by citizen activism. Started in the late 1980s, the movement took a big step forward in 1988 when a Plain Language Centre was established in Toronto by the Canadian Legal Information Centre (CLIC). It received initial funding from legal, corporate, and consumer groups and has been self-sustaining since 1991.[24] A report by Dykstra characterizes the Centre's mission as creating awareness about the movement and providing tools, training, and research needed to adopt the plain language approach (1991, p. 43).

[24] Reported in Kimble (1992, pp. 46–47).

The quality of legal documents has been a prominent catalyzing force behind plain language in Canada (for a discussion, see Jordan, 1994). In 1991, Saskatchewan became the first province to begin a government-wide program in clear language. In British Columbia the Plain Language Institute commissioned research on legal writing and sponsored a conference for legal experts (Coe, 1992). To date, plain language has been supported mainly by businesses involved in creating legal, financial, or insurance documents.

University and industry research labs have been at the forefront of Canadian work that goes beyond plain language to broader considerations of document design. For example, researchers at McGill University's Center for Cognitive Science have been tracking the process of producing technical documents collaboratively (Breuleux & Bracewell, 1994). Faculty from the department of English at the University of Waterloo in Ontario sponsored several international conferences on issues of quality in document design.[25] Cultural, rhetorical, and linguistic approaches to document design are under study by members of the Canadian Association of Teachers of Technical Writing (CATTW), a group that holds an annual conference and also publishes the informative journal *TechnoStyle*. And Bell Northern Research (now called Nortel) has made use of the findings of recent work in document design and has sponsored innovative research.

[25] Canadian conferences about document design issues continue to grow in number. Researchers and practitioners in computer documentation came to Ottawa in 1992 for the Association for Computing Machinery's Special Interest Group on Documentation (SIGDOC) Conference. Banff was the site for the 1994 Institute for Electronics and Electrical Engineers (IEEE) conference on Professional Communication.

Style 1: Extra leading between paragraphs, no indentation, and ragged right.

[23] In the United States, a similar contest, "The Worst Manual of the Year," was sponsored in 1993 by The Communication Circle, a company owned by author and teacher Jonathan Price.

agreements to compete for Plain English Awards. At the same time, the public is invited to nominate examples of the worst documents for Golden Bull Awards.[23] Even the government has endorsed the efforts of the campaigners for plain language. In 1985, for example, the Civil Service and the Plain English Campaign cosponsored a Plain English exhibition, attended by Prime Minister Margaret Thatcher. And in 1986, the exhibit was displayed in the House of Commons (Kimble, 1992, p. 53). Clearly, such backing from the U.K.'s highest officials has been instrumental in keeping plain language before the public eye. This sort of official endorsement, helping to ensure the movement's momentum, has not occurred in the United States since the Carter administration.

For several decades, researchers in the U.K. have guided plain language campaigners away from pithy prescriptions about short sentences and simple words and have encouraged them instead to evaluate empirically readers' understanding of documents (Wright, 1980, 1988a). For an illustration of this "document design approach" in practice, see Cutts (1993), who describes the redesign of a legal document.

Plain Language in Australia. In Australia, the plain language movement began in 1976 when the NRMA insurance company, a subsidiary of the National Road Motorists Association, issued its first *Plain English Car Insurance Policy*. Eagleson (1991) suggests that unlike the movements in the U.K. and the United States, the Australian movement developed in established organizations in the private and public sector, mainly insurance companies, real estate agencies, and, to a lesser extent, government, particularly the Victoria Law Reform Commission (p. 36).

Once plain language documents were introduced, Australian businesses and government agencies found that they yielded considerable economic benefits. In the insurance industry, for example, companies that revised their forms and contracts using plain language principles discovered that the number of invalid claims fell, procedures were followed more efficiently, and employees who processed forms were more productive. It also took much less time to train staff and to provide accurate advice to customers. In government, the revision of one poorly designed summons led to the equivalent of a savings of $400,000 per year (Eagleson, 1991, p. 39). Moreover, litigation declined, demonstrating that plain language could work successfully in law. Plain language documents drew writers and readers together, simultaneously solving the different problems of each.

Plain language issues continue to be debated in Australia (Penman, 1993). For example, the Centre for Plain Legal Language hosted a conference in 1994 on plain language, during which researchers discussed the

impact of taking a plain language approach to text revision on the quality of documents. This thorny issue has also been under investigation in Australia by the Communications Research Institute of Australia (CRIA). Since 1985, the CRIA has been contributing to knowledge about what makes documents work. Their studies suggest that plain language legal documents are not always superior to quasi-legal writing. CRIA researchers have been developing a set of principles that they believe will help writers produce legal texts that are more usable than those produced using plain language guidelines (Penman, 1990).

Plain Language in Canada. The plain language movement in Canada has been shaped largely by government action rather than by citizen activism. Started in the late 1980s, the movement took a big step forward in 1988 when a Plain Language Centre was established in Toronto by the Canadian Legal Information Centre (CLIC). It received initial funding from legal, corporate, and consumer groups and has been self-sustaining since 1991.[24] A report by Dykstra characterizes the Centre's mission as creating awareness about the movement and providing tools, training, and research needed to adopt the plain language approach (1991, p. 43).

[24] Reported in Kimble (1992, pp. 46–47).

The quality of legal documents has been a prominent catalyzing force behind plain language in Canada (for a discussion, see Jordan, 1994). In 1991, Saskatchewan became the first province to begin a government-wide program in clear language. In British Columbia the Plain Language Institute commissioned research on legal writing and sponsored a conference for legal experts (Coe, 1992). To date, plain language has been supported mainly by businesses involved in creating legal, financial, or insurance documents.

University and industry research labs have been at the forefront of Canadian work that goes beyond plain language to broader considerations of document design. For example, researchers at McGill University's Center for Cognitive Science have been tracking the process of producing technical documents collaboratively (Breuleux & Bracewell, 1994). Faculty from the department of English at the University of Waterloo in Ontario sponsored several international conferences on issues of quality in document design.[25] Cultural, rhetorical, and linguistic approaches to document design are under study by members of the Canadian Association of Teachers of Technical Writing (CATTW), a group that holds an annual conference and also publishes the informative journal *TechnoStyle*. And Bell Northern Research (now called Nortel) has made use of the findings of recent work in document design and has sponsored innovative research.

[25] Canadian conferences about document design issues continue to grow in number. Researchers and practitioners in computer documentation came to Ottawa in 1992 for the Association for Computing Machinery's Special Interest Group on Documentation (SIGDOC) Conference. Banff was the site for the 1994 Institute for Electronics and Electrical Engineers (IEEE) conference on Professional Communication.

Style 2: Identical leading within paragraphs and between them, paragraphs indented, and ragged right.

[23] In the United States, a similar contest, "The Worst Manual of the Year," was sponsored in 1993 by The Communication Circle, a company owned by author and teacher Jonathan Price.

agreements to compete for Plain English Awards. At the same time, the public is invited to nominate examples of the worst documents for Golden Bull Awards.[23] Even the government has endorsed the efforts of the campaigners for plain language. In 1985, for example, the Civil Service and the Plain English Campaign cosponsored a Plain English exhibition, attended by Prime Minister Margaret Thatcher. And in 1986, the exhibit was displayed in the House of Commons (Kimble, 1992, p. 53). Clearly, such backing from the U.K.'s highest officials has been instrumental in keeping plain language before the public eye. This sort of official endorsement, helping to ensure the movement's momentum, has not occurred in the United States since the Carter administration.

For several decades, researchers in the U.K. have guided plain language campaigners away from pithy prescriptions about short sentences and simple words and have encouraged them instead to evaluate empirically readers' understanding of documents (Wright, 1980, 1988a). For an illustration of this "document design approach" in practice, see Cutts (1993), who describes the redesign of a legal document.

Plain Language in Australia. In Australia, the plain language movement began in 1976 when the NRMA insurance company, a subsidiary of the National Road Motorists Association, issued its first *Plain English Car Insurance Policy*. Eagleson (1991) suggests that unlike the movements in the U.K. and the United States, the Australian movement developed in established organizations in the private and public sector, mainly insurance companies, real estate agencies, and, to a lesser extent, government, particularly the Victoria Law Reform Commission (p. 36).

Once plain language documents were introduced, Australian businesses and government agencies found that they yielded considerable economic benefits. In the insurance industry, for example, companies that revised their forms and contracts using plain language principles discovered that the number of invalid claims fell, procedures were followed more efficiently, and employees who processed forms were more productive. It also took much less time to train staff and to provide accurate advice to customers. In government, the revision of one poorly designed summons led to the equivalent of a savings of $400,000 per year (Eagleson, 1991, p. 39). Moreover, litigation declined, demonstrating that plain language could work successfully in law. Plain language documents drew writers and readers together, simultaneously solving the different problems of each.

Plain language issues continue to be debated in Australia (Penman, 1993). For example, the Centre for Plain Legal Language hosted a conference in 1994 on plain language, during which researchers discussed the

impact of taking a plain language approach to text revision on the quality of documents. This thorny issue has also been under investigation in Australia by the Communications Research Institute of Australia (CRIA). Since 1985, the CRIA has been contributing to knowledge about what makes documents work. Their studies suggest that plain language legal documents are not always superior to quasi-legal writing. CRIA researchers have been developing a set of principles that they believe will help writers produce legal texts that are more usable than those produced using plain language guidelines (Penman, 1990).

Plain Language in Canada. The plain language movement in Canada has been shaped largely by government action rather than by citizen activism. Started in the late 1980s, the movement took a big step forward in 1988 when a Plain Language Centre was established in Toronto by the Canadian Legal Information Centre (CLIC). It received initial funding from legal, corporate, and consumer groups and has been self-sustaining since 1991.[24] A report by Dykstra characterizes the Centre's mission as creating awareness about the movement and providing tools, training, and research needed to adopt the plain language approach (1991, p. 43).

[24] Reported in Kimble (1992, pp. 46–47).

The quality of legal documents has been a prominent catalyzing force behind plain language in Canada (for a discussion, see Jordan, 1994). In 1991, Saskatchewan became the first province to begin a government-wide program in clear language. In British Columbia the Plain Language Institute commissioned research on legal writing and sponsored a conference for legal experts (Coe, 1992). To date, plain language has been supported mainly by businesses involved in creating legal, financial, or insurance documents.

University and industry research labs have been at the forefront of Canadian work that goes beyond plain language to broader considerations of document design. For example, researchers at McGill University's Center for Cognitive Science have been tracking the process of producing technical documents collaboratively (Breuleux & Bracewell, 1994). Faculty from the department of English at the University of Waterloo in Ontario sponsored several international conferences on issues of quality in document design.[25] Cultural, rhetorical, and linguistic approaches to document design are under study by members of the Canadian Association of Teachers of Technical Writing (CATTW), a group that holds an annual conference and also publishes the informative journal *TechnoStyle*. And Bell Northern Research (now called Nortel) has made use of the findings of recent work in document design and has sponsored innovative research.

[25] Canadian conferences about document design issues continue to grow in number. Researchers and practitioners in computer documentation came to Ottawa in 1992 for the Association for Computing Machinery's Special Interest Group on Documentation (SIGDOC) Conference. Banff was the site for the 1994 Institute for Electronics and Electrical Engineers (IEEE) conference on Professional Communication.

Style 3: Extra leading between paragraphs, paragraphs indented, and ragged right.

◀ **Figure 5.43** *Three two-page spreads used to determine the paragraph style readers preferred for continuous body text. When given the choice among these paragraph styles, readers preferred Style 3, the one with extra vertical space (leading) between paragraphs, paragraphs indented, and ragged right.*

SUMMARY: DESIGNING THE TEXT WITH TYPE AND SPACE

In this chapter, I've explored a range of typographic and spatial options for designing documents that enable readers to see the text. Among the conclusions we can draw are the following:

- Readers are influenced by typographic cues. They respond to differences among typefaces and are especially sensitive to contrast among typographic elements. Typography helps to create the mood, look, and feel of a document.

- The time that document designers spend considering the interactions among x-height, point size, line length, and use of leading is time well spent. When these features are well orchestrated, documents can be both easy to read and aesthetically pleasing. Legibility is a serious issue, especially when people are reading online.

- The typography that readers prefer depends on what they are reading. The reader's purpose as well as the document's genre may significantly influence the reader's expectations for typographic cueing.

- In selecting a set of typefaces for everyday purposes, three criteria need to be considered: flexibility, contrast, and distinctiveness. Choosing typography is a rhetorical decision. Document designers must consider the context in which people will read the type and their reasons for engaging with the content.

- The design of a document can influence a person's perception of the design of products and services. Good document design plays a positive role in how people think and feel about products and services.

- By applying Gestalt principles of visual perception, document designers can better structure spatial cues to help people navigate and use complex documents. Changes in the visual organization of a document can lead to changes in how people perceive its content.

- Spatial cues such the size, position, and value of the major graphic elements must be carefully integrated. Document designers may employ symmetric or asymmetric layouts. In using either way of organizing a design, the important goal to strive for is visual balance. Keep in mind that a symmetrical layout can be balanced along a vertical axis or a diagonal axis. Above all, any principle of organization, symmetrical or asymmetrical, must reinforce the rhetorical aims of the text.

- Modular grids can be useful tools for integrating horizontal and vertical spatial cues in documents. Taking the time to develop a grid that suits the content can have a dramatic influence on how the content will speak to people—on how they interpret the structure and on what they perceive as important. Grids can help document designers meet their rhetorical goals for the reader by unifying the visual field and articulating the structure of the content.

The evidence that I have reviewed in this chapter makes it clear that there are very strong interactions between the visual and verbal features of documents. To be sensitive to the needs of readers, document designers should make use of what we now know about visual and verbal rhetoric and about how the two are intimately related.

upon the environment in which it is used. Where you place the base phone determines the sound quality of the cordless phone. The following guidelines and illustration will help you have interference-free phone conversations.

Away from noise sources such as a window by a street with heavy traffic.

your radio
uld have the
on.

Away from heat sources, such as radiators, airducts, and sunlight.

Away from a microwave oven.

Away from excessive moisture, dust, mechanical vibration, or shock.

Away from a personal computer.

6

The Interplay of Words and Pictures

In this chapter, I explore how words and pictures work together. There are four sections. ✦ Section 1 raises issues about the interpretation of words and pictures by highlighting cognitive, social, and cultural dimensions of constructing meaning. ✦ Section 2 presents studies of people searching documents and shows how words and pictures influence what they do. The first study reveals patterns of search for solving computing problems. The second examines the unnerving sense of fragmentation people may experience as they try to put together the "big picture" of World Wide Web sites. ✦ Section 3 characterizes five ways that words and pictures may interact and offers examples of each. ✦ Section 4 analyzes the ways in which readers' values may come into play as they interpret prose and graphics—reminding us that a picture is only sometimes worth a thousand words. ✦ Taken together, Chapter 6 provides a window on the very difficult problem of integrating words and pictures in order to help readers meet their goals.

Left-hand page. *An enlargement of an illustration for an instruction guide for a cordless telephone system. The drawing shows the best locations in the house for placing the telephone system so that they can avoid interference while using the cordless phone. The original drawing, on which this is based, is shown in Figure 7.10 (p. 468). Drawing by Carlos Peterson for Karen Schriver Associates, Inc.*

Most experienced document designers have developed their expertise primarily in writing or design, but rarely in both. Historically, writers and designers were viewed as different types of communicators—writers as "word" people and designers as "image" people. As we saw in Chapter 2, writers and graphic designers took very different academic and professional paths (see "Professional Development in Document Design," pp. 69–97, and *The Timeline,* pp. 106–149). However, in the 1980s and 1990s, changes in technologies and in the organization of the workplace had a dramatic influence on document design practice. The traditional separations between the activities of word and image people began to erode. Increasingly, both writers and designers were expected to create both words and pictures—to integrate the visual and the verbal, whether using print, video, or multimedia. Today's professional must be flexible enough to cross the disciplinary gulch between writing and design. Though individuals may still emphasize their talents with words or images, they must be able to solve complex communications problems by applying knowledge of both visual and verbal rhetoric.

Increasingly, professionals have voiced interest in knowing more about the interplay of prose and graphics. Although document designers have been looking for new ideas to inform their thinking, most of the available literature has been disappointing. Indeed, there is a worrisome trend to answer the field's questions about bringing together words and pictures by turning only to technology. The popular literature tends to focus on how technology can be used to combine prose and graphics instead of on how to choose the words and pictures that people need, want, or prefer. When document designers focus their energies on technological issues for organizing and displaying documents without first figuring out how the prose and graphics will be experienced by readers, they increase the likelihood of creating vibrantly colorful documents that are disjointed, hard to understand, and ugly. Compare the reviews of two similar CD-ROM products in Figure 6.1.

[1] Katherine and William Horton (1995) argue that when it comes to moving paper documents online, there should be "no dumping allowed."

The reviewer's negative comments about the second CD-ROM stem from problems created by simply "dumping online" every word and picture that was available (the whole compost heap) rather than trimming and pruning the content to suit the reader's interests.[1] Recent capabilities for integrating prose and graphics sometimes offer such a forest of digital possibilities that it is easy to forget that better technology doesn't equal better communication. Document designers need to resist what Johnson (1994) calls "romancing the hypertext." They need to step back from the glow of the screen and focus on how readers interact with documents; that is, on how people create meaning from the visual and verbal content.

◀ **Figure 6.1** *A screen from a CD-ROM about garden plants. Illustration reprinted from* The Garden Encyclopedia *with the permission of Books That Work. Article reprinted from* Newsweek, *May 22, 1995, p. 8 (used with permission).*

In this chapter, I hope to encourage document designers to move away from the dull vision of our field which says we are merely "information decorators" who specialize in using the latest technologies for making prose and graphics pretty—sprinkling documents with icons, clip art, and color. I contend that learning the latest technologies for assembling and displaying documents is not the most important thing for professionals to do.[2] Instead, I want to push the idea of document designers as *communications architects*. With more information about how people interpret words and pictures, document designers can be visionaries in the design of prose and graphics. To paraphrase Marcel Proust: The real voyage of discovery consists not in seeking new landscapes but in having new eyes.

Here, I explore the relationship between words and pictures, focusing on the often subtle interactions between readers and documents. This

[2] Thus, I won't talk about choosing authoring tools, scripting, SGML, HTML, WinHelp, RoboHelp, OS/2, single-sourced documents, Java, VRML, information reuse, or any of the soon-to-be-replaced technology-driven conceptions that pervade the field. Although technological considerations are no doubt important, they are not the most critical issues for document designers to spend time thinking about.

chapter has four major sections that explore the interplay between prose and graphics.

- *Section 1* explores how people construct meaning from prose and graphics—highlighting some of the cognitive, social, and cultural dimensions of interpretation.

- *Section 2* examines the issue of searching for information in documents. It points to problems that poor writing and design can create for readers as they attempt to find what they need. To portray these issues, I present two cases. The first shows some typical ways in which people look for information as they try to solve computing problems, particularly when they have available to them a variety of information sources from which to choose. The second examines the disconcerting sense of fragmentation that people may experience as they try to put together the words and pictures when searching World Wide Web sites.

- *Section 3* describes how prose and graphics may interact in documents and presents five ways to integrate words and pictures for various purposes. This discussion shows us that in order for document designers to achieve their rhetorical goals for readers, they must be deliberate in how they bring together words and pictures, anticipating the particular kind of relationship prose and graphics should have with one another.

- *Section 4* evaluates the ways in which readers' values and beliefs interact as they interpret prose and graphics. It presents a case study which shows that readers' values and beliefs may influence their interpretation as much if not more than their ability to understand the text. It underscores how document designers must anticipate the range of readers' possible engagements with prose and graphics.

These four sections are designed to help document designers make more deliberate decisions as they bring together prose and graphics for readers.

SECTION 1
FREEDOM AND CONSTRAINT IN READING

To understand reading, we must recognize and deal with an apparent paradox: Reading is a social act in that it depends on a community that shares meanings; yet it is also an individual act in that it depends critically on the reader's unique knowledge, attitudes, and values. This paradox is captured eloquently by Louise Rosenblatt (1978):

> Part of the magic—and indeed the essence—of language is the fact that it must be internalized by each individual human being, with all the special overtones that each

unique person and unique situation entail. Hence language
is at once basically social and intensely individual. (p. 20)

More recently, Steve Witte (1992) put it this way: "meaning-making
can be represented at a fundamental level as an interplay between self and
other" (p. 281). The shared aspects of language are dramatically reflected
in language communities: the French, the Japanese, the Navajo. Within
each language community, individuals share an incredible variety of
connections between signs and meanings. According to Benjamin Lee
Whorf, the early twentieth-century linguist, these communal connections
reflect a shared world view. He put it this way:

> We dissect nature along lines laid down by our native
> languages.... We cut nature up, organize it into concepts,
> and ascribe significances as we do, largely because we are
> parties to an agreement to organize it in this way—an
> agreement that holds through our speech community and is
> codified in the patterns of our language. (1956, pp. 213–214)

But the enormous amount of commonality within a language community does not negate the importance of the differences among individuals.
Each reader brings a lifetime of unique experience to documents—
experience which comes into play each time he or she interprets visual or
verbal language. As shown in Chapters 3 and 4, experience plays a role in
how people approach documents, in whether they read them, and in how
they may think about themselves as readers and comprehenders. We saw
in the drug education study that readers may make radically different
interpretations of the same text because of differences in their experience.

The literature on reading suggests that it is important to consider both
the individual differences among readers and the shared ways that people
experience documents. Rather than focusing on[3] the often unpredictable
ways that readers may engage with prose and graphics—a major preoccupation in some academic circles these days—document designers need to

---

[3] Over the past few years, a lively debate has ensued in the document design community about
the ways in which readers construct meaning from documents. Some have focused on the
impossibility of shared meaning among readers—celebrating misreading as part of a political
argument about diversity and difference. Others have also recognized the inherent ambiguity in
language, but approach the issue of what to do rather differently. They argue that although
there is no "rhetoric of neutrality" for document designers (Kinross, 1989), we can still
articulate a vision of design which focuses on "the social, common world, and on the
possibility of shared meanings" among readers (Kinross, July 13, 1995, email post to the
InfoDesign Forum). In this book, although I point to the diverse ways that readers experience
texts, I do so with the intent of making readers' shared ways of constructing meaning more
apparent. (To get involved in such discussions, subscribe to the InfoDesign Forum; send email
to majordomo@fwi.uva.nl and in the body of your message type: subscribe InfoDesign.)

ask how the design of prose and graphics can contribute to the possibility of shared meanings. But there is a further complication. Reading is a situated activity. It is influenced by the contexts in which it occurs (Seely Brown, Collins, & Duguid, 1989). For example, a set of instructions for operating a device (e.g., a copier or a vacuum cleaner) may be hard to understand if the device is absent but perfectly clear if it is present (Suchman, 1987). A satisfactory account of reading must characterize those aspects of reading that are shaped by (1) the text; (2) the reader's unique knowledge, attitudes, and values; and (3) the reader's context.

Just how can document designers get a better understanding of this basically social and intensely individual process called interpretation? One of the best ways is to be alert for opportunities to learn about how people understand and interpret prose and graphics—to see firsthand what helps and what hurts.

In 1936, I. A. Richards argued that "rhetoric should be a study of misunderstanding and its remedies" (p. 3). As part of modern rhetoric, document design must take up the challenge of studying how readers of documents come to understand or misunderstand them.[4] This implies two things. First, it means that we must learn more about how understanding is influenced by knowledge, experience, or values. Second, it means that we must learn more about how the design of prose and graphics can enable or disable readers as they attempt to construct meaning from documents.

Fortunately, document designers don't have to do this entirely on their own. There is a considerable body of theory and research that summarizes more than a century of observations about what people do as they engage with prose and graphics. These observations are drawn from a variety of disciplines that study how people construct meaning from language—disciplines such as rhetoric, psychology, reading, semiotics, linguistics, discourse analysis, and artificial intelligence. Although these disciplines neither share assumptions about what communication is nor about how it should be studied, taken together they offer very useful ideas about what is going on during interpretation. In the next section, I distill some of this literature to offer a sketch of what interpreting prose and graphics requires of readers.

[4] This chapter is dedicated to Richard Leo Enos, a classical rhetorician and Professor of Rhetoric at Texas Christian University, who introduced me to rhetoric and who encouraged me to continue in its study. Thanks, Rich.

THE PROCESS OF INTERPRETATION:
THE ULTIMATE WORKOUT

To understand what happens during the interpretation of documents, we must consider how people read—a complex knowledge-driven and text-driven process. By *knowledge-driven*, I mean what the reader brings to bear during interpretation—knowledge, experience, feelings, social awareness, and culture. By *text-driven,* I suggest the reader's interaction with visual or verbal signs. The first kind of process has been called "top-down" and the second "bottom-up" by cognitive psychologists and members of the artificial intelligence community.

A key idea of recent work is that the reader arrives at an interpretation of a text on the basis of evidence from interacting multiple cues.[5] Some of these are text-driven (or bottom-up) cues that come from the prose or graphics—word meanings, sentence structures, pronoun references, pictures, diagrams, charts, graphs, and so on. Others are knowledge-driven (or top-down) cues that come from the reader's experience, attitudes, and beliefs. Readers use everything in the perceptual field to make their judgments about words and pictures under consideration. They draw on their beliefs about the author's intention, their knowledge of the topic, their representation of the text so far (Hayes, 1989a), their memories of other texts of the same genre or other texts on similar topics (visual or verbal), and their recollection of other textual experiences (such as video, music, or face-to-face interactions). All of these act as *resources for interpretation* (Moll & Greenberg, 1993; Witte, 1992). With these cues, the reader is able to resolve ambiguities at the lexical, grammatical, and semantic levels, to fill in missing information, and to reduce the cognitive load required for comprehension. In short, multiple cues allow readers to make quick decisions on-the-fly about what is going on.

When readers use the cues that are available to them, they don't arrive at "The meaning" but rather at a best guess for a meaning appropriate to the situation. These judgments apply to many aspects of the interpretation, from identifying signs and symbols to making estimates of the author's probable intent. Which cues readers rely on and how deeply they attend to the text depend on situational variables such as the readers' moods and interests as well as the cultural, social, physical, and technological setting. As people build a representation of what the text means, they derive their ideas from a *"dynamically changing knowledge state ... [which] ... can vary*

---

[5] Interactive theories of interpretation began in 1977 with Rumelhart's landmark paper, "Toward an Interactive Model of Reading." Bottom-up theories such as those of Gough (1972) or LaBerge and Samuels (1974) formalized the idea that reading comprehension begins with the perception of print and ends with the construction of a representation of meaning. According to Danks and Hill (1981), the difficulty with bottom-up theories is that they fail to account for the fact that readers and listeners can frequently anticipate parts of a linguistic message before bottom-up processing is completed. As evidence, researchers point to the ways that people compensate for poorly written text during reading. For example, skilled readers can generate an intended meaning for a text even if it is riddled with typographical errors or ambiguities in sentence construction.

depending on the particular text, the reader's knowledge about the topic, the reader's enduring interests, and the reader's momentary reading goals" [italics added] (Just & Carpenter, 1987, p. 21). Rumelhart and McClelland (1981) describe it this way:

> Roughly speaking, processing in an interactive model of reading proceeds in the following way: The reader begins with a set of expectations about what information is likely to be available.... These expectations, or initial hypotheses, are based on our knowledge of the structure of letters, words, phrases, sentences, and larger pieces of discourse, including nonlinguistic aspects of the current contextual situation. As visual information from the page begins to become available, it strengthens those hypotheses that are consistent with the input and weakens those that are inconsistent. The stronger hypotheses, in turn, make even more specific predictions about the information available. (p. 37)

Much of the research on how people read unfamiliar material, that is, stuff they've never seen before, shows that they sometimes rely more on the text to figure out the meaning (Danks & Hill, 1981) and at other times rely more on their own knowledge (Perfetti & Roth, 1981).

So what does all this mean for document designers? By implication, we need to make textual moves in our documents that will help readers with both their knowledge-driven and text-driven constructions of the text and graphics. On one hand, most books about professional writing have suggested that the reader's understanding of the sentences is the main thing to worry about. On the other, books about visual design have tended to concentrate on the relationships among design elements from the designer's point of view. Both traditional foci fail to emphasize the reader's knowledge, attitudes, values, and culture as potent resources for interpretation. Writers should not abandon their attention to style and linguistic precision. Similarly, graphic designers need not give up their interest in form and visual tension. But both writers and designers need to widen the focus of their lens in order to learn more about how people actually interact with graphics and typography.

The theory and research that has been developing in rhetoric and the psychology of reading can help us understand the reader's world. As Waller[6] puts it, "theory and research gives us evidence to back up our ideas when faced with the situation of a client who doubts our judgment." Perhaps more importantly, it can help us to correct the faulty assumptions we might have about what readers are doing with our texts and why.

[6] Robert Waller's comment was posted on the InfoDesign List Serve Bulletin Board on May 12, 1995.

The Immediacy of Interpretation:
Constructing Representations through Syntax and Semantics

Just and Carpenter (1980) posit that people deal with the sequential nature of language (particularly of prose) by trying to interpret each successive word of a text as soon as they encounter it, integrating the new information they have gleaned with what they already know about the text and its subject matter. Although there is often no fixed sequence in which to examine graphics, readers try to form an immediate representation of the meaning of visual displays as well (Larkin & Simon, 1987). Just and Carpenter (1987) refer to people's tendency to make rapid judgments about the meaning of the text as the *immediacy of interpretation* (p. 16). This interpretative strategy lies in marked contrast to the *wait-and-see* strategy proposed by others (see Kimball, 1973; Marcus, 1980), in which readers postpone interpreting the meaning of a sentence (or a nonlinguistic symbol) until they have read a sentence (or graphic) that follows it or that is positioned in spatial relation to it. In other words, readers wait-and-see so they can use the full textual context to make their interpretation.

Just and Carpenter (1987) argue that "the evidence is overwhelming that readers don't wait-and-see unless they have to" (p. 16). Instead, they rely on everything in their perceptual field—the syntax and semantics of the prose and graphics—to construct an idea of the meaning as quickly as possible. Readers still take advantage of the textual context to constrain the meaning, but they do so by elaborating or amending an interpretation "already under construction" rather than waiting for sufficient context before interpretation begins in earnest.

In fact, interpretation typically happens so fast that readers are unaware of the complex processes that are involved. Readers may become aware of these processes only when something goes wrong. Consider, for example, the following "garden path" sentence: "Having stuffed himself at dinner, the taxidermist became a monument to his own art." It is only at the end of the sentence that readers become aware that they made a choice in interpreting the word "stuffed" and that it doesn't fit with the rest of the sentence. (See Daneman & Carpenter, 1983, for a discussion). We can even imagine "garden path" visuals. For example, look back at Figure 5.31 in the previous chapter (p. 320). Whether we start reading the figure from the top or the bottom, the interpretation we make at first doesn't fit with the rest of what we see.

Americans visiting China or Japan quickly realize how culturally constrained interpretation is and how difficult it is to assign appropriate meanings to signs without cultural knowledge. Conversely, when Americans read texts in English that have been composed by nonnative English speakers, they may interpret more meanings than the speaker intends. In fact, the linguistic and nonlinguistic cues that native speakers of English (or any language) interpret "without thinking" draw on sophisticated knowledge of their language and their culture. To illustrate this point, Figure 6.2 presents the lighter side of cross-cultural miscommunication. Most of these examples are one-sentence procedural instructions. Yet even the act of interpreting these simple sentences calls on readers to draw upon their cultural and linguistic knowledge in order to figure out what is going on. These sentences were found in hotels around the world and were aimed, we must presume, at English-speaking tourists.

Let's look at one of these examples in Figure 6.2: sentence 9. The reader who makes sense of the sign posted above the door of a shop in Hong Kong must do much more than recognize five words:

> Ladies have fits on second.

In addition to finding word meanings and discerning grammatical relations, the reader must recognize that the following is true:

- There is more than one meaning for the word "fits." In order to appreciate the intended significance of the sign, the reader uses linguistic and cultural knowledge to disambiguate its possible meanings within the context. (Readers are usually not aware of multiple meanings even though they are frequent.)
- The writer is *not* aware of the multiple meanings. Readers who interpret this sign as funny (i.e., who chuckle at the idea of a group of ladies on the second floor throwing fits) recognize that the writer doesn't see the alternative interpretations one could construct.

Sophisticated inferences such as these are made between the time reading begins and the time the reader "gets the joke." This simple example, modeled on work by reading researcher Philip Gough (1984), shows that even the reading of mundane street signs can call on people to perform complex feats of interpretation. To be sure, what readers do in interpreting sentences such as those in Figure 6.2 accounts for only some of the mental gymnastics that individuals must engage in when they make sense of complex documents.

What can document designers learn from this example? One thing is that when we design prose or graphics, we always bring a frame of reference with us, a frame that may not be shared by our readers and that

1. In a Tokyo hotel: It is forbidden to steal hotel towels please. If you are not person to do such thing please not read notis.

2. In a Bucharest hotel lobby: The lift is being fixed for the next day. During that a time we regret that you will be unbearable.

3. In a Belgrade hotel elevator: To move the cabin, push button for wishing floor. If the cabin should enter more persons, each one should press a number of wishing floor. Driving is then going alphabetically by national order.

4. In a Paris hotel elevator: Please leave your values at the front desk.

5. In a hotel in Athens: Visitors are expected to complain at the office between the hours of 9 and 11 A.M. daily.

6. In a Yugoslavian hotel: The flattening of underwear with pleasure is the job of the chambermaid.

7. In an Austrian hotel catering to skiers: Not to perambulate the corridors in the hours of repose in the boots of ascension.

8. On the menu of a Swiss restaurant: Our wines leave you nothing to hope for.

9. Outside a Hong Kong tailor shop: Ladies have fits on second.

10. In a Rhodes tailor shop: Order your summers suit. Because is big rush we will execute customers in strict rotation.

11. In an East African newspaper: A new swimming pool is rapidly taking shape since the contractors have thrown in the bulk of their workers.

12. A sign posted in Germany's black forest: It is strictly forbidden on our black forest camping site that people of different sex, for instance, men and women, live together in one tent unless they are married together for this purpose.

13. In a Rome laundry: Ladies, leave your clothes here and spend the afternoon having a good time.

14. Advertisement for donkey rides in Thailand: Would you like to ride on your own ass.

15. On the box of a clockwork toy made in Hong Kong: Guaranteed to work throughout its useful life.

16. In a Bangkok temple: It is forbidden to enter a woman even a foreigner if dressed as a man.

17. In a Vienna hotel: In case of fire, do your utmost to alarm the hotel porter.

◀ **Figure 6.2** *The lighter side of cross-cultural miscommunication. Source: Anonymous (widely circulated on the Internet and broadcast on National Public Radio in 1995).*

we ourselves may not perceive. Our frame of reference comes from various sources which interact during document design, including:

- Personal knowledge, beliefs, attitudes, and values
- Cultural knowledge about how signs (visual or verbal) typically work, both in particular contexts and among various groups of people
- Knowledge about writing and design
- Knowledge of the topic about which we are writing or visualizing
- Knowledge of our organization/client and its goals for the content
- Textual and graphic knowledge of documents that may be similar in genre or content
- Knowledge of the capabilities and limitations of technology

Paradoxically, each of these can be a source of strength or weakness in document designers' efforts to communicate effectively. When we fail to take the reader's frame of reference into account, we may, like the writers of the sentences in Figure 6.2, inadvertently invite alternative constructions of the text that we don't intend. But unlike the writers in Figure 6.2—whose prose comes off as funny—document designers who misunderstand the audience and their frames of reference can create documents that evoke confusion, and in some cases even anger.

Making Sense of Graphics Requires Knowledge

Larkin and Simon (1987) show that the *sequence in which people read* a prose text or a graphic makes a difference in how quickly they can form a representation of the content and what kind of representation they form. With prose, there are more constraints on the order of reading than there are with graphics. People engage with prose linearly, one word at a time, in sequences that make clauses, sentences, and so on. Depending on one's culture, prose asks us to read left to right, top to bottom, right to left, or boustrophedon—right to left, and then left to right.

Compared to prose, most graphics place many fewer constraints on how people read them, allowing knowledgeable searchers to go straight to the content they want or need. If the reader knows what he or she may be looking for, it can be quicker to search a graphic than prose because prose requires a sequential search. Conversely, if readers are not knowledgeable searchers, complex graphics (particularly instructional, quantitative, and scientific) may pose significant problems for them, for they call on a different way of reading that has few ground rules about when to look at what (Kosslyn, 1994; Winn, 1991). In these cases, readers may need help in the form of supplementary prose or even a supplementary graphic to guide them in their interpretation of the primary graphic. For example, Hegarty, Carpenter, and Just (1991), who studied people reading technical diagrams of a pulley system, found that readers with low-mechanical ability had serious troubles in making heads or tails of the diagrams. By contrast, high-mechanical ability readers could go straight to the key parts of the diagram, and in fact could even build a useful representation of the text when the prose that went with the diagram was presented in a scrambled order. Hegarty and her colleagues conclude that even though graphics may have few inherent sequential constraints on their processing, that does not mean that they are necessarily easy to understand (p. 650).

Some Problems in Designing Instructional Graphics that Must Bridge Cultural Boundaries

Research in cross-cultural document design supports both the idea that graphics are not always obvious and that the order in which people read matters. Zimmerman and Perkin (1982), for example, provided a fascinating case study that bears on these issues. They described an effort to develop a range of paper-based educational materials for poor people in Bangladesh, Botswana, and Guatemala. They found that efforts to design instructions using a combination of words and pictures for audiences in third-world countries often meet with failure because these materials depend on the audience being able to read the words (in 1982, when they conducted their study, 75 percent of the men in Bangladesh could not read or write, and, although it is not reported, probably a higher percentage of women). In the past, these audiences were "written off." Organizations did not want to waste limited resources on brochures and pamphlets for a population who could not read. To address this issue, Zimmerman and Perkin developed culturally appropriate pictorial materials for nonreaders by involving them directly in the design process.

By using feedback-driven audience analysis (discussed in Chapter 3), Zimmerman and Perkin gained insight into the knowledge, beliefs, and concerns of their audience and used what they learned to select symbols that were meaningful for their intended audiences. In particular, they created documents designed to help people who could not read understand topics such as nutrition, farming, family planning, or controlling mosquitoes through a "pictures-only" document design strategy. They provide convincing evidence that visual messages need to be revised depending on the local culture. Here is an example of what they found:

In Mexico, Bangladesh, and the Philippines, one of the symbols developed, tested, and retested was the symbol for menstruation. In Mexico it was found that women associated a roll of cotton with menstruation; a Kotex [brand of sanitary napkins] box was originally tested, but it proved to be a satisfactory symbol only among urban women. In the Philippines, a red dot on the front of a woman's dress was tested as the symbol for menstruation.... Although the red dot on the dress was deemed distasteful by population program managers, it was the symbol clearly understood by rural semiliterate women, the target audience. In Bangladesh, the most widely recognized symbol for menstruation was a red spot at the back of a woman's sari. (p. 122)

The work of Zimmerman and Perkin identified two problems in creating pictorial instructions that must cross cultural boundaries:

- *First,* document designers must visualize familiar objects and symbols that make direct contact with the specific local culture, requiring detailed study of the culture prior to designing the visuals.[7] They found, for instance, that when designers pictured a tractor in a brochure about farming for readers who used hand plows or bullocks, the visual both detracted from the intended message and confused the reader. Moreover, they found that their assumptions about the best graphics for a particular country always needed to be tested and refined.[8]

- *Second,* a key hurdle lies in choosing the best sequence for instructional pictures so that the reader builds a complete and coherent understanding of the message. The sequence is crucial because the order in which people interpret visual instructions shapes their understanding. They found that to constrain readers' interpretations of instructional graphics, document designers must guide readers' visual inspections of the document through the use of space, size, position, proximity, and clarity of image (I discussed these issues in Chapter 5; see also Meggs, 1992a).

Zimmerman and Perkin approached learning about the order in which people read visual instructions by using what they called the *picture-ordering*

[7] This point has been made again and again by authors concerned with designing messages for international audiences; for example, see Axtel (1990), Horton (1994), or Jones, Kennelly, Sweezy, Thomas, and Velez (1992).

---

[8] Using focus groups, interviews, and comprehension tests, Zimmerman and Perkin (1982) assessed their instructional documents with villagers in rural and remote areas of Bangladesh and other developing countries. This allowed them to redesign based on feedback from the audience. They found some messages required as many as six revisions before their message was clear. Their iterative process sometimes led them to design one document, while at other times two final versions were created, one with pictures only and another with pictures and minimal print using the local language and village vocabulary (p. 121). However, in the versions using print as a supplement to the pictures, the pictures still had to stand alone for members of the audience who could not read the words. This was truly a hard document design task.

procedure. They first illustrated each procedure separately. Then they asked readers to put the individual pictures into a sequence that seemed most logical to them and describe what the flow of the pictures meant. Zimmerman and Perkin found the picture-ordering procedure useful as a prototyping device to see what audiences already know about a topic (or what misconceptions they may have) before the document is designed.[9] The procedure can also be employed to evaluate the quality of the final document by assessing whether readers can remember the correct order of the pictures after they've read the document. Moreover, this research suggests that in evaluating graphics, it is essential to explore their appropriateness in relation to the readers' knowledge and cultural context.

SECTION 2
SEARCHING PROSE AND GRAPHICS ON PAPER OR ONLINE

Research on reading suggests that the effective navigation of complex documents is a learned skill, whether the documents are primarily verbal or primarily visual.[10] We learn to understand the structure of complex documents by relying on familiar visual and verbal features. Through practice in using a particular genre of document, we learn the *conventions* of that genre and of the media in which that genre is usually presented. Let's take a familiar example: reading the newspaper. Ask yourself for a moment, how do you decide which parts of the text to read and in what order to read them?

If you are like most practiced newspaper readers, you have honed a navigation strategy that suits your interests and motivations for getting news. Some of us start with the sports section and move to the business section; others begin with the horoscopes and move to the comics. Still others focus only on the national and international news, paying most attention to page-one stories. During a television program[11] about the role of media in structuring public opinion, a reporter asked top magazine editors from around the United States to share their thoughts on how they read newspapers (all of them read several every day). Interestingly, one said, "I always start with the *Washington Post* Op-Ed page, then I read page one, then I read the *New York Times* Op-Ed page and go from there." Another, Hendrick Hertzberg, editor for the *New Yorker*, explained:

> Before I even look at other newspapers, I pay attention to the front page of the *New York Times*. Not only do I look at what is on that page, but the relative position of one story to another. After all, the structure of the front page is the ontology of what newsmakers think is important,

[9] The picture-ordering procedure provides some of the same benefits as the Wizard-of-Oz procedure used in prototyping the design of computer interfaces (Brennan, 1990; Thomas, 1976; Vertelney & Booker, 1990). In the Wizard-of-Oz procedure, the user's keyboard input is intercepted by an experimenter, who sits "Oz-like behind the curtain" of the computer, where he or she simulates the system's responses. This allows designers to mock up what people will see on a computer screen (e.g., menus, words, pictures, icons, buttons, and so on), allowing users to try out ideas before limited financial resources are spent on ideas that don't work. By prototyping, document designers can learn (before incurring major costs) what people like and don't like about a design.

[10] See, for example, Guthrie and Dreher (1990), Guthrie, Weber, and Kimmerly (1993), or Leinhardt, Zaslavsky, and Stein (1990).

[11] The television program, called *The Editors*, aired on the Cable Satellite Public Affairs Network (C-SPAN) on Jan. 9, 1995.

the Zeitgeist of the day. Then I read the rest with this frame in mind.

For these expert newspaper readers, the visual structure of the text, the position of one story in relation to another, the amount of space devoted to one story or another, all provide rhetorical clues about what the editor of the newspaper thinks is important. These clues suggest not only what to read but also how to navigate the content. Even highly skilled newspaper readers admit, however, that the design of most newspapers may make it hard to figure out what the editor had in mind. In Figure 6.3, I present former newspaper editor Max Frankel's account of just what a chore it can be to read the newspaper according to the way most editors design it.

As Frankel points out, the practice of making readers "jump" to somewhere inside the newspaper by following the annoying "continued on page 12" may make some people "quit rather than leap." Unfortunately, this inconsiderate rhetorical convention (i.e., "continued on page 4") has also been adopted by designers of newsletters. Frankel's recommendation to reinvoke the old convention called the "refer"—in which a sentence, caption, or short paragraph refers the reader to an elaboration elsewhere in the paper—would be a welcome reader-centered renovation to newspaper and newsletter design. In effect, the refer acts as an executive summary and supports readers in making navigation easier, allowing them to avoid the jumping-pages syndrome.

This example helps to make clear that readers learn to navigate complex documents by learning the rhetorical conventions of genres (whether they like the design or not). However, not all textual conventions used in the design of documents are obvious; some must be learned. When readers don't know the conventions, they may experience troubles. For instance, Leinhardt, Zaslavsky, and Stein (1990) review a number of studies which show that in order to make reasonable interpretations of quantitative graphics, readers need to know which graphic conventions to pay attention to. In interpreting line graphs, for example, readers must evaluate global features such as the general shape of the graph (e.g., increases, decreases, or dramatic changes in slope or direction). They must also assess the local features, such as the use of scales, units of measure, lines in relation to one another, or lines in relation to the axes. Readers who don't know the graphic conventions may not only miss the main point but also feel less competent in their ability to evaluate data-based claims made through graphic displays more generally.

There are many accounts in the research literature that suggest that interpreting the rhetorical conventions of prose and graphics is a learned skill. For example, Dobrin (1994) recounts an anecdote of teaching adults

Jumpers vs. Refers by Max Frankel

Sometimes, as a former editor, I read the front pages of The Times—or The Washington Post or the Los Angeles Times—the way editors have designed them to be read. Quite an exercise.

I begin at the top right corner, the now-conventional (though hardly logical) place where the editors of large-size papers display their choice of the most important article of the day, called the "lead" but spelled "lede." After reading the page 1 portion of the lede, I move to the left-most column to read the off-lede, or second most important article, and then similarly work my way through the opening paragraphs of the other articles at the top of the page, those "at the fold" and finally those at the bottom.

En route, I may be interrupted or distracted by assorted pictures, word boxes, or charts. But assuming that I reach the bar code at the bottom by the intended route, I would then, as on a recent Thursday with The New York Times, have to plunge inside the paper with the following half-thoughts like these somehow embedded in my mind:

> In the past the Clinton Administration had declined to put strong pressure on the Bosnian Government, citing the suffering of Muslim civilians at the hands of the
>
> ———————
>
> *Continued* on Page A10, Column 1

> The degree to which American youth encounter peril at the hands of other American youths is reflected in 1992 Justice Department Statistics: 55 percent of all
>
> ———————
>
> *Continued* on Page B14, Column 1

Newspaper layout requires that I carry this baggage of six, seven or eight articles interrupted in midsentence or midword until, here and there, I encounter the continuation of each one. I will not, of course, encounter them in the order in which I left them; they were arrayed on page 1 in their presumed order of importance, but their continuations are neatly arrayed inside with articles on related subjects—starting with the international news, then national, metropolitan and so on.

Because The Times is by no means unique in its devotion to this bizarre design, a nasty choice awaits tens of millions of readers. They can:

(a) Read the front-page articles only to the point of interruption and just forget about the rest;

(b) Select one, perhaps two, front-page articles whose continuations they will immediately seek out, as directed, skipping the other front-page news and leaping over a good deal of the news inside;

(c) Not read the front page at once in its entirety but rather pursue the continuation of each article as directed, repeatedly returning to page 1 to pick up the next;

(d) Take page 1 and renew acquaintance with the topless bottom of each article wherever they find it, vaguely recalling where they left off or occasionally peeking back at page 1 to pick up the thread. Or simply abandon the interrupted passage and press shakily forward.

Small wonder, given the perversity of this routine, that there is no good English word to describe the process of continuations and, as far as I can determine, no good history of how it came to be. In the jargon of journalism, the interrupted articles are said, accurately enough, to "jump" to an inside page and the second portion of the article is widely called "the jump"…

….Experience, anecdote and surveys persuaded me some time ago that readers are annoyed by the jumping and that perhaps half never bother to follow the front-page article inside; they'd rather quit than leap…. [T]here exists a device that would perfectly preserve the traditional appearance of any paper's front page while eliminating the barbaric ripping in two of every day's most important reports.

The device at hand is a summary and signpost of a longer article, which we call a "reefer" but spell "refer" since it is a sentence, caption, or short article "referring" the reader to some kind of elaboration elsewhere in the paper.

As soon as tomorrow morning, with hardly a change in their appearances, The Timeses of New York or Los Angeles or The Washington Post or The Philadelphia Inquirer could produce front pages of "refers"—meaning concise and well-written summaries that resemble, and occupy the same space as the top of the now interrupted articles. But instead of screeching to an awkward halt in midsentence, the refers would end coherently and then advise the reader to see a "Detailed Account on Page 13."

USA Today often uses this device…. the same reporter writes and signs both the page 1 summary and the detailed acount inside.

…. The reader who is content with a summary of any matter would obtain a coherent one; the reader who wants a fuller account would be directed inside, as always. The reader stumbling upon a dispatch inside would no longer find it is topless. And newspapers would run a better race against more fluid media if, replacing jumpers with refers, they finally call off the annoying morning calisthentics.

▲ **Figure 6.3** *An excerpt from an article published in the* New York Times Magazine, *Dec. 11, 1994 (used with permission). (Newspaper names were not italicized in original.)*

with low literacy skills how to read newspapers and magazines. He reports that because these readers didn't know the rhetorical conventions of these genres, they had "difficulty distinguishing between advertisements and articles in magazines and they had trouble figuring out the relationship between a sidebar, an italicized introduction, and the text of an article" (p. 306). We can imagine that any reader, experienced or not, may encounter some disorientation when navigating a complex new genre for the first time.

However, we can also imagine that when documents are designed to intentionally erase the differences among the rhetorical conventions that typically distinguish one genre from the next, even the best of readers might be fooled. Indeed, an old typographic trick in newspapers is to use the same typeface for stories and ads.[12] The idea was to deliberately blur the genres of narrative and sales, enabling ads to gain the authority of fact-based stories. Unfortunately, this practice still is alive and well in tabloids, in infomercials on television, and even in respected newspapers such as the *New York Times*. Frankel (1996) calls these gimmicks *advertorials,* magazine ads that masquerade as editorial content.

12 For a pointer to this dubious practice of blending ads and fact-based stories, see *The Timeline* in Chapter 2, the first entry in the 1920s under the strand "Education and Practice in Graphic Design" (p. 110).

An advertorial that has run several times in the *Times* features promotional messages about New York hotels positioned next to a George Plimpton essay celebrating New York's cultural attractions. Plimpton's prose was at least plainly labeled "advertisement" and set in a distinctive typeface. Other publishers, especially those on the World Wide Web, have not been so careful. Indeed, they have been trying to lure children "with puzzles, prizes, and personal messages from the Nabisco Thing, the Colgate Tooth Wizard … or with KidsKash for redemption in the Loot Locker" as long as children report what brand of athletic shoes they wear (Frankel, 1996, p. 22). The growth of kidpitch on the Web is yet another new low for the advertising industry. Educators need to teach students how to ask questions of the content they read on the Web. More than ever, students need critical reading skills. More than ever, readers need honest document design.

Even without the use of such unscrupulous tactics, some of the problems people experience with paper-based genres may worsen when they read the same genre online. One of the prime candidates for disorientation in today's online compendium of information sources are those large bodies of linked texts and graphics called *hypertexts.* Although readers of paper-based newspapers may dislike hopping from the front of the paper to its middle, they have to acquiesce when they get to hypertexts, because its "links are made for jumping."

Jumping, Skipping, and Surfing: Helping Readers Navigate Complex Documents

Dobrin (1994) conjectures that teaching people to read hypertexts may amount to teaching them how to read the textual conventions of a new text form. He posits that if the conventions of hypertext are new, people need to be taught how to read them, just as conventions of magazine layout need to be taught. But as Charney (1994) astutely points out, it will be hard for teachers to instruct students in the conventions of hypertext if the conventions don't exist. Because the rhetorical conventions of hypertext are currently under construction (some would say destruction), we are experiencing a period in which we document designers are groping through the design space and inventing as we go. One characteristic of hypertext that is substantially different from paper is that "hypertext accepts as strengths those very qualities—the play of signs, intertextuality, the lack of closure—that deconstruction poses as the ultimate limitations of literature and language" (Bolter, 1991, p. 166).

With most genres, readers can rely on familiar cues provided by the document designer. By contrast, when reading hypertexts, "readers cannot avoid writing the text itself, since every choice they make is an act of writing" (Bolter, 1991, p. 144). In a sense, the roles of writer and reader blur, with readers' personal preferences guiding their path through the information structure. However, Pat Wright (1987b) cautions that not all people will reap the benefits of constructing their own text: "Increased freedom for readers to integrate information in their own preferred order may be beneficial, but only if readers are skillful in selecting their information order" (p. 46). That most people will generate good questions which will enable them to search productively for the information they need, select what to read from that pool of information, choose the best order in which to read it, and then put their own text together as a coherent story is an untested assumption of more than trivial importance. As Marvin Minsky (1995) predicts, "the traffic jam on the information highway will be right in front of our eyes and hands."

SEARCHING FOR INFORMATION: A CASE STUDY OF HOW PEOPLE SEARCH FOR ANSWERS TO COMPUTING PROBLEMS

When people look for information that will help them to fix a computing problem, they have a variety of options. They can try to figure it out on their own, ask another person for help, or consult a document, either online or hardcopy. As people make their choices, they often do so with at least a general idea of the costs and benefits of one information source over another. They know that some of the time when they look for information they won't find it and, if they do, they may not understand it.

The study I discuss next is about how people search for answers to computing problems when they have many information sources to choose from. It explores how search is influenced by factors such as the user's experience and the task being performed. Although the study was done over a decade ago with computer systems rather different from the ones in current use, it illustrates some very important principles about the information search process. I argue that in looking for information to solve computing problems, users' actions may depend not on any predisposition about the intrinsic goodness of one media over another (e.g., even users who prefer to use online documents may feel that hardcopy documents are better for some purposes). Rather, most people choose an information source based on their assessment of the situation at hand; they make their best guess about what kind of information may suit their task and what source in their immediate context might give them the best information most quickly.

A few years ago, my colleagues and I[13] observed a user community in an academic environment over a four-month period as they carried out their day-to-day work. There were more than 200 people in this community, most of whom were affiliated with the psychology department at Carnegie Mellon University—including students, faculty, postdocs, visiting researchers, secretaries, office managers, computing staff, engineers, operators, maintenance technicians, and technical gurus. The community had their own computing system, which networked together IBM PCs, high-end UNIX and Sun workstations, LISP machines, graphics terminals, and printers. It was also well-connected to other computing environments (e.g., to a distributed networked environment called Andrew and to a Digital Equipment Corporation TOPS-20 mainframe system) and to the Internet. Since it was a relatively small user community, it was possible to collect data from the full range of people who used the system—from novice users to system wizards.

We explored how people looked for information and the kinds of information sources they relied on. Among the questions we asked were the following:

- Where do people look for information when they need it?
- Are there systematic differences among user groups?
- How does the task individuals want to accomplish influence the way they seek information?
- Do people prefer to read documents presented on paper or online?

[13] My collaborators in this 1986 study were John R. Hayes, Carol Danley, Wendie Wulff, Karen Cerroni, Lisa Davies, Debra Graham, Edward Flood, Eric Bond, Robert Berkowitz, Thomas Duffy, John Legelis, and Kerim Nitku. We thank Janet Thomas of IBM (Endicott, NY) for inspiring us to conduct this study and Diane Langston for her expert advice about online help systems. This study has not been published previously; it had been classified as proprietary. Another output of this research was a 330-page review of the hardcopy and online literature that had been conducted up to 1986 (see Schriver et al., 1986).

To address these questions, we "roamed" offices and computing clusters to observe people as unobtrusively as possible as they did their work, attending to patterns of search and to the tasks people were trying to accomplish when they needed help. We also surveyed[14] the community about their attitudes and preferences for documents and their experience in using computers. In addition, with the permission of members of the user community, we conducted random system checks to learn which software applications people tended to work with most often and the kinds of online documents and help files they requested.[15] These multiple qualitative and quantitative data sources gave us complementary vantage points from which to identify the information sources the users accessed and their attitudes toward these sources.

Our onsite observations revealed that users had available quite a variety of formal and informal sources from which to acquire information—from asking a friend to sending email to an online user consultant to checking a hardcopy reference manual. The random system checks gave us a sense of the applications people used most frequently. The information about the applications people were using dovetailed with the onsite observations; together, these data provided a detailed picture of the routine tasks people carried out (in fact, we identified 21 typical tasks for users in this environment). We used this information to create the questions for our survey. We gave participants a list of the sources from which they might get information (e.g., online manuals, user consultants, hardcopy manuals) and a list of typical tasks that people often carried out in this research-oriented academic environment (e.g., use a wordprocessor to create a technical report, run a spreadsheet to calculate a budget, replace the toner in a laser printer). We asked participants to think back over their use of documentation over a four-month period to identify how they had searched for information (if they did) when they ran into a problem while performing any of 21 computing tasks; 13 were associated with software applications and 8 with hardware.

On the basis of the participants' responses to our survey questions about the frequency with which they used computers and their years of experience in doing so, we applied cluster analysis[16] and identified six distinct user groups. The main difference among these groups appeared to be their sophistication in using computers. The groups varied from

[14] Of the 200+ people with accounts on this computing system, 113 volunteered to participate in the survey; others agreed to be observed as long as we did not interfere with their work.

[15] Note that it is not possible to tell what task a person was doing with only information about their application. Thus, someone using a wordprocessor could also be working on ideas for creating a chart or graph. Furthermore, even if an application was running, it did not mean anyone was using it (we found users often left their desks, sometimes for hours, and left their software running and that many people ran batch jobs at night when the system load was lighter).

[16] Cluster analysis is a statistical method that allows one to examine the relationships among multiple variables at the same time. We employed it here to determine whether individuals in this computing environment were similar enough to fall into groups or clusters. We explored variables such as participants' computing experience, the kinds of applications they used, their background in programming (if at all), the types of publications they read (e.g., magazines about computers), and the like.

▶ Table 6.1 *How different groups of computer users estimated how frequently they solved computing problems by figuring it out on their own or by asking someone else. Users with little experience tend to ask someone else. As they gain experience, users tend to prefer solving problems on their own.*

The Relationship Between User Group and Tendency for Solving Computing Problems

Computing Experience	User Group	Solve Myself	Ask Someone Else for Help
Novice	1	10	43
	2	20	34
Intermediate	3	18	26
	4	21	25
Expert	5	28	24
Guru	6	38	13

Note. This table shows tendencies *only* for problems users tried to solve when they did not try online or hardcopy manuals. Values indicate responses in percentages for each user group; because rows exclude the use of documentation, they do not total 100% for each group (n = 113).

rank novices (Group 1) to computer gurus (Group 6). The first two columns of Table 6.1 show these different groups of computer users.

Participants' self-reports of their information searches as they tried to solve computing problems revealed several patterns. As summarized in Table 6.2, across all six user groups and all 21 tasks, participants tended to "ask another person" or "solve it on their own" 53 percent of the time. When they did use documentation, they relied on hardcopy about twice as often as online help. These findings are consistent with previous research (Kern, 1985; *PC Magazine,* 1988; Sticht, 1985).

Our analysis also showed that when users did not use any documentation, they either "figured it out on their own" or "asked someone else for help." Moreover, their choices about what to do depended on their user group. We found that users' preferences for information sources varied systematically across these six groups. As shown in Table 6.1 (see columns 3 and 4), the more sophisticated groups preferred to solve computing problems on their own, while the less sophisticated were more likely to rely on another person. In addition, the more sophisticated groups were more likely to use online and hardcopy documentation than the less sophisticated users (not shown in the table).

In interviews, many people mentioned hating to read hardcopy documents that had been simply "dumped" online. In addition, this user

Searching for Information: Where Do Computer Users Look?

◀ Table 6.2 *How computer users reported they searched for information over a four-month period.*

	Frequency	Percent
Another Person	385	28
On My Own	334	25
Hardcopy Manual	253	19
Online Help	139	10
Informal Notes	62	5
Online User Consultant	46	3
Hardcopy Handouts	39	3
User Consultant on Duty	38	3
Online Manual	37	3
Total Searches	1333	

Note. 113 people reported where they searched for information for problems experienced with 13 software and 8 hardware tasks.

community seemed not to favor asking user consultants for help, reporting they got better, more direct, and more understandable answers from friends. Our onsite observations revealed that many people (even system wizards such as experts in high-end computing and artificial intelligence applications programming) had created their own "cheat sheets" in the form of hardcopy handouts and informal lists of key commands. Some users photocopied these documents for friends and took on the role of "resident expert." These users acted much like the resident experts observed by Mirel (1989) in her study, which portrayed how office workers avoid using computer manuals by relying on other people in their office to help them out.

How Readers' Tasks Shape Their Decision-Making About Searching for Information

We examined how often people in this computing environment reported using the primary information channels in performing several high-frequency computing tasks for which we knew the same content was available in both hardcopy and online. Table 6.3 presents how people used the highest-scoring information sources (asking someone else, solving it on your own, hardcopy manual, or online help) to get information about various tasks.

▶ Table 6.3 *Where users reported looking for information the last time they encountered a problem while carrying out four high-frequency computing tasks. The same information was available in hardcopy and online.*

Searching for Information: Patterns for Typical Computing Tasks

	Type of Program				Frequency	Percent
	Word Processing	Sending Mail	Serving Files	Financial/ Statistical		
Ask Another Person	35	32	29	23	96	31
Solve On Your Own	15	16	10	6	47	15
Hardcopy Manual	45	1	2	40	88	28
Online Help or Documentation	5	43	26	4	78	25
Total Searches	100	92	67	73	309	

Note. Values indicate the number of searches made by 113 people. Due to rounding, the percentage column may not equal 100%.

Responses show that people were consistent with their earlier reporting in that about 30 percent of the time, they tended to ask someone else for help (see Table 6.2). Importantly, when people used documentation, the type of document they chose depended on the task they were doing. For tasks such as wordprocessing and running financial programs, users preferred hardcopy; for sending mail and serving files (e.g., running a file transfer program such as FTP), they preferred online.

In interviews with members of the user community, we found that most people preferred hardcopy when they thought one or more of the following might fit their situation:

- The task they wanted to accomplish would be time consuming, forcing them to refer back to the hardcopy now and then over the course of a few hours of work.

- There would be so much online documentation that finding the necessary information would be annoying and time consuming.

- The online information would interfere with the text they were working on, either by forcing them to get out of their file, by increasing the memory load on their machine, thus slowing it down and perhaps crashing it, or by covering up part of the text they were working on.

- The problem was conceptual, one in which they wanted to spend a little extra time thinking over the big picture, the definitions, or the relationships among tasks.

- They wanted pictures, technical illustrations, or graphics—reporting that the visuals in hardcopy were easier to read, more crisp in appearance, and less of a hassle to display.

In contrast, users tended to prefer online documents when they thought one or more of the following might be the case:

- The task would take little time and would allow them to "get in and out" of online help quickly.

- The help file would be short and would allow them to control the size of the help window and its rate of display.

- Displaying the help file or online document would not destroy the context of their work (the integrity of their files was much more important than getting help).[17]

- The help would be procedural rather than definitional. This finding aligns with observations made by Kern, Sticht, Welty, and Hauke (1976), who found that people using technology to carry out their jobs require *task-oriented information* (that is, procedural, tailored to the unique situation) rather than *topic-oriented information* (that is, definitional, such as found in an encyclopedia).

Interviews with users revealed that although they usually relied on other people and hardcopy manuals, they were not necessarily wedded to these information sources. In our survey, we probed the idea that people might not be using the information source they most preferred by asking them to imagine they could get high-quality information from each of their usual sources for information. We suspected that more people might want to use the hardcopy and online documents if they thought that reading them would be as intelligible as asking another person. To explore this issue, we asked the 113 users to rank their preferences if they knew they could get *equally good information* from each information source.

[17] Most of the users in this community had standard 13-inch monitors. The size of the help window was about 6 inches wide; thus it almost always covered up part of the screen. Unfortunately, the system did not allow users to resize the help window. The problems of fixed-size windows and of covering up the main window have been solved in more recently developed help systems, but many people still use 13-inch monitors.

▶ Table 6.4 *Where people preferred to look for answers to their computing problems.*

Searching for Information: Sources Computer Users Preferred

---

1. Online Help
2. Hardcopy Manual
3. Ask Another Person
4. Online Manual
5. Hardcopy Handouts
6. Informal Notes
7. Online User Consultant
8. User Consultant on Duty

Note. 113 participants ranked the sources in the order they would prefer to use them, assuming they could get the same information from each documentation source.

Table 6.4 shows that, given the assumption of equally good information, users chose online help as their preference, followed by hardcopy. That users would prefer online was somewhat surprising, given its fourth rank in the patterns of search they had reported elsewhere in the same survey and that we had observed in our onsite observations. The patterns of search reported elsewhere (see Tables 6.2 and 6.3) suggested that if people used documents at all they favored hardcopy. The discrepancy between the documents people were using (hardcopy) and what they preferred (online) prompted us to evaluate the quality of the hardcopy and online documents users had available.

[18] Quality is a critical issue for the design of both hardcopy and online computer documentation. Just because online information is cheaper for organizations to create and maintain doesn't mean it is any better than paper. Industry standards for excellence in online or hardcopy must be defined by users. As Shirk (1988) points out, online documentation is written specifically for access only by means of a computer; it is not simply paper-based documentation placed online (p. 312).

[19] For a discussion of the limitations of expert judgment, see Schriver (1989a).

Surprisingly, much of the early work comparing online and hardcopy did not mention the quality of the documentation. Instead it tended to focus only on the medium, usually promoting online as a panacea.[18] Often good hardcopy documents were compared to poor online or vice versa. Although researchers did not purposely mislead document designers, they wrongly drew conclusions about what designers should do because their results were confounded with the quality of the texts. *It appears that the most important issue is not paper or screen, but how the communication is designed—that is, whether it has been written and visualized in a clear and engaging way for the particular audiences who want to use a given medium for accomplishing specific tasks.*

To better understand the relationship between what people were using and what they preferred to use, we evaluated a sample of the 280 hardcopy and 115 online documents available for users in this environment. We selected at random 38 hardcopy manuals and 36 help topics to see how well they were designed. Given the number of texts we wanted to assess, we chose to employ expert judgment[19] and to make only a crude global-level assessment of the documents. We did not, for example, rate separately the tutorials, user guides, specifications manuals, reference guides, and the like, but sampled randomly from all categories and evalu-

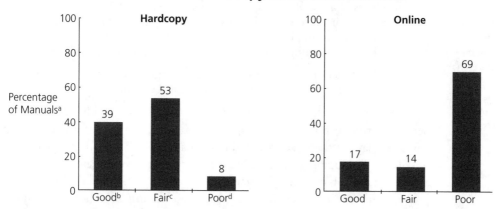

How Document Designers Rated
the Hardcopy and Online Manuals

Hardcopy — Good[b] 39, Fair[c] 53, Poor[d] 8

Online — Good 17, Fair 14, Poor 69

Percentage of Manuals[a]

[a] Experienced document designers rated 38 hardcopy manuals and 36 online help topics.

[b] Minor revisions were required to make the document excellent.

[c] Considerable revisions were required to make it excellent, but much of the text and graphics could be saved.

[d] Major revisions were required to make it excellent and little of the text could be saved—calling for major rewriting and redesigning.

▲ **Figure 6.4** *When users searched for information in documents, they tended to look in hardcopy (see Tables 6.2 and 6.3), even though they reported a preference for using online help (see Table 6.4). The graphs presented here show how experienced document designers rated a random sample of the hardcopy and online documents users had available. The high frequency of poorly designed online documents may explain (at least in part) why users were reluctant to search for information in a medium they preferred.*

ated each one against criteria for that genre (e.g., if a tutorial, how good of a tutorial was it?). We also did not rate the prose and graphics separately, but asked the general question: How well do the words and pictures work together for the user? Three experienced document designers rated the sample documents as "good" (i.e., minor revisions required to make the document excellent for a user), "fair" (i.e., considerable revisions required to make it excellent for a user, but much of the text could be saved), or "poor" (i.e., major revisions were required, calling for substantive rewriting and redesigning in order to make it excellent).

The results of our evaluation, presented in Figure 6.4, indicate that the bulk of the hardcopy documents were judged to be good or fair while most of the online documents were rated fair or poor (raters agreed in 88 percent of the cases). We found that more than half of the hardcopy manuals *did not*

- Specify the intended audience.
- Give readers alternative paths through the information.
- Provide overviews in prose or graphics.

20 A running header (also
called running head) is a line
of text that appears at the
top of each page or screen in
a fixed horizontal position. It
signals to readers the author's
name, the part, chapter,
section, or subsection they
are looking at.

- Offer well-chosen typographic cues for helping readers access information. Poor typography made it hard to distinguish first-level headings from subheadings. The manuals had no tabs, running headers,[20] or footers. Their cues consisted mainly of boldfaced headings set in uppercase, which were centered over a single column or a two-column body text using justified-right, block-style margins.

- Employ functional and aesthetically pleasing graphic design (inconsistent grid system, crowded pages, and haphazard signaling).

Although the hardcopy manuals were not ideal, they did have a number of positive features. For example, they had a predictable format and a consistent layout that readers could easily navigate. The headings, while not always intelligible to non-UNIX programmers, were legible and alphabetized (not an optimal organization, but at least familiar). The procedures were accurate and many had useful examples. There were also well-chosen cross-references to other content. Most of the instructions were written in active voice with simple sentence patterns (e.g., subject-verb-object). For the most part, the troubleshooting information was helpful.

In our evaluation of online help, we found only two positive features: there was consistent formatting of the help screens 94 percent of the time (even though judges didn't like the format, at least it was consistent) and the help messages had cross-references to other topics 61 percent of the time.[21] The screens used none of the principles that have become standard in online information design[22] and violated most of the Gestalt principles I discussed in Chapter 5. Comprehension of the text on the screens was made difficult by complicated sentence structures (27 percent) and jargon (23 percent). Rarely did document designers attempt to make their instructions visual; in fact, less than 5 percent of the documents we sampled contained charts, graphs, screen displays, or technical illustrations. The worst problem was the length of the help topics. Only 30 percent were between 1 and 10 screens in length; 36 percent of the screens were 11 to 20 or more panels of information, and 34 percent were topics consisting of 21 screens or more. The ideas of modularizing the content so that users could anticipate the length of help files and of giving readers cues about how much of the file remained to be read (e.g., through percent-done indicators or even with simple phrases such as "1 of 42") were not part of the vocabulary of the designers of these documents.

---

21 This study was conducted before there were many commercially available hypertext help systems on the market. For this reason we rated traditional cross-referencing of online documents as a positive feature.

22 See, for example, Brockmann (1990), Duffy, Mehlenbacher, and Palmer (1992), Dumas (1988), Galitz (1989), Horton (1991, 1994); Mullet and Sano (1995), and Shneiderman (1987).

Some Implications about Users and Their Preferences for Online and Hardcopy Documents

We can believe that users' reluctance to use the online documents in this computing environment may have been related, at least in part, to their poor document design. *These findings suggest that users' preferences for a medium may be overridden by their perception of the quality of documents available in that medium.*

Research by Hendry (1995) suggests that online documents still cause users problems. He evaluated an online document that had been structured for online presentation using a Standard Generalized Markup Language (SGML).[23] He found that the way the online manual displayed information made it hard for readers to understand how prose examples fit into the text's structure—that is, they could not get the "big picture" of the text elements that came before and after the examples, a picture required for the examples to make sense. Hendry cautions communicators that SGML has not been designed from the user's perspective and requires extensive hand-tweaking to create effective online documents. He argues that communicators need a rhetorical markup language that will allow interactive computing systems to deploy online texts in a way that preserves the rhetorical cues about the relations among structural pieces of a document.

We can conclude from our study of computer users that before document designers make judgments about why people do or do not read their documents, they must understand the *situational context for reading.* Important parts of that context include the reader's tasks, the competing information sources available, the reader's beliefs about the quality of documents, the media employed for presenting the document, and the readers' past experiences with using various media. This study reminds us that the design of documents can influence the paths people take in their search for information. Once people opt for a document as their information source,

---

[23] SGML is an international computing standard for describing documents by their structure. In using SGML, the document designer inserts what are called tags into a document which specify the structure and parts of a document, such as "this is a paragraph," "this is an example," or "this is a bulleted list." SGML allows for the creation of electronic and print documents from a single source (or database) of information. It also allows the database to be used in many ways, with options for combining and recombining the source material to make customized documents. For this reason, "document reuse" became the SGML buzzword of a few years ago. SGML also offers portability across computing platforms. Because SGML offers a technological solution for managing large databases of information and allows organizations to reuse the same text in different ways, many organizations have jumped on the SGML bandwagon. However, almost no research from the writing or design community has considered the impact on readers of using SGML. Hendry's (1995) study is one of the first to examine the rhetorical impact of SGML.

they face the problem of finding what they want within the document. In the next section, I discuss some of these navigational issues by considering how people search hypertexts on the World Wide Web.

FRAGMENTATION ON THE WEB: A CASE STUDY OF THE VIRTUAL TOURIST ("I CAN'T GET A SENSE OF THE BIG PICTURE")

In the past few years, many organizations and individuals have become enthusiastic about the potential of communicating through the World Wide Web. However, in the rush to design home pages and databases of linked information, not many have spent time thinking about how people will actually experience their Web designs: that is, how people will understand and make use of the prose and graphics they find. In fact, although there are now dozens of cookbooks on everything from designing home pages to managing your GIFs and JPEGs, there are almost no books that present empirical evidence about how people read and interpret what they encounter on the Web. Without an understanding of what people do, books that claim to provide design strategies about what people need or want are merely armchair speculation. Document designers have an important role to play in defining what it means to be effective when integrating prose and graphics on the Web. I contend that the foundation for making these contributions lies in research about the human side of the Web.

The case study I discuss in this section was carried out by Daphne van der Vlist, a student at the University of Utrecht in Holland.[24] In her research, Van der Vlist examined how people read and interpret the *Virtual Tourist,* a site designed to give the "inside scoop" on dozens of cities around the world. The idea underlying the *Virtual Tourist* is that users can call up a world map and then click on a country they'd like to visit. Once connected to a country, users select among different regions to visit, getting more specific with each click, until finally users can find suggestions about where to eat, shop, or drink coffee in particular cities.

Evaluating the Document Design of a Web Site: Goals and Methods

Participants in Van der Vlist's study were seven native speakers of Dutch in their early twenties; participants were fluent in English as well as several other languages. Their task: to visit Paris via the *Virtual Tourist* and provide commentary about what they found en route.[25] Users were told their comments would be used to improve the design of future Web sites.

[24] I had the pleasure of meeting Daphne van der Vlist and other exceptional students during my 1995 stay at the University of Utrecht as a visiting professor. Daphne took my graduate course, "The Nature of Expertise in Document Design." She conducted this case study of reading on the Web as part of her final project for the course. I thank Daphne for allowing me to draw from and extend her work.

[25] In particular, users were asked to first explore the *Virtual Tourist's* links about the culture of Paris, then to check out the Parisian café scene, and finally to end up on a page that provided the address of the Dutch Embassy.

In evaluating the document design of this Web site, Van der Vlist had three goals:

- *First,* to investigate how users responded to the visual and verbal design of the *Virtual Tourist.*

- *Second,* to learn what they thought about the quality of the content and how it was presented.

- *Third,* to compare the ideas that the names of the links suggested to users with the actual content of the link.[26]

To understand how people reacted to the *Virtual Tourist,* users provided think-aloud protocols as they navigated the Web site. After they were finished, they answered a set of open-ended survey questions. Because there were more than 1,000 screens available at this site, participants were asked to explore a set of 16 links that were chosen in advance.[27] Figure 6.5 shows eight of the links she asked users to visit.

To explore whether the naming of the links helped users to anticipate their content accurately, Van der Vlist employed a prediction task in which users were asked to look at a screen with its optional visual or verbal links and to make guesses about what might come next if they clicked on that link (e.g., if you see a heading, "What does it suggest about the content you will find?" or a picture, "What does it make you think of?"). Users' guesses about the content were compared with what was actually presented. For example, in Screen 5 of Figure 6.5, there are four icons arranged in a horizontal row from left to right. Users were prompted to consider what words and pictures they thought would be linked to "The City" or "Paris Kiosque." In addition, users were asked what came to mind as they read various word and picture combinations. In Screen 6, for instance, there is a picture of a little map which is associated with the label "Interactive Map" (see the horizontal row, the fourth picture and the label below it). Van der Vlist questioned users about what they thought an interactive map was and how they would expect to engage with one. She compared the features of the map readers imagined with the map users were actually shown. *The idea here is that document designers who create Web sites should be aware of the range of expectations, connotations, and resonances that icons or key words may suggest to readers.* The prediction task proved a useful method for assessing two key aspects of the document design of the Web pages:

1. It provided information about what icons, pictures, and words suggest and do not suggest to users.

2. It identified situations in which two or more icons, pictures, or words (designated as links) suggested to users the same or overlapping meanings. This is important for document designers to know because if users don't know which icon or word has the closest

[26] The question of how well the name of a link gives a sense of the content is similar to the issue of whether a heading or subheading provides an accurate forecast of content that follows it.

[27] By constraining which links readers saw, it was not possible to learn about what people explored on their own. That was not a goal for this study. In designing studies to evaluate the human side of the Web, it is important to focus one's goals. No single study can examine all issues.

It looks like it is easy to use. But there are screaming colors and the letters aren't very clear to see. The green used for the title, "Virtual Tourist," is very striking, but the letters are not striking because of their shape.

The heading, "Virtual Tourist" is nice, modern, glossy, there are nice globes in the background which I didn't see at first. But the whole heading is maybe a bit too disorderly.

The map of the Europe is nice, not too colorful. It's useful that the names of the countries are in it.

The phrase, "Select a country from the map below" is in bold typeface, that is good. The map is great; even the small countries are on it. It really looks professional.

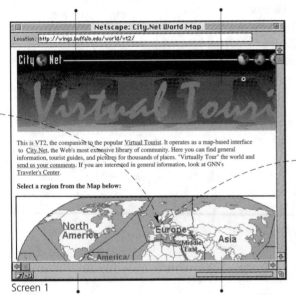

Screen 1

Screen 2

I prefer reading magazines and books, but for short texts a computer screen is OK. The advantage is that you can search a lot faster and select more of interest. OK, now I guess I just click on a country to select it, I don't see any more instructions about how to use the map.

It takes some time before the pictures appear on the screen. When you want specific information it might take awhile before you get the information you want. However, when you have been working with this system for a while, I think you will be able to access the information quickly.

This map looks less organized than the prior screen. I wonder how you should click on Jersey. Do you click on the name or on the place where the country should be? The names of the countries are outside of the countries a lot of times, this is a little disturbing.

I had trouble figuring out what to do with the map, so I looked down the page. It said, "Information about the maps used, and how to use them on your own is available." But when I read it, there was no information about how to use these maps, but how to make them yourself!

▲ **Figure 6.5** *Participants' comments while following a series of links through the World Wide Web Site,* Virtual Tourist II, *which provides information about places of interest from around the world. Reprinted from City Net's* Virtual Tourist II *with the permission of Brandon Plewe, Buffalo, NY, and Norman Barth, San Diego, CA. Netscape windows reprinted with the permission of Netscape Communications Corp., Mountain View, CA.*

There are those small letters again. I won't read them this time. They're irritating.

I don't understand the categories, "Home, Contents, Regions, Countries, Index, Search," but I just want to click right away to find out. Are the categories opportunities to get to other screens?

This looks well organized because of the headings. The categories are very clear, you can scroll quckly through the document and find what you like. But there's not much to choose from under the headings. Where's all the good stuff, all the details?

There are too many links on this screen, but you won't be reading all of this and it looks well organized. So, maybe it is OK.

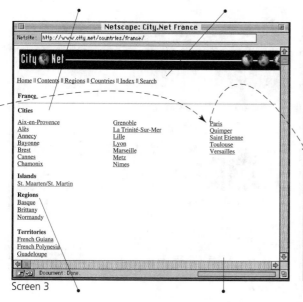

Screen 3

Screen 4

I thought France had a lot more regions. Where are they? Why aren't they here?

I miss the pictures, but I'd also like some explanations, you know, some interesting content, some ideas about what each section of France is like. I'd like to see more information about what to expect if I chose one of these links. I don't want to read them all to know what is there, that would take years.

I like the way the French and English translations of of "the Paris Pages" and the "Subway Navigator for Paris" are separated. I think it's confusing when the same information is repeated on the same page in a different language.

This is not very clear. Maybe it would be useful to put the topics next to each other at the top of the screen, because now you have to scroll through the whole screen to see the possibilities.

I like the French quote, but I don't think people who only speak English will understand it. There should be an English translation of the quote.

I don't like the pictures of the statues here, they are not in a box like the other pictures on the page.

Nice architecture, but I don't think of that when I think of 'culture.' Something more famous would be better ... an overview of modern city life, like the center of the city, you know, some places you really want to go to. I can't get a feel for Paris from this.

There is not much information. It's almost not worth reading it. I'd like to see more general facts or the history. This really needs some interesting detail.

Screen 5

Screen 6

I like the icons, the graphics are nice, but why are there two photographs and two drawings? It looks to me like they just want to fill the page. The last photograph is best, the first one is a bit hidden. The 'i' for tourist information really stands out, it is so different from the other icons.

I would like to know what the Paris Kiosque is about. I don't know what a kiosque is supposed to be. Is it a place where you get newspapers and magazines? Or is it a round building with announcements tacked to the outside and a toilet inside? The picture above the text reminds me of buildings I've seen all over Europe.

The first picture isn't too good. This could be better if it were an aerial photograph of a central part of Paris or a picture with the most famous monuments and museums together. People see things that they know; then they associate them with Paris.

Those little letters are really ugly and not readable. I won't read them. It looks like a mess. When you really take your time, you can work your way through, but it is a bit small.

I think that an interactive map is a map on a computer screen. When I want to go to a certain location I can type the name, then the map will show me where it is. You can type the names of streets, hotels, or tourist attractions. OK, that's not how this interactive map works.

The color is very tiresome for your eyes and everything is printed so close together it is hard to find anything. Can't the museums and monuments be ordered alphabetically or something?

I tried to click on the picture of the Basilique, but nothing happened. I clicked on other pictures and went to other pages, now how do I go to another page? But it is a nice picture, really dresses up the page a bit.

How did I end up here? Basilique du Sacré Coeur? What's that? I thought I was going to Palais de la Découverte, listed as 18 under museums. I don't understand how I got here.

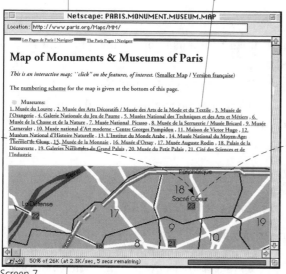

Screen 7

Screen 8

I like this map, you can see very easily what lies nearby, in which district and if it's in the center of Paris. But I think you have to understand the numbering scheme to understand what is what.

This is very illogical. They say it is a "map of monuments and museums," but then they list the museums, then the map, and finally the monuments. They should at least present the monuments first before the museums to be at all consistent.

A lot of this information is useful. The information under "where," the telephone number, and so on is interesting. Plus, it is good to know how to get there on the metro. The word 'sanctuary' is misspelled.

At least this text is almost legible. I didn't like trying to read the text that was small and in italics. It's too hard.

meaning to the content they are looking for, they waste time by having to search through more than one link, thus increasing the likelihood of exiting the Web site when they don't find what they want on their first look.

As we just saw in Figure 6.5, the Paris pages of the *Virtual Tourist* prompted an interesting blend of positive and negative comments, many of which highlight the "On one hand, I love it, but on the other hand, it stinks," emotional seesaw that users may experience as they cruise Web sites. The comments that readers made as they jumped from link to link suggest that they had three major concerns as they engaged with the prose and graphics:

- *Concern 1:* The effectiveness of the content
- *Concern 2:* The graphic integrity and legibility of the typography and the visual images
- *Concern 3:* The integration of the prose and graphics

Though the readers' concerns were specific to these particular Web pages, they raise issues that are relevant to writing and visualizing the content for any Web site.

Reader Concern 1:
The Effectiveness of the Content of Web Pages

On many occasions during their online visit to Paris via the *Virtual Tourist,* readers commented favorably on the colorful pictures and mentioned how interesting and beautiful they were to look at. As one man said of Screen 8, "It really looks like Sacré Coeur. I love that place." But as much as the readers enjoyed the pretty pictures, they expected more. Much more.

Problems of Pretty Pictures Combined with Low-Information Prose

For the most part, the prose of the *Virtual Tourist* took the form of tedious lists. The content was so spare that readers were left wondering, "Where's all the good stuff, all the details?" (see Screen 4). Content items were often underdeveloped or had significant gaps, prompting readers to comment, "There's not much information. It's almost not worth reading" (see Screen 6). On some screens, users resisted connecting to links because in their words, "I'd like to see more information about what to expect if I chose one of these links. I don't want to read them all to know what is there; that would take years" (see Screen 3). These comments suggest that Web designers need to make the content of their sites as rich and meaningful for users as possible. When content is low in information, pretty pictures won't save the day. The dazzle-them-with-pictures approach may have attracted inexperienced users to content-challenged sites on the Web a few years ago, but today's users want content, not fluff.

Problems created by headings. The headings that previewed the links didn't always help readers form a thoughtful representation of the topic. For example, the headings in Screen 4, "Arts and Entertainment," "City Guides," "Food and Drink," "Maps," "Other Guides," and "Transportation" do not comprise a logically coherent family. The items are neither complete (e.g., what happened to topics such as architecture, museums, culture, or lodging?) nor are they at the same level of abstraction (e.g., "Food and Drink" could be a subcategory of "Arts and Entertainment").

Contrary to popular opinion, readers wanted not less prose but more. Importantly, though, they didn't want just any prose (i.e., not an encyclopedic core dump). They hoped for well-written prose that had been designed to accommodate reading on the screen. Readers' responses suggested that they expected each Web page to have a rhetorical purpose (e.g., "What is this here for?" "How does this screen relate to that one?"). Instead, readers seemed disconcerted as they moved from screen to screen and complained that they were getting a piecemeal view of Paris (e.g., "This doesn't add up").

Problems created by the choice of content. Readers commented that the *Virtual Tourist's* depiction of Paris sometimes clashed with their personal experience. They raised questions about why some of the content was chosen. For example, at the time these pages were tested, the only link available in Screen 4 under the heading "Arts and Entertainment" was to Disneyland Paris. However, most Europeans don't go to Paris to see Disneyland and it is likely that most Americans don't either. Not surprisingly, readers wanted to know about permanent museums collections, upcoming art shows, burlesque at the Moulin Rouge, or poetry readings along the West Bank. They didn't want to read canned text about Disneyland. The content violated readers' expectations for what would be there and was inconsistent with their prior knowledge of the French art and entertainment scene. In actuality, these topics were covered at the *Virtual Tourist* site, but they were distributed over many headings and hard to locate in synoptic form. Thus, the Web designer could argue "the content is in there, the user just has to find it." The problem is, the user won't wait long enough to find it.

Readers predicted the category "Arts and Entertainment" would contain subcategories at a general level of specificity (e.g., museums, dance, film, parks, theater). Thus, Disneyland could have been a reasonable item if it had been nested under a heading such as "amusement parks," but by itself, it stood out as an odd link (even further emphasized by its position as the first item on the screen). As discussed in Chapter 5, the reader's eye is drawn to items of spatial prominence and to visual clusters that contrast with others (e.g., short lists in relation to long, light type in relation to dark type, big pictures in relation to small ones). It may be that presenting "Arts and Entertainment" first was simply an artifact of using a default alphabetical arrangement for the headings. But few readers will take the time to study the principle of organization and rationalize why an impoverished category would be placed first.

Problems created by underdeveloped content. Document designers should assess the usefulness to the reader of every bit of cyberspace they stake out. This requires, of course, some sense of what readers really want to know. It also means resisting the tempting but rhetorically lame strategy of collecting everything available about a topic and simply adding it to the database. Links in which content is not yet developed or of questionable value should be placed "on hold" until they are truly ready for human consumption. Some users in Van der Vlist's study felt that the *Virtual Tourist* seemed to have links for the sake of having them. Although adding links to someday-to-be-developed nodes may be a quick way to build an impressive number of nodes and links to one's Web site, the number of nodes and links has no necessary relationship to the quality of the information the site offers. If a category has only a few elements, document designers should combine the category with another and generate a new name for the consolidated category that suggests the new content as well as the old.

Similarly, if the content available about a topic is essentially a picture-file, the names of the categories should accurately reflect this. Avoid the pretense of providing content through prose when either (1) the knowledge of the topic is limited, or (2) there is not time to artfully compose and skillfully adapt the text for presenting it on a screen. Just as readers have come to expect high-quality visuals, they have come to assume they will get interesting and well-written prose. Most people want the prose to be as concise as possible, but not so short that it becomes cryptic and ambiguous. Readers of the *Virtual Tourist* remarked that paperback travel guides were more detailed, often funny, gave a sense of the author's personality, and evoked a personal feeling they did not experience online.

If readers feel the content for a Web site is disorganized and choppy, it may raise doubts in their minds about the utility of the information itself. And we saw in Chapters 3 and 4, it may also cast a negative shadow on the organizational identity of the group who put the information out there. Document designers have the opportunity to bring a new rhetorical credibility and sensitivity to the Web, a concern for quality in content that has been missing.

***Problems created by pictures that inappropriately narrow the
topic.*** Document designers for the Web need to worry about what
rhetorician I. A. Richards (1936) called "interanimation"—that is, words
in context talking to other words, pictures to other pictures. Symbols
work together to help orchestrate a sense of the meaning. As people read,
neighboring symbols animate one another, allowing readers to construct
meanings that are more than the sum of the individual words or pictures.
When visual or verbal symbols are placed in dynamic relation, at least four
things can happen: (1) the meanings can be enriched—what readers
construct during reading expands their prior understanding of the topic;
(2) the meanings can be constrained in ways that lead a majority of readers
to construct a similar (though never the same) understanding of the topic;
(3) the meanings can be constrained but the meanings individual readers
construct may be at odds with the ways that others understand the topic;
or (4) the meanings can be narrowed inappropriately—the representation
readers are able to construct wrongly reduces their representation of the
topic.

How does this idea about interanimation relate to the Paris pages?
Readers wondered why the Web designer chose to depict the culture of
Paris (the city of lights and the city of love) by presenting mainly pictures
of statues and monuments (see Screens 5 and 6). Several readers felt that
pictures of architecture narrowed the way that a person new to Paris
would imagine the city, pointing out, "I don't think about buildings
when I think of Paris; these pictures are not the right symbols." Since
photographs of architecture dominated the landscape, the sense of culture
evoked by the collage of visuals wasn't very rich. One reader felt that the
similarity among the photos could make the reader lose interest; "I'd
probably stop here, it doesn't look that inviting to go on." Convincing
the reader to maintain interest is an important rhetorical consideration in
designing Web pages.

Perhaps even more consequential is inviting readers to suspend their
impulse to nail down the content by choosing visuals that invite them to
think about the content more deeply. To evoke a complex idea credibly,
document designers must carefully select examples (both visual and verbal)
that typify the range of alternatives that cover the terrain of the idea.
Better not to visualize than to encourage the reader to form a reductive or
one-dimensional image of a topic. By considering the likely
interanimation of symbols—how their orchestration may enrich an idea,
constrain it suitably, or narrow it inappropriately—document designers
can make better choices for words and pictures that shape readers' impressions of the content.

Problems created by inadequate structuring of content in lists.

A list is a good way to preview a document's available content, but the positive effects of using them can be diminished if there are too many lists or if they are not arranged in a visually consistent manner. In reading screens from the *Virtual Tourist,* readers noticed a lack of consistency in the layout of the lists (some were oriented horizontally like a paragraph in English, others vertically). Readers didn't like either style very much. They reported having troubles scanning the items when lists were formatted horizontally (see Screen 6), and they were annoyed by the need to scroll through long vertical lists formatted as single columns (see Screen 4). Readers of these one-column vertical lists tended not to bother to scroll down to see what was below their visible screen. They preferred lists that were presented in arrays of three short vertical columns as in the top of Screen 3, appearing to respond to the discrete visual chunks. (For similar findings in people's reactions to tabular displays, see Wright, 1982.) The shorter lists were easier to digest at a glance.

Document designers need to be careful not to present screen after screen filled with lists. Readers may grow weary of this approach—get "listed out"—paying little attention to later screens and to the individual items they present.[28] Readers in Van der Vlist's study who were bored with the lists increased the rate of their clicking, suggesting they were skipping much of the available content.

To keep the reader's attention, document designers must make each cluster of information a rhetorically effective package. This means that headings for lists are very important; they must call out the name of the family of ideas in a clear and interesting way. Moreover, the visual organization of the rhetorical cluster (in this case, the headings, subheadings, and listed items) should make it easy to see the structure; that is, to see which lists are related, which are embedded, and so on. (For a discussion of rhetorical clusters, see Chapter 5, "A Heuristic for Decision-Making in Constructing Grids," pp. 341–357).

In creating lists, the document designer needs to establish a consistent layout, but more important is the quality of the content itself. Readers in Van der Vlist's study were very positive about the concept of *Virtual Tourist,* but expressed misgivings about the content they actually found. Readers noted that some lists omitted content they expected. For example, Screen 3 presents the category "regions" of France (see the third heading in the first column), but the list is incomplete. As one reader asked, "What happened to Alsace, Lorraine, Burgundy, Loire, Côte d'Azure, and other regions?" Another reader put it this way, "I thought France had a lot more regions. Where are they?" In fact, all of the Dutch readers noticed the conceptual holes in the list of regions of France. We

[28] In their monthly column "Jargon Watch," reporters for *Wired* (May, 1996) describe a similar phenomenon called the "Dorito Syndrome." It has to do with feelings of emptiness and dissatisfaction triggered by addictive substances that lack nutritional content: "I just spent six hours surfing the Web, and now I've got a bad case of Dorito Syndrome" (p. 52).

can believe that the Web designer left out the other regions not because he didn't know they existed, but because he had not yet developed their content. But the "say nothing strategy" was rhetorically unwise because it made readers question his knowledge of the subject matter. It would have been better to list all of the regions and to point out which links were still under development.

Each item in a list should be selected in order to stand alone as well as to work in concert with other items. Moreover, each item should present content at the same level of abstraction. When listed items are parallel and conceptually complete, they allow readers to see how the parts of the content add up. (For more ideas about grouping elements in itemized lists, see Appendix C, pp. 506–517).

Problems created by a lack of visual consistency in signaling the links to access the content. All of Van der Vlist's participants liked the appearance of the world map (Screens 1 and 2) and the map of Paris (Screen 7). The maps were colorful but not garish, crisp in resolution, and at the right level of detail. Although the design of the maps made users enthusiastic about using them, participants had problems figuring out where to click and what was going to happen next. Since there were no instructions about how to use the maps, most readers tried to click on the name of a country, city, or place, but this didn't always produce the result they expected. Sometimes what they clicked on was actually a link and other times it was not. For example, in identifying the links on the world map shown in Screen 2, readers wondered, "If the name of the place is too long to fit inside the picture of the place, should I click on the place or on its name?" (See the labels for Jersey and Guernsey in Screen 2.) What was missing was a consistent visual cue that meant "click here" as well as a consistent pattern for the location of links within regions.[29]

Reader Concern 2:
The Graphic Integrity and Legibility
of the Typography and the Visual Images

As we saw in Chapter 5, two critical features of well-chosen typefaces are (1) legibility and (2) rhetorical appropriateness. Van der Vlist found that readers noticed how easily they could see the type and make out the images when exploring the Web (just as they do in using paper documents). Readers' comments spoke not only to these features but also to the graphic integrity of images (such as icons, photographs, and maps). That is, readers made judgments in which they evaluated the graphics by comparing their quality to others they had seen before or to those which appeared on the same Web page (see readers' comments on Screens 1, 2,

[29] If physical limitations of a graphic prevent visual consistency in signaling the links, provide supplementary verbal cues to help readers decide where to click. Display these cues on the portion of the Web page most likely to be called up first (most Web pages are much longer than what users see on their first click). Put the labels in places with maximum contrast so the typography is distinct from the background.

5, 6, and 7). Although readers' criteria for quality was not very specific, they were sensitive to issues such as color, detail, level of resolution, proximity, and shape.

Problems with Legibility and Rhetorical Appropriateness

The comments made by readers in this study tended to support the findings of earlier research which showed people may have problems with reading typography on a computer screen (Haas & Hayes, 1986).[30] While some typefaces on a computer screen have an ugly jagged look, others have a tight and small appearance (especially those with small x-heights). Although technical limitations related to HTML (defined and discussed in Appendix C, pp. 506–517) may prohibit Web designers from controlling which typefaces will be displayed on users' computer screens, the parts of the design they do control should employ typographic and spatial cues that are legible and that help readers perceive, organize, remember, and enjoy those messages.

The Web designers of the *Virtual Tourist* had no control over the actual fonts displayed on users' machines as they read the Paris pages. It was a standard HTML file, which gives little control over the typography. Thus, unlike designers using the latest version of Netscape Extensions or Adobe Acrobat—products that enable Web designers to control the fonts displayed, even if the user's machine does not have the same fonts installed— it was not possible to employ typography as a key design feature. The font users saw as they read the Paris pages depended on the font they selected in the menu of their Web browser. Users in Van der Vlist's study read the Paris pages in 10-point Adobe Garamond (chosen by default; it was already set when users logged on). Unfortunately, because Adobe Garamond has a small x-height, readers found it difficult to read, mentioning that much of the text had a rough look (even with Adobe Type Manager on). They were most bothered by the text set in italics, which caused the space between letters to shrink, giving the type a scrunched look (see readers' comments about Screens 3, 6, 7, and 8). The problem with the type, however, was limited to the onscreen version of the text. When the text was downloaded, legibility was excellent.

Although antialiasing techniques for getting rid of the "jagged look" of typography on the screen (see Chapter 5, footnotes 45 and 48, p. 282) are rapidly improving the legibility of the type users read online,[31] document designers still need to worry about the legibility of type under less-than-terrific "normal" conditions. The conditions under which most users access the Internet include: (1) using a slow 14.4-kilobytes-per-second modem, making it hard to download graphic files quickly; (2) working

[30] See the research cited in Chapter 5, the sections, "What Research Says about the Legibility of Typography," and "Legibility and Online Documents" (pp. 274–275 and pp. 282–283, respectively).

[31] For a discussion of antialiasing and of decision-making in designing custom typefaces, see Taylor (1996a). For research on some of the variables of typefaces that may make a difference in readers' performance and preferences (such as size, line length, leading, proximity, similarity, emphasis, and sequence) see Van der Waarde (1993).

with an average to below-average resolution 14-inch color monitor (which gives a 10.5" to 12.4" viewable display area); (3) working without type manager software such as Adobe Type Manager, and (4) working in a room at school or in an office where the screen is subject to overhead glare.

Presently it looks as though using sans serif fonts will work best with the many low-resolution monitors users have available (designers for television have used mainly sans serif for years, and the resolution on current televisions, at least in the United States, is below that of computer monitors, making sans serif a wise choice).[32] As organizations and individual computer users gradually acquire monitors with improved resolutions, it will be easier for them to read a range of typefaces and styles on the screen. Indeed, there are already many legible serif fonts designed for low-resolution electronic environments.[33] Even when all users get high-resolution monitors, the size of type will matter, as will its style, word spacing, line spacing, line length, and so on (for some guidelines about these issues, see Appendix C, pp. 506–517).

Despite the lack of control over the fonts, the designer of *Virtual Tourist* did a fine job in presenting strikingly beautiful visuals without a lot of clutter (see readers' comments about Screens 1, 2, and 8). Overall, unlike some Web sites which vibrate with color and garishly textured backgrounds, this site was orderly and pleasantly subdued. Readers noticed this feature and made comments such as, "It doesn't shout at you. I like that."

Reader Concern 3:
The Integration of the Prose and Graphics

Readers on the Web are confronted with prose and graphics that are presented in various ways. Some of the time, words and pictures are used in pairs to evoke an idea, such as an icon and its label. Other times, words are used to annotate graphics, often functioning as links to other Web pages. But most of the time, prose and graphics are integrated as part of the body text in order to help users represent the content. In each of these situations, the integration of the prose and graphics has a direct influence on how readers respond to the Web page, whether they understand the icons, whether they click on the links, and whether they are able to form a coherent representation of the content.

Problems with Ambiguous Mappings between Icons and Labels

It is a good idea to pair icons and labels (that is, to double signal[34] an idea by giving the reader multiple ways to represent the same idea), but taken

[32] High-definition TV (HDTV) will change all of this, but it is unclear how soon this will happen.

[33] See Black (1990) for a discussion of the relationship between choosing a face and its output medium. Also see back issues of the *Adobe Type Catalog,* for descriptions of new faces designed for digital environments.

[34] By double signal, I mean providing two cues to call attention to the same text element. For example, an icon of a trashcan with the word "trash" written below it is a double signal.

together, the icons and words should constrain the meanings readers may infer. Well-designed icons use semantic redundancy to limit the meanings readers construct as much as possible. For example, in Screen 6, most users did not know what the Paris Kiosque was, even though there was an icon and a label for the idea. Users' expectations for its content ranged from a ticket outlet to a place to get newspapers such as *Le Monde* to a round building with billboards plastered all over the outside and a WC (a bathroom) inside. Although the Paris Kiosque might be all of these things, the icon did not clarify this and neither did the label. Readers commented that when they didn't understand a graphic or label, they lost interest in clicking on it. This may, however, depend on the quality of the graphic and its topic. We can imagine people clicking on graphics that seem interesting even if they are incomprehensible.

Problems Created by Inconsistent Patterns in the Pairing of Words and Pictures

Readers noticed incongruities in how the prose and graphics mapped onto one another. In Screen 6, for example, readers liked the idea of providing the four icons to match the choices they could click on; however, upon looking closely, readers discovered five choices, not four. The last one, "calendar," is not illustrated. The problem here is that Web designers set up a visual rhythm for the reader's eye (see an icon, map it to its label) and then stopped the pattern abruptly (see no icon, only a label). This mismatch between prose and graphics increases the likelihood that readers may not see the calendar option. Document designers need to maintain consistency in the visual/verbal patterns they set up. Otherwise, they may inadvertently lead users to overlook some items.

Problems Created by Difficult-to-Follow Organizational Patterns and Numbering Schemes

To help readers identify the location of monuments and museums in Paris, a colorful city map is presented, but the internal organization of the map is chaotic. It uses three numbering schemes, making it difficult to separate one scheme from another and tricky to map the verbal descriptions to the numbers. Moreover, it is hard to tell whether all numbers on the map are links. Figure 6.6 presents the full Web page available to users who click on Screen 7. This page caused so many problems that it warrants a closer look.

Each monument and museum is assigned a number which corresponds to a number on the map. Numbers are double signaled using shape and color[35] (filled red circles stand for museums and blue squares for monu-

[35] The use of color was important to this map; users who did not have a color monitor had trouble distinguishing the little squares and circles because of poor contrast with the background (for a discussion of the discriminability of symbols, see Chapter 5, the section, "Legibility and Quantitative Graphics," pp. 279–281). Document designers must consider the needs of users who do not have state-of-the-art technology to display their Web pages.

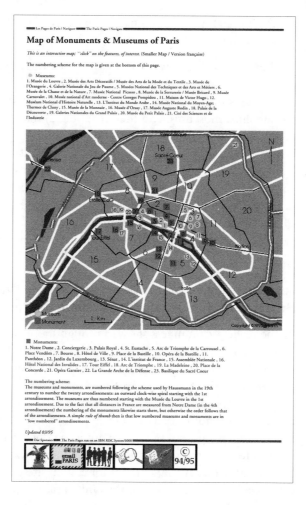

◀ **Figure 6.6** *The full text that is available in Screen 7 (in Figure 6.5) by scrolling the text.*

ments). Numbers for monuments and museums are links, taking the user to a page such as Screen 8. However, the map also presents a third set of numbers which are explained in a confusing way at the bottom of the Web page: "The museums and monuments are numbered following the scheme used by Haussmann in the 19th century to number the twenty arrondissements: an outward clockwise spiral starting with the 1st arrondissement." Readers disliked having to figure out this scheme. They found the map an interesting historical curiosity but for their purposes, congested and chaotic, especially when it was overlaid with two other numbering systems.

From the users' perspective, the third numbering system was also not of help because the arrondissements were not clickable. This annoyed users who predicted that the label "Interactive Map" (see the subheading in italics under the main heading of Figure 6.6) would mean that all numbers were clickable. Some users didn't want to click on preset regions, but thought the program would allow them to type in a destination and automatically go to it. Users' expectations went largely unfulfilled.

Users' expectations were also violated by the organization of this Web page itself. In predicting the contents of the heading "Map of Monuments & Museums of Paris," readers expected one of two orders, either (1) monuments, museums, and then map; or (2) map, monuments, and then museums. What is presented is museums, then map, then monuments. Users with a standard 14-inch monitor cannot fit the map onto their screen easily and are forced to view it in segments as in Screen 7. The same is true for the world map shown in Screens 1 and 2. This choppiness in presentation adds to the readers' sense of fragmentation. Obviously not all graphics can be redesigned for the small screen, but the most important part of the graphic should appear first on the user's monitor.

Lessons Learned about Designing on the Web: Helping Readers Avoid the Problem of Fragmentation

As the readers' comments show, although there was much they liked about the *Virtual Tourist,* there were a number of design features that caused them problems and that together contributed to a sense of fragmentation. If the *Springtime for Your CD-ROM* advice on gardening needed a Weedwacker (shown in Figure 6.1), this Web site needs some fertilizer. And not just any Miracle Gro will do. The *Virtual Tourist* appears to have grown up like an amoeba, a big arm here, a little arm there, a foot over there. It appears the content was simply added on as it became available. As the content for a Web site grows, it should be developed coherently so that it fits into a plan, a plan that readers can infer by the structure of the links. In some cases, adding new content will require wholesale reorganization. Document designers ought not to expect readers to guess which topics are complete and which ones are under construction, which items are clickable and which are not.

Moreover, the reader should not have to search through list upon list in order to get a sense of the options. This will mean document designers have serious work ahead in the form of organizing Web documents and of making categories of information meaningful, semantically distinct, conceptually coherent, and visually prominent. To do so in a rhetorically effective way calls on good writing and design skills. It also calls for feedback-driven audience analysis (described in Chapter 2), for little is known about how people actually interact with Web pages. Thus we have almost no knowledge about how to best structure the relationships between words and pictures on the Web. At the risk of repeating myself, too much time in document design circles is being spent arguing over the details of HTML code, GIFs, JPEGs, frames, browsers, and so on. Although anyone designing on the Web must know these things, they are not the most important thing for document design professionals to worry about. It's the interplay of prose and graphics that ought to concern us.

Too many companies are rushing to get their information on the Web without giving much thought to whether the information is worth reading or whether it is presented in a way that makes the experience—of searching, reading, and using—enjoyable. Most of the available Web sites have been designed without an understanding or even a passing thought about how people might navigate them. Academics who write about the Internet are inclined to represent it in binaries: as either evil or wonderful. Business and organizations have tended to see the Internet as just another medium for selling. In the words of *Newsweek,* companies just want to know, "How much bang for the buck?" (1996, April 1). Given the competing ideological, educational, and economic agendas, it is not surprising that the Internet hasn't yet lived up to users' expectations.

If experiences elsewhere on the Web are like those of Van der Vlist's users, people are not building a very coherent image of the content presented on the Web. Although getting a sense of the big picture is not always necessary, it doesn't hurt (and it always helps if you are trying to learn something). Once document designers know more about what readers are actually doing as they engage with the Internet, they will be in a more informed position to employ visual and verbal moves that will deliver on the promise of a new medium for communication.

SECTION 3
HOW PROSE AND GRAPHICS INTERACT

In this section, I first discuss some of the advantages and disadvantages of combining words and pictures. Then I describe five relationships between words and pictures that readers encounter frequently.

When Pictures Help and When They Don't

The maxim "A picture is worth a thousand words" reflects a common belief about the expressive power of visuals. Like many maxims, this one contains an element of truth that has been oversimplified. Cognitive research has shown that memory for pictures tends to be better than memory for words (Shepard, 1967).[36] Pictures can arouse the reader's interest and curiosity and are often well remembered even long after people see them (Nickerson, 1968).

[36] Shepard (1967) asked participants to view a series of 612 pictures from sources such as magazine advertisements. He gave people a test in which they decided whether they (1) had seen the picture before or (2) had never seen it before. People were 98.5 percent accurate, even after they had participated in viewing some 10,000 slides over a five-day period.

Levie and Lentz (1982) evaluated the research literature that compared text only, illustrations only, or both text and illustrations. They found that of the 46 experimental studies they reviewed, in all but one learning was better with text and illustrations than with text alone. Further, in 81 percent of these cases the differences in favor of text and illustration combinations were significant. The largest benefits were found for people with poor reading skills, who on average performed 44 percent better with text and illustrations than with text only. By contrast, more skilled readers performed 23 percent better. These results clearly indicate that the text plus illustrations combination is typically superior to text alone.[37] Further, the results suggest that if the audience consists of less able readers or reluctant readers, it is especially important to combine well-designed visuals with the text and to avoid a text-only approach.

When words and pictures are working well together, there is little doubt that they afford the reader better information than either one alone. Figure 6.7 presents an example that illustrates the point. This text and picture combination comes from a college textbook about cognitive psychology and problem solving (Hayes, 1989a). Notice that the text asks the reader to take on the role of the waiter in the picture. By showing the reader how we lose information from short-term memory in an everyday setting, the reader may find it easy to understand the concept of displacement. The picture without the words requires special knowledge to guess its meaning. The words without the picture don't provide the same degree of vividness and specificity as they do with it.

Larkin and Simon (1987) discussed what words or pictures may offer readers when the two representations are informationally equivalent, that is, "all of the information in the one is also inferable from the other, and vice versa" (p. 67). They found that whether a picture is the best representation depends on the nature of the idea depicted, on the spatial

---

[37] In a well-designed study, Westendorp (1995) compared seven different picture-text combinations as people carried out a set of instructions for using a multifeatured telephone system. Surprisingly, the "words-only" condition enabled users to use the procedures more quickly and more accurately than either "static pictures" or "animated instructions accompanied by prose." Westendorp's results stand in contrast to those which suggest that prose plus pictures lead to best performance. One explanation for Westendorp's findings may be that people are very familiar with the spatial array of telephones and don't really need the extra spatial information provided by pictures (as we saw in Chapter 4, readers tended to use the telephone manual least; see Table 4.2, p. 214). A more complex or less familiar product might lead to very different results. Differences among studies such as these remind document designers of the importance of carefully analyzing the function of the words or pictures, asking what the particular situation will demand of the reader and what role the words and pictures should play in order to help readers meet their goals.

FORGETTING AND SHORT-TERM MEMORY

There are two ways we can lose information from short-term memory: by *displacement* and by *decay*.

Displacement

Imagine yourself as a novice waiter who believes that good waiters keep orders in short-term memory. You take the order of your first customer: mussels, borscht, spaghetti, rice, asparagus, pickles, and cocoa. "Very good, ma'am," you say, not really meaning it, but confident that the order is safely stored in short-term memory. As you walk away, the customer says, "And a side of zucchini, waiter!" Now you're in trouble. Your short-term memory holds seven chunks and zucchini makes eight. You remember the zucchini, but it has pushed something else out of STM. You have no idea what it was. But you know that at some point the customer is going to say, "Waiter, where is my _____?"

This is forgetting by *displacement*. Because short-term memory holds a limited number of chunks, putting a new chunk in when it is full will push an old chunk out.

◀ Figure 6.7 *An example of a well-integrated text and illustration. Together they convey the idea about short-term memory better than either alone.* From The Complete Problem Solver (1989) *written by John R. Hayes and illustrated by Joan E. Krejcar. Reprinted with the permission of Lawrence Erlbaum Associates, Hillsdale, NJ.*

organization of the display, and on the grouping within the visual. For example, they note that in a diagram "often much of the information needed to make an inference is present and explicit at a single location" (p. 65). In addition, whether words or pictures are better depends on the knowledge and skills of the reader (who must know how to take advantage of the structure of the display). Hegarty and her colleagues (Hegarty, Carpenter, & Just, 1991; Hegarty & Steinhoff, 1994) showed that readers with high-spatial ability were better at using technical diagrams of pulley systems than readers with low-spatial ability.

Wright and Reid (1973) compared the speed and accuracy with which people could use a flowchart, a table, and an itemized list. They found that the advantage of either format depended on the difficulty of the task people needed to do. When the task was simple, readers performed the fastest with the table, followed by the list, and slowest with the flowchart. When the task was hard, readers were more accurate with the flowchart, then the table, and worst with the list. Wright and Reid conclude that the most appropriate format for presenting information will depend on the characteristics of the readers and on the complexity of the task.

Tables, matrices, and flowcharts may pose problems for readers unfamiliar with the spatial cues these formats use. Wright (1982) argued that people need special skills to interpret tabulated materials and that redundancy can be an important aid in reducing the reader's cognitive load. For example, people often find it easier to use tables organized as lists than tables organized as matrices. (With a matrix format, readers must scan a column and a row to locate a particular cell; in a list format, they have only one dimension to deal with). Similarly, some people do poorly with flowcharts because they aren't familiar with their conventions (e.g., what triangles, diamonds, and rectangles may mean) and may be averse to learning from them. By contrast, experts have been found to use diagrammatic information more efficiently than prose because they know where to look (Hegarty et al., 1991).

However, visuals are not always helpful. In some situations, pictures may even get in the way, especially if they merely decorate the text, distracting readers from engaging fully with the content they most need (Peeck, 1987). For example, in studies about how people understand broadcast television news, researchers have found that viewers need to pay attention to both the words and pictures. In particular, viewers need to concentrate on the narrative structure of the text (presented orally) in order to understand the story and its causal connections (e.g., who did what to whom and why). A striking picture may weaken the listener's attention to the words, leading to a shallow and disjointed understanding of the content (Berry, 1983a, 1983b; Gunter, 1987). Similarly, in an interview with the cast and managers of the television newsmagazine *60 Minutes,* the producer offered these words about the integration of words and pictures: "In designing our news segments, we usually create the words first and then the pictures. Listening to the story is more important than a flag-waving graphic. Since graphics are so powerful, they may take over the story" (CNN, *Larry King Live Show,* August 17, 1996).

Researchers have been concerned with whether people learn more from prose, pictures, or combinations, but they also want to know which medium readers prefer. Although document designers' lives would be made simpler if what readers preferred matched what they performed best with, this is often not the case.

Psychologists suggest there may be dramatic *performance-preference tradeoffs,* that is, people may prefer a medium they do not perform well with. They may like pictures, but learn little from them. They may prefer words but learn more from pictures, or they may prefer pictures but do just as well with words and pictures. An interesting illustration comes from Swedish research on people watching television news programs. Studies of broadcast news show that although viewers prefer to view the news with as much "live footage" as possible, the impact of still photos, graphics, or schematic drawings can be *just as good* in enhancing learning from the news (Findahl, 1971; Findahl & Hoijer, 1976, Gunter, 1987, p. 248). Just as on television, we can imagine that having full-motion video on the Web won't necessarily enhance learning.

There is little argument about the power of pictures to make ideas vivid.[38] The continuing controversy is over how to bring words and pictures together in harmonious ways so that readers can use the information to fit their unique purposes—whether their goal is to enjoy the text, to learn from it, to assess its relevance, to use it directly in carrying out a task, or to learn from it in order to lay the foundation for accomplishing a long-term goal.[39]

The evidence indicates that the decisions document designers make about the relationships between prose and graphics can have a major impact both on the clarity of the message and on how engaging the message is. To help insure that the impact is positive, document designers should take time to learn about the audience—their preferences, expectations, and biases for one format or another. In the section that follows, I will provide some suggestions that can help document designers make these decisions with greater rhetorical sensitivity. However, in designing combinations of prose and graphics, it is important to recognize that readers are an independent lot. They decide what they are going to read and in what order. If we want our readers to read in a certain way, we need to provide them with clear and interesting cues to guide them. (Even then, though, there is no guarantee that readers will use the cues we provide.)

Making Words and Pictures Work Together: The Basics

Obviously, documents that make a reader struggle to get the main points because of poorly designed picture-prose combinations waste the reader's time. When prose and pictures that are intended to work together are

[38] Not only is vividness important to pictures, but it is also highly desirable in choosing words. Research shows that words which readily evoke images are better remembered than abstract ideas that are less easily visualized (Bower, 1970; Paivio, 1969). Similarly, in studies of narratives, concrete passages are remembered and understood better than passages filled with abstract terminology (Philipchalk, 1972; Yuille & Paivio, 1969).

[39] These goals for reading were discussed in Chapter 5. See the "Typeface Under Duress Study" (pp. 288–303).

poorly written, poorly visualized, contradictory, or when one mode makes a point prominently that the other tends to obscure or fails to mention, readers must spend extra effort figuring out the intended relationship (Benson, 1994; Gunter, 1987; Levin, Anglin & Carney, 1987). We've seen examples of these sorts of problems in the previous chapter (see Figures 5.16 and 5.32, pp. 308, 321) and in the case study of the *Virtual Tourist*.

But the quality of the writing and design is not the only aspect of picture–prose combinations that can give readers troubles. Words and pictures can also create difficulties for readers when they are physically separated from one another in space or time; for example, charts or graphs that are positioned at the end of a report instead of in proximity to their mention (Winn, 1991) or animations that are presented after a prose explanation in a multimedia program instead with the explanation simultaneously (Mayer & Sims, 1994). When words and pictures appear in separate places, readers are forced to split their attention between the two modes and mentally integrate the disparate sources of information before the content can be intelligible (Chandler & Sweller, 1991). This not only annoys the reader but also, and more important, distracts the reader from thinking about the message of the text (Sweller, Chandler, Tierney, & Cooper, 1990).

Moreover, the research literature suggests two important characteristics of prose and graphic combinations: (1) the quality of the writing and the design and (2) the spatial relationship (in time or space) between the prose and graphics. Even when these two characteristics are well orchestrated, there are many sorts of relationships that might exist between the prose and graphics. Next I describe five of the most common relationships.

FIVE WAYS TO INTEGRATE PROSE AND GRAPHICS

Previous research has characterized three key relationships among prose and pictures: redundant, complementary, and supplementary (Hegarty, Carpenter, & Just, 1991; Willows & Houghton, 1987a, 1987b). To these three I add two more: juxtapositional and stage-setting. Let's look at each briefly and then in more detail.

- *Redundant*—characterized by substantially identical content appearing visually and verbally, in which each mode tells the same story, providing repetition of key ideas

- *Complementary*—characterized by different content visually and verbally, in which both modes are needed in order to understand the key ideas

- *Supplementary*—characterized by different content in words and pictures, in which one mode dominates the other, providing the main ideas, while the other reinforces, elaborates, or instantiates the points made in the dominant mode (or explains how to interpret the other)

- *Juxtapositional*—characterized by different content in words and pictures, in which the key ideas are created by a clash or a semantic tension between the ideas in each mode; the idea cannot be inferred without both modes being present simultaneously

- *Stage-Setting*—characterized by different content in words and pictures, in which one mode (often the visual) forecasts the content, underlying theme, or ideas presented in the other mode

These do not necessarily constitute a complete set of all the relationships readers may experience or that document designers may want to establish. Further, in some cases a prose and graphics combination may fall on the boundary of two categories. This set simply represents some of the more common ways words and pictures work together.

Redundant

A first way that prose and graphics can work together effectively is through redundancy, the repetition or paraphrasing of key ideas. Redundancy is often achieved in document design by presenting similar ideas in alternative representations (e.g., visually and verbally), in alternative media (e.g., paper and online), or through different senses (e.g., sight and sound).

Redundancy has a Jekyll and Hyde nature. It appears as the evil Mr. Hyde when the author tells us or shows us things that we already know very well. However, it appears as the good Dr. Jekyll when we are struggling to understand a concept fully. In using redundancy, document designers must exercise judgment about the difficulty of the topic and the audience's level of skill and interest. The more difficult the topic, the more likely it is that the audience will welcome redundancy.

Research shows that people's comprehension may be improved if key points are presented both in words and pictures, allowing readers to acquire new information both visually and verbally, a process that Paivio (1990) calls "dual coding." The idea is that when pictures reformulate what is presented in prose or vice versa, the reader can generate another representation of the content. Taking in information in more than one way increases the likelihood that readers will understand and remember it. Multiple representations may have important benefits, helping people build stronger and more elaborate connections about the subject matter in memory.

A study by Atman and Puerzer (1995) tested four ways of presenting information about the process of global warming:

1. A continuous prose paragraph

2. An itemized list

3. A flowchart with a prose paragraph

4. A diagram with a prose paragraph

Figure 6.8 shows the alternative versions used in the Atman and Puerzer study. Notice that Examples 3 and 4 are fully redundant conditions, giving the same ideas in both visual and verbal form. Example 3 offers a mental model of the relationships among the content by showing the structural relationships in the form of a flowchart. Example 4 provides the more traditional redundant pair, a schematic diagram with a prose explanation that repeats the ideas.

Each participant read one of these versions and answered a set of comprehension questions. After the comprehension test, participants evaluated all four formats and chose the one they preferred. Atman and Puerzer found no significant differences in readers' comprehension of the main points about global warming across these four ways. However, readers overwhelmingly preferred the diagram with the prose paragraph (Example 4 in Figure 6.8). Participants reported feeling more comfortable with the pictures and words, preferring the more literal diagram over the flowchart. But keep in mind that their preference for the diagram did not increase their understanding. As I noted earlier, what people may prefer to

▼ Figure 6.8 *Four different ways of presenting information about global warming.*

GLOBAL WARMING

What Is The Greenhouse Effect?

Energy from the sun (mainly light) passes through the earth's atmosphere. Some of it is reflected back into space by clouds and light-colored parts of the earth (like snow). Most of the energy is absorbed by the atmosphere and the earth's surface. The earth and atmosphere warm up and try to radiate heat energy back to space.

Greenhouse gases in the atmosphere trap this energy for a time in the earth's atmosphere. Greenhouse gases include water vapor, carbon dioxide, methane, nitrous oxide and chlorofluorocarbons (CFCs). This process is called the greenhouse effect because the greenhouse gases trap heat in the atmosphere in the same way that glass traps heat in a greenhouse.

Example 1: Continuous prose format.

GLOBAL WARMING

What Is The Greenhouse Effect?

• Energy from the sun (mainly light) passes through the earth's atmosphere.

• Some of it is reflected back into space by clouds and light-colored parts of the earth (like snow). Most of the energy is absorbed by the atmosphere and the earth's surface.

• The earth and atmosphere warm up and try to radiate heat energy back to space.

• Greenhouse gases in the atmosphere trap this energy for a time in the earth's atmosphere. Greenhouse gases include water vapor, carbon dioxide, methane, nitrous oxide and chlorofluorocarbons (CFCs).

• This process is called the greenhouse effect because the greenhouse gases trap heat in the atmosphere in the same way that glass traps heat in a greenhouse.

Example 2: Itemized list format.

read may offer them no better information, but may keep them reading long enough to get the most from a document.

Complementary

Words and pictures that complement one another employ different visual and verbal content, and both modes are designed to work together in order to help the reader understand the same main idea (the same referent). Together, the two modes render the idea more fully than either does alone because each provides different information about the idea. For example, a complementary text and diagram combination about how a motor works might offer a 3-D presentation of the spatial features of the motor, a representation that would be cumbersome to provide in prose. On the other hand, details about the purpose of the motor and its practical uses might be best presented in words. Each form makes a unique contribution to strengthen and clarify the reader's understanding of the main idea.

Complementary relationships also help readers integrate the content from words and pictures. Each mode has a mutually constraining effect on the meanings readers are likely to generate for the main idea. For instance, a headline of a newspaper may suggest how to interpret the front-page photo. Let's examine some differences in what readers may understand from words only, from pictures only, and from a complementary text and graphic combination. Figure 6.9 (on the next spread) shows three ways of presenting instructions. The example was created by a former graduate student of mine, Tamara Sargeant, in the class "Integrating Visual and

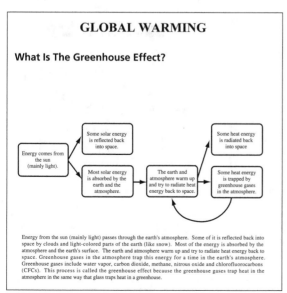

Example 3: Flowchart and prose format.

Example 4: Diagram and prose format.

Verbal Texts." This assignment required that students document a procedure for "removing, inserting, and verifying batteries" in three ways:

1. Words only (with a modular grid and typography to signal the textual hierarchy)

2. Pictures only, including icons or directional symbols such as arrows (numbers and minimal headings were also included)

3. Words and pictures (designed to instantiate a relationship between prose and graphics, such as complementary or supplementary)

Sargeant documented the procedures for a pocket translator that converted English to Japanese and vice versa. In her words-only version (see Example 1), Sargeant employed a simple grid with enumerated steps (in which the numbers "hang" in the margin) and "cautions" and "tips" are outdented. Sargeant's straightforward action-oriented writing style is clear and concise. Notice, however, that the words-only version neither allows the user to envision exactly where the battery tray is nor how it slides open.

In the pictures-only version (see Example 2), she arranges the six steps in a three rows, reading left to right. To promote coherence and visual repetition, each procedure is enclosed with a retaining box of the same size. Note that the hands and the arrow give positional and orientation information not available in the word-only version. But notice that the information about how to position the batteries so the positive (+) signs are facing up is not available in the pictures-only version. There is also a procedural gap between steps 3 and 4 in that there is no visual information

▼ Figure 6.9 *The original and revised versions of instructions for inserting batteries into a pocket translator. In the revised versions the numbered pictures help readers visualize the steps of the task they are trying to accomplish. Created by Tamara Sargeant, who holds a master's degree in professional writing.*

How to Change the Batteries

You will need two SONY CR2025 lithium batteries.

◆ Caution: Do not expose batteries to open flame or intense heat.

Removing old batteries

① Turn the translator off by pressing the OFF, the top key on the right hand side.

② Turn the unit over.

③ Using a sharp-pointed object, such as a fine tip pen, press the small circle labeled PUSH. It is on the left hand side under the diagram.

④ While still pressing the circle, grip the slot to the left with your finger nail and slide the battery tray out to the left.

⑤ Tip the tray to remove the old batteries.

Inserting new batteries

▲ Tip: It is best not to combine a new battery with an old one

① Place the new CR2025 lithium batteries on top of the circles in the battery tray making sure the writing and + signs are facing up.

② Slide the tray back into the unit. Push it until a click is heard.

Verifying the batteries

Turn the translator on by pressing the J→E Key located on the front right hand side. The words that appear in the display screen should be very clear.

If the translator does not come on or if the words are faint, press the RESET circle located on the bottom at the back.

Example 1: Words only.

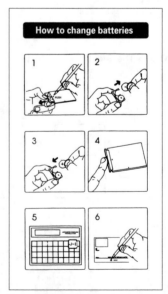

Example 2: Pictures only.

about how to slide the tray back into the unit. The verbal instructions say "Push it [the tray] until a click is heard." This information perhaps could have been conveyed visually, but it would be difficult to do so without using the word "click."

The words and pictures version (see Example 3) is mainly text with selected complementary word and picture relationships. The illustrations provide spatial cues about where to press, how to slide open the battery tray, and how to insert the batteries, while the prose offers explicit procedures about where to look, what to do, and when to do it. These complementary words and pictures together provide complete information about the actions to take.

In an informal usability test of these alternatives, Sargeant found that readers preferred Example 2 (the pictures-only version) but performed more accurately with Example 3 (the words and pictures version). Notice how difficult it is to provide information about verifying the batteries using only pictures. As Bieger and Glock (1986) point out, a diagram is useful for spatial, contextual, and configural information, but prose may be a better source of procedural details.

Let's look at a final example to see why prose and graphics in complementary combinations can be better than words or pictures alone. Figure 6.10 (on the next page) shows how a diagram can help make abstract textual content more concrete and understandable.

The topic of Figure 6.10 is from Salvadori's (1980) book about architecture, which in his words is "for those who love beautiful buildings and wonder how they stand up" (p. 13). The book is mainly text with diagrams that complement or supplement the prose. The excerpt shown in Figure 6.10 is from a section about how roofs are built in which he discusses dome roofs and flat roofs. Here Salvadori discusses two types of surfaces from which roofs can be built: developable and non-developable. For those of us who are not architects, these concepts

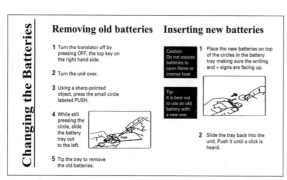
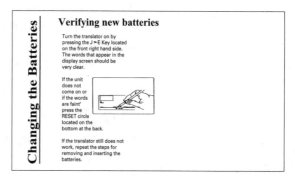

Example 3: Words and pictures.

▶ **Figure 6.10** *An example of how text and illustrations can work together to make an idea clearer. Reprinted from Mario Salvadori,* How Buildings Stand Up: The Strength of Architecture, *with the permission of W. W. Norton & Company, Inc., New York. Copyright © 1980 by W. W. Norton & Company, Inc.*

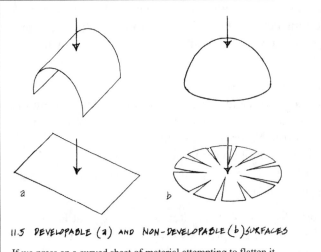

11.5 DEVELOPABLE (a) AND NON-DEVELOPABLE (b) SURFACES

If we press on a curved sheet of material attempting to flatten it, depending on its shape, the sheet will flatten by itself of have to be stretched or sliced before is can be made flat. For example, a sheet of paper bent into a half-cylinder and then released flattens by itself (Fig. 11.5a). It is said to be a developable surface (from the idea "to unfold" contained in the verb "to develop"). But if we cut a rubber ball in half, producing a small spherical dome, the dome will not flatten by itself if we lay it on a flat surface. Neither will it become flat if we push on it. It only flattens if we cut a large number of radial cuts in it or if, assuming it is very thin, it can be stretched into a flat surface (Fig. 11.5b). The dome (and actually all other surfaces except the cylinder) are non-developable, unflattening surfaces. Because they are so hard to flatten, they are also much stiffer than developable surfaces. (It will be more obvious why non-developable surfaces are better suited to build large roofs once we learn how such roofs sustain loads.)

are neither intuitive nor transparent. In fact, the meanings of "developable" and "non-developable" are counterintuitive; developable seems like a good thing, a surface that could be developed; while non-developable suggests it could not be developed. However, as the complementary diagram makes clear, non-developable surfaces tend to hold themselves up because flattening them requires distorting or tearing them. Thus, they are better suited for building large roofs than are developable surfaces. Salvadori's diagram and text complement one another because each provides essential information not provided by the other that allows the reader to understand the distinction.

Supplementary

A third way words and pictures may be arranged is in a supplementary relationship, in which one mode is dominant, providing the main ideas and most of the content, while the other shores up and elaborates the points made in the dominant mode. Integrating words and pictures through supplementary relationships has been studied more than any of the other ways of bringing prose and graphics together (see Willows & Houghton, 1987a). Words or pictures that supplement one another often occur in the form of examples—a picture may illustrate a point or a sidebar may unpack a picture.

The literature on problem solving suggests that examples can be useful for learners, particularly if they are used actively in thinking through an idea (VanLehn, Jones, & Chi, 1992). A number of studies suggest that supplementary words or pictures may enhance learning. For example, Bernard (1990) found that extended captions can improve learning from instructional illustrations, suggesting that document designers may need to consider ways to more effectively elaborate captions to prompt readers to process the content more thoughtfully. Smillie (1985) studied the effects of illustrated job-performance aids in United States military contexts (e.g., documents intended for enlisted personnel who carry out jobs in which they "read to do," such as reading a manual to fix an Army Jeep). He found that to get someone to understand a complex procedure that involves flipping a switch or turning a knob requires a picture that makes the action as explicit as possible, showing only the part of the object needed for the step.

A few examples of supplementary relationships reveal how they work. Lest we think that a well-designed supplementary relationship is a recent invention, Figure 6.11 (on the following page) shows a few excerpts from the 1915 *Singer Sewing Machine Manual*. Even with its rather crude layout (fully justified text with perfectly symmetrical arrangement of text and picture combinations), there is little doubt that the illustrations are a very helpful supplement to the procedural instructions. The picture in the first panel allows the user to make a comparison between the body of her machine (in 1915, it was her machine) and the photo; even sewing machines had a variety of slightly different models from which to choose.

In the second panel of Figure 6.11, the user learns how to raise the presser foot in order to make a stitch. Notice how the procedures are linked to the machine parts. The figure illustrates what to do, amplifying ideas already stated in the text with a concrete embodiment of the thing itself. In the third panel, the user is provided close-ups of how to hold the bobbin. These give a sense of scale, orientation, and position that is not captured in the prose, even though one could argue that the information is there. These illustrations both elaborate the points made in the proce-dures and reinforce them by pointing at the same referent.

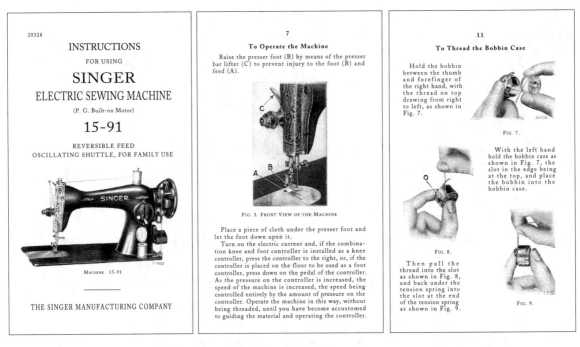

▲ **Figure 6.11** *Pages from a 1915 Singer sewing machine manual offer a combination of airbrushed drawings and realistic pictures to document the procedures for using the machine. The pictures supply information not available in the text, such as spatial cues about how to hold the bobbin case in relation to the bobbin and what the slot of the bobbin case looks like. Reprinted from the* Instuctions for Using the Singer Electric Sewing Machine, Model 15-91 *with the permission of the Singer Sewing Company, Edison, NJ.*

A different sort of supplementary relationship is shown in Figure 6.12, an excerpt from a psychology textbook written by John Hayes (1989a). The text describes how the research method "protocol analysis" can be used in studying problem solving. Importantly, the text also suggests that there is much the method cannot help researchers to see, for "the mental process, like the porpoise, runs deep and silent." But even with these words, which are concrete and allow the reader to imagine the scene the author paints, the idea of just how little researchers can see when using protocol analysis becomes vivid only after we see the picture of the porpoises jumping in and out of the water. The picture reminds us that the porpoise is in the water much deeper and longer than his occasional leaps above the waves. Unlike just reading the words, this gives the reader a feel for the seascape—for the advantages and limitations of protocol analysis.

We can see that supplementary relationships can be employed to elaborate key points that need to be "driven home" for the reader. When the reader may have trouble imagining what is intended, supplementary prose or pictures often help to clarify and expand how the reader construes the main ideas.

◀ Figure 6.12 *A page from a psychology textbook that describes the research method called protocol analysis. Reprinted from* The Complete Problem Solver *(1989), written by John R. Hayes and illustrated by Joan E. Krejcar. Reprinted with the permission of Lawrence Erlbaum Associates, Hillsdale, NJ.*

PROTOCOL ANALYSIS MORE GENERALLY CONSIDERED

As we have seen, protocol analysis can be used as an aid in understanding a wide variety of tasks from simple problem solving by apes to complex performances such as solving algebra word problems and playing chess. Typically though, protocols are incomplete. Many processes occur during the performance of a task which the subject can't or doesn't report. The psychologist's task in analyzing a protocol is to take the incomplete record provided by the protocol, together with his knowledge of human capabilities, and to infer from these a model of the underlying psychological processes by which the subject performs the task.

Analyzing a protocol is like following the tracks of a porpoise. Occasionally, the purpose reveals itself by breaking the surface of the sea. Its brief surfacings are like the glimpses of the underlying mental processes which the protocol affords us. Between surfacings, the mental process, like the porpoise, runs deep and silent. Our task is to infer the course of the process from these brief traces.

It is important for document designers to plan carefully how a supplementary prose and graphic combination should function within the structure of a document. As we have seen, unneeded additions can be distracting and unsystematic additions can be confusing. Moreover, randomly added pictures may inappropriately lead readers to believe that the topics with pictures are more important than those without pictures.

▶ **Figure 6.13** *A page from the J. Peterman Company Catalog for Christmas 1992. Reprinted with the permission of J. Peterman, owner of the J. Peterman Company, Lexington, KY.*

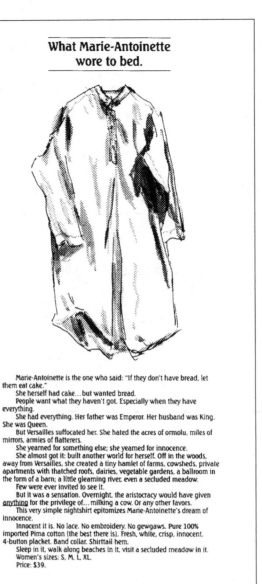

What Marie-Antoinette wore to bed.

Marie-Antoinette is the one who said: "If they don't have bread, let them eat cake."

She herself had cake…but wanted bread.

People want what they haven't got. Especially when they have everything.

She had everything. Her father was Emperor. Her husband was King. She was Queen.

But Versailles suffocated her. She hated the acres of ormolu, miles of mirrors, armies of flatterers.

She yearned for something else; she yearned for innocence.

She almost got it: built another world for herself. Off in the woods, away from Versailles, she created a tiny hamlet of farms, cowsheds, private apartments with thatched roofs, dairies, vegetable gardens, a ballroom in the form of a barn; a little gleaming river, even a secluded meadow.

Few were ever invited to see it.

But it was a sensation. Overnight, the aristocracy would have given anything for the privilege of…milking a cow. Or any other favors.

This very simple nightshirt epitomizes Marie-Antoinette's dream of innocence.

Innocent it is. No lace. No embroidery. No gewgaws. Pure 100% imported Pima cotton (the best there is). Fresh, white, crisp, innocent. 4-button placket. Band collar. Shirttail hem.

Sleep in it, walk along beaches in it, visit a secluded meadow in it. Women's sizes: S, M, L, XL.

Price: $39.

101

Juxtapositional

A fourth way that prose and graphics may interact is through a juxtapositional relationship, in which the main idea is created by a clash, an unexpected synthesis, or a tension between what is represented in each mode. With juxtapositional relationships, the reader cannot infer the intended idea unless both prose and graphics are present simultaneously. In *Type and Image,* design historian Philip Meggs (1992a) says "that type can bind an image, directing the viewer toward a specific meaning…. A headline or a title is often on equal level with the image…. Headlines and titles often interact with images to clarify, modify, or extend their meanings…. Visual-verbal synergy is the cooperative action of words and pictures used together to create a meaning that is greater than the signification of the parts" (pp. 41–64).

The most common environment for juxtapositional relationships is advertising, which as a matter of course operates by conjoining rather disparate visual and verbal elements. Take, for example, Figure 6.13, "What Marie Antoinette Wore to Bed," an ad from the *J. Peterman and Company Catalog*. What is interesting about this ad is that what the reader imagines depends fully on the synthesis of the two modes rather than on the interpretation of one or the other. On its own, the nightshirt looks ordinary. No big deal. But when coupled with the idea of Marie Antoinette, the ordinary cotton takes on a regal, romantic air.

As a way to talk about juxtapositional relationships with my students, I have used this ad in my classes. In doing so, I copy the ad and duplicate the picture of the nightshirt on one sheet of paper and the body copy on another. I give half the class the nightshirt and the other half the body copy. Then I ask each group to fill in the missing mode—visual or verbal, asking students who get the "nightshirt only" to write the body copy that might accompany such a product and the students who get the "body copy only" to draw a picture of the product. Inevitably, students in the nightshirt-only group write copy that sounds as if it came straight from New England outfitting companies such as L.L. Bean or Lands End. Students in the copy-only group tend to create pictures of an elegant lady in a long white flowing gown, no embroidery or lace but definitely romantic. Afterwards, students share their creations and discuss what actually appeared in the catalog. Students were often horrified to find that their "first-impulse original idea" was nearly identical to those of many other people in their group. For example, in almost every class (I tried this many times) a good proportion of students in the shirt-only group would not only describe the shirt as made of 100-percent pima cotton, but would also provide the consumer with an optional tartan plaid pattern.

When they are done well, juxtapositional relationships have a way of surprising the reader. Consider Figure 6.14 (on the next page). The idea of a nun selling "conversion techniques" is a humorous mix of the profane and the sacred. Notice that if we saw the picture of the nun with only the logo "Pittsburgh Type," the ad wouldn't work. Similarly, if we saw just the words "Some conversion techniques are better than others," it would be just more of the same old same old. The dynamic interaction between the picture and the words creates a meaning that is different from and more interesting than the meaning of either alone.

▶ **Figure 6.14** *An example of a juxtapositional relationship between the prose and graphics. This ad won a 1993 advertising award for black and white photography for a business or trade publication in Pittsburgh, PA. The copywriters were Bill Garrison and Cathy Bowen, the art director was David Hughes, and the photography was by Rieder & Walsh, Inc. Reprinted with the permission of Pittsburgh Type, Pittsburgh, PA.*

Juxtapositional relationships between prose and graphics are most often employed in advertising design, poster art, book jackets, CD-cover design, and cartoons. In general, document designers have been a bit conservative in their picture-prose combinations, tending to stick mainly with supplementary relationships. Clearly there is much more room for exploration and creativity in combining word and image.

Stage-Setting

A fifth way that prose and graphics may interact is through a stage-setting relationship, in which one mode provides a context for the other mode by forecasting its content or soon-to-be presented themes. A stage-setting text or graphic may enhance what follows it by providing a contextual framework in which the verbal content can be understood (Bransford and Johnson, 1972). Researchers have explored the effects of stage-setting text features such as outlines, lists of instructional objectives, flowcharts, summaries, and advance organizers. The advance organizer was defined by Ausubel (1960) as a brief prose paragraph which precedes a detailed text and which is at a higher level of abstraction than a summary. An advance organizer is intended to provide a framework for learning new material. Stage-setting prose or pictures have been found to be helpful as long as they don't give the reader a narrow impression of the topic and encourage them to selectively ignore parts of the text that are not previewed.

Kieras and Bovair (1984) studied how learning to operate a mechanical device can be facilitated by providing a stage-setting pictorial model that helps learners understand how the device works. They found that the users who learned procedures with the initial help of a pictorial model (they called it a "device model") could learn new procedures with the same equipment much faster. They proposed that providing readers with a mental model of complex devices could help readers in significant ways. Their work is consistent with earlier research on mental models, advance organizers, summaries, and previews—all of which serve to help readers get a sense of the "big picture" before they begin.

One context in which document designers often present stage-setting relationships is at the beginning of chapters in multi-chaptered documents. It is common to conjoin the title of a chapter with an evocative illustration in the chapter's opening spread. The idea in joining an image with the title is to give the reader a feel for the theme of the content. Although it is most typical simply to repeat a key visual that appears within the chapter, at other times the stage-setting relationship does more than simply provide a visual anchor of what the reader is about to read. Sometimes a stage-setting relationship aims to shape the reader's attitude about the content in a particular way. In Figures 6.15 and 6.16 (on the next spread), I present two illustrations that were designed as chapter dividers for a VCR manual.[40] The purpose of the illustrations was to preview the content and give the reader the impression that the information about the VCR would not be hard to understand.

Figure 6.15 appeared as a left-hand page that accompanied a chapter (which began on a right-hand page) entitled "Learning Advanced Tasks: How to Get the Most from Your VCR." The topics in this chapter ranged from "getting rid of picture distortion in a videotape" to "editing tapes with two VCRs." One of the goals of the opening spread was to give the reader a sense of how simple even advanced tasks could be. The manufacturer of the VCR, a large Japanese consumer electronics company, wanted to emphasize the VCR's advanced recording features. Shown in Figure 6.15 is illustrator Burton Morris' interpretation of an image that readers would find easy to understand and that would convey the idea that

40 These illustrations were created as part of a larger project by my colleagues and me (described in Chapter 7). My colleagues were Michele Matchett, Norma Pribadi Polk, Mary L. Ray, Dan Boyarski, Carlos Peterson, Daniel Lepore, Burton Morris, James Adams, and Ilene Lederer.

▶ **Figure 6.15** *An Illustration for a chapter divider in a VCR Manual. Designed by Burton Morris for Karen Schriver Associates, Pittsburgh, PA.*

the user could tape a show, even while they were sleeping. This drawing was one that our document design team liked a lot; we felt it met our goals for previewing the content and for setting the mood. We were not sure, however, about whether the image of the children sleeping on the rug would give readers the idea that the VCR was taping a show on the TV.

Figure 6.16 was designed to accompany a chapter entitled "Trouble-shooting." Our intent with this illustration was to give the reader a whimsical image of "things going wrong" (on the left page) with "here's what to do" on the right page. We sought a direct but humorous approach to the topic of troubleshooting. Our document design team thought this drawing established the right tone for the chapter.

Let's look at what readers thought about Figures 6.15 and 6.16. To learn about how readers would interpret these drawings, I conducted an informal evaluation in which I asked 25 undergraduate and graduate students (ages eighteen to thirty-seven) to provide some feedback about how well the illustrations worked for them. Students were writing and design majors in my class "Integrating Visual and Verbal Texts." To elicit their feedback I copied the two illustrations without their chapter title, just as they are shown in Figures 6.15 and 6.16. On a separate sheet of paper, I listed the table of contents for the VCR manual. Each student looked at the two pictures and chose which chapter title the picture best suited. I also asked students to (1) describe the goal of the picture and (2) to say whether they liked it. Students did not know that my colleagues and I had designed it and so were very generous with their criticisms.

Of the 25 students, 23 correctly identified Figure 6.15 as coming from a chapter on "Advanced Features" and 25 of 25 guessed accurately that

◀ **Figure 6.16** *An illustration for a trouble-shooting section of an instruction guide for a VCR. The illustration was intended to present a humourous and light-hearted approach to troubleshooting. Unfortunately, the client did not interpret the illustration in this way. Designed by Burton Morris for Karen Schriver Associates, Pittsburgh, PA.*

6.16 was linked with "Troubleshooting." Students were quite familiar with the functionality of VCRs and readily described the goal of Figure 6.15 in words such as the following: "programming a VCR to tape a show," "recording a show while you're out," or "taping a program with the TV off." Students had no problem figuring out the intended content of the illustration. However, in judgments students made about whether they liked the illustration, we found that 18 students liked it while 7 disliked it. Surprisingly, those who disliked it had the same reason, a reason that no one on our team had considered. Students felt the picture showed an irresponsible mother and father who were "sneaking out to go somewhere and leaving the VCR and dog at home as babysitters." This response took our design team by surprise. We thought it looked as though the kids had simply fallen asleep in front of the TV and that the mom might be whispering to the dad, "sh-h-h … the kids are asleep." Those students who disliked the picture thought it was a bad idea to include it in a revision. As one student put it, the company should not be presenting the message, "We'll keep the kids company even when you go away."

By contrast, students liked the illustration for the Troubleshooting chapter (Figure 6.16). They thought it was funny and many of them mentioned that they "really liked the dog's eyes." In fact, 24 of 25 students liked it; the one who didn't thought it was dumb.

But as I discussed in Chapter 3, the intended audience for a document is not the document designer's only audience. When our document design team showed these illustrations to our client, we got yet another response. The client felt that Figure 6.15 was quite appropriate for their manual and thought it would work well in their various markets, particularly VCRs aimed at consumers in the middle range of their target markets. Their only worry was that they felt the television looked as though it came from the 1950s. We explained that the TV was not the focus of the picture nor would readers remember its details. Since the company also makes televisions, they were concerned that readers might think their TVs looked like the one in the picture. But after further consideration, the client decided that Figure 6.15 was a success. When the client team saw Figure 6.16, however, it was a different story. Our client felt that the picture showed the VCR exploding—frightening everyone in the family including the poor dog. Everyone on the client's team hated this picture and thought it opened up the issue of product liability. Back to the drawing board.

My point in these examples is to show that we document designers need to exercise judgment in the stage-setting combinations we create. Any visual or verbal cue we present may be considered important and revealing to some readers while the same cue will be ignored by others (e.g., none of the students noticed the TV in Figure 6.15 that so concerned our client). Although it's not possible to please everyone even some of the time, getting feedback does help. Designing prose and graphic combinations on intuition alone runs the risk of pleasing only ourselves. Next is an example that shows what can happen if a document designer doesn't think through the details of integrating the visual and verbal text when setting the stage.

Setting the Wrong Stage

Figure 6.17 is a page from a book on "roadside geology" written for a layperson. The prose and picture combination shown here is an example of stage-setting gone wrong. This combination comes very early in the text, appearing on pages two and three of a 350-page book. The reader might expect it to provide an initial visual Gestalt which will be filled out as the chapters unfold. Look at the paragraph below the diagram. It tells the reader that the scale used to characterize geological time is divided in the following way: "its basic units ... periods ... are lumped ... into eras, and subdivided into ... epochs."

However, the diagram—the Geological Time Scale—does not follow this organization. The first unit of time mentioned in the text, "the period," is not the first heading in the diagram but the third. The reader is encouraged to use "period" as an anchor for interpreting the diagram and to see eras as larger than periods. Thus, instead of reading the diagram left

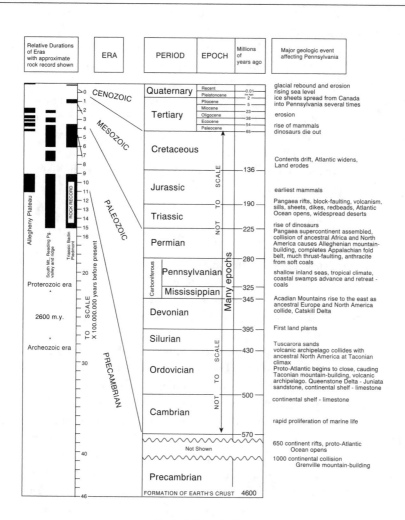

Geologic Time Scale

◀ **Figure 6.17** *Oops, this picture is worth only about 250 words. Illustrations can be difficult to follow if the description of the illustration presented in prose does not match the organization of the illustration. Reprinted from* Roadside Geology of Pennsylvania (1990), *written by Bradford B. Van Diver, with the permission of Mountain Press Publishing Company, Missoula, MT.*

The combined data derived from relative and absolute dating, and correlation for rock records from all over the world, yield the modern Geologic Time Scale, a kind of calendar of Earth history. Its basic units, called periods, are divided according to the appearance or extinction of certain life forms. Periods are lumped into larger units called eras, and subdivided into smaller ones called epochs.

The rock record of Pennsylvania spans an unusually broad range of geologic history. In guiding you through its corridors of time, I refer repeatedly to ages of the rocks in terms of the periods, eras, and epochs of the Geologic Time Scale. Don't try to memorize all these strange names, but do refer to the chart from time to time. This is your map to navigate the vast seas of geologic time.

to right, the reader must start in the middle and read left, then turn around and read right again. This might be an unnatural reading sequence for most Western readers. In addition, the little black rectangles that look like bar code are never mentioned in the text. The author's comments, though clearly intended to be friendly, suggests that he believes the reader needn't understand the diagram. This seems to send conflicting messages to the reader about the role of the text in foreshadowing the picture (and the role of this prose and picture combination in setting the stage for the whole book). The graphic is rich with potential information, but it is unclear how readers will take advantage of what it has to offer, since they must figure it out without help from the prose.

A Word about Scientific Visualization

In discussing prose-picture combinations, I have used examples in which the document designer's purpose was to explain or persuade. Here, I will show how activity in the area of scientific visualization can be instrumental not only in explaining an idea to an audience, but also in creating knowledge within the scientific community. Researchers in the sciences use visual displays such as tables, graphs, photographs, drawings, and flow diagrams to communicate their knowledge to a variety of audiences, one of the most important of which is the audience of their peers. Scientific visualization helps readers—both experts and novices in scientific and technical domains—understand the intricacies of chemical, biological, and physical processes that are almost impossible to describe in prose, processes such as how the sun's radiation influences the solar system. In fact, in some cases, the prose hasn't even been written when scientific illustrators are asked to begin visualizing. Thus, unlike the clichéd view of document design as a "clean up" activity, the work of scientific and technical illustrators can help catalyze thinking about a new idea by articulating its form, contouring its shape, and giving it visual presence.

The rhetorical role of scientific visualization on scientific thinking has only recently been considered. In the short time it has been studied, researchers have put to rest the naive view that data are somehow obvious or speak for themselves, that the scientist need only "put them out" and the reader will see their transparent significance and readily embrace the claims the scientists make. In their study of the practices of scientists working in advanced topics in biochemistry, Gilbert and Mulkay (1984) explored how scientists use data to argue for their positions. In the context of this work about the nature of scientific knowledge building, they made a number of observations about the role that scientific illustration may play in shaping scientists' thinking:

Pictures are part of and are embedded in a conceptual argument. Accordingly, the nature of the picture changes as the argument changes.... The character of the pictorial representation varies in accordance with the interpretational work being carried out in the text as a whole.... Because scientists' interpretative work tends to vary from one social context to another, pictures are also to some extent context-dependent. For example, pictures in research reports tend to differ from those in reviews. And pictures in textbooks and popular accounts of recent developments, although in some cases copied directly from the research literature, are often supplemented by pictures devised specifically for the context of teaching.... The relationship between the biological phenomena under study and their pictorial representation is treated as highly contingent.... However, the relationship is not regarded as entirely arbitrary. (pp. 146–157)

Scientific illustrators working with researchers doing cutting-edge work must often visualize a complex idea when there are no previous models upon which to draw (see Figure 6.18). In early phases of high-stakes

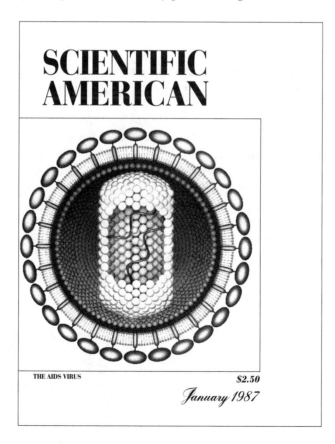

◄ Figure 6.18 *A reproduction of the first technical illustration of the AIDS virus. The original magazine cover was printed in four color. In the original drawing, the black spiral-like structure inside the rectangular shape in the center of the drawing was red. The spiral structure depicts the RNA helix, the most important feature of the inner core of the virus (For more detail, see Kelvin, 1992). Illustrated by George V. Kelvin in 1987. Reprinted with his permission.*

research, for example, the scientific discourse about the subject matter is largely oral. Such was the case for George Kelvin, scientific illustrator of the first visualization of the AIDS virus. Under the guidance of leading medical experts in the field, Kelvin painted the first illustration using the research data that was available at the time. In generating the illustration, Kelvin collaborated extensively with scientists, working with notes and slides of other viruses, and carrying out extensive face-to-face interviews. Information about the shape, size, and structure of the virus had been gathered by molecular biologists using electron microscopy and x-ray diffraction patterns. Figure 6.18 shows Kelvin's first visualization of the AIDS virus as it appeared on the cover of the *Scientific American* in 1987. The illustration depicts the virus at one million times its actual size.

Kelvin collected information that had been represented by the scientific team's "key players" in different forms, such as oral texts (i.e., conversations and interviews), visual texts (i.e., data tables, drawings, slides, graphs), and written texts. He then reconstructed these different forms by shaping them into a single representation, a visualization that could enable inferences that would not otherwise be available to scientists. Kelvin's illustration is now on exhibit at Epcot Center in Orlando, Florida.

SECTION 4
HOW READERS' VALUES AND BELIEFS INTERACT AS THEY INTERPRET PROSE AND GRAPHICS

Earlier in this chapter, I discussed how linguistic and cultural knowledge may come into play as readers interpret words (e.g., Figure 6.2). I close the chapter with an example that explores how readers' values and beliefs may interact as they interpret visuals. In the following example, I present a case study illustrating a document and the responses of a group of highly motivated readers. It shows what may happen if document designers fail to consider how an illustration may appear to someone who does not share their point of view.

What's Wrong with This Picture?

Let's Visit a Research Laboratory is a poster created by the U.S. Department of Health and Human Services in the early 1990s (see Figure 6.19 on the next spread). The poster was distributed free of charge to elementary school teachers for use in their classrooms with children in grades two through five. It was part of a package that, in addition to the poster, included sample lesson plans, a student brochure, and a teacher's guide. The original poster, about twice the width and three times the height of that displayed in Figure 6.19, is printed in four colors with a glossy finish.

Let's look at the writing and design of this poster to ask how well the prose and graphics work together for young readers. There are few words in this poster, mainly presented in the post-it–like notes at the bottom. The sentences are written in simple declarative form; for example, "This is a technician. A technician is a trained...." Most are in the affirmative. Not many are long or heavily embedded. The labels which appear at the bottom of the pictures of each room of the research lab match the labels on the post-its. So far, so good.

In terms of the poster's graphic design, depicting the research lab by presenting a cutaway view of the building gives the reader the feeling of getting to peek behind the walls—quite a nice idea. The cartoon-style illustrations are bright and colorful, probably evoking a positive response from children. A few pictures that present conceptually difficult material are explained in the notes at the bottom of the poster. For example, the picture of the monkey called Baby Lester in the incubator in Room 9 is explained in note 9, item B.[41]

[41] Though the typesize in the 13 notes looks tiny as it is reproduced here, its actual size was quite generous (about 18 points), posing no problems of legibility.

The poster may cause problems for students, however, in mapping the numbers and letters that appear within the illustrations to those that appear in the post-it notes. The lettering within the pictures, A, B, C, and so on, is randomly ordered, neither clockwise or counterclockwise, making for chaotic mapping between the points on the notes and the illustrated items. Some of the letters appear to the left of the object they label, some to the right; see, for example, Room 6, the labels C, D, and A—all could refer to the pharmacologist. Since students of this age might follow the alphabet quite literally, the haphazard labeling scheme may lead them to skip some of the items pointed out. A lesser problem, but still one that makes for inconsistency, is the mapping between the room labels and the post-it labels. In the labels for the rooms, the room numbers are the same size as the room name; in the labels for the post-its, the room numbers are large and the room names appear in a centered position in relation to the number. There appears no reason for this change in the visual display. These problems, while irksome, do not pose major difficulties for children or their teachers in comprehending the message.

However, if we take the words and the pictures together, document designers must ask a larger question: What message does this poster present about the topic? What does it say about what goes on in research laboratories that use animals in experiments? Is this image honest? Is this

▶ Figure 6.19 *This poster was part of an educational packet produced by the U.S. Department of Health and Human Services (under the auspices of the former Alcohol, Drug Abuse, and Mental Health Administration). Writers and designers at the Department of Health and Human Services skillfully crafted the poster to appeal to its audience (children in grades two to five), but in doing so, they oversimplified an extremely complex and controversial topic. The result was that some adult readers felt the poster significantly distorted the topic and presented children with biased information. In fact, animal rights groups called on the U.S. President to discontinue its publication.*

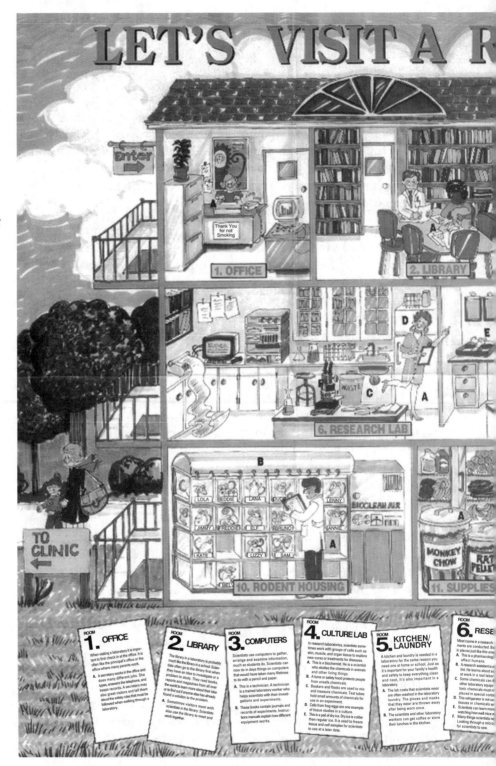

SEARCH LABORATORY

3. COMPUTERS

4. CULTURE LAB

5. KITCHEN/LAUNDRY

QUIET!

7. TESTING LAB

8. TREATMENT

Baby Lester

9. NURSERY

ACME CAGE WASHER

PLEASE DON'T FEED THE HUMANS

12. CAGE WASHER

13. MONKEY HOUSING

ROOM 7. TESTING LAB

Scientists also study animals closely related to humans, such as monkeys. Some monkeys are trained to do activities much like video games which are actually experiments. They usually work in a room of their own so as not to be disturbed.

A. This is a neuroscientist. He is a scientist who studies how the brain works.

B. When animals are needed in an experiment, scientists most often use mice or rats. When scientists want to learn more about the human brain they often work with monkeys because the brains of monkeys are very much like the brains of humans.

C. Special chairs are made for the monkeys that allow them to see the T.V. Monitor and move about comfortably, but keep them from running around the room.

D. Monkeys solve problems while looking at T.V. monitors. These monitors are connected to computers that record the monkey's answers which scientists will study later.

E. Sometimes video cameras are used to keep track of the monkey's actions.

ROOM 8. TREATMENT

Most laboratories have a room just like a doctor's office to care for animals if they become ill or get injured. Just like kids, monkeys can play and sometimes bite one another. They need treatment for cuts and scrapes.

A. This is a veterinarian. He works at the laboratory and treats sick or injured animals.

B. When people work with animals they wear lab coats, masks, and gloves to prevent the spread of any germs between animals and humans.

C. Just as in a doctor's office, there are cupboards to store medicines, ointments and creams that the veterinarian will need when treating the animals.

D. Like humans, monkeys are not always happy to be in a doctor's office.

ROOM 9. NURSERY

Baby monkeys are kept in a nursery which is somewhat like a daycare center.

A. This is a nurse. He watches over the young monkeys to be sure they are healthy and comfortable.

B. Very young monkeys get cold easily and need to stay in specially heated, covered beds called incubators. These incubators are similar to those used in hospitals for human infants. Incubators keep monkeys warm until their fur grows in.

C. Monkeys live in clean, comfortable cages big enough for them to play in. Just like children, monkeys like to play with toys, hold blankets or towels, and swing on ropes.

ROOM 10. RODENT HOUSING

All animals in the laboratory are provided proper shelter. Mice live in cages such as these when they are part of an experiment. Scientists can easily watch how well they are doing. Many laboratories raise their own rats and mice in similar cages.

A. This is a physiologist. He is a scientist that studies all the vital life processes of an organism.

B. In some experiments rats and mice must be protected from germs that might be in the air. A clear plastic tent covers this entire set of cages. Under it a machine called a flowhood blows clean air.

ROOM 11. SUPPLIES/ STORAGE

All food for laboratory animals is kept in a separate room and stored properly to be sure it stays fresh.

A. Animals are fed nutritious foods. Rats mostly eat net pellets but monkeys like to have fruits and special treats with their monkey chow. Some monkeys even enjoy popsicles served in cups.

ROOM 12. CAGE WASHER

A. This is an animal care worker. He is one the many people who is trained to help scientists take care of the animals. Animal care workers check to be sure the animals are healthy, clean the cages, feed the animals and often play with them.

B. Entire cages can be washed in special machines. Just like a kitchen dishwasher, this machine sterilizes what it cleans.

ROOM 13. MONKEY HOUSING

Every effort is made to safeguard the well-being of laboratory monkeys.

A. This is an ethologist or behavioral scientist. She is a scientist who tries to learn more about why animals act in certain ways. For example, how do female monkeys learn to be good mothers.

B. Some laboratories have space for monkeys to play outside. Video cameras may be used to record the monkey's activities.

What's Wrong with This Picture?

Government Lab-animal Poster Concerns HSUS

A poster produced by the U.S. Department of Health and Human Services (HHS) entitled "Let's Visit a Research Laboratory" [is] a full-color, cartoon-style poster [which] shows a building with thirteen different rooms and features people, animals, and equipment. The building purports to be a research laboratory, but certainly no invasive research is taking place there. The animals and people are all smiling. In Room 7, the testing lab, a happy monkey presses buttons on a computer panel.... Room 13, the monkey housing, is not a collection of grim cages, but a delightful jungle-gym affair in which many children would no doubt enjoy playing....

The poster's cartoon art is not in keeping with the seriousness of the controversial and emotionally charged issue of animal experimentation. It is, however, very much in keeping with the preferences of an audience of young children. Why might cartoon art have been selected? "Because a more realistic portrayal would frighten children and be unacceptable to teachers," says Ms. Finch [former classroom teacher and executive director of HSUS's National Assocation

for Humane and Environmental Education (NAHEE)]. "When we cannot be truthful about an issue without scaring young children, then the issue itself is inappropriate for that age group...."

The reality—that there exists a broad spectrum of beliefs regarding this highly controversial topic—was not addressed. This approach is highly questionable from the educator's standpoint. Both the student and teacher guides dismissed the concept of "alternatives" to animal experimentation.

.... [T]he HSUS Scientific Advisory Council ... members agreed that the bias in the materials was unjustified and recommended that the HSUS invoke the federal Freedom of Information Act to learn how many of the posters and accompanying materials had been distributed nationwide. Such a request was made; the HSUS is awaiting a response.

... HSUS President Paul G. Irwin explained the HSUS position in letters to President Bill Clinton and Donna Shalala, secretary of HHS. It is hoped that, under President Clinton's administration, the HHS will discontinue publication of these materials.

—Willow Ann Soltow

NAHEE director, Special Programs

▲ Figure 6.20 *An excerpt from an article which detailed the Humane Society's concerns with the poster "Let's Visit a Research Laboratory" (Soltow, 1993, pp. 6–8).*

image accurate? Are students and their teachers presented with a realistic portrayal of the treatment of rodents and monkeys in research labs? These are questions that were raised in 1993 by the Humane Society of the United States (HSUS), the largest organization in the United States dedicated to the humane treatment of animals. Figure 6.20 presents the highlights of the Humane Society's interpretation of the poster. Figure 6.21 is an excerpt from a position statement about the design of elementary educational materials. The statement was sent to President Bill Clinton and to the Secretary of Health and Human Services, Donna Shalala.

In reporting the opinions of various teachers who received *Let's Visit a Research Laboratory*, the HSUS (Soltow, 1993) offers these impressions from one first-grade teacher:

> When I first saw it [the poster], I thought it was laughable. All those happy, smiling monkeys in cages. [See blowup of Room 13: Monkey Housing in Figure 6.22.] Then I said to myself, 'this poster is printed with government money!' That really bothered me because it's completely biased and the subject is not age appropriate at all. (p. 6)

HSUS Position Statement on Elementary Education Materials Distributed by the Department of Health and Human Services

[The] … shortcomings of these materials are totally inconsistent with the level of integrity and fairness that should be observed in government-sponsored educational materials. We find these materials to be both biased and pejorative in as much as they:

1. fail to address the inherently controversial nature of the subject;

2. exploit children's natural love of animals and attempt to persuade children that laboratories are places in which research animals engage in playful and enjoyable activities;

3. fail to provide a balanced discussion of the ethical considerations relating to the potential suffering of animals used in research;

4. attempt to polarize the issue of the use of animals in research by characterizing

people concerned about animal suffering as "extremists";

5. seek to relegate sentient creatures to the same level of importance as the inanimate objects used by scientists in their research;

6. reject the mainstream concept of "alternatives" to the use of animals in research and education;

7. fail to mention animal-welfare and animal protection groups in listings of possible resource agencies and materials;

8. inadequately advise teachers regarding the care and maintenance of animals used in classroom studies.

Because the subject of the use of animals in biomedical research is highly controversial and complex and therefore inappropriate for young children, and because of the blatant bias and propaganda evident in the above-named materials, we strongly oppose the use of public funds for the future production, distribution, and promotion of these materials by the United States government and its agencies.

Patty Finch, executive director of the HSUS's National Association for Humane and Environmental Education (NAHEE) and a former classroom teacher, was deeply concerned when she saw the poster and accompanying materials. "Teachers often receive biased materials in the classroom," she observes. "But we don't expect our government to be the source of blatantly biased materials" (Soltow, 1993, p. 7).

Other readers who are quoted in support of the Humane Society's point of view found the "lucky mice" with names such as Jimmy, Lizzy, and Baby Lester—names just like family pets—to be grossly misleading (see blowup of Room 10: Rodent Housing in Figure 6.23). Moreover, they found the text and illustrations to be biased, skirting the serious nature of the controversial topic of animals in biomedical research. For example, the issue of using monkeys in experiments is sugarcoated with a cartoon of a monkey good-naturedly playing the role of hacker (see blowup of Room 7: Testing Lab, in Figure 6.24). *Although the monkey looks to be the "happy camper" in a usability study, there's a big difference: It's not the product or the manual the researcher is testing, it is the monkey.* The comments the Humane Society makes in Figures 6.20 through 6.24 (in the text and captions) portray vividly how readers' values and beliefs can interact as they interpret documents.

▲ **Figure 6.21** *An excerpt from a 1993 HSUS position statement about the package of elementary education materials entitled "Let's Visit a Research Laboratory" (poster and lesson plans), "Animals and Science" (student brochure), and "Animals and Science" (teacher's guide). These materials, produced by the Department of Health and Human Services (under the auspices of the former Alcohol, Drug Abuse, and Mental Health Administration), were distributed by the Department of Health and Human Services' National Institute of Mental Health.*

▶ **Figure 6.22** *In the poster created by the U. S. Department of Health and Human Services, cheerful monkeys housed in Room 13 frolic in jungle-gym enclosures. Their real life counterparts often languish, isolated, in grim cages. Caption composed by HSUS (Soltow, 1993, p. 7).*

It is unlikely that the document designers who worked on this poster consciously composed it with the idea of glorifying the fun experience of laboratory animals. (Although clearly the Department of Health and Human Services does have a vested interest in biomedical research using animals.) One plausible explanation is that document designers went overboard in their enthusiasm to simplify the topic and make "science look like fun." In the process, they emphasized only positive features of the content.

In addition, document designers wrote and visualized in a way that made other opinions seem unimportant or nonexistent. In the brochure for students that was included with this package, people who did not support the use of animals in biomedical research were labeled as "extremists." Document designers took an unfortunate name-calling strategy rather than articulating clearly the moral dilemma that all drug developers face. To wit: If humans want better drugs, who should the new drugs be

▶ **Figure 6.23** *The lucky mice of Room 10, the rodent-housing area, have been given names like Jimmy, Freddie, and Lizzy, just like beloved family pets. Caption composed by HSUS (Soltow, 1993, p. 7).*

◀ Figure 6.24 *In Room 7, the poster's testing lab, a happy monkey presses buttons on a computer panel as a smiling researcher watches the monkey in action. Caption composed by HSUS, Washington, DC (Soltow, 1993, p. 7).*

tested on—animals or people? Had they represented the problem fairly, their visual and verbal moves would not seem so willfully resistant to other points of view. These textual clues tend to support the Humane Society's contentions of bias and of a pejorative attitude toward those who do not agree with using animals in research.

Whether we agree or disagree with the Humane Society's perspective about the treatment of animals in biomedical research is not the point. Rather, it is that document designers did not take seriously the frame of reference of the various reader groups who might encounter the document. The result was a poster that did a disservice to animal rights advocates, to employees in biomedical research labs, and to the children they hoped to educate. Animal rights advocates are painted as extremists, while people who work for research labs appear "clueless" about a topic of international controversy. Document designers took a sensitive topic and treated it as though they were visualizing a trip to the local zoo.

The Humane Society's response to this poster also makes evident that readers may interpret not only what is visually or verbally present in a document but also what is absent. In their interpretations of the pictures, for example, they make judgments about illustrations depicted (happy monkeys) and those omitted (monkeys under the knife). In deciding what to picture or not to picture, document designers need to keep in mind that what they leave out may be as important to the reader as what they leave in (see Sims-Knight, 1992). Failing to come to terms with readers' perspectives, even when we disagree with them, may bias decision-making in document design in ways that could turn a potentially interested audience into a hostile one.

This case from the Humane Society and the study I presented in Chapter 3 ("Just Say No to Drugs and Other Unwelcome Advice," pp. 165–203) show us that readers bring their knowledge, experience, values, and beliefs to bear *as* they interpret the words and pictures. Readers may even use their knowledge to interpret textual cues that document designers deem insignificant; for example, the hair of a teenager in the drug education study (see Figure 3.1, p. 173) and the smile of a monkey in the animal lab poster (see Figure 6.24). Although document designers may not have considered these graphic choices to be resources for interpretation, readers saw them differently. As readers brought their point of view to bear in interpreting the main ideas of these documents, the representation of the content they formed was radically different from the one document designers had hoped they would construct. But because document designers did not fully consider how their graphic choices might be interpreted from other points of view, they opened the door to interpretations they did not intend.

SUMMARY: SOME ADVICE ABOUT INTEGRATING WORDS AND PICTURES

This chapter has described some ways that words and pictures may work together. We've seen that in order to orchestrate prose and graphic combinations that enable readers to meet their goals, document designers need information about the process of interpretation itself—about reader's knowledge-driven and text-driven understanding of documents. This chapter has presented a number of studies that suggest we must help readers:

- Search for the information they want in prose and graphics.
- Make sense of it once they find it.
- Construct a coherent interpretation of the prose and graphics.
- Generate connections between the words and pictures.
- Put the information to personal use.

Although we don't know all there is to know about these areas, document designers can take advantage of the work done up to this point. Research suggests a number of principles for enhancing people's ability to search, understand, and make use of documents. The work that I've presented in this chapter on how people interpret words and pictures suggests the following tentative guidelines:

- Help readers interpret prose and graphic combinations by focusing their attention on the relationships between the content presented visually and verbally.

- Consider the reader's task when choosing between presenting information in hardcopy or online.

- Enable readers to construct a consistent story about the content through the design and integration of prose and graphics.

- Reinforce difficult concepts for readers by using redundant prose and picture combinations.

- Strengthen and constrain the meaning for readers by using complementary prose and graphic combinations.

- Amplify ideas for readers by supplementing prose or graphics with other prose or graphics

- Violate readers' expectations for the topic with juxtapositional relationships between the prose and graphics.

- Give readers advice about what to pay attention to by using stage-setting prose and graphic combinations.

- Display graphics shortly after they are referred to in the text.

- Use verbal cues in the body text to guide the reader to examine graphics and to notice their key features.

- Use captions that help readers interpret the main points of the graphic; make the organization of the prose map onto the structure of the graphic or visual display.

- Take care in creating itemized lists; make certain that the content is written in parallel fashion and that the listed items form a conceptual family.

- Avoid pretty pictures combined with low-information prose.

- Evaluate how the words and pictures may animate one another when placed in proximal relation to one another; choose combinations that enrich readers' understanding of the topic rather than those which narrow the topic inappropriately.

We need to know much more about the interplay of words and pictures—about how people search for information, about how they understand what they find, about how they use information when it is presented in different formats, and about how their understanding of the information may change as they move from one media to the next. Here, I've tried to illuminate some of the issues that document designers need to pay attention to in bringing together words and pictures. But if we are to have the "new eyes" that Marcel Proust spoke of, we've got a lot of looking yet to do.

WE AWAIT FURTHER INSTRUCTIONS, YOUR GRACE...

PART THREE

RESPONDING TO READERS' NEEDS

7

What Document Designers Can Learn from Readers

The central focus of this book has been the reader. I've emphasized how important it is for document designers to attend carefully to their audiences. In this last chapter, I describe two studies that dramatically illustrate the gains that can be achieved by designing with the reader in mind. ❧ The first reveals the power of readers' feedback for broadening the designer's awareness of what audiences need and for improving the quality of documents. ❧ The second is an evaluation of "protocol-aided audience modeling" (PAM), a teaching method that uses commentary from the audience to help designers build a better model of the reader. This study demonstrates that using PAM can significantly improve document designers' ability to anticipate problems that readers may have with poorly written and poorly visualized documents. ❧ Finally, I make some observations that bring the book to a close, calling on document designers to build a strong research community to meet the challenges that still confront our field.

Throughout this book I have argued that document designers need to understand how people think and feel as they engage with documents and that doing so involves more than relying on intuition and experience. A skeptic could argue, however, that I haven't provided compelling evidence that documents designed on the basis of the ideas I've presented are substantially better than those that could be produced by building on intuition and experience. Nor have I elaborated the benefits for the document designer of taking a reader-oriented perspective, benefits that might extend beyond the design task at hand. In other words, I haven't shown that all of this actually works. In this chapter, I demonstrate the practical benefits of taking a reader-oriented rhetorical stance. I show that "taking the reader seriously" can make a substantial difference in people's ability to use documents. Moreover, I establish that experience in feedback-driven audience analyses can make document designers better at what they do.

In order to make these arguments, I present two final studies. The first shows that feedback-driven audience analysis alerts document designers to a range of problems that readers may experience—problems that even veteran document designers do not anticipate. This study also suggests that the insights provided by readers enable document designers to create documents that are substantially better than those produced without such insights. The second study assesses a teaching method for improving document designers' ability to anticipate readers' problems. It offers clear evidence that practice in evaluating how people enage with poorly written and poorly visualized documents can significantly improve document designers' sensitivity to readers' needs. This study suggests that there are substantial long-term benefits associated with observing readers in action.

WHY WRITING AND GRAPHIC DESIGN MATTER: THE INFLUENCE OF TEXT QUALITY ON READERS' COMPREHENSION AND USE OF DOCUMENTS

In Chapters 4, 5, and 6 of this book, I presented examples of documents from the world of consumer electronics—manuals for stereos, VCRs, and telephone answering machines. The documents I showed were part of a larger study that was intended to assess whether good writing and good graphic design actually matter to readers. I describe that study here. I will show that revisions made on the basis of readers' feedback can lead to marked improvements in documents. More importantly, I will illustrate why modern empirical methods, particularly iterative evaluation methods in which the audience actively participates, enable document designers to do a better job than they could by relying solely on intuition and experience.

Evaluating the Quality of Document Design Through Usability Testing

To provide the context out of which this usability study grew, I revisit the background I presented in Chapter 4 for the "Blame Study." This study developed in the same way as most studies of usability: It grew from a practical need. The corporate sponsor of our research, a large Japanese consumer electronics company, had received complaints that its VCRs and stereo systems were hard to use and that its manuals were difficult to follow. To understand why people were having so many problems, the company chose two of their biggest selling models for usability testing: a VCR intended for the United States market and a stereo system intended for both American and European markets. There were three goals for the study:

- To learn as much as we could about why users found the company's manuals hard to follow and the products hard to use.

- To employ readers' feedback in the redesign of the instruction guides and in the creation of recommendations for improving the interface design of the products.

- To see if people performed better with the revised guides than with the original guides.

Participants in the Usability Test

Although people of any age could use the VCR or stereo system, the company had a special interest in users between twenty and forty years of age. For the VCR, the company was interested in people who spoke American English. For the stereo, they asked us to recruit Americans who spoke only English, as well as people who were bilingual in English and French, English and German, and English and Spanish.

We tested the original instruction guides, our initial revisions, and our final revisions. To test the guides, we recruited a pool of potential participants from which we randomly selected people who fit the profile. (Limited funding for the research necessitated a smaller sample than we would have liked.) For the VCR, 17 people participated in the evaluation: six who tested the original instruction guide, six who tested the initial revision, and five others who tested the final revision. For the stereo, 41 people participated: 17 who tested the original instruction guide (three English-only speakers, five French bilinguals, four German bilinguals, and five Spanish bilinguals), 12 who tested the initial revision, (three English-only, three French bilinguals, three German bilinguals, and three Spanish bilinguals), and 12 who tested the final revision (three English-only, three French bilinguals, three German bilinguals, and three

Spanish bilinguals). All participants were paid $25 for their time (which was about an hour and fifteen minutes).

Methods and Constraints in Carrying Out the Usability Test

A constraint on our work was that for the stereo guide, all four languages—English, French, German, and Spanish—had to be presented on every two-page spread. The manufacturer insisted that we test the bilinguals with both English and their native language present on the same page. We collected think-aloud user protocols from participants who read the text written in their native tongue and commented on it in English. This proved to be very easy for bilingual participants.

Participants involved in the testing of the VCR instruction guide were asked to perform seven tasks, including setting the date and the time on the VCR, watching one channel while recording another, and setting the timer to record a show in five minutes. Stereo participants engaged in ten tasks, including connecting the four system components (a radio, a cassette player, a CD player, and a set of speakers), recording a sequence of songs on a cassette tape, and programming the CD player to play songs in a certain order.

A few details about my collaborators in this research are also relevant in understanding the project.[1] In total, there were 11 members on the document design team, each of whom was an experienced document designer.[2] The team consisted of two writers, two graphic designers, two technical illustrators, three commercial artists, a video editor, and a research director.

David O'Connor, a document designer, observes a new computer user trying out some procedures. Thanks to photographer Ken Andreyo of Carnegie Mellon University, Pittsburgh, PA.

Bill Wrbican, a usability test participant, tries to understand UNIX programming with the help of a manual.

---

[1] My colleagues in this project were Michele Matchett (managing, writing, editing, and testing), Mary L. Ray (writing, editing, and testing), Norma Pribadi Polk (graphic design and survey research), Dan Boyarski (graphic design); Ann Steffy Cronin (video editing and data analysis); Carlos Peterson (technical illustration); Daniel Lepore (technical illustration); Burton Morris (illustration); Ilene Lederer (illustration), and James Adams (illustration). Without the talents and efforts of these people, this research could not have taken place. I thank them. Most of all, we thank the people who participated in this study.

[2] All team members had college degrees (the writers had master's degrees, the designers MFAs; similarly, the technical illustrators and commercial artists had advanced degrees). Each person on the team was also a seasoned professional, having completed document design projects for a variety of international clients. In addition, two of the team members were professors (Boyarski and Schriver) and had developed courses in document design and interface design. Given that the team had 70+ years of collective experience and that several of the team members had won awards for graphic design or writing, it seems safe to say the team was comprised of expert document designers. By "document designer," I refer to writers, designers, and illustrators on the team.

The team began the project by evaluating the instruction guides on the basis of our document design experience. In this evaluation, we scrutinized the visual and verbal design of the texts, paying special attention to the text features of the instruction guides that we thought would create problems for readers. This evaluation is called a *features analysis,* a formal critique of the integration of the visual and verbal features employed in the document (here, we assessed everything from the design of the grid to the construction of the sentences). The features analysis was followed by usability testing of the guides. Drawing on the features analysis and readers' feedback, our team redesigned the guides. We iterated this process of evaluation, usability testing, and redesign through the creation of two revisions of the original document. Altogether, the project involved the following stages:[3]

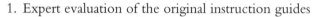

Jim Palmer, a usability test coordinator, monitors the quality of the audio and video as the test is in progress.

1. Expert evaluation of the original instruction guides

2. Usability testing of the original instruction guides

3. Creation of initial revisions of the original guides

4. Expert evaluation of the initial revisions

5. Usability testing of the initial revisions

6. Improvement of the initial revisions to produce final revisions

7. Usability testing of the final revisions

The illustrations shown in this spread give an idea of how usability testing is carried out in a formal laboratory-like setting. Shown here are a few photographs from a usability test conducted by my former students at Carnegie Mellon. In traditional usability testing, the participant sits in one room (the testing room) and the usability tester observes from another room through a one-way mirror. In addition, a second person on the testing team usually monitors the recording of the audio and video as it progresses.

Jim Palmer edits the video tape from the usability test.

Although this type of formal arrangement can work quite well, it tends to be somewhat expensive to set up. Fancy test rooms and editing equipment are not critical to usability evaluations. In fact, using separate rooms for tester and participant may create an uncomfortable (and artificial) distance between the observer and the observed, which may make the participant feel as though he or she is the one being tested rather than the text or product.

---

[3] We conducted three rounds of testing because there were several contrasts we wanted to make in our data analysis. Generally speaking, usability specialists find two rounds of testing to be sufficient, a test of an original and a revised version. We designed our study in order to make two major comparisons: one between the original instruction guides and the initial revisions, and another between the original instruction guides and the final revisions.

We chose instead to conduct our usability test of the consumer electronics equipment in a more relaxed and informal setting. Thus, we did not use a testing room with a one-way mirror and did not pretend to be absent. Rather, we sat in the same room as participants as they tried out the stereo or VCR. Ideally, a test of this sort should be carried out in the actual context in which people need to use the equipment—in this case, in someone's living room. In fact, we did carry out several pilot tests with participants in the privacy of their own homes. The photos on this spread were taken in living rooms of our pilot test participants; notice the little girl Kaitlyn (bottom right) steals the stage as her mom tries to hook up the VCR. However, because we had a lot of equipment to set up, we carried out the main study in an office setting.

Ruth and Jim use a manual to set the switches on their VCR.

How Usability Testing Broadened Experts' Vision

Both expert judgment and usability testing revealed a variety of problems—some verbal, some visual, some related to translation from one language to another, and still others related to the design of the products. In the sections below, I discuss the kinds of problems discovered in each of these areas. To highlight the contribution made by usability testing, I first present problems that were identified through expert judgment. I then discuss the additional problems that were identified through usability testing.

Problems of Poorly Written Prose

As one might expect, document designers were concerned with the verbal presentation of the manuals. Their evaluation identified a variety of organizational and stylistic problems, including:

Jim checks the back panel of the VCR to make sure the connections are right.

- Poorly designed tables of contents and missing indices.
- Nonparallel grammatical construction of tasks and subtasks.
- Ambiguous information about how to recover from errors.
- Weak sentence structures and excessive use of passive voice.
- Use of engineering jargon and acronyms.

Usability testing provided document designers with additional information about how well the prose was operating. Readers' feedback detailed not only problems that the team had already identified but also problems such as these:

- Poorly organized tasks in which procedures were sequenced in ways that disoriented readers. Look back at Figure 5.33 (p. 322), which presents an excerpt from the usability test of Spanish-English participant Martha. Notice that the manual elaborates how to improve the reception of the radio signal before describing how to connect the antenna to the radio. As Martha put it, "Why are they telling me this stuff about improving the radio's reception? At this point, I don't want to improve anything. I just want to make it work."

- Badly chosen task names that reflected an engineer's model of the equipment and made it difficult for users to imagine the tasks that were involved. Users could neither infer the context in which doing the task was appropriate nor understand why they would want to do it; for example, the VCR task "insert editing" mystified most participants, as did the stereo task "edit playback."

- Information that irritated and frustrated users, such as calling components by their model numbers instead of by their common name (for example, the tape deck for the stereo was referred to as the ZBT49 instead of as the tape deck).

Problems of Poor Visual Design

Document designers were as concerned with the visual presentation of the instruction guides as they were with the verbal. In their evaluation, they concentrated on issues such as these:

Mary explains to her son Kenny how to use the remote control.

- Poorly designed layouts that made it difficult to scan the text and generated a chaotic path for the reader's eye to follow.

- Haphazard use of icons and visual symbols.

- Inconsistent typographic cues such as the use of reverse type and bold type for content at the same level of the information hierarchy.

- Mismatches between illustrations and accompanying text.

However, usability testing showed document designers that they had just begun to identify the problems that the graphics and typography would create for users. Readers' feedback revealed other difficulties that document designers had not identified, problems such as these:

- Competing navigational cues, which made it difficult to locate key information because much of the text was "oversignaled"—too much bold type, reverse type, bulleting, underlining, indenting, boxing, shading—making everything seem important.

Kaitlyn helps her mom connect their VCR to the television.

- Legibility problems with the typeface, which was set at 10 point with very tight leading. In addition, the line length was inconsistent; text with the same rhetorical function had two or more line lengths.

- Missing captions, labels, and color codes for technical illustrations, which made it hard for readers to ascertain which part of the product they were inspecting, and without references to the colors of wires, buttons, or connectors, mapping picture-to-product proved to be extremely difficult.

- Ambiguities in the rendering of technical illustrations, making it hard to tell which parts of the illustrations were wires and which parts were components (the use of engineering-style drawings led to unfortunate visual similarities between edges of product components and wires; for an example, look back at Figure 5.32, p. 321).

Problems of Translation

Monique tries to use the index of the stereo manual, but finds there isn't one.

Although the members of this document design team were quite experienced, their training did not prepare them to attend to difficulties caused by poor translation. For the most part, the translation problems they identified were limited to lexical choices that were not part of standard American English. For example, the company had chosen to call the remote control for the VCR and stereo "remote commander" (see the first of the three displays shown in Figure 7.7, p. 464). Document designers thought this phrasing sounded as if they were making reference to a leader of a South American army. During testing, however, especially of the stereo manual, bilingual speakers identified several other translation difficulties, including the following:

- Poor phrasings and ungrammatical sentences.

- Missing or misplaced punctuation, which created pronoun reference problems and syntactic ambiguities.

- Unidiomatic expressions and infrequently used words (bilinguals often reported, "We would never say it this way; we hardly ever use that word").

Problems of Product Design

Jacques searches for information about using the remote control to operate the CD player but has trouble locating the procedures because the steps are not formatted in a way that makes them visually distinct.

Although the document designers did identify a few product design problems—such as buttons that were too small or that were crowded together—they tended to spend most of their time evaluating the text. During usability testing, however, they realized that many of the problems were caused by inconsistencies in product design and by poor mapping between the product and the instruction guides. Users pointed to difficulties such as these:

- Meaningless labels on device parts that were not explained in the instruction guides.

- Buttons for some tasks that appeared on the remote control but not on the equipment, thus forcing users to complete some tasks with the remote control even if they did not want to.

- Use of confusing symbols (e.g., the symbol > 12 was used to indicate how to select a song on the CD that was higher than track number 12; the same > symbol was also used to mean "advance" and a similar one was used for "play").

Overall, the usability evaluation prompted document designers to attend to problems they would have otherwise missed or ignored. In predicting problems they believed might be caused by the prose or graphics, document designers did not have access to the information they needed to anticipate difficulties created by content that was out of order, misplaced, or missing. And although they were sensitive to issues related to the integration of the text and graphics, they typically were unable to diagnose the specific difficulties that readers would have with mapping the relations among text, graphics (especially technical illustrations), and product design. Usability testing provided document designers with a perspective that was simply unavailable when they drew on their years of practice in writing and graphic design.

Paul reads a VCR manual in an effort to get the clock to stop blinking 12:00, 12:00, 12:00. But the manual leaves out an important step and so the procedure doesn't work.

Assessing the Effectiveness of the Revisions

To assess the effectiveness of our revision process, my colleagues and I compared the accuracy and the speed with which participants completed tasks using the original instruction guides and the final revisions. Results indicated that the revised versions significantly improved participants' accuracy in performing VCR and stereo tasks. For the VCR, some participants using the original guide failed five or six of the seven tasks, while all participants who used the revised instruction guide completed all seven tasks without failures.[4]

To provide an indication of the overall direction of these results, we collapsed the success rate over the two products for the original and the revised versions. We found that on average, the original instruction guides allowed readers to perform their tasks accurately about 56 percent of the time while the final revisions produced an accuracy rate of 97 percent.

We obtained similar results for the speed with which participants completed tasks using the original and revised instruction guides. For the VCR, we found that the time participants needed to complete the seven

Nora checks the instruction manual in order to connect the antenna to the TV and VCR, but the connectors on her antenna do not look like any of the pictures in the manual.

---

[4] These findings were significant at the .002 level by the Wilcoxon-Mann-Whitney test. A similar improvement was found for the stereo instruction guide (p = .0005 by the Wilcoxon-Mann-Whitney test).

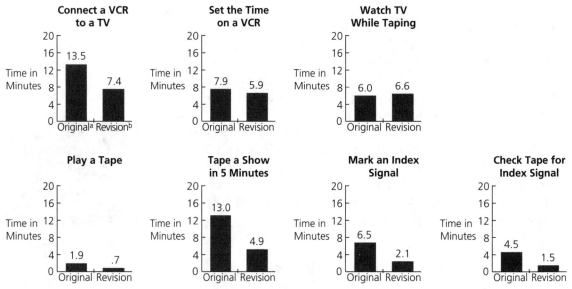

Average Time Spent on VCR Tasks: Original vs. Revision

Note. Values represent participants' mean time per task.
[a] Six participants completed seven tasks using the original instruction guide.
[b] Five participants completed seven tasks using the revised instruction guide.

▲ Figure 7.1 *The relationship between participants' time on task and the version of the instruction guide used. Participants were generally able to complete tasks more quickly using the revised guide than the original.*

[5] These results are significant at the .002 level, using the Wilcoxon-Mann-Whitney test.

[6] This improvement is significant at the .002 level, using the Wilcoxon-Mann-Whitney test.

tasks was reduced significantly[5] (see Figure 7.1). With one exception, the revised instruction guides improved participants' speed in completing tasks. Results for the stereo (shown in Figure 7.2) were much the same. We found an advantage for the revised instruction guide in completing tasks more quickly in nine out of ten cases.[6] When we collapsed participants' task completion times for the VCR and stereo tasks, we found that on average, the new manuals reduced participants' task completion time by roughly 44 percent (from an average of 7.7 minutes per task to 4.3 minutes per task).

Comparing Reader-Focused Methods with More Traditional Methods of Editing and Revision

Although we have demonstrated that our revisions did improve the instruction guides, the critical reader should ask, "Do reader-focused testing procedures offer more than the traditional methods based on intuition and experience?" Indeed, this was the challenge that my colleagues and I posed for ourselves. To what extent could we, as experi-

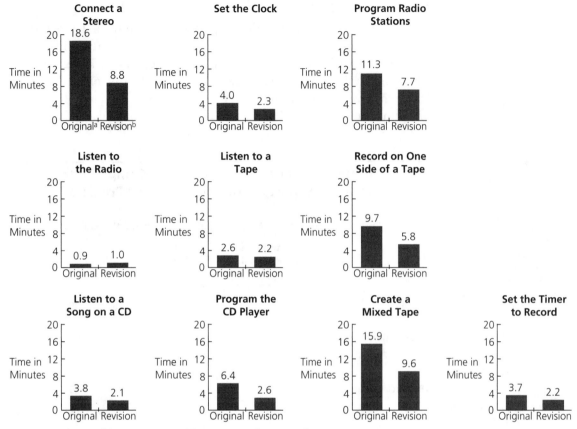

Average Time Spent on Stereo Tasks: Original vs. Revision

Note. Values represent participants' mean time per task.

a 17 participants (three English-only speakers, five French bilinguals, four German bilinguals, five Spanish bilinguals) completed 10 tasks using the original instruction guide.

b 12 participants (three English-only speakers, three French bilinguals, three German bilinguals, three Spanish bilinguals) completed 10 tasks using the revised instruction guide.

▲ Figure 7.2 *The relationship between participants' time on task and the version of the instruction guide used. Participants were generally able to complete tasks more quickly using the revised guide than the original.*

enced writers and designers, predict the problems that readers would experience when they used the instruction guides? To address this question, we compared (1) the expert evaluations of the original guides with the results of testing those original guides (see the upper half of Table 7.1 on the next page) and (2) the expert evaluations of the initial revisions with the results of testing those initial revisions (see the lower half of Table 7.1). The data in Table 7.1 suggest that the experts did rather poorly in predicting the problems that readers experienced. The experts accurately predicted more problems with the prose than problems in the other categories across the original and the initial revision. However, in separate analyses, we discovered that they also falsely predicted more verbal problems than problems in other categories.

It is important to note that the original manual and the initial revision were not comparable because the problems caused by poorly written prose, poor visual design, and poor translation were somewhat different. Although many of the problems readers discovered in the original manual had been solved in the initial revision, readers in the second test discovered problems that readers on the first test did not, and unfortunately, the

▶ Table 7.1 *Prior to usability testing, expert writers and graphic designers predicted the problems they believed the instruction guides would create for readers. This table shows the relationship between the problems experts predicted and the problems readers experienced with the original and initial revision of the VCR and stereo instruction guides. It shows that expert judgment is not enough. Usability testing provides experts with an important window on readers' problems. Most of the problems that experts missed were solved in their final revisions; the improvements in the guides led to significantly enhanced performance for users. (An earlier version of this analysis appeared in Schriver, 1995.)*

Problems Participants Experienced Compared to Problems Expert Document Designers Predicted

Problems Predicted and Missed in the Original Instruction Guides[a]

	Participants Experienced	Experts Predicted		Experts Missed	
	(N)	(N)	(%)	(N)	(%)
Verbal	23	15	65	8	35
Translation	6	2	33	4	67
Visual	12	6	50	6	50
Product Design	8	2	25	6	75
TOTAL	49	25	51	24	49

Problems Predicted and Missed in an Initial Revision of the Guides[a]

	Participants Experienced	Experts Predicted		Experts Missed	
	(N)	(N)	(%)	(N)	(%)
Verbal	16	5	31	11	69
Translation	4	0	0	4	100
Visual	5	0	0	5	100
Product Design	11	2	18	9	82
TOTAL	36	7	19	29	81

[a] To enable comparision, the problems participants experienced and the problems experts predicted are collapsed for the VCR and stereo manuals. Numbers indicate problem categories rather than absolute numbers of problems; for example, the problem that participants may have experienced related to the "poor legibility of the typeface" in an instruction guide was counted as one visual problem even if all participants experienced difficulties with it. Similarly, one problem was scored as predicted if the team of experts noted the problem.

revision had also introduced some problems of its own. Table 7.1 offers a rough benchmark of the problems that readers experienced and that experts predicted and missed in four main problem categories: verbal, translation, visual, and product design.

A striking contrast that the data in Table 7.1 make evident is that the experts predicted relatively more of the problems in the original instruction guides than in the initial revisions (51 percent vs. 19 percent). There are a number of possible explanations for this large difference. First, it is possible that most of the obvious problems were dealt with in the process of revising the original instruction guides. Thus, there may have been fewer problems that were easy to identify in the initial revisions than in the original guides.

Another possibility is that because the expert judges were also the authors of the initial revision, they may have been unable to see the problems in their own work; their knowledge of the text's content may have allowed them to fill in gaps that readers without such knowledge would readily notice (for a discussion of the "knowledge effect" in revision, see Hayes, 1989b). Possibly a second independent panel of experts would have been able to predict more than 19 percent of the problems in the first revisions.

In any event, a best case estimate on the basis of these data is that experts are unlikely to predict more than half of the problems that readers will experience, and perhaps they will predict substantially less. Studies by Benson (1994), Lentz and Pander Maat (1992), and Lentz and De Jong (1995) provide a similar view of the limitations of relying solely on expert opinion to guide document design. Taken together, research makes it apparent that expertise in writing and graphic design is not always enough to make textual choices that will matter from the reader's point of view.

Using the Original and Revised Instruction Guides: Does Native Language, Gender, or Experience Make a Difference?

To determine if there were differences among the various language groups, we examined the stereo data (shown in Table 7.2 on the next page). Although the number of participants from each group was too small for meaningful statistical comparison, we found no substantial differences among language groups in either speed or accuracy of completing tasks. What is evident is that all language groups perform better with the revised instruction guide, succeeding on average 70 percent of the time with the original and 94 percent of the time with the revised version.

Success Rate by Native Language and Version of the Stereo Instruction Guide

	Original[a]	Revised[b]
English-only	73	100
French-English	66	90
German-English	82	97
Spanish-English	60	90

Note. Values represent percentages of accurately completed tasks.

[a] 17 participants (three English-only speakers, five French bilinguals, four German bilinguals, five Spanish bilinguals) completed 10 tasks using a stereo with the original instruction guide.

[b] 12 participants (three English-only speakers, three French bilinguals, three German bilinguals, three Spanish bilinguals) completed 10 tasks using a stereo with the revised instruction guide.

▲ Table 7.2 *Participants' average success rate according to language.*

Consuela explains that the technical illustration for connecting the components of the stereo does not look like the equipment. She reports that she's run out of wires and can't proceed.

Russ tries to get the answering machine to quit repeating the annoying phrase, "Friday 9 A.M." Even after he pushes "stop" nothing happens. The manual gives no advice about what to do.

Success Rate[a] by Gender and Version of the VCR and Stereo Instruction Guides

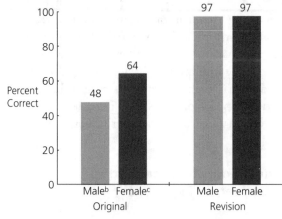

Note. Numerical values indicate the average percent correct in completing VCR and stereo tasks (combined over all tasks for the two guides).

[a] Both male and female VCR participants completed 7 tasks per person; stereo participants completed 10.

[b] 20 males participated in testing the original and revised instruction guides.

[c] 20 females participated in testing the original and revised instruction guides.

▲ Figure 7.3 *The relationship between men and women and their success rate in completing VCR or stereo tasks depending on the instruction guide they used. Both men and women are "hurt" by poor design, and both men and women improve in their success rate when using the revised instruction guides.*

Our next question was whether men and women differed in either the accuracy with which they completed tasks or their speed. We examined the data by collapsing the success rate by gender across the VCR and stereo instruction guides. We found no differences between men and women, but again saw that both men and women improved dramatically with the revised instruction guides (see Figure 7.3). (I changed the representation of the data from a tabular display in Table 7.2 to a bar chart in Figure 7.3 to emphasize visually the similarity between men and women in using the revised instruction guides.)

We then examined whether participants who differed in experience with using consumer electronics equipment might differ in their success rate (see Table 7.3). This analysis revealed no significant differences due to experience. However, I feel that this result should be interpreted with caution. There were only six participants who described themselves as having "little" experience with consumer electronics; three who used the original manual and three who used the revised manual. The three who used the original manual had an average success rate of only 41 percent. It is possible, therefore, that if we had tested a larger sample, we might have found that users with little experience are especially disadvantaged by poor manuals. The issue is important enough to warrant further study.

Henrik avoids using the manual and connects the equipment on his own, explaining that he had a stereo system just like this one in his apartment in Munich.

Success Rate by Experience and Version of the VCR and Stereo Instruction Guides

	Experience[a]	
	Much (n = 15)	**Some/Little** (n = 8)
Original[b]	63	55
	Much (n = 11)	**Some/Little** (n = 6)
Revised	95	96

Note. Values represent mean success rate in percentages. N means number of participants who rated themselves as having "some/little" or "much" experience for each version.

[a] Participants rated their experience on a survey prior to testing. "Much" experience indicates that the participant used a VCR or stereo at least three times per week and connected at least one time; "some/little" indicates that the participant used a VCR or stereo roughly once every other week and connected at most one time.

[b] Different participants tested the original and revised versions of the instruction guides: 23 people participated in testing the original VCR and stereo instruction guides; 17 people participated in testing the revised guides.

▲ **Table 7.3** *The relationship between the version of the instruction guide participants used, their experience, and their accuracy in performing VCR and stereo tasks. Participants of all experience levels improved with the revised instruction guides. Participants with little or some experience had more difficulty with the original guides than did those with much experience.*

Antoinette checks the manual in order to set the function on the stereo to record a radio broadcast onto a cassette tape.

Across the various data analyses, we found consistent evidence that the most important factor in learning to use new technology was not a person's native language, sex, or previous experience with using similar equipment. Rather, the most important factor was the quality of the writing and graphic design of the instruction guide. Similar results were found by Jansen and Steehouder (1991), who compared a set of original and revised government forms. They found no influence of variables such as sex, education, or experience with filling out forms. All participants benefited from the revised forms because they were simply easier to fill out. Research is beginning to provide converging results which show that the quality of the text may be the single best predictor of how well people will be able to use a document.

Dispelling the Myth that Confused Readers Are Lazy Readers

Some may believe that people who have trouble understanding instruction guides are simply not working hard enough—that is, they are not attending carefully to the text, or they are failing to read enough to get the main points. To test this hypothesis, we made use of the protocols from the usability tests of the original VCR and stereo instruction guides along with protocols we collected for the telephone answering machine instruction guide (discussed in Chapter 4). We focused our attention on users' activities as they began their tasks. We wanted to know how they searched for the information they needed to complete a task and how much they read *before they actually started carrying out a task, that is, before they began using the procedures.* We were interested in what people did as they began their tasks because we observed that how participants oriented themselves as they got started often influenced their success.[7] The video protocols[8] allowed us to determine how readers searched the instruction guides and how much they read as they oriented themselves to the tasks. In particular, we wanted to know three things:

[7] See the discussions of information search by Dreher and Guthrie (1990), Guthrie et al. (1993), Kirsch and Mosenthal (1990), Larkin and Simon (1987), and Wright and Lickorish (1994).

- How many pages users looked at before starting their task
- How many words they read before starting their task
- Their success or lack of success in carrying out the task

[8] Because we had some difficulties with the audio portion of some of our video tapes, we could analyze the data for only 28 of the 35 people. We limited our attention to three basic tasks and three advanced tasks. Basic tasks are those which are fundamental to elementary setup and use of a consumer product. In this case, basic tasks included "inserting a cassette tape into a telephone answering machine," "connecting a VCR to a television and an antenna," and "connecting stereo components." Advanced tasks are optional, carried out only occasionally; these included "recording a conversation with a telephone answering machine," "marking an 'index signal' on a video tape," and "recording two songs from a CD to a cassette tape, one song on one side of the tape and the second song on the other side."

We hypothesized that people who were unsuccessful might, as did participants in a study by Kieras (1985), fail to read enough of the instructions to fully understand them.[9] Kieras found that participants tended to stop reading too soon, that they gave up before coming to important details that would help them carry out procedures correctly.

However, in analyzing the activities of participants in our study,[10] we found quite a different pattern (see Table 7.4). Taking basic tasks and advanced tasks together, we found that participants who were unsuccessful in completing tasks searched nearly twice as many pages (on average 4.7 as opposed to 2.5) and read more than twice as many words (on average 46 instead of 21) as those who were successful. As I discussed in Chapter 6, searching lengthy documents can be an intrinsically difficult task for many people. Researchers and practitioners should resist concluding that people who have difficulties with search tasks are not trying very hard.

Participants who were effective in their searches used key words from the task scenarios to guide them, readily derived synonyms for words they could not match, and could often guess what a related task might be. If they didn't find what they were looking for in one place, they had heuristics

[9] Participants in his study used a hierarchical menu system to examine step-by-step instructions and had the option of selecting menu choices that allowed them to move to lower levels of the hierarchy in order to see the details of specific operations.

[10] I thank Ann Steffy Cronin for her collaboration in this analysis.

Average Number of Pages Searched and Words Read Before Beginning Tasks

Basic Tasks[a]	Successful (n = 20)	Unsuccessful (n = 8)
Pages[b]	2	3
Words[c]	16	49
Advanced Tasks[d]	Successful (n = 17)	Unsuccessful (n = 11)
Pages[e]	3	6
Words[f]	27	44

[a] Basic Tasks: Inserting a cassette tape into a telephone answering machine, connecting a VCR to a television and antenna, connecting stereo components together.

[b] For basic tasks, the range of pages searched by successful participants was 0 to 4; for unsuccessful participants the range was 0 to 6. (Note: There were 27 pages in the answering machine instruction guide; 60 pages in the VCR guide; and 75 pages in the stereo guide.)

[c] For basic tasks, the range of words read by successful participants was 0 to 64; for unsuccessful participants the range was 0 to 176.

[d] Advanced Tasks: Recording a conversation with a telephone answering machine, marking an "index signal" on a videotape, recording a song from a CD on one side of a cassette tape and another song on the other side.

[e] For advanced tasks, the range of pages searched by successful participants was 0 to 6; for unsuccessful participants the range was 2 to 14.

[f] For advanced tasks, the range of words read by successful participants was 0 to 72; for unsuccessful participants the range was 5 to 121.

◀ Table 7.4 *The relationship between the number of pages participants searched, the number of words they read, and their accuracy in performing basic and advanced tasks with instruction guides for consumer products. Successful participants searched fewer pages and read fewer words before beginning their tasks than unsuccessful participants. Participants who were unsuccessful in carrying out tasks searched more pages and read more words, countering the assumption that users who fail at tasks usually do not try very hard. These data suggest that searching for information can be a hard task and that users may need to be taught effective search strategies.*

for finding the information elsewhere. In contrast, poor searchers rarely restated the task to themselves in their own words. They did not formulate alternative names for tasks and did not guess when a task might be a subtask of another. When they found information that they thought might be useful, they tended to read and not be able to recognize when their reading was not giving them relevant information. They had trouble monitoring whether they were finding what they wanted and sometimes went back to the task scenarios and started over. Of course, if the manual itself was poorly written and poorly visualized, it just made matters worse. Figure 7.4 presents an excerpt from a usability test participant who was trying to connect the VCR to a TV and an antenna.

▶ Figure 7.4 *Jeff, a usability testing participant, who tries to connect a VCR to a TV and an antenna. Because the instruction guide is written and illustrated in an ambiguous way, he has trouble finding the right procedures and is unable to make the right connections. He winds up starting all over again after considerable effort and frustration.*

"I'm going to have to use the manual to connect the VCR to the TV and antenna. Let's see."
Jeff opens the VCR manual to pages 2 and 3, looks at the section titled, Warning.
"I never read the cautions."
He turns to pages 4 and 5, Precautions and Introduction, and reads the first of the Introduction.
"Introduction. How to use this manual. This manual is arranged to help you quickly find the information. . ."
Jeff skips to the next paragraph and reads the first sentence.
"First, look through the table of contents before you begin."
He stops reading and looks up.
"I'm confused already."
Jeff turns the page to the next section, Identifying Operational Parts.
"Identifying operational parts, let's try that. This is the front (he indicates the picture of the VCR in the manual). We're looking at the back (the VCR on the table). OK."
Jeff silently compares the picture of the VCR in the manual to the actual VCR on

the table, then asks a question.
"Are you sure this is the same machine (VCR on the table) as is in here (VCR in the manual)?"
He shakes his head in disbelief and turns to pages 8 and 9, Identifying Operational Parts.
"OK, here we are, page 8, 'identifying operational parts.' One ... connect to the VHF/ UHF connectors on your TV referring to the 'connections' section. Onscreen displays are output via the VHF/UHF OUT connector. Two, control S in jack (minitype). Connect to the control S output jack of another product for systematic operations such as synchronized editing ... which I won't be doing. Three ... connect to the video/audio output jacks of other VCR. Four ... connect to the video/ audio input jacks of other VCR. Five, monitor out video jacks. Connect to the video/ audio input jacks on a TV. On- screen displays are via this connector. Six, AC outlet supplies AC power to video or audio equipment. Do not connect any equipment with power consumption exceed-

ing 400 watts. Seven ... connect the supplied AC power cord. Number eight, RF unit selector, use to select the channel for VCR playback ... number eight, is that direction for the remote control? I hope it is, I'm not quite sure about connecting yet. If it is, then that's the instructions on how to use the remote, which I don't want to use yet. Why do these pictures read sideways? You know, like a comic book. You have to read across and see stuff and then read down and then across ... It's weird."
Jeff turns the page and looks at pages 10 and 11, Connections.
"Connections. Before you begin turn off the power to the VCR and the TV. Disconnect the AC power cord of the VCR and the TV from the wall outlet. Do not connect the AC power cords until all of the connections are completed. First check your TV. If your TV does not have video and audio input jacks ... check the antenna terminals on your TV."
He looks at the bottom left corner of the back of the TV, then goes back to the manual.

These data suggest that there is an important role that document designers can play in helping users navigate lengthy texts by building documents with appropriate and consistent rhetorical cues that make navigation more intuitive, and less of a linguistic and perceptual guessing game. These data also remind us that if readers experience problems with searching linear hardcopy texts, where discourse cues are presumably more familiar and easier to see, these problems may escalate considerably when reading hypertext and online documents. As a number of researchers have cautioned (see, for example, Charney, 1994; Van der Geest, 1994; Wright, 1994), the assumption that searching large bodies of networked information is easy and unproblematic may be wrong.

"If your TV does not have video and audio input jacks. Check for antenna terminal. Well, this TV has the old kind of connectors for a rabbit ears antenna."
Jeff looks at the back of the television and reads the labels on the controls.
"VHS output? Vertical hold, hmm ... I hate to say it, but I don't know how to hook this thing up. It doesn't have those video and audio input jacks."
He reads page 11 again.
"If it doesn't have jacks check the antenna terminals."
Jeff looks at the television and pulls the antenna wire off the back of the television.
"Well, I don't know if this is it or not. This is the antenna and that must be the terminal because it was hooked up to that. Well I am going to guess that this is where it goes."
Jeff reattaches the antenna to the television.
"I'm not going to blow this up, I hope."
Jeff returns to the manual, open to pages 10 and 11. He begins reading another part of page 11.

"Now, connection example 1 to connect a 'combination VHF/UHF antenna.' When did I decide I had to do that? Is this out of order?"
He glances back at page 10.
"Go through connection examples one to five to find the appropriate connections."
He reads example one, step one on page 11.
"Disconnect the TV antenna cable from the TV receiver and connect it to the VCR. "
Jeff repeats the procedure slowly, deliberately.
"Disconnect the TV antenna cable from the TV receiver and connect it to the VCR."
He looks at the page for a moment and then decides that the second example is the one he should read. The second example is a drawing of an antenna connector that is similar to the one connected to the TV. Jeff again removes the antenna cable from the TV.
"This is the correct connection, example 2, to connect a VHF antenna only. This is what I have. Disconnect the antenna cable from the TV and connect it to the VCR. If the antenna cable is a 75-ohm coaxial,

round-type, use an F-type connector, optional. "
Jeff rolls his eyes and sets the antenna cable on the desk.
"F-type connector. Ha-ha-ha! This is very confusing to me because I really don't have any idea of how to do it. It's sort of like hit or miss, maybe I looked in the wrong place."
Jeff pauses a moment takes a deep breath and picks up the antenna cable again.
"OK, now, if I have this cable it says to connect it. But where? F-type connector, optional. I don't know if I have an F-type connector."
He picks up the F-type connector on the table and studies the back of the TV.
"So this little gizmo is it, something I actually use?"
Jeff compares the back of the VCR and the TV once more.
"How is it gonna make any sense to hook this (F-type connector) up to that (TV)?"
Jeff looks at the illustration at the bottom of page 11.
"How to attach the TV antenna cable and an F-type connector, see page 15."
Jeff turns to page 15 and reads.

"Strip a quarter of an inch from the end of the cable. It says I have to strip the wire. Great, there has to be an easier way to do this. I guess I'm gonna need tools just to connect a lousy antenna."
He scans the headings on page 15.
"Attaching the optional separator/mixer."
Jeff looks at page 14.
"To connect a cable TV system."
He looks over pages 12 and 13.
"I think I might have to read this over again, but I don't know if this is where to look. Maybe I should start over."
Jeff pages through the manual to page 5 and begins reading the section titled, Introduction.
"OK, introduction. I already read how to use this manual. This manual is arranged to help you quickly find the information ... Well it does not help me find the information. OK, the manual consists of the four following sections. I have to admit if this was mine—at this point—it would go back to the store. If I had to hook it up myself, it would be gone!"

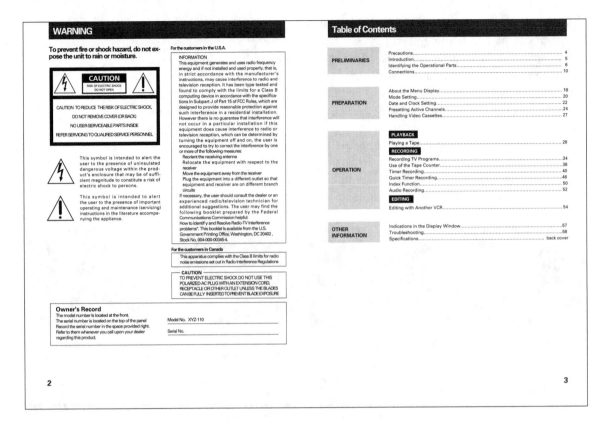

WARNING

To prevent fire or shock hazard, do not expose the unit to rain or moisture.

For the customers in the U.S.A.

CAUTION
RISK OF ELECTRIC SHOCK
DO NOT OPEN

CAUTION TO REDUCE THE RISK OF ELECTRIC SHOCK,
DO NOT REMOVE COVER (OR BACK)
NO USER-SERVICEABLE PARTS INSIDE
REFER SERVICING TO QUALIFIED SERVICE PERSONNEL

This symbol is intended to alert the user to the presence of uninsulated dangerous voltage within the product's enclosure that may be of sufficient magnitude to constitute a risk of electric shock to persons.

This symbol is intended to alert the user to the presence of important operating and maintenance (servicing) instructions in the literature accompanying the appliance.

INFORMATION
This equipment generates and uses radio frequency energy and if not installed and used properly, that is, in strict accordance with the manufacturer's instructions, may cause interference to radio and television reception. It has been type tested and found to comply with the limits for a Class B computing device in accordance with the specifications in Subpart J of Part 15 of FCC Rules, which are designed to provide reasonable protection against such interference in a residential installation. However there is no guarantee that interference will not occur in a particular installation if this equipment does cause interference to radio or television reception, which can be determined by turning the equipment off and on, the user is encouraged to try to correct the interference by one or more of the following measures:
 Reorient the receiving antenna
 Relocate the equipment with respect to the receiver
 Move the equipment away from the receiver
 Plug the equipment into a different outlet so that equipment and receiver are on different branch circuits
If necessary, the user should consult the dealer or an experienced radio/television technician for additional suggestions. The user may find the following booklet prepared by the Federal Communications Commission helpful:
How to Identify and Resolve Radio-TV Interference problems". This booklet is available from the U.S. Government Printing Office, Washington, DC 20402, Stock No. 004-000-00345-4.

For the customers in Canada
 This apparatus complies with the Class B limits for radio noise emissions set out in Radio Interference Regulations

— CAUTION —
TO PREVENT ELECTRIC SHOCK DO NOT USE THIS POLARIZED AC PLUG WITH AN EXTENSION CORD, RECEPTACLE OR OTHER OUTLET UNLESS THE BLADES CAN BE FULLY INSERTED TO PREVENT BLADE EXPOSURE

Owner's Record
The model number is located at the front.
The serial number is located on the top of the panel
Record the serial number in the space provided right.
Refer to them whenever you call upon your dealer regarding this product.

Model No. XYZ-110

Serial No.

Table of Contents

PRELIMINARIES
Precautions...4
Introduction...5
Identifying the Operational Parts...............................6
Connections...10

PREPARATION
About the Menu Display..18
Mode Setting...20
Date and Clock Setting..22
Presetting Active Channels...24
Handling Video Cassettes...27

PLAYBACK
Playing a Tape...28
RECORDING
Recording TV Programs..34
Use of the Tape Counter..38
Timer Recording..40
Quick Timer Recording..48
Index Function...50
Audio Recording..52
EDITING
Editing with Another VCR...54

OTHER INFORMATION
Indications in the Display Window..............................57
Troubleshooting..58
Specifications..back cover

2   3

▲ Figure 7.5 *An original version of a Table of Contents for a VCR manual.*

Moving from Usability Test to Revision

To provide a sense of the documents that readers in this study used, I present a number of before-and-after examples from the instruction guides in Figures 7.5 through 7.13. Following is brief commentary on each.

Figure 7.5 is the original version of a table of contents for a VCR manual; this spread is the first of the manual. Notice that it opens with a forbidding set of warnings and cautions. Our testing revealed that users disliked this way of introducing the product, making them feel as though something might go wrong even before they got started. Interestingly, warning labels on devices have a rather mixed effect. Sometimes they serve to make a person take notice and be more careful; at other times they make the user feel reluctant to try out the device; and at still other times warnings are simply ignored. Research shows that whether or not people take warning labels seriously depends on the context. Furthermore, how much attention they pay depends on whom is doing the warning and on the content of the warning itself. Surprisingly, it has been found that the more authoritative-sounding the person doing the warning, the more likely people are to deliberately disobey the warning. For example,

Choosing what to read based on your VCR experience

Table of contents

If you are an . . .	You should read . . .	Hints
inexperienced user— a first-time or infrequent user of VCRs	*Chapter 1: Setting up Your VCR* *Chapter 2: Learning Basic Tasks*	Once you have your VCR connected, it may be helpful for you to: • watch the demo to learn about the options which are available to you with the menus • set the clock so you are not frustrated by the flashing "12:00" To learn about the advanced features (after you have learned the basic tasks) read *Chapter 3: Learning Advanced Tasks*.
experienced user— a frequent VCR user who is familiar with features on VCRs	*Chapter 1: Setting Up Your VCR* *Chapter 3: Learning Advanced Tasks*	It may be helpful for you to look at the connection section of Chapter 1 when you are setting up your VCR.

Bushman and Stack (1996) studied warning labels designed for parents to monitor the violent programs their children may watch on television (e.g., "This film contains some violent content. The United States surgeon general has concluded that television violence has harmful effects on young viewers"). They found that warning labels actually *increased* viewers' interest in watching violent programs; participants who saw the warning had more desire to see violent films than did participants in a no-label condition. Document designers have much more to learn about the effects of warning labels on thinking, motivation, and action.

▲ **Figure 7.6** *A revision of the Table of Contents shown in Figure 7.5. By Michele Matchett (writing), Burton Morris (illustration), and Norma Pribadi Polk (graphic design) for Karen Schriver Associates, Inc., Pittsburgh, PA.*

In our revision of the VCR manual (shown in Figure 7.6), we moved the warnings next to the procedures at the points in the text at which they were needed. This shift allowed us to change the opening spread in tone and layout. Our revision employs the same style of drawings shown earlier in Figures 6.15 and 6.16 (pp. 426–427). Our intent with this picture was to invite readers to pause for a moment in order to decide which chapters of the VCR manual to read. As shown, we present an if-then table to suggest which chapters are appropriate for users of various levels of experience. Notice also that the table of contents takes a task-oriented approach and uses active verbs in the headings rather than verbs turned

11 A helpful treatment of sentence-level writing issues can be found in Kolln (1996), who discusses grammar from a rhetorical point of view; Williams (1989), who offers advice on style; or Lanham (1992), who suggests ways to revise long-winded sentences.

into nouns; that is, nominalizations.[11] For example, instead of saying "preparation," in which the verb "prepare" has been turned into the noun "preparation," we say "connecting the VCR."

Figure 7.7 shows three versions of a remote control device for a VCR. The first version is the original, designed by the client's team. The second two are the initial and final revisions created by our team. Notice that the client's document designers employed shading as a way to make the devices stand out from the background. As I discussed in Chapter 5, making figure–ground relationships apparent to the reader can be very helpful. However, a problem with the rendering shown in the original version is that document designers chose the wrong visual element to highlight. They should have been focusing the reader's attention on the buttons, not on the edges of the devices. Readers already know what the devices look like. At this point in the manual, the reader needs to recognize the different input jacks on the back of the VCR or the different buttons on the remote control.

In the initial revision (shown as Version 2 in Figure 7.7), there are a number of changes. First, we limited the visual content to one electronic device per spread; here we depict only the remote control (not the VCR

▼ **Figure 7.7** *Three versions of a page that identifies the buttons on a remote control for a VCR. Versions 2 and 3 were designed by Norma Pribadi Polk, Michele Matchett, Daniel Lepore, and Mary L. Ray for Karen Schriver Associates, Inc., Pittsburgh, PA.*

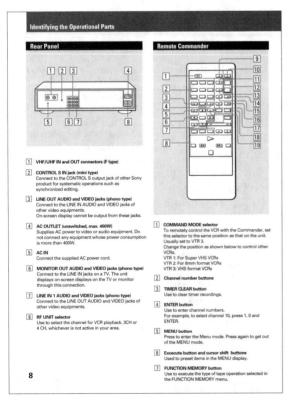

Version 1: The Original

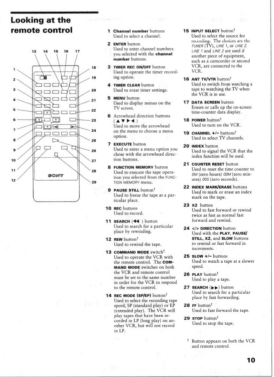

Version 2: The Initial Revision

and the remote). Second, we changed the drawing of the remote control. We set a goal not to use horizontal leader lines to call out the buttons. Participants in our initial usability test found that the horizontal lines extending from the buttons of the device in the first example made it difficult to track the line and find the right button. Since the leader lines took the same angle as the buttons, they tended to blend in with adjacent horizontal lines, making it hard to distinguish between the lines and the edges of the buttons. Furthermore, the numbers at the end of each leader line were enclosed in a square, adding yet another set of boxes to look at.

In our initial revision (see Version 2), we angled the leader lines so that none mirrored the edges of the buttons. This made the leader lines easier to see; however, the drawing was still problematic because the buttons themselves were crowded and our drawing looked somewhat like a spider. Norma Pribadi Polk then came up with the idea that we use the buttons as the figure and the remote control itself as the ground, which led us to darken the color of the buttons so that they would stand out from the device (shown in the final revision, Version 3 in Figure 7.7). In addition, our final version uses circles instead of squares to enclose the numbers of each button, a small but aesthetically pleasing change.[12]

[12] Special thanks to Daniel Lepore, who drew the technical illustrations for the VCR manual.

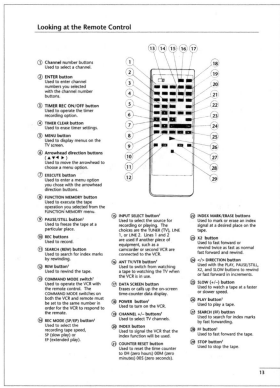

Version 3: The Final Revision

▶ **Figure 7.8** *The original version of a telephone answering machine manual. These instructions were about how to install a microcassette tape in order to make recordings. Notice that the part of the device the user should look at is too small and that the instructions are unclear. This is the same manual (and same spread) that confused the participant whose protocol was excerpted earlier in Figure 4.2 (p. 221).*

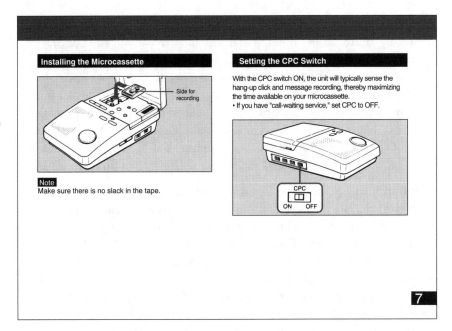

Usability testing showed that people could easily locate the buttons when they used the final version of the guide. In contrast, almost every person who had trouble finding the right buttons to press on the remote control read the original guide. Of course all three versions would have been much better if the remote control didn't have so many buttons to document in the first place.

In Figure 7.8, I show the original version of a spread from a telephone answering machine manual; it offers instructions for installing a cassette tape into the device and setting a switch. This particular page is the same one read by participant Muriel in Figure 4.2 (p. 221).

Our team's revision is presented in Figure 7.9 (a built-in telephone had been added to the answering machine, but the procedures required hadn't changed much). As shown, we changed the grid completely and took an action-oriented approach to the procedures. We added a small gray highlighted area to many of the illustrations in order to show which part of the device was important to look at while carrying out the procedures. In addition, instead of presenting the procedures as a running paragraph as in Figure 7.8, we enumerated each step, calling out what to do en route to setting up the device.

Earlier in this book, we saw that participant Muriel could not understand how to get rid of slack in the cassette tape used for recording incoming messages with the answering machine. She commented, "all

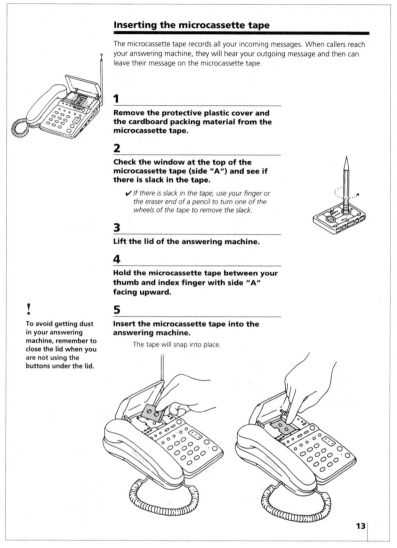

Inserting the microcassette tape

The microcassette tape records all your incoming messages. When callers reach your answering machine, they will hear your outgoing message and then can leave their message on the microcassette tape.

1

Remove the protective plastic cover and the cardboard packing material from the microcassette tape.

2

Check the window at the top of the microcassette tape (side "A") and see if there is slack in the tape.

✔ *If there is slack in the tape, use your finger or the eraser end of a pencil to turn one of the wheels of the tape to remove the slack.*

3

Lift the lid of the answering machine.

4

Hold the microcassette tape between your thumb and index finger with side "A" facing upward.

5

Insert the microcassette tape into the answering machine.

The tape will snap into place.

!

To avoid getting dust in your answering machine, remember to close the lid when you are not using the buttons under the lid.

13

◀ **Figure 7.9** *A revision of the telephone answering machine manual shown in Figure 7.8. This page is part of the same revised manual shown earlier in Figure 5.18 (p. 311). Document design by Mary L. Ray, Dan Boyarski, Carlos Peterson, and Norma Pribadi Polk for Karen Schriver Associates, Inc. Pittsburgh, PA.*

they say is make sure there is no slack in the tape" (see the "note" below the first picture in Figure 7.8). In our revision of the guide, we employed a complementary visual-verbal relationship to instantiate what to do. We described the idea in words and visualized it by showing a pencil tightening up the slack in the tape (see the second drawing in Figure 7.9). In addition, we supplemented our procedures with drawings that showed how to place the tape into the tape well (see the bottom two drawings in Figure 7.9). Here, to make a more friendly impression, we show a hand placing the tape into the device. We think the proportions, the sense of scale, and the tone work fairly well.[13]

[13] Special thanks to Dan Boyarski for his keen sense of the visual.

▶ **Figure 7.10** *An original version of a spread from an instruction guide for a combination "cordless phone with a regular phone." The regular phone is called a "base" phone. These instructions describe where to place the base phone so that it will not create interference while using the cordless.*

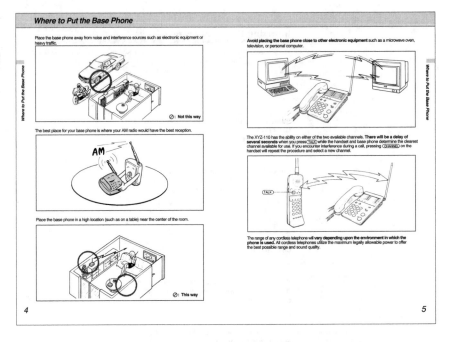

In Figure 7.10, I present the original version of a spread from an instruction guide for a cordless telephone. The visuals illustrate "where to put the base phone"; the base phone is the main unit of a combination cordless phone and regular phone. The spread gives advice about where to position the main unit in order to avoid interference while using the cordless. Notice that each of the five main ideas is separated by a box and that it uses a mixed illustration style, with cartoons and line drawings. The boxes, which frame the procedures, were intended to chunk the advice. However, these ideas are related and should not be separated. Notice that the first and third illustrations show a bird's eye view of an interior of a living area. These two illustrations are oddly separated from each other by a cartoon of two radios talking to one another. The fourth picture is a realistic drawing that gives information about potential sources of interference such as a microwave, and the fifth provides a note about how the range of the cordless varies as a function of the environment in which it is used.

Figure 7.11 is a new version of the "Where to put the base phone" spread, revised based on usability testing. In our revision, we elaborated on the idea of using a bird's eye view of a living area by refining the drawing, grouping relevant content items, emphasizing particular parts of the living area, highlighting the 3-D aspect of the living area, and increasing the size of the drawing. The new drawing included all of the information presented in the old version as well as some new information.

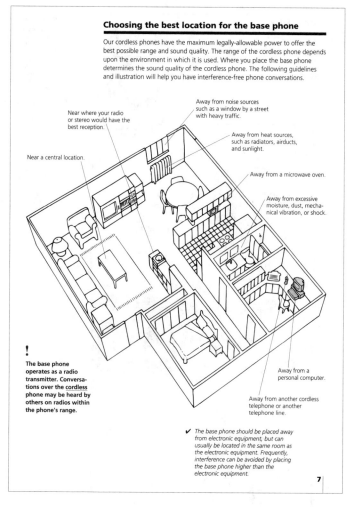

Figure 7.11 *A revision of the spread from the instruction guide for the "cordless phone and regular phone" shown in Figure 7.10. Document design by Carlos Peterson (illustration), Dan Boyarski (graphic design), Norma Pribadi Polk (graphic design), and Mary L. Ray (writing) for Karen Schriver Associates, Inc, Pittsburgh, PA.*

What had been separate boxes for each idea in the original version were now unified by a single visual frame (the living area).

Other features of the revision (Figure 7.11) include a consistent illustration style. As readers look at the page, they don't see the hand of many illustrators, but of one. The diagram is large enough to enable seeing the details of the living space without squinting. In addition, the revision employs a more appropriate typeface, type size, leading, and line length for the captions. Note that the angled leader lines add some visual interest to the page. Another aspect of the design that warrants attention is the shift from a boxy organization in the original to the asymmetrical one shown in the revision. The revision is not only more functional but is also more aesthetically pleasing, setting up relationships among the visual and verbal elements instead of segregating them.

▶ **Figure 7.12** *An example of a chapter divider from a stereo system manual that was intended for a European audience. Document design by Ilene Lederer (illustration), Norma Pribadi Polk (graphic design), and Mary L. Ray (writing) for Karen Schriver Associates, Inc., Pittsburgh, PA.*

CD Player
Lecteur CD
CD-Spieler
Reproductor de discos compactos

3

In this chapter you will learn about the CD player and about how it works as part of the stereo system. You will learn how to play compact discs (CDs) in three play modes: normal, shuffle and program. The modes allow you to decide which tracks (that is, songs or recordings) you will listen to. You will also learn to specify the order in which order the tracks will be played. (For information on recording CDs onto cassette tapes, see *Recording a CD in Chapter 4*.)

The topics presented in Chapter 3 are:

• Playing a CD (normal play)
• Playing tracks in random order (shuffle play)
• Playing tracks in specific order (program play)
• Playing tracks repeatedly

❖ Whenever you are using the stereo, remember to press and release SYSTEM POWER on the Tuner to turn the stereo on. Also press and release POWER on the CD Player and Tape Player to turn the components on. If you want, you can leave the CD Player and Tape Player POWER on all the time and use the SYSTEM POWER to turn the stereo on and off.

38

Figure 7.12 is a chapter divider for a stereo manual; it introduces a section that describes the operation of a compact-disc (CD) player. The original manual did not use chapter dividers. In fact, chapters started randomly, either on a left page or on a right page without any special attention to making one different than the next, a practice that disoriented users as they tried to navigate the manual. Furthermore, because the manual had only engineering-style technical illustrations, it was dry and lifeless. This was unfortunate because the product was fun to use; in the words of one of our usability participants, "the sound from this equipment is fantastic, but they don't even hint about this. It's all so technical, you know."

To get away from an overly technical approach, our team worked with illustrator Ilene Lederer to create fanciful escapist drawings that would set the stage for each component of the stereo system. Figure 7.12 invites the user to learn about the CD player. This drawing, we think, reinforced a positive image of the product and of the company, suggesting that the product is fun and not hard to learn. Unfortunately, our client rejected this drawing on the basis that it suggested one could put "CDs in the sand." The client felt that if users put CDs in the sand, they could melt or get warped and that the company could be held liable for damage to personal property that was encouraged by the picture in the manual. Sigh...

Figure 7.13 presents a revised version of a spread from the stereo manual. It is the same one shown earlier in Figures 5.16, 5.27, and 5.28 (pp. 308, 317). The main thing to notice is the grid design. We employed a three-column grid (six across a spread), in which columns one and two on the first spread of each chapter were reserved for a chapter divider picture; after the first spread, columns one and two were employed for technical illustrations while columns three through six were for the text, one column for each of the four languages. In this way, users didn't have to guess which picture was associated with their language because all language groups used the same pictures. Usability testing showed that users preferred this version over the old one and could use the instructions more quickly and with greater accuracy.

▼ **Figure 7.13** *A revision of a spread from a stereo manual, the same multi-language manual for European audiences shown in Figure 7.12 and earlier in Figures 5.16, 5.27, and 5.28 (pp. 308, 317). Document design by Mary L. Ray, Norma Pribadi Polk, Carlos Peterson, Michele Matchett, and Dan Boyarski for Karen Schriver Associates, Inc., Pittsburgh, PA. The translation was carried out by a European contract firm hired by the client.*

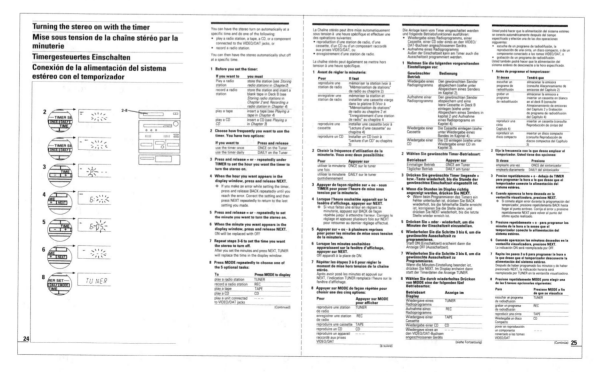

Although we have evidence that this manual is definitely better than the old one, we think it could still use more work. Unfortunately, in the redesign, we were severely constrained by space limitations. The client decided against increasing the page count, even though usability testing indicated that many of the most important features had not been documented in the original, making it impossible for users to complete their tasks. This meant that the new manual had to include more content than the old one in the same number of pages. This constraint led us to choose a type size of 9-point Univers Condensed with 11 point leading. Although Univers is a highly legible type (as we saw in the study of "Typography Under Duress" in Chapter 5), even a legible face will suffer if it is presented at a small size and in a condensed version. In retrospect, we would never choose this again—it is uncomfortably small.

In addition, there were problems created by the blowups of the buttons which appeared in column one on each spread. Because the blowups were physically distant from the procedures (especially from the fifth and sixth columns), they sometimes gave readers troubles. Unlike the close links we had established for the answering machine manual (see Figure 5.18, p. 311), users of the stereo manual had a lot of back and forth mapping to do. Thus, even though everything users needed was on the spread, they tended to ignore the blowups because it was a nuisance to track the step to the picture. In the end, while the revision did enhance people's ability to use the stereo system, our design team knew we could have done a better job with fewer constraints. C'est la vie.

Implications

Looking back over this study and reflecting on readers' tendencies to blame themselves (reported in Chapter 4), I would like to highlight a number of issues. The findings of the "Blame Study" in Chapter 4 revealed that readers tend to blame themselves when products and instruction guides mislead them. The "Blame Study" suggested that the cumulative effect of peoples' experiences with poorly designed products and badly written instruction guides may convince them that they are incompetent both as readers and as users of technology. However, as the usability study reported in this chapter makes evident, the majority of the confusions that readers experienced resulted from a combination of poor writing and poor visual design.

Moreover, the study described in this chapter suggests that, contrary to popular belief, problems in using instruction guides are distributed roughly evenly across age, gender, and nationality groups. All groups benefited from the improved quality of the revised texts. Indeed, for participants in these studies, the most important factor in learning to use new technology was not a person's previous experience, sex, or even how hard he or she tried. Rather, the most important factor was the quality of the writing and visual design of the instruction guide.

The results of this study suggest that the revision process, guided by reader-focused evaluation, can produce a very substantial improvement in text quality. Furthermore, this study showed that the results of usability testing are not simply "what any expert would predict." In fact, the experts in this study predicted less than half of the problems that readers experienced when using the texts. This research indicates clearly that revisions based on expert judgment together with user protocols can lead to substantial improvement in text quality. However, the research does not tell us which specific revisions were important for readers and which had little effect. The next step in this research program is to compare readers' performance with documents in which a set of visual and verbal text features have been systematically varied. Studies of this type will allow us to identify the textual moves that may have the most impact on readers.

This study indicates the important practical and scientific gains to be made through studies of readers' interactions with texts and of document designers at work. Studies such as this one show, I think, that document design research can have an invigorating effect on the study of visual and verbal rhetoric in the humanities and fine arts. Studies in document design are grounded in problems of society and are responsive to the needs of people. Indeed, through its focus on principled rhetorical action, document design research has the potential to improve the quality of our everyday lives by improving the texts we use to make sense of our world.

WHAT CAN DOCUMENT DESIGNERS LEARN FROM USABILITY TESTING?

As we have seen, usability testing routinely reveals important problems that document designers, even expert ones, may fail to detect. Involving the audience as active participants in document design provides substantial benefits—by both improving the documents that people use and broadening the scope of problems that document designers can attend to during revision. However, these benefits come at a modest financial cost—one that makes some organizations balk. Although the gains of employing human-centered design are clear, organizations have tended to shy away from the idea of usability as a permanent feature of their development process. Clearly, it would be beneficial to all if there were an educational method that could help document designers predict the problems that readers might have with documents without actually having to carry out a usability test for every poorly designed document (or product). A method that sensitizes writers and designers to the typical problems that people may experience with poorly written or badly visualized documents could go far in closing the gap between designers' intuitions and readers' needs.

In this section, I will describe a teaching method I call *protocol-aided audience modeling (PAM)*. Students taught by this method significantly increased their ability to diagnose readers' problems as compared to students taught by traditional methods.

14 For a more extensive discussion, see Schriver (1987, 1992b).

The idea for the protocol-aided audience-modeling method (PAM)[14] grew out of research I conducted at Carnegie Mellon University's former Communications Design Center (CDC)—a nonprofit organization that was dedicated to basic and applied research in document design (see Chapter 2, "Early Research Centers in Document Design," pp. 73–75). During the 1980s, researchers at the CDC developed and elaborated a method called *protocol-aided revision* (Swaney, Janik, Bond & Hayes, 1981/1991; Schriver, 1984, 1991). Its purpose—as we saw in the first study of this chapter—is to enable writers to employ direct feedback from readers to guide revision activity. By asking readers to think aloud as they work with a document and a machine, writers are able to capture readers' real-time cognitive processing of the text and identify the aspects of functional texts that create difficulties for readers.

In the mid-1980s, there was a core of writers at the CDC who had taken part in much of the document design and usability testing research at Carnegie Mellon and who for a number of years had been using protocol-aided revision to evaluate functional texts. I observed that these experienced writers and usability testers seemed to be much better at planning and revising text than were writers who had years of on-the-job editing experience. (I made this comparison between CDC writers and students who were enrolled in Carnegie Mellon's graduate program in professional writing, some of whom entered the program with substantial experience in professional editing.) I wondered why the CDC writers were so good and thought that perhaps their keen rhetorical awareness had to do with their extensive involvement in watching readers-in-action. My hunch was that perhaps the CDC writers' repeated experiences with "catching users in the act" as they grappled with poorly written prose and badly designed graphics had increased their sensitivity to audiences' needs more generally. They seemed to know what to expect from readers, often anticipating their moves even before they saw readers actually engage with a document.

To explore this intuition, I designed the PAM teaching method, which involves a sequence of ten lessons for document designers, each with the following format:

1. First, the document designer reads a sample document with the goal of making a list of any problems that he or she believes the prose or graphics will create for the intended audience.[15]

2. Second, the document designer reads a transcript of a think-aloud protocol from a member of the intended audience who is trying to understand the sample document. With the help of the transcript, the document designer generates a second list of problems that he or she believes the prose or graphics will create for the audience.

My idea was that once document designers had some practice in using PAM, they might be able to anticipate problems on their first pass (without the reader's feedback) that they could detect only after seeing reader's feedback early in the sequence of lessons. To assess whether PAM could be employed to improve document designers' sensitivity to readers' needs, I explored the following questions:

- Would PAM help document designers predict problems that texts create for readers?

- Would PAM work as well or better than more familiar methods such as audience-analysis heuristics, peer-response methods, or role playing?

- Would the sensibilities that document designers acquire through PAM transfer to new texts and to new genres?

IMPROVING DOCUMENT DESIGNERS' SENSITIVITY TO READERS: PROTOCOL-AIDED AUDIENCE MODELING (PAM)

To test the effectiveness of PAM, I compared it to more traditional methods of teaching audience analysis used in the professional writing classroom. In particular, I asked 117 college juniors and seniors from ten classes in "writing in the professions" to participate in an evaluation of PAM. Five classes served as an experimental group and five as a control group. Students were enrolled in a variety of degree programs in humanities, engineering, or business management. The course was an elective, and class size ranged from 12 to 22 students. In total, there were 43 students in the experimental classes and 74 students in the control classes.[16]

Evaluating Protocol-aided Audience Modeling

A pretest was given to both experimental and control classes early in the semester (see Figure 7.14 on the next page). During the semester, students were taught to anticipate readers' needs through either PAM or through a combination of methods, including audience-analysis heuristics, collaborative peer-response groups, and role-playing activities.[17] Teaching for

[15] Prior to the first lesson, students are provided a profile of the audience (knowledge, background, and experience).

[16] Roughly equal numbers of students volunteered to participate (75 students in the experimental classes and 85 in the control classes). However, there was an unequal distribution of English majors across the two groups, with more in the experimental classes. Because English majors may have had an advantage over other students, the major analyses I report here were carried out on the data from 117 students who were not English majors, 43 students in the experimental classes and 74 students in the control classes.

[17] For descriptions of these methods for analyzing the audience, see the textbooks of Lannon (1985); Lauer, Montague, Lunsford, and Emig (1985); and Mathes and Stevenson (1976).

▶ Figure 7.14 *Overview of the study design.*

Experimental Classes	Pretest	Protocol-aided Audience Modeling (PAM)	Posttest
Control Classes	Pretest	Audience analysis heuristics and peer-response teaching	Posttest

both experimental and control classes took place over about six weeks. Both groups were posttested about three-quarters of the way through the semester.

The study required that I develop teaching, testing, and validation materials, each of which is described below.

The teaching materials for the PAM method consisted of ten lessons, each containing two parts:

1. *A "problematic" document, that is, a poorly written and poorly visualized text that will cause comprehension difficulties for the intended audience.*
   I selected ten problematic instructional documents; each text was one to four pages in length. The documents were elementary lessons in operating a university computing system and were intended for freshmen, secretaries, and university staff who had never used a computer before. An important feature of these texts was that they did not contain spelling or grammatical errors. Rather, they had incomplete forecast statements, poor stage-setting relationships between prose and graphics, cryptic definitions, unclear procedures, missing examples, misleading headings, ambiguous goal statements, weak summaries, and other "beyond the word-level or phrase-level" problems. Some of the documents had been composed by student writers;[18] others had been generated by the computer scientists who wrote the software. Each text introduced a new topic (e.g., sending mail, formatting a report, creating a table, using an online card catalogue for the campus library).

2. *A think-aloud reading protocol of a person trying to understand the text.*
   For each of the ten texts, a reading protocol was collected from a different member of the actual audience—freshmen and secretaries learning to use a computer. The protocols revealed a wide variety of understanding and usability problems—problems that poorly written instructions often create for readers. The ten protocols were formatted so that students could easily distinguish readers' responses from the original text.

[18] Students who created the documents were not enrolled in the classes in the study.

The ten lessons were culled from a set of more than 20 texts on which think-aloud reading protocols had been collected. Figure 7.15 presents an excerpt from one of the problematic texts (written by a computer scientist) and Figure 7.16 (on the following page) is a think-aloud reading protocol collected on that text. I chose the lessons based on how well they highlighted the ways in which instructional texts can create problems for readers and make comprehension a painful process (Schriver, 1984).

Pretest and Posttest Materials

Materials for the pretest and posttest were six naturally occurring expository science texts, each approximately one-half page in length. The six texts were excerpts from the "science" and "medicine" sections of *Time* and *Newsweek* magazines; thus, they were intended for a general U.S. audience with an average reading level of grade 11. These elementary scientific texts were not altered in any way. (They were, in fact, a subset of the texts used in the Thibadeau, Just, and Carpenter, 1982, eye movement studies of the reading process.) The texts covered topics in physiology, human development, engineering, and the like. Like the texts used in the ten lessons, the testing materials did not contain grammatical, spelling, or mechanical errors. Rather, they caused comprehension problems for readers because the writers failed to provide necessary contextual information, left out examples, presented confusing metaphors

---

An Excerpt from a Problematic Software Manual

Commands for English Text

EMACS enables you to manipulate words, sentences, or paragraphs of text. In addition, there are commands to fill text, and convert case.

Editing files of text in a human language ought to be done using Textmode rather than Fundamental mode. Invoke M-X Text Mode to enter Text mode. See section 20.1 [Major Modes], p. 85. M-X Text Mode causes Tab to run the function ^R Tab to Tab Stop, which allows you to set any tab stops with M-X Edit Tab Stops (See section 11.3 [Indentation], p. 46). Features concerned with comments in programs are turned off except when explicitly invoked. Automatic display of parenthesis matching is turned off, which is what most people want. Finally, the syntax table is changed so that periods are not considered part of a word, while apostrophes, backspaces and underlines are.

If you are editing input for the text justifier TEX, you might want to use TEX mode instead of Text mode. See the file INFO: ETEX. INFO.

◀ Figure 7.15 *This example shows a portion of a set of instructions from the* EMACS User's Manual *written by a computer scientist from MIT. It provided a very detailed and technical discussion of* EMACS, *one of the early text editors for wordprocessing while connected to a mainframe. Fortunately, software manual design has come a long way since this early user's guide. Most of today's software manuals are not nearly this bad, but vestiges of the bad old days are still alive and well in the design of many manuals for modems and hardware.*

▶ **Figure 7.16** *A transcript of the think-aloud protocol of a new user who participated in a usability test of the EMACS computer manual. The think-aloud protocol was provided by an undergraduate student. The excerpt from which he is reading is shown in Figure 7.15. His comments are in boldfaced italics.*

An Excerpt from a Think-aloud Usability Protocol

Ok, now I'm going to try … Commands for English Text. EMACS enables you to manipulate words, sentences, or paragraphs of text. *These commands sound like ones I'd use all the time—good. In addition, there are commands to fill text, and convert case. I don't know what it means to fill text, I guess it means putting data from one text into another … that is, filling the text with what you want in it. Well, I guess I'll soon find out.*

Editing files of text in a human language *human language? Boy that sounds strange, what could they be distinguishing here? Maybe computer language or machine language from human language?* ought to be done using Textmode rather than Fundamental mode. *Well, I don't know what textmode or fundamental mode is, so how will I know which I'm in? Let's see* … Invoke M-X Text Mode to enter Text mode. *I won't do that because I do not have time to see the other section. That's terrible to tell me to* … See section 20.1 [Major Modes], p. 85. M-X Text Mode causes Tab to run the function ^R Tab to Tab Stop, *Now wait a minute, what is all this stuff? Sounds important, but I have no idea what it could mean. I know what tabs on a typewriter are, and I see a tab key here, but what the heck does running the function ^R Tab to Tab stop mean? Oh God, now they want me to look up another section* … which allows you to set any tab stops with M-X Edit Tab Stops (See section 11.3 [Indentation], p. 46).… *Just to get started in this one. No I think I'll skip that. I'll deal with it when I have to use it. I thought this section was on how to edit; what does setting tab stops have to do with editing?* Features concerned with comments in programs are turned off except when explicitly invoked. *Hmm … a feature? Wonder what a comment feature is? How do they get turned off? Do I have to turn them off? Well I guess I can't turn them off if I don't know what they are.* Automatic display of parenthesis matching is turned off, which is what most people want. *What does that mean? How do I know if I'm like most people and want them turned off? I wish they'd tell me why I need to know all these hacker terms!* Finally, the syntax table is changed so that periods are not considered part of a word, while apostrophes, backspaces and underlines are. *Syntax table … no idea. Of course, I do know what the syntax of sentences are, so maybe it means something to do with certain commands EMACS considers acceptable … maybe certain actions in a row produce a correct syntax.*

If you are editing input for the text justifier TEX, you might want to use TEX mode instead of Text mode. See the file INFO: ETEX. INFO. *Well, I don't want to edit input for the text justifier mode, I just want to figure out how to manipulate words and paragraphs—like it says up here (points to the top of section). This stuff is too complicated and it's aggravating to read …*

---

or analogies, provided illogical transitions, or packed information too densely. Here is an example of one of the six texts; its topic is holography.

> Lights, mirrors and nozzles are the tools of holography—the reconstruction of light waves to create a three-dimensional image. Unlike photography, holography produces no negative. It produces a hologram, a recording of light waves reflected from a laser-illuminated object. First, the laser's light is split into two beams. One is

reflected by a mirror onto a photographic plate; the other is directed at the subject. When the laser strikes the subject, it is fractured by the uneven surface and reflected back to the plate. Thus, the plate records a superimposed pattern of both sets of light waves—the pure ones from the mirror and the jumbled ones from the subject itself. Then another laser beam is directed through the photographic plate to release a three-dimensional image.

Validation Materials

To evaluate the accuracy of experimental and control writers' predictions of readers' responses during the pretest and the posttest, I identified the problems the testing materials created for an audience of lay readers. I collected reading protocols from 30 freshmen trying to understand each of the six texts used in the pretest and posttest. The order in which the 30 freshmen read the six texts was counterbalanced. Two raters, who were graduate students in English,[19] independently evaluated each of the 180 protocols provided by the freshmen and analyzed the problems freshmen experienced in trying to understand the passages. I established the criterion that any problem that was experienced by three or more of the freshmen would be designated as a problematic text unit. Thus, if 10 percent of the 30 freshmen had a problem at the same text unit, I considered it enough of a problem to warrant a document designer's attention.

Three types of problems emerged: local (problems at the word-level), sentence-level (problems within sentences), and global (problems beyond the sentence, e.g., "this text needs an example here").[20] Frequently, the same text area would cause problems of more than one type—problems that ranged from vocabulary difficulties to those of integrating new information within the context of given information.

I used the information about the text locations at which readers experienced problems to create templates for scoring writers' predictions.

[19] Thanks to Daniel Medvid and Christina Carey for their generous help in this analysis; both hold master's degrees in professional writing.

[20] In more than 90 percent of cases, the problems that the freshmen readers experienced had an identifiable location in the text, such as "this section here makes the idea too hard to understand." Being able to identify a location allowed judges to classify reader's problems as word-level, sentence-level, or global (above the sentence-level). I call problems such as these "referable problems." In contrast, "nonreferable problems" did not have such a locus; rather, they appeared to reflect cumulative effects of many parts of the text, such as, "This whole thing is confusing." Two raters categorized the problems in the protocols as "referable" and "nonreferable." Interrater reliability in judging referability was .914 (using a statistic called Cohen's Kappa). I used only the referable problems as a measure against which to judge experimental and control writers' predictions of reader problems. Nonreferable problems accounted for less than 10 percent of the problems experienced.

Figure 7.17 is an example of one of the texts I used, *Artificial Heart*. The underlined text units are the places at which readers noticed they were having difficulties (these locations don't pinpoint where the problem started or stopped, just when readers realized something had gone awry). In coding the protocols, a problem was defined as any statement that signaled confusion or misunderstanding of the text. The freshmen readers made statements like the following three:

> I do not understand how a baby could have an "inward growing grin." Why would a psychiatrist study such a thing as grins? (The freshman was reading the text *Babies' Smiles,* which contained a discussion that described "sleepy smiles" as those in response to "external stimuli" and then distinguished the "sleepy smiles" from those referred to as "inward growing grins.")

> A "miniature nuclear furnace!" Why would you use nuclear power inside a human being? Is this one of those metaphors or something? (The freshman was reading the text *Artificial Heart,* which presented a statement that said artificial hearts use a "miniature nuclear furnace" to keep them going.)

> Thus the plate records a superimposed pattern of both sets of light waves—the pure ones from the mirror and the jumbled ones from the subject itself … I guess there's an image of the person in the mirror, and one of the lights from the laser, or one of the beams, is directed toward the image and one is directed toward the person, I guess the subject. And the reflection coming off the subject is a lot more jumbled than the one coming off the mirror. Okay, but I'm still not sure what the photographic plate does. Why don't they have a picture? (The freshman was reading the text *Holography,* which described the process of fracturing a laser.)

Using the summaries of readers' problems, such as the example in Figure 7.17, we scored writers' predictions of readers' difficulties.

How the Study Was Carried Out

The professional writing classes took place in their usual manner with a few exceptions. At the beginning of the semester, all students took a pretest, predicting readers' problems with three of the six testing texts, such as *Artificial Heart*. Classes proceeded with either the protocol-aided audience modeling method or the audience analysis heuristics methods.

Places in the Text at which Readers Noticed Comprehension Difficulties[a] While Reading

Artificial Heart

A <u>miniature nuclear furnace</u> is needed to keep an
16
<u>artificial heart</u> beating. The artificial system consists of
3
the synthetic heart chambers and valves them-

selves, an <u>engine</u> to make the chambers pump, and
4
the fuel source to run the engine.

The <u>nuclear source</u> is a two inch capsule containing
3
<u>Plutonium-238</u> with a <u>half life of 89 years</u> and a
3   5
very slow rate of decay. The capsule surface is 360

degrees Fahrenheit so a <u>metal "carrier"</u> was designed
7   6
to <u>conduct excess heat</u> out of the body. This carrier
7   6
<u>is attached</u> to the <u>aorta</u> by means of a
4   4
<u>titanium tube</u>. First, a two inch segment of the aorta
10
is unclamped to allow the blood to flow

through the tube. The <u>nuclear capsule</u> then is
3   4
<u>placed in the carrier</u>.
9

"A miniature nuclear furnace" powers "a heart," that's a weird image! It doesn't sound like something that would ... should be involved in any human device. I think maybe they should have shown some sort of a link between the two. In reading this you can sort of visualize it but they should give you something a little bit more concrete, to help start the ideas going.

Well, I'm not quite sure what a "titanium tube" is—I assume titanium is some kind of metal. But what is it for?

Here again I am not sure what they mean by "carrier." Is that part of the furnace, the artificial heart, or is that involved with veins or parts of the body? At first, I thought the carrier just went out to a readout. Instead it's attached to the aorta, which doesn't make sense.

Now I have never heard of this kind of artificial heart before. We have studied things like this, and the artificial hearts that are in use now are nothing like this because they're not powered by this kind of motor.

Sounds rather scientific. I'm not sure what a half life is. It's probably self-explanatory, though.

I'm to picture the capsule and metal carrier ... I don't know what a "carrier" might look like. I'm not really sure, so the surface is pretty hot. Guess I'll read on because they'll probably tell me.

I'm not sure what the "aorta" is. Is that part of the heart or part of the human body surrounding the heart? Maybe they need a diagram.

I still don't understand why the person doesn't get burned by the heat of the metal capsule. I really don't understand this. They should explain why you need this stuff. This doesn't make it clear.

This isn't a very good explanation. And there's no graphics. It's not exactly what I thought an artificial heart was. I didn't know they used a nuclear source. I guess they do.

[a] Underlined words and phrases show the point in the text at which participants noticed a problem in the text. The numbers underneath the lines show the number of the 30 participants who noticed a problem at that point.

▲ Figure 7.17 *A paragraph taken from a "Science and Medicine" section of a magazine. Shown here are comments made by readers who were freshmen in college.*

Teaching Procedure for Experimental Classes

On the first day, students in the experimental classes were presented with one of the ten problematic texts and told that the intended audience consisted of freshmen in college who had not used computers before, that is, readers unfamiliar with the topic of the text. Students were prompted to decide how well the text met the needs of the audience by employing the following procedure.

First, students read the text and underlined or bracketed words, phrases, sentences, sections, or graphics—any size text unit that they felt would cause a lay reader trouble in understanding the text. To discourage students from underlining the whole text, they were asked to try to be certain that any text area they underlined or bracketed would cause only one problem for a reader. Then students were asked to assess each part of the text they marked and to diagnose what they thought the reader's problem would be. Students diagnosed problems by writing a one-sentence characterization of the reader's probable difficulty. For instance, a student might respond "the reader needs a definition of this concept." Students were not provided with any instruction in diagnosing readers' problems but were asked to phrase their characterizations in a way that would allow another person in the class to understand the problem they thought the reader would have.

Next, students were given the second half of the lesson: a think-aloud protocol transcript of a member of the audience reading and attempting to understand the text. Students were asked to read the protocol with the goal of using it to help them detect and diagnose additional problems that were made evident by the reader. During their second pass, students were encouraged to pay special attention to those problems they missed on their first pass, additional problems the reader feedback helped them to see and describe. To summarize, the teaching method for each of the ten lessons had two parts:

Part One

1. Read the draft document.
2. Predict the reader's problems with the document (*detection* phase).
3. Characterize the reader's potential problems with the document (*diagnosis* phase).

Part Two

1. Read the think-aloud protocol transcript.

2. Use the reader's responses to identify additional problems (*detection* phase).

3. Use the reader's responses to characterize the additional problems (*diagnosis* phase).

During their first pass, students predicted and diagnosed problems on the basis of their intuition; during their second pass, they detected and diagnosed new problems revealed by the readers who were attempting to understand the texts. Students worked in this manner through each of the ten lessons. At no time during the course of the ten lessons did students receive feedback about the quality of their performance.

Teaching Procedure for the Control Classes

Writers in the control classes were taught to anticipate the reader's needs through a variety of audience-analysis heuristics and peer-response methods, including peer critiquing, role playing, and purpose-oriented audience pedagogies. Students were taught using mainly small-group exercises. Once or twice a week, they critiqued one another's papers, worked in collaborative groups, role played, or examined a variety of "good" and "bad" model texts of the sort written in the professions, such as reports, proposals, memos, and so on. Teachers were rigorous in providing students with detailed feedback about how well their papers reflected the needs of the audience. All assignments in the course were written for audiences other than the teacher. For each paper, students were advised to elicit comments from members of their intended audience. Teachers reported that most students participated fully in classroom activities. Teachers who taught the course had been using this combination of methods for a number of years.

Pretest and Posttest Procedure

Writers in both experimental and control classes were tested using the six texts described above as "validation materials." The six testing texts were divided into two groups: three texts labeled A and three labeled B. Half of the participants, both experimental and control, were pretested on the A texts and posttested on the B texts. The other half were pretested on the B texts and posttested on the A texts. For each of the six texts, writers were asked to predict the location and nature of problems that a freshman reader might have with the text. In this way, the testing procedure mirrored the detection and diagnosis phases of the PAM lessons. The essential difference between testing and training was that neither group (experimental nor control) was provided with reading protocols during pretest or posttest.

Results

I compared experimental and control classes to evaluate their improvement in accurately predicting readers' problems. An accurate prediction is one in which writers predict problems that readers actually had as measured by the reading protocols collected from the freshmen. Results, graphed in Figure 7.18, indicate that writers in the experimental classes improved dramatically from the pretest to the posttest, increasing in accuracy by 62 percent, while writers in the control classes remained essentially unchanged. Analysis of variance indicates that the experimental classes' gain scores were significantly greater ($F = 26.037$; $df = 1, 8$; $p \leq .001$) than those of the control classes. In addition, there was no significant difference between the accuracy of experimental and control classes' pretest scores ($F = .685$; $df = 1, 8$; $p = .432$). At posttest, average scores for writers in the control classes were lower than at pretest, but not significantly so.

▶ Figure 7.18 *The effect of protocol-aided audience modeling (PAM) on writers' ability to anticipate readers' problems accurately.*

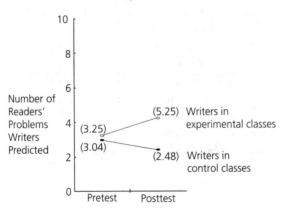

In addition to asking whether writers improved in their accuracy of predictions, I was concerned with whether writers in the experimental and control classes had changed in their ability to differentiate actual reader problems from nonproblems. One can imagine that a teaching method of this sort could make writers hypersensitive to text problems, leading them to say that everything is a problem. Consequently, it was important to determine whether problems writers predicted were, in fact, problems for readers.

An analogous situation is that of judging the quality of a book reviewer. A reader evaluating a book reviewer's performance would want to know more than that the reviewer recommended a high proportion of the good books on the *New York Times* book list that were published during the year. If that were enough, we could all become good book reviewers simply by recommending every book that is published. We would praise every good book, but we could hardly be described as discriminating. We would display no sensitivity to the differences between good and bad books. What we want in a good book reviewer, then, is someone who praises good books but not bad ones.

Similarly, it is not enough that writers accurately predict a high proportion of readers' problems. If that were enough, we could all become good predictors of readers' problems simply by identifying every text unit as problematic. Writers must be able to discriminate between textual moves that will or will not cause a problem for most readers.

The desirable situation is one in which the writer identifies a higher proportion of potential reader difficulties in text units that are problematic than in text units that are not. In other words, we want the probability that a writer says that an element is problematic when in fact it is (the probability of a hit) to be greater than the probability of saying that an element is problematic when it is not (the probability of a false alarm).

To analyze the relationship between writers' accurate and inaccurate predictions, I used signal detection analysis because it takes into account both the hit rate and the false alarm rate in evaluating the sensitivity of performance. Signal detection analysis focuses on a measure, called D^1, which reflects the differences between the probability of a hit and the probability of a false alarm. I found that writers in the experimental classes were not "problem happy" but in fact had increased their ability to differentiate problems from nonproblems significantly more than had control writers.[21] These results suggest that writers taught with protocol-aided audience modeling improved significantly in their ability to anticipate readers' needs and that the sensitivities writers developed are helpful in discriminating problems that readers actually have. These findings raised the question, "What sorts of readers' problems are writers getting better at anticipating?"

[21] These findings are based on conducting an analysis of variance on the gain scores in D^1 ($F = 8.752$; $df = 1, 8$; $p \leq .018$).

Writers' Diagnoses of Readers' Problems

To answer this question, I evaluated the kinds of problems writers diagnosed and how the diagnoses differed from pretest to posttest. A sample of 100 diagnoses from the pretest and 100 from the posttest for both the experimental and control groups (a total of 400 diagnoses) was evaluated from the more than 2,800 diagnoses writers made. My goal was to determine whether protocol-aided audience modeling affected the kinds of problems writers noticed from pretest to posttest. To capture the various dimensions of writers' diagnoses, I created three coding schemes that were designed to view the data in complementary ways. All 400 diagnoses were coded three times, once for each scheme.

Problems Focused on the Reader, Self, or Text

- *Reader-focused diagnosis*—characterized by an explicit mention of the reader, as in "A freshman student may not have an understanding of photography and would probably get confused when reading the analogy between photography and holography."

- *Self-focused diagnosis*—characterized by the use of "I," for example, "How do I know what causes 'inward growing grins?' From my point of view, 'inward growing grins' are ridiculous. This text doesn't have a clear purpose to me."

- *Text-focused diagnosis*—characterized by their similarity to stylistic maxims and grammatical rules, as in "You should always define concepts the first time they are mentioned in a paragraph."

Problems of Commission versus Omission

- *Problems of commission*—created by what the document says, that is, problems caused by what is on the page. This category includes anything that can be diagnosed by looking at the text as written and or visualized calling attention to a potential problem it creates, such as "This is written in passive voice and that is bad" or "That format is ugly."

- *Problems of omission*—caused by what is *not* on the page. This category involves diagnoses of potential problems that are caused by what the document is missing. Problems of omission are brought about by missing content, underdeveloped ideas, gaps in logic, incomplete procedures, nonexistent transitions, or missing graphics. For example, one student diagnosed a problem in this way: "First it talks about 'vitreous humor' and tries to define it, and then it switches to things like what causes blindness. I think something needs to be 'put in' to help the reader see why things like blindness and diabetes are related to vitreous humor somehow. Something is left out. A picture would help too."

Problems at the Global or Local Level

- *Global diagnosis*—characterized by a description of a reader's problem conveying that the writer is attending to text elements larger than a sentence, such as "This whole description of holography doesn't flow. It seems kind of jumbled up like those 'jumbled laser beams.'"

- *Local diagnosis*—characterized by a description of a reader's problem that shows the writer is focusing on text units of a sentence or smaller, as in "This word 'nozzle' sounds easy but it's not. Is it like a hose? They should pick a better word."

These coding schemes were derived from the research literature on revision (Flower et al., 1986; Hayes et al., 1987; Hull, 1987; Scardamalia & Bereiter, 1983) and from the freshmen readers' problems in comprehending the testing materials. Results from analyzing the diagnoses along these three dimensions—reader, self, or text; omission versus commission; and global or local—provided converging results.

Table 7.5 displays the changes in percentages of reader-, self-, and text-focused diagnoses from pretest to posttest. At pretest, writers in both groups frequently made text-focused and self-focused diagnoses. These results are not surprising, given the traditional emphases in writing classes. However, at posttest, the percentages of text-focused diagnoses declined for both groups, the control group by 7 percent and the experimental by 21 percent. Writers in both groups made more diagnoses that reflected a concern for the reader; the main difference was that the experimental writers did so more often.

It appears that both PAM and the traditional methods made students more aware of optional ways to diagnose text problems. At posttest, writers in both experimental and control classes increased in their "self-focused" diagnoses. They more frequently monitored their own

Writers' Diagnoses of Readers' Problems Focused on the Reader, Self, or Text

	Pretest	Posttest	Change
Experimental Classes (n = 43)			
Reader	17	33	+ 16
Self	38	43	+ 5
Text	45	24	- 21
Control Classes (n = 74)			
Reader	9	13	+ 4
Self	32	35	+ 3
Text	59	52	- 7

Note. Values represent students' responses in percentages.

◄ Table 7.5 *At pretest, writers in both groups tended to focus more on their own problems with the text and on stylistic problems. At posttest, writers in the experimental and control classes increased in their reader-focused diagnoses, but those who took part in the protocol-aided audience modeling increased much more.*

comprehension to predict what might trouble another reader, as the following diagnosis of *Vitreous Humor* suggests:

> When I read the title "vitreous humor," I thought it was talking about a type of new joke. Now that I read the whole thing, I still don't understand it. And I bet others won't figure out this part about people going blind from diabetes either.

In addition to using themselves as a model of the reader, writers in the experimental classes made more diagnoses in which they distinguished themselves from the reader with statements such as the following, from a diagnosis of *Artificial Heart*:

> I read about artificial hearts when William Shrader got his, and I think some guy from Louisville got one too. But a freshman who hasn't read that story would never get this stuff. It's too complicated and the "plutonium" reference is scary. What if the "metal carrier" comes open? Is that why they seem to croak off so soon?

As Table 7.5 shows, writers in the experimental classes showed the largest increases in reader-focused diagnoses. At posttest, writers taught with the PAM method were much more prone than writers in control classes to make diagnoses such as the following based on *Artificial Heart*:

> A freshman might take the phrase "a miniature nuclear furnace keeps an artificial heart beating" too literally. They might think doctors put radioactive stuff in your body. The writer is being too metaphorical for freshmen, too much like I'm a new hip reporter from *Discover* magazine.

An analysis of the increases in writers' diagnoses that involved an explicit mention of the reader revealed a significantly greater increase for writers in experimental classes than for those in control classes.[22] These results suggest that PAM heightened writers' awareness of the audience more than did the conventional pedagogy.

Table 7.6 summarizes writers' diagnoses of omission and commission. Again, at pretest, writers attended closely to the text-as-written, spending most of their diagnostic activity describing errors of commission. However, at posttest, writers in the experimental classes increased in their diagnoses of how missing information might create problems for readers.[23]

At posttest, writers in the experimental classes seemed especially adept at perceiving gaps in the logic of the text or in detecting missing content.

[22] These findings are based on conducting an analysis of variance ($F = 26.133$; $df = 1, 8$; $p \leq .001$).

[23] An analysis of variance indicated that the experimental classes' shift toward diagnosing problems of omission is significantly greater than that of the control classes ($F = 48.133$; $df = 1, 8$; $p \leq .001$).

Writers' Diagnoses of Readers' Problems: Omission and Commision

Experimental Classes (n = 43)	Pretest	Posttest	Change
Omission	18	51	+ 33
Commission	82	49	- 33
Control Classes (n = 74)			
Omission	17	30	+ 13
Commission	83	70	- 13

Note. Values represent students' responses in percentages.

◀ Table 7.6 *At pretest, writers in the experimental and control groups spent most of their time diagnosing the text-as-written. At post-test, writers with experience in analyzing readers' think-aloud protocols paid more attention to missing information.*

They made diagnoses such as the following:

> By the time the reader gets to this idea, you have forgotten the main point. Something is missing here. There is a leap in what is said. The writer should restate the big picture of the flywheel idea. I do not know why I am being told this stuff—I need the purpose said again, if it was ever said to start with (diagnosis of *Flywheels*).

> What this eyeball passage needs is a diagram of an eye. Why would you write this without a picture? The writer must have forgot it or else he doesn't care if the reader knows what's going on (diagnosis of *Vitreous Humor*).

It is important to point out that writers in the control classes also made such diagnoses at posttest; the essential difference was that they made far fewer.

Table 7.7 presents the relationship between global and local diagnoses for writers in the experimental classes and control classes. Previous research in revision would predict the pretest results; that is, writers in both groups started out with a tendency to focus on local problems. Local diagnoses, as one would expect, concentrated on diction and style. By the posttest, the experimental group increased significantly more than the control group in the number of global diagnoses they made.[24] Most writers' global diagnoses concerned issues of coherence, logic, and organization. This finding suggests that the PAM pedagogy helped writers in the experimental classes to perceive more problems at the global level of the text, an important advantage for initiating effective revision activity.

[24] These results are based on conducting an analysis of variance ($F = 38.4$; $df = 1, 8$; $p \leq .001$).

▶ Table 7.7 *The relationship between global and local diagnoses writers made.*

Writers' Diagnoses of Readers' Problems: Global and Local

	Pretest	Posttest	Change
Experimental Classes (n = 43)			
Global	21	51	+ 30
Local	79	49	- 30
Control Classes (n = 74)			
Global	24	31	+ 7
Local	76	69	- 7

Note. Values represent students' responses in percentages.

Implications of Using PAM to Improve Document Designers' Sensitivity to Readers

This study has several interesting implications for education in document design. First, it has shown that protocol-aided audience modeling can improve students' ability to identify problems that a text will create for readers. Second, it has shown that PAM works significantly better in improving this ability than do traditional teaching methods. Third, it has shown that the positive effects of PAM can generalize from one genre (procedural manuals) to another (expository science writing). At a more detailed level, the study showed that PAM enabled writers to become

- Better able to diagnose problems from the reader's point of view.
- More sensitive to problems caused by visual and verbal omissions.
- Increasingly aware of problems at the global level of the document.

On the negative side, this study found little evidence that traditional methods of teaching had much of an impact on students' ability to detect problems, at least over the six-week duration of the study. Further investigation of teaching methods that aim to improve writers' abilities to notice and solve problems is necessary. Teachers of document design need more ways to teach the process of imagining the reader. The focus of much of our teaching, particularly about revising prose, has been on finding what is wrong the text as written and fixing it rather than on evaluating what the reader needs and providing it. Yet most teachers would agree that perhaps the biggest problem with student writing lies not in what they say but in what they fail to say.

Although I've shown that PAM can improve students' ability to perceive text problems that may give people difficulties, we don't know if this method influences writers' ability to revise. This study did not examine the effects of PAM on writers' revisions. Research that brings together the thinking that document designers engage in as they plan a revision with the actual changes they make is a necessary next step. As Hayes and Nash (1996) point out, linking process to product is critical if we are to understand the nature of planning and revising.

Perhaps the most important finding of this study is that document designers who engage in usability testing may improve their ability to anticipate readers' problems with texts for which they have no reader feedback. These results suggest that there may be important cognitive advantages for document designers who employ reader-focused methods to guide their revision of prose and graphics.[25] The protocol-aided audience modeling method helped expand writers' consideration of the needs of audiences generally, changing both the nature of the problems writers noticed and their ability to characterize them. Several students who participated in the PAM method reported that after going through the training they could not read their drafts anymore without hearing "readers in their heads" saying, "I'm confused! What do you mean by that?" The PAM method helped writers acquire a model of the reader at work—a critical awareness for document design.

Writers and graphic designers can conclude, then, that to gain the most from usability testing they should work to consolidate their experience, asking, "What have we learned from these readers and this rhetorical situation that can be used to guide planning and revision of other documents?" When document designers are able to answer this question for themselves, they will recognize that usability testing is not an end in itself—it can be an opportunity for building a model of the ways that people engage with prose and graphics.

[25] For a discussion of other reader-focused methods, see Dumas and Redish (1993), Nielsen and Mack (1994), Raven and Flanders (1996), Schriver (1989a), and Schuler and Namioka (1993).

CONCLUSION

As we saw in Chapter 2, document design has made substantial progress in this century. When the century was new, document designers worked in isolation. There were neither professional societies nor journals through which they could exchange ideas or provide each other with support. There were no academic programs to teach novices or to foster research about writing and design. As the century draws to a close, the situation is much improved. There are professional societies with thousands of members (e.g., the Society for Technical Communication alone has more than 20,000 members[26]). There are also many journals that publish

[26] Based on an estimate of membership by the STC Communication Director Maurice Martin (June 30, 1996; e-mail correspondence).

document design articles (look back at Figure 2.11, pp. 98–99). In addition, there are hundreds of academic programs that teach writing, graphic design, or both.

Despite these advances, document design still faces some very serious problems. In Chapter 2, I described some of the difficulties that document designers have experienced in gaining recognition and respect in industry and academia. In industry, document design is often construed as requiring little special knowledge and few skills beyond the ability to speak and see. In the academy, the field is typically accorded low status compared to other areas of study. Document design has only occasionally been able to establish itself as an intellectual discipline on par with other disciplines. All too often, document design is seen as unimportant, as intellectually uninteresting, as having no theory or research, and as addressing only trivial problems.

As I argued in Chapter 2, such views of document design may have had their origin in the craft tradition that has dominated much of the teaching in writing and design. But whatever their origin, these views are very much out of date. Document design can no longer be viewed as the application of rules of grammar and format. Modern document design addresses problems that are as important, as complex, and as intellectually challenging as any faced by other disciplines.

To dramatize the point, let us imagine the kinds of problems we might face in carrying out a document design task such as designing a drug brochure or a VCR manual and the kinds of knowledge it would be useful to have to solve those problems.

1. One early concern would be to make sure that the audience could understand our prose. We might do this by using ourselves to model the audience, assuming that "if it's clear to me, it must be clear to them." However, if our knowledge differs substantially from that of the audience, we may be very poor judges of what the audience will understand. A consumer electronics manual written by an industrial engineer may be very clear to the engineer but quite opaque to the general public.

   Another approach to assuring that audiences could understand the document would be to collect think-aloud protocols from the intended audience. This approach will almost always be useful, but it may not always be practical. Even when it is practical, the work of writing will progress more quickly the better the document designer can predict readers' responses to the first draft. What kind of knowledge would help the document designer to do this? First, it would be useful to have knowledge about readers in general. For example, it would be helpful to know what kinds of text features are liable to cause confusion, such as complex conditionals, missing examples, and so on. This sort of information would probably be most helpful and accessible if it were organized into a theory of reading.

In addition, it would be useful to have a compendium of ways in which special audiences, such as senior citizens, seventh-graders, and the learning disabled, differ from the generality of readers.

The "Monster in the VCR" study in Chapter 4 shows that in order to understand many practical reading problems, document designers must consider much more than the clarity of what's on the page. Missing information created a problem of enormous complexity for the readers. The problem of textual omissions was also important in the scientific texts discussed in this chapter. In addition to problems created for readers by the text, we saw that it is crucial to understand how people move back and forth between text and product—among reading, thinking, and doing. It is important to understand the nature of the problem-solving process in which the reader is engaging if we are to create texts and user interfaces that facilitate that process.

2. A second early concern in our example of designing a drug education brochure or a VCR manual would be to make sure that the audience could understand the graphics. In assessing the graphics, we could rely on our intuition to guide visualizing or we could employ reader-feedback methods (discussed in Chapters 3 and 7). However, these procedures have the same limitations for assessing graphics as they have for assessing prose. And just as with prose, a model of graphic comprehension such as is provided in part by Gestalt principles (in Chapter 5) would make our task substantially easier.

3. In carrying out document design tasks, it is not enough to produce clear prose and clear graphics. It is also necessary to make them work together as an integrated whole. In designing, we need to strike a balance between too few graphics and too many; between too few words and too many. We need to answer questions such as "Will this graphic add enough to be worth the effort of switching attention from prose to graphic and back again?" and "Will the reader be able to make the connection between the prose and the graphic?" At present, there is very little research that bears on these issues. I have tried to lay out some of the relationships in Chapter 6, but document designers would benefit from a comprehensive model of the relationship between prose and graphics.

4. So far, we have been concerned with evaluating the clarity of prose and graphics, that is, how well they enable the reader to construct the message or the content of the document. However, as we've seen, readers infer much more from the document than the author's

message. They also draw conclusions about the author's character and competence and about the rhetorical situation; for example, "Are these people trying to con me?" In many cases, the reader's perception of the writer and of the rhetorical situation is more important than the clarity of the document. For example, in the "Just Say No to Drugs" study (Chapter 3) and in the "Let's Visit a Research Lab" case (Chapter 6), both the students reading the drug education brochures and the members of the Humane Society reading the research lab poster understood the document's messages quite well. However, their acceptance of these messages was strongly determined by their judgments about the document designer's knowledge, character, and attitude toward them.

Although there is valuable research that relates to judgments of a writer's character (e.g., see the work of O'Keefe, 1990), there is still much that we need to understand. For example, it would be very useful if we understood what it was in the "Just Say No" study that led readers to characterize the writer as "a white hippie who thinks he is cool, but he's not," a person "who may know the facts, but nothing of real life," "a 'big nurse' type," or "someone who would never come to my neighborhood." As yet, there is no adequate theory that would allow us to predict these responses. If there were such a theory, it would be very useful to document designers.

5. In carrying out document design activity, we need to be concerned with the reader's emotions, feelings, and motivations as well as with their cognitive processes. Even if a document is quite clear, the intended audience may not read it if it *appears* forbidding or unattractive. In attempting to create attractive documents, designers often use themselves as models of the audience. The results can be disastrous when there are major differences between the writer and the audience. Graphics that were intended to be engaging (Figure 3.1, p. 173), amusing (Figure 3.4, p. 178), or evocative (Figure 6.5, Screens 5 and 6, p. 394) were viewed by readers as offensive in the first case, seriously out-of-date in the second, and inappropriately narrow in the third. Studies of how people feel and of what they prefer as they interpret prose, graphics, and typography can serve a valuable role in avoiding such disasters.

It would be useful to have a model, even a crude one, that would allow us to anticipate readers' preferences for typeface, text density, and graphic design. As yet, such a model is not available. The research I presented in Chapter 5 suggests some of the contextual issues—such as the relationship between genre and typeface—that ought to be considered in building such a model.

In reviewing the variety of problems that we have to face in designing documents and the varieties of knowledge that would be helpful to us in solving those problems, it becomes very clear that document design is definitely not a trivial field. In its fully developed form, document design must include accounts of the following areas:

- Prose comprehension
- Graphic comprehension
- Interaction of prose and graphics
- Problem solving
- Perception of the author's persona and the rhetorical situation
- Aesthetic preferences for prose, graphics, and typography
- Impact of technology and interface design on human understanding and motivation
- Culture and situational context in guiding thinking, feeling, and action

Some of these topics, such as reading comprehension and problem solving, are being actively explored by researchers in other fields. Indeed, much information is already available on these topics. For other topics, though, such as the interaction of prose and graphics, readers' perception of the writer's persona and the rhetorical situation, and readers' aesthetic preferences for prose and graphics, it seems likely that document design must take the lead in doing the research and constructing the theory.

I believe that the greatest challenge that faces document design today lies in creating knowledge that is uniquely relevant to document designers. To meet this challenge, we have to act together. No single individual, no matter how talented or experienced, is going to solve our problems. The Romantic tradition of individual action is a dead end for document design. Instead, we need to build on the strengths we have in our professional organizations and our journals. We need to develop a powerful research community in which knowledge is created through dialogue, in which research results and theoretical ideas are subjected to rigorous scrutiny, and in which the ideas that survive the critique can form a solid foundation for an increasingly rich and dynamic discipline of document design.

Appendices

The author gratefully acknowledges the publishers listed in Appendix A

for granting permission to reprint the covers of their publications pictured in

Chapter 2, Figure 2.11. ❧ In composing documents typographically, it is

important to consider the standard character set for the typefaces that may

be employed, that is, their alphabet and numbers. In addition, it is a good

idea to evaluate typefaces for any special characters and symbols that may

be available. Appendix B explains the uses of some common symbols that

document designers may use in formatting body text, itemized lists, and

quoted material. ❧ Appendix C supplements the discussion of designing

documents typographically, spatially, and pictorially that is presented in

Chapters 5 and 6. It gives a set of guidelines for designing online docu-

ments and describes the special issues that need to be considered in

creating documents for computer or television screens, including documents

that will be presented on the World Wide Web.

◀ **Left-hand page.** *A segment of a financial report about the Seligman Common Stock from the Morningstar Report. Courtesy of Morningstar, Inc., Chicago, IL.*

Publications of Interest to Document Designers

American Educational Research Journal (AERJ) carries original reports of empirical and theoretical studies and analyses in education.

The American Educational Research Association, 1230 17th Street NW, Washington DC 20036-3078

American Institute of Graphic Arts (AIGA) Journal of Graphic Design (not pictured) explores the history, theory, and practice of graphic design.

American Institute of Graphic Arts, 164 Fifth Avenue, New York, NY 10010

American Medical Writers Association (AMWA) Journal publishes news and articles of interest to members of the American Medical Writers Association.

American Medical Writers Association, 9650 Rockville Pike, Bethesda, MD 20814

Cognitive Science publishes articles on such topics as knowledge representation, inference, memory processes, learning, problem solving, planning, perception, natural language understanding, connectionism, brain theory, motor control, intentional systems, and other areas of multidisciplinary concern.

Ablex Publishing Corporation, 355 Chestnut Street, Norwood, NJ 07648

College Composition and Communication (CCC): Journal of the Conference on College Composition and Communication provides a forum for critical work on the study and teaching of reading and writing at the college level.

National Council of Teachers of English, 1111 W. Kenyon Road, Urbana, IL 61801-1096

College English (CE) addresses a broad cross-section of the profession. Appropriate subjects are literature (including nonfiction), linguistics, literacy, critical theory, reading theory, rhetoric, composition, pedagogy, and professional issues.

National Council of Teachers of English, 1111 W. Kenyon Road, Urbana, IL 61801-1096

Communication Arts (not pictured) publishes articles on creativity for graphic designers, art directors, copywriters, photographers, illustrators and multimedia designers.

Communication Arts, 410 Sherman Avenue, PO Box 10300, Palo Alto, CA 94303

Communication News: Newsletter of the Communications Research Institute of Australia (CRIA) publishes articles dedicated to improving the quality of human communication through research, training, and debate. CRIA is a major center for independent research in Australia, exploring all aspects of communication.

Prof. David Sless, Communications Research Institute of Australia, 1st Floor, The Old School Hall, Maitland Street, Hackett ACT 2602, Applelink, Australia 0383; Phone 06 257 3155; Fax 06 247 5056

Computers and Composition explores the use of computers in writing classes, writing programs, and writing research. It provides a forum for discussing issues connected with writing and computer use.

Prof. Cynthia Selfe (Michigan Technological University) and Prof. Gail Haiwisher (University of Illinois), Humanities Dept., Michigan Technological University, Houghton, MI 49931

Design Issues: History, Theory, Criticism provides a scholarly forum for history, theory, and criticism of design.

The MIT Press, 55 Hayward Street, Cambridge, MA 02142

Design Methods: Theories, Research, Education and Practice is devoted to education and communication in the fields of design methodology and applied design method, and the fields of study of theories of design and theories of designing.

The Design Methods Institute, PO Box 3, San Luis Obispo, CA 93406

Design Quarterly covers architecture, design, and contemporary graphics.

MIT Press for the Walker Art Center, Circulation Dept., MIT Press Journals, 55 Hayward Street, Cambridge, MA 02142-1399

Design Studies approaches an understanding of design from comparisons of its application in all areas including engineering, architecture, planning, and industrial design. The journal reports on new developments, techniques,

▲ **Appendix A.** *To order these publications, contact the addresses listed below the statement about editorial policies. The covers of most of these publications are pictured in Figure 2.11 (pp. 98–99); those not pictured are so indicated.*

knowledge, and applications in the practice of design as well as design education: how design techniques may be taught, the approach to ill-defined problems, and the impact of new technologies.

Butterworth-Heinmans, Linacre House, Jordan Hill, Oxford OX2 8DP UK

Discourse Processes: A Multidisciplinary Journal (not pictured) provides a forum for cross-fertilization of ideas from diverse disciplines which share a common interest in discourse.

Ablex Publishing Corporation, 355 Chestnut Street, Norwood, NJ 07648

Graphis (not pictured) provides information about design, graphics, and illustration.

B. Martin Pedersen Graphis Press, Corp., Dufourstr 107, CH 8008 Zurich, Switzerland

Human Factors publishes original articles about people in relation to machines and environments, including evaluative reviews of the literature, definitive articles on methodology, quantitative and qualitative approaches to theory, and empirical articles reporting original research.

Human Factors and Ergonomics Society, Box 1369, Santa Monica, CA 90406-1369

Human-Computer Interaction coalesces the best research and design work from diverse fields into a distinct new field of human-computer interaction, covering the theoretical, empirical, and methodological issues of (1) user science and (2) computer system design as they affect the user.

Lawrence Erlbaum Associates, 365 Broadway, Hillsdale, NJ 07642

I.D.: Magazine of International Design (not pictured) targets corporate and independent designers of business and consumer products.

Magazine Publications L.P., I.D., PO Box 11247, Des Moines, IA 50340-1247

IDeAs: Newsletter of the Information Design Association features articles of interest to professionals and educators from fields interested in how information can be designed with the reader's needs in mind.

Conrad Taylor, 5 Arlesford Road, London, UK SW9 9JS
Phone/fax: (44) 171 207 2493
E-mail: ida@alexand.demon.co.uk

IEEE Transactions on Professional Communication: A publication of the Institute of Electrical and Electronics Engineers (IEEE) publishes articles that address a variety of issues including communication education and training, communication technology, corporate and organizational communication, graphic and visual communication, international communication, and speech communication.

Institute of Electrical and Electronics Engineers Professional Communication Society, 345 East 47th Street, New York, NY 10017

Information Design Journal (IDJ) explores a wide range of topics related to information design, particularly the design of communications of information of social, technical, and educational significance. These may be research reports, design evaluation reports, reviews, and theoretical papers. Articles are written with a multidisciplinary readership in mind.

Prof. Paul Stiff, Dept. of Typography and Graphic Design, University of Reading, PO Box 239, Reading, UK RG6 2AU

International Journal of Human-Computer Studies publishes papers on human-computer interaction, the person-computer interface, mathematical and engineering approaches to the study of people, and artificial intelligence approaches to computing.

Academic Press division of Harcourt Brace, 24-28 Oval Road, London NW1 7DX UK

*Journal of Computer Documentation: A Publication of SIGDOC (Special Interest Group for Documentation of the Association for Computing Machinery) provides a forum dedicated to advancing computer documentation toward greater technical artistry.[a]

Association for Computing Machinery Press, PO Box 12115, Church Street Station, New York, NY 10249

Journal of Advanced Composition (JAC) provides an advanced forum for scholars of rhetoric and composition theory, especially those interested in the general field of advanced composition, including advanced expository, business and technical writing, and writing across the curriculum.

Association of Teachers of Advanced Composition, Prof. Gary A. Olson, Editor, Department of English, University of South Florida, Tampa, FL 33620-5550

---

[a]Asterisk (*) is part of the title of the *Journal of Computer Documentation*.

**The Journal of Business Communication (JBC):
A Publication of the Association for Business Communication** (not pictured) publishes manuscripts from new as well as from established scholars and practitioners of business communication. Explores a variety of theoretical, philosophical, and methodological approaches to business communication.

Association for Business Communication, 100 English Building, 608 South Wright Street, Urbana, IL 61801

Journal of Business and Technical Communication (JBTC) discusses communication practices, problems, and trends in business, professional, scientific, and governmental fields.

Sage Publications, 2455 Teller Road, Thousand Oaks, CA 91320

Journal of Design History publishes new research, provides a forum for dialogue and debate, and addresses current issues of interest. The journal aims to help consolidate design history as a distinct discipline.

Oxford University Press/Oxford Journals, Walton Street, Oxford, OX2 6DP UK

Journal of Experimental Psychology: Applied (not pictured) provides a forum for empirical investigations in experimental psychology that bridge practically oriented problems and psychological theory. It also seeks articles that test models of cognitive processing in applied situations. Areas of interest include the applications of perception, attention, decision making, reasoning, information processing, learning, and performance. Settings may be industrial (such as human-computer interface design), academic (such as intelligent computer-aided instruction), or consumer oriented (such as applications of text comprehension theory to the development or evaluation of product instructions).

American Psychological Association, 750 First Street, NE, Washington, DC 20002-4242

Journal of Technical Writing and Communication (JTWC) contains essays on oral as well as written communication for purposes from pure research to needs of business and industry.

Baywood Publishing Company, Inc., 26 Austin Avenue, PO Box 337, Amityville, NY 11701

Metropolis: The Magazine of Architecture and Design covers trends and concepts in architecture and design with emphasis on metropolitan areas.

Bellerophon Publications, 177 East 87th Street, New York, NY 10128

Print: America's Graphic Design Magazine (not pictured) disseminates projects and portfolio pieces from practicing designers. Offers ideas on visual communication such as film, animation, environmental, and computer graphics.

RC Publications, Inc., 3200 Tower Oaks Boulevard, Rockville, MD 20852

Proceedings of the Council for Programs in Technical and Scientific Communication (CPTSC) promotes programs and research in technical and scientific communication; develops opportunities for the exchange of ideas and information concerning programs research; and assists in the development and evaluation of new programs in technical and scientific communication.

Council for Programs in Technical and Scientific Communications, Prof. Stephen A. Bernhardt, Dep't. of English, New Mexico State Univ., Las Cruces, NM 88003

Proceedings of the Conference on Computer-Supported Cooperative Work (CSCW 88) presents multidisciplinary perspectives on the role of the computer in group work, especially on the potential of computer technologies in enhancing socially organized work.

Association for Computing Machinery Press, 11 West 42nd Street, New York, NY 10036

Reading Research Quarterly (RRQ) provides a forum for the exchange of information and opinion on theory, research, and practice in reading.

International Reading Association, Headquarters Office, 800 Barksdale Road, PO Box 8139, Newark, DE 19714-8139

Research in the Teaching of English (RTE) publishes original research on the relationships between language teaching and language learning at all levels, preschool through adult. Articles reflect the variety of methodologies and modes of inquiry in the disciplines that contribute to our field, such as anthropology, history, linguistics, psychology, philosophy, sociology, and rhetoric.

National Council of Teachers of English, 1111 W. Kenyon Road, Urbana, IL 61801-1096

Rhetoric Review (RR): A Journal of Rhetoric and Composition publishes scholarly and historical studies, theoretical and practical articles, provocative pieces on the profession, humorous repartee, substantial review essays of professional books and textbooks, personal essays, and poems. The editors believe that rhetoric belongs at the center of the course in composition; they see *Rhetoric Review* as a theoretical and pedagogical resource for both new and experienced teachers and scholars, and a platform for a lively exchange of opinion within our discipline.

Rhetoric Review Association of America, Prof. Theresa Enos, Editor Rhetoric Review, Department of English, University of Arizona, Tucson, AZ 85721

SIGCHI: Journal of the Special Interest Group on Computer-Human Interaction of the Association for Computing Machinery (ACM) provides a forum for articles on the study of human factors in the human-computer interaction process, including research, design, development, and evaluation of interactive computing systems. The focus is on human communication and interaction with computer systems.

Association for Computing Machinery Press, SIGCHI Bulletin, 1515 Broadway, New York, NY 10036

Technical Communication (TC): Journal of the Society for Technical Communication (STC) publishes articles of professional interest to technical communicators—including writers, editors, artists, teachers, managers, consultants, and others involved in preparing technical documents.

Society for Technical Communication (STC), 901 North Stuart Street, Arlington, VA 22203

Technical Communication Quarterly (TCQ): Journal of the Association of Teachers of Technical Writing (ATTW) includes articles on research, theory, and teaching methods relevant to the education of students in the fields of scientific and technical communication. The ATTW encourages research and writing that reflect on the improvement of teaching and the advancement of knowledge in technical and scientific communication.

Prof. Billie J. Wahlstrom, Department of Rhetoric, 202 Haecker Hall, 1364 Eckles Avenue, University of Minnesota, St. Paul, MN 55108-6122

Technostyle deals with subjects of interest to readers involved in business, technical, academic, professional, scientific, and governmental communication, as teachers, practitioners, or researchers. A wide range of approaches to the study of nonliterary communication is entertained by Technostyle—rhetorical, linguistic, sociological, cultural, and ethnographic (published in French and English).

Prof. Diane Wegner, Dept. of English and Communication, Douglas College, PO Box 2503, Westminster, British Columbia, Canada V3L 5B2

tekst[blad] publishes articles for professional writers, providing news, discussions, research outcomes, interviews, critiques, and literature reviews. Topics of focus include text structure and style, genres, design, pretesting, and "the profession."

tekst[blad] is published by Bohn Stafleu Van Loghum Publishers, Postbus 246, 3990 CA Houten, The Netherlands (published in Dutch).

Intermedia, P.O. Box 4, 2400 MA Alphen aan den Rijn, The Netherlands

The Technical Writer provides a forum for exchanging ideas about technical writing in Japan; 44 issues were published ending in November 1993. At the time of publication a date for this journal to resume printing had not been set (published in Japanese).

ID Corporation, Kagurazaka Bldg. 5F, 42 Kagurazaka 6-chome, Shinjuku-ku, Tokyo 162 Japan

Visible Language (VL) discusses research and ideas that help define the unique role and properties of written language. It is a basic premise of the journal that writing/reading form an autonomous system of language expression that must be defined and developed on its own terms.

Sharon Poggenpohl, Rhode Island School of Design, 2 College Street, Providence, RI 02903

Written Communication (WC): An International Quarterly of Research, Theory, and Application publishes theory and research in writing from fields including anthropology, English, history, journalism, linguistics, psychology, and rhetoric.

Sage Publications, 2455 Teller Road, Thousand Oaks, CA 91320

Common Typographic Symbols

Character		Uses	Keystrokes	
			Mac	**PC**
ellipsis (less than a sentence deleted)	a ... a	Denotes, in quoted material, that less than a sentence has been left out. Put one space on either side to set off the ellipsis from the rest of the text. Avoid manually spacing an ellipsis because the width of the space made by the space bar is for words, not characters; it is too wide for characters and draws too much attention to the ellipses. Another benefit of the ellipsis character is that the three dots which comprise the ellipsis operate as a single character and will not separate if they fall at the end of a line (as they will if manually spaced). Ellipses are also used as a stylistic device to catch the reader's attention. In this case, including space on either side of the ellipsis is optional (e.g., "Just when you thought your hard drive would never let you down...crash!").	Op-;	Alt-Ctrl-period
ellipsis (more than one sentence deleted)	a.... a	Denotes, in quoted material, that a sentence or more has been left out. Type a period followed by the ellipsis character. Insert one space after the last period.	period, Op-;	period,
One space after a period, question mark, exclamation point, or colon	end. Begin	Indicates a sentence or idea has ended. Use one space (not two) after these punctuation marks, as the practice of using two spaces is just another holdover from using a typewriter.	space	space
fixed space (nonbreaking space)	Mr. Ed	Connects two words when a line break between them is undesirable. A fixed space is the same width as the regular space, but it will not break at the end of a line. For instance, if the name of a company is two words, it is important that the words appear on the same line (e.g., Rand McNally). Thus, inserting a fixed space between the two words insures they will not be accidentally separated.	Op-space	Ctrl-Sh-space
double open quotes ("curly quotes")	"	Indicates the beginning of a quoted passage. Use in place of straight up and down quotation marks (double straight quotes mean inches).	Op-[	Ctrl-Sh-[
double close quotes ("curly quotes")	"	Ends a quoted passage.	Op-Sh-[	Ctrl-Sh-]
single open quotes ("curly quotes")	'	Opens a quote within a quote. Use in place of a straight quote which means foot (i.e., 12 inches).	Op-]	Ctrl-[
single close quotes ("curly quotes")	'	Ends a quote within a quote, a quote in a title or subtitle, or acts as an apostrophe.	Op-Sh-]	Ctrl-]

Using these symbols. Op = Option key; Alt = Alt (Alternate) key; Sh = Shift key; Ctrl = Control key. A hyphen between two keystrokes indicates "press the two keys at the same time" (e.g., for "Ctrl-9," press Control and 9 at the same time). A comma between two keystrokes means "press the keys in consecutive order" (e.g., for "Ctrl-1, Sh-A," press Control and 1 then press Shift and A). A bolded keystroke indicates "hold down the first key while pressing the other keys" (e.g., for "**Alt**-0177," hold down the Alt key while typing 0177; bolded keystrokes appear on pp. 504–505). The keystrokes presented here apply to programs such as Microsoft Word. Consult a user's guide for the appropriate keystrokes for programs such as Pagemaker or Quark XPress. **PC users note:** To create a character for which the keystrokes include a minus sign (e.g., Ctrl-Alt-minus) or numbers (e.g., **Alt**-0210), you must use a numeric keypad instead of the numbers on the top row of the keyboard. If you do not have a separate numeric keypad, you can turn on a numeric keypad through your keyboard by holding down the *Function* key while pressing *Numlock* and then *Padlock*.

▲ Appendix B. *Using typographic cues appropriately is one of the many things that "add up" in creating well designed documents.*

Common Typographic Symbols

Character		Uses	Keystrokes	
			Mac	**PC**
em dash (the width of an uppercase "M")	a — a a—a	Sets off parenthetical expressions. Can be used with spaces on each side of the em dash or with no spaces. Most publications close up the spaces around em dashes because the extra space can draw too much attention to the dash itself. However, the position of em dashes differs slightly from typeface to typeface, an important consideration in making the decision to close up the spaces or not. If the em dash touches the letters on either side and interferes with the cross-strokes of the letterforms (e.g., e—e) then consider using the spaces to insure legibility (e.g., e — e). Never use two hyphens instead of an em dash as it is a vestige of the typewriter. Exception: em dashes may not work in e-mail.	Op-Sh-hyphen	Ctrl-Alt-minus **PC users:** Do not use a hyphen instead of the minus sign; the minus key is located on the numeric keypad (see the note at the bottom of p. 502).
en dash (half the width of an em dash)	pp. 33–75	Connects continuing or inclusive numbers, dates, pages, or times (e.g., 8 A.M. – 5 P.M.). An en dash is shorter than an em dash (which is too long for purposes such as citing page numbers) and longer than a hyphen (which is too short).	Op-hyphen	Ctrl-minus
hyphen (the shortest dash)	e-mail	Joins words that consist of two or more parts working together as a unit to express a specific concept (e.g., blue-pencil, ex-president, an FDA-approved drug). If a hyphenated compound falls at the end of a line, avoid hyphenating the compound further by dropping the last word of the compound to the next line.	hyphen	hyphen

Hyphens are also used to break lines of type. When hyphenation is overused, the document will have an ugly right-hand margin. Avoid having more than two consecutive lines hyphenated. (A stricter guideline, and one that many document designers prefer, is to avoid all consecutive hyphens.) Generally speaking, try to use no more than three hyphens per paragraph. These parameters will give the document a "soft ragged-right" appearance, a look that is pleasing to the eye. It is also a good idea to avoid hyphenating headings and subheadings altogether.

☞ **Tip:** When using page layout programs such as Pagemaker, set the hyphenation to "off" for headings and subheadings. Set it to "manual + dictionary" and "limit consecutive hyphens to 1" for body text. These parameters eliminate hyphens in headings and subheadings. They will also format the body text to use any hyphens inserted manually (as in compound nouns), break words according to the dictionary stored in the program, and prevent the hyphenation of two or more lines in a row.

Common Typographic Symbols

Character		Uses	Keystrokes	
			Mac	**PC**
copyright symbol	©	Used to indicate the material has been copyrighted and may not be used without the express permission of the author or copyright holder. Legally binding with or without the word *copyright* in conjunction with the symbol.	Op-G	Alt-Ctrl-C
registration symbol	®	Indicates a registered symbol or service mark with the United States patent office. Also used are trademarks (see below).	Op-R	Alt-Ctrl-R
trademark symbol	™	Designates a name of a product, service, or brand-name that is the proprietary use of a company or organization that developed it. Generally speaking, trademarks are used as adjectives rather than nouns. For example, use: In this project, we need to purchase 50 new SyQuest™ removable hard disk cartridges for a good price. Instead of: In this project, we need to purchase 50 new SyQuests for a good price. For publications that have many references to trademarked or registered items, it is common to write a single statement that acknowledges the trademarks as a group (as is used for this book; see the copyright page). In situations in which a blanket copyright statement is employed, it is still necessary to use initial capitalization, uppercase, or small capitals for in-text citations of the trademarked items.	Op-2	Alt-Ctrl-T
dagger[a]	†	An alternate symbol to an asterisk (*). Used for notes or footnotes that qualify, explain, or provide additional information. The dagger should be formatted as a superscript.	Op-T	**Alt**-0134
bullet (typographic cue that signals a list; can be a dot, square, triangle, or other symbol)	•	Draws the reader's attention to a series of items in a list. Compared to the format of typical paragraphs, bulleted items stand out from their surroundings because they employ extra horizontal and vertical space. Items that require two or more lines of type should be set off further by using "hanging indents." That is, the second line and subsequent lines of text in the item do not wrap out to the margin of the bullet but to the internal margin of the text; thus, the bullets hang. (Note: The same principle of using hanging indents should be used for enumerated lists as well.) When formatting bulleted items, avoid wide margins between the bullet and the text as the bullets may appear to form their own column. Generally speaking, use no more than five character spaces between the bullet and the item (two or three character spaces is preferred). This format allows the reader to scan the list quickly and to see immediately that the bullets and the items are related.	Op-8	Crtl-Sh-8

[a] **PC users note:** The dagger symbol will work only for fonts that have complete character sets, such as Times Roman.

Zapf Dingbats: Useful Symbols

Symbol	Keystrokes		Symbol	Keystrokes	
	Mac	**PC**		**Mac**	**PC**
☛	Sh-8	Sh-8	③	Sh-Op-'	**Alt**-0174
☞	Sh-=	Sh-=	④	Sh-Op-O	**Alt**-0175
✍	hyphen	hyphen	⑤	Op-5	**Alt**-0176
✓	3	3	⑥	Sh-Op-=	**Alt**-0177
✔	4	4	⑦	Op-,	**Alt**-0178
✕	5	5	⑧	Op-.	**Alt**-0179
✖	6	6	⑨	Op-y	**Alt**-0180
✗	7	7	⑩	Op-m	**Alt**-0181
✘	8	8	❶	Op-d	**Alt**-0182
✚	Sh-B	Sh-B	❷	Op-w	**Alt**-0183
●	l	l	❸	Sh-Op-P	**Alt**-0184
○	m	m	❹	Op-p	**Alt**-0185
■	n	n	❺	Op-b	**Alt**-0186
❑	o	o	❻	Op-9	**Alt**-0187
❐	p	p	❼	Op-0	**Alt**-0188
❒	q	q	❽	Op-z	**Alt**-0189
❏	r	r	❾	Op-'	**Alt**-0190
▲	s	s	❿	Op-o	**Alt**-0191
▼	t	t	①	Sh-Op-/	Ctrl-`, Sh-A
◆	u	u	②	Op-1	**Alt**-0193
❖	v	v	③	Op-L	**Alt**-0194
❛	Sh-[	Sh-[	④	Op-V	**Alt**-0195
❜	Sh-\	Sh-\	⑤	Op-F	**Alt**-0196
❝	Sh-]	Sh-]	⑥	Op-X	**Alt**-0197
❞	Sh-`	**Alt**-0126	⑦	Op-J	**Alt**-0198
❄	Op-N	**Alt**-0247	⑧	Op-\	**Alt**-0199
→	Op-]	**Alt**-0212	⑨	Sh-Op-\	**Alt**-0200
→	Sh-Op-]	**Alt**-0213	⑩	Op-;	**Alt**-0201
↔	Op-/	**Alt**-0214	❶	Op-space	**Alt**-0202
↕	Sh-Op-V	**Alt**-0215	❷	Op-`, Sh-A	**Alt**-0203
↗	Sh-Op-1	**Alt**-0218	❸	Op-N, Sh-A	**Alt**-0204
➔	Sh-Op-2	**Alt**-0219	❹	Op-N, Sh-0	**Alt**-0205
→	Sh-Op-3	**Alt**-0220	❺	Sh-Op-Q	**Alt**-0206
→	Sh-Op-4	**Alt**-0213	❻	Op-Q	**Alt**-0207
→	Sh-Op-5	**Alt**-0222	❼	Op-hyphen	**Alt**-0208
➤	Sh-Op-R	**Alt**-0228	❽	Sh-Op-hyphen	**Alt**-0209
①	Op-u	**Alt**-0172	❾	Op-[	**Alt**-0210
②	Op-=	**Alt**-0173	❿	Sh-Op-[	**Alt**-0211

☞ **Troubleshooting tip.** In programs such as Pagemaker for the Macintosh, you may find that some of these symbols will not appear on the screen and/or print correctly. If you have problems using these characters, try this: After you select *Print*, the Print Window will display. At the right side of this window, click on *Options*. A new set of choices will appear. At the bottom of the window there is a section titled *Font;* if the option *"use symbol font for special characters"* is checked, deselect it. Otherwise, Pagemaker will substitute the Symbol font for some of these characters.

Like other industries, aircraft companies have been moving toward paperless maintenance manuals. A technician for a B-2 bomber used to require a small wagon-load of binders and manuals to service and repair the airplane. Now, the same information is presented via a portable display device, complete with online text and graphics. The U.S. Air Force estimates this system will reduce the time maintenance technicians spend searching for the correct procedures by 30 percent. Courtesy of Northrop Corporation, B-2 Division, Pico Rivera, CA.

[1] In particular, I bring together the ideas from researchers in human factors, rhetoric, and psychology. I also distill the advice of expert practitioners in graphic design, interface design, and typography (e.g., see the guidelines derived from Heid, 1996a, 1996b; Horton, 1994; Mullet & Sano, 1995; Taylor, 1996b; and Tschichold, 1967). Guidelines that are not referenced are based on my interpretation of the available research and on my experience in observing people trying to use online documents.

GUIDELINES FOR DESIGNING ONLINE DISPLAYS

The literature about the design of computer displays or television screens suggests a number of provisional guidelines, which I summarize below. This advice is based on empirical research and extensive practical experience. As I've said in earlier chapters, the field of document design can be enriched by the insights of research and expert practice. Here I interpret and integrate the previous literature from a document design perspective.[1] I exclude technical issues of building online information systems, user interfaces, help systems, or Web sites—there are many excellent books already available on these topics. These guidelines are intended to supplement ideas presented in Chapters 5 and 6 about the ways that document designers can orchestrate the visual design of documents to enhance their rhetorical goals. The guidelines concern macrolevel issues as well as microlevel details, both of which work in concert to create an impression of the content.

Choosing a Typeface

- Choose either serif or sans serif type families, but make sure the particular families are uniform in the thickness of the strokes and cross strokes of the letterforms. Avoid condensed or stretched faces in either serif or sans serif faces (Human Factors Society, 1988).

- Limit the variation of typography to a few sizes from one or two typeface families. When using two type families, avoid using two serif fonts or two sans serif fonts. Instead, use one serif and one sans serif for contrast (Mullet & Sano, 1995, p. 70).

Choosing a Type Size

- When choosing a size for body text, headings, or other content elements readers will want to scan through, consider the user's probable distance from the screen as a factor in legibility. For example, if users sit from 20" to 24" inches away from the screen, 10 to 11 point type (or higher) for body text and 14-point type (or higher) for display text will be legible under ideal conditions—that is, good light and no distortion from the screen angle (American National Standards Institute, 1979). It is wise to use bigger point sizes for serif faces as they tend to have a tighter word spacing than sans serif faces.

▲ Appendix C. *Intended as a supplement to Chapters 5 and 6, this appendix consolidates the advice from researchers and practitioners about the design of online displays.*

- Typography that is legible onscreen may not necessarily be comfortable to the eye. Many people prefer to read text set at larger sizes when they are reading online than when they are reading text on paper (e.g., 12 to 14 point for online rather than the typical 10 to 12 point on paper). When designing for the partially sighted or visually impaired, use 14 to 16 point[2] (Bruce, McKennell, & Walker, 1991; Shaw, 1968, 1969).

- In making choices about the font size for online documents, carefully consider the characteristics of the typeface itself (e.g., x-height, letter-spacing) and how the text will be spaced (line width and leading). Make these choices in relation to the characteristics of the audience (e.g., age, eyesight, level of motivation, or willingness to read continuous text). When in doubt, it is better to err in the direction of bigger rather than smaller type as more readers find larger type to be not only legible but also soothing to their eyes.

- Consider the needs of users who are age sixty-five or older; this community is getting larger and will continue to do so over the next 20 years or so (largely due to the postwar baby boom). Older adults have been found to experience significantly more difficulty in learning to use a computer than have younger adults (Kelley & Charness, 1995). But little work has assessed the design of hardcopy or online information for this population. Several studies suggest that spatial ability is a good predictor of success in computing tasks.[3] Thus, less-able users may need stronger, more explicit spatial cues to help them navigate a series of screens. For a discussion of designing for the elderly, see Hartley (1994) and van Hees (1994).[4]

- Keep in mind that many users wear glasses or contact lenses and that 5 percent to 10 percent of the population is colorblind.[5]

Using Serif Typefaces

- When using serif type families, which are acceptable for online displays as long as they are well chosen, consider those with square or slab endings (Rehe, 1974, p. 41). (For an example of a classic slab face, Serifa, see Figure 5.1, Example 1, p. 253). Typefaces with delicate serifs may display irregularly because serifs that fall on pixel boundaries may not display at all (Horton, 1991, p. 186).

- When using serif type families, choose those with distinct ascenders and descenders (Galitz, 1989). Like the serifs, ascenders and descenders may break apart when light shines from behind them (Rehe, 1974, p. 41). Beware of faces with either too much thick and thin contrast in the

[2] This research was carried out with partially sighted people using paper documents; for online, it is best to go with the higher end of this range, 16 point or even higher, depending on the characteristics of the typeface and the line length.

[3] For a review of the relationship between spatial ability and computing (as well as other factors), see Kelley and Charness (1995).

[4] Van Hees' work (a master's thesis) is written in Dutch. Surprisingly, there are almost no studies of elderly readers in the document design literature.

[5] Regrettably, this book omits discussion of color in document design. Due to publishing constraints, I was not able to use color for this book and it did not seem helpful to talk about color without being able to show color examples.

strokes of the letterforms (e.g., Bodoni, Times Bold) or faces with set width (e.g., Avant Garde) (Taylor, 1996b).

Using Sans Serif Typefaces

- When using sans serif—the preferred style of type for online because of its simple, highly legible, modern appearance—employ type families such as Univers, Frutiger, Helvetica, or Futura. Consider the medium weight or the bold version of these typefaces, especially if the stroke thickness is thin—the strokes may appear thinner on a screen than on paper.[6]

[6] For elaboration about the characteristics of sans serif typefaces, see, for example, Bass (1967, 1971), Frutiger (1980), Rehe (1974), Reynolds and Simmonds (1981), McVey (1985), or Schmandt (1987).

Making Decisions about How the Type Will Be Displayed

- Consider typeface families designed by typographers for high legibility, such as ITC Stone Sans Serif (called Stone Sans) and ITC Stone Serif or Adobe's Lucida Roman and Lucida Sans Serif (called Lucida Sans). These have been designed for low-resolution laser printers, fax machines, and computer screens (Adobe Systems, 1989).

- When designing online documents that must cross computing platforms such as IBM and Macintosh, choose typefaces that are common to all systems or carefully select equivalent typefaces. Typefaces of the same name are not always the same on different systems. Windows TrueType fonts, for example, are not always the same size as Macintosh TrueType fonts (Horton, 1994).

- In striving for typographic contrast, carefully consider the weight of the face (e.g., light, medium, bold, black, and extra black). The best contrast within the same family is usually found in the use of two weights that differ by more than one "step" on the scale (Mullet & Sano, 1995, p. 81). For example, the contrast between light and medium, medium and bold, or bold and black is often weak and unnoticeable online. Better results are achieved using the stronger cue (a bigger perceptual jump in darkness) such as light and bold, medium and black, light and black, or medium and extra black.

Employing Italic and Underlining

- Avoid italics as it is hard to read online (McVey, 1985), especially in seriffed faces (Rehe, 1974). As on paper, avoid underlining for styling text within paragraphs or headings (Galitz, 1989) unless, of course, the system requires it. Underlining is a throwback to the days of typewriters. Similarly, steer away from stylized, decorative, and cursive typefaces (Tschichold, 1967).

Using Uppercase Letterforms

- As in hardcopy, do not use uppercase letterforms (e.g., ALL CAPS) for styling paragraphs. Instead, use uppercase and lowercase, as it allows the text to be read more quickly and more accurately. When more emphasis is needed than uppercase and lowercase can provide, try other cues such as changing the position of the type, increasing the weight of the type, or moving to a larger point size.[7]

- Uppercase letterforms can be employed effectively for labels. Uppercase labels have been found to enable users to search the screen faster than labels using lowercase (Vartabedian, 1971). Keep in mind that uppercase letterforms stacked over four or more consecutive lines of type may suggest a heavy and serious paragraph; use only when the rhetorical situation calls for it.

[7] Many authors have discussed the problems associated with reading uppercase letterforms (e.g., Paterson & Tinker, 1946; Tinker & Paterson, 1939; Rehe, 1974; Shneiderman, 1987; Wheildon, 1995).

Choosing a Typeface Based on Its Letterspacing

- Proportional spacing—that is, letterspacing proportional to the shape and contour of the letterform—is read faster, with fewer and wider eye fixations than fixed-width (or monospaced) type—that is, letterspacing which is the same for all characters regardless of their shape or width. With proportional spacing, the letter "i" takes up less space than the letters "m" or "w." Traditional typewriter characters have a fixed width and are monospaced. Proportional spacing is rated higher in visibility, ease of reading, and contrast (Helander, Billingsley, & Schurick, 1984).

Specifying the Justification of the Margins

- As in hardcopy, use justified left, ragged-right margins rather than fully justified text (i.e., with straight edges on both the right and left margins) as justification can reduce online reading speed by about 10 percent (Trollip & Sales, 1986). If justification is necessary, take every step to ensure the word spacing is equal across the text area (Campbell, Marchetti, & Mewhort, 1981).

Choosing the Vertical and Horizontal Space

- Specify the vertical space (leading) so that it is 115 percent of the body text size. That is, leading should add about 15 percent to the point size of the face used for the body text (Human Factors Society, 1988). This is about 5 percent tighter than the leading recommended for paper documents (which is typically 120 percent of the body text, adding about 20 percent to the face's point size). If space permits, use 20 percent leading because legibility tends to be poorer onscreen.[8]

- Signal breaks in ideas by employing more leading between the paragraphs of online text than within them (Dumas, 1988). To avoid a "busy" look, minimize the number of alignment points, that is, the number of separate margins or tabs between the left and right margins (Tullis, 1988). Strive for a clean alignment of major text elements by using sufficient horizontal space between columns of text as well as clear vertical space between groups of items (Mullet & Sano, 1995).

- Avoid the use of bounding boxes (i.e., putting borders around the content elements in order to visually cluster them). Instead, align the content by using the edges of the content elements themselves (e.g., elements with hard margins align easily). Employ strong vertical and horizontal cues in order to create visual clusters (Mullet & Sano, 1995).

- Align text blocks, pictures, buttons, radio controls, and labels both horizontally and vertically. When horizontal and vertical cues are misaligned, the screen can become unnecessarily difficult to scan.

- When positioning a column of labels or buttons (many of which are designed using rectangles, squares, or ovals as a frame), there are at least two considerations. First, align the edges of the frames on the left (make sure the frames used for parallel items are sized equally). Second, align the words within the frame. In this way, both the edge of the frame and the text itself are aligned, making it easier to scan.

- Never "center" items in a vertical list on a screen. It creates an irregular margin on both left and right, making it hard to scan. Its irregular shape can also create an unintended visual pattern. Just as it is a bad idea to center itemized lists on paper, it is a bad idea to do so online. Instead, left justify each listed item and use hanging indents (described in Appendix B) so that the items maintain a strong left margin.

---

[8] To calculate the point size of the desired leading, first take the point size for the body text and multiply it by 15 percent. Use that number as the estimate for the number of points of leading needed between the lines of type. Second, add the point size of the body text and the desired number of points of leading together. This gives an estimate of what the baseline-to-baseline measurement of the leading should be set at. Let's take an example. If the body text is set at 11 point, one would take 11×15 percent = 1.65. This means that roughly 1.5 points of leading are needed (leading is generally specified in increments of half-points and whole points). Next add the number of points needed to the point size of the face (11 + 1.5 = 12.5). Thus, the leading should be specified as 11/12.5 (that is, 11-point body text over 12.5-point leading, which gives 1.5 points of leading).

Revealing the Structure of the Content

- Reinforce the structure of the content by placing common elements (i.e., elements with the same rhetorical function such as overviews, descriptive text, procedures, examples, navigational aids) in the same position/margin from screen to screen. In doing so, standardize the size, shape, color, texture, line weight, orientation, alignment, and spacing of the key features. Structural repetition is important to online information because it unifies a sequence of screens and enables efficient navigation (Mullet & Sano, 1995, p. 154). To assist in the placement of items, employ a modular grid (described in Chapter 5, Section 4, pp. 336–356).

- To increase the efficiency with which people can navigate an online document or a Web site, it is important for users to be able to predict both where they will see information from one screen to the next and what rhetorical function that information will serve. Establish a visual and verbal rhythm across a series of screen displays by using consistent visual language (e.g., typographic cueing via typefaces, sizes, weights, colors, line lengths, leading) and parallel verbal language (e.g., strong verbs written in the active voice, key ideas placed high in the structure of paragraphs, the purpose of the content made explicit, similar content items composed of similar lengths). Place key rhetorical clusters[9] in prominent positions and repeat the pattern over the sequence of screens. This will help to create continuity both within and across the screens. It can also give identity and distinctiveness to a display.

  [9] For a discussion of rhetorical clusters, see Chapter 5 (pp. 342–345).

- Plan the path for the user's eye to travel by positioning structural elements in a way that invites scanning (i.e., elements positioned as a sequence that could be read left-to-right, top-to-bottom, or in some other predictable direction). Use the same pattern from screen to screen with occasional deviations for pages with special content that deserves contrast. (For an example of how a user's eye travels in hardcopy text, see Figures 5.27 and 5.28, p. 317). These visual repetitions become perceptual landmarks for users. Test the path users take with members of the intended audience.

Considering the Density of the Screen

- Screens should not appear crowded to the reader. A generous use of blank space is not a waste of space but a way to increase the intelligibility of the text. Try to maintain overall density[10] levels no higher than 25 to 30 percent of the screen area (Dodson & Shields, 1978; Tullis, 1988). The density on paper should be no more than 50 percent of the text area (Tinker, 1963). However, to reduce the

  [10] The overall density of a screen refers to the percentage of character positions on the screen containing data (Galitz, 1989, p. 69).

density, do not increase the use of abbreviations and acronyms because this will be counterproductive (Galitz, 1989).

Grouping Elements with Itemized Lists

- Break up blocks of text by using itemized lists, numbered steps, and specific examples. Logically group items within the lists to aid learning and speed up the visual search process (Card, 1982; Treisman, 1982). Provide meaningful headings and subheadings to lists.

- Avoid combining unrelated items in a list. Items should form a family or group. Don't make the reader work to figure out the structure. As we saw in the case study of the *Virtual Tourist* World Wide Web site in Chapter 6, when a list introduces a set of subtopics, people study the list to decide how well it covers the main topic and whether it looks interesting (see pp. 399–401). Signal the content of lists with well-written headings or previews which capture the gist of the itemized content elements.

- Avoid lists that contain items whose meanings overlap so much that readers might interpret two items as equally likely to signal the same content. This is especially important in offering users a list of choices for moving from one screen to the next. If the choices overlap, then users are forced to look up two items instead of one, increasing their likelihood of quitting before finding the desired item (Mullet & Sano, 1995; Shneiderman, 1987).

- Do not use an itemized list when the order of the information is important (e.g., in procedures). Instead, use numerals or letters.

- Balance the use of lists with content-rich paragraphs as readers tend to grow weary of too many lists. The overuse of lists defeats their rhetorical purpose—that is, to draw attention to ideas which preview, itemize, point at, consolidate, or summarize. If every sort of content is equally likely to be a list, then the benefits of using lists as "typographic segmentation" to signal changes in the structure of the content are lost because everything looks the same (Waller, 1980). Gestalt psychologists suggested that the eye is attracted to areas of high contrast. When things look different from their surround, we notice them. Itemized lists stand out because they employ vertical blank space between items more frequently than do paragraphs of continuous text. If, of course, everything is itemized, the list has nothing to contrast with.

- Use a parallel syntactic structure when composing items for a list. Be consistent in how each item is formatted. Convention suggests that either lowercase or uppercase can be employed to format the first letter of the first word of items in a list. If the items in the list complete the sentence which introduces them, lowercase should be employed to format the first word. However, if the items are complete sentences, the first word should start with an uppercase letter and include internal punctuation (commas, semicolons) and closing punctuation (periods).

- If listed items are short, no internal or terminal punctuation is needed. If the items contain commas or other internal punctuation, they should terminate with a closing punctuation mark. An exception to terminal punctuation can be made if the internal punctuation falls within parentheses or brackets.

- It may be disconcerting for readers to see lists formatted using lowercase and uppercase alternately in the same document (however, I could find no studies about this topic). There has been an editorial trend toward capitalizing the first word of each item in lists whether the list is comprised of single words or of complete sentences (Tarutz, 1992). In using this strategy, one maintains the same rules about internal and closing punctuation, that is, short items don't get punctuation while longer ones or already punctuated items do. It is also important to write the sentence that precedes the list so that it stands alone as a complete sentence. However, in some rhetorical contexts, capitalizing individual words and short phrases may give them too much rhetorical prominence and may give the impression of being oversignaled. Mixing the two styles (using both uppercase and lowercase to introduce lists) in the same document can work if both types of lists don't appear on the same spread or screen. The important goal to strive for is consistency. (See also Appendix B).

Grouping Elements on the Screen

- Keep in mind that the Gestalt principles of figure-ground relations, proximity, similarity, continuity, and closure[11] work together to foster visual groupings on a screen (Galitz, 1989; Mullet & Sano, 1995).

- Align all numbers using a justified-right format. In this way, the number 10 will align properly under the number 1904. Decimal numbers should be aligned on their decimal points.

[11] I discuss principles of Gestalt psychology and their application to document design in Chapter 5 (pp. 303–326). See also Mullet and Sano's (1995) discussion of using Gestalt principles to design the user interface.

- When using rules to divide screen areas, use thicker rules at the top of the screen and lighter ones after the first one. The thick-thin contrast will help guide the reader's eye through the display. One can also vary the length of rules to reinforce the textual hierarchy. Take care not to overuse rules. (Excessive use of rule lines should also be avoided in the design of paper documents because it can make the text too segmented.) In online and hardcopy design, rule lines can be used profitably to signal rhetorical chunks. But when used haphazardly, rule lines can make the text feel choppy and incoherent. Do not assume the reader who opens the text in the middle of a hardcopy document will notice the thicker rule lines on previous pages (which signaled that the content being looked at is subordinate to that earlier content). Do not assume users of online documents will have accessed previous screens that set up the visual hierarchy and flow of the content. Try to plan each spread or screen to function as a self-contained module in which the hierarchy of the content is clearly signaled through the design.

- When setting columns of short lists onscreen (e.g., lists of options, commands, menu choices), an important consideration is the column width. Avoid the common error of making the columns too close together. In choosing a width for columns, first find the longest item that needs to be displayed in each column. Then add roughly four to six character spaces to its character count to specify the column width. Avoid reducing columns to the minimum number of character spaces needed to display the widest item (Mullet & Sano, 1995, p. 44). Why? Because the resulting column will have an irregular right margin that may make the longer words seem to organize the shorter ones. Longer words should blend in with the list, not act as subheadings within the list. As the Gestalt psychologists showed, size matters.

Orienting the Online Page

- Design pages for the screen using a landscape (horizontal orientation) rather than portrait (vertical orientation), as the majority of computer monitors are wider than they are tall (Taylor, 1996b). Consider designing online pages for smaller 13" to 14" monitors.

Choosing a Line Length

- Keep line length short: 40 to 60 characters (Tullis, 1988). But take care to choose a length that is long enough so that the syntactic groups of sentences are preserved, usually no fewer than 20 characters per line (Wheildon, 1995).

- Don't forget that line length interacts with point size and leading. When lots of text is needed, consider shortening the line length and using two columns (Galitz, 1989).

- If different parts of the text serve different rhetorical purposes, consider cueing the distinctions with different line lengths. For example, overview and explanatory text often have the longest line lengths on a screen, while procedures and examples often have the shortest.

- Avoid formatting two or more consecutive lines of type with hyphenation (Dumas, 1988). The problem of too many hyphens is more noticeable onscreen (see also pp. 269–271 and Appendix B).

Considering Graphic Cueing

- Avoid typographic or graphic cueing that reduces the legibility of the information being emphasized. For example, do not use blinking to turn a message off and on (Dumas, 1988).

- Strive for the use of thinner rather than thicker rule lines. Try 1-point rules for onscreen segmentation before moving to thicker ones; avoid rules four points and higher as these amount to graphic excess (Mullet & Sano, 1995, p. 29). Avoid using vertical rules to separate columns; use space instead (Tufte, 1983).

- Avoid gratuitous use of 3-D (e.g., drop shadows) on borders, boxes, and quantitative graphics. These techniques often distort the integrity of information, particularly of quantitative graphics (Beattie & Jones, 1992; Kosslyn, 1994; Tufte, 1983). Save 3-D for rendering objects for which the third dimension adds information over its 2-D equivalent (Mullet & Sano, 1995, p. 35). Consider the ideas presented in Chapter 5 on Gestalt principles for instances when using 3-D is not only a good idea, but a better one (pp. 303–326).

- Avoid the use of boxes to cluster key elements of the screen (i.e., boxes drawn as borders around clusters of elements). The information readers want to see is inside the box; bounding it with an edge introduces an unnecessary level of complexity and visual noise in the perceptual field (Mullet & Sano, 1995). Instead, employ precise alignment of the elements themselves without the boxes. As the Gestalt psychologists have shown, grouping elements in the visual field is a powerful way to make readers see their relationships (see Chapter 5, pp. 303–313). Position has been found to be a more powerful way to form perceptual clusters than drawing boxes around them (Bertin, 1983).

- If a graphic (picture, icon, or symbol) has a variety of meanings and it is important to constrain the user's interpretation, it may be helpful to double signal the meaning by placing a word or phrase below the picture in order to suggest the intended idea more explicitly (e.g., putting the word *trash* below the trash icon).

- Avoid icons or graphics that are culturally dependent. Always test icons with members of the intended language/culture.

- Avoid sexist, offensive, or suggestive imagery or gestures. Images of death, injury, sex, or violence are almost never appropriate in public documents.

Positioning Subheadings

- Position subheadings to the left of body text for Western cultures, where reading generally proceeds from left to right, top to bottom. Place the headings for other languages, such as the cursive group (e.g., Arabic, Urdu, and Hebrew), to the right, as these languages are read from right to left. The display of headings should be organized in accordance with the reading habits of the culture of the intended audience (Spencer, 1985, p. 191).

- Changes in *position* on the screen may be more visible to the eye than *size* or *value* (that is, the intensity of the shade or the weight) (Bertin, 1983; Mullet & Sano, 1995).

- When designing subheadings, consider double signaling as a possible strategy. Use position and weight (or color) for emphasis. Consider formatting headings to appear in a separate margin so they stand off from the text, making them easier to scan (Taylor, 1996b).

Designing Type and Graphics for the World Wide Web[12]

- In making choices about pictures and diagrams, always consider the time it will take for the screen to redraw the images. Keep in mind that complex art often takes a long time to render on the screen. Avoid graduated fills for special-effects "gee-whiz" backgrounds and mood setting. Use them only when needed for the precision of the image. This will increase the speed with which users can load and display the document (Taylor, 1996b).

- When creating graphics with hot spots[13] that allow users to navigate to other links by clicking on them (these graphics are called *image maps*),

[12] The presentation of information on the Web requires some special considerations beyond those I've mentioned so far. Here I present a few technical concerns about designing for the Web to maximize the legibility of screens and the speed with which users can retrieve information from pages. I discussed content issues and suggested ways to create rhetorically effective text and graphics in Chapter 6 (see the section "Fragmentation on the Web," pp. 390–407).

[13] A *hot spot* is a clickable area on a Web page (button, icon, word, or image) that connects the user to another place (page, link, or site) on the Web. A hot spot on the Web works like a hypertext link.

standardize the typography employed on "clickable" buttons, icons, and words. This way users will know which words are clickable and which ones are dead areas on the screen. Don't vary the type size of hot spots unless the bigger elements are actually more important to the structure of the document. When users are forced to "click around" without a sense of priority and without knowing which buttons are actually hot spots, they can rapidly become frustrated (Heid, 1996a).

- Beware of using image maps (i.e., graphics with hot spots) to design the whole page as a single graphic (Taylor, 1996b). Although doing so allows the designer to maintain control over how the document will look when displayed, the capaciousness of image maps strains the network's bandwidth, often taking several minutes to load. Users may become impatient with the time it takes to display the whole image map and may exit the site before exploring it fully.[14]

- Keep in mind that about 5 percent of users still use text-only browsers such as Lynx. A larger number use 14.4-Kbps[15] modems and turn off the browser's graphic-loading option. For these groups, it's good to provide text-only navigation options, such as a bar of words-only options below the image map (Heid, 1996a, p. 127).

- In considering how the document will be displayed on the Web, keep in mind that with HTML,[16] users can choose their own typography and it is not possible to anticipate how the user's Web browser will be set up. Thus, document designers cannot predict how their texts will be displayed. The most a designer can do is to set up the defaults in a manner which best suits the material (Taylor, 1996b). This technological limitation is changing and will probably be obsolete by the time you read this book.

[14] When designing image-maps for Web pages, use client-side image maps (a special type that puts the burden of figuring out "where to go" on the browser that sends the server a URL rather than on the server itself. (URL means Uniform Resource Locator; it is a set of instructions that tells the browser how to find and access information). Image maps that depend on the server are called server-side image maps. Client-side image maps have the benefit for users of showing the exact address of each hot spot and link as the mouse pointer moves over it so that users can better navigate where they are going. They also have the advantage of distinguishing hot spots from dead areas. Current browsers that support client-side image maps are Netscape Navigator, Microsoft Internet Explorer, and Spyglass Mosaic. For a discussion of image maps, both client-side and server-side, see Heid (1996a, 1996b).

[15] Kbps means kilobytes per second; it refers to the speed with which the modem sends the data over the phone wires.

[16] HTML stands for Hypertext Markup Language. It enables World Wide Web page designers to tag text elements (e.g., plain, boldface, and italics) in order to define how a browser will display the type and graphics. (A browser is an application such as Netscape Navigator designed to view HTML documents on the World Wide Web.) However, in using HTML, the designer loses most of the special typographic formatting. Companies have been developing tools to allow HTML authors more control over the way their texts will display (e.g., Netscape Extensions or Adobe Acrobat). Such products are designed to ensure that a document will be displayed with the intended typography, even if the user's machine does not have the same fonts installed. For more information about these issues, visit the following sites on the World Wide Web: http://home.netscape.com or http://www.adobe.com.

Ranks of Europe's Emplo

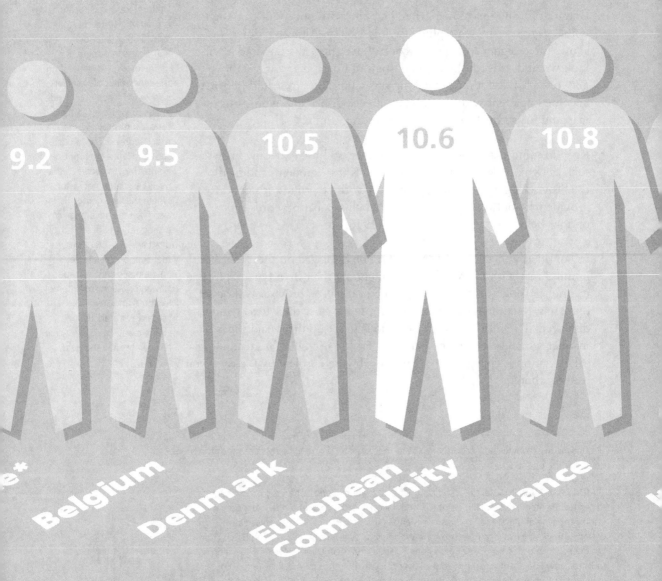

e*   Belgium   Denmark   European Community   France

9.2   9.5   10.5   10.6   10.8

Germany's is estimate for July; Greece's is for Decem

Bibliography

AAA Academy. (1911). *Rules governing the use of aeronautical apparatus*. Washington, DC: AAA Academy, Engineering and Manufacturing Branch.

Ackerman, J. M. & Oates, S. (1996) Image text and power in architectural design and workplace writing. In A. H. Duin & C. J. Hansen (Eds.), *Nonacademic writing: Social theory and technology* (pp. 81–121). Mahwah, NJ: Lawrence Erlbaum.

Adams, K. H. (1993). *A history of professional writing instruction in American colleges: Years of acceptance, growth, and doubt*. Dallas, TX: Southern Methodist University Press.

Adobe Systems. (1989, Fall). Face fax. *Font & Function: The Adobe Catalog*, p. 12.

Adobe Systems. (1995, Winter). The possibilities are endless: Now for Macintosh and Windows, Adobe multiple master typefaces. *Font & Function: The Adobe Catalog*, pp. 6–7.

Aizu, I., & Amemiya, H. (1985). The cultural implications of manual writing and design. In *Proceedings of the Society for Technical Communication* (pp. WE–33–WE–35). Houston, TX: Society for Technical Communication.

Alebeek, H., van. (1995, June). Amerikaanse prof. Schriver bepleit betere gebruiksaanwijzing voor apparaten: Slechte handleiding electronica leidt tot frustraties. *Brabants Dagblad*, pp. 3–4.

Allen, J. (1989). Breaking with a tradition: New directions in audience analysis. In B. E. Fearing & W. K. Sparrow (Eds.), *Technical writing: Theory and practice* (pp. 53–62). New York: Modern Language Association.

Allen, J. (1995). More results from the ATTW survey. *ATTW Bulletin, 5*(3), 2–3.

Althusser, L. (1971). *Lenin and philosophy*. London: New Left Books.

American Institutes for Research. (1979). *Fine Print*. Washington, DC: American Institutes for Research.

Anders, P. L., & Evans, K. S. (1994). Relationship between teachers' beliefs and their instructional practice in reading. In R. Garner & P. A. Alexander (Eds.), *Beliefs about text and instruction with text* (pp. 137–153). Hillsdale, NJ: Lawrence Erlbaum.

Anderson, P. V. (1995). Evaluating academic technical communication programs: New stakeholders, diverse goals. *Technical Communication, 42*(4), 628–633.

Anderson, P. V., Miller, C. R., & Brockmann, R. J. (Eds.). (1983). *New essays in technical and scientific communication*. New York: Baywood Press.

Apple Computer. (1992). *Localization for Japan*. Cupertino, CA: Apple Computer.

Apple Computer. (1993, Summer). *The Apple catalog*. Clearwater, FL: Apple Computer.

Apple, M. W. (1992). The text and cultural politics. *Educational Researcher, 21*, 4–11, 19.

Applebee, A. R. (1974). *Tradition and reform in the teaching of English*. Urbana, IL: National Council of Teachers of English.

Aristotle. (1975). *The "art" of rhetoric*. Freese, J. H. (Trans.), G. P. Goold, (Ed.). Cambridge, MA: Harvard University Press. (Translated from Aristotle's original work composed in 330 B.C.)

Arnheim, R. (1969). *Visual thinking*. Berkeley and Los Angeles, CA: University of California Press.

Arnot, R. (1993, June 15). *Eye on your health, CBS Evening News* [Television program]. New York: CBS.

◀ **Left-hand page.** An isotype graph showing employment trends in Europe. For a discussion of the pros and cons of this type of display, see Neurath (1974) and MacDonald-Ross (1977).

Associated Press. (1990, September 12). Professor takes gibberish out of Mitsubishi manuals. *Japan Times,* p. 5.

Atman, C. J., & Puerzer, R. (1995). *Reader preference and comprehension of risk diagrams* (Tech. Rep. No. 95-8). Pittsburgh, PA: University of Pittsburgh, Department of Industrial Engineering.

Ausubel, D. P. (1960). The use of advance organizers in the learning and retention of meaningful verbal material. *Journal of Educational Psychology, 51,* 267–272.

Axtel, R. E. (1990). *Do's and taboos around the world.* New York: John Wiley & Sons.

Bain, A. (1866). *English composition and rhetoric.* New York: D. Appleton & Company.

Baird, J. W. (1917). The legibility of a telephone directory. *Journal of Applied Psychology, 1,* 30–37.

Baker, R. P. (1924). *The preparation of reports: Engineering, scientific, administrative.* New York: Ronald Press.

Ballay, J., Graham, K., Hayes, J. R., & Fallside, D. (1984). *CMU/IBM Usability study: Final report* (Tech. Rep. No. 11). Pittsburgh, PA: Carnegie Mellon University, Communications Design Center.

Barker, H. (1988). Typographic points on the desktop. *Visible Language, 22* (2/3), 343–367.

Barry, J. A. (1991). *Technobabble.* Cambridge, MA: MIT Press.

Barton, B. F., & Barton, M. S. (1993). Modes of power in technical and professional visuals. *Journal of Business and Technical Communication, 7* (1), 138–162.

Barton, B. F., & Barton, M. S. (1985). Toward a rhetoric of visuals for the computer era. *The Technical Writing Teacher, 12,* 126–145.

Bartram, D. (1982). The perception of semantic quality in type: Differences between designers and non-designers. *Information Design Journal, 3* (1), 38–50.

Bass, R. (1967). The development of CBS news 36. *Journal of Typographic Research, 4*(Spring), 147–167.

Bass, R. (1971). The development of vidifont. *Visible language, 1*(Winter), 5–12.

Bayer, H. (Ed.) (1953).*World geo-graphic atlas.* Chicago, IL: Container Corporation of America.

Bazerman, C. (1980). A relationship between reading and writing. *College English, 41*(6), 656–661.

Bazerman, C. (1983). Scientific writing as a social act: A review of the literature of the sociology of science. In P. V. Anderson, R. J. Brockmann, & C. R. Miller (Eds.), *New essays in technical and scientific communication* (pp. 156–184). Farmingdale, NY: Baywood Press.

Bazerman, C. (1985). Physicists reading physics: Schema-laden purposes and purpose-laden schema. *Written Communication, 2*(1), 3–23.

Bazerman, C. (1988). *Shaping written knowledge: The genre and activity of the experimental article in science.* Madison, WI: University of Wisconsin Press.

Beale, L. (1990, October 2). Technological advances bring a brave, rude world. *San Jose Mercury News,* p. C–1.

Beattie, V., & Jones, M. J. (1992). *The communication of information using graphs in annual reports* (Certified Research Rep. No. 13). Available from the Chartered Association of Certified Accountants, 29 Lincoln's Inn Fields, London WC2A 3EE.

Beck, I. L., McKeown, M. G., & Gromoll, E. W. (1989). Learning from social studies texts. *Cognition and Instruction, 6,* 99–158.

Beck, I. L., McKeown, M. G., & Worthy, M. J. (1993, April). *Questioning the author: An approach to enhancing students' engagement to text.* Paper presented at the annual meeting of the American Educational Research Association, Atlanta, GA.

Becker, D., Heinrich, J., van Sichowsky, R., & Wendt, D. (1970). Reader preferences for typeface and leading. *Journal of Typographic Research, 1* (Winter), 61–66.

Benedikt, M. (Ed.) (1991). *Cyberspace: First steps.* Cambridge, MA: MIT Press.

Benson, P. J. (1994). *Problems in picturing text.* Unpublished doctoral dissertation, Carnegie Mellon University, Pittsburgh, PA.

Bentley, M. (1921). Leading and legibility. *Psychological Monographs, 30,* 48–61.

Berke, R. L. (1995, September 13). Red Cross tones down AIDS material. *New York Times,* p. A20.

Berke, R. L. (1995, September 17). Dole defends wife's role at Red Cross. *New York Times,* p. 26.

Berkenkotter, C. (1981). Understanding a writer's awareness of audience. *College Composition and Communication, 32*(4), 388–399.

Berkenkotter, C., & Huckin, T. N. (1995). *Genre knowledge in disciplinary communication: Cognition/culture/power.* Hillsdale, NJ: Lawrence Erlbaum.

Berlin, J. (1984). *Writing instruction in nineteenth-century American colleges.* Carbondale, IL: Southern Illinois University Press.

Berlin, J. (1987). *Rhetoric and reality: Writing instruction in American colleges, 1900–1985.* Carbondale, IL: Southern Illinois University Press.

Berlin, J. (1990). *A short history of writing: From ancient Greece to twentieth-century America* J. J. Murphy, (Ed.). Davis, CA: Hermagoras Press.

Bernard, R. M. (1990). Using extended captions to improve learning from instructional illustrations. *British Journal of Educational Technology, 21,* 215–225.

Bernhardt, S. A. (1986). Seeing the text. *College Composition and Communication, 37*(1), 66–78.

Bernstein, L., & Paschall, S. (1993, August 9–15). Consumer contracts now must meet plain-language rules under state law. *Pittsburgh Business Times,* p. 15.

Berry, C. (1983a). A dual effect of pictorial enrichment in learning from television news: Gunter's data revisited. *Journal of Educational Television, 29,* 407–419.

Berry, C. (1983b). Learning from television news. *Journal of Broadcasting, 27*, 359-370.

Bertin, J. (1983). *Semiology of graphics*. Madison, WI: University of Wisconsin Press.

Bieger, G. R., & Glock, M. D. (1986). Comprehending spatial and contextual information in picture-text instructions. *Journal of Experimental Education, 54*(4), 181–188.

Bill, M. (1945). *Modern Swiss architecture 1925–1945*. Basel, Switzerland: Verlag Karl Werner.

Bizzell, P. (1982). Cognition, convention, and certainty: What we need to know about writing. *PRE/TEXT, 3*, 213–243.

Bizzell, P., & Herzberg, B. (1990). *The rhetorical tradition: Readings from classical times to the present*. Boston: Bedford Books of St. Martin's Press.

Black, A. (1990). *Typefaces for desktop publishing: A user guide*. London: Architecture, Design and Technology Press.

Black, B. (1981). A model plain language law. *Stanford Law Review, 33*(2), 255–300.

Blakeslee, A. M. (1993). Readers and authors: Fictionalized constructs or dynamic collaborations. *Technical Communication Quarterly, 2*(1), 23–35.

Bobbitt-Nolen, S., Johnson-Crowley, N., & Wineburg, S. S. (1994). Who is this "I" person, anyway: The presence of a visible author in statistical text. In R. Garner & P. A. Alexander (Eds.), *Beliefs about text and instruction with text* (pp. 41–55). Hillsdale, NJ: Lawrence Erlbaum.

Bolter, J. D. (1991). *Writing space: The computer, hypertext and the history of writing*. Hillsdale, NJ: Lawrence Erlbaum.

Bond, S. J. (1985). Protocol-aided revision: A tool for making documents usable. In *Proceedings of the IBM Academic Information Systems University AEP Conference* (pp. 327–334). Alexandria, VA: IBM.

Bond, S. J., Hayes, J. R., & Flower, L. (1980, April). *Translating the law into common language: A protocol study* (Document Design Project Tech. Rep. No. 8). Pittsburgh, PA: Carnegie Mellon University

Bonsiepe, G. (1968). A method of quantifying order in typographic design. *Journal of Typographic Research, 3*, 203–220.

Booth, W. C. (1961). *The rhetoric of fiction*. Chicago, IL: University of Chicago Press.

Boring, E. G. (1929). *A history of experimental psychology* (2nd ed.). New York: Appleton-Century-Crofts.

Bosley, D. S. (1993). Cross-cultural collaboration: Whose culture is it, anyway? *Technical Communication Quarterly, 2*, 51–62.

Bossard, J. H. S., & Dewhurst, J. F. (1931). *University education for business: A study of existing needs and practices*. Philadelphia: University of Pennsylvania Press.

Bovair, S., & Kieras, D. E. (1991). Toward a model of acquiring procedures from text. In R. Barr, M. L. Kamil, P. B. Mosenthal, & P. D. Pearson (Eds.), *Handbook of reading research: Vol. 2* (pp. 206–229). New York: Longman.

Bowen, B., Duffy, T. M., & Steinberg, E. R. (1991). Analyzing the various approaches of plain language laws. In E. R. Steinberg (Ed.), *Plain language: Principles and practice* (pp. 19–29). Detroit, MI: Wayne State University Press.

Bower, G. H. (1970). Organizational factors in memory. *Cognitive Psychology, 1*, 18–46.

Braddock, R., Lloyd-Jones, R., & Schoer, L. (1963). *Research in written composition*. Champaign-Urbana, IL: National Council of Teachers of English.

Brady, F. (1996). Fine tune your type for a perfect fit: Multiple master typefaces offer ultimate control. *Font & Function: The Adobe Catalog, 17*(Spring), 16–17.

Brandt, D. (1990). *Literacy as involvement: The acts of writers, readers, and texts*. Carbondale, IL: Southern Illinois University Press.

Bransford, J. D., & Johnson, M. K. (1972). Contextual prerequisites for understanding: Some investigations of comprehension and recall. *Journal of Verbal Learning and Verbal Behavior, 11*(6), 717–726.

Breland, K., & Breland, M. K. (1944, April). Legibility of newspaper headlines printed in capitals and in lower case. *Journal of Applied Psychology, 28*, 117–120.

Brennan, S. E. (1990). Conversation as direct manipulation: An iconoclastic view. In B. Laurel (Ed.), *The art of human-computer interface design* (pp. 393–404). Reading, MA: Addison-Wesley.

Brent, D. (1992). *Reading as rhetorical invention*. Carbondale, IL: National Council of Teachers of English.

Breuleux, A., & Bracewell, R. J. (1994, April). *Cooperation, sharing, and support between specialists in producing technical documentation*. Paper presented at the annual meeting of the American Educational Research Association, New Orleans, LA.

Britton, B. K., Gulgoz, S., & Glynn, S. M. (1993). Impact of good and poor writing on learners: Theory and practice. In B. K. Britton, A. Woodward, & M. Binkley (Eds.), *Learning from textbooks: Theory and practice* (pp. 1–46). Hillsdale, NJ: Lawrence Erlbaum.

Britton, J. (1975). *The development of writing abilities (11–18)*. London: Macmillan Education.

Britton, W. E. (1975). What is technical writing? A redefinition. In D. H. Cunningham & H. A. Estrin (Eds.), *The teaching of technical writing* (pp. 9–14). Urbana, IL: National Council of Teachers of English.

Brockmann, R. J. (1983). Bibliography of articles on the history of technical writing. *Journal of Educational Technology Systems, 13*(2), 155–165.

Brockmann, R. J. (1990). *Writing better computer user documentation: From paper to hypertext, version 2.0*. New York: John Wiley & Sons.

Brockmann, R. J. (1996). *From Millwrights to shipwrights to the twenty-first century: Explorations in a history of technical communication in the United States*. Creskill, NJ: Hampton Press.

Brubach, H. (1993, November 21). Mail-order America. *New York Times Magazine*, pp. 54–61, 68–70.

Bruce, I., McKennell, A., & Walker, E. (1991). *Blind and partially sighted adults in Britain: The RNIB survey Vol. 1*. London: HMSO.

Bruffee, K. (1984). Collaborative learning and the conversation of mankind. *College English, 46* (7), 635–652.

Buchanan, R. (1985). Declaration by design: Rhetoric, argument, and demonstration in design practice. *Design Issues: History, Theory, Criticism, 2*(1), 4–22.

Buchanan, R. (1990). Myth and maturity: Toward a new order in the decade of design. *Design Issues: History, Theory, Criticism, 6*(2), 70–80.

Buchanan, R. (1992). Wicked problems in design thinking. *Design Issues: History, Theory, Criticism, 8*(2), 5–21.

Burke, K. (1950). *A rhetoric of motives*. New York: Prentice-Hall.

Burt, C. L. (1959). *A psychological study of typography*. Cambridge, UK: Cambridge University Press.

Burtis, P. J., Bereiter, C., Scardamalia, M., & Tetroe, J. (1983). The development of planning in writing. In G. Wells & B. M. Kroll (Eds.), *Explorations in the development of writing* (pp. 153–174). Chichester, UK: John Wiley & Sons.

Bush, V. (1945, July). As we may think. *Atlantic Monthly, 176,* pp. 101–108.

Bushman, B. J., & Stack, A. D. (1996). Forbidden fruit versus tainted fruit: Effects of warning labels on attraction to television violence. *Journal of Experimental Psychology, 2*(3), 207-226.

Cable News Network. (1996, February 21). *CNN Prime News* [Television program]. Atlanta, GA: Turner Broadcasting.

Campbell, A. J., Marchetti, F. M., & Mewhort, D. J. K. (1981). Reading speed and text production: A note on right justification techniques. *Ergonomics, 24*(8), 633–640.

Campbell, K. S. (1995). *Coherence, continuity, and cohesion: Theoretical foundations for document design*. Mahwah, NJ: Lawrence Erlbaum.

Card, S. K. (1982, March 15–17). User perceptual mechanisms in the search of computer command menus. In *Proceedings of the Human Factors in Computer Systems* (pp. 190–196). Gaithersburg, MD.

Carson, R. (1962). *The silent spring*. Boston: Houghton Mifflin.

Carter, J. (1979). Improving government regulations: Statement on Executive Order 12044, March 23, 1978. In *Public papers of the Presidents of the United States, Book I* (pp. 563–564). Washington, DC: U.S. Government Printing Office.

Carter, R., Day, B., & Meggs, P. B. (1985). *Typographic design: Form and communication*. New York: Van Nostrand Reinhold.

Caruso, D. (1990, April 8). A new art form comes of age. *San Francisco Examiner*, p. D–14.

Casey, S. M. (1993). *Set phasers on stun and other true tales of design, technology, and human error*. Santa Barbara, CA: Aegean.

Chall, J. S. (1958). *Readability: An appraisal of research and application*. Columbus, OH: Bureau of Educational Research.

Chall, J. S., & Squire, J. R. (1991). The publishing industry and textbooks. In R. Barr, M. L. Kamil, P. B. Mosenthal, & P. D. Pearson (Eds.), *Handbook of reading research: Volume 2* (pp. 120–146). New York: Longman.

Chandler, P., & Sweller, J. (1991). Cognitive load theory and the format of instruction. *Cognition and Instruction, 8*(4), 293–332.

Charney, D. (1993). A study of rhetorical reading: How evolutionists read 'The Spandrels of San Marco'. In J. Selzer (Ed.), *Understanding scientific prose* (pp. 203–231). Madison: University of Wisconsin Press.

Charney, D. (1994). The effect of hypertext on processes of reading and writing. In C. L. Selfe & S. J. Hilligoss (Eds.), *Literacy and computers: The complications of teaching and learning with technology* (pp. 238–263). New York: Modern Language Association.

Charrow, R., & Charrow, V. R. (1979). Making legal language understandable: Psycholinguistic study of jury instructions. *Columbia Law Review, 79*, 1306–1374.

Chase, S. (1953). *The power of words*. New York: Harcourt Brace Jovanovich.

Chase, S., & Schlink, F. J. (1927). *Your money's worth: A study in the waste of the consumer's dollar*. New York: Macmillan.

Chen, L. (1982). Topological structure in visual perception. *Science, 218*, 699–700.

Chi, M. T. H., Bassock, M., Lewis, M., Reimann, P., & Glaser, R. (1989). Self-explanations: How students study and use examples in learning to solve problems. *Cognitive Science, 13*, 145–182.

Chomsky, N. (1957). *Syntactic structures*. The Hague, Netherlands: Mouton.

Cleveland, W. S., & McGill, R. (1984). The many faces of a scatterplot. *Journal of the American Statistical Association, 79*, 807–822.

Clive, M., & Russo, F. (1981). The plain English movement in America: A view from the front. *Information Design Journal, 2*(3/4), 208–214.

Cognition and Technology Group at Vanderbilt University. (1991). Technology and the design of generative learning environments. *Educational Technology, 31*(5), 34–40.

Cole, B. (1993). Multimedia–The technology framework. *IEEE Spectrum, 30*(3), 32–39.

Coleridge, S. T. (1983). *Biographia literaria*. (J. Engell & W. J. Bate Eds.). Princeton, NJ: Princeton University Press. (Original work published in 1817)

Coles, P., & Foster, J. J. (1975). Typographic cuing as an aid to learning from typewritten text. *Programmed Learning and Educational Technology, 12*, 102–108.

Coles, W. E., Jr. (1978). *The plural I*. New York: Holt, Rinehart, & Winston.

Combies, P. (1987). *The struggle to establish a profession: An historical survey of the status of college composition teachers 1900–1950*. Unpublished doctoral dissertation, Carnegie Mellon University, Pittsburgh, PA.

Communications Research Institute of Australia. (1992). Research update: Designing information for people—Proceedings from the symposium. *Communication News, 5*(2), 10–11.

Coney, M. B. (1987). Contemporary views of audience: A rhetorical perspective. *Technical Writing Teacher, 14*, 319–336.

Coney, M. B. (1992). Technical readers and their rhetorical roles. *IEEE Transactions on Professional Communication, 35* (2), 58–63.

Conklin, J. (1987). Hypertext: An introduction and survey. *IEEE Computer, 20*(9), 17–41.

Connors, R. J. (1981). The rise and fall of the modes of discourse. *College Composition and Communication, 32*, 444–463.

Connors, R. J. (1982). The rise of technical writing instruction in America. *Journal of Technical Writing and Communication,12*, 329–352.

Connors, R. J. (1985). Mechanical correctness as a focus in composition instruction. *College Composition and Communication, 36*(1), 61–72.

Connors, R. J. (1988). The rise and fall of the modes of discourse. In G. Tate & E. P. J. Corbett (Eds.), *The writing teacher's sourcebook* (pp. 24–34). New York: Oxford University Press.

Connors, R. J., Ede, L. S., & Lunsford, A. A. (1984). The revival of rhetoric in America. In R. J. Connors (Ed.), *Essays on classical rhetoric and modern discourse* (pp. 1–15). Carbondale, IL: Southern Illinois University Press.

Consumers Union. (1986, January and February). 50 years ago. *Consumer Reports, 51* (1 and 2), pp. 8–10 and pp. 76–79.

Consumers Union. (1986, April and May). 50 years ago. *Consumer Reports, 51* (4 and 5), p. 228 and pp. 283–284.

Consumers Union. (1986, August and September). Memo to members and Setting film speed. *Consumer Reports, 51* (8 and 9), pp. 495–497 and pp. 561–562.

Consumers Union. (1986, October and November). 50 years ago. *Consumer Reports, 51* (10 and 11), p. 652 and p. 709.

Consumers Union. (1992, July). Wasted healthcare dollars. *Consumer Reports, 57* (7), pp. 435–449.

Consumers Union. (1992, October). Food labels: New and improved? *Consumer Reports, 57* (10), pp. 654–655.

Cook, K. J. (1990). Reminiscences: A personal history of the STC—Lessons from a technical publisher. *Technical Communication, 37* (2), 195–196.

Corbett, E. P. J. (1965). *Classical rhetoric for the modern student.* New York: Oxford University Press.

Corina, M. (1975). *Trust in tobacco: The Anglo-American struggle for power.* New York: St. Martin's Press.

Council for Programs in Technical and Scientific Communication. (1995). Application for Council for Programs in Technical and Scientific Communication (CPTSC) program review and guidelines for self-study to precede CPTSC visit. In M. Cooper (Ed.) *Proceedings of the CPTSC Annual Meeting* (pp. 119–130). Houghton, MI: CPTSC.

Couture, B. (1986). Effect ideation in written text: A functional approach to clarity and exigence. In B. Couture (Ed.), *Functional approaches to writing: Research perspectives* (pp. 69–92). Norwood, NJ: Ablex.

Cowan, R. S. (1983). *More work for mother.* New York: Basic Books.

Craig, J. (1980). *Designing with type: A basic course in typography.* New York: Watson-Guptill.

Craig, J., & Barton, B. (1987). *Thirty centuries of graphic design.* New York: Watson-Guptill.

Craig, J., & Bevington, W. (1989). *Working with graphic designers.* New York: Watson-Guptill.

Craig, R. (1990). Ideological aspects of publications design. *Design Issues: History, Theory, Criticism, 6*(2), 18–27.

Creek, H. L. (1939). Teachers of English in engineering colleges: Selection and training. In *Proceedings of the Society for the Promotion of Engineering Education* (pp. 300–313). Pittsburgh, PA: Office of the Secretary.

Creek, H. L., & McKee, J. H. (1931). English in colleges of engineering. *English Journal, 21*, 819.

Cringely, R. X. (1992). *Accidental empires: How the boys of Silicon Valley make their millions, battle foreign competition, and still can't get a date.* Reading, MA: Addison-Wesley.

Cross, N., Naughton, J., & Walker, D. (1981). Design method and scientific method. *Design Studies, 2*(4), 198–201.

Crowley, S. (1990). *The methodical memory: Invention in current-traditional rhetoric.* Carbondale, IL: Southern Illinois University Press.

Cunningham, D. H., & Harris, J. G. (1994). Undergraduate technical and professional writing programs: A question of status. *Journal of Technical Writing and Communication, 24*(2), 127–137.

Cunningham, D. J., Duffy, T. M., & Knuth, R. A. (1993). The textbook of the future. In C. McKnight, A. Dillon, & J. Richardson (Eds.), *Hypertext: A psychological perspective* (pp. 19–50). Chichester, UK: Ellis Horwood.

Current, R. N. (1954). *The typewriter and the men who made it.* Urbana, IL: University of Illinois Press.

Cutts, M. (1993). Unspeakable acts. *Information Design Journal, 7*(2), 115–120.

Cutts, M., & Maher, C. (1986). *The plain English story.* Stockport, UK: Plain English Campaign.

Daneman, M., & Carpenter, P. A. (1983). Individual differences in integrating information between and within sentences. *Journal of Experimental Psychology, 9*, 561–583.

D'Angelo, F. J. (1975). *A conceptual theory of rhetoric.* Cambridge, MA: Winthrop.

Daniels, M. (1980). The ingenious pen: American writing implements from the eighteenth century to the twentieth. *The American Archivist, 43*, 312–324.

Danks, J. H., & Hill, G. O. (1981). An interactive analysis of oral reading. In A. M. Lesgold & C. A. Perfetti (Eds.), *Interactive processes in reading* (pp. 131–153). Hillsdale, NJ: Lawrence Erlbaum.

Dautermann, J. (1993). Negotiating meaning in a hospital discourse community. In R. Spilka (Ed.), *Writing in the workplace: New research perspectives* (pp. 98–110). Carbondale, IL: Southern Illinois University Press.

Davis, B. (1983, November 30). Hundreds of Coleco's Adams are returned as defective: Firm blames user manuals. *Wall Street Journal*, p. A4.

De Tienne, K. B., & Smart, K. L. (1995, November 13–15). The battle of paper documentation versus online documentation. In *Proceedings of the Disappearing Borders*. Dortmund, Germany: International Council for Technical Communication (INTECOM).

Del Sesto, S. L. (1981). The science journalist and early popular magazine coverage of nuclear energy. *Journal of Technical Writing and Communication, 11*, 315–327.

Design Issues. (1990). Educating the designer. *Design Issues: History, Theory, Criticism, 7*(1).

Dewey, J. (1916). *Democracy and education*. New York: Macmillan.

Dewey, J. (1938). *Experience and education*. New York: Macmillan.

Diehl, W. A., & Mikulecky, L. (1980). The nature of reading at work. *Journal of Reading, 24*(3), 221–228.

Dieli, M. (1986). *Representing the user: Evaluation strategies of expert writers*. Paper presented at the annual meeting of the American Educational Research Association, San Francisco, CA.

Dijk, T. A., van. (1980). *Macrostructures*. Hillsdale, NJ: Lawrence Erlbaum.

Dijk, T. A., van, & Kintsch, W. (1983). *Strategies of discourse comprehension*. New York: Academic Press.

Dobrin, D. N. (1983). What's technical about technical writing? In P. V. Anderson, R. J. Brockmann, & C. R. Miller (Eds.), *New essays in technical and scientific communication: Research, theory, practice* (pp. 227–250). Farmingdale, NY: Baywood Press.

Dobrin, D. N. (1989). *Writing and technique*. Urbana, IL: National Council of Teachers of English.

Dobrin, D. N. (1994). Hype and hypertext. In C. L. Selfe & S. J. Hilligoss (Eds.), *Literacy and computers: The complications of teaching and learning with technology* (pp. 305–315). New York: Modern Language Association.

Dodson, D. W., & Shields, N. L., Jr. (1978). Development of user guidelines for ECAS display design. Vol. 1 (Rep. No. NASA-CR-150877). Huntsville, AL: Essex Corp.

Doheny-Farina, S. (1992). *Rhetoric, innovation, technology: Case studies of technical communication in technology transfers*. Cambridge, MA: MIT Press.

Dole, J. A., & Sinatra, G. M. (1994). Social psychology research on beliefs and attitudes: Implications for research on learning from text. In R. Garner & P. A. Alexander (Eds.), *Beliefs about text and instructions with text* (pp. 245–264). Hillsdale, NJ: Lawrence Erlbaum.

Doordan, D. P. (1990). Design at CBS. *Design Issues: History, Theory, Criticism, 6*(2), 4–17.

Dragga, S. (1996). Is this ethical? A survey of opinions on principles and practices in document design. *Technical Communication, 43*(1), 29–38.

Dreher, M. J., & Guthrie, J. T. (1990). Cognitive processes in textbook chapter search tasks. *Reading Research Quarterly, 25*, 323–339.

Duffy, T. M. (1985). Readability formulas: What's the use? In T. M. Duffy & R. H. W. Waller (Eds.), *Designing usable texts* (pp. 113–143). New York: Academic Press.

Duffy, T. M., & Jonassen, D. H. (1991). Constructivism: New implications for educational technology? *Educational Technology, 31*(5), 7–12.

Duffy, T. M., & Langston, M. D. (1985). *Online help: Design issues for authoring systems* (Tech. Rep. No. 18). Pittsburgh, PA: Carnegie Mellon University, Communications Design Center.

Duffy, T. M., & Waller, R. H. W. (Eds.). (1985). *Designing usable texts*. Orlando, FL: Academic Press.

Duffy, T. M., Mehlenbacher, B., & Palmer, J. E. (1992). *Online help systems: Design and evaluation*. Norwood, NJ: Ablex.

Duffy, T. M., Post, T. A., & Smith, G. (1987). An analysis of the process of developing military technical manuals. *Technical Communication, 34*(2), 70–79.

Duffy, T. M., Trumble, J., Isenberg, T., Janik, C. J., & Rogers, K. (1987). *Learning with online and hardcopy tutorials* (Tech. Rep. No. 32). Pittsburgh, PA: Carnegie Mellon University, Communications Design Center.

Dumas, J. S. (1988). Designing user interfaces for software. Englewood Cliffs, NJ: Prentice-Hall.

Dumas, J. S., & Redish, J. C. (1993). *A practical guide to usability testing*. Norwood, NJ: Ablex.

Durbin, M. F., Wahl, L. E., Molony, S. T., Klein, S., & Wade, C. (1993). And now, from the company that brought you the seven-eyed trout: Risk communication in action. In *Proceedings of the International Technical Communication Conference* (p. 78). Arlington, VA: Society for Technical Communication.

Dykstra, G. (1991). A Plain Language Centre for Canada. In E. R. Steinberg (Ed.), *Plain language: Principles and practice* (pp. 43–50). Detroit, MI: Wayne State University Press.

Eagleson, R. D. (1991). The plain English movement in Australia and the United Kingdom. In E. R. Steinberg (Ed.), *Plain language: Principles and practice* (pp. 32–36). Detroit, MI: Wayne State University Press.

Eagleton, T. (1983). *Literary theory: An introduction*. Minneapolis, MN: University of Minnesota Press.

Eames, C., & Eames, R. (1973). *A computer perspective*. Cambridge, MA: Harvard University Press.

Ede, L. S., & Lunsford, A. A. (1984). Audience addressed/audience invoked: The role of audience in composition theory and pedagogy. *College Composition and Communication, 35*(2), 155–171.

Ehrenberg, A. S. C. (1977). Rudiments of numeracy. *Journal of the Royal Statistical Society, 140*(3), 277–297.

Elbow, P. (1973). *Writing without teachers*. New York: Oxford University Press.

Elbow, P. (1981). *Writing with power: Techniques for mastering the writing process*. New York: Oxford University Press.

Elbow, P. (1987). Closing my eyes as I speak: An argument for ignoring audience. *College English, 49*, 50–69.

Elbow, P. (1994). Introduction. In P. Elbow (Ed.), *Landmark essays in voice and writing* (pp. xi-xlvii). Davis, CA: Hermagoras Press.

Elmer-Dewitt, P. (1993, April 12). Electronic superhighway. *Time*, pp. 50–58.

Englebart, D. C. (1963). A conceptual framework for the augmentation of man's intellect. In P. D. Howerton & D. C. Weeks (Eds.), *Vistas in information handling: Vol. 1* (pp. 1–29). Washington, DC: Spartan Books.

Enos, R., & Lauer, J. M. (1992). The meaning of heuristic in Aristotle's *Rhetoric* and its implications for contemporary rhetorical theory. In J. L. Kinneavy (Ed.), *A rhetoric of doing* (pp. 79-87). Carbondale, IL: Southern Illinois University Press.

Ericsson, K. A., & Simon, H. A. (1991). *Protocol analysis: Verbal reports as data* (2nd ed.). Cambridge, MA: MIT Press.

Ernst, U. (1986). The figured poem: Towards a definition of genre. *Visible Language, 20* (1), 8–27.

Fabrizio, R., Kaplan, L., & Teal, G. (1967). Readability as a function of the straightness of right-hand margins. *Journal of Typographic Research, 1*, 90–95.

Faigley, L. (1985). Nonacademic writing: The social perspective. In L. Odell & D. Goswami (Eds.), *Writing in nonacademic settings* (pp. 231-248). New York: Guilford Press.

Faigley, L., & Miller, T. (1982). What we learn from writing on the job. *College English, 44*(6), 557–569.

Fatout, P. (1948). Growth of the humanistic stem. *Proceedings of the American Society for Engineering Education, 55*, 715–717.

Fearing, B. E., & Sparrow, W. K. (1989). Part one: On the history and theory of technical writing. In B. E. Fearing & W. K. Sparrow (Eds.), *Technical writing: Theory and practice* (p. 1). New York: Modern Language Association.

Felker, D. B. (1980). *Document design: A review of the relevant research.* Washington, DC: American Institutes for Research.

Felker, D. B., Pickering, F., Charrow, V. R., Holland, M., & Redish, J. C. (1981). *Guidelines for document designers.* Washington, DC: American Institutes for Research.

Felsenfeld, C. (1991). The plain English experience in New York. In E. R. Steinberg (Ed.), *Plain language: Principles and practice* (pp. 13–18). Detroit, MI: Wayne State University Press.

Fenton, E. (1996). *The Macintosh font book: Typographic tips, techniques and resources* (3rd ed.). Berkeley: Peachpit Press.

Findahl, O. (1971). *The effects of visual illustrations upon perception and retention of news programmes.* Stockholm: Swedish Broadcasting Corporation, Audience and Programme Research Department.

Findahl, O., & Hoijer, B. (1976). *Fragments of reality: An experiment with news and TV visuals.* Stockholm: Swedish Broadcasting Corporation, Audience and Programme Research Department.

Findeli, A. (1990). Moholy-Nagy's design pedagogy in Chicago (1937-46). *Design Issues: History, Theory, Criticism, 7*(1), 4–22.

Fisbein, M. (1967). *Reading in attitude theory and measurement.* New York: John Wiley & Sons.

Fitting, R. U. (1924). *Report writing.* New York: Ronald Press.

Fleming, D. (1996a). Professional-client discourse in design: Variation in accounts of social roles and material artifacts by designers and their clients. *Text, 6* (2), 133-160.

Fleming, D. (1996b). The rhetoric of design: Argument, story, picture, and talk in a student design project. Unpublished doctoral dissertation, Carnegie Mellon University: Pittsburgh, PA.

Flexner, S. B. (1982). *Listening to America.* New York: Simon and Schuster.

Flipczak, B. (1994). Technoliteracy, technophobia, and programming your VCR. *Training, 31*(1), 48–52.

Flower, L. (1979). Writer-based prose: A cognitive basis for problems in writing. *College English, 41*, 19–37.

Flower, L. (1989). Rhetorical problem solving: Cognition and professional writing. In M. Kogan (Ed.), *Writing in the business professions* (pp.) 3-36). Urbana, IL: National Council of Teachers of English and the Association for Business Communication.

Flower, L., & Hayes, J. R. (1981). A cognitive process theory of writing. *College Composition and Communication, 32*, 365–387.

Flower, L., Hayes, J. R., & Swarts, H. (1983). Revising functional documents: The scenario principle. In P. V. Anderson, R. J. Brockmann, & C. R. Miller (Eds.), *New essays in technical and scientific communication* (pp. 41–58). New York: Baywood Press.

Flower, L., Hayes, J. R., Carey, L., Schriver, K. A., & Stratman, J. F. (1986). Detection, diagnosis and the strategies of revision. *College Composition and Communication, 37*(1), 16–55.

Flower, L., Schriver, K. A., Haas, C., Carey, L., & Hayes, J. R. (1992). Planning in writing: The cognition of a constructive process. In S. P. Witte, N. Nakadate, & R. D. Cherry (Eds.), *A rhetoric of doing: Essays on written discourse in honor of James L. Kinneavy* (pp. 181–243). Carbondale, IL: Southern Illinois University Press.

Fogarty, D. J. (1959). *Roots for a new rhetoric.* New York: Russell & Russell.

Foley, J. (1876). *History of the invention and illustrated process of making Foley's diamond pointed gold pens, with complete illustrated catalogue.* New York: Mayer, Merkel, and Ottoman.

Foss, S. K., Foss, K. A., & Trapp, R. (1991). *Contemporary perspectives on rhetoric* (2nd ed.). Prospect Heights, IL: Waveland Press.

Foster, J. J. (1979). The use of visual cues in text. In P. A. Kolers, M. E. Wrolstad, & H. Bouma (Eds.), *Processing of visible language: Vol. 1* (pp. 189–203). New York: Plenum Press. printed text.

Foster, J. J., & Bruce, M. (1982). Reading uppercase and lowercase on Viewdata. *Applied Ergonomics, 13*(2), 145–149.

Foster, J. J., & Coles, P. (1977). An experimental study of typographic cuing in printed text. *Ergonomics, 20*, 57–66.

Fountain, A. M. (1938). *A study of courses in technical writing.* Nashville, TN: George Peabody College.

Frankel, M. (1994, December 11). Jumpers vs. Refers. *New York Times*, pp. 46, 48.

Frankel, M. (1996, June 2). Media mongrels. *New York Times Magazine*, pp. 20, 22.

Frascara, J. (1995). Graphic design: Fine art or social science? In V. Margolin & R. Buchanan (Eds.), *The idea of design* (pp. 44–55). Cambridge, MA: MIT Press.

Freedman, S. W. (1994). *Exchanging writing, exchanging cultures: Lessons in school reform from the United States and Great Britain*. Cambridge, MA and Urbana, IL: Harvard University Press and National Council of Teachers of English.

Frutiger, A. (1980). *Type sign symbol*. Zurich, Switzerland: ABC Edition.

Gagné, R. M., & Briggs, J. L. (1979). *Principles of instructional design* (2nd ed.). New York: Holt, Rinehart, & Winston.

Galitz, W. O. (1989). *Handbook of screen format design* (3rd ed.). Wellesley, MA: QED Information Sciences.

Garner, R., & Alexander, P. A. (Eds.). (1994). *Beliefs about text and instruction with text*. Hillsdale, NJ: Lawrence Erlbaum.

Garner, R., & Hansis, R. (1994). Literacy practices outside of school: Adults' beliefs and their reponses to "street texts". In R. Garner & P. A. Alexander (Eds.), *Beliefs about text and instruction with text* (pp. 57–73). Hillsdale, NJ: Lawrence Erlbaum.

Garner, R., Alexander, P. A., Gillingham, M. G., Kulikowich, J. M., & Brown, R. (1991). Interest and learning from text. *American Educational Research Journal, 28*, 643–659.

Garofalo, K. M. (1988). Typographic cues as an aid to learning from textbooks. *Visible Language, 22*(2/3), 273–298.

Geest, T., van der. (1994). Hypertext: Writing and reading in a non-linear medium. In M. Steehouder, C. J. M. Jansen, P. van der Poort, & R. Verheijen (Eds.), *Quality of technical documentation* (pp. 49–66). Amsterdam, Netherlands: Rodopi Press.

Gentner, D., & Gentner, D. R. (1983). Flowing waters or teeming crowds: Mental models of electricity. In D. Gentner & A. L. Stevens (Eds.), *Mental models* (pp. 99–129). Hillsdale, NJ: Lawrence Erlbaum.

Geonetta, S., Allen, J., Curtis, D., & Staples, K. (1993). *Academic programs in technical communication* (4th ed.). Arlington, VA: Society for Technical Communication.

Giard, J. R. (1990). Design education in crisis: The transition from skills to knowledge. *Design Issues: History, Theory, Criticism, 7*(1), 23–28.

Gibson, W. (1950). Authors, speakers, readers, and mock readers. *College English, 11*, 265–269.

Gibson, W. (1966). *Tough, sweet & stuffy: An essay on modern American prose styles*. Bloomington, IN: Indiana University Press.

Gibson, W. (1969). *Persona: A style study for readers and writers*. New York: Random House.

Gilbert, G. N., & Mulkay, M. (1984). *Opening Pandora's box: A sociological analysis of scientists' discourse*. Cambridge, UK: Cambridge University Press.

Giscard d'Estaing, V. (1993). *Inventions and discoveries 1993: What's happened, what's coming, what's that?* New York: Facts on File.

Glenberg, A. M., Wilkinson, A. C., & Epstein, W. (1982). The illusion of knowing: Failure in the self-assessment of comprehension. *Memory and Cognition, 10*(6), 597–602.

Glushko, R. J., & Bianchi, M. H. (1982). Online documentation: Mechanizing development, delivery, and use. *Bell System Technical Journal, 61*(6), 1313–1323.

Glynn, S. M., Britton, B. K., & Tillman, M. H. (1985). Typographical cues in text: Management of the reader's attention. In D. H. Jonassen (Ed.), *Technology of text: Principles for structuring, designing, and displaying text: Vol. 2* (pp. 192–209). Englewood Cliffs, NJ: Educational Technology Publications.

Goldsmith, E. (1987). The analysis of illustration in theory and practice. In H. A. Houghton & D. M. Willows (Eds.), *The psychology of illustration. Vol. 2. Instructional issues* (pp. 53–85). New York: Springer-Verlag.

Golsby-Smith, T. (1996). Fourth order design: A practical perspective. *Design Issues: History, Theory, Criticism, 12*(1), 5–25.

Gombrich, E. H. (1961). *Art and illusion*. Washington, DC and New York: National Gallery of Art, Bollingen Foundation, and Pantheon.

Goswami, D., Redish, J. C., Felker, D., & Siegel, A. I. (1981). *Writing in the professions: A course guide and instructional materials for an advanced composition course*. Washington, DC: American Institutes for Research.

Gottschall, E. M. (1989). *Typographic communications today*. Cambridge, MA: MIT Press.

Gough, K. (1968). Implications of literacy in traditional China and India. In J. Goody (Ed.), *Literacy in traditional societies* (pp. 69–84). New York: Cambridge University Press.

Gough, P. B. (1972). One second of reading. In J. Kavanagh & I. Mattingly (Eds.), *Language by ear and eye* (pp. 331–358) Cambridge, MA: MIT Press.

Gough, P. B. (1984). Word recognition. In P. D. Pearson (Ed.), *Handbook of reading research: Vol. 1* (pp. 225–253). New York: Longman.

Gould, J. D., & Grischkowsky, N. (1984). Doing the same work with hardcopy and with cathode-ray tube (CRT) computer terminals. *Human Factors, 26*(3), 323–337.

Gould, J. D., Alfaro, L., Finn, R., Haupt, N., & Minuto, A. (1987). Reading from CRT displays can be as fast as reading from paper. *Human Factors, 29*(5), 497–517.

Gragson, J., & Selzer, J. (1990). Fictionalizing the readers of scholarly articles in biology. *Written Communication, 7*(1), 25–58.

Graves, R., McFadden, J., & Moore, S. (1994). Technical communication programs at Canadian post-secondary institutions. *Journal of Business and Technical Communication, 24*(3), 237–250.

Grech, C. (1992, April). Computer documentation doesn't pass muster. *PC Computing, 5*(4), 212–214.

Greene, S., & Ackerman, J. M. (1995). Expanding the constructivist metaphor: A rhetorical perspective on literacy research and practice. *Review of Educational Research, 65*(4), 383–420.

Grego, R. C. (1987). Science, late nineteenth-century rhetoric, and the beginnings of technical writing instruction in America. *Journal of Technical Writing and Communication, 17*, 63–78.

Gregory, M., & Poulton, E. C. (1970). Even versus uneven right-margins and the rate of comprehension in reading. *Ergonomics, 13*, 427–434.

Gribbons, W. M. (1992). Organization by design: Some implications for structuring information. *Journal of Technical Writing and Communication, 22* (1), 57–75.

Gross, A. G. (1990). *The rhetoric of science*. Cambridge, MA: Harvard University Press.

Grun, B. (1991). *The timetables of history* (3rd ed.). New York: Touchstone and Simon & Schuster.

Gunter, B. (1987). *Poor reception: Misunderstanding and forgetting broadcast news*. Hillsdale, NJ: Lawrence Erlbaum.

Guthrie, J. T., & Dreher, M. J. (1990). Literacy as search: Explorations via computer. In D. Nix & R. Spiro (Eds.), *Cognition, education, multimedia* (pp. 65–113). Hillsdale, NJ: Lawrence Erlbaum.

Guthrie, J. T., Weber, S., & Kimmerly, N. (1993). Searching documents: Cognitive processes and deficits in understanding graphs, tables, and illustrations. *Contemporary Educational Psychology, 18*, 186–221.

Haas, C. (1996). *Writing technology: Studies on the materiality of literacy*. Mahwah, NJ: Lawrence Erlbaum.

Haas, C., & Hayes, J. R. (1986a). *Pen and paper vs. the machine: Writers composing in hard copy and computer conditions* (CDC Tech. Rep. No. 16). Pittsburgh, PA: Carnegie Mellon University, Communications Design Center.

Haas, C., & Hayes, J. R. (1986b). What did I just say? Reading problems in writing with the machine. *Research in the Teaching of English, 20*(1), 22–35.

Hackos, J. T. (1994). *Managing your documentation projects*. New York: John Wiley & Sons.

Hackos, J. T. (1995). Trends forum explores future of technical communication. *Intercom, 42*(4), 4–5, 16–17.

Halliday, M. A. K., & Hasan, R. (1976). *Cohesion in English*. London: Longman.

Hansen, F. (1972). *Consumer choice behavior*. New York: Free Press.

Harmon, J. E., & Gross, A. G. (1996). The scientific style manual: A reliable guide to practice? *Technical Communication, 43* (1), 61–72.

Harrington, E. W. (1948). Rhetoric and the scientific method of inquiry. *University of Colorado Studies: Series in Language and Literature, 1*, 1–64.

Hartley, J. (1994). *Designing instructional text* (3rd ed.). New Brunswick, NJ: Nichols Publishing.

Hartley, J., & Burnhill, P. (1971). Experiments with unjustified text. *Visible Language, 5*, 265–278.

Hartley, J., & Rooum, D. (1983). Sir Cyril Burt and typography. *British Journal of Psychology, 74* (2), 203–212.

Hartzog, C. P. (1986). *Composition and the academy: A study of writing program administration*. New York: Modern Language Association.

Hatch, J. A., Hill, C. A., & Hayes, J. R. (1993). When the messenger is the message: Readers' impressions of writers' personalities. *Written Communication, 10* (4), 569–598.

Hawisher, G. E., LeBlanc, P., Moran, C., & Selfe, C. L. (1996). *Computers and the teaching of writing in American higher education, 1979–1994: A history*. Norwood, NJ: Ablex.

Hayes, J. R. (1989a). *The complete problem solver* (2nd ed.). Hillsdale, NJ: Lawrence Erlbaum.

Hayes, J. R. (1989b). Writing research: The analysis of a very complex task. In D. Klahr & K. Kotovsky (Eds.), *Complex information processing: The impact of Herbert A. Simon* (pp. 209–234). Hillsdale, NJ: Lawrence Erlbaum.

Hayes, J. R., & Flower, L. (1980). Identifying the organization of writing processes. In L. W. Gregg & E. R. Steinberg (Eds.), *Cognitive processes in writing: An interdisciplinary approach* (pp. 3–30). Hillsdale, NJ: Lawrence Erlbaum.

Hayes, J. R., Flower, L., Schriver, K. A., Stratman, J. F., & Carey, L. (1987). Cognitive processes in revision. In S. Rosenberg (Ed.), *Advances in applied psycholinguistics: Vol. 2: Reading, writing, and language processing* (pp. 176–240). Cambridge, UK: Cambridge University Press.

Hayes, J. R., & Nash, J. G. (1996). On the nature of planning in writing. In C. M. Levy & S. Ransdell (Eds.), *The science of writing: Theories, methods, individual differences, and applications* (pp. 29–55). Mahwah, NJ: Lawrence Erlbaum.

Hayhoe, G. F., Kunz, L. D., Southard, S. G., & Stohrer, F. (1993). *Growing to fit the future: Academic programs in technical communication* (White Paper). Alexandria, VA: Society for Technical Communication.

Hayhoe, G. F., Stohrer, F., Kunz, L. D., & Southard, S. G. (1994). The evolution of academic programs in technical communication. *Technical Communication, 41*(1), 14–19.

Hays, R. (1975). What is technical writing? In D. H. Cunningham & H. A. Estrin (Eds.), *The teaching of technical writing* (pp. 3–8). Urbana, IL: National Council of Teachers of English.

Hees, M., van. (1994). Oud geleerd, oud gedaan: Optimalisering van handleiddingen voor ouderen. Unpublished master's thesis, University of Utrecht, Center for Language and Communication, Netherlands.

Hegarty, M., Carpenter, P. A., & Just, M. A. (1991). Diagrams in the comprehension of scientific text. In R. Barr, M. L. Kamil, P. B. Mosenthal, & P. D. Pearson (Eds.), *Handbook of reading research. Vol. 2* (pp. 641–668). New York: Longman.

Hegarty, M., & Steinhoff, K. (1994, April). *Use of diagrams as external memory in a mechanical reasoning task*. Paper presented at the annual meeting of the American Educational Research Association, New Orleans, LA.

Heid, J. (1996a, July). Making image maps for web sites. *MacWorld,* pp. 125–127.

Heid, J. (1996b, August). Server-friendly image maps. *MacWorld,* pp. 135–137.

Helander, M. G., Billingsley, P. A., & Schurick, J. M. (1984). An evaluation of human factors research on visual display terminals in the workplace. In *Proceedings of the Human Factors Review* (pp. 55–129). Santa Monica, CA: Human Factors Society.

Hellemans, A., & Bunch, B. (1991). *The timetables of science*. New York: Touchstone and Simon & Schuster.

Hendry, D. G. (1995). Breakdowns in writing intentions when simultaneously deploying SGML-marked texts in hard copy and electronic copy. *Behavior & Information Technology, 14*(2), 80–92.

Herrmann, R. O. (1970). *The consumer movement in social perspective* (Discussion Paper No. 88). University Park, PA: Penn State University.

Heskett, J. (1989). *Philips: A study of the corporate management of design*. London: Trefoil.

Hidi, S., & Baird, W. (1988). Strategies for increasing text-based interest and students' recall of expository texts. *Reading Research Quarterly, 23*, 465–483.

Higgins, A. S. (1989). Reminiscences: A personal history of the STC—The editor speaks. *Technical Communication, 36*(3), 261–262.

Higgins, D. (1986). The corpus of British and other English-language pattern poetry. *Visible Language, 20*(1), 28–51.

Higham, S. C. F. (1918). *Scientific distribution*. New York: Alfred A. Knopf.

Hilgard, E. R. (1987). *Psychology in America: A historical survey*. Orlando, FL: Harcourt Brace Jovanovich.

Hillocks, G. (1986). *Research in written composition: New directions for teaching*. Urbana, IL: ERIC Clearinghouse on Reading and Communication Skills and National Conference on Research in English.

Hoft, N. L. (1995). *International technical communication: How to export information about high technology*. New York: John Wiley & Sons.

Holland, V. M. (1981). *Psycholinguistic alternatives to readability formulas* (Document Design Project Tech. Rep. No. 12). Washington, DC: American Institutes for Research.

Holland, V. M., & Rose, A. M. (1981). *A comparison of prose and algorithms for presenting complex instructions* (Document Design Project Tech. Rep. No. 17). Washington, DC: American Institutes for Research.

Hollis, R. (1994). *Graphic Design: A concise history*. London: Thames and Hudson.

Holmes, G. (1931, June). The relative legibility of black print and white print. *Journal of Applied Psychology, 15*, 248–251.

Horton, W. (1991). *Illustrating computer documentation: The art of presenting information graphically on paper and online*. New York: John Wiley & Sons.

Horton, W. (1994). *Designing and writing online documentation: Hypermedia for self-supporting products*. New York: John Wiley & Sons.

Horton, K. W., & Horton, W. (1995). No dumping allowed: The right way to put documents online. In *Proceedings of the Annual Conference of the Society for Technical Communication* (p. 455). Washington, DC: Society for Technical Communication.

Houp, K. W., & Pearsall, T. E. (1968). *Reporting technical information*. New York: Macmillan.

Huey, E. B. (1968). *The psychology and pedagogy of reading* (1st ed.). Cambridge, MA: MIT Press. (Original work published in 1908 by Macmillan, New York)

Hull, G. A. (1987). The editing process in writing: A performance study of more skilled and less skilled college writers. *Research in the Teaching of English, 21*(1), 8–29.

Hunt, P. (1993). The teaching of technical communication in Europe: A report from Britain. *Technical Communication Quarterly, 2*(3), 319–330.

Hvistendahl, J. K., & Kahl, M. R. (1975, January 17). Roman v. sans serif body type: Readability and reader preference. *ANPA News Research Bulletin*, 3–11.

Information Design Journal. (1993). Special issue on maps and diagrams. *Information Design Journal, 7* (1).

Iser, W. (1978). *The act of reading: A theory of aesthetic response*. Baltimore, MD: Johns Hopkins University Press.

James, H. (1934). *The art of the novel*. New York: Charles Scribner's Sons.

Janik, C. K., Swaney, J. H., Bond, S. J., & Hayes, J. R. (1981). Informed consent: Reality or illusion? *Information Design Journal, 2* (3/4), 197–207.

Jansen, C. J. M. (1992). *Research in technical communication: A Dutch perspective*. Paper presented to International Technical Communications Conference, Atlanta, GA.

Jansen, C. J. M. (1994). Research in technical communication in the Netherlands. *Technical Communication, 41* (2), 234–239.

Jansen, C. J. M., & Steehouder, M. (1991). Formuleren als bron van taalverkeersproblemen. *Tijdschrift voor Taalbeheersing, 13*(1), 30–45.

Jansen, C. J. M., & Steehouder, M. (1992). Forms as a source of communication problems. *Journal of Technical Writing and Communication, 22*, 179–194.

Japan Times. (1990, September 12). Professor takes gibberish out of Mitsubishi manuals. *Japan Times*, p. 15.

Jean, G. (1992). *Writing: The story of alphabets and scripts*. New York: Harry N. Abrams.

Jenks, I. H. (1989). Reminiscences: A personal history of the STC—Some predecessor societies. *Technical Communication, 36*(3), 82–84.

Johnson, R. R. (1994). The unfortunate human factor: A selective history of human factors for technical communicators. *Technical Communication Quarterly, 3*(2), 195–212.

Jonassen, D. H. (Ed.) (1982). *The technology of text: Vol. 1*. Englewood Cliffs, NJ: Educational Technology Publications.

Jonassen, D. H. (Ed.) (1985). *The technology of text: Vol. 2*. Englewood Cliffs, NJ: Educational Technology Publications.

Jonassen, D. H., Hannum, W. H., & Tessmer, M. (1989). *The handbook of task analysis procedures*. New York: Praeger.

Jones, C. (1970). *Design methods: Seeds of human futures*. New York: John Wiley & Sons, Interscience.

Jones, C., & Thornley, D. G. (Eds.). (1963). *Conference on design methods.* Oxford: Pergamon Press.

Jones, S., Kennelly, C., Mueller, C., Sweezy, M., Thomas, B., & Velez, L. (1992). *Developing international user information.* Bedford, MA: Digital Press.

Jordan, M. P. (1994). Plainer legal language: Definitions and requirements in acts. *Journal of Technical Writing and Communication, 24* (3), 333–352.

Just, M. A., & Carpenter, P. A. (1980). Theory of reading: From eye fixations to comprehension. *Psychological Review, 87* (4), 329–354.

Just, M. A., & Carpenter, P. A. (1987). *The psychology of reading and language comprehension.* Boston: Allyn and Bacon.

Kallet, A., & Schlink, F. J. (1933). *100,000,000 guinea pigs: Dangers in everyday foods, drugs, and cosmetics.* New York: Grosset & Dunlap.

Kalmbach, J. (1988). Reconceiving the page: A short history of desktop publishing. *Technical Communication, 35*(4), 277–281.

Kantor, K. (1975). Creative expression in the English curriculum. *Research in the Teaching of English, 9* (Spring), 5–29.

Kawasaki, G. (1993). The Akihabara syndrome. *MacWorld, 110*(6), 316.

Kelley, P. (1985). *Academic programs in technical communication* (3rd ed.). Washington, DC: Society for Technical Communication.

Kelley, C. L., & Charness, N. (1995). Issues in training older adults to use computers. *Behaviour and Information Technology, 14*(2), 107–120.

Kelvin, G. V. (1992). Illustrating for science. New York: Watson-Guptill.

Kendall, P. J. (1988). Implications of technical documentation in European industry. *The Communicator* (77), 2–3.

Kern, R. P. (1985). Modeling users in their use of technical manuals. In T. M. Duffy & R. H. W. Waller (Eds.), *Designing usable texts* (pp. 341–375). Orlando, FL: Academic Press.

Kern, R. P., Sticht, T. G., Welty, D., & Hauke, R. N. (1976). *Guidebook for the development of Army training literature.* (HUMRRO Tech. Rep.). Alexandria, VA: U.S. Army Research Institute for the Behavioral and Social Sciences, Human Resources Organization.

Keyes, E. (1993). Typography, color, and information structure. *Technical Communication, 40* (4), 638–654.

Keyes, E. (1995, April 25). *Verbalizing about the visual: Visual analysis tools for design evaluation and group communication.* Paper presented at the annual meeting of the Society for Technical Communication, Washington, DC.

Keyes, J. (1995). *Solving the productivity paradox: TQM for computer professionals.* New York: McGraw-Hill.

Kidwell, P. A., & Ceruzzi, P. E. (1994). *Landmarks in digital computing: A pictorial history.* Washington, DC: Smithsonian Institution.

Kieras, D. E. (1985). *The role of prior knowledge in operating equipment from written instructions* (Tech. Rep. No. 19). Ann Arbor, MI: University of Michigan.

Kieras, D. E., & Bovair, S. (1984). The role of a mental model in learning to operate a device. *Cognitive Science, 8,* 255–273. (Original article published as Tech. Rep. No. 13 UARZ/DP/TR-83/ONR-13, University of Arizona)

Killingsworth, M. J., & Palmer, J. S. (1992). *Ecospeak: Rhetoric and environmental politics in America.* Carbondale, IL: Southern Illinois University Press.

Kimball, J. P. (1973). Seven principles of surface structure parsing in natural language. *Cognition, 2,* 15–47.

Kimble, J. (1992). Plain English: A charter for clear writing. *Thomas M. Cooley Law Review, 9*(1), 1–58.

Kinneavy, J. L. (1983). Contemporary rhetoric. In W. B. Horner (Ed.), *The present state of scholarship in historical and contemporary rhetoric* (pp. 167–213). Columbia, MO: University of Missouri Press.

Kinross, R. (1989). The rhetoric of neutrality. In V. Margolin (Ed.), *Design discourse: History, theory, criticism* (pp. 131–143). Chicago: University of Chicago Press.

Kinross, R. (1992). *Modern typography: An essay in critical theory.* London: Hyphen Press.

Kintsch, W. (1990, January). *How readers construct situation models for stories: The role of syntactic cues and causal inferences.* Paper presented at the First Winter Text Conference, Jackson Hole, WY.

Kintsch, W., & Dijk, T. A., van (1978). Toward a model of text comprehension and production. *Psychological Review, 85,* 363–394.

Kirkman, J. (1992). CNAA courses in technical communication. *The Communicator*(3.7/8), 1–6.

Kirsch, I. S., & Mosenthal, P. B. (1990). Exploring document literacy: Variables underlying the performance of young adults. *Reading Research Quarterly, 25*(1), 5–30.

Kitagawa, M. M., & Kitagawa, C. (1987). *Making connections with writing: An expressive writing model in Japanese schools.* Portsmouth, NH: Heinemann.

Kitzhaber, A. (1953). *Rhetoric in American colleges, 1850–1900.* Unpublished doctoral dissertation. Seattle, WA: University of Washington.

Klare, G. R. (1963). *The measurement of readability.* Ames, IA: Iowa State University Press.

Klare, G. R. (1974). Assessing readability. *Reading Research Quarterly, 10* (1), 61–102.

Klare, G. R. (1976). Judging readability. *Instructional Science, 5* (1), 55–61.

Klare, G. R. (1984). Readability. In P. D. Pearson (Ed.), *Handbook of reading research* (pp. 681–744). New York: Longman.

Klaus, C. (1976). Public opinion and professional belief. *College Composition and Communication, 27,* 335–339.

Kleinman, P. (1989). *Saatchi & Saatchi: The inside story*. Lincolnwood, IL: NTC Business Books.

Kniffin, J. D. (1979). The new readability requirements for military technical manuals. *Technical Communication, 26*, 16–19.

Koffka, K. (1935). *Principles of Gestalt psychology*. New York: Harcourt, Brace and Company.

Köhler, W. (1947). *Gestalt psychology*. New York: Liveright.

Kolers, P. A., Wrolstad, M. E., & Bouma, H. (1979). *Processing of visible language: Vol. 1*. New York: Plenum Press.

Kolers, P. A., Wrolstad, M. E., & Bouma, H. (Eds.). (1980). *Processing of visible language: Vol. 2*. New York: Plenum Press.

Kolln, M. (1996). *Rhetorical grammar (2nd ed.)*. New York: Macmillan.

Kosslyn, S. M. (1994). *Elements of graph design*. New York: W. H. Freeman.

Kostelnick, C. (1994). From pen to print: The new visual landscape of professional communication. *Journal of Business and Technical Communication, 8* (1), 91–117.

Kostelnick, C. (1996). Supra-textual design: The visual rhetoric of whole documents. *Technical Communication Quarterly, 5* (1), 9–33.

Kotovsky, K., Hayes, J. R., & Simon, H. A. (1985). Why are some problems hard? Evidence from the Tower of Hanoi. *Cognitive Psychology, 17* (2), 248–294.

Kramer, R., & Bernhardt, S. A. (1996). Teaching text design. *Technical Communication Quarterly, 5*(1), 35–60.

Kreppel, M. C. (1995). Wanted: Tenure and promotion for technical communication faculty. *Technical Communication, 42* (4), 603–606.

Krueger, R. A. (1988). *Focus groups: A practical guide for applied research*. Newbury Park, CA: Sage.

Kurzweil, R. (1990). The age of intelligent machines. Cambridge, MA: MIT Press.

LaBerge, D., & Samuels, S. J. (1974). Toward a theory of automatic information processing in reading. *Cognitive Psychology, 6*, 293-323.

Landauer, T. K. (1995). *The trouble with computers: Usefulness, usability, and productivity*. Cambridge, MA: MIT Press.

Lanham, R. A. (1992). *Revising business prose*. New York: Macmillan

Lannon, J. M. (1985). *Technical writing* (3rd ed.). Boston: Little, Brown.

Larkin, J. H., & Simon, H. A. (1987). Why a diagram is (sometimes) worth ten thousand words. *Cognitive Science, 11*, 65–99.

Larson, M. S. (1977). *The rise of professionalism: a social analysis*. Berkeley: University of California Press.

Lauer, J. M., Montague, G., Lunsford, A. A., & Emig, J. (1985). *The four worlds of writing* (2nd ed.). New York: Harper & Row.

Legenza, A., & Knafle, J. D. (1978). *The effective components of children's pictures* (ERIC ED No. 165 134). Alexandria, VA: ERIC Clearinghouse.

Leinhardt, G., Zaslavsky, O., & Stein, M. K. (1990). Functions, graphs, and graphing: Tasks, learning and teaching. *Review of Educational Research, 60* (1), 1–64.

Lentz, L., & de Jong, M. (1995). *The evaluation of text quality: Expert-focused and reader-focused compared*. (Working Paper). Utrecht and Enschede, Netherlands: Utrecht University, Centre for Language and Communication, and Twente University.

Lentz, L., & Pander Maat, H. (1992). Evaluating text quality: Reader-focused or text-focused? In H. Pander Maat & M. Steehouder (Eds.), Studies of functional text quality (pp. 101–114). Amsterdam: Rodopi Press.

Levie, W. H., & Lentz, R. (1982). Effects of text illustrations: A review of research. *Educational Communication and Technology Journal, 30* , 185–232.

Levin, J. R., Anglin, G. J., & Carney, R. N. (1987). On empirically validating functions of pictures in prose. In D. M. Willows & H. A. Houghton (Eds.), *The psychology of illustration: Vol. 1. Basic research* (pp. 51–85). New York: Springer-Verlag.

Levy, R. (1990). Design education: Time to reflect. *Design Issues: History, Theory, Criticism, 7* (1), 42–52.

Linder, S. (1970). *The harried leisure class*. New York: Columbia University Press.

Lively, B. A., & Pressey, S. L. (1923). A method for measuring the 'vocabulary burden' of textbooks. *Educational Administration and Supervision, 9*, 389–398.

Livingston, A., & Livingston, I. (1992). *The Thames and Hudson encyclopedia of graphic design and designers*. London: Thames and Hudson.

Lönberg-Holm, K., & Sutnar, L. (1944). *Catalog design: New patterns in product information*. New York: Sweet's Catalog Service.

Lönberg-Holm, K., & Sutnar, L. (1950). *Catalog design progress: Advancing standards in visual communication*. New York: Sweet's Catalog Service.

Long, R. C. (1980). Writer-audience relationships: Analysis or invention? *College Composition and Communication, 31*, 221–226.

Long, R. C. (1990). The writer's audience: Fact or fiction? In G. Kirsch & D. H. Roen (Eds.), *A sense of audience in written communication* (pp. 73–84). Newbury Park, CA: Sage.

Luke, C., de Castell, S., & Luke, A. (1983). Beyond criticism: The authority of the school text. *Curriculum Inquiry, 13*, 111–127.

Lundgren, R. (1994). *Risk communication: A handbook for communicating environmental, safety, and health risks*. Columbus, OH: Battelle Press.

Lunsford, A. A., & Ede, L. S. (1996). Representing audience: "Successful" discourse and disciplinary critique. *College Composition and Communication, 47* (2), 167–179.

Macdonald, N. H., Frase, L. T., Gingrich, P. S., & Keenan, S. A. (1982). The writer's workbench: Computer aids for text analysis. *Educational Psychologist, 17*(3), 172–179.

Macdonald-Ross, M., & Waller, R. H. W. (1975). Criticisms, alternatives, and tests: A framework for improving typography. *Programmed Learning and Educational Technology, 12*, 75–83.

MacDonald-Ross, M. (1977a). Graphics in text. In L. S. Shulman (Ed.), *Review of research in education* (pp. 49–85). Itasca, IL: F. E. Peacock.

MacDonald-Ross, M. (1977b). How numbers are shown: A review of research on the presentation of quantitative data in texts. *A.V. Communication Review, Winter*, 359–409.

Macrorie, K. (1978). *Telling writing*. Rochelle Park, NJ: Hayden.

Mansnerus, L. (1996, September 15). Don't Smoke. Please. Pretty please. *New York Times*, p. E–5.

Marchand, R. (1990). A review of John Heskett's book *Phillips: A study of the corporate management of design*. *Design Issues: History, Theory, Criticism, 7*(1), 83–84.

Marcus, M. P. (1980). A theory of syntactic recognition for natural language. Cambridge, MA: MIT Press.

Margolin, V. (1989a). Introduction. In V. Margolin (Ed.), Design discourse: History, theory, criticism (pp. 3–28). Chicago, IL: University of Chicago Press.

Margolin, V. (1989b). Postwar design literature: A preliminary mapping. In V. Margolin (Ed.), *Design discourse: History, theory, criticism* (pp. 265–287). Chicago, IL: University of Chicago Press.

Matchett, M., & Ray, M. L. (1989). Revising IRS publications: A case study. *Technical Communication, 36*(4), 332–340.

Mathes, J. C., & Stevenson, D. W. (1976). *Designing technical reports: Writing for audiences in organizations*. Indianapolis, IN: Bobbs-Merrill.

Mayer, R. E., & Sims, V. (1994). For whom is a picture worth a thousand words? Extensions of dual-coding theory of multimedia learning. *Educational Psychology, 86* (3), 389–401.

Mayer, R. N. (1989). *The consumer movement: Guardians of the marketplace*. Boston: Twayne Pub. of G.K. Hall & Company.

Maynes, E. S. (1976). *Decision making for consumers*. New York: Macmillan.

McCormick, K. A. (1994). *The culture of reading and the teaching of English*. New York: St. Martin's Press for Manchester University Press.

McCoy, K. (1990). Professional design education: An opinion and a proposal. *Design Issues: History, Theory, Criticism, 7* (1), 20–22.

McKee, J. H. (1936). Portrait of a department. *English Journal, 25*, 752–759.

McVey, G. (1985). Legibility in film-based and television display systems. Technical Communication, 32 (3), 21–28.

Meggs, P. B. (1983). *The history of graphic design*. New York: Van Nostrand Reinhold.

Meggs, P. B. (1992a). *Type & image: The language of graphic design*. New York: Van Nostrand Reinhold.

Meggs, P. B. (1992b). *The history of graphic design* (2nd ed.). New York: Van Nostrand Reinhold.

Meij, H., van der. (1994). Catching the user in the act. In M. Steehouder, C. J. M. Jansen, P. van der Poort, & R. Verheijen (Eds.), *Quality of technical documentation* (pp. 201–210). Amsterdam, Netherlands: Rodopi Press.

Millar, H. (1996, August). The electronic scriptorium. *Wired,4* (8) pp. 94-104.

Miller, C. R. (1979). A humanistic rationale for technical writing. *College English, 40*(6), 610–617.

Miller, C. R. (1984). Genre as social action. *Quarterly Journal of Speech, 70*, 151–167.

Miller, C. R. (1985). Invention in technical and scientific discourse: A prospective survey. In M. G. Moran & D. Journet (Eds.), *Research on technical communication* (pp. 117–162). Westport, CT: Greenwood Press.

Miller, C. R. (1989). What's practical about technical writing? In B. E. Fearing & W. K. Sparrow (Eds.), *Technical writing: theory and practice* (pp. 14–24). New York: Modern Language Association.

Miller, G. A. (1956). The magic number seven, plus or minus two: Some limits on our capacity for processing information. *Psychological Review, 63*, 81–97.

Miller, J. (1978). *Writing and reality*. New York: Harper & Row.

Miller, S. (1991). *Textual carnivals: The politics of composition*. Carbondale, IL: Southern Illinois University Press.

Mills, G. H., & Walter, J. A. (1954). *Technical writing*. New York: Holt.

Milroy, R., & Poulton, E. C. (1978). Labeling graphs for improved reading speed. *Ergonomics, 21*, 55-61.

Minsky, M. (1995, January 15). *Future quest: The information superhighway* [Television program]. New York and Washington, DC: Public Broadcasting Service.

Mintzberg, H. (1975, July/August). The manager's job: Folklore and fact. *Harvard Business Review*, 54–59.

Mirel, B. (1989). The politics of usability: The organizational functions of an in-house manual. In S. Doheny-Farina (Ed.), *Effective documentation: What we have learned from research* (pp. 277–297). Cambridge, MA: MIT Press.

Mitchell, J. H. (1989). Reminiscences: A personal history of the STC—The more things stay the same. *Technical Communication, 36* (4), 418–419.

Moholy-Nagy, L. (1947). *Vision in motion*. Chicago, IL: Paul Theobald.

Moll, L. C. & Greenberg, J. (1993). Creating zones of possibilities: Combining social contexts for instruction. In L. C. Moll (Ed.), *Vygotsky and education: Instructional implications and applications of sociohistorical psychology* (pp. 319–348). New York: Cambridge University Press.

Moore, P., & Fitz, C. (1993a). Gestalt theory and instructional design. *Journal of Technical Writing and Communication, 23* (2), 137–157.

Moore, P., & Fitz, C. (1993b). Using Gestalt theory to teach document design and graphics. *Technical Communication Quarterly, 2* (4), 389–410.

Moran, M. G., & Journet, D. (Eds.). (1985). *Research in technical communication: A bibliographic sourcebook*. Westport, CT: Greenwood Press.

Morris, C. W. (1938). *Foundations of the theory of signs*. Chicago, IL: University of Chicago Press.

Moss, W. (1987). The plain English campaign: An interview. *Research and Practice in Adult Literacy (RaPAL) Bulletin No. 4*, pp. 1–6.

Müller-Brockmann, J. (1985). *Grid systems in graphic design* (Revised ed.). New York: Hastings House.

Mullet, K., & Sano, D. (1995). *Designing visual interfaces: Communication oriented techniques*. Mountain View, CA: SunSoft Press.

Muter, P., Latremouille, S. A., Treurniet, W. C., & Beam, P. (1982). Extended reading of texts on television screens. *Human Factors, 21*, 529–540.

Nader, R. (1993, June 21). *CNBC Late Night News* [Television program]. New York: Consumer News and Business Channel.

Nakamura, R. L. (1990, November 19). The X Factor. *InfoWorld*, pp. 51–55.

Neel, J. (1988). *Plato, Derrida, and writing*. Carbondale, IL: Southern Illinois University Press.

Nelson, D. (1974). Scientific management, systematic management, and labor, 1880–1915. *Business History Review, 48*, 479–500.

Nelson, J. R. (1931). English, engineering and technical schools. *English Journal, 20*, 495.

Nelson, J. R. (1940). *Writing the technical report* (2nd ed.). New York: McGraw-Hill.

Neurath, O. (1974). Isotype. *Instructional Science, 3*, 127-150.

New York Times. (1977, February 6). As per paragraph (i) (2) (ii) (B) or (D). *New York Times*, p. 14E.

New York Times. (1982, December 26). Some plain-speaking Britons get last word on gibberish. *New York Times*, p. 12L.

Newell, A., & Simon, H. A. (1972). *Human problem solving*. Englewood Cliffs, NJ: Prentice-Hall.

Newsweek. (1996, March 4). Now you see 'em, now you don't. *Newsweek*, p. 55.

Nickerson, R. S. (1968). A note on long-term recognition memory for pictorial material. *Psychonomic Science, 11*, 58.

Nielsen, J., & Mack, R. L. (Eds.). (1994). *Usability inspection methods*. New York: John Wiley & Sons.

Nilsson, J. D. (1990). Reminiscences: A personal history of the STC—Huntsville, Alabama history. *Technical Communication, 37* (1), 91–93.

Noble, D. F. (1977). *America by design: Science, technology, and the rise of corporate capitalism*. New York: Oxford University Press.

Norman, D. A. (1988). *The psychology of everyday things*. New York: Basic Books.

Norman, D. A., & Draper, S. W. (Eds.). (1986). *User centered system design*. Hillsdale, NJ: Lawrence Erlbaum.

North, S. M. (1987). *The making of knowledge in composition: Portrait of an emerging field*. Upper Montclair, NJ: Boynton/Cook.

Nussbaum, B., & Neff, R. (1991, April 29). I can't work this thing: Frustrated by high tech? Designers are getting the message. *BusinessWeek*, pp. 58–66.

Nystrand, M. (1986). *The structure of written communication: Studies in reciprocity between writers and readers*. New York: Academic Press.

O'Connell, J. (1971). *The injury industry and the remedy of no-fault insurance*. Champaign-Urbana, IL: University of Illinois Press.

O'Hara, F. M. (1989). Trends in STC. *Technical Communication, 36*(4), 91–93.

O'Keefe, D. (1990). *Persuasion: Theory and research*. Newbury, CA: Sage Publications.

Odell, L., & Goswami, D. (1982). Writing in a non-academic setting. *Research in the Teaching of English, 16*(3), 201–223.

Odell, L., & Goswami, D. (Eds.). (1985). *Writing in nonacademic settings*. New York: Guilford Press.

Ong, W. (1975). The writer's audience is always a fiction. *PMLA, 90*, 6–21.

Orman, F. (1918). *A vital need of the times*. New York: F. Orman.

Ornatowski, C. M. (1992). Between efficiency and politics: Rhetoric and ethics in technical writing. *Technical Communication Quarterly, 1*(1), 91–103.

Osborne, D. J., & Holton, D. (1988). Reading from screen versus paper: There is no difference? *International Journal of Man-Machine Studies, 28* (1), 1–9.

Ovink, G. W. (1965). 100 years of book typography in the Netherlands. In K. Day (Ed.), *Book typography* (pp. 230–271). Chicago: University of Chicago Press.

Paine, A. B. (1912). *Mark Twain, a biography: The personal and literary life of Samuel Langhorne Clemens*. New York: Harper & Row.

Paivio, A. (1969). Research at the Children's Television Workshop. *Educational Broadcasting Review, 3* , 43–48.

Paivio, A. (1990). *Mental representations: A dual coding approach*. New York: Oxford University Press.

Palmer, G. (1912). Culture and efficiency through composition. *English Journal, 1*, 488.

Palmer, R. (1995). *Rock & roll: An unruly history*. New York: Harmony Books.

Paradis, J., Dobrin, D. N., & Miller, R. (1985). Writing at Exxon ITD: Notes on the writing environment of an R & D organization. In L. Odell & D. Goswami (Eds.), *Writing in nonacademic settings* (pp. 281–307). New York: Guilford Press.

Pardoe, A. O. (1990). Reminiscences: A personal history of the STC—An artist remembers. *Technical Communication, 37* (2), 188–190.

Park, D. (1982). The meanings of 'audience'. *College English, 44*, 247–257.

Parker, W. R. (1988). Where do English departments come from? In G. Tate & E. P. J. Corbett (Eds.), *The writing teacher's sourcebook* (pp. 3–15). New York: Oxford University Press. (Original article published in 1967, *College English, 28,* 339–351)

Paterson, D. G., & Tinker, M. A. (1932). Studies of typographical factors influencing speed of reading: VIII. Space between lines or leading. *Journal of Applied Psychology, 16*(August), 388–397.

Paterson, D. G., & Tinker, M. A. (1940). Influence of line width on eye movements. *Journal of Experimental Psychology, 27*(November), 572–577.

Paterson, D. G., & Tinker, M. A. (1942). Influence of line width on eye movements for six point type. *Journal of Educational Psychology, 33*(October), 552–555.

Paterson, D. G., & Tinker, M. A. (1946). Readability of newspaper headlines printed in capitals and lower case. *Journal of Applied Psychology, 30*(April), 161–168.

Patton, P. (1993, May/June). The big book: Put out to pasture. *I.D.*, pp. 21–22.

PC Magazine. (1988). Users survey. *PC Magazine*, pp. 40–41.

Pearsall, T. E. (1969). *Audience analysis for technical writing*. Beverly Hills, CA: Glencoe.

Pearsall, T. E., & Sullivan, F. (1976). *Academic programs in technical communication*. Washington, DC: Society for Technical Communication.

Pearsall, T. E., Sullivan, F., & McDowell, E. (1981). *Academic programs in technical communication* (2nd ed.). Washington, DC: Society for Technical Communication.

Peeck, J. (1987). The role of illustrations in processing and remembering illustrated text. In D. M. Willows & H. A. Houghton (Eds.), *The psychology of illustration: Vol. 1. Basic research* (pp. 115-151). New York: Springer-Verlag.

Peirce, C. S. (1934). *Collected papers of Charles Saunders Peirce. Vol. 5* C. Hartshorne & P. Weiss, (Eds.). Cambridge, MA: Harvard University Press.

Penman, R. (1985). What's wrong with plain English? *Communication News, 5*(2), 4.

Penman, R. (1990). *Comprehensible insurance documents: Plain English isn't good enough* (Occasional Paper No. 14). Canberra, Australia: Communications Research Institute of Australia.

Penman, R. (1993). Unspeakable acts. *Information Design Journal, 7*(2), 121–131.

Perelman, C., & Olbrechts-Tyteca, L. (1969). *The new rhetoric: A treatise on argumentation* (J. Wilkinson & P. Weaver, Trans.). Notre Dame, IL: University of Notre Dame Press.

Perfetti, C. A., & Roth, S. F. (1981). Some of the interactive processes in reading and their role in reading skill. In A. M. Lesgold & C. A. Perfetti (Eds.), *Interactive processes in reading* (pp. 269–297). Hillsdale, NJ: Lawrence Erlbaum.

Petroski, H. (1993). *The pencil: A history of design and circumstance* (3rd ed.). New York: Alfred A. Knopf.

Philipchalk, R. P. (1972). Thematicity, abstractness, and the long-term recall of connected discourse. *Psychonomic Science, 27,* 361–362.

Phillips, R. A. (1979). Making maps easy to read–A summary of research. In P. A. Kolers, M. E. Wrolstad, & H. Bouma (Eds.), *Processing of visible language* (pp. 165–174). New York: Plenum Press.

Pinelli, T. E., Cordle, V. M., & McCullough, R. (1986). A survey of typography, graphic design, and physical media in technical reports. *Technical Communication, 33,* 75–80.

Pinelli, T. E., Glassman, M., & Cordle, V. M. (1982). *Survey of reader preferences concerning the format of NASA technical reports* (NASA TM-No. 84502). National Aeronautics and Space Administration: Washington, DC.

Porter, T., & Goodman, S. (1988). *Designer primer: For architects, graphic designers, and artists*. New York: Charles Scribner's Sons.

Poulton, E. C. (1955, April). Letter differentiation and rate of comprehension of reading. *Journal of Applied Psychology, 49,* 358–362.

Poulton, E. C. (1967). Searching for newspaper headlines printed in capitals of lowercase letters. *Journal of Applied Psychology, 51,* 417–425.

Prelli, L. J. (1991). *A rhetoric of science: Inventing scientific discourse*. Columbia, SC: University of South Carolina Press.

Presidential Commission. (1905–1913). *Records of the President's commision on economy and efficiency, 1905–1913* (Record Group No. 51). Washington, DC: Bureau of the Budget, National Archives Building.

Printers' Ink. (1939, July 14). Sicken 'em; sell 'em. *Printers' Ink*, pp. 21–22.

Purvis, A. W. (1992). *Dutch graphic design, 1918–1945*. New York: Van Nostrand Reinhold.

Pyke, R. K. (1926). Report on the legibility of print (Special Rep. Series No. 110). London: Medical Research Council.

Rainey, K. T., & Kelly, R. S. (1992). Doctoral research in technical communication, 1965–1990. *Technical Communication, 39* (4), 552–570.

Ramey, J. (1995a). User's guide to the literature of usability testing: A selected bibliography. In C. Velotta (Ed.), *Practical approaches to usabilty testing for technical documentation* (pp. 89–105). Arlington, VA: Society for Technical Communication.

Ramey, J. (1995b). What technical communicators think about measuring value added: Report on a questionnaire. *Technical Communication, 42* (1), 40–51.

Rand, P. (1993). *Design form and chaos*. New Haven, CN: Yale University Press.

Rand, P. (1993, May 2). Failure by design. *New York Times*, p. E19.

Raven, M. E., & Flanders, A. (1996). Using contextual inquiry to learn about your audiences. *The Journal of Computer Documentation, 20* (1), 1–27.

Redish, J. C. (1985). The plain English movement. In S. Greenbaum (Ed.), *The English language today* (pp. 125–138). New York: Pergamon Press.

Redish, J. C. (1989). Reading to learn to do. *IEEE Transactions on Professional Communication, 32*(4), 289–293.

Redish, J. C. (1993). Understanding readers. In C. M. Barnum & S. Carliner (Eds.), *Techniques for technical communicators* (pp. 14–41). New York: Macmillan.

Redish, J. C. (1995). Adding value as a professional technical communicator. *Technical Communication, 42*(1), 27–39.

Redish, J. C., & Selzer, J. (1985). The place of readability formulas in technical communication. *Technical Communication, 32*(4), 46–52.

Rehe, R. F. (1974). Typography: *How to make it most legible*. Carmel, IN: Design Research International.

Rettig, M. (1991, July). Nobody reads documentation. *Communications of the Association for Computing Machinery (ACM), 34* (7), pp. 19–24.

Reynolds, J. F., Matalene, C. B., Magnotto, J. N., Samson, D. C., Jr., & Sadler, L. V. (1995). *Professional writing in context: Lessons from teaching and consulting in the worlds of work*. Hillsdale, NJ: Lawrence Erlbaum.

Reynolds, L., & Simmonds, D. (1981). *Presentation of data in science*. Amsterdam: Martinus Nijhoff.

Rhodes-Marriott, T. (1990). Reminiscences: A personal history of the STC—Reflecting on STC in Canada. *Technical Communication, 37* (3), 303–305.

Richards, I. A. (1936). *The philosophy of rhetoric*. New York: Oxford University Press.

Rickards, E. C., & August, G. J. (1975). Generative underlining strategies in prose recall. *Journal of Educational Psychology, 67*, 860–865.

Rivers, W. E. (1994). Studies in the history of business and technical writing: A bibliographical essay. *Journal of Business and Technical Writing, 8* (1), 6–57.

Robinson, D. O., Abbamonte, M., & Evans, S. H. (1971). Why serifs are important: The perception of small print. *Visible Language, 4*, 353–359.

Rogers, M. (1991, January 7). The right button: Why machines are getting harder and harder to use. *Newsweek*, pp. 46–47.

Rosenblatt, L. (1978). *The reader, the text, the poem: The transactional theory of the literary work*. Carbondale, IL: Southern Illinois University Press.

Roth, R. (1977). The evolving audience: Alternatives to audience accommodation. *College Composition and Communication, 38*, 47–55.

Rubens, P. M. (1985). Technical and scientific writing and the humanities. In M. G. Moran & D. Journet (Eds.), *Research in technical communication: A bibliographic sourcebook* (pp. 3–23). Westport, CT: Greenwood Press.

Rubin, E. J. (1921). *Visuell wahrgenommene figuren: Studien in psychologischer Analyse (pt. 1)*. Copenhagen: Gylendal (original work published 1915)

Rubin, J. (1994). *Handbook of usability testing: How to plan, design, and conduct effective tests*. New York: John Wiley & Sons.

Ruder, E. (1982). *Typographie* (4th ed.). Niederteufen, Germany: A. Niggli.

Rüegg, R. (1989). *Basic typography: Design with letters*. New York: Van Nostrand Reinhold.

Rumelhart, D. E. (1977). Toward an interactive model of reading. In S. Dornic (Ed.) *Attention and performance (Vol. 6*, pp. 573–603). Hillsdale, NJ: Lawrence Erlbaum.

Rumelhart, D. E., & McClelland, J. L. (1981). Interactive processing through spreading activation. In A. M. Lesgold & C. A. Perfetti (Eds.), *Interactive processes in reading* (pp. 37–60). Hillsdale, NJ: Lawrence Erlbaum.

Russell, D. R. (1991). *Writing in the academic disciplines: 1870–1990*. Carbondale, IL: Southern Illinois University Press.

Sageev, P. (1994). *Helping researchers write so managers can understand*. Columbus, OH: Battelle Press.

Sanders, T. (1992). *Discourse structure and coherence: Aspects of a cognitive theory of discourse representation*. Published doctoral dissertation, Tilburg University, Netherlands.

Sauer, B. A. (1996). Communicating risk in a cross-cultural context: A cross cultural comparison of rhetorical and social understandings in U.S. and British mine safety training programs. *Journal of Business and Technical Communication, 10*(3), 306–329.

Scardamalia, M., & Bereiter, C. (1983). The development of evaluative, diagnostic, and remedial capabilities in children's composing. In M. Matlew (Ed.), *The psychology of written language: A developmental approach* (pp. 67–95). London: John Wiley & Sons.

Schilb, J. (1989). Composition and poststructuralism: A tale of two conferences. *College Composition and Communication, 40*, 422–443.

Schmandt, C. (1987). Color text display in video media. In *Color and the Computer* (pp. 255–266). Boston, MA: Academic Press.

Schriver, K. A. (1984). *Revising computer documentation for comprehension: Ten exercises in protocol-aided revision* (Tech. Rep. No. 14). Pittsburgh, PA: Carnegie Mellon University, Communications Design Center.

Schriver, K. A. (1987). *Teaching writers to anticipate the reader's needs: Empirically-based instruction*. Unpublished doctoral dissertation, Carnegie Mellon University, Pittsburgh, PA.

Schriver, K. A. (1989a). Evaluating text quality: The continuum from text-focused to reader-focused methods. *IEEE Transactions in Professional Communication, 32*(4), 238–255.

Schriver, K. A. (1989b). Document design from 1980 to 1989: Challenges that remain. *Technical Communication, 36*(4), 316–331.

Schriver, K. A. (1989c). *Writing for expert or lay audiences: Designing text using protocol-aided revision* (Tech. Rep. No. 43). Pittsburgh, PA: Carnegie Mellon University, Communications Design Center.

Schriver, K. A. (1991a). Plain language through protocol-aided revision. In E. R. Steinberg (Ed.), *Plain language: Principles and practice* (pp. 148–172). Detroit, MI: Wayne State University Press.

Schriver, K. A. (1992a). Teaching writers to anticipate readers' needs: What can document designers learn from usability testing? In H. Pander Maat & M. Steehouder (Eds.), *Studies of functional text quality* (pp. 141–157). Amsterdam: Rodopi Press.

Schriver, K. A. (1992b). Teaching writers to anticipate readers' needs: A classroom-evaluated pedagogy. *Written Communication, 9*(2), 179–208.

Schriver, K. A. (1993a). Quality in document design: Issues and controversies. *Technical Communication, 40*(2), 239–257.

Schriver, K. A. (1993b). Revising for readers: Audience awareness in the writing classroom. In A. M. Penrose & B. M. Sitko (Eds.), *Hearing ourselves think: Cognitive research in the writing classroom* (pp. 147–169). New York: Oxford University Press.

Schriver, K. A. (1995, June 13). *Document design as rhetorical action*. Belle van Zuylen Professor Oratory Series. Utrecht, Netherlands: University of Utrecht (Available from Faculteitsbureau, Kromme Nieuwegracht 46, 3512 HJ, Utrecht, NL).

Schriver, K. A., Hayes, J. R., & Steffy Cronin, A. (1996). *"Just say no to drugs" and other unwelcome advice: Exploring the creation and interpretation of drug education literature* (Final Rep.). University of California at Berkeley and Carnegie Mellon University, National Center for the Study of Writing and Literacy: Berkeley and Pittsburgh, PA.

Schriver, K. A., Hayes, J. R., Danley, C., Wulff, W., Davies, L., Cerroni, K., Graham, D., Flood, E., & Bond, E. (1986). *Designing computer documentation: A review of the literature—hardcopy, online, general applications* (Tech. Rep. No. 31). Pittsburgh, PA: Carnegie Mellon University, Communications Design Center.

Schrodt, P. (1982, April). The generic word processor. *Byte*, pp. 32, 34, 36.

Schroeder, J. J. (1970). Introduction. In J. J. Schroeder (Ed.), *The miniature reproduction of the Sears, Roebuck & Company 1900 catalog* (pp. iii–v). Northfield, IL: DBI Books.

Schuler, D., & Namioka, A. (Eds.). (1993). *Participatory design: Principles and practices.* Hillsdale, NJ: Lawrence Erlbaum.

Schumacher, G. M., & Waller, R. (1985). Testing design alternatives: A comparison of procedures. In T. M. Duffy & R. H. W. Waller (Eds.), *Designing usable texts* (pp. 377–403). New York: Academic Press.

Schutte, W. M., & Steinberg, E. R. (1983). *Communication in business and industry*. New York: Holt, Rinehart, & Winston.

Schutz, H. G. (1961). An evaluation of methods for presentation of graphic multiple trends—Experiment III. *Human Factors, 31*, 108–119.

Scott, F. N. (1901, June). College-entrance requirements in English. *School Review, 9*, 365–378.

Scott, F. N. (1922). English composition as a mode of behavior. *English Journal, 11*, 467–472.

Scott, W. D. (1908). *The psychology of advertising*. Boston: Small, Maynard.

Seely Brown, J. S., Collins, A., & Duguid, P. (1989). Situated cognition and the culture of learning. *Educational Researcher, 18*(1), 32–42.

Selber, S. A. (1994). Beyond skill building: Challenges facing technical communication teachers in the computer age. Technical Communication Quarterly, 3 (4), 365–390.

Selzer, J. (1992). More meanings of audience. In S. P. Witte, N. Nakadate, & R. D. Cherry (Eds.), *A rhetoric of doing* (pp. 161–177). Carbondale, IL and Edwardsville, IL: Southern Illinois University Press.

Shannon, C. E., & Weaver, W. (1948). A mathematical theory of communication. *Bell System Technical Journal, 27*, 379–423, 622–656.

Shannon, C. E., & Weaver, W. (1949). *The mathematical theory of communication*. Urbana, IL: University of Illinois Press.

Shaw, A. (1968). Print for poor vision readers. *The Penrose Annual, 61*, 92–101.

Shaw, A. (1969). *Print for partial sight*. London, UK: The Library Association.

Shelley, P. B. (1991). A defense of poetry. In A. D. F. Macrae (Ed.), *Selected poetry and prose*. London: Routledge and Kegan Paul (previously published 1821)

Shepard, R. N. (1967). Recognition memory for words, sentences, and pictures. *Journal of Verbal Learning and Verbal Behavior, 6*, 156–163.

Shimberg, H. L. (1989). Reminiscences: A personal history of the STC—The Washington chapter: Genesis and growth. *Technical Communication, 36* (3), 264–267.

Shirk, H. N. (1988). Technical writers as computer scientists: The challenges of online documentation. In *Text, context, and hypertext: Writing with and for the computer* (pp. 311–327). Cambridge, MA: MIT Press.

Shneiderman, B. (1987). *Designing the user interface*. Reading, MA: Addison-Wesley.

Shrage, M. (1990, October 22). It's them—Those people with voice mail. *San Jose Mercury News,* p. C–4.

Shulman, J. J. (1960). The anonymous technical writer in history. *STWP Review, 7*, 22–26.

Shushan, R., & Wright, R., & Lewis, L. (1996). *Desktop publishing by design: Everyone's guide to Pagemaker 6* (4th ed.). Redmond, WA: Microsoft Press.

Simon, H. A. (1981). *The sciences of the artificial* (2nd ed.). Cambridge, MA: MIT Press.

Sims-Knight, J. E. (1992). To picture or not to picture: How to decide. *Visible Language, 26* (3/4), 324–387.

Sinclair, U. (1906). *The jungle*. New York: Doubleday.

Smillie, R. J. (1985). Design strategies for job performance aids. In T. M. Duffy & R. H. W. Waller (Eds.), Designing usable texts (pp. 213–243). New York: Academic Press.

Smith, B. (1979). Design history and the visual language of design. *Information Design Journal, 1*(1), 23–32.

Smith, F. R. (1988). The challenges we face. *Technical Communication, 35*(2), 84–88.

Smith, H. J. (1989). From caveat emptor to caveat venditor: Some legal concerns for technical communicators. In *Proceedings of the International Technical Communication Conference* (pp. MG-49–MG-52). Washington, DC: Society for Technical Communication.

Smith, J. (1990, June 17). Expertise at CMU helping Japanese with write stuff. *Los Angeles Times Magazine,* p. 6.

Smith, J. M., & McCombs, E. (1971). The graphics of prose. *Visible Language, 4*(Autumn), 365–369.

STC Manitoba, STC Alberta, & STC West Coast. (1994a). *Study and report on current and desirable standards for technical communication in western Canada.* Winnipeg, Manitoba: Society for Technical Communication Canada and Western Economic Diversification Canada. (Available from STC-Manitoba, 135 Lawndale Ave., Winnipeg, MB R2H1T2).

STC Manitoba, STC Alberta, & STC West Coast. (1994b). *Understanding the western Canadian market for technical communication services.* Winnipeg, Manitoba: Society for Technical Communication Canada and Western Economic Diversification Canada.

Society for Technical Communication. (1993). Introduction. *Technical Communication Special Edition, 1.40*(3–A), 2.

Society of Typographic Arts. (1987). *Herman Zapf and his design philosophy.* Chicago, IL: Society of Typographic Arts.

Soltow, W. A. (1993, Spring). What's wrong with this picture? *HSUS News,* pp. 6-8.

Southard, S. G. & Reeves, R. (1995). Tough questions and straight answers: Educating technical communicators in the next decade. *Technical Communication, 42* (4), 555–565.

Souther, J. W. (1957). *Technical report writing* (1st ed.). New York: John Wiley & Sons.

Souther, J. W. (1963). Design that report! In H. A. Estrin (Ed.), *Technical and professional writing* (pp. 225–229). New York: Harcourt, Brace and World.

Souther, J. W. (1989). Teaching technical writing: A retrospective appraisal. In B. E. Fearing & W. K. Sparrow (Eds.), *Technical writing: Theory and practice* (pp. 2–13). New York: Modern Language Association.

Spencer, H., Reynolds, L., & Coe, B. (1974). Typographic coding in lists and bibliographies. *Applied Ergonomics, 5,* 136–141.

Spencer, H., Reynolds, L., & Coe, B. (1975). Spatial and typographic coding within bibliographical entries. *Programmed learning and educational technology, 12,* 95–101.

Spencer, R. H. (1985). Computer usability testing and evaluation. Englewood Cliffs, NJ: Prentice-Hall.

Spiro, R. J., Feltovich, P. J., Jacobson, M. J., & Coulson, R. L. (1991). Cognitive flexibility, constructivism, and hypertext: Random access instruction for advanced knowledge acquisition in ill-structured domains. *Educational Technology, 31*(5), 24–33.

Spring, J. (1986). *The American school: 1642–1985.* New York: Longman.

Spyridakis, J. H. (1989a). Signaling effects: Part I. *Journal of Technical Writing and Communication, 19*(1), 227–239.

Spyridakis, J. H. (1989b). Signaling effects: Part II. *Journal of Technical Writing and Communication, 19*(4), 395–415.

Stanberg, S. (1993, June 4). *NPR Morning Edition* [Radio program]. Washington, DC: National Public Radio.

Stankowkski, A. (1966). *Visual presentation of invisible processes.* Teufen AR: Verlag Arthur Niggli AG.

Starch, D. (1966). *Measuring advertising readership and results.* New York: McGraw-Hill.

Steinbeck, J. (1969). *Journal of a novel: The East of Eden letters.* New York: Viking Press.

Steinberg, E. R. (1986). A pox on pithy prescriptions. *College Composition and Communication, 37*(1), 96–100.

Steinberg, E. R. (Ed.) (1991). *Plain language: Principles and practice.* Detroit, MI: Wayne State University Press.

Stevenson, H. W., Lee, S. Y., & Stigler, W. (1982). Classroom behavior and achievement of Japanese, Chinese, and American children. In R. Glaser (Ed.), *Advances in instructional psychology: Vol. 3* (pp. 153–191). Hillsdale, NJ: Lawrence Erlbaum.

Stewart, D. C. (1985). Some history lessons for composition teachers. In G. Tate & E. P. J. Corbett (Eds.), *The writing teacher's sourcebook* (pp. 16–23). New York: Oxford University Press.

Sticht, T. G. (1977). Comprehending reading at work. In M. A. Just & P. A. Carpenter (Eds.), *Cognitive processes in comprehension* (pp. 221–246). Hillsdale, NJ: Lawrence Erlbaum.

Sticht, T. G. (1985). Understanding readers and their uses of text. In T. M. Duffy & R. H. W. Waller (Eds.), *Designing usable texts* (pp. 315–340). New York: Academic Press.

Stoughton, B., & Stoughton, M. R. (1924). Education in English for engineering students. *Proceedings, SPEE, 21,* 144–147.

Stratman, J. F. (1988). *The rhetorical dynamics of appellate court persuasion: An exploratory comparison of advocates' brief composing process with court clerks' brief reading and review process.* Unpublished doctoral dissertation, Carnegie Mellon University, Pittsburgh, PA.

Stratman, J. F. (1990). Theories of the appellate court brief: Implications for judges and attorneys. In G. Kirsch & D. H. Roen (Eds.), *A sense of audience in written communication* (pp. 115–139). Newbury Park, CA: Sage.

Stratton, C. R. (1979). Technical writing: What it is and what it isn't. *Journal of Technical Writing and Communication, 9,* 9–16.

Strong, E. K. (1926, March). Values of white space in advertising. *Journal of Applied Psychology, 10,* 107–116.

Strunk, W., Jr., & White, E. B. (1959). *The elements of style.* New York: Macmillan.

Suchman, L. A. (1987). *Plans and situated actions: The problem of human machine communication.* Cambridge, UK: Cambridge University Press.

Sullivan, P. A., & Flower, L. (1986). How do users read computer manuals? Some protocol contributions to writers' knowledge. In B. T. Petersen (Ed.), *Convergences: Transactions in reading and writing* (pp. 163–178). Urbana, IL: National Council of Teachers of English.

Sutherland, I. E. (1968). A head-mounted three-dimensional display. In *Proceedings of the Fall Joint Computer Conference (FJCC)* (pp. 757–764). Washington, DC: Thompson Books.

Sutnar, L. (1961). *Visual design in action: Principles, purposes*. New York: Hastings House.

Swaney, J. H., Janik, C. J., Bond, S. J., & Hayes, J. R. (1991). Editing for comprehension: Improving the process through reading protocols. In E. R. Steinberg (Ed.), *Plain language: Principles and practice* (pp. 173–203). Detroit, MI: Wayne State University Press. (Original article published in 1981 as Document Design Project Tech. Rep. No. 14, Pittsburgh, PA: Carnegie Mellon University)

Swann, C. (1991). *Language and typography*. New York: Van Nostrand Reinhold.

Swarts, H., Flower, L., & Hayes, J. R. (1980). *How headings in documents can mislead readers* (Document Design Project Tech. Rep. No. 9). Pittsburgh, PA: Carnegie Mellon University, Communications Design Center.

Sweigert, R., Jr. (1956). A technical writing course that works. *Proceedings, American Society for Engineering Education, 63*, 262–266.

Sweller, J., Chandler, P., Tierney, P., & Cooper, M. (1990). Cognitive load as a factor in the structuring of technical material. *Journal of Experimental Psychology, 119*(2), 176–192.

Sypherd, W. O. (1939). Thirty years of teaching English to engineers. *Proceedings, SPEE, 47*, 162–164.

Sypherd, W. O., & Brown, S. (1933). *The engineer's manual of English*. New York: Scott, Foresmen.

Tarutz, J. A. (1992). *Technical editing: The practical guide for editors and writers*. New York: Addison-Wesley.

Taylor, C. D. (1934). The relative legibility of black and white print. *Journal of Educational Psychology, 25*(November), 561–578.

Taylor, C. (1996a, March 15). Custom type design. *IDeAs*, pp. 12–19.

Taylor, C. (1996b). *Designing for the screen*. (Available from the author: 4 Wyatt Close, Rotherhithe, London SE16 1UL UK)

Taylor, F. W. (1911). *Principles of scientific management*. New York: Harper & Row.

Tebeaux, E. (1991a). Visual language: The development of format and page design in English Renaissance technical writing. *Journal of Technical Writing and Communication, 5* , 246–274.

Tebeaux, E. (1991b). Ramus, visual rhetoric, and the emergence of page design in medical writing of the English Renaissance: Tracking the evolution of readable documents. *Written Communication, 8* (4), 411–445.

Tebeaux, E., & Killingsworth, M. J. (1992). Expanding and redirecting historical research in technical writing: In search of our past. *Technical Communication Quarterly, 1* (2), 5–32.

Tebeaux, E. (Ed.) (1995). *Issues for promotion and tenure for faculty in technical communication: Guidelines and perspectives*. St. Paul, MN: ATTW Publications.

Tebeaux, E. (1996). Nonacademic writing into the 21st century: Achieving and sustaining relevance and research and curricula. In A. H. Duin & C. J. Hansen (Eds.), *Nonacademic writing: Social theory and technology* (pp. 35–55). Mahwah, NJ: Lawrence Erlbaum.

Therrien, L. (1991, October 25). Motorola and NEC going for glory. *Business Week*, p. 60.

Thibadeau, R., Just, M. A., & Carpenter, P. A. (1982). A model of the time course and content of reading. *Cognitive Science, 6*, 157–203.

Thomas, J. C. (1976). *A method for studying natural language dialogue* (IBM Research Rep. No. RC 5882). Yorktown Heights, NY: IBM T. J. Watson Research Center.

Thorndike, E. L. (1921). *The teacher's word book*. New York: Teachers College, Columbia University.

Tinker, M. A. (1955). Prolonged reading tasks in visual research. *Journal of Applied Psychology, 39* (December), 444–446.

Tinker, M. A. (1963). *Legibility of print*. Ames, IA: Iowa State University Press.

Tinker, M. A., & Paterson, D. G. (1939). Influence of type form on eye movements. *Journal of Experimental Psychology, 25*(November), 528–531.

Tinker, M. A., & Paterson, D. G. (1942, February). Reader preferences and typography. *Journal of Applied Psychology*, 38–40.

Tompkins, J. (Ed.) (1980). *Reader-response criticism: From formalism to post-structuralism*. Baltimore, MD: Johns Hopkins University Press.

Treisman, A. (1982). Perceptual grouping and attention in visual search for features and for objects. *Journal of Experimental Psychology, 8,* 194–214.

Trollip, S., & Sales, G. (1986). Readability of computer-generated fill-justified text. *Human Factors, 28,* 159–164.

Tschichold, J. (1987). *The new typography*. Berkeley and Los Angeles: University of California Press. (Original work published 1928)

Tschichold, J. (1967). *Asymmetric typography*. New York: Van Nostrand Reinhold. (Original work published 1935)

Tufte, E. R. (1983). *The visual display of quantitative information*. Cheshire, CT: Graphics Press.

Tullis, T. S. (1988). Screen design. In M. G. Helander (Ed.), *Handbook of human-computer interaction* (pp. 377–411). Amsterdam: Elsevier Science.

Twyman, M. (1970). *Printing 1770–1970: An illustrated history of its development and uses in England*. London: Eyre & Spottiswoode.

Twyman, M. (1979). A schema for the study of graphic language (tutorial paper). In P. A. Kolers, M. E. Wrolstad, & H. Bouma (Eds.), *Processing of visible language: Vol. 1* (pp. 117–150). New York: Plenum Press.

Twyman, M. (1981). Typography without words. *Visible Language, 15*(1), 5–12.

Tyler, A. C. (1995). Shaping belief: The role of audience in visual communication. In V. Margolin & R. Buchanan (Eds.), *The idea of design* (pp. 104–112). Cambridge, MA: MIT Press.

U.S. Bureau of Naval Personnel. (1955). *Draftsman 3*. Washington, DC: U.S. Government Printing Office.

U.S. Department of Commerce. (1984). *How plain English works for business: Twelve case studies*. Washington, DC: U.S. Government Printing Office.

U.S. Department of Health. (1984). *Pretesting in health communications: Methods, examples, and resources for improving health messages and materials* (NIH Publication No. 84-1493). Washington, DC: U.S. Department of Health and Human Services.

VanLehn, K., Jones, R. M., & Chi, M. T. H. (1992). A model of the self-explanation effect. *The Journal of Learning Sciences, 2* , 1–59.

Varnedoe, K., & Gopnik, A. (1990). *High & low: Modern art & popular culture*. New York: Museum of Modern Art.

Vartabedian, A. G. (1971). The effects of letter size, case, and generation method on CRT display search time. *Human Factors, 13*(4), 363–368.

Velotta, C. (Ed.) (1995). *Practical approaches to usabilty testing for technical documentation*. Arlington, VA: Society for Technical Communication.

Vertelney, L., & Booker, S. (1990). Designing the whole-product user interface. In B. Laurel (Ed.), *The art of human-computer interface design* (pp. 57–63). New York: Addison-Wesley.

Veysey, L. R. (1965). *The emergence of the American university*. Chicago, IL: University of Chicago Press.

Veysey, L. (1979). The plural organized worlds of the humanities. In A. Oleson & J. Voss (Eds.), *The organization of human knowledge in modern America* (pp. 51–106). Baltimore: Johns Hopkins University Press.

Vitanza, V. J. (1987). Rhetoric's past and future: A conversation with Edward P. J. Corbett. *PRE/TEXT, 8*, 247–264.

Vliet, A., van. (1995, June 12). De terreur ven de onbegrijpelijke gebruiksaanwijzing 'Goede handleiding pure reclame'. *Nieuwsblad,* pp. 1–2.

Waarde, K., van der. (1993, September). *An investigation into the suitability of the graphic presentation of patient package inserts*. Unpublished doctoral dissertation, University of Reading, Department of Typography and Graphic Communication, Reading, UK.

Wadsworth, G. B. (1913). *Principles and practices of advertising*. New York: G. B. Wadsworth.

Walker Art Center. (1989). *Graphic design in America: A visual language history*. New York: Harry N. Abrams.

Waller, R. H. W. (1980). Graphic aspects of complex texts: Typography as macropunctuation. In P. A. Kolers, M. E. Wrolstad, & H. Bouma (Eds.), *Processing of visible language 2: Vol. 13* (pp. 241–253). New York: Plenum Press and NATO Scientific Affairs Division.

Waller, R. H. W. (1982). Text as diagram: Using typography to improve access and understanding. In D. H. Jonassen (Ed.), *The technology of text: Principles for structuring, designing, and displaying text* (pp. 137–166). Englewood Cliffs, NJ: Educational Technology Publications.

Waller, R. H. W. (1985). Using typography to structure arguments: A critical analysis of some examples. In *The technology of text: Principles for structuring, designing, and displaying text: Vol. 2* (pp. 105–125). Englewood Cliffs, NJ: Educational Technology Publications.

Waller, R. H. W. (1987). Typography and reading strategy. In B. K. Britton & S. M. Glynn (Eds.), *Executive control processes in reading* (pp. 81–106). Hillsdale, NJ: Lawrence Erlbaum.

Waller, R. H. W. (1996, May). The origins of the IDA. *Information Design Association*, pp. 2–3.

Walvoord, B. E., & McCarthy, L. P. (1990). *Thinking and writing in college: A naturalistic study of students in four disciplines*. Urbana, IL: National Council of Teachers of English.

Washington Post. (1986, March 12). Technical fields hiring more women to rewrite jargon. *Washington Post,* p. 31.

Weiss, E. H. (1993). The technical communicator and ISO 9000. *Technical Communication, 40* (2), 234–238.

Wenzel, J. W. (1963). *The rhetoric of science*. Unpublished doctoral dissertation, University of Illinois, Champaign, Urbana.

Wertheimer, M. (1922). Untersuchungen zur Lehre von der Gestalt: 1. prinzipielle bemerkungen. *Psychologische Forschung, 1,* 47–58.

Wertheimer, M. (1923). Untersuchungen zur Lehre von der Gestalt: 2. *Psychologische Forschung, 4,* 301–350.

Westendorp, P. (1995, June 28). *Testing pictures, texts, and animations for procedural instructions*. Paper presented at the Conference on Verbal Communications in Professional Settings, Utrecht, Netherlands.

Wheildon, C. (1995). *Type & layout: How typography and design can get your message across—or get in the way*. Berkeley, CA: Strathmoor Press.

White, J. V. (1982). *Editing by design: A guide to effective word-and-picture communication for editors and designers*. New York: Bowker.

White, J. V. (1987). *The grid book: A guide to page planning*. Paramus, NJ: Letraset USA.

White, J. V. (1988). *Graphic design for the electronic age: The manual for traditional and desktop publishing*. New York: Watson-Guptill.

Whorf, B. L. (1956). Science and Linguistics. In J. B. Carroll (Ed.), *Language, thought and reality: Selected writings of Benjamin Lee Whorf* (pp. 207–219). Cambridge, MA: MIT Press.

Williams, J. M. (1989). *Style: Ten lessons in clarity and grace* (3rd ed.). New York: HarperCollinsPublishers.

Willows, D. M., & Houghton, H. A. (Eds.). (1987a). *The psychology of illustration: Vol. 1. Basic research*. New York: Springer-Verlag.

Willows, D. M., & Houghton, H. A. (Eds.). (1987b). *The psychology of illustration: Vol. 2. Instructional issues*. New York: Springer-Verlag.

Wilson, A. (1993). *The design of books*. San Francisco: Chronicle Books.

Wilson, J. H. (1955). Our colleges can teach writing—If they are made to. *Proceedings, American Society for Engineering Education, 62*, 431–435.

Wineburg, S. S. (1991). Historical problem solving: A study of the cognitive processes used in the evaluation of documentary and pictorial evidence. *Journal of Education Psychology, 83*, 73–87.

Winn, W. (1991). Learning from maps and diagrams. *Educational Psychology Review, 3*(3), 211–247.

Winterowd, W. R., & Blum, J. (1994). *A teacher's introduction to composition in the rhetorical tradition*. Urbana, IL: National Council of Teachers of English.

Wired Magazine. (1996, January). CD-ROMs that suck. *Wired Magazine*, pp. 166-167.

Witte, S. P. (1992). Context, text, intertext: Toward a constructivist semiotic of writing. *Written Communication, 9* (2), 237–308.

Witte, S. P., & Faigley, L. (1981). Coherence, cohesion, and writing quality. *College Composition and Communication, 32*, 189–204.

Wright, P. (1980). The criterion for designing written lanugage. In P. A. Kolers, M. E. Wrolstad, & H. Bouma (Eds.), *Processing visible language: Vol. 2* (pp. 183–206). New York: Plenum Press.

Wright, P. (1982). A user-oriented approach to the design of tables and flowcharts. In D. H. Jonassen (Ed.), *The technology of text: Principles for structuring, designing, and displaying text: Vol. 1* (pp. 317–340). Englewood Cliffs, NJ: Educational Technology Publications.

Wright, P. (1987a). Writing technical information. In E. Z. Rothkopf (Ed.), *Review of research in education: Vol. 14* (p. 327–385). Washington, DC: American Educational Research Association.

Wright, P. (1987b). Reading and writing for electronic journals. In B. K. Britton & S. M. Glynn (Eds.), *Executive control processes in reading* (pp. 23–55). Hillsdale, NJ: Lawrence Erlbaum.

Wright, P. (1988a). Functional literacy: Reading and writing at work. *Ergonomics, 31*, 265–290.

Wright, P. (1988b). The need for theories of NOT reading: Some psychological aspects of the human-computer interface. In H. Bouma & B. Elsendoorn (Eds.), *Working models of human perception* (pp. 319–340). London: Academic Press.

Wright, P. (1988c). Beyond plain English. *Research and Practice in Adult Literacy (RaPAL) Bulletin No. 5*, 15–17.

Wright, P. (1994). Quality or usability: Quality writing provokes quality reading. In M. Steehouder, C. Jansen, P. van der Poort, & R. Verheijen (Eds.), *Quality of technical documentation* (pp. 7–38). Amsterdam: Netherlands: Rodopi Press.

Wright, P., & Lickorish, A. (1983). Proof-reading texts on screen and paper. *Behaviour and Information Technology, 2*(3), 227–235.

Wright, P., & Lickorish, A. (1984). Ease of annotation in proofreading tasks. *Behaviour and Information Technology, 3*, 185–194.

Wright, P., & Lickorish, A. (1988). Color cues as location aids in lengthy texts on screen and paper. *Behaviour and Information Technology, 7*, 11–30.

Wright, P., & Lickorish, A. (1994). Menus and menu load: Navigation strategies in interactive search tasks. *International Journal of Human-Computer Studies, 40*, 965–1008.

Wright, P., & Reid, F. (1973). Some alternatives to prose for expressing the outcomes of complex contingencies. *Journal of Applied Psychology, 57*, 160–166.

Wright, P., Creighton, P., & Threlfall, S. M. (1982). Some factors determining when instructions will be read. *Ergonomics, 25*, 225–237.

Wulff, W. (1989). *Collaboration in document design: A case study of process and product*. Unpublished doctoral dissertation, Carnegie Mellon University, Pittsburgh, PA.

Wurman, R. S. (1989). *Information anxiety*. New York: Doubleday.

Yankelovich, N., Landow, G. P., & Cody, D. (1986). *Creating hypermedia materials for English literature students*. (Tech. Rep.). Providence, RI: Brown University, Institute for Research in Information and Scholarship.

Yates, J. (1989). *Control through communication: The rise of system in American management*. Baltimore, MD: Johns Hopkins University Press.

Young, R. E. (1976). Invention: A topographical survey. In G. Tate (Ed.), *Teaching composition: 10 bibliographic essays* (pp. 1–43). Ft. Worth, TX: Texas Christian University Press.

Young, R. E. (1980). Arts, crafts, gifts, and knacks: Some disharmonies in the new rhetoric. *Visible Language, 14*(4), 341–350.

Young, R. E. (1995). "Tracing round the frame": Thinking about writing in departments of English. In R. J. Gabin (Ed.), *Discourse studies in honor of James L. Kinneavy* (pp. 149–167). Potomac, MD: Scripta Humanistica.

Young, R. E., & Goggin, M. D. (1993). Some issues in dating the birth of the new rhetoric in departments of English: A contribution to a developing historiography. In T. Enos & S. C. Brown (Eds.), *Defining the new rhetorics: Vol. 7* (pp. 22–43). Newbury Park, CA: Sage.

Young, R. E., Becker, A. L., & Pike, K. L. (1970). *Rhetoric: Discovery and change*. New York: Harcourt Brace Jovanovich.

Youngblood, C. T. (1990). Reminiscences: A personal history of the STC—Captain Youngblood reports. *Technical Communication, 37*(2), 193–194.

Yuille, J. C., & Paivio, A. (1969). Abstractness and the recall of connected discourse. *Journal of Experimental Psychology, 82*, 467-471.

Zachrisson, B. (1965). *Studies in the legibility of printed text*. Stockholm: Almqvist & Wiksell.

Zappen, J. P. (1987). Historical studies in the rhetoric of science and technology. *The Technical Writing Teacher, 14*, 285–298.

Zijlmans, M. (1995, June 17). Na de aanschaf volgt de gebruiksaanwijzing. *De Volkstrant*, pp. 5–6.

Zimmerman, M. L., & Perkin, G. W. (1982). Instructing through pictures: Print materials for people who do not read. *Information Design Journal, 3*(2), 119–134.

Zoglin, R. (1992, November 23). Can anybody work this thing? *Time*, p. 67.

Zook, L. M. (1989). Reminiscences: A personal history of the STC—Memories of STC. *Technical Communication, 36*(4), 414–416.

	Time to Deliver	Kind of Oral/Written Messages Required by the Rhetorical Context
Summary Level	9-20 seconds	Oral Message: *CNN Sound bite Level* One "Take Home" Message (1 sentence + 1 image)
Integration	9 seconds to 2 minutes	Oral Message: *Snapshot Level* One Main Message Elaborated with 1 or 2 S Charts, Graphs, Posters, or Video Clips (roughly 3 sentences)
Interpretation	9 seconds to 15 minutes	Oral Message: *Spin Level* Very Concise; Addresses Only Questions One may b About; Audience Driven Charts and Graphs, (Length = 3-5 sentences to 2 pages + charts/g
Condensation	15 minutes to 30 minutes	Oral Message: *Executive Summary Level* Minimal Elaboration of Key Data Points, Sev and Graphs with Data Reduction (Length = 1-5 pages)
Extraction	20 minutes to 1 hour	Written Message: *Technical Report Level* Supporting Data, Detailed Charts, Graphs, M Appendixes, References (Length = 5-30 pages)
Comprehensive Knowledge base	2 hours to 4 hours	Written Message: *Exhaustive Technical Repor* Comprehensive Treatment-Details, Laws, St or Testimony, Raw Data, Appendices, Refere (Length = 1-50 documents; 50-200 pages per

Author and Subject Indexes

Author Index

A

Abbamonte, M. 274, 275, 276, 534
Abbott, T. viii
Ackerman, J. M. 165, 203, 519, 527
Adams, J. 446
Adams, K. H. 62, 66, 519
Aiken, H. 119
Aizu, I. 140, 141, 519
Albers, J. 80
Alebeek, H., van. 241, 519
Alexander, C. 87
Alexander, P. A. 224, 225, 521, 524, 526
Alfaro, L. 282, 526
Allen, J. 95, 149, 156, 519, 526
Althusser, L. 185, 519
Amdahl, G. 129
Amemiya, H. viii, 140, 141, 519
Anders, P. L. 226, 519
Anderson, P. V. 68, 71, 97, 137, 519, 524, 525
Anglin, G. J. 411, 530
Anisson, J. 251
Apollinaire, G. 108
Apple, M. W. 519
Applebee, A. 109, 117, 119, 123, 125, 127, 519
Aristotle 58, 59, 519
Armstrong, E. H. 115
Armstrong, N. 130, 131
Arnheim, R. 338, 519
Arnot, R. 149, 519
Arunachalam, M. 288
Astaire, F. 116
Atanasoff, J. V. 117
Atman, C. J. 288, 413, 414, 415, 520

Auerbach, M. viii
August, G. J. 274, 534
Ausubel, D. 425, 520
Axtel, R. E. 374, 520
Ayer, A. 116

B

Backus, J. 123
Bain, A. 61, 520
Baird, J. W. 109, 520
Baird, W. 224, 528
Baker, M. L. ix
Baker, R. P. 112, 520
Ballay, J. 75, 520
Bardeen, J. 125
Barker, H. 43, 143, 520
Barr, R. 521, 522, 528
Barry, J. A. 125, 139, 520
Bartlett, F. C. 114
Barton, B. 86, 87, 107, 109, 115, 117, 119, 121, 123, 125, 127, 129, 131, 133, 137, 523
Barton, B. F. 6, 284, 304, 520
Barton, M. S. 6, 284, 304, 520
Bartram, D. 259, 287, 288, 303, 520
Bass, R. 128, 508, 520
Bass, S. 122
Bassock, M. 226, 522
Battison, R. 534
Bayer, D. ix
Bayer, H. 80, 120, 338, 340, 520
Bayer, L. ix
Bazerman, C. 47, 69, 139, 144, 180, 520
Beale, L. 147, 520
Beam, P. 282, 532
Beck, I. L. 224, 226, 520
Becker, A. L. 58, 65, 69, 162,

163, 274, 539
Becker, D. 520
Bell, A. G. 111
Benedikt, M. 131, 520
Benson, P. J. 224, 411, 455, 520
Bentley, M. 274, 520
Bereiter, C. 36, 487, 522, 534
Berger, H. 113
Berke, R. L. 168, 520
Berkenkotter, C. 158, 162, 166, 180, 188, 288, 520
Berkowitz, R. 380
Berlin, J. 24, 58, 67, 107, 109, 113, 119, 125, 129, 520
Bernard, R. M. 419, 520
Bernhardt, S. A. 6, 251, 284, 304, 338, 339, 520, 530
Bernstein, L. 28, 520
Berry, C. 410, 520
Bertin, J. 310, 311, 515, 516, 521
Bevington, W. 87, 144, 145, 523
Bianchi, M. H. 247, 526
Bieger, G. R. 417, 521
Bill, M. 118, 521
Billingsley, P. A. 509, 528
Bilotti, L. ix
Binkley, M. 521
Bizzell, P. 58, 139, 521
Black, A. 272, 273, 279, 289, 403, 521
Black, B. 521
Black, S. D. 111, 135
Blakeslee, A. M. 180, 521
Bloch, F. 113
Bloom, A. 142
Blum, J. 61, 539
Bobbitt-Nolen, S. 180, 521
Bolter, J. D. 115, 379, 521
Bond, E. 75, 380, 535
Bond, S. J. 74, 75, 521, 528, 537
Bonsiepe, G. 274, 521
Bonstingl, J. J. ix

Left-hand page. *Document designers often create a variety of texts from a single database of information. This chart illustrates the movement from a comprehensive knowledge base through various stages of condensation, interpretation, and integration. I created this visual to portray the tasks of report writers at the U.S. General Accounting Office (GAO). Thanks to Catherine and John Smith for allowing me to observe their stimulating seminars on "Writing Testimony" for GAO report writers.*

Subject Index

Colophon

The body text is set in Bembo, a typeface that was originally used in Cardinal Bembo's book *De Aetna*, published by the Venetian scholar and printer Aldus Manutius in 1495. Bembo is known as an Old Style face, a Renaissance style of typography in which designers attempted to capture some of the visual properties of writing with a pen. As the first Old Style face, Bembo provided a model for European typographic design over the next two centuries. More recently Bembo has been remastered for digital typesetting by the Monotype Corporation. ❧ The chapter numbers are set in Garamond, another Old Style face, designed by the Parisian engraver and typefounder Claude Garamond in 1531 and redrawn for the computer by Adobe Systems, Incorporated. ❧ The heads and sidematter are set in Frutiger, a sans serif typeface created in 1976 by Swiss typographer Adrian Frutiger. It too has been created for the computer by Adobe Systems, Incorporated.